Appalachia

Social Context Past and Present

Fourth Edition

Edited by
Phillip J. Obermiller
Michael E. Maloney

Formerly edited by
Bruce Ergood
Bruce E. Kuhre

KENDALL/HUNT PUBLISHING COMPANY
4050 Westmark Drive Dubuque, Iowa 52002

ISBN 0-7872-9136-6

Printed in the United States of America
10 9 8 7 6 5 4 3 2 1

To Katie Brown
organizer of the Frank Foster Memorial Library
on Appalachian Migrants
and still working to clear
the air around urban Appalachians.

Contents

IV Appalachian Stereotypes 109

V The New Appalachian Culture 137

VI Health and the Environment 191

VII The Political Economy of Appalachia 215

Foreword to the Fourth Edition

by Loyal Jones

I used the three previous editions of *Appalachia: Social Context Past and Present,* edited by Bruce Ergood and Bruce Kuhre, for some seventeen years in a course called Appalachian Problems and Institutions. It was a good text. In my opinion, the second edition was better than the first, and the third was better than the second. Now, under the editorship of Phillip Obermiller and Michael Maloney, we have a new edition for a new century and in many ways a new Appalachia. There have been many changes in the region since the first edition appeared in 1976, just as there has been a change in the ranks of those who write about the region. While many of us old scholars are still hanging around, a new generation has come on the scene, seeing a changing region with a whole lot of improvements but also with a whole rash of new issues and concerns.

The new editors have sought recent essays by these new scholars, while retaining some of the ageless themes that impart an understanding of the Appalachian past. This edition also includes articles that show the growth in, and the maturing of, Appalachian Studies as a discipline. The volume should be effective as a text in a variety of courses relating to sociology, education, community and regional development, political science and government, regional economics, community organizing, leadership, resource management, and the like. The articles are by knowledgeable persons who have tried to describe and analyze the region and its people in relation to inevitable forces and influences from the nation and the world.

Appalachia—land and people—is one of the most complex subjects any writer ever attempted to understand, let alone explain to others. John C. Campbell, one of the earliest writers to take on the task, said that more is known about the place *that isn't so* than about any other place, and many Appalachian stereotypes had not fully taken hold at the time he wrote. Since then various newspaper and magazine articles, several popular movies, numerous television shows and hundreds of brochures from "helping" agencies have appeared, telling interesting but not always accurate stories about us mountaineers. Such material keeps coming. For complex reasons these people have presented their views on mountaineers, and for equally complex reasons, readers and viewers have accepted these images with little critical adjustment. Mainstream Americans have been fascinated by Appalachian people for more than a century, and have avidly read or watched widely disparate descriptions of us. Thus, they carry pictures in their heads derived from the various media, and it has been difficult for them to take a new look, unencumbered by the distorted pictures, at the facts and at our own description of ourselves.

This new edition of *Appalachia: Social Context Past and Present* presents an opportunity to study the region anew. The essays reflect thoughtful definitions and analyses by natives of the region, as well as newcomers, who have risen on the Appalachian scene in fairly recent years. It also contains sophisticated theoretical analyses of the region and of similar places worldwide, showing the influence of academic enclaves from which some of the writers observe the region. Together, these essays show not an isolated region and insular people but rather Appalachia as a part of the global order, or disorder as the case may be. The careful reader cannot escape the truth that the industrial world still depends on Appalachian coal, oil, and gas, builds with Appalachian wood, and utilizes Appalachian intellect and labor. The reader will also grasp the fact that the problems of Appalachia are the problems of the industrial system and of governmental policies, and that the best solutions most often come from Appalachians themselves. Appalachia is a part of the modern world with all of its advantages and problems. Many Appalachians have prospered along with advantaged people elsewhere, but conversely, like disadvantaged people throughout the country and the world, many here in the mountains, especially single-parent families and children, have lost ground and are very poor by American standards. Some Appalachian workers have rejoiced at new jobs with decent wages while others have seen their well-paid industrial jobs go to Third World countries, and have had to accept lower paying service work. They have also seen their unions decline in power and influence. Some Appalachian states and counties offer at least adequate government, good schools, and enough support payments to provide minimum shelter and food. Others, depending on how political or how inept, offer services that would be unacceptable in other parts of the country.

We Appalachians are in ways distinctive—perhaps more traditional than some others, more personal in our relationships, and more willing to mind our own business even to the point of letting others run things in a way that serves some better than others. Describing the distinctive qualities of Appalachians gets us writers in trouble. In order to show how we are different, we generalize. When we do, we also create stereotypes. Scholars try to devise interviewing instruments to elicit information in an objective way, in the hope of settling certain controversial subjects. Even these studies, however, do not always bring agreement because we each have differing ideological orientations and seek information for differing reasons, seeing facts, data or opinion through our own biases, ideology, and needs. Even if we were objective, however, there is no single book or essay (although I am frequently asked to recommend one) that can give us the real and true Appalachia. We must examine an expanding literature, written by people with varying views, in order to understand that this region is complex and that we must form our own views after diligent study.

Many students come to class with their biases well in place. Some see the "problems" of Appalachia as being the result of Appalachian culture. If people are unemployed, then they must be "sorry," that is, lazy, and whatever problems they face must be their own fault. Don't we all know numerous people who have overcome difficulties with the right values and hard work? Others come to class seeing Appalachian natives as victims of a rapacious industrial system or of bad government. One of the first points we must teach is that this region—any region—is more complicated than any one theory suggests. Many factors bear on Appalachian poverty. What is the effect of the region being treated as a raw materials colony? What is the effect of outside ownership? What is the effect of the disparity in development capital between rural and urban areas? What happens to initiative if there are not enough jobs in a county? What effect does bad or inadequate education have on the culture? How can the effects of poor medical care be computed? How are people affected by vicious stereotypes and by being classed as inferior because of their accents or manner?

This book will lead students into considering some of these difficult questions. They will consider different descriptions and definitions of the region. They will explore recent trends in Appalachian migration and urbanization. They will learn about Appalachian history and diversity, and about the region's culture, economy, and environment. They will take a new look at some old stereotypes, consider regional policy issues, and become familiar with community-based organizations that are tackling those issues.

Preface to the Fourth Edition

"Appalachia" is a fugitive concept. It has many disguises—cultural gem, economic hinterland, literary motif, energy colony, retirement haven, ecological disaster, recreational oasis, common stereotype, and all-American archetype to name a few. The region is often reported lurking at the intersection of history and social change. Eye witnesses argue about its age and actual location, and they disagree about the most likely suspects in any lineup of Appalachian cultural characteristics. Some expert witnesses say that there actually is no "Appalachia," that the name just represents a figment of the academic imagination.

Yet Appalachia is not nothing. It is not New England, although a portion of the geological region extends through New England to Nova Scotia. It is not the Mississippi Delta, the Midwest, or the Piedmont although the federally designated Appalachian region overlaps some of these regional designations. John Shelton Reid has asked why we do not just consider Appalachia part of the South. That approach would not be particularly attractive to the Appalachian residents of Ohio, Pennsylvania, or New York. Others say that the region makes more sense if you lop off its northern tier and focus on Southern Appalachia. The descendants of miners, loggers and steel workers in Pennsylvania and Ohio will justifiably ask why their communities were left out. So will the residents of New York's hill country and the uplands of Western Maryland.

If Appalachia is not nothing, what is it? For many it is the 406-county region designated by Congress in the Appalachian Development Act of 1965 as amended at various times, most recently in the 1990s. There are countries whose boundaries make no more sense than Appalachia's federally designated boundaries. Their boundaries were determined by wars, treaties, and other acts no more rational than an act of the United States Congress. Some studies may legitimately require the Appalachian Regional Commission's definition be expanded or contracted. For example, historians and folklorists might reasonably consider it "the back country" that lay east of the original coastal settlements. Certain environmental studies would be concerned about patterns of deforestation or species extinction disregarding county and state definitions. Bioregionalists would define their areas of study by rivers and their drainage basins. Cultural geographers may draw a map of "the upland South" which includes parts of Ohio and even southern Indiana and Illinois as part of Appalachia. They will note similar cultural regions in the Ozarks and East Texas and even western Washington state where migrants from Appalachia have settled. Musicologists might be surprised to find the center of Bluegrass music to be somewhere north of Cincinnati in Ohio's Miami Valley. Students of Appalachia must become comfortable with flexible definitions, an approach that is key to working with a fugitive concept.

Harry Emerson Fosdick once spoke of the beauty of being used by great ideas, and Appalachia is an idea that uses us well. Even if Appalachia were just a mental construct, it nonetheless would be a valuable one. We live in a world of regions—Wales in Britain, Italy's Mezzogiorno, and Spain's Basque region for example. In the United States we have not only Appalachia, but also New England, the Great Lakes, the Great Plains, the Mississippi Delta, and the Borderlands of the Southwest. Naming regions is simply a way of talking about a place and its people. That a region or its residents are at times ignored and at other times wildly misunderstood does not undermine the usefulness of regionalism as a concept. Regionalism forms a very practical context for unveiling the social, political, and economic dynamics of a place and how the people living in that place interact with those dynamics. This book provides a means of learning about a specific region, Appalachia, while at the same time pointing to much larger issues in the context of that region.

It is only fair to tell readers how we went about compiling this edition. Our strategy was to be as inclusive as possible given the fact that our search was limited to social science materials by the nature of the previous editions. We surveyed members of the Appalachian Studies Association, teachers of Appalachian courses, and directors of academic, governmental, and community-based Appalachian organizations. We placed queries on appropriate Internet listservers and bulletin boards, as well as in regional newsletters. We reviewed every reading mentioned in the Appalachian course syllabi posted by Emily Satterwhite on the Appalachian Studies Association's website, and in Chris Baker's most recent edition of "Appalachian Studies Syllabus Guide and Teaching Materials" published by the American Sociological Association. We also examined the articles published since 1990 in five key serials: the *Appalachian Journal*, the *Journal of Appalachian Studies, Now and Then, Appalachia,* and *Appalachian Heritage.*

An analysis of the survey responses, the course syllabi, and the journal articles guided us in developing an expanded outline for the fourth edition. We incorporated the original forty-five articles from the previous edition into this new table of contents, along with over three hundred new entries that we had identified for possible inclusion. At that point we had assembled some 5,000 pages of material for a 450-page text. In weekly editorial sessions stretching over a period of several months, we read and discussed the material at hand until we had winnowed the manuscript down to about one-fifth its original size. A second, more arduous, selection process brought the volume to its current size.

In almost every case we were faced with two or three excellent candidates for every entry we finally selected. We obviously considered many fine entries which, due to the constraints of space, we could not include in the final volume. But space limitations were not our primary concern. We strove to identify and include entries that reflected the best Appalachian scholarship with a particular emphasis on works that have appeared during the decade since the last revision. In those cases where we thought there were no satisfactory candidates, we invited colleagues to write entries specifically for this reader.

We have worked hard to make this revision a useful and representative volume. Nevertheless, we know that some of the entries in the previous editions will be missed by those who have used them in the past, while others will point to materials they believe more suitable than the ones we have selected. This is as it should be, because we believe the field of Appalachian Studies has matured to the point where we can rightfully call each other to ever higher standards. The editorial process has been long and arduous, but not without reflection and careful judgement. We look forward to the healthy discussions the publication of this volume may entail.

In compiling this volume we did not seek to impose a particular orthodoxy or overarching theme on the material, looking instead for quality scholarship and goodness-of-fit in relation to the text as a whole. There is some unavoidable repetition of issues, but readers should look for no governing interpretation of the Appalachian region or its people presented here. We have tried to present the cases of both the defenders and the prosecutors of various perspectives on the region. The users of this volume will consequently find differing, sometimes conflicting, theories and evidence in each topical area covered in the following pages. Readers are invited to judge for themselves the value of these materials, because the jury is still out on the concept of Appalachia.

Many people have had a hand in making this volume: Ohio University Professors Emeriti Bruce Ergood and Bruce Kuhre who produced the first three editions; Chad Chandlee and his colleagues at Kendall/Hunt without whom there would have been no fourth edition; Appalachian research assistants Bonnie Hood Smith and Phyllis Shelton and data base manager Martha Murphy; Jeff Dey, keyboarder extraordinaire; the sixty-eight activists and academics who took the time to respond to our questionnaire; and in particular Ron Eller and Steve Fisher who provided equal parts of encouragement, insight, and admonition. Whatever organization, quality, and usefulness readers may find in this volume are due to the combined efforts of all of these people, and we thank each of them most sincerely. Given the selection process described above, errors of omission and commission are clearly ours alone.

Phillip J. Obermiller
Michael E. Maloney
Cincinnati, Ohio

I

What Is Appalachia?

In this section, we present the ideas of several leading interpreters of the region and its people as we enter the 21st Century. Most would agree that the physical region could be somewhat loosely described as "the eastern mountains of the United States," but after that the qualifications would have to begin. The area is not all mountainous—there are hills and plateaus as well as mountains—and one of the region's largest features is a valley. Similar complexity abounds when we begin discussion of the region's people. There was a time when the debate centered around whether Appalachians were mostly Scots Irish or Anglo Saxon. Here and in the sections on diversity and on stereotypes the reader will come to understand that the people of Appalachia belong to no single ethnic, racial or socioeconomic designation, nor can their culture be reduced to a simple list of traits.

The first article, written by Richard Couto and titled simply "Appalachia," uses the federal definition of Appalachia to discuss its geographic subdivisions, describe its demographics, and present a critique of how its people have been described in cultural terms. The second article, by David Walls and Dwight Billings, was written in 1977 and represents an early effort to formulate a sociological approach to Appalachia. This article begins with images of Appalachia presented by novelists, then moves through analyses based on genetic theory, models based on a subculture of poverty, and theories of regional development and internal colonialism, to a more comprehensive view based on an analysis of industrial capitalist development. Their article is followed by one written sixteen years later by Alan Banks, Dwight Billings, and Karen Tice outlining the postmodern trends in Appalachian studies. Overviews are given in this article of historian Henry Shapiro's radical deconstruction of Appalachian concepts, and Stephen Foster's image of culture as a discursive forum rather than something that can be defined in a fixed and final way. We close this section with an article by Henry Shapiro that traces the evolution of the image of Appalachia from 1870 into the early twentieth century.

1

by Richard A. Couto

Appalachia

The Appalachian region has had many different boundaries. Currently, the Appalachian Regional Commission (ARC) uses a specific geopolitical definition of 406 counties in 13 states. Previously, social scientists used several different sets of boundaries to delineate the region. In addition to geographic boundaries, Appalachia denotes a distinct cultural region of contradictory and incorrect popular conceptions focusing on quilts, dulcimers, and images of universal poverty and hardship. All these elements of the popular conception of the region can be found in Appalachia; none of them describes the entire region or all the people who live there. These cultural images offer conflicting interpretations of the region but only a small sense of the diversity to be found there. It is difficult to make a safe generalization about the Appalachian region. This chapter offers an overview of the region that explains why generalizations are difficult. It examines geographic and cultural boundaries of Appalachia and offers an analytical framework to understand cultural representations of the region.

Defining the Geographic Regions

Different researchers have used various geographic boundaries for the region. Early sociologists, like Campbell (1921) and Kephart (1913), established boundaries, such as the southern highlands, that united a group of people with some common cultural characteristics. Kephart's study incorporated an uncertain number of counties in the Great Smoky Mountains region of North Carolina, Georgia, and Tennessee. Campbell's study offered a much broader definition—210 counties in 9 states extending north of Kephart's region. A 1960 study by the Maryland Department of Economic Development expanded the boundaries of the region to 11 states from New York to Alabama (Ford 1962). A survey conducted by Ford (1962) included 205 counties in just 6 states. By the mid-1960s, a half-century of analysis had provided several different geographic boundaries for Appalachia.

In 1965, the Appalachian Regional Development Act, which created the Appalachian Regional Commission, drew the boundaries of the region once again. These boundaries, the most expansive to date, have become widely accepted. They follow the spine of the Appalachian Mountains from the southern tier of New York counties to a tier of northeast Mississippi counties. The region encompasses 406 counties and 13 states, including all of West Virginia and portions of Alabama, Georgia, Kentucky, Maryland, Mississippi, New

Source: From *Sowing Seeds in the Mountains: Community-Based Conditions for Cancer Prevention and Control* by Richard Couto, Nancy Simpson & Gale Harris. NIH Publication #94-3779, National Cancer Institute, 1994.

York, North Carolina, Ohio, Pennsylvania, South Carolina, Tennessee, and Virginia.

The current definition, like that of ARC, came from a national sense of acute human need within a region and a national commitment to do something about it. It also resulted from an effort of state and congressional leaders to include their jurisdictions in an area of special federal initiatives. Federal administrators welcomed this initiative. They built much congressional support for the Appalachian Regional Commission, a fledgling agency of the Kennedy administration, which was a precursor of "War on Poverty" programs in the 1960s. Geography interacted with centers of power in Washington, D.C., to push the region's boundaries farther and farther. Initially, the ARC region included only 11 states. New York was added because it was contiguous. Mississippi was added also because it was contiguous and contained two senior U.S. senators who could be powerful friends to a federal program (Raitz and Ulack 1984). The region continued to change at its edges. It gained one Ohio county in 1991 and a Mississippi county in 1992.

Thus, the Appalachian Mountains are only part of the logic of this broad geographic definition. Other parts of that logic include economic similarities, contiguity, measures of low income and human well-being, and congressional representation of 26 senators and 59 members of the House of Representatives. That logic continues with some changes. The region now has 60 House members, an increase of 1 despite slower population growth than the rest of the nation. Some Appalachian states lost congressional representation (e.g., New York), and others gained (e.g., Georgia). More than 25 years of programs and reports create additional reasons to accept ARC's geographic boundaries. In addition, local political and business elites in 406 counties are now organized into economic development areas and provide local support, giving the region an additional unique feature. In some ways, this geographic definition continues former definitions but adds specific political and administrative criteria.

Nearly all geographic definitions of Appalachia encompass an area with diverse economies and populations that make generalizations difficult. ARC's definition compounds this difficulty. It includes areas that forged the heart of the Industrial Revolution with steel and coal. Areas of the region demonstrated the possibility of mass production of goods and textiles and pioneered in the development of chemicals and plastics. Other parts of Appalachia with economic bases of agriculture and tourism remain only indirectly touched by the Industrial Revolution. This part of the region includes numerous rural counties with populations of less than 10,000. On the other hand, the region includes Pittsburgh and Birmingham and is contiguous to other major metropolitan areas including Atlanta, Cincinnati, Harrisburg, Lexington, Memphis, and Montgomery. Other major cities, including Albany, Baltimore, Buffalo, Cleveland, Columbus, Nashville, New York, Philadelphia, and Washington, D.C., are within an hour's drive of ARC's Appalachian boundaries.

Analysts concede the diversity within the Appalachian region by use of subregions: Northern, Central, and Southern Appalachia. The northern subregion takes in most of the older industrial area of the region and the nation, including all the Appalachian counties in Maryland, New York, Ohio, and Pennsylvania. In addition, counties in Virginia and West Virginia are included in Northern Appalachia. Central Appalachia, the smallest of the subregions, includes all the counties of eastern Kentucky and some of the Appalachian counties of Tennessee, Virginia, and West Virginia. Southern Appalachia includes the remainder of Appalachian counties of Tennessee and Virginia as well as all the Appalachian counties of Alabama, Georgia, Mississippi, North Carolina, and South Carolina. As discussed later, measures of socioeconomic well-being and the economies of these subregions vary widely. There are profound differences among counties in the same subregion as well.

Another distinction among the counties of Appalachia involves their urban or rural status. Two hundred and sixty-six counties (67 percent) of the region are rural. Thirty-two percent of the Appalachian population resides in these rural counties, whereas only 15 percent of the total U.S. population lives in rural counties. Central Appalachia has the fewest number of urban counties. Figure 1 offers a view of the boundaries of Appalachia, and sets off the three subregions. Obviously, this geographic region is not the hidden, socioeconomically homogeneous, remote, and distinct region that may reside in the popular imagination.

Demographics

Population changes have occurred differently among the subregions of Appalachia. The entire region increased its population by a mere 1.6 percent from 1980 to 1990 compared with a national increase of 9.8 percent. Southern Appalachia increased its population during this period by 9.4 percent—mostly in the urban counties, which grew by 10.8 percent. These figures obscure the incredible growth in suburban Atlanta. There, the population growth of one country—Gwinnett County—accounts for 56 percent of all of Appalachia's increased population between 1980 and 1990.

Northern Appalachian counties had a population decline (3.1 percent) from 1980 to 1990, especially among the urban counties of that subregion (3.9 percent). Central Appalachian counties lost more population (4.7 percent). Rural counties in both Northern and

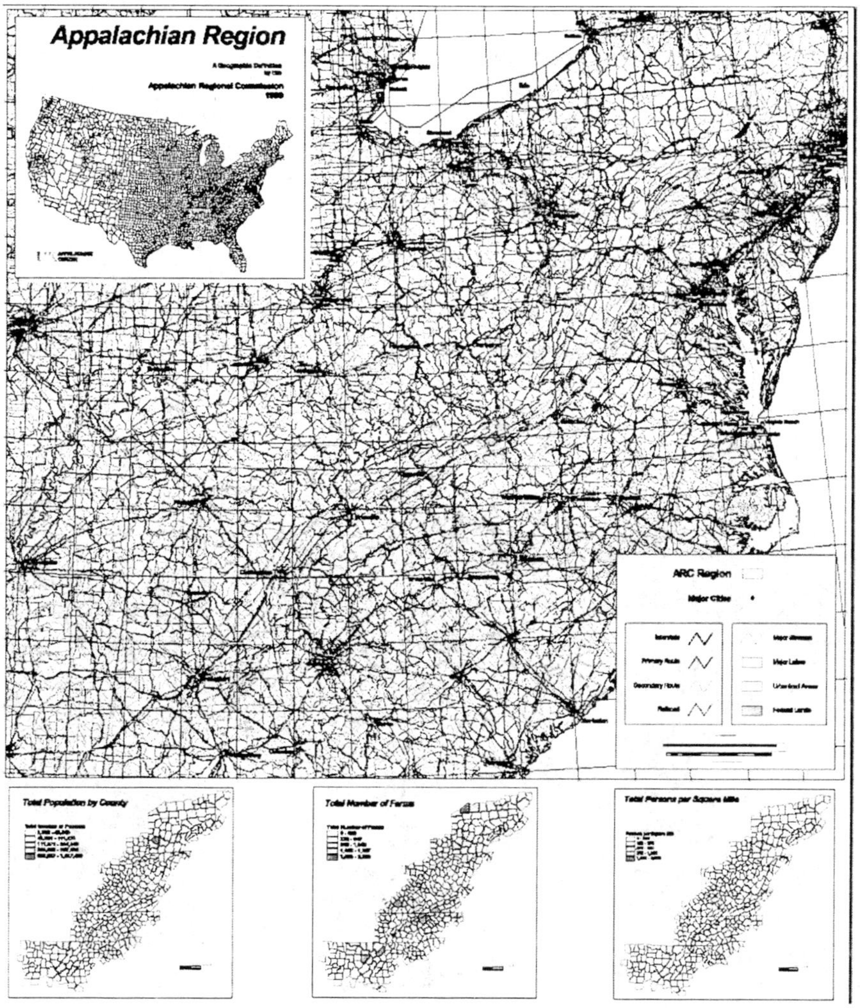

Figure 1. The Appalachian Region

Central Appalachia decreased in population (0.3 percent and 5.1 percent, respectively). These losses compare with the national average gain in rural areas of 2.7 percent in the same decade. Table 1 compares 1980 and 1990 population figures for the Appalachian portions of each state.

Figures from the 1990 census indicate that 20.7 million or 8 percent of all Americans live in Appalachia. Fifty percent of them live in only three states—Alabama, Pennsylvania, and Tennessee. African Americans constitute 7.3 percent of the region's population but a much larger segment of the Appalachian populations of Alabama, Mississippi, and South Carolina. Native Americans make up less than 1 percent of the population of the region and are concentrated primarily in western North Carolina. Table 2 provides a breakdown of the 1990 Appalachian population by race and state.

What We Know About Appalachia

After the boundaries have been set and the people counted, the question occurs: What is special and unique about the Appalachian region? Writers, journalists, and video and camera crews have visited specific places within Appalachia's boundaries to explain mistakenly how the characteristics of the people found there express a variation of American experience: dialect, a specific rural lifestyle and subsistence agriculture, godlessness, godliness, violent family feuds, excessive parental affection, industrial work, exploitation of labor, organized resistance of workers to exploitation, or poverty in large amounts and severe forms.

TABLE 1 Appalachian population* by state, 1980 and 1990

Appalachian Part	***Population***		***Change***	
	1980	***1990***	***Total***	***Percent***
Alabama	2,430,244	2,529,623	99,379	4.1
Georgia	1,103,971	1,508,030	404,059	36.6
Kentucky	1,077,095	1,045,357	–31,738	–2.9
Maryland	220,132	224,477	4,345	2.0
Mississippi	498,374	510,400	12,026	2.4
New York	1,083,241	1,088,470	26,874	0.5
North Carolina	1,217,732	1,306,682	88,950	7.3
Ohio	1,376,130	1,372,893	–3,237	–0.2
Pennsylvania	5,994,240	5,769,410	–224,830	–3.8
South Carolina	793,040	888,057	95,017	12.0
Tennessee	2,073,834	2,146,992	73,158	3.5
Virginia	549,888	517,816	–32,072	–5.8
West Virginia	1,950,183	1,793,477	–156,706	–8.0
Appalachia	20,368,104	20,701,684	333,580	1.6
United States	226,545,805	248,709,873	22,164,068	9.8

*Data for 399 Appalachian counties.
Source: Appalachian Regional Commission

TABLE 2 **1990 Appalachian population* by race and state**

Appalachian Part	*White*†	*Percent White*	*African-American*	*Percent African-American*
Alabama	2,026,236	80.1	503,387	19.9
Georgia	1,413,612	93.7	94,418	6.3
Kentucky	1,029,300	98.5	16,057	1.5
Maryland	215,592	96.0	8,885	4.0
Mississippi	353,169	71.2	142,520	28.8
New York	1,068,223	98.1	20,247	1.9
North Carolina	1,187,852	90.9	118,830	9.1
Ohio	1,344,130	97.9	28,763	2.1
Pennsylvania	5,537,522	96.0	231,888	4.0
South Carolina	738,341	83.1	149,716	16.9
Tennessee	2,027,240	94.4	119,752	5.6
Virginia	504,505	97.4	13,311	2.6
West Virginia	1,737,182	96.9	56,295	3.1
Total:	19,182,904	92.7	1,504,069	7.3

*Data for 398 Appalachian counties.
†White population figure includes all other race/ethnicities that total less than 1 percent.
Source: Appalachian Regional Commission, unpublished data

Even the early, more focused studies of Appalachia conducted by Kephart (1913) and Campbell (1921) cautioned against generalizations concerning the residents of the region. Campbell explained that the people of Appalachia were socially heterogeneous, despite being white in overwhelming numbers and living in a specifically defined contiguous area. Moreover, he understood that statements about people in the remote rural areas of his study could not be applied with equal accuracy to the people in the same region who lived in towns and valleys (Campbell 1921).

As the boundaries of Appalachia expanded, the differences among people within the region also grew, making generalizations about residents in the region even more difficult. For example, how do residents in Ithaca, New York, and Tupelo, Mississippi, share an Appalachian culture; or residents of Pittsburgh and the Atlanta suburbs; or Binghamton, New York, and Estill County, Kentucky?

Generalizations about the residents of the Appalachian region and their culture come primarily from disregard of cautions about extrapolating from one set of people to another, from one place to another, or from one time to another. Very few studies encompass the entire region and its many issues. Most studies deal with Central Appalachia—eastern Kentucky and contiguous portions of east Tennessee, southwestern Virginia, and southern West Virginia. Other studies are even more limited to a particular community in a particular county in Central or Southern Appalachia.

Caudill's influential book (1962), *Night Comes to the Cumberlands: A Biography of a Depressed Area,* is still a widely read classic and a very good historical introduction. However, it addresses only a portion of the coalmining counties in eastern Kentucky. There are problems extrapolating Caudill's work to other coalmining counties, as well as to the noncoal counties, of eastern Kentucky. Based on Caudill's work, it is simply impossible to generalize, for example, to the anthracite coalfields of Pennsylvania, to the portion of Central Appalachia that is not coal mining, or to the rest of the region as defined by ARC.

Caudill's book mixes two strong but distinct interpretations of the problems of the Central Appalachian region. Caudill blames the social origins and inbreeding of the region's residents for its political, social, and economic problems. In this, he resembles those who have used a culture-of-poverty analysis to explain the region. Weller's (1965) prominent work, *Yesterday's People,* illustrates this approach as do numerous other studies most often written by helping professionals, including mental health workers. Cunningham (1987) has taken up the cultural interpretation most recently in his book—*Apples on the Flood: The Southern Mountain Experience*—although much more adroitly than others and without victim blaming. Caudill's work is so rooted in victim blaming that psychologist Arthur Jensen, in a television interview with journalist William Buckley in the early 1970s, averted charges that his studies of IQ and African Americans were racist by appealing to Caudill's work.

On a more popular front, *The Foxfire Book* (Wigginton 1972) emphasized Appalachian culture in a much more positive manner. These accounts of folklore and folkways portray a self-reliant, talented, and intelligent group of rural people. However, generalizations can no more be made from this work, done primarily in rural, northern Appalachian Georgia, than they can from Caudill's work.

As a result of numerous studies and reports, Appalachia conjures up conflicting and inaccurate images of people who live there. On the one hand, we have television's "The Waltons," offered as a model in the 1992 Republican presidential campaign on family values; on the other hand, we have the Hatfields and the McCoys, commercialized as bumbling bumpkins or fiendishly cruel, like the residents of rural Georgia portrayed in the film *Deliverance.* Similarly, popular images suggest the cartoon indolence and innocence of Li'l Abner and Snuffy Smith and news coverage of the grueling work and militancy of nameless coal miners.

Scholarly examinations trace the popular concepts of Appalachia and their origins back to national trends in markets for literature and social interventions. Literary magazines seeking short stories of local color found them in descriptions of parts of Appalachia. Social workers in settlement schools found contributions for their work in responses to their descriptions of the needs of the residents of the region whom they served and the many more they did not (Shapiro 1978). Later, political and social activists looking for places that needed change found them in the conditions of poverty in Appalachia as well (Batteau 1990). People outside the Appalachian region often have defined the region in terms of their commercial, financial, social, or political needs. This is not to say there is no accuracy in the accounts that we have. It does suggest an additional reason why the generalizations we have of the Appalachian region may be misguided as well as misinformed.

In addition to his emphasis on the characteristics of the Appalachian people in his study, Caudill (1962) also interpreted the region's problems in terms of corporate control and related political collusion. Others have built on this interpretation to place Appalachian events and conditions into the mainstream of American life and processes of industrialization and economic development. In these studies, Appalachian conditions of poverty and human need are more the consequence of economic decision making by coal companies, textile mills, the timber industry, and absentee landowners. The region's extractive industry sends minerals and timber to wealthier areas and receives as little in return as possible. Legislation to benefit the companies developing the raw materials of the region left local and state governments with little tax base to provide essential services such as education, medical care, and public health. The political corruption that went into forming this legislative inequity left reformers with few avenues to justice (Appalachian Land Ownership Task Force 1983; Eller 1982; Gaventa 1980; Lewis et al. 1978). One study reinterprets the feud of the Hatfields and the McCoys, which has stimulated so many stereotypes of "hillbillies," in terms of the economic transformation going on at the time (Waller 1988).

Unlike the cultural interpretations of Appalachia, these studies emphasize what national economic and political forces have done to the region. Likewise, rather than an interpretation of a culture that incapacitated citizens to resist negative influences, these studies suggest how people fought back against such forces. When taken together, even these studies of the Appalachian region are limited in providing an overview of the region broadly defined by the Appalachian Regional Commission. They also focus on a particular set of counties, once again most often in Central Appalachia; a particular time; or a particular industry (e.g., coal, textiles, steel).

In sum, what we "know" about Appalachia is largely extrapolated from case studies, most often from Central or Southern Appalachia; from historical studies of a set of counties, an industry (e.g., coal), or labor union efforts; and from cultural descriptions and interpretations of very specific places or practices. What we "know" often obscures the fact that Appalachian residents, regardless of subregion, are average and ordinary human beings, who under a given environment will develop like other human beings. Part of the problem of Appalachia is what we "know" about it and have to unlearn. In this regard, Appalachian social problems resemble other social problems such as race (Du Bois 1935, p. iii).

Addressing the social problems of Appalachia, no less than any other region, requires knowledge of the social and historical factors that have shaped those problems and the cultural responses that residents of a particular place have fashioned. If there is a culture of poverty, it is in large part a response to the poverty in which people found themselves living and a reasonable response to their prospects of escaping it. Likewise, if there are cultural traits like fatalism, they are likely, in large measure, to be a response to the lack of resources required to improve a condition. Much of the historical and social analysis of the region provides only for safe generalizations of particular places at particular times. As with any other region, we have to accept change over time in the same place and differences among places even in the same region. The expanse of the Appalachian region and the conflicting standards used in defining it make these cautions about generalizations essential. We have become especially cautious in making generalizations about Appalachian culture, the topic to which we now turn.

The Cultural Representation of Appalachia

Few areas of Appalachia attract more attention today than the area of culture. Caudill's (1962) and Weller's (1965) emphases on unique characteristics such as fatalism remain popular, especially among helping professionals who are new to the region and seek to adapt to the culture. Caudill and Weller offer handy hooks on which it is easy to hang innovative interventions and expressions of concern. Their interpretations allow helping professionals to portray the region as beyond the mainstream waiting to be brought in with the tools of professional intervention.

Work following that of Caudill and Weller explains Appalachian culture in positive terms and the seemingly differentiating negative characteristics as expressions of differentiating economic circumstances. Prominent among these later cultural treatments, Appalshop, a media collective in Whitesburg, Kentucky, tells the virtues of Central Appalachia in film, video, radio broadcast, and theater. Individual Appalachians contributed the major portion of this recent work on the positive cultural traits of Appalachians. Often their studies begin with a narrative account in which they acquire their Appalachian identity only upon contact with institutions, such as colleges, away from their home; this acquisition imparts shame for their origins and their low circumstances; they reclaim their pride in the virtues of their unique, no longer suppressed identity; and they present their current work as one variant of the valuable multicultural American experience (Blair 1993).

In some cases, these authors defiantly assert the superiority of Appalachian ways over others. For example, Grigsby (1993) contrasted his working-class background of the coalmining region of eastern Kentucky with the middle-class, academic culture of which he is now a part as a college teacher. In particular, he recalled his chagrin at the conduct of his departmental chair who expressed anger that Grigsby had not attended a party and had not responded with his intention to come or not to come. That anger was coupled with disbelief and disdain that Grigsby did not know what RSVP means. Grigsby then counterattacked in this conflict of cultures.

> I don't like "RSVP" invitations. I don't like being forced to decide early to attend an event and then be forced to go later if I don't want to, and I'm convinced that the working-class approach to such functions ("Come if you want and can and bring something to eat or drink") is a more logical way to conduct "parties," or to use the working-class word—"get-togethers"—which is again more logical (Grigsby 1993, p. 8).

This form of cultural counterattack comes with deep resentment—"dismay and venom" (Speer 1993, p. 12)—over the continued assumption of inferiority of Appalachian culture. Tracing their intellectual protest back to work of Branscome, Seltzer, Whisnant, and others in the early 1970s, these recent accounts testify to the staying power of pejorative stereotypes of "hillbillies." Other ethnic groups have exemptions from comic books; for example, one does not find comic books on Hasidic Jews, Mormons, or Latinos. Likewise, it is hard to imagine finding a book on how to speak "eastern" as easily as one finds books on speaking "southern" and "hillbilly." We continue to caricature Appalachia, however, in whole and in part, in comic strips, television shows and reruns, movies, and even in countless souvenir shops at interstate exits throughout the region.

It is simply inconceivable that after the civil rights movement we would base our understanding of African Americans on blackface comedy, such as television reruns of "Amos and Andy." Social and political change has come with cultural changes regarding race. This has spilled over into other areas such as gender. Thus a "Women's Joke Book" would be funny to more people if it contained jokes told by women instead of jokes told by men about women. These changes contrast sharply with the unchanged status of Appalachian cultural stereotypes (Crawford 1993). In the mid-1980s, John Shelton Reed affirmed the continuation of what others had pointed out in the early 1970s: "Hillbillies appear to be the last acceptable ethnic fools" (Speer 1993, p. 18).

These observations illustrate a much larger background of cultural representation that has been addressed by other writers. For example, Batteau assumes that stereotypes are images made in the context of intergroup relationships in which "different groups seek to impose their will on others" (Batteau 1990, p. 199). Similarly, Whisnant (1983, p. 6) relates Appalachian cultural representation to the politics of culture. In the latter, misleading concepts of local people are disseminated to people with influence and wealth as part of the interaction of very different cultural systems. The distant cultural systems (e.g., centers of industrial capital in the United States in the late 19th century) focus on parts of the local culture. By separating parts of local culture from the broader social, political, and economic history that explains local culture, the distant cultural systems obscure the political implications of their own efforts to change local culture (Whisnant 1983, p. 16). In doing so, these distant cultural systems assume the superiority of their own cultural forms and establish the justification for their efforts at change.

Cunningham (1987) places Whisnant's work in an intermediary range of cultural conflict. Cunningham views culture, politics, and economics as a seamless web woven from the interactions of three groups: the metropolitan core region or civilized group, the outside region or savage group, and the intermediate region that lies between the two other groups. He applies his analytical framework to the interaction of Rome (civilized, metropolitan core), the Celts and Scottish highlanders (the savage outside region), and the Scottish lowlanders and Ulster Irish (the intermediate region). Cunningham applies this same analysis to the Appalachian region as well: the American east coast, Appalachia, and Native Americans. His analysis has the limits of any effort that attempts to connect events and conditions 19 centuries apart and of most efforts to explain Appalachia by focusing on one part of it.

Cunningham's analysis, on the other hand, provides a framework to analyze cultural representations of Appalachia. Figure 2 represents that framework. Between the core and intermediate regions is an economic boundary that the core region penetrates sufficiently to develop economic relations. Between the intermediate and outside regions lies a more rigid political and cultural boundary, like Hadrian's wall demarcating Roman boundaries on the British Isles. The first boundary is permeable. Culture flows from the core region to the intermediate region primarily, and economic goods flow from the intermediate region to the core region primarily. The second boundary is far less permeable and represents the border where, the core group believes, commercial and cultural exchanges are not useful and perhaps dangerous. People venture from the intermediate region and the core region to the outside region primarily to verify the savage nature of the region, the need for rigid boundaries, and the superiority of the other two regions. Virtue is bestowed on those in the outside region who pass the boundaries into one of the other two regions.

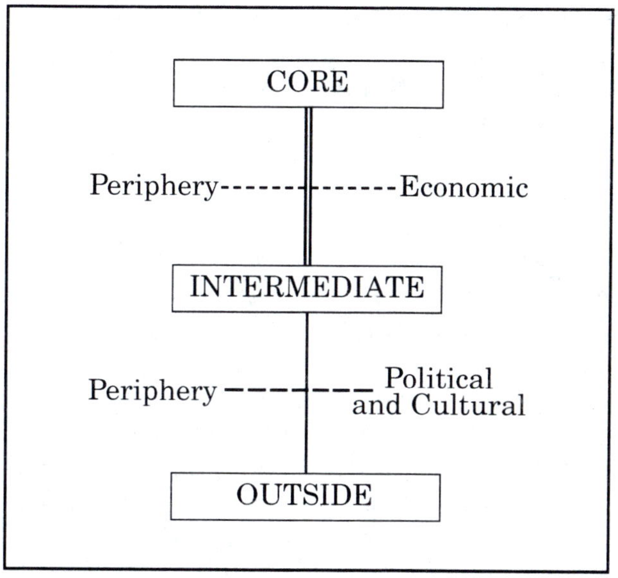

Figure 2. Portrayal of Cunningham's regions and boundaries

Cunningham's borders and regions apply to much of what we already have discussed about Appalachian cultural representation. If we keep in mind the economic borders as well as the political and cultural borders disputed by the core and outside regions, we can understand the feud between the Hatfields and the McCoys as a conflict over the permeability of the economic border and the reinforcement of the rigid cultural and political border. Waller's (1988) interpretation of the feud certainly supports this. Cunningham also helps us understand the work of Caudill and Weller. On the one hand, they provide a permeable boundary for the expression of concern of the core region for the intermediate region. On the other hand, Caudill and Weller provide an intermediate region by portraying an outside region where "savages"—insufficiently civilized human beings—have been replaced with "dolts"—insufficiently intelligent or motivated human beings.

Similarly, Cunningham helps explain the shame so many Appalachian professionals feel when they come into contact with the metropolitan core. They are mistaken for "savages" from the outside region. They work hard to pass through the cultural border to the intermediate region as well as through the border to the core. Cunningham ascribes an impaired identity to such people, of which he is one: "a peripheralized people . . . victims of (among other things) distorted rites of passage which reinforce these insecure ego-boundaries and ego-foundations" (Cunningham 1987, p. xxiii).

However useful, Cunningham's analysis has its limits as well. The boundaries, for example, are defined from the core region out. Although this is accurate in terms of power relations, an essential part of culture, it assumes the cultural superiority established by those power relations. Similarly, those boundaries and the individual and collective identities that culture imparts are not static. Even Hadrian's wall was tested, breached, and reinforced.

Like some members of any group, some Appalachians protest their pejorative portrayal: the boundaries of culture that others establish. They may do so vociferously as the coal operator did in the film *Rich Land, Poor People.* He complained on camera to the camera crew about media portrayals that focused on poverty exclusively. Other Appalachians may protest modestly as one Appalshop character explains in *Strangers and Kin,* a film about negative stereotypes in Appalachia. He recalled being called to the school auditorium to select a pair of shoes from the hundreds of pairs sent in reaction to a televised documentary on poverty in eastern Kentucky. His father's face expressed disappointment in himself, as provider, and in his son, for accepting someone else's assessment of his need. He never wore those shoes. More recently, local Appalachian residents have used cultural protest in their efforts to block waste dumps or water projects in their communities. They interpreted these projects' premises as assumptions that the people and communities to be affected by the dumps and projects were worth little and better off moved to another location (Cable 1993; Foster 1993).

In addition to challenging the cultural borders established by others, Appalachians also use them and thus reinforce them. Town residents may deny the truth of stereotypes when applied to them, but they may assert their validity when applied to residents outside of town. Likewise, the professional class of the region may accept and extend pejorative portrayals of working-class and low-income residents, as a portion of Caudill's work did. Thus, Cunningham's distinction of a core and outside culture has a counterpart within the intermediate cultural region among people who assert their identity with core values by distinguishing themselves from those whom core values brand "hillbilly" with debilitating human characteristics. Thus, interregional cultural differences have a counterpart in intraregional cultural differences. As Campbell (1993, p. 1) has concluded, "Some Appalachians . . . exhibit modernity by accepting the prevailing stereotypes as valid but only for a certain segment of the population—a segment to which they do not belong."

Despite the negative characteristics embedded in Appalachian stereotypes, some Appalachians embrace them occasionally. For example, the Appalshop film "Strangers and Kin" shows us "Hillbilly Days" in Pikeville, Kentucky, in which men and women dress up as the media caricatures them and their forebears. Similarly, Hazard, Kentucky, welcomed with open arms, or at least with a downtown parade, the characters of the prime-time television show "The Dukes of Hazzard." If anything could dispel the premise of simple generalizations of Appalachian cultural representations, it would certainly be this event. A coal town of eastern Kentucky, which came within one "z" of the fictional county, feted the cast of a television series filmed in California, set in northern Alabama, but without any African Americans. Hazard, Kentucky, proudly identified with the bungling corruption and tantrums of the political officials and with the bumpkin common sense and decency of the protagonists of the series. Such events portray the human capacity to deflect the shame embedded in stereotypes. Members of a stereotyped group often take the humor aimed at them and laugh at or with those who make the jokes.

More important, such events invite the question, which Batteau (1990) recently examined: "Whose Appalachia is this?" Obviously, as Cunningham and Whisnant make clear, Appalachian cultural representation is a field in which two different cultures conflict. Batteau, Cunningham, and Whisnant make clear that those within the intermediate region learn how to market their culture and that of the outside region. The economic boundary of the core and intermediate regions is permeable to the flow of cultural exchange in both directions when related to economics. Local officials of Columbiana County, Ohio, demonstrated that recently. Originally, they declined to be included among Appalachian counties but reversed themselves in 1991. The switch from concern with stigma to an assertion of "hillbilly" identity came in part with the lost opportunity for federal funds available through participating in programs of the Appalachian Regional Commission. At least one person embraced kinship with West Virginia, a "hillbilly" personality, as well as a "river rat" identity upon the county's entrance into the Appalachian region (Tribe 1993, p. 26).

In answer to his own question, Batteau asserts that Appalachia is a social invention like the cowboy or the Indian. It is one part positive virtues such as self-sufficiency, pioneering spirit, patriotism, independence, and the dignity of making one's humble way despite adversity. It is one part negative images of dependency, failure, retarded economic and human development, and the dismay of humble people having lost their way because of adversity. Appalachian cultural representation is also one part new and one part old. The old part is virulent racism of the 1890s. Appalachia seemed a pool of Anglo-Saxon genes to develop and thus to prove this group's superiority to African Americans and immigrants. The new part is whatever representation seems appropriate to market in a proposal for funding from federal or foundation sources. The region is also both profane and sacred—profane for the human need and environmental destruction in the region and sacred because people and land have been sacrificed for the greed of some and for the well-being of the nation.

Positives & Negatives

In this regard, Galbraith, in his pathbreaking book, *The Affluent Society* (1958), and in his later reflection on American life, *The Culture of Contentment* (1992), uses Appalachia as a test of America. His latter book offers a cultural interpretation of America to explain the poverty of the Appalachian region. America's "culture of contentment" entails a majority who are fortunate and favored or who hope to be so, who act on behalf of their own immediate short-term benefit, and who willingly tolerate the need for increased and improved social welfare policies, apparent in places like Appalachia, without doing anything to meet those needs or to achieve those policies (Galbraith 1992). Galbraith illustrates Batteau's conclusion about Appalachian cultural representations: "'Appalachia' is a frame of reference, not a fact." It is a willful association "with a broad array of other texts" (Batteau 1990, p. 200).

Conclusion

The practical implications of the cultural representation of Appalachia are made evident throughout this book. After all, projects of the Appalachia Leadership Initiative on Cancer (ALIC) emanate from the core region, Washington, D.C., and the National Cancer Institute. They can entail cultural conflict—for example, efforts to change unhealthy behaviors. In addition, the effect of cultural stereotypes on residents of the same Appalachian community will affect their capacity to work together and the membership of coalition efforts. After people learn the painful experience of culture's role in exploitation, they have the opportunity to learn from it and to do better. Two primary strategies deal with negative cultural stereotypes: to protest those that others use and to do better ourselves (Speer 1993).

Behind these practical difficulties are the profoundly complex factors that create, maintain, and adapt a wide assortment of Appalachian cultural representations. Obviously, any community-based, problem-solving intervention needs to start with the history and culture of the community in which it is occurring. In Appalachia, as in every other region, this means inquiring about and uncovering those specifics. Communities in Appalachian New York vary widely from those in Appalachian Mississippi. Similarly, adjoining counties may vary as well and require different approaches in community-based problem solving because of different histories and cultural adaptations.

2

by David S. Walls and Dwight B. Billings

The Sociology of Southern Appalachia

Sociologists have been fascinated by the Appalachians ever since George Vincent of the University of Chicago took a four-day horseback ride through Breathitt, Perry, and Knott Counties in eastern Kentucky in 1898. Urging study of "this curious social survival . . . now being modified so rapidly," Vincent concluded his descriptive and impressionistic account, "Let students of sociology leave their books and at first hand in the Cumberlands deal with the phenomena of a social order arrested at a relatively early state of evolution."[1] Setting aside questions about the accuracy of Vincent's characterization of the region as a retarded frontier, we can see in his article two themes which predominate in sociological studies of Appalachia from his day to ours: social change and social problems.

Vincent acknowledged his debt to such writers of the "local color movement" as Mary Murfree and John Fox, Jr., for being the first to recognize the Southern Mountains as a distinctive subcultural region. The "discovery" of the Southern Appalachians is itself a problem in the sociology of knowledge and has been addressed by historian Henry Shapiro in *Appalachia on Our Minds,*[2] a brilliant interpretation of the emergence of a national consciousness of Southern Appalachia in the period from 1875 to 1920. Herbert Blumer's comment could well apply to Vincent (and many others) in regard to Appalachia: "Sociological recognition follows in the wake of societal recognition, veering with the winds of the public identification of social problems."[3]

Theories of Social Change and Social Problems

The themes of social change, social problems, and the response of private and public social policy underlie the major social surveys of the Southern Appalachian region: John C. Campbell's *Southern Highlander and His Homeland* in 1921, the U.S. Department of Agriculture's *Economic and Social Problems and Conditions of the Southern Appalachians* in 1935, the section on the "Southern Appalachian Coal Plateaus" in the Study of Population Redistribution in 1936, the Ford Foundation supported study *The Southern Appalachian Region: A Survey* in 1962, and the various studies and annual reports of the Appalachian Regional Commission since 1965.[4] These studies illustrate a major accomplishment of the sociology of Appalachia: the analysis of demographic data from census

Source: Reprinted from *Appalachian Journal,* Vol. 5, No. 1 (Autumn 1977), pp. 131–144.

statistics, including population changes, fertility rates, incomes, unemployment, housing, health, and so on.

Surprisingly, little systematic attention has been devoted by sociologists of Appalachia to fundamental theories of social change or models that explain regional poverty and underdevelopment. Tacit assumptions about the process of social change are more common than explicit models of the roots of regional problems and strategies to overcome the area's difficulties. Description, explanation, and prescription are intertwined in many studies and are not often clearly distinguished. Yet over the years a variety of arguments have been advanced to account for what is variously described as the backwardness, poverty, underdevelopment, and resistance to change of the Appalachian region and its people.

Genes vs. Environment. In the late nineteenth century, historian John Fiske implied a genetic basis for Appalachian poverty and backwardness by suggesting the poor class of mountaineers were the descendants of convicts and indentured servants. The argument of genetic deficiency was elaborated in the 1920s by Arthur Estabrook and Nathaniel Hirsch and revived recently by Harry Caudill.[5] In contrast, the geographic circumstances of isolation and poor communication were emphasized at the turn of the century by William Frost and Ellen Semple.[6] One objective of John Campbell in *The Southern Highlander* was to refute Fiske's argument by providing a correct record of the origins and current status of mountain people and by emphasizing an environmental explanation of mountain problems.[7] In recent years genetic and geographical explanations have generally been superseded by sociocultural and economic theories. During the 1960s, three models were drawn upon to explain Appalachian poverty and underdevelopment: the subculture of poverty, regional development, and internal colonialism models. Each of these three current models was first discovered in the context of underdevelopment in the Third World and applied by analogy to the Appalachian case.

Three Models

Subculture of Poverty. The subculture of poverty model identifies the internal deficiencies of the lower-class subculture as the source of the problem. Oscar Lewis is the social scientist most closely identified with this model, and the most widely read exposition of the model applied to Appalachia is Jack Weller's *Yesterday's People,* which borrows an analytic framework from Herbert Gans.[8] The subculture of poverty model suggests remedial programs of education, social casework, and clinical psychology. Other studies of Appalachian culture in these terms include David Looff's *Appalachia's Children,* Norman Polansky's *Roots of Futility,* and various articles by Richard Ball.[9]

This model in general has been subjected to devastating criticism, and Steve Fisher has criticized Weller's application of this model to Appalachia.[10] In an empirical test, sociologist Dwight Billings has shown the model to be of little value in explaining the lack of economic development in the mountain section of North Carolina and the contrasting industrialization of the piedmont. Ironically, it was just when the distinctiveness of the Southern Appalachian traditional subculture was fading that the subculture of poverty model was popularized and applied to the region.[11]

The pejorative viewpoint on Appalachian culture has been answered by an affirmative approach in works from John and Olive Campbell through Loyal Jones' essay on Appalachian values. Mike Maloney and Ben Huelman have contrasted the affirmative and pejorative approaches in their essay, "Humanism, Scientism, and the Southern Mountaineer."[12] With the humanistic tradition, in their terms, are Robert Coles, John Fetterman, Tony Dunbar, Kathy Kahn, and John Stephenson, who use their subjects' own words to characterize Appalachian lifeworlds.[13] Their descriptions of individuals and families manage to capture the strengths as well as the shortcomings of mountaineers and the diversity of personality types within some common subcultural themes.

The subculture of poverty model can be seen as only one approach within a broader framework of explanations rooted in the tradition of cultural idealism. Affirmative cultural approaches toward Southern Appalachia, as exemplified by Frost and the Campbells, are the obverse side of the coin from the pejorative tradition of the subculture of poverty school. The regionalism of the 1930s, as personified by Howard Odum and others, followed in the tradition of affirmative cultural idealism and looked to ties to the land and a sense of place, combined with planning, for regional revitalization. As John Friedmann points out, the new regionalism of the 1960s discarded the grounding in cultural idealism in favor of a regional development model resting within the contemporary technocratic image and ideology of science.[14]

Regional Development. Although the literature on development includes disciplines from social psychology to social ecology, the most influential stream derives from neoclassical economics as amended by central place theory.[15] The resulting regional development model is concerned with providing economic and social overhead capital, training people for skills for new industrial and service jobs, facilitating migration, and promoting the establishment or relocation of privately-owned industries through a growth center. Niles Hansen is probably the best known academic proponent of this approach. The major attempt to apply the model within the United States is the work of the Appalachian Regional Commission (ARC) and its associated programs.[16]

A major sociological contribution to the regional development model is the notion of a modernizing elite as the agent of the developmental process. H. Dudley Plunkett and Mary Jean Bowman elaborate this idea in *Elites and Change in the Kentucky Mountains.* They identify the "interstitial person" as the "cultural bridge" between traditional and modernizing groups and investigate such key occupational groups as bankers, lawyers, public officials, clergy, physicians, and schoolteachers to determine their relative commitments to change. In general, Plunkett and Bowman found the "ministering professionals"—clergy, physicians, and teachers—to have the most modern outlook: businessmen to be intermediate; and the local administrative elite, the "gerontocracy" of bankers, lawyers, and politicians to be the most traditional.[17] The ARC strategy appears to follow the Plunkett and Bowman suggestion of cooperating with the modernizing professionals to coopt or outmaneuver the traditional business elites and the old county political machines. The basic structure for this strategy on the local level is the multi-county Local Development District, which serves as a mechanism for arriving at consensus among regional elites. Through the dual federal-state structure of the ARC, the interests of regional and national elites are reconciled.

With its emphasis on mainstream economic theory and the technical aspects of development, the regional development model lays claim to being a scientific, value-free, non-controversial approach. As such, it is an effective means of providing additional resources to the region without affecting the existing structure of resource control. Actions taken by regional and national planners are defended as technical decisions, rather than political choices among alternative courses of development. Political sociology calls attention to the possibility that the most important decisions may be the "non-decision": the questions that are never raised and the subjects that never make the public agenda. Examples include public ownership of the region's natural resources and worker or community owned and controlled industry.[18]

Internal Colonialism. The issues of power and privilege in Appalachia are seldom faced squarely by the subculture of poverty and regional development advocates. In reaction to this obvious shortcoming, academics and activists looked for a model that emphasized inequality and exploitation. They hit upon the internal colonialism model for reasons that had much to do with the focus of the New Left in the 1960s—imperialism abroad and oppression of racial minorities at home. As applied to Appalachia, the internal colonialism model has been used to examine the process by which dominant outside industrial interests established control and continue to prevent autonomous development of the subordinate internal colony. The model suggests the need for an anticolonial movement and a radical restructuring of society, with the redistribution of resources to the poor and powerless.

In his best selling 1962 study *Night Comes to the Cumberlands,* Harry Caudill makes only a passing reference to colonialism; by 1965 he begins to use the *internal* colonial designation. The theme was quickly picked up by activists and radical intellectuals in the Central Appalachian area, particularly the group associated with the Peoples' Appalachian Research Collective and its journal, *Peoples' Appalachia.*[19]

Helen Lewis and her associates have attempted a detailed application to Appalachia of Robert Blauner's model of the process of internal colonization of black Americans. In this analysis, such institutions as the Appalachian family and church emerge as not simply survivals of an earlier traditional subculture but also as defensive institutions whose "closed" characteristics are in part formed in resistance to the process of colonization. By emphasizing such values as "equality, non-competitiveness, and family-neighborhood solidarity," the family and the church resist the social change that would integrate the region into the American mainstream.[20]

Much of the attraction of the internal colonialism model, including its application to Appalachia, derives from its powerful analysis of the destruction of indigenous culture in the process of establishing and maintaining domination over the colonized group. It has also performed a valuable service by focusing attention on the acquisition of the raw materials of the region by outside corporate interests and on the exploitation of the local work force and community at large resulting from the removal of the region's natural resources for the benefit of absentee owners.

Although the internal colonialism model has raised important questions about wealth, power, and exploitation in central Appalachia, it may not offer the most satisfactory characterization of the situation of the region. The analogy with racial minorities in America has serious limitations in any strict definition of internal colonialism.[21] The involuntary entry into the United States of enslaved blacks from Africa or the conquered Native American tribes and the Mexican people of the Southwest presents a substantially different situation from that of most Appalachians. Barriers to the assimilation of Appalachians into mainstream society—prejudice against "hillbillies"—are based on bias against the lower classes, not against all the people of the region. The historical development of Appalachia since the expansion of industrial capitalism may present a better example of class domination than Colonial domination.[22]

Toward a More Comprehensive Theory of Social Change in Appalachia. A comprehensive theory of social change in Appalachia must synthesize and integrate a humanistic approach to culture, the technical aspects of regional development, and an appropriate critique of domination at the present period. Some outlines of such a theory emerge from the work of Frankfurt School theorist Jürgen Habermas. For Habermas there are three fundamental conditions or media through which social systems are maintained: interaction, work, and power or domination. All human societies use these means to resolve the problems of preserving life and culture. Corresponding to each of these media are the human "interests" in mutual understanding, technical control, and "emancipation from seemingly 'natural' constraint."[23] A solution to the problems of Appalachian poverty and underdevelopment would have to be concerned with each of the three modes of culture, technique, and domination. Habermas' distinction provides a basis for viewing cultural adaptation, technical development, and redistribution of power as potentially complementary aspects of social development.

We suggest the history of the Appalachian region is best understood in the context of industrial capitalist development. Currently, Appalachia must be analyzed in the context of advanced capitalism in the United States. In some instances (analyzing the role of the Japanese steel industry in providing capital for opening new coal mines in the region, for example), we may have to expand our horizon to the framework of the world capitalist system. In a recent work Habermas analyzes advanced capitalist societies in terms of their economic, administrative (state), and legitimation systems and the resulting class structures. This framework prompts us to examine the competitive and monopolistic sectors of private industry, the role of state expenditures, the legitimation of the system and the containment of rebellion, and the full complexity of the class structure of the region.[24] It may be fruitful to view Southern Appalachia as a peripheral region, rather than an internal colony, within an advanced capitalist society.[25]

"Middle-Range" Issues in the Sociology of Southern Appalachia

At a less comprehensive level of social theory, in the "middle-range" of sociological investigation, base-line studies have been made in several areas. We have substantial knowledge of kinship and community structures, cultural configurations, and demographic changes. We have much less complete knowledge of Appalachian patterns of social stratification and politics. It is useful to summarize these studies and to point out deficiencies in our knowledge.

Class, Status, and Power in Appalachia. As noted above, the subculture model and the regional development model of Appalachian change have both diverted attention away from certain aspects of social structure and politics and redirected attention to issues of cultural and psychological "modernity"—this, despite the fact that Appalachia was born modern. Two misconceptions about the traditional subculture deserve comment. The traditional subculture of the Southern Appalachians should not be characterized as either a poverty subculture or as a peasant culture. The pre-industrial, pioneer way of life cannot be equated with a subculture of poverty as described by Oscar Lewis; there is no evidence that traditional mountain families felt helpless, dependent, or inferior.[26] The analogy to a peasantry has been used in two senses, both in reference to the traditional subculture and to the type of domination during the company town era.[27] Neither analogy is accurate. Nineteenth-century mountaineers were not descendants of a peasant people, but the children and grandchildren of eighteenth century colonists, most of whom had been landless wage-earners from an agricultural and mercantile capitalist country about to enter into the industrial revolution. In sharp contrast to the *Gemeinschaft* solidarity of traditional peasant society, the Appalachian mountaineer was already the quintessential modern individualist. Further, the situation of the miner in the company town is typical of social relations in the early stage of oligopoly capitalism and should be designated as such, not as a condition of peasantry.

Inappropriate cultural models—as they fix attention on "rich Appalachia" and "poor Appalachia," on "traditional Appalachia" and "modern Appalachia"—obscure the region's complex pattern of social stratification. The expansion of state expenditures has helped create sizeable intermediate groupings of public workers (in education, local government, and public services) and workers in industries heavily subsidized by public funds (health services particularly). These elements of the "new working-class" have taken their places alongside such long-established groups as coal miners, workers in small factories, small farmers, country merchants, county-seat retailers, bankers, professionals, independent coal operators, and managers for the nationally-based coal companies in the monopolistic sector, in addition to the household workers, the welfare poor, and others outside the standard labor force. The occupational structure is obviously complex, and its changes need to be analyzed over time, particularly in relation to changes in the coal industry and the growth of state expenditures.

We have no studies of industrial communities in the mountains and, consequently, we have few accounts of stratification in mining communities and county-seat towns. Rural stratification has frequently been over-looked as well,[28] but some good studies have been made. John Stephenson has pictured a four-level structure in "Shiloh," and Schwarzweller, Brown, and Mangalam[29] have identified a clearly developed stratification system in "Beech Creek," despite the fact that they were studying poor families. Social status differences in Beech Creek were manifested in family reputation, visiting, marital exchanges, and territorial locations. Lower status people retained their ascribed family status—in the authors' words their "inherited stigma"—despite personal achievements. This suggests that social factors which influence interaction in mountain communities across status boundaries have not been sufficiently studied. Such factors have important consequences for power and participation in local communities and thus for social and economic mobility.

One of the authors of this essay (Billings) first encountered the *process* of stratification when he attended grade school in a Southern West Virginia county-seat town. School property included two buildings and students were segregated by their fathers' occupations. "Coal Camp" students were routinely assigned to an annex, ostensibly because of "special learning difficulties," although every year two or three were assigned to the main building. In the fourth grade, Billings observed that one of these children always turned red and buried her face in her hands when the teacher called on her to participate in class. This same child was once stood up before the class and her chapped hands were shown to her classmates. The teacher explained that her father could not afford to buy her handcream and, in missionary language, she asked if one of the other children would share her bounty and bring her some cream. The undertaker's daughter did. Later, in her absence, the class was told that this was the same child who brought lice into the classroom.

This story suggests that being poor involves a social identity which is learned early and enforced by informal relationships in the local community. We know little about the rule-governed interactions—in the school, the work place, the welfare office, the voting place—which condition the performances of those defined as "the poor" in the mountains. Nor do we know much about the group with whom they have the most direct contact, the mountain middle class, for the latter have been rarely studied. Sociologists who have studied the middle class, such as Plunkett and Bowman, have been chiefly interested in their attitudes. The mountain middle class is typically viewed as a "cultural bridge" between the rural community and mass society. Their role as "gatekeeper," a better functional analogy, has been ignored and their influence on education, social services, political participation, and the economy has not been fully grasped. In fact, community power structure studies in Southern Appalachia are practically non-existent, although we have had Floyd Hunter's work as an exemplar for over 20 years, and a vast amount of subsequent literature.[30]

Richard Ball reported on the power structure of a northern West Virginia mining county; Rod Harless reported on a county in southern West Virginia.[31] Harless found that the county political elite, consisting of bankers and lawyers, were also on retainer for absentee corporations. Harless, however, used only the positional study method, not the reputational or decision-making case study methods. His work is of limited use for understanding the actual exercise of power and influence although it suggests a political structure similar to those found in other economically peripheral or dependent regions.[32] The middle-class role in county politics has also been discussed by Harry Caudill, Richard Couto, Tony Dunbar, and in Huey Perry's "They'll Cut Off Your Project," a description of confrontation in West Virginia during the War on Poverty.[33]

Scholars who developed the colonial model have focused attention on another social group, absentee owners, who are influential in the life of the region, and in the politics of natural resource development. For example, Harless tried to identify a West Virginia ownership establishment and Richard Diehl[34] described an "Appalachian Energy Elite." A field of growing importance is the sociology of natural resource use. The social impact of the Army Corps of Engineers' dam building is beginning to be studied. The social and economic costs of

Appalachian coal production have been explored in a series of reports by the Appalachian Resources Project at the University of Tennessee. Si Kahn has opened a discussion of the impact of Forest Service policies on the region.[35] Sue Johnson and Rabel Burdge have outlined a methodology for sociologists making contributions to Environmental Impact Statements under the National Environmental Policy Act of 1969. Another avenue for investigating the social impact of a disaster is explored by Kai Erikson's study of the destruction of community in the wake of the Buffalo Creek Flood.[36]

For the most part, these studies, like the community literature, fail to analyze the actual use of power and influence by absentee owners. An important exception is John Gaventa's analysis of the American Association, an English land-holding corporation in eastern Kentucky and Tennessee.[37] On a related theme, the increasing coordination of government and business in resource development has been described by David Whisnant and by Harry Caudill in the *Watches of the Night*.[38]

Surprisingly little attention has been paid to racial and ethnic minority groups, a shortcoming which has bolstered the old stereotype of Appalachia as a bastion of Anglo-Saxon stock. Racial minorities in Southern Appalachia include blacks, Native Americans, and mixed-race groups. Blacks numbered approximately 1.3 million of the total Appalachian population of 18.2 million according to the 1970 census, some 7.3 percent of the population in the 13-state region as defined by the ARC.[39] The few studies that have been made concerning black Appalachians have been concerned primarily with their participation in the coal industry.[40] Blacks composed a substantial proportion of the work force in coal mining in the Southern states between 1890 and 1930. Since that time the proportion of black miners has declined. The mechanization of the industry that began in the 1950s hit particularly hard at the black miner, who did not receive an equal share of the jobs operating continuous miners and other heavy equipment. As employment in the coal industry declined, blacks were laid off in disproportionate numbers. The increase in strip mining also worked against blacks, who rarely obtained jobs with stripping firms. Black Appalachians have been migrating out of the region at a greater rate than whites.

The Eastern Band of Cherokee Indians is the only organized group of Native Americans living in the Southern Appalachian region. Until recently, the only thorough study of the Eastern Cherokees had been conducted in the late 1950s by the Cross-Cultural Laboratory at the University of North Carolina. The Special Cherokee Issue of the *Appalachian Journal* in 1975, edited by Burt Purrington, has added considerable new material on the Eastern Cherokees.[41] The four counties in western North Carolina which include the Eastern Cherokee reservation lands had a total Indian population of 3,937 in the 1970 census. Several hundred additional Indians live in the North Carolina Piedmont and eastern Tennessee.

Ten major mixed-race or triracial (white, black, and Native American ancestry) groups have been identified in the eastern United States. Two of these, the "Melungeons" and the "Guineas," reside within the Southern Appalachian region. The Melungeons of Tennessee continue to give rise to a considerable quantity of mythology, despite the sober scholarship of Edward Price in the early 1950s. There is little up-to-date information on either group, although a study is underway on the Guineas of West Virginia.[42] An attempt was made to count the mixed-race peoples in the 1950 census, but the figures are highly suspect.[43] Research is needed to determine to what extent these groups have been maintained or have been assimilated.

As with blacks, studies of European ethnic groups in Southern Appalachia have been conducted mainly in terms of their association with the coal industry.[44] And with the notable exception of Kathy Kahn's *Hillbilly Women,* little systematic attention has been given to mountain women.

Finally, in the last few years some excellent theoretical work on social movement organization has been done by sociologists, and we have two exemplary case studies of CORE and SDA.[45] But for Appalachian social movements, social scientists have not kept up with the journalists in describing how occupants of class and status positions organize for cooperative and political action. Brit Hume's *Death and the Mines* provides information on the Black Lung Association and the Miners for Democracy movements. The War on Poverty in Appalachia has prompted many books.[46] David Whisnant has provided historical interpretations of the Council of the Southern Mountains and the Congress for Appalachian Development, and Frank Adams has written a history of the Highlander Center.[47] Most of the literature on the Tennessee Valley Authority written since Philip Selznick's classic *TVA and the Grass Roots* has been historical rather than analytical.[48] Little evaluative research has been done on either the War on Poverty programs or the Appalachian Regional Commission. Attempts by community organizers to create an Appalachian identity among unemployed out migrants in urban contexts and to adapt their communities to the model of inner-city ethnic group politics also deserve more attention.[49]

Culture and Community in Appalachia. Since the time of Frost and the Campbells, students of the Southern Appalachians have been attempting to characterize the subculture of the region. In the major effort to survey the extent to which the traditional subculture has persisted, Thomas Ford in 1962 defined four themes: individualism and self-reliance, traditionalism, fatalism, and fundamentalism. Of these, the people questioned showed a significant difference from national norms only in the direction of greater fundamentalism.[50] It is not clear whether subcultural differences that still persist are distinctive of Southern Appalachia rather than of the rural South, of the rural United States generally, or, as a cultural geographer has suggested, of the Upland South.[51]

Too often, social scientists have erroneously sought to measure Appalachian culture against some standard of urban, middle-class values. This is especially a problem when the former is pejoratively pitted against the latter which is seen as an indicator of "modernity" and, implicitly, of moral health. This prevents an understanding of Appalachian culture in its own terms. In Eugene Genovese's *Roll, Jordon, Roll,* an analysis of slave culture in the American South, and in Richard Sennett and Jonathan Cobb's *The Hidden Injuries of Class,* an analysis of ethnic, working-class culture in contemporary Boston, we have exemplary treatments of the dialectical relationship between class position and culture in history.[52] Unfortunately we lack such a comprehensive historical study of Appalachian culture and society, although James Brown and Helen Lewis have provided much insight.

Brown summarizes the orientation of the preindustrial Appalachian culture in three themes: familism (social interaction), puritanism (belief system), and individualism (personality system).[53] In *Mountain Families in Transition* the authors abstract cultural traits from their behavioral expressions which exactly counter the pathogenic qualities so often attributed to the culture of "yesterday's people." In a brilliant article entitled "Family, Religion and Colonialism in Central Appalachia; or Bury My Rifle at Big Stone Gap," Helen Lewis, Sue Kobak, and Linda Johnson interpret more recent developments in Appalachian culture as a response to "the process of colonialization as it occurred in the Central Appalachians."[54] Family and church institutions, in particular, "became defensive and reverted inward in order to protect members from the sudden influence which came with the development of industrialization." Their work suggests that seen in this context, as a localized response beginning at the turn of the century to the national mobilization of population and resources in America to achieve maximum capitalist industrial development, contemporary Appalachian culture can no longer be seen as that of an "arrested frontier." Rather, one sees functional parallels between contemporary Appalachian culture and other such reactive movements as populism in the South, the emergence of ethnic communities in the industrial Northeast, the flight of the white middle class to suburbia in the 1950s in order to preserve the values of small town and family living,[55] the emergence of a "counterculture" among their children in the 1960s, the subsequent flight of many of these children underground or to Canada to avoid the Vietnam War, the recent protest among working-class communities against busing, and even the opposition to imposed textbooks in the rural sections of West Virginia's Kanawha Valley industrial region. All these may be seen as responses to centralizing tendencies of mobilization and massification.

Studies of communities in Southern Appalachia are less advanced than is first apparent. We have some excellent studies of isolated agricultural communities: Marion Pearsall's *Little Smokey Ridge,* Brown's "Beech Creek." But we also have studies of very poor communities presented as typical: Rena Gazaway's "Duddie's Branch," and Bill Surface's *The Hollow.*[56] And then we have three studies of Celo, North Carolina, done in the early and mid-1960s which make little or no reference to each other.[57]

Studies by John Stephenson, Helen Lewis, and others demonstrate the variety of occupational groupings and life-styles within rural communities.[58] Art Gallaher has suggested a typology of communities ranging from extremely isolated rural, less isolated rural with some stores and services, company towns, county seat towns, and major urban areas.[59] The diversity of family, life style, and community types is apparent, in contrast to the stereotypes of the uniform subculture of poverty on the one hand, and the polarization of Appalachian society into the rich and the poor on the other.[60] Among aspects of Appalachian culture and community, family organization has received much attention. The importance of the extended family and kinship groups has been noted in most studies of rural regions in Appalachia, in comparison with the relative isolation of the nuclear family in mainstream society. Brown's study of "Beech Creek" over a thirty-year period has made the greatest contribution to the study of mountain families during the great migration out of the region between 1940 and 1970.

The presentation and analysis of census data on the Appalachian region has long been used to describe the characteristics of the population, the differences within the region, and its lag behind the rest of the nation. Campbell presents data from the 1910 census in *The Southern Highlander;* the USDA study presents data through the early 1930s; the Ford study analyzes the data from 1940 to 1960, and Brown has analyzed the 1970 census.[61] Gordon DeJong has made the most detailed analysis of fertility decline in the region.[62] The *Annual Reports* of the ARC bring the income and employment figures up to date. Recently efforts have been made to assess changes in the "quality of life" in the region.[63]

The study of migration out of and into the Appalachians has been developed in considerable detail. Migration from the region has been a feature since the early 1800s; overlooking this pattern contributes to an exaggerated sense of the isolation of the region during the mid-1800s. People left the mountain areas of Kentucky, Tennessee, and the Carolinas and made their way to the Ozarks, southern Illinois, and Oklahoma.[64] A long-standing migration stream from two sources in the Southern Appalachians to two areas of settlement in western Washington state, two thousand miles away, has been described in detail in Woodrow Clevinger.[65] The migration began around 1880, in connection with the timber industry, hit a peak between 1900 and 1917, and continues to a limited extent even to this day. During the 1930s the central Appalachians experienced a net in-migration stream.[66] The work of Clevinger, Brown, and others has demonstrated the importance of the family system in the migration process. While the major migration streams from the region are known, much remains to be done to identify the streams on a detailed, local, or county level. Related to the literature on Appalachian migration is a variety of material on occupational adjustment to industrial work.[67]

An obvious deficiency in the sociological literature on the Appalachian community is the analysis of work. Despite the growing literature on the "single industry community," we have no good studies on industrial communities in the mountains. The only study of a coal mining community in the United States is Herman Lantz's "Coal Town" in southern Illinois.[68] With the exception of the work of Lewis and Knipe, and studies by Ronald Althouse and Keith Dix, little has been done on the industrial sociology of the coal industry by social scientists. Investigative journalists have accomplished far more in analyzing developments in the coal industry, mine disaster, and the everyday life of coal miners.[69] A fascinating problem in this area of industrial sociology is explaining the success of unionization in the coalfields and its failure in the textile mills. No comparative studies of coal and textile communities have been made, despite the assertion that both share similar subculture and situation of domination.[70]

Toward a Sociology of the Appalachian Future. Much of the research on Southern Appalachia has sought either to discover a romantic past or to proclaim "the eve of an astonishing development."[71] Instead, we need hard sociological thinking about an Appalachian future. For this we need a more adequate historical society in order to recover an authentic mountain past and to gain a critical perspective on current developments. We also need a more comprehensive sociology of culture in order to articulate the values and goals of Appalachian people, especially those who otherwise lack an institutional basis from which to be heard. Such people have not often been listened to by missionaries, developers, and bureaucrats. Finally, we urgently need a study of the landowning and energy-getting elites in Appalachia whose plans, about which we are always so ignorant, often seem inexorable. The likely emergence of a national energy policy and the importance of coal in that policy make this research agenda and the timely voice of Appalachian people all the more imperative.

3

by Alan Banks, Dwight Billings, and Karen Tice

Appalachian Studies, Resistance, and Postmodernism

John Gaventa's remarks, made at the first annual meeting of the Appalachian Studies Conference, were a call for a more constructive relationship between activists and scholars.[1] They were a challenge to produce knowledge useful for democratic empowerment. Gaventa's remarks were also intentionally exaggerated. Good writing about the region was never the exclusive property of a small, committed group of nonacademics. But Gaventa's observations were nonetheless important. They helped give identity to the emerging Appalachian Studies Association (ASA) and shape relations among activists and scholars in and around the region.

Designed from the beginning to "coordinate analysis of the region's problems across disciplinary lines" and to "relate scholarship to regional needs and the concerns of the Appalachian people," the ASA has provided an important context for those who seek to overcome the separateness of regional activists, citizens, and academicians. As the program of the sixth annual ASA meeting in 1984 proudly recalled: "The Appalachian Studies Conference was formed in 1977 by a group of scholars, teachers, and regional activists who believed that shared community has been and will continue to be important for those writing, researching and teaching about things Appalachian." At its best, the ASA has provided a social space where oppositional discourse has flourished. Despite tensions between their goals, the ASA has served as a forum where activists and academics can talk with each other, rather than at each other. It has been a meeting place for people with very different daily pressures and role obligations.

This chapter falls into two main sections. First, we examine the emergence of Appalachian Studies and the Appalachian Studies Association. We argue that both have contributed to grassroots dissent in the region, but we also address intellectual and organizational tendencies that threaten to constrain the ASA's role as an important region-wide forum. Then, we explore the emergence of a new direction in Appalachian Studies—postmodernism. Our objective is to focus upon the political implications that postmodernism may have for those of us in Appalachian Studies who want to build upon

Source: From the Chapter "Appalachian Studies, Resistance and Postmodernism" by Alan Banks, Dwight Billings, and Karen Tice, as it appears in Fighting Back in Appalachia: Traditions of Resistance and Change edited by Stephen L. Fisher. Reprinted by permission of Temple University Press.

the activist traditions that have long sustained our work.

Oppositional Discourse and Appalachian Studies

In Appalachian Studies, research and action have always had an important connection. This is not to say that all perspectives on Appalachia contribute equally to an effort to understand or abolish social inequalities in the region. But ameliorative impulses have predominated, rather than scholarly detachment. Put differently, the research carried out by many Appalachian scholars has not come primarily from the intellectual agenda of academic disciplines, but rather from a regional conversation among activists and scholars. Even the much criticized "culture of poverty" musings in *Yesterday's People* were popularized by a minister working to improve the lives of Appalachian people. Though wrongheaded, Jack Weller's book, like Harry Caudill's *Night Comes to the Cumberlands,* had an important audience among educators, church people, and community development workers. Indeed, Weller's book was handed out among young Appalachian Volunteers and Vista workers entering the region in the late 1960s as a sort of handbook for understanding regional woes, a Peterson's field guide for recognizing Appalachian people on the wing. What concerned subsequent Appalachian scholars, of course, was the way Weller's book stereotyped the region's people as backward folk who existed outside industrial America.[2]

Beginning about 1970, many people began to understand the "problem" of Appalachia in a new way—not as "fatalism," as Weller had maintained, but as "the coal industry." Writing in *Mountain Life & Work,* Helen Lewis helped pioneer an alternative discourse on Appalachia as an economically exploited, politically dominated, and culturally denigrated "internal colony." This new discourse was not the exclusive property of any particular audience. Rather, the colonial interpretation of Appalachian problems had great appeal among scholars, activists, and community people within the region. It helped us see ourselves in a larger social context and visualize a path for collective struggle and resistance.[3]

Over the past twenty years, Appalachian scholars and activists have formed an alliance that has yielded some very impressive results. While this alliance, understandably, has had its uneasy moments, Appalachian activists and scholars have documented a complex history of both "resistance" to and "complicity" with capitalist development in the mountains. Some writers have explored how Appalachian coal miners in the 1920s and 1930s grew into one of the most militant and class-conscious workforces in the United States, building a strong oppositional culture in the mountains and providing national leadership for industrial unionism in the CIO.[4] Other writers have examined a different response to domination and exploitation: quiescence and complicity.[5] Still others have provided important analyses of how both these trends developed in specific mountain communities.[6]

In the context of the ASA, such studies institutionalize a memory of resistance and dissent that otherwise would be erased from the region. They provide a link between research and the grassroots that recognizes the importance of historical struggles in our personal and collective growth. These studies nurture an understanding of social change that rejects the attempts of historical winners to justify the losers' fate as the inevitable result of personality flaws or geography or impersonal market conditions. Such an understanding portrays regional inhabitants as actors with history-making potential. Knowledge that leads to this sort of self-understanding is an important part of what has sustained the regional conversation among intellectuals and activists. It is also the sort of discourse that is indispensable if oppositional movements are to flourish.

In addition to helping preserve the region's history of dissent, Appalachian scholars have also worked with community people to expand current knowledge about the region. One important example comes from the late 1970s. In 1977 the Tug River, located on the Kentucky–West Virginia border, flooded and left thousands homeless. Angered at being forced to live in crowded flood plains because of absentee ownership and frustrated by governments' inability to find alternative sites for relocation, local activists called for support from other regional groups to create a federation of grassroots organizations known as the Appalachian Alliance. In addition to providing an important regionwide forum and publishing educational materials, members of the Alliance helped to launch the Appalachian Land Ownership Task Force. The task force, consisting of both activists and academics, trained indigenous researchers to investigate mineral rights, land ownership, and taxation on over 20 million acres of land in eighty counties spanning six states in the region.[7]

The task force's documentation of vast amounts of minimally taxed land and mineral resources owned by absentee firms spearheaded tax reform efforts in Tennessee and Virginia. It also led to challenges to mineral leasing practices in North Carolina, and was used to persuade the state supreme court in West Virginia to rule that inequitable school funding in that state was unconstitutional. In Kentucky, the information, skills and attitudes gained from the land study helped form the Kentucky Fair Tax Coalition (KFTC). Numbering more than twenty-three hundred members statewide, KFTC (now Kentuckians For The Commonwealth) has helped to reform policy on unmined mineral taxes and won passage of a constitutional amendment prohibiting the use of the notorious "broad form deed" that formerly allowed mineral owners to mine surface owners' property without permission or compensation. Moreover, the indigenous researchers were empowered with new knowledge, new skills, and a new confidence to battle local political and economic elites.

Another constructive example of a scholar-activist partnership can be found in the cultural arena. Many people have worked to overcome the often romantic and contrived characterizations of Appalachian culture and produce an understanding that is supportive of regional identity yet sensitive to the realities of inequality in a world capitalist system. Their general orientation has been to preserve a focus on cultural identity and regional pride while incorporating this understanding into an analysis of the position of Appalachia within a larger political economy.

Knowledge about the region's culture as well as its traditions of dissent and its current problems has been widely disseminated through a proliferating number of Appalachian Studies courses on college campuses across the region. Growing respectability as a multidisciplinary intellectual field has helped to legitimate the development of majors and minors in Appalachian Studies, while student internships have helped to link classroom learning with community needs and realities. The increasing number of Appalachian centers devoted to teaching, research, and service among the region's colleges and universities is another indicator of important new commitments that at least begin to counter the prior neglect of Appalachia by academic institutions.

An off-campus illustration of the benefits of the scholar-activist partnership can be found at Appalshop, a grassroots-based, multimedia production collective located in Whitesburg, Kentucky. Appalshop operates a public radio station and produces documentary films for classroom and community use, musical recordings of important regional talent that otherwise might go unnoticed, and traveling plays that portray positive images of the region and its traditions of dissent. Appalshop artists have made it a policy to work closely with scholars and educators to produce representations of the region that nourish positive identities and broaden political awareness.

Beyond the actual content of research and writing, Appalachian Studies conferences also provide a significant forum for discussing the region's current problems and possibilities. A recent meeting of the ASA included in excess of five hundred participants and a hundred presentations from both grassroots and academic organizations. Institutionalized conversations among activists and scholars provide an important social space for discussions about the region's future. In the same way that shelters for battered women provide a feminist presence in rural Appalachian communities, and community-based mental health centers provide a "meeting place, a public space, and a forum for discussion and decision-making regarding programs for the community,"[8] Appalachian Studies conferences provide a context for important political conversations. In the absence of regionwide organizations that once served to connect grassroots struggles, such as the now defunct Appalachian Alliance and the Council of the Southern Mountains, conferences play a crucial role.

For academics, especially, the Appalachian Studies conferences are a welcome alternative to the high-pressure and intensely specialized meetings of the various academic disciplines. They not only help to sustain scholars' commitment to study Appalachia—a topic often marginalized in the academic disciplines—but also encourage them to relate their professional interests and skills to political issues. The conferences permit broader interdisciplinary conversations than those of other academic associations and help to inform academics about concerns and developments at the grassroots. In addition to formal panels and sessions, informal gatherings of academics, activists, artists, and musicians at the conferences nurture interpersonal connections that help to overcome the insularity and myopia of academic work.

At the same time, however, the increasing academic respect that has been won for Appalachian Studies threatens to undermine some of what has been most unique and healthy about the Association. Most recent participants would agree, and many would regret, that the annual conferences are becoming increasingly academicized. While providing an important outlet for academic studies of Appalachia, recent conferences have begun to give less and less attention to grassroots struggles, and we believe activists have begun to feel less at home there and to find the conferences less relevant to their concerns. Success contributes to this problem, since the proliferation of sessions forces selective participation. With many competing sessions, it is now possible to attend only sessions devoted to one's specialty, whether poetry, social science, or politics. Other than dinner keynote speeches, there are few sessions that compel broad participation and focus attention on the common concerns that originally motivated the establishment of the Association.

From its inception, the ASA has been structured to bridge academic and community terrains. For example, annual meetings alternate between regional college campuses and public parks in the hope that nonacademic participants will be encouraged to attend. An annual Appalachian Youth Conference involving several hundred youths and parents occurs at the same time as the ASA conference and includes several sessions that are integrated with the ASA. Nominations for leadership roles in the ASA have been made to reflect the diversity in the region and the Association. The first African American president of the ASA has recently finished his term in office, and in 1991 members for the first time chose a public school teacher as president. They will hold an upcoming annual conference on the campus of one of the region's high schools.

Such efforts address problems of elitism and racism and show that the collaboration between regional citizens, activists, and academicians is valued by ASA members. But the tendencies toward academicization and compartmentalization will require continuing attention. Such tensions parallel those occurring in other movement-based groups such as Women's Studies that are similarly committed to broad-based struggles against exploitation, domination, and cultural denigration. For example, members of the Women of Color Caucus formally walked out of a recent meeting of the National Women's Studies Association because of institutionalized racism. Trisha Franzen and Lois Helmbold report: "The NWSA leadership acted as if the organization had already done its anti-racism work, and the trust that NWSA was committed to anti-racism was like a title granted for life, not something which could be re-examined."[9] The

ASA, too, must consciously struggle to sustain itself as a forum for oppositional politics.

Not only will the ASA have to address the problems of academicization and the politics of gender, race, and class, but it will need to confront the possibilities and pitfalls engendered by the turn toward postmodernism. Just as Teresa Ebert asserts that "postmodernism has become an unavoidable issue for feminists—activists and theorists alike,"[10] we believe that postmodernism, primarily because of its stress on difference and diversity, is beginning to open up new possibilities for thinking and writing about Appalachia. At the same time, postmodernism complicates the politics of coalition-building within the ASA and the region.

What Is Postmodernism?

The meaning of "postmodernism" is hotly debated in the arts, literature, philosophy, and social sciences. Some writers view postmodernism as an entirely new era of history and a new form of society.[11] They picture a society marked by fragmentation and heterogeneity, where Star Wars and Disney World replace social reality and substitute for meaning. Others interpret postmodernism less grandly as the ideological expression of the "cultural logic" of mass-consumer capitalism.[12] Still others view postmodernism even more narrowly as simply as artistic or narrative style. We choose to think about postmodernism as a new sensibility that involves a heightened and healthy skepticism about truth claims. "Postmodernism," as the feminist scholar Michelle Barret puts it, "is a cultural climate as well as an intellectual position, a political reality as well as an academic fashion."[13] This way of understanding postmodernism has important implications for how people think and write about the world, including Appalachia.

The postmodern sensibility calls into question common-sense notions about thinking (reason) and how thoughts are expressed (representation). With Clifford Geertz, we take postmodernism to be a new "way of thinking about the way we think." This new sensibility entails "not just another redrawing of the cultural map . . . but an alteration of the principles of mapping."[14] In Appalachian Studies, such new mapping principles have important political implications for how we think about and represent Appalachian regional identities as well as for the relationship between scholars and grassroots activism.

The modern understanding of thinking—which postmodernism leaves behind—came into being most fully during the eighteenth-century Enlightenment. It took the objectivity of reason as an article of faith. Enlightenment philosophers assumed that human reason was the vehicle that would lead to progressive social change, the means through which people could throw off their chains. For example, when Thomas Jefferson and the other signers of the Declaration of Independence justified the American colonies' secession from Great Britain in terms of "truths" they held "to be self evident," they expressed the belief that reason's truths were readily apparent to all who could think for themselves—all those, that is, freed from the blinders of dogma and tradition.[15]

What we are calling "postmodernism" signals an end to this faith in reason and its effects. As the authors of *Brave New World* and *1984* depict, and as Hiroshima and Auschwitz symbolize, rationality has deeply penetrated most aspects of life in modern society, yet it has failed to secure life, liberty, and happiness. We are left in a position where rationality without reason permeates all aspects of social life, where schooling is informative but not enlightening, where work is sustaining but not humanizing, and agriculture is efficient but not sustainable.[16]

As early as the late nineteenth century, Friedrich Nietzsche, whose ideas were a precursor to postmodernism, challenged the "god's eye" view of truth that was taken for granted by the Enlightenment in general and science in particular, noting that it presupposes "an eye such as no living creature can imagine, an eye required to have no direction, to abrogate its active and interpretive powers—precisely those powers alone that make seeing, seeing something." Thus, according to Nietzsche, "all seeing is essentially perspective, and so is all knowing."[17] Since Nietzsche, the idea that truth is always and inevitably relative to one's cultural standpoint has been widely advanced. We have come to understand, for instance, that the natural sciences do not operate with an objective god's eye. Scientific "facts" are not independently existing realities waiting "out there" to be discovered but rather are produced through the application of theories, assumptions, conventions, methods, procedures, and beliefs held by the scientific community.[18] In this view, science, no less than any other art or discipline, is understood to be a culturally conditioned way of acting upon the world, of seeing as well as not seeing. In large measure, "what we call postmodern philosophy today is precisely about questioning the fundamental authority of science."[19] Consequently, as science loses the aura of absolute certainty that once seemed to privilege it among other ways of knowing, the demarcations between science, the humanities, the arts, and other cultural belief systems become unsure. These fields, as Geertz notes, become "blurred genres."[20]

Besides making explicit the cultural givens and practices that make thinking possible, postmodernism also refutes the naive idea that meaning precedes representation. Rather than being transparent vessels that convey truths without influencing their content, representations help to shape what can be seen and thus accepted as true. As Hayden White observes, "in any account of reality"—whether its genre is science, history, or fiction—"narrativity is present." He adds that "every narrative, however seemingly full, is constructed on the basis of a set of events which might have been included but were left out."[21]

One example of the importance of narrativity is a recent representation of Appalachia by David Cattell-Gordon as "a [regionwide] culturally transmitted traumatic stress syndrome."[22] Heavily indebted to the views of Appalachia espoused by Caudill and Weller, this account of "the effects of [Appalachian] history" as social trauma "bred in the bones of the people of the region" is flawed because it constitutes Appalachians solely as "victims" and obscures the potentiality of diverse subjects' making history. In particular, oppositional movements and actions are excluded from the narrative, thereby minimizing the possibilities for agency and empowerment. Such an account leaves unquestioned pardigmatic views of Appalachia that have the effect of either marginalizing and excluding Appalachians as fully human beings or else treating them as a monolithic category. In contrast to Cattell-Gordon's clinical portrait, a postmodern sensibility would suggest that a more kaleidoscopic view of culture and history is essential for capturing the complexity of Appalachia's past and potential.

Many writers are troubled by postmodernism's abandonment of the unitary vision of objective truth in favor of unapologetically partial viewpoints. Some interpret postmodernism as "cultural helplessness," claiming that "postmodernism is above all post-1960s. . . . It is post–Viet Nam, post–New Left, post-hippie, post-Watergate . . . [where] belief has become difficult."[23] Others are even more critical, claiming that the "corrosive skepticism and nihilism" of most postmodernist thinking "disables both theoretical inquiry and political practice."[24] We reject such harshly critical views of postmodernism. Like Geertz, we discern "a distinctly democratic temper" in postmodernism's "fluid, plural, uncentered, and ineradicably untidy" approach.[25] Thus, we see postmodernism as having the potential to point Appalachian Studies in some important new directions. In particular, we believe that a cautious use of postmodern insights can guide our efforts in making sure that Appalachian Studies continues to be one of the region's voices of dissent.

The Postmodern Challenge: Avoiding Universalism and Essentialism

Appalachian Studies and Women's Studies both emerged as prominent features of university life in the 1970s in response to democratic impulses at the grassroots level in the late 1960s. Both have struggled with how to critique widespread stereotypes, accommodate the plurality of experiences and perspectives among participants, and further the common goals of academics and activists in struggles for social justice. We believe that the feminists' extensive wrestling with postmodernism, its political implications for feminist practice, and its place in the academy has much to contribute to Appalachian Studies. Applications include not only how to incorporate an understanding of gender into our work on Appalachia, but also how to think about regional identities in new and less restrictive ways.

Increasingly, many feminists are beginning to represent the social world in a postmodern manner in order to avoid explanations that are universalistic. These feminists question the validity of any unitary ways of knowing that claim to understand and describe the complexity of social relations in a totalistic fashion. Such universalistic knowledge claims and truth assertions—"metanarratives"—are rejected as reductionistic and ahistorical. As Nancy Fraser and Linda Nicholson note, feminists are calling into question "the dominant [modernist] philosophical project of seeking objectivity in the guise of a god's eye view which transcends any situation or perspective."[26]

As power conversations or privileged discourses, metanarratives are the ideological manifestations of inequitable social relations. In the case of gender, they falsely universalize white male expressions and experiences and, at the same time, peripheralize the diverse experiences of women. Instead, many feminist scholars are taking a more kaleidoscopic point of view that does not collapse the multiplicity of women's experiences, preoccupations, and expressions into the universal woman. They debunk descriptions that lump women into a monolithic category by exploring not only commonalities but differences among women.[27]

Thus, as postmodernists, feminist scholars have grown deeply suspicious of any descriptions of women and men, minorities, or humanity in general—and here we should add regions and regional populations—that rely on a universal image, model, norm, or method. They challenge as ideological assertions that repress multiplicity and diversity. Feminists also advocate a "deconstructive strategy" that takes apart falsely unified conceptions such as "women"—or, in our case, "Appalachians"—in order to reveal the internal diversity and plurality that such representations mask.

These feminist scholars are calling for approaches that are non-universalistic, self-conscious about perspective and values, and open to the multiplicity and diversity of experiences. If applied to Appalachian Studies, this approach would challenge us to replace unitary notions of Appalachians and Appalachian identity with plural and complexly constructed conceptions of social identity. The paradigmatic Appalachian would thus be replaced by a conception that represents Appalachian regional identities—these being decidedly plural—as "one strand among others, attending also to class, race, ethnicity, age, and sexual orientation . . . in short . . . more like a tapestry composed of many threads of many hues than one woven in a single color."[28]

Internal Heterogeneity

In addition to a critique of universalistic thinking that represses the diversity of experiences among Appalachian peoples, postmodern feminist scholars can also teach us to challenge essentialistic thinking about Appalachia. "Essentialism" is the tendency to treat historical and social constructions as "fixed, natural, and absolute."[29] Essentialistic thinking further tends to reduce complex relations to fixed, and often binary, oppositions that are hierarchically ordered. In Appalachian Studies, we are accustomed to thinking in terms of such oppositions as Appalachian/non-Appalachian, insider/outsider, scholars/activists, culture folk/action folk. In such cases, interrelatedness is reduced to sets of either/ors. Postmodernism challenges us to rethink these taken-for-granted categories and to ask instead how they are constituted in historically situated social relations.

Taken together, opposition to universalistic and essentialistic thinking provides Appalachian Studies with avenues to transform our knowledge base and inform our practice of regional politics. In the remainder of this chapter, we wish to highlight steps in this direction already evident in Appalachian Studies.

Postmodern Directions in Appalachian Studies

Several recent contributions to the Appalachian literature advance a postmodern sensibility. Herbert Reid, for instance, challenges the either/or of class versus culture in Appalachian Studies by suggesting how a "critical and viable concept of [Appalachian] regionalism" can be developed that does not obscure the continuities between regional and national cultural life as well as cultural and class differences within the region. Ron Lewis and Sally Maggard discount, respectively, the either/ors of class versus race and class versus gender in studies of the interplay of the lived experiences of gender, race, and class stratification in the Appalachian coalfields. John Gaventa, Barbara Smith, and Alex Willingham connect struggles for economic justice and alternative forms of economic development in Appalachia to similar grassroots struggles in other parts of the South and to national patterns of deindustrialization.[30]

Perhaps the earliest and, in many ways, still the most radically postmodern study of Appalachia is Henry Shapiro's *Appalachia on Our Mind*. Shapiro's intellectual history of the "idea of Appalachia" does much to deconstruct the "mythic system" that interprets Appalachia as "a coherent region with a uniform culture and homogenous population." Shapiro shows that the representation of the Appalachian population as "a distinct people with distinct and describable characteristics" owes much to a stereotyped tradition of writing about life in the southern mountains that originated in late nineteenth-century local color fiction as well as in missionaries' accounts depicting Appalachia as "a strange land and a peculiar people."[31]

The radical implications of Shapiro's work for Appalachian Studies are overlooked when his text is read simply as providing empirical support for an essentialistic and reductionistic understanding of Appalachia as a "colony." In such accounts, an essentialistic understanding of Appalachia as a traditional or poverty subculture is replaced by an equally essentialistic understanding of Appalachia as an exploited colony. But Shapiro does much more than simply document the imperialistic practices of missionaries and social workers in the region's past. By remaining skeptical about the existence of any essential Appalachian experience or unitary Appalachian identity, Shapiro calls attention to how mythical versions of Appalachia are produced every day in discursive representations of the region. Thus he highlights the fact that activists and scholars produce partial versions of reality every time they write about or act in the name of Appalachia. The obvious shortcoming of Shapiro's work, however, is that there is more to Appalachia than simply language about the region.[32] Thus, his work overlooks the nondiscursive realities in the region: real-life events such as death and injury in the mines; black lung and brown lung; economic exploitation, poverty, and unemployment; gender and racial oppression. The problem that Shapiro's study of representation raises is how to deconstruct universalizing and essentializing myths of Appalachia while sustaining viable forms of regional politics.

A partially successful effort in this direction combines Shapiro's stress on how Appalachia is represented in discourses with large narratives about changes in social organization. Rodger Cunningham's *Apples on the Flood* is a sophisticated and deeply probing application of the colonial model of Appalachia and an extended essay on the cultural and psychological consequences of peripheralization.[33] Its thesis is that the internalization of pejorative discourses and opinions about Appalachia by Appalachians results in their infantilization and the development of damaged selves. Such a "psychological heredity" would undoubtedly have important negative implications for contemporary Appalachians' ability to make their own history and organize themselves collectively to resist exploitation and oppression. Floating like apples on the tide of historical circumstances, today's

Appalachians are tragically portrayed by Cunningham as damaged souls—in the final analysis, victims of the pernicious effects of modernity itself—who are overidentified with their oppressors and closed off from an authentic and self-centered existence.

In style—but not in substance—Cunningham's work partakes of the new postmodern sensibility we have been describing. The author deliberately blurs the genres of anthropology, history, psychology, folklore, sociology, and comparative literature to produce an ambiguous and challenging text that defies categorization as factual social history, social science, fiction, or autobiography. He calls attention to the power of representations by showing how they operate through internalization in the social psychology of colonialism, and he directs attention toward their operation in his own text by pointing out his own narrative strategies and the effects he hopes them to have upon his readers. But in marked contrast with postmodern writers who deliberately produce ambiguous, contradictory, and open-ended texts in order to "destabilize stable ways of looking at the world" and to include the reader as an active participant in constructing the various meanings a text may come to have,[34] Cunningham supplies fixed and final answers in his portrayal of a paradigmatic Appalachia. In doing so, he subverts his own wish for Appalachian peoples to be the authors of their own identities by succumbing to the temptation of writing a metanarrative from a god's eye perspective no less Olympian than that of Caudill and Weller, of whom he is critical.

Whereas Shapiro critically examines the pejorative discourses that constitute the "myth of Appalachia," Cunningham's exploration of the psychological consequences of the internalization of such discourses has the effect of universalizing and essentializing his understanding of the Scotch-Irish experience in a manner that reduces the complexity and openendedness of Appalachian experiences to a static and bleakly pessimistic caricature: Li'l Abner with a severely neurotic personality.[35]

Just as women, blacks, and the Eastern European miners of West Virginia and eastern Kentucky are erased from Cunningham's narrative of Appalachian history, so too is the likelihood of resistance and dissent. And having presented a deterministic account of "the present mainly as a product of past forces" and admittedly told "only half the story," Cunningham's only way out lies in "the liberating power of true myth." Thus an author "repelled . . . by [Appalachian] social activists' tendency to dismiss, ignore, or pigeonhole cultural questions" in the early seventies dispatches activism to the "realm of imagination."[36]

We believe that the solution to Cunningham's dilemma—how to convey the interrelationship of politics and culture in Appalachia—lies in adopting a postmodern view of culture. In contrast to Cunningham's essentialistic understanding of culture as a singular "structure of meanings," we suggest the value of Jerome Bruner's conceptualization of culture as "a forum for negotiating and renegotiating meaning." According to Bruner, "it is the forum aspect of culture that gives its participants a role in constantly making and remaking the culture—an active role as participants rather than as performing spectators who play out their canonical roles according to rule when the appropriate cues occur."[37] This nonessentialistic view of culture allows for multiplicity and diversity at the same time that it recognizes culture as providing ample resources for its participants to engage in the sort of "identity politics" modeled above by contemporary feminists.

Stephen Foster's recent study, *The Past Is Another Country,*[38] makes exemplary use of such a model of culture in an investigation of grassroots resistance in Appalachia that is premised on an appreciation of Appalachia's cultural diversity. Rather than presenting a fixed image of local culture as a set of collective traits, Foster documents the "politics of culture" in Ashe County, North Carolina—that is, the changing and strategic discourses of self- and community representation. From this perspective Foster remarks that the local culture "appears in this context as extraordinarily fluid and changeable; it operates as a placeholder, a representation that shifts, deviates, and often wobbles in an unstable and quixotic fashion, depending on the desires, options, constraints, and interventions operating at the crossroads of the present."[39]

In his analysis of the successful efforts of local citizens in 1975 to prevent the Appalachian Power Company from damming a portion of the New River to create a reservoir that would have displaced 287 families, Foster examines local resistance as a "politics of representation." In stark contrast to Cunningham's interpretation that the "mountaineer's notorious 'present-orientation'" is evidence of his "being cut off from the past," Foster highlights the practices whereby Ashe County citizens objectified a version of their culture and their past to planners and outside policymakers as a way of life worth preserving. Here, the "domination of imposed discourses of economic necessity and economic interest" by elites were countered by local folk festivals that served both to mobilize support to "save the river" and to objectify local culture. Ironically, however, by choosing to represent their threatened way of life in terms of stereotyped images, folk-culture artifacts, and music, grassroots activists opened the door to the commodification of a partial version of their culture and thus potentially to further elite domination. Foster returned to Ashe County nearly ten years later to find that the embrace of mythic forms of ethnic identify that had served to stop the dam project had also begun to change the rhetorical forms through which local people understood themselves, their history, and their community.

Foster's image of culture as a discursive forum rather than a configuration of traits or a unitary structure of meaning should alert us in Appalachian Studies to the variety of discourses that constitute social identity as well as to the diversity of subjects actively involved in making history in Appalachia. Further, his refusal to describe local culture the way it "really" is, in any fixed or final way—that is, his refusal to write a "metanarrative"—exemplified the postmodern ethnographic ideal of "apprehend[ing] and inscrib[ing] 'others' in such a way as not to deny or diffuse their claims to subjecthood."[40] As such, his study provides not only important insights into problematic aspects of grassroots activism but also a model for how Appalachian scholars can learn to write about the region without succumbing to the temptation of speaking like the invisible, know-it-all "over-voice" that is a commonplace in television advertising and mass media broadcasting.

Conclusion

In challenging the notion that writers can attain a god's eye view of truth and represent reality in its totality, postmodernism has the potential to make all of us, activists and scholars, more humble and reflective about what we claim and assert. From the recognition that "truths" are always "truths for some particular person or group," it follows that our commonsense notions of what "Appalachia" is, or who "Appalachians" are, can always be opened up to include more diversity or, as postmodernists like to say, more "difference." Yet, as many feminists have been forced to admit, the recognition of difference and diversity is a political challenge. As Teresa Ebert notes, the recognition of differences among women "opens up the multiplicity of differences among (within) women, but in doing so it undermines the unity or collectivity of women and gender as categories on which an oppositional politics can be based."[41] The achievement of diversity and unity can only result from political effort.

The recognition of difference—indeed, the positive valorization of difference—that postmodern thinking encourages should help us to appreciate that what we have been doing in the Appalachian Studies movement and in the Appalachian Studies Association has been a positive yet fragile accomplishment. Still, if the Appalachian Studies movement is to fulfill its promise of "help[ing] to reconstruct a public sphere through which people can participate in democratizing the structures of political economy and everyday life,"[42] difference and diversity must be further embraced and accommodated. Mythical images of a homogeneous Appalachia must not be allowed to suppress the important class, race, ethnic, and gender differences that figure in the life of the region. Likewise, the organizational structures and processes of the ASA must be revised in ways that support such diversity.

Ours, as we have seen, is not the only scholarly association to face new organizational tensions that result from growth and success and raise concerns about how to remain connected to founding ideals—the grassroots basis of our common identity and purpose. Many current tensions in the ASA mirror those in other movement-based organizations that are likewise committed to supporting democratic struggles. For instance, Lisa Hall has observed that the linkages between community- and academically based participants in women's studies and ethnic studies have weakened. "Academic feminism and ethnic studies as a whole," she says, "have not maintained the direct connections with the communities that helped to create them."[43]

Organizational reforms within the ASA itself may help to combat the trend toward academicization and contribute to the preservation and strengthening of ties between the Appalachian Studies movement and the grassroots. If ASA conferences are becoming too large and its sessions too specialized, then noncompetitive plenary sessions, arranged to include scholarly activists and activist scholars, can be used to front-stage important conversations that have regionwide implications. Ideally, annual conferences—now typically coordinated by local colleges—could be cosponsored by local grassroots organizations that would conduct off-site sessions highlighting local issues and struggles and thus challenging the ASA to reaffirm its original goal of relating scholarship to regional needs and the concerns of Appalachian people. The steering committee that governs the association, increasingly peopled by academicians, can change its membership criteria to create formal slots for individuals representing grassroots organizations, while caucuses can be organized to reflect and encourage diversity within the general membership. We hope that such small but self-conscious efforts can help to keep alive an important form of cooperation in the region that has great potential to contribute further to Appalachian and American public life.

4

by Henry D. Shapiro

Appalachia and the Idea of America: The Problem of the Persisting Frontier

Since the 1870s, Americans have regarded Appalachia as a strange land inhabited by a peculiar people. Defined by its culture as well as by geography, Appalachia has seemed an anomaly in an otherwise unified and homogeneous nation, a discrete region, in but not of America. As such it has generally been ignored, or at most viewed as a quaint and interesting land where moonshiners and feudists live in log cabins and speak the stately language of Elizabethan England, while their wives spin and weave and sing traditional ballads of kings and queens and ravens sitting on fences. From time to time, however, the existence of Appalachia has been brought more or less forcibly to the attention of Americans living outside the region. At such times the peculiarities of mountain life, in whatever terms they are defined at the particular moment, have become troublesome facts requiring explanation, and Americans have been forced to consider the possible implications of Appalachia's existence for their own understanding of the nature of American civilization.

Our own is such a time, of course. In the context of our recent discovery of poverty in the United States, Appalachia has come to epitomize that "other America" of which Michael Harrington wrote, the antithesis of an America defined by economic growth and technological achievement. As a symbol of the existence of pockets of poverty in an affluent society, Appalachia has in fact had a clear advantage over more ephemeral examples of the same phenomenon—those populations which we designate in statistical rather than human terms as "the poor" and to which we thereby deny any existence except that in the minds of demographers. Appalachia is physically real as well as statistically real. It has location and a history—and a history of poverty. Its poverty too has a history and, like Appalachia, can not be expected to disappear with increasing national prosperity.

In the last decade, as a consequence, we have rediscovered Appalachia, and have been faced once again with the need to explain the persistent discrepancy between life in the Southern mountain region and life in the rest

Source: Reprinted from *An Appalachian Symposium,* J. W. Williamson (ed.). Copyright Appalachian State University Press, 1977, pp. 43–55. Used by permission.

of the United States. Such explanation has been easy, however. Having defined Appalachia as a land characterized by permanent poverty, we may regard the disparity between Appalachia and America as a difference of degree, not of kind. In Appalachia there is less money, less opportunity for the accumulation of money, and consequently less of what money can provide, to individuals and to the community, than is normal in the rest of the nation. Seen in these terms, Appalachian culture becomes the culture of a depressed area and hence a temporary phenomenon, however permanent the conditions which create it may be. We are thus obliged to deal only with the historical causes of Appalachia's poverty, and with the anomaly of pockets of poverty in an affluent society. Because we have so severely restricted our vision of the relationship of Appalachia and America, in other words, we need not face the kind of situation which might challenge our conception of America as a land of opportunity, where economic growth is natural, or of American civilization as unified and homogeneous.[1]

America's relationship with Appalachia has not always been so simple, however. From the late nineteenth century, when the mountainous portions of eight Southern states were first recognized as composing a discrete region, at least through the 1920s, the existence of this strange land and peculiar people raised questions about the nature of American civilization itself. Discovered in the 1870s by local color writers who used it as a neutral ground against which to set their stories of upper-class romance and lower-class passion, by the end of the century Appalachia had come to seem a stubborn outpost of that quintessentially American way of life which industrialism and urbanism were destroying. Indeed, Appalachia was unique among the "little corners" of the nation which came to the public's attention via the local color movement, in that its peculiarities, although identified as characteristic of the American past, were observed in the American present. The tendency to glorify America's past, which has been the typical accompaniment of our most assiduous efforts to abandon that past, gave the peculiarities of Appalachian life a rather special meaning and value during the last years of the century, to the degree that these were identified with the culture and customs of earlier days. From this point of view, the transformation of Appalachia by the forces of modernization and homogenization could only be regarded with ambiguity or downright despair, while the persistence of pioneer virtues among the isolated mountaineers made them seem a rebuke to an effete generation and a possible leaven for the nation.[2]

It was the absence of modern economic institutions and modern social patterns which had first attracted the local color writers to Appalachia—physically for purposes of rustication at the resort areas of the New South and imaginatively as a field to be mined for literary material.[3] Between 1870 and 1890, at the very beginning of the literary exploitation of the region, at least one hundred twenty-five short stories and more than ninety sketches dealing with the nature of mountain life were published.[4] As one of the areas of the nation "least affected by the progress of a growing national unity"[5] and yet within close proximity to the very centers of the nationalizing process, Appalachia seemed inherently interesting, even while its topography and natural history, and the peculiar folkways of its inhabitants, made it seem romantic and picturesque.

The dominance of the literary imagination in this first discovery of Appalachia was of great significance. Not only did it establish as conventional an essentially literary vision of the Southern mountain region as a strange land inhabited by a peculiar people, over the view of those who saw in the mountains only unlimited possibilities for economic development,[6] but it made literary criteria primary in analyses of mountain life and of the relationship of Appalachia and America. Even such non-literary types as Nathaniel Southgate Shaler, the Kentucky-born Harvard geologist, and George E. Vincent, a University of Chicago sociologist, directed their efforts more at achieving an elegance of style than at careful and complete discussion of mountain conditions. Among the literary folk, on the other hand, Charles Dudley Warner, from the security of an established literary reputation and with an image as Connecticut sophisticate to maintain, was virtually alone in daring to admit that mountain poverty was as dull and unpleasant as any other kind of poverty, from the point of view of participants and observers both.[7] In the literature of Appalachia, as a consequence, metaphor characteristically did the work of exposition. Because it was more interesting, the "as if" was preferred to the "is," and came eventually to be identified as reality.

It was this tendency which may be said to have given America's image of Appalachia its particular form. Those first on the scene noted with some surprise that the mountaineers lived under the rude conditions of a pioneer generation. Those next on the scene sought to turn a literary trick, and in emphasizing the picturesque qualities of life in the region suggested that a journey there was like a journey into America's past—"you detach yourself from all that you have experienced, and take up the history of English speaking men and women at the point it had reached a hundred or a hundred and fifty years ago."[8] It was an easy next step to the identification of the Appalachian present with the American past as a matter of fact, not merely of metaphor. By the end of the century, the literature on Appalachia asked with all seriousness how this enclave of pioneer culture has been preserved against the ravages of time and of progress, and how most effectively to assist the mountaineers in leaping a hundred years from their present to the present of the rest of the nation. The mountaineers had become "our pioneer ancestors."[9]

It is at this point that one may speak of the emergence of a tension between Appalachia and America. Appalachia had come to represent America's past, a past of heroism and self-sacrifice, hard work and commitment, by which independence had been won and preserved, the Union defended, a continent subdued. It was a past in which giants walked the earth, with axe and Bible in hand. It was in any case America's own past, and hence not to be discredited lightly. From the late 1880s on, as a consequence, one may see a persistent ambiguity toward the peculiarities of mountain life in the literature on Appalachia. To the degree that these were conceived as the undesirable consequences of poverty and isolation, they were regarded with contempt, or with that "sympathetic understanding" which precedes remedial action. To the degree that they were conceived as survivals of an earlier pattern of culture, however, they were respected as different but acceptable, or even held up for emulation by a modern generation out of touch with its past and hence with the essential national temper. Ambiguity towards the peculiarities of Appalachian life involved more than America's response to the existence of this particular region, however. Ultimately it precipitated a confrontation with the fact of social and geographic diversity in the present.

Perhaps the most striking aspect of Appalachia's strangeness to those Americans who discovered the region at the end of the nineteenth century was the apparent absence in mountain culture of conceptions of law and order, and of "correct" notions of the relationship of the individual and society, as manifested by the apparent prevalence of feuding and the manufacture of blockade or "moonshine" whiskey. The disregard for duly constituted authority which these phenomena implied was an overt indication of the disparity between mountain life and the more normal life of the rest of America. "A shock falls across the . . . mind to realize that such a community of lawlessness should exist in a country that calls itself civilized," one commentator noted after reading John Fox, Jr.'s fictional reconstruction of "A Cumberland Vendetta."[10] More important, the occurrence of feuding and moonshining helped crystallize a growing sense, based originally on the impressionistic accounts of travellers and short-story writers, that Appalachia was indeed a discrete region, in but not of America.

Conflicts between mountaineers and revenue officers over enforcement of the excise tax on whiskey were reported in the periodical press as early as 1867. It was in the next two decades, however, as the more general interest in Appalachia developed, that real attention was paid to moonshining as one of the peculiarities of mountain life.[11] At issue was not so much the illegality of unlicensed distilleries, however, but the quaintness of this aspect of domestic economy as it persisted in the mountains. By the 1890s, moonshining had become so integral an element in the popular concept of Appalachia that discussion of the phenomenon, often coupled with a defense of such illegal activities on historical grounds, became virtually a requirement in descriptive pieces dealing with the region, while an escape from, or an attack by "revenooers" similarly became a conventional incident in mountain fiction. Suggestive of conventional literary images of banditti or outlaws caught in a historical process which they could neither understand nor control, these fictional confrontations between moonshiners and "foreigners" representing the legal and social standards of the larger community functioned to epitomize the tension between Appalachia and America, while reinforcing the accepted notion of Appalachia's historical character.

Feuds in the Southern mountains aroused less interest outside the region during this early period, at a time when such private wars could be dismissed as natural extensions of hostilities engendered by the Civil War. By the mid-1880s, feuding incidents began to appear with some frequency in short fictional pieces set in the mountains, as well as in descriptive sketches of mountain life, and by the end of the century the prevalence of feuding had become a conventional element in the popular conception of Appalachia as a strange land inhabited by a peculiar people. Like moonshining, feuding was viewed as a picturesque if somewhat unfortunate aspect of life in that isolated region of the nation, and was explained in historical terms as the result of the persistence of primitive social conditions and a correspondingly primitive form of social control, or else as the result of a persisting tendency toward violence among Southerners.

The outbreak of a new series of family wars around the turn of the century, and the subsequent extension of what had first appeared as private conflict into the arena of public affairs, involving local and then state and interstate politics, brought feuding as an aspect of mountain life to the attention of the nation in a new way.[12] Like moonshining, this new outbreak of feuds involved the mountaineers in a direct confrontation with the world of more normal American behavior, and in particular with the outsiders' institutions of social control. While the possibility of romanticization existed, then, to the degree that the feuds involved persons outside the immediate mountain community, the requirements of the social order in maintaining its viability demanded that this particular aspect of mountain life be defined pejoratively as "lawlessness," even as it demanded that the feudists themselves be convicted as lawbreakers and sentenced to terms in the penitentiary. More important from our point of view, however, accounts of the feuds which flourished around the turn of the century, when combined with the widely accepted notion of the prevalence of illegal distilling in the mountains, precipitated a redefinition of Appalachia as a land of violence and lawlessness.[13]

In and of itself this new emphasis involved nothing more than a more sharply focused conception of the nature of Appalachian otherness. A kind of aesthetic distance continued to separate the mountaineers as objects of popular interest from the writers and social workers who went among them and described their peculiar habits to the rest of America. In the context of a conventional description of the mountaineers as "our contemporary ancestors" and of mountain violence as a survival from an earlier stage of historical development, however, the identification of Appalachia as a lawless land created a dilemma within the American dialogue on the meaning of Appalachia's existence, and raised questions concerning the nature of American civilization as well. Over against an idyllic vision of mountaineers as hard-working pioneers, dependent on their own resources and initiative, was placed what seemed to be a more realistic picture, of pioneer individualism as anarchy, and self-help as anti-social behavior. If private justice yielded public chaos, if private enterprise involved the rejection of public morality, were our pioneer ancestors like our "contemporary ancestors," merely brawlers and brigands?

By the beginning of the twentieth century, of course, there were many who were quite prepared to admit that America's pioneer past was one of violence and anarchic individualism, preferring for that very reason the more civilized present in which egoism had given way to altruism. Indeed, that may well be said to have been the point of much of the rhapsodizing over vanishing frontiers which took place around the turn of the century. It was in any case a position commonly taken by writers on Appalachia in the early years of the twentieth century, and especially by those connected with agencies of social uplift for whom the persistence of the past into the present created irony rather than ambiguity. To them the historical character of mountain life was kind of bad joke on the mountaineers, as well as a sign of their pressing need for assistance so that they might cast off a discredited or at least a useless past, and join the rest of the nation in the present.[14]

The identification of violence and lawlessness in the Southern mountains as a survival of the American past, which consistent definition of the mountaineers as "our contemporary ancestors" demanded, did create a dilemma nonetheless. What this meant in practice was that explanation of feuding and moonshining by reference to an historical situation came to be seen as inadequate or, to the degree that it unbalanced the equation of a known present and a presumed past, unsatisfactory. In the early twentieth century, as a consequence, two new emphases appeared in discussions of mountain life, which may be seen as responses to the conceptual dilemma which conditions of lawlessness in Appalachia created. The first of these involved identification of the more violent aspects of mountain life as European rather than American in origin, thus permitting continued utilization of the doctrine of survivals while maintaining a traditional conception of the American past as rude but law-abiding. The second involved abandonment of the doctrine of survivals entirely and a new emphasis, in accord with general trends of early twentieth-century social theory, on environment as the determinant of social and cultural patterns. In these terms, Appalachia was seen to be characterized by frontier conditions but was no longer defined as The Frontier.

From the publication in 1878 of Rev. James Craighead's *Scotch and Irish Seeds in American Soil,*[15] the mountaineers of Appalachia were conventionally assumed to be the descendants of Scottish and Scotch-Irish settlers from western North Carolina and Pennsylvania. This was a view which appealed particularly to the home-mission propagandists of the Presbyterian Church, who were enabled thereby to add the responsibilities of blood relationship to the humanitarian appeal of need in requesting funds for benevolent work among the mountaineers. Non-Presbyterians found the notion equally appealing, however. In part this was because it agreed with conventional notions about the patterns of westward migration during the eighteenth century, but in part this was also the case because it identified the independent mountaineer with that group of colonists conventionally assumed to be the most "independent" in America's eighteenth-century population. The definition of mountain life as a survival of pioneer life was thus reinforced, albeit in a slightly different way.

It was with particular reference to the occurrence of feuds in the mountains that the somewhat ambiguous designation of the mountaineers as "American Highlanders" occurred, however, in an address by Secretary Charles J. Ryder of the Congregationalist American Missionary Association. "No other term so aptly describes these mountaineers as does Highlanders," Ryder noted in 1897:

> They have Highland clans with Highland chieftains at the head of them. Highland feuds flame out now and again, often bringing death and ruin. Not only topographically but also socially the term of the American Highlanders fittingly describes these mountaineers. The relationship between the Lowlanders of the South and the Highlanders is also much the same as that which obtained [N.B.] between the same classes in Scotland. . . . In general

> character and in physical endurance the comparison between the Highlanders of Scotland and America holds good.[16]

During the early years of the twentieth century, an increasing consciousness of violence as a characteristic of mountain life facilitated the transformation of Ryder's metaphor into a picture of reality, and the mountaineer as Highlander took his place alongside the mountaineer as contemporary ancestor in discussions of Appalachia. By 1916, John M. Moore's classic mission-study text, *The South To-Day,* could complain that "the peculiarities of an individualistic people have been interpreted as hideous deficiencies." In fact, Moore asserted, the mountaineer was "the pure Scotch-Irishman, and in manners, beliefs, and speech his lineage can be traced. . . . I found that Scott and Stevenson in their tales of the Campbells and MacGregors were describing the parties that were appearing in the later roles of feudists in Kentucky. The heads of feuds were no more ordinary men in Kentucky than in Scotland."[17] Feuding and moonshining, and a general proclivity to violent and lawless behavior, were thus explained as the result of a particular ethnic heritage rather than of an essentially lawless strain in the American national character, which the identification of violence as a survival of pioneer ways seemed to suggest. More desirable aspects of mountain life might continue to be identified with the American past, and hence be seen as quintessentially American, while the mountaineer himself was maintained in the morally neutral ground of middle-class romanticism.

The use of an environmental explanation for the peculiarities of Appalachia functioned in a similar way, as response to the dilemma which the occurrence of feuds and moonshining presented. Unlike explanation in terms of survivals, however, it did not emerge from within the American dialogue on the meaning of Appalachia as a result of the transformation of metaphor into a statement of reality. It involved instead the introduction of a kind of cultural relativism as a point of view into the literature on Appalachia, and of a new model of social change as a matter of adaptation rather than of development pure and simple. For the environmentalists, as a consequence, while "normal" American culture remained preferable, the legitimacy of a peculiar and indigenous mountain culture was neither denied nor denigrated by its identification with some earlier phase in the evolution of the normal American form. In "The Anglo-Saxons of the Kentucky Mountains: A Study in Anthropogeography," for example, Ellen Churchill Semple argued in what was to become the characteristic way that the apparent persistence of historical forms in the mountains might be better understood as a matter of adaption to a particular environment. Utilitarian ethics, an independence of spirit bred by isolation and the necessity for self-reliance, an economy "severely limited in its possibilities" by lack of transportation facilities, were the circumstances in which feuding and moonshining developed as appropriate means of obtaining justice and disposing of a corn crop, respectively. "The same conditions which have kept the ethnic type pure have kept the social phenomena primitive," she noted "with their natural concomitants of primitive ethics and primitive methods of social control."[18]

For the environmentalists, the critical fact which set Appalachia off from America was not the occurrence of feuding and moonshining, the peculiarities of speech which had received such attention from the local color writers, the persistence of traditional folk song and traditional handicrafts, or even the log cabins which dotted the hillsides, but the absence of community. This was the cause from which all else, including the prevalence of violence in the region, followed. "Lack of good roads has caused an undue isolation, has prevented cooperative activity and the realization of the ideals of a modern community life," one commentator argued. An "overdeveloped individualism" has resulted "where there is no cohesive community life . . . [and] where local agencies are non-existent and non-local agencies inoperative," said another.[19] Especially in the hands of Warren H. Wilson of the Presbyterian Department of

Church and Country Life and John C. Campbell, Secretary of the Russell Sage Foundation's Southern Highland Division, the use of an environmentalist explanation for the peculiarities of Appalachia facilitated a redefinition of the region as "hyper-rural" and the perception of fundamental similarities among all such hyper-rural sections of the nation. "The question of the mountain dwellers is a national question," Campbell told the Home Missions Council in 1916. "You have it in your New England Hills, with less hope of solution it is sometimes felt, and although it is a larger question in the South, it is, after all, only a question of intensified rural conditions."[20]

In such terms, the conflict between Appalachia and America became not a conflict between past and present but between rural and urban ways, and the occurrence of feuds and moonshining became social problems of a kind to be expected in rural regions where community was absent. Although substantial disagreement over how the much-needed sense of community might be provided in Appalachia characterized the environmentalists' discussion of the region—Campbell and Wilson for example urged education appropriate to rural conditions in order to establish a viable mountain culture, while Walter Hines Page, like Wilson a former member of Roosevelt's Country Life Commission, favored removal of the mountaineers to the industrial centers of the New South where the development of community would be natural rather than artificial[21]—so far as feuding and moonshining were concerned there was agreement. Unfiltered through the haze of romance, private justice was seen to yield public chaos, and individualism, in the absence of the controls which community provides, to breed lawlessness. The occurrence of violence in the Southern mountains, when explained as adaptation to environment, thus became an undesirable yet ultimately a temporary and remediable phenomenon, a distortion of the more basic and desirable qualities of independence and self-reliance characteristic of rural life generally and of that special case of rural life which was Appalachia.

Resolution of the dilemma which the occurrence of feuding and moonshining in the Southern mountains posed did not eliminate violence from mountain life, of course, any more than it resolved the tension which the very existence of this strange land and peculiar people generated. Feuding and moonshining persisted as social problems, becoming in fact more acute as prohibition made the manufacture of whiskey increasingly profitable and as the so-called clan wars were complicated by the emergence of class conflict in the region during the later 1920s.[22] Violence continued as a consequence to point up the distance between Appalachia and America. Even after the era of violence had ended, however, Appalachia remained an "other" America in the American consciousness, defined now in terms of one set of characteristics, now in terms of another. And as such, Appalachia has continued to prick our consciences and to challenge the notions of what American civilization is and what it ought to be. If we continue to respond ambiguously, it is better than that we fail to respond at all.

II

Appalachian Diversity

In the previous edition of this reader, various authors advocated for more studies of racial and ethnic minorities in the Appalachian population. During the 1990s the literature in this branch of Appalachian studies expanded considerably. *Colored People: A Memoir* by Henry Louis Gates, Jr. and Cornel West gained national attention. John Inscoe's *Race in Appalachia* was published in 2001. William Turner and Edward Cabbell's 1985 collection, *Blacks in Appalachia,* is no longer the sole book-length treatment of the subject of race in Appalachia. Numerous scholarly articles now challenge some of the conventional wisdom and document the existence of slavery, the Ku Klux Klan, and other elements of individual and institutional racism in the region. Articles and books on other racial and mixed race people in Appalachia appeared; Cherokees, Melungeons, and Black Cherokees are receiving new attention in the literature.

Appalachian women's studies have also advanced with the publication of Carol Giesen's *Coal Miners' Wives: Portraits of Endurance* and Barbara Ellen Smith's *Neither Separate Nor Equal: Women, Race, and Class in the South.* Other books and articles with feminist themes continue to appear, and Appalachian women play major leadership roles at Appalachian Centers across the region, in the Appalachian Studies Association, and in publishing encyclopedias and handbooks on Appalachia. During this same period, gay and lesbian issues became topics at Appalachian Studies Association conferences, and *The Journal of Appalachian Studies* began publishing articles on these subjects.

We have included material on diversity throughout this edition, but have selected four articles here as representative of the literature. Betty Duggan's article, "The Eastern Cherokees of Southern Appalachia," describes the struggle of the Cherokee to survive as a viable culture in Appalachia. An article by historian John Inscoe describes racism in 19th century Appalachia. Judith Ivy Fiene's article looks at gender and class issues related to self-image. The article by Kate Black and Marc Rhorer focuses on the experiences of gays and lesbians in the mountains and in migrant centers.

5

by Betty J. Duggan

The Eastern Cherokees in Southern Appalachia: Principal People, Persistent People

Throughout the spring of 1838 people of the Cherokee Nation—families, farmers, craftspeople, ferry operators, planters, village leaders, statesmen—continued daily life while resisting, through political and legal means, compliance with the Indian Removal Act of 1830. Populations in what is now eastern Tennessee, western North Carolina, and northeastern Alabama were already swollen by refugees from northern Georgia, where Cherokee lands had been confiscated and sold in a state lottery. On May 23 Major General Winfield Scott, following the dictate of the federal government, led 7,000 U.S. soldiers and volunteers into field operations to remove all Cherokees from their southern Appalachian homeland. Beginning that day and continuing into the summer, 16,000 Cherokees were taken into custody at gunpoint from homes and fields, often with no time to gather necessities or family.[1]

Some 8,000 to 12,000 Cherokees survived the ravages of disease and climate on brutal marches through beloved mountains, along familiar creeks and rivers to departure points on the Tennessee River. For those who survived one of the subsequent 800 mile journeys west to an unknown Indian Territory, this awful and momentous event was memorialized forever in the Cherokee phrase, *Nunna daul Tsuny,* "The Trail Where We Cried."[2] The U. S. government called this event "Emigration," but a more accurate term is "Removal." Left behind when it ended, largely in less accessible parts of the southern Appalachian mountains in western North Carolina, were no more than 1,100 Cherokees; perhaps another 300 remained in Tennessee, Alabama, and Georgia combined.[3]

Members of today's Eastern Band of Cherokee Indians are descendants of these determined survivors. In 2001 there are approximately 12,500 enrolled Eastern Cherokees, of whom about 7,400 reside in several long-standing communities and dispersed neighborhoods located on 56,574 acres of tribal land in western North Carolina. Many of the nonresident members live in nearby non-Indian communities, or work "away" in metropolitan areas, such as Ashveville, Knoxville, Oak Ridge, and Atlanta.[4] Politically headquartered in the town of Cherokee, the Eastern Band of Cherokee is the only federally recognized American Indian group in the southern Appalachian region.[5] Anthropologist Sharlotte Neely, borrowing a concept developed by ethnologist Edward Spicer, believes that contemporary Eastern Cherokees have survived as a distinct ethnic group, a "persistent people," because they have resisted absorption into Euro-American civilization in important arenas—personal life, family life, and society.[6] Like their ancestors, the Eastern Cherokees continue to abide, at times setting themselves apart and being set apart by non-Indians, through more than 150 years of political, cultural, and social change. They are a remnant of an ancient indigenous people and an ethnic minority in both Appalachia and in America.

The Principal People

Early Spanish military expeditions under Hernando De Soto (1540) and Juan Pardo (1566–1568) passed through Cherokee lands, penetrating into the ridge and valley section of East Tennessee on the far side of the Unaka or Great Smoky Mountains.[7] When relations with the British were first established around 1670, the Cherokees controlled over 40,000 square miles of river bottoms, valleys, ridges, hill country, and mountain lands which are now part of Virginia, Tennessee, Kentucky, North Carolina, South Carolina, Georgia, and Alabama. By the eighteenth century, the Cherokees were the most politically powerful and populous of the Southeastern tribes, fitting well their own name for themselves, *Ani-Yunwiya,* "the principal people."[8]

Eighteenth century Cherokee towns, villages, and associated hamlets centered in five upland South locales tagged by the British as the Lower, Valley, Middle, Out, and Overhill Towns. These settlement concentrations were situated on or near the Savannah, Hiwassee, Tuckasegee and Little Tennessee Rivers and their tributaries. The Cherokee settlements varied in size from a few families to nucleated settlements with 100 to 600 inhabitants.[9] Although linked socially and culturally, there were ancient distinctions between the Cherokee subregions, including different Cherokee language dialects (Lower Towns—Eladi; Valley and Overhill Towns—Atali; Middle and Out Towns—Kituhwa) and stylistic preferences within certain crafts traditions.[10]

With extensive displacement of native peoples in the Southeast occurring during the eighteenth century, several other Indian groups—the Natchez, Yuchis, and Catawbas—established settlements among the Cherokees that varied in length of duration and success; the last few Natchez Indian families removed to Indian Territory with their Cherokee hosts. The Principal People also suffered temporary and permanent displacements within their own territory. Many Cherokee villages and agricultural fields were torched repeatedly between the 1750s and early 1790s during the French and Indian and Revolutionary wars and subsequent American frontier conflicts.[11]

At the time of European contact to be a Cherokee meant that one was born to a Cherokee mother and therefore a member of her matriclan. All of one's kin, and one's responsibilities to them and other Cherokees, were defined through a Crow-type matrilineal kinship system that distinguished between the matriclans of one's mother, father, mother's father, and father's father. A typical Cherokee household consisted of an older adult couple, their daughters and unmarried sons, the spouses and unmarried children of married daughters, and so on into the next generation in the female line.[12]

At the beginning of the eighteenth century the Principal People were an egalitarian society, joined as a jural community through social and cultural ties. All seven clans were ideally represented in one's home village. Local clan segments regulated land use, marriages, crimes, and ruled on revenge killings for murders involving its members. In times of war and crisis, all Cherokee villages could be linked together through the clan network. Ordinarily each village (along with dependent hamlets) was politically independent and under the direction of a local council composed of male elders, heads of clans, and White (peace) and Red (war) representatives. Labor was often, though not exclusively, divided along gender and kinship lines, and communal labor groups called *gadugi* carried out the more arduous agricultural and community tasks in each town or settlement. The Cherokee ethos stressed harmonious relations through the avoidance of direct conflict as well as generosity with one's time and goods with other Cherokees, adopted Cherokees, and guests. The ideal of harmony was symbolized and restored to balance each fall during the season of the Green Corn or harvest festival, when all Cherokees participated in ritual purification ceremonies and the sacred fire in each village's public meeting place (town house) was extinguished and rekindled.[13]

Between 1700 and 1730, the Cherokees became in a sense employees in a world-wide cottage industry that supplied the European leather, fur, and hat-making industries, thereby participating in the first incursion of the world market economy into the southern Appalachians.[14] Millions of deerskins and other pelts, most likely prepared by Cherokee women or family groups, were traded by the men, primarily to the British, in exchange for manufactured goods such as firearms, metal tools, housewares, salt, rum, mirrors, pigments, jewelry, cloth, and kaolin pipes. Initially Cherokee traders took their products to the Carolina forts or coastal towns, but very soon British traders became residents in several Cherokee towns. By the 1790s overharvesting of fur-bearing animals and overreliance on monocultural trade, coupled with land losses related to trade debts, war, and deaths from European diseases led to economic and military domination of the Principal People first by the British, and then by the Americans.[15]

Around 1800, the United States government and various missionary societies collaborated on "civilization programs" designed to enculturate the Cherokees in Western values and domestic and mechanical skills, aiming to convert them to productive farmer-citizens and Christians for the young American republic. In less than three decades the Cherokees made remarkable strides in adopting and adapting Western agrarian and domestic practices along with Western models for politics, religion and education to their own cultural, social, and political needs.[16] The Choctaws, Chickasaws, Creeks, and Seminoles were also targeted by similar programs, but the Cherokees are still at times called the most civilized of the Five Civilized Tribes of the Southeast. In the final analysis the Cherokees' accomplishments mattered little; after two decades of impassioned debate and opposition in the U.S. Congress, judiciary, and citizenry, the principle of Manifest Destiny triumphed and all Indians east of the Mississippi River became legally subject to the Indian Removal Act.[17]

Historians William McLoughlin and Walter Conser's analysis of an 1835 federal census of the Cherokees, taken in anticipation of Removal, found an emerging, three-tiered class system among the Principal People: a tiny, Anglo-Cherokee planter elite (50 out of 2,637 families); a sizeable Cherokee middle class; and a large cadre of poor, culturally conservative Cherokees.[18] As anthropologist Marshall Sahlins points out, however, in situations of interethnic and especially of colonial domination and contact, "cultural meanings are revalued as they are practically enacted."[19] Studies by archaeologist Brett Riggs and cultural geographers Richard Pillsbury and Leslie Hewes indicate that while Anglo-American technological innovations did make headway even in remote mountain villages by the 1830s, the vast majority of Cherokees remained culturally and socially conservative even as they adapted selected Western innovations and technologies. Almost all continued to speak Cherokee solely or by preference. Many learned to read and write in the Sequoyah syllabary, practiced traditional Cherokee crafts alongside introduced crafts and trades, and attended Baptist or Methodist services while still consulting with traditional medicine men and conjurers. Most located and maintained their introduced log cabins, individual farmsteads, and livestock herds along traditional lines of kinship, labor relations, and settlement patterns. This was done in association with the farmstead of a local headman, who often kept a townhouse on his property for public meetings. This newer type of dispersed Cherokee community might stretch for miles along creeks and river valleys. By the 1830s, Anglo-American squatters and settlers were sometimes near neighbors, and some even attended religious services at missions and preaching stations within the Cherokee Nation.[20]

Becoming the Eastern Band of Cherokee Indians

Popular accounts often attribute the Eastern Cherokees' escape from Removal to their hiding out in the mountains, or the self-sacrifice of the resisters *Tsali* (Old Charlie), two of his sons, and his brother who were executed for killing two soldiers and wounding a third during an escape from an Army detail that had captured them.[21] Anthropologist Duane King believes it was the actions of their Cherokee executioners in compliance with a bargain offered by General Scott, that really saved two local bands from deportation to Indian Territory. The executioners, including the local headman, *Euchella,* all lived on the Nantahala River in the Middle Towns as did the *Tsali* family, and may have been neighbors and kin. This suggests, perhaps, that they followed prescribed Cherokee legal traditions as much as Scott's orders. The two protected groups then fused, forming the geographic center and largest group of the future Eastern Band of Cherokee Indians.[22] The other group, the Oconoluftee or Citizen Cherokees, lived in the Out Towns locale under the leadership of another headman, *Yonaguska.* Historians point out that they were probably exempted from Removal because they had resided since 1819 as citizens and private landholders just outside the boundary of the Cherokee Nation in North Carolina on the Oconoluftee River.[23]

How other Cherokees avoided exile to Indian Territory is more complex. Some, like the *Tsali* family, did flee deeper into the mountains, hiding until the danger was past. On a case by case basis some frail elders or gravely ill people and their care-givers received special dispensations from the Army. Some members of the Cheoah and Buffalo settlements, located in the Snowbird Mountains near Robbinsville, North Carolina, were initially pursued and captured, but due to bad weather and road conditions combined with epidemic diseases they were allowed to return to their own homes. Many other Cherokees escaped from internment camps or along the Trail of Tears, journeying in secret, often at night, until they reached familiar territory. One Georgia community escaped by other means. Before Removal, 22 wealthy Anglo-Cherokee planter families on the Chattahoochee River in Georgia were granted immunity from expulsion by that state's government in compensation for several male members' assistance and signatures during Removal treaty negotiations. Nevertheless they eventually lost their property and incurred the wrath, revenge, and disdain of fellow Cherokees.[24]

In 1842 prominent western North Carolinia landholder and trader, William Holland Thomas, whom *Yonaguska* had adopted by Cherokee custom when Thomas was a boy, estimated that between 1,000 and 1,200 Cherokees remained in North Carolina, Tennessee, Alabama, and Georgia. Historian John Finger puts the total number of Cherokees then in the East at about 1,400 people, including 300 individuals who remained in the latter three states. The threat of another removal loomed large for decades, even though government efforts to persuade remaining Cherokees to emigrate to Indian Territory ceased in 1842. Their own traumatic personal experiences surely kept such fears alive, but a trickle of letters and petitions to federal and state governments from a few irate settlers and legislators demanding total deportation continued for decades. As a precautionary measure Will Thomas, in his role as their legal and business advisor, urged all Eastern Cherokees to join the Oconoluftee and Nantahala groups on their marginal mountain lands.[25]

In the aftermath of Removal, there were three major concentrations of Eastern Cherokees. At the Qualla Town settlement (near modern Cherokee) there were about 700 people, mostly from *Yonaguska*'s Oconoluftee band and *Euchella*'s smaller Nantahala band, along with some refugees from widely-scattered pre-Removal communities. This is the group of Eastern Cherokees over whom Will Thomas held sway, and about whom most has been written. Separate settlements quickly emerged at Qualla Town, although it is not yet clear whether this occurred through traditional Cherokee community-making actions or Thomas' efforts to settle clan members together. All but one survive today: Yellow Hill (Cherokee), Raven Place (Big Cove), Wolf Town, Bird Town, Paint Town, and Pretty Woman Town (extinct). Most Qualla Town landholdings were contiguous and difficult to reach. As a result, the people of Qualla Town enjoyed considerable cultural isolation until the 1880s, even though adjacent parts of the Oconoluftee Valley had long been settled by non-Indians. Because Indians had been excluded as land owners by the state the Qualla town farms and thousands of other acres in western North Carolina were paid for by Eastern Cherokees, but registered in Will Thomas' name.[26]

About fifty miles south, in the Snowbird Mountains was the Cheoah settlement where between 100 and 200 Cherokees remained. Almost all were pre-Removal residents of Cheoah or the nearby Buffalo settlements, temporarily joined by a smattering of refugees from the Middle and Valley Towns as well as from the Ducktown Basin settlements of southeastern Tennessee. Shortly after Removal three non-Indian sympathizers managed to buy up over 1,200 acres of confiscated Cherokee lands for the Cheoah Cherokees. These new Cheoah holdings ran along several mountain creeks among lands bought by non-Indian settlers. This culturally conservative group, today know as the Snowbird Cherokees, remained unstudied until anthropologist Sharlotte Neely began ethnographic work among them late in the twentieth century.[27]

The third group, another 100 to 200 people, was concentrated near Murphy, North Carolina, in the historic Valley Town subregion about 80 miles south of Qualla Town. Some scholars have lumped both pre-and-post Removal Cherokees of this area with some more acculturated communities further south in the Georgia hill country, perhaps due to the establishment of a Baptist mission and school at the Peachtree settlement on the Hiwassee River in the 1820s. Period documents, however, indicate that this was actually a stronghold of cultural conservatives, including several prosperous Anglo-Cherokee families who were traditionalists and Removal resisters. The author's own research on outlying post-Removal communities substantiates there was considerable variation in the nature and composition of Eastern Cherokee communities in (old) Cherokee County until the mid-1880s, when an exodus of full-blood and Anglo-Cherokee conservatives from the area began after one of their own, N.J. Smith, was elected Principal Chief and moved to the Qualla Boundary. In recent decades, mainly descendants of the culturally and genetically marginal "white Indians" who remained behind in Cherokee County have reasserted their ties with the Eastern Band as the Tomotla community.[28]

Several other smaller, culturally conservative Eastern Cherokee communities emerged in outlying areas. The Ducktown Basin settlements of southeastern Tennessee and Sandtown in Macon County, North Carolina, were resettled by returning refugees shortly after the Trail of Tears. They peaked in population before the Civil War and a few Cherokee families remained in these areas in the early twentieth century. The Long Ridge Cherokee settlement in the mountains northwest of Murphy and a tiny Cherokee farming settlement in Loudon County, Tennessee, developed between the 1870s and 1890s and then quickly declined. Another post-Removal settlement, known to Eastern Cherokees of the day as the "Nantahala Indians," was relocated near the site of the historic Middle Town of Alarka. This community reached its zenith between the 1890s and 1910s, ending only with another federal relocation caused by dam construction.[29]

During the first two decades after Removal the internal political organization of the Eastern Cherokees followed traditional lines. Settlements had a "lead man" and a council of 12 men who handled civic, legal, and social matters for the community. They also had one or more *gadugi*, or work parties/mutual aid societies which were a branch of the village council. Public town houses for council use and for traditional ceremonies and social dances were maintained in many Eastern Cherokee communities until after the Civil War, possibly into the 1880s at Yellow Hill (Cherokee) or even later in the Snowbird Mountains.[30]

For external political, business, and legal matters the Eastern Cherokees looked to Will Thomas. Shortly after the Civil War, however, Thomas' health began to decline and his business dealings became hopelessly entangled in lawsuits. Because many Eastern Cherokees kept accounts at Thomas' general stores and because he held title to much of their land, this turn of events was of critical importance to the remnant. In 1868 several Cherokee settlements selected representatives for their first general council since Removal. They met in the town house at Cheoah—the only Cherokee settlement remaining in its historic location—where they drafted a constitution and discussed the group's land ownership problems. A year later, the council met again at Cheoah to hold tribal elections and to ratify a constitution. In 1889 the Eastern Band of Cherokee Indians was chartered as a legal corporation in the state of North Carolina, an unusual action taken to clarify their still confused state and federal relationships and to resolve the property rights issues.[31]

For most Cherokees who avoided Removal or eventually returned, traditional lifeways and practices were the rule. Beginning in the 1880s, however, the Qualla Town settlements experienced increased pressure to assimilate by federal agents and officials of a new boarding school at Yellow Hill (first Quaker and later government-run). Tribal size became inflated by the inclusion of many people of minimal Cherokee genetic heritage or with non-Indian spouses. Many were believed eager to receive anticipated allotments of Eastern Cherokee lands (which did not occur), with some even moving onto tribal lands. The Cheoah settlement was probably not significantly affected by these changes until considerably later. As early as the 1870s, however, the smaller, fledgling settlements in outlying areas experienced other kinds of tensions, as non-Indian populations increased, and racial tensions heightened throughout the South during and after Reconstruction.[32]

It was in the 1880s that ethnologist James Mooney began his detailed studies of traditional Cherokee lifeways, myths, and language. While much of Mooney's fieldwork was conducted in and around Cherokee, a number of his informants had grown up in other pre-Removal or outlying post-Removal settlements. Most notably, Principal Chief N.J. Smith, assisted him and served as a primary source for many Cherokee myths and linguistic translations.[33]

Mooney's works revealed much about traditional Cherokee lifeways and cultural practices, pre-and-post-Removal tribal history, and Removal era events. Subsequent studies by anthropologists of the Eastern Band during the twentieth century continued to examine traditional culture and change through ethnographic research. Two major historical works about the Eastern Band by John Finger focus on the tribal level and on Cherokee responses to federal interventions.

Until the author's research began, few studies existed on the nature of community and family life in outlying settlements or on relations between these Eastern Cherokee populations and local non-Indians during the post-Removal era.[34] This work reports complex, shifting economic and social interactions between the Ducktown Basin Cherokees and local non-Indians in southeastern Tennessee that appear to stand in marked contrast to the relative isolation that the Qualla Town and Cheoah settlements experienced through the 1880s. In 1843 refugee families returned to their home locale in the Basin; a major copper reserve was discovered there leading to widespread land speculation and industrial development by the early 1850s. The Cherokees who reestablished communities in the Basin, and other Cherokees drawn in as peripheral industrial workers during the copper boom of the 1860s, were profoundly affected by the changing nature of local non-Indian society and by shifting perceptions about "Indianness" in the South and in America.[35]

The Ducktown Cherokees obtained land in their own names, established matrilocal settlements they treated as community property, and often lived in sight of non-Indian neighbors. Initially, there was considerable interaction and goodwill between the Ducktown Basin Cherokees and their non-Indian neighbors, although throughout its post-Removal history this enclave remained very traditional in native language use, community formation and maintenance, and social interaction. A few examples of this interaction are: a local Cherokee labor gang (possibly a *gadugi*) helped build a new road for copper export; a Baptist congregation invited the monolingual Cherokees to join their church; some Cherokees worked for the copper processors by cutting timber and making charcoal; barter of traditional Cherokee basketry for staples took place routinely between the groups; and Cherokee males sometimes hired themselves out as day laborers to local non-Indian and Cherokee farmers. After the Civil War, however, increased competition for limited agricultural lands in this mountainous location, population growth, and increased ethnic, social, and economic stratification in the industrialized sector of the local, and increased non-Indian population served to heighten racial awareness. In the 1880s and 1890s the growth of local and regional inter-racial tensions and violence eventually led to the gradual withdrawal of the Ducktown Basin Cherokees—first to more and more remote locations within the Basin, then to the culturally conservative Long Ridge settlement, next into the traditionalist Nantahala Indian settlement, and finally into the Cherokee and Snowbird areas after the Nantahala settlement was displaced by dam-building in the 1910s.[36]

Tradition, Crafts, and Tourism

The indigenous crafts produced by the Cherokees at the beginning of the eighteenth century reflected the group's traditional economic base of hunting and fishing, slash-and-burn agriculture, and gathering wild plant foods. This was a material culture rooted in the natural environment and the ritual paraphenalia adjunct to maintaining their spiritual well-being.[37] The Principal People's entry into the deerskin trade and subsequent acquisition of European trade goods quickly resulted in the decline of a number of traditional crafts, including stone tools, blowguns, and featherwork. A few crafts—notably doubleweave rivercane basket, stone pipe, and blanket production—flourished as European and colonial markets developed. Some exotic trade goods—items wrought in brass, tin, silver, and iron, as well as glass trade beads—became raw material sources, being refashioned into traditional and introduced crafts, especially arrowheads, tools, and jewelry. A hundred years later, the "civilization" programs fostered several introduced crafts, including loom weaving, spinning, and blacksmithing.[38]

Barter of some crafts items to neighboring frontier settlers began at least by the early nineteenth century. After Removal the barter of traditional and introduced crafts—especially baskets, handmade chairs, and wooden cooking utensils—became a critical part of many Eastern Cherokee families' economic strategies. Periodic forays by Eastern Cherokee women and children, and sometimes whole families, became commonplace. This continued well into the twentieth century until the southern Appalachian region's dependence on subsistence agriculture declined and with it the demand for utilitarian crafts. Stories about such trips are still told in Cherokee and non-Indian communities in southern Appalachia, and more than a few non-Indian families in the region cherish heirloom Cherokee baskets and other crafts, along with stories about the traveling groups of Indians from whom they were acquired. Peddling trips also provided an important opportunity for interaction between Cherokees and non-Indians in homes and general stores throughout the region. Aggie Ross Lossiah, a great-granddaugher of John Ross, last Principal Chief of the old Cherokee Nation, remembered as a girl practicing her

English, learning new games, and eating unusual foods (like biscuits) on family peddling trips through Loudon County, Tennessee, between the 1880s and early 1900s.[39]

In the late nineteenth century as a trickle of wealthy tourists from posh mountain health resorts ventured into their communities, a few Eastern Cherokees began making and selling fake "Indian artifacts." Many other Eastern Cherokees sold new and used craft items to a series of ethnologists sent out from the nation's premier museums.[40] Emergence of an *in situ* public market for crafts, however, really began between 1908, when a new railroad spur line into Cherokee opened, and 1914, the year that automobiles appeared in western North Carolina and the first annual Cherokee Indian Fair was instituted.[41]

Mass tourism was now beginning on the Qualla Boundary. With it came much needed cash and involvement in emerging handicraft and tourist markets. The international Arts and Crafts movement and the Settlement School movement were at a peak during these early decades of tourism. America's nostalgic city dwellers bought up handmade objects they believed either reproduced or continued colonial era and regional craft traditions. Creating demand and appreciation, these movements introduced major changes in production methods, materials, designs, and forms to suit the tastes of customers and meet mass marketing quotas. This was true of both Appalachian and Cherokee craftspeople. For instance, the traditional Cherokee singleweave rivercane basketry tradition underwent significant changes as new shapes and eye-popping design fields crowded with brightly colored repetitions of traditional design elements appeared for sale.[42]

In the 1930s, the Great Depression hit the Eastern Cherokees especially hard; many barely eked out a subsistence on tiny, subdivided and worn-out farms. Bureau of Indian Affairs records indicate, however, that craftspeople still had incomes during these difficult times. "Indian New Deal" programs opened up other job opportunities and led to the construction of new tribal offices and buildings at the Cherokee Boarding School. In line with New Deal philosophy and with traditional Cherokee economic and labor patterns, a cooperatively-owned tribal hotel, a crafts outlet at the boarding school, a trading post, a gas station, a store, a canning factory, and camping facilities were opened. Some non-Indian landowners and businessmen objected to these developments, viewing them as threats to their own hopes for tourist dollars from the Great Smoky Mountain National Park.[43]

In 1946, fifty-three Cherokee craftspeople organized the Cherokee Indian Crafts Co-op, an organization which in 1954 incorporated as the Qualla Arts and Crafts Mutual, Inc. Over the next half century, Qualla Arts and a number of its members became world renowned in ethnic and folk art circles. As an official tribal enterprise, Qualla Arts has been viewed by the Eastern Band and by the Co-op's membership as a critical tribal institution, responsible for encouraging and insuring continuation of Cherokee crafts. As one Eastern Cherokee said, "it [Qualla Arts] was about the best thing we ever done." Direct income and annual dividends have provided economic stability for many families, especially because until recently most jobs on the Qualla Boundary were low-paying, seasonal tourism work.[44]

Today, the Qualla Arts and Crafts cooperative and Cherokee crafts traditions face radically different challenges. Now more Eastern Cherokees have access to year-round jobs in the manufacturing, service, and tourism sectors, both on and off the reservation. There are increased tribal benefits derived from several successful enterprises such as gaming, and fewer people have the economic incentive or time to devote to making labor-intensive, handmade crafts. Time will tell which crafts will survive or emerge among the Eastern Cherokees as valued cultural or ethnic symbols—in the future they may be produced for personal reasons or artistic expression only. Nor is it known how this longstanding tribal cooperative, world famous for fostering quality traditional crafts and ethnic art among the Eastern Cherokees and other American Indian groups, will adjust to changing markets and tastes.

cultural traits

?

Being Eastern Cherokee Today

Annual visitation in the Great Smoky Mountains National Park, of which Cherokee, North Carolina, is the eastern gateway, reached ten million visitors in the 1990s.[45] The casual tourist driving through Cherokee today confronts an historic progression of touristic scenes: an aging Santaland; a glittering Vegas-style tribal casino and hotel complex; stereotypic "chiefing" tepees and "Indian" souvenir shops; chain motels and older motorcourts; fast-food restaurants; a culturally-sensitive reenactment of early Cherokee village life; "hillbilly" themed adventure stops and storefronts; and generic shop-till-you-drop minimalls. While some of the oldest businesses are under long-term leases to non-Indians, Cherokee-owned tourist businesses are steadily increasing.

In the middle of this surreal landscape is Cherokee center (formerly Yellow Hill) and geographical heart of tribal government for the Eastern Band of Cherokee Indians. Here one finds small clusters of community buildings and facilities—tribal administrative offices, ceremonial grounds, a museum, a crafts cooperative, schools, the Cherokee Boys Club (another tribal cooperative enterprise), and a few modest homes and churches. The physical and visual juxtapositioning of the touristic and tribal within modern Cherokee is emblematic of the predominant role that tourism has played in the daily lives of many Eastern Cherokees. One recent estimate links nearly 75 percent of current Eastern Band revenues to tourism, creating an incredible boon for the moment, but also a monocultural dependence always vulnerable to national economic crises, trends, and tastes.[46]

Beyond Cherokee center, the other Qualla Boundary communities—Big Cove, Painttown, Birdtown, and Wolftown and several younger neighborhoods—are affected to varying degrees by the presence of tourists. In Graham County, the Snowbird Cherokee community, and further south in Cherokee County, the resurgent "white Indian" Tomotla community have felt the first-hand effects of tourism much less. This may soon change. With the opening of the Cherohala scenic highway through the Snowbird community increased tourism and development will surely become issues of concern in the not too distant future. Indeed, people in Tomotla recently began pressing for construction of a bingo hall in their community.[47]

In 1982 Cherokee Bingo opened and the Eastern Band of Cherokee Indians turned to gaming as a way to bring year-round tourist dollars and jobs into their community. In 1997 a new tribal venture, Harrah's Cherokee Casino, was created in cooperation with an outside gambling conglomerate. The casino complex, with attendant restaurants and a child care facility, generated millions of dollars in new revenue for the Eastern Band during its first year, and by the year 2000 provided about 1,500 jobs (500 for Eastern Cherokees and 1,000 for non-Indians from the surrounding locale). Annual visitation to the casino in 2000 was about 3.6 million people.[48] Each year half of the Eastern Band's share of profits from the casino goes into tribal coffers to fund programs providing social welfare, health, and educational opportunities for tribal members. This distribution plan for shared community betterment builds on the foundation laid by older Cherokee institutions and tribal enterprises, such as the Cherokee Boys Club, Qualla Arts and Crafts, Qualla Housing Authority, and Tsali Manor seniors' center. The other half of casino profits (in 2000 this amounted to $5,000 per individual) is distributed annually among Eastern Band members on a per capita basis and is quickly raising the standard of living for many families. Increased spending by casino visitors and Eastern Cherokees and related new jobs have meant revenue enhancement for nearby counties such as Swain and Jackson. The Eastern Band also donates significant sums to the area's non-Indian civic and health organizations.[49]

Yet contention within the tribe about gaming was and still is considerable, with some Eastern Band members refusing to cash their distribution checks on religious grounds. Others oppose the casino because of important changes it might have on the Eastern Cherokees' sense of community and way of life. When the casino was still only an idea, a Cherokee elder spoke about the controversial issue on the grounds of the Tsali Manor seniors' center, after completing a lunch time interview with the author. She pulled her sweater closer and gestured upward toward the mountains towering over us and outward along the constricted Oconoluftee River bottom, saying that she had a dream recently. In a voice tinged with regret, or perhaps bitterness, she said that she had seen every bit of land in Cherokee, every place that she had known so intimately in her 70 plus years, covered up in new construction, even to the mountain tops, leaving no room for her people. In North Carolina as well some citizens and local governments, eager for new revenue sources, initially voiced opposition to the casino citing fairness concerns about allowing gaming only on Indian lands.

Today, Cherokee is experiencing a construction boom, fueled by casino revenues and tourist spending. Some of this development is aimed at improving tourist services and facilities, but much serves Cherokee community needs such as supermarkets, roads, buildings, and added tribal programs and services. A partial listing of projects scheduled for completion soon includes: renovation of the Ginger Welch complex to house an expanded tribal library and genealogical research facility and some 20 other tribal offices; addition of an infant care facility at the Dora Reed Children's Center (tribal Headstart headquarters); a new building for the tribal Travel and Promotion office; additions to the Cherokee Fair Grounds ("Ceremonial Grounds"); and the development of a large convention center and five-story hotel at the casino complex. With each expansion the Eastern Band's Office of Culture Resources is there to assess, study, and preserve Cherokee archaeological resources. Increased tribal revenues have also meant programmatic expansion for this office into historical and cultural studies, with current projects including a Cherokee language preservation program and oral history projects.[50]

In the 1950s and early 1960s extensive anthropological research, conducted in Big Cove and Paint Town (then polar opposites, culturally) by a team of researchers under sponsorship of the University of North Carolina, yielded detailed information about individual and community expectations of Eastern Cherokee identity and values. The late Western Cherokee anthropologist Robert Thomas posited a range of expected behaviors that generally correlated with social and/or socioeconomic groups, ranging from culturally conservative to fully acculturated, but varying contextually by the ways and situations in which individuals enacted them. The range included: (a) "Cultural Conservatives," who emphasized Cherokee language use, traditional practices and behaviors; (b) "Generalized Indians," who self-identified as Eastern Cherokee, but had both Cherokee and non-Indian values; (c) "Rural-white Indians," who genetically were minimally Eastern Cherokee and socially similar to non-Indian peoples of southern Appalachia and; (d) a very small group of "Middle-class Indians," business owners or their employees who identified more closely with co-workers than other Eastern Cherokees. Anthropologist John Gulick, in his overview of the larger group's research, coined the term "Harmony Ethic" to describe the cluster of traditional values and behaviors still embraced by culturally conservative Eastern Cherokees who made up about one-quarter of the population.[51]

In the 1990s historian John Finger referred to modern Eastern Band members as "Cherokee Americans," suggesting further acculturation and an added dimension to their collective and individual identities.[52] Today Eastern Cherokees share much in common socially and culturally with their non-Indian, southern Appalachian neighbors, as well as other Americans. Most speak a local Appalachian dialect of English with a distinctively melodic Cherokee accent. A growing number of Cherokee students elect to attend non-Indian schools located off the reservation. Shared casino revenues and individual disbursements mean more Eastern Cherokees will attain middle class economic status.

Non-Indian spouses are not uncommon, even among Snowbird families, many of whom still speak the Atali dialect of Cherokee at home and live in neighborhoods of matrilineally-related kin or even in matrilocal households. Community and neighborhood fund-raising, parades, support activities, and commemoration ceremonies, sometimes rapidly organized, now extend beyond family and reservation needs to regional and national crises—medical emergencies, natural disasters, the Gulf War, and the World Trade Center attacks for example.

It is important, however, to understand that contemporary Cherokee identity is syncretic—layered, nuanced, and by no means homogenous—and is certainly influenced by centuries of adaptation, but is still often underpinned by ancient meanings and values. It is sometimes hard for non-Indians to understand why many American Indian peoples, including the majority of Eastern Cherokees, continue to live together in ethnic enclaves, even on poverty-stricken reservations. Anthropologist Raymond Fogelson recently discussed three primary attributes of traditional Native American identity that cut across individual tribal identities—blood and descent, relationship to the land, and sense of community. The Cherokees have endured European contact, epidemics, wars, missionization, being rent in two by the Trail of Tears, years of poverty and racism, the blessing and curse of tourism, and countless government policy reversals. For the Eastern Cherokees the three primordial sentiments expressed through shared Cherokee genealogical connections and history, attachment to their southern Appalachian homeland, and shared values (especially the Harmony Ethic) signify what anthropologist Fredrik Barth refers to as the "unit of continuity in time" that is key to understanding ethnic identity.[53]

While Eastern and Western Cherokees remain politically and socially distinct, contact between these groups has been continuous since 1838. In 1984, for the first time since the Trail of Tears, the tribal councils of the Cherokee Nation of Oklahoma and the Eastern Band of Cherokees, with their respective Principal chiefs, met in joint session at Red Clay, Georgia, the site of the last general council of the old Cherokee Nation held before the Trail of Tears. This has evolved into an semi-annual event, with joint councils alternating between Cherokee and Tahlequah, the respective capitals of the Eastern Band and the Cherokee Nation of Oklahoma. Many other Eastern Cherokees have for years attended events or spent vacations with relatives in Oklahoma. Oklahoma Cherokees attend the annual Fall Festival in Cherokee to share in powwow and traditional dances, pan-Indian foods, traditional Cherokee stickball games, and juried crafts displays. For a number of years, the Snowbird Cherokee community has hosted an annual "Trail of Tears Singing," an event at which Oklahoma Cherokees are special guests. This is a time when Cherokee language, traditional foods, and ceremony co-mingle with gospel quartet music sung in Cherokee and English. Both events draw non-Indian visitors and participants as well. More recently, a group of culturally conservative Eastern Cherokees, with the assistance of traditional Western Cherokee religious practioners, consecrated a stomp ground in the Big Cove community, creating a private space for the most traditional of dances and ceremonies away from the hubbub of tourism in nearby Cherokee.[54]

The Principal People, divided geographically and politically by Removal more than 150 years ago, still persist symbolically and in spirit. Many of their descendants, including the Eastern Band of Cherokee Indians, maintain a shared sense of historical origins and memory, as well as cultural heritage and values. One Oklahoma Cherokee expressed this common thread succinctly and elegantly:

> Being a Cherokee is a way of thinking and a way of knowing. The Cherokees in bright cars and neat suits are still men [and women] of the eagle race, the people of the eternal fire. And we are still a proud people who have kept alive a great spirit. The eternal fire still burns brightly for my people, the Cherokees.[55]

Acknowledgments

Special thanks to Eastern Cherokees James Bird, Marina Catt, Joyce Dugan, Shirley Jackson Oswalt, and David Redmond, and to colleagues Sharlotte Neely, Jeff Gardner, JoLee Gardner, and Bret Riggs for their assistance or encouragement in developing this essay. The author is also indebted to many Eastern Cherokees, to several residents of western North Carolina and East Tennessee, and to colleagues and mentors who over the years have shared memories or insights which continue to inform my understanding and interpretations of things Cherokee.

6

by John C. Inscoe

Race and Racism in Nineteenth-Century Southern Appalachia: Myths, Realities, and Ambiguities

David Whisnant, one of the premier chroniclers of Appalachia, recently noted that whenever he read books that generalized about "the South," he amused himself by checking their generalizations against what he knows of the mountain South. Rarely, he said, was the congruence very great. Nowhere, in fact, has the incongruence between the highland and lowland South been more apparent than on matters of race. In one of the most celebrated regional generalizations, U. B. Phillips in 1928 argued that racism—or more specifically the quest for white supremacy—was the central theme of southern history. While that claim has been debated ever since, few scholars have objected to the basic premise behind it: that, as Phillips put it quite simply, the Negro was an essential element in "the distinctive Southern pattern of life."[1]

For a significant section of the South, the southern Appalachians, however, the African American presence has not been central, perhaps not even essential, to its distinctive pattern of life. That so integral a factor to southern life elsewhere is peripheral to highland society no doubt accounts for the fact that, despite increasingly sophisticated analysis of the complexities of both southern race relations and Appalachian society, the two fields have not yet intersected to any significant degree. Perhaps as a result, no other aspect of the Appalachian character has been as prone to as much myth, stereotype, contradiction, and confusion as has the matter of race relations and racial attitudes among mountaineers.

Historians have often skirted the question, but none have yet tackled it nearly so directly as have literary interpreters of the region. Two works of early twentieth-century fiction are particularly striking in their portrayals of the contradictory assumptions regarding racism among southern highlanders.

Both works, one a short story and one a novel, use the Civil War as a catalyst through which mountain whites confront not only blacks for the first time, but their own racist proclivities as well. In so doing, they give dramatic form to the deep-seated discrepancies that have long plagued popular and scholarly ideas regarding the relationship between these two groups of southerners.

In his immensely popular 1903 novel, *The Little Shepherd of Kingdom Come,* John Fox chronicled a young orphan boy's move from Kentucky's Cumberland mountains to the Bluegrass. Chad Buford had never seen a black person until he left his home and moved to a nearby valley, where he encountered two slaves. Dazed, he stared at them and asked his companion Tom, "Whut've them fellers got on their faces?" "Hain't you nuver seed a nigger afore?" his friend asked. When Chad shook his head, Tom said, "Lots o'folks from yo' side o' the mountains nuver have seed a nigger. Sometimes hit skeers 'em." "Hit don't skeer me," Chad replied. A few years later, when the outbreak of the Civil War forced Kentuckians to take a stand for or against the Union, Chad, by then a teenager fully exposed to slavery and plantation society as they existed in central Kentucky, chose to fight for the Union, despite pressure from his Confederate guardians. Yet his attitude toward slavery or blacks was not central to his decision. His exposure to it had been brief, and the defense of slavery, Fox wrote, "never troubled his soul. . . . Unlike the North, the boy had no prejudice, no antagonism, no jealousy, no grievance to help him in his struggle."[2]

Nearly thirty years after the publication of Fox's novel, William Faulkner examined highland racial attitudes from another, far more dramatic angle. In a 1932 short story, "Mountain Victory," he wrote of a Confederate major from Mississippi and his slave, who in heading home from Virginia just after the end of the Civil War, came upon a Tennessee mountain family and asked to spend the night in their cabin. The bulk of the story involves the varied reactions of members of this family to their two strange guests and their racial identity. Only well into the story does it become apparent that the Tennesseans assumed that Major Weddel, of French and Creole ancestry, was black as well, which prompted him to taunt his hosts as the source of their hostility: "So it's my face and not my uniform. And you fought four years to free us, I understand." Ultimately their revulsion toward the black and the close relationship he enjoyed with his master led to a violent denouement, an ambush by the mountain men that left both Mississippians and one of the Tennesseans dead.[3]

This powerful but little-known Faulkner story and Fox's far more widely read saga of Civil War Kentucky offer enlightening comparisons on a number of levels. Both are studies of the culture clashes between plantation aristocrats and poor white mountaineers, and both examine the tensions between Confederate and Unionist values that set southerner against fellow southerner. But perhaps most significantly, both Faulkner and Fox depicted highlanders' ignorance—or to use Faulkner's term, innocence—of the biracial character of the rest of the South and described very different responses by highlanders suddenly exposed to the reality of another race.

While more subtle in delineating the reactions of their mountain characters than many, Faulkner and Fox both relied on one of the most basic assumptions regarding preindustrial Appalachian society—the absence of blacks. This essay explores the implications of that demographic given in terms of both the myths and realities of a far more elusive factor—the racial attitudes of white southern highlanders resulting from that minimal or nonexistent contact with blacks and what, if anything, made their brand of racism unique. Which was a more accurate reflection of mountain racism: John Fox's young humanitarian hero or Faulkner's vicious and violent Tennesseeans?

Part of the romanticization of Appalachia that accompanied its "discovery" in the late nineteenth century lay in its perceived racial and ethnic homogeneity. "Nowhere will be found purer Anglo-Saxon blood," a journalist wrote of the northern Georgia mountains in

1897.[4] Ethnogeographer Ellen Semple extolled the mountain populace of Kentucky on the same grounds. Not only had they kept foreign elements at bay, she observed in 1901, but they had "still more effectively . . . excluded the negroes. This region is as free from them as northern Vermont."[5] After geological expeditions through the Blue Ridge and the Alleghenies in the late 1880s, Harvard professor Nathaniel S. Shaler wrote that there were "probably more white people who have never seen a negro in this part of the United States than in all New England." He was amused at the intense curiosity his own black servants evoked among highland men and women, some of whom traveled over twenty miles to stare at them.[6]

Appalachian residents contributed to the myth. In 1906 East Tennessee minister Samuel Tyndale Wilson, then president of Maryville College, stated categorically that the mountain region is "the only part of the South that is not directly concerned with the race problem." He even suggested that the commonly used term "mountain whites," which he found pejorative (too much like "poor white trash"), be replaced with simply "mountaineer," with no need for any designation by race. In *The Hills Beyond,* his semifictional interpretation of his region's history, Asheville native Thomas Wolfe claimed that the mountain people had not owned slaves and that in many counties, "Negroes were unknown before the war."[7]

Even Flannery O'Connor based one of her most celebrated stories, "The Artificial Nigger," on the premise that mountaineers had no contacts with blacks. The 1950 story, which O'Connor once said was her favorite, centers on an elderly northern Georgia man who brings his ten-year-old grandson on an excursion to Atlanta in order to expose him to the world beyond their isolated backwoods existence. The experience becomes one of continual encounters with blacks, which alternately baffle, intrigue, repel, and traumatize the two highlanders, whose backgrounds have left them totally unprepared for this strange race of people. Once safely back home, the young boy sums up his introduction to the biracial urban South: "I'm glad I've went once, but I'll never go back again."[8]

While O'Connor (like Faulkner and Fox) drew upon the assumption of a pure white mountain South to explore more universal racial themes, more recent scholars have made much of the propangandistic effects of that image. James Klotter has argued convincingly that it was the region's perceived "whiteness" that so appealed to northern interests at the time and inspired them to divert their mission impulses toward deserving highlanders after their disillusionment with similar efforts on behalf of southern blacks during Reconstruction. More recently, Nina Silber has suggested that northerners found postwar reconciliation more palatable with the mountain South, due to its racial purity and its loyalty to the Union during the war. These traits provided northerners with identifying links less apparent in poor whites elsewhere in the South, still unreformed rebels caught up in the biracial complexities of the lowland South.[9]

This basic demographic assumption, which Edward Cabbell has called Appalachia's "black invisibility" factor, is simple enough to refute and a number of studies in recent years have effectively demolished the myth that African Americans were a negligible presence in Appalachia.[10] Slavery existed in every county in Appalachia in 1860, and the region as a whole included a black populace, free and slave, of over 175,000. Freedmen and -women continued to reside in most areas of the mountain South by century's end, when their numbers totaled over 274,000.[11] Most of the region's few urban areas, such as Chattanooga, Knoxville, Asheville, and Bristol, saw a dramatic influx of blacks in the decades following the Civil War, and communal experiments, such as North Carolina's "Kingdom of the Happy Land" and Kentucky's Coe Ridge, were established by freedmen and -women moving into the region from antebellum plantation homes elsewhere.[12] From the 1880s on, the coalfields of Kentucky, Virginia, Tennessee, and especially West Virginia attracted thousands of southern blacks and drastically changed the racial demographics of substantial areas of central Appalachia.[13]

There were, however, rural areas of the southern highlands from which former slaves drifted away. At least ten Appalachian counties lost their entire black population between 1880 and 1900, due to a combination of push (scare tactics) and pull (economic opportunity elsewhere) factors.[14] Thus by the end of the century there were large numbers of mountain residents whose contacts with blacks were negligible. It was they who served as the models of racial purity—or to use Faulkner's term, "innocence"—to both contemporary observers and later generations. But the nature of the racial attitudes spawned by this void, whether real or perceived, has proven a difficult aspect of the mythology to come to terms with. Like W. J. Cash's *The Mind of the South,* most treatments of mountain racism have characterized it as a single and simple mentality. But unlike Cash, who took over 400 pages to describe the regional "mind" as he saw it, most of what has been written about southern highlanders' racial views has been consigned to slight and usually casual references, based on conjecture, exaggeration, and overgeneralization. More often than not, the topic is mentioned only in passing in works with other concerns or priorities. Much is taken for granted, and no one to date has subjected the issue to either serious scrutiny, systematic analysis, or substantial documentation.

What makes the topic so intriguing is the sharp dichotomy that characterizes opinions as to how white mountaineers viewed blacks. On the one hand is the assumption on which Faulkner drew heavily—highlanders' inherent fear of and intense hostility toward the race that they alone among southerners did not know or control. Conversely there is the more extensively supported notion that the mountains were a southern oasis of abolitionism and racial liberality. Despite the pervasiveness of both schools of thought, proponents of one never seem to have acknowledged the other, much less made any direct effort to discredit it.

Cash's *Mind of the South* had much to do with giving widespread credence to the idea of mountain hostility to blacks. At least his one relevant statement is among the most often quoted. "Though there were few slaves in the mountains," Cash wrote, the mountaineer "had acquired a hatred and contempt for the Negro even more virulent than that of the common white of the lowlands; a dislike so rabid that it was worth a black man's life to venture into many mountain sections."[15] This was a belief to which mountain residents and chroniclers of the region had long adhered. Just after the Civil War, John Eaton, as commissioner of Tennessee's Freedmen's Bureau, noted that even though there were far fewer blacks in the state's eastern highlands, "the prejudice of the whites against the Negro was even more acute" there than in areas overrun with "colored" refugees, such as Memphis or Vicksburg.[16]

John Campbell, perhaps the region's most influential twentieth-century chronicler, presented a somewhat more judicious view of its racism but confirmed that there were counties "without a single Negro inhabitant and where it was unpleasant if not unsafe for him to go." Muriel Shepherd quoted a North Carolina highlander who, in explaining why there were no blacks, free or slave, in the Rock Creek section of Mitchell County, stated that "colored people have a well-founded belief that if they venture up there they might not come back alive."[17]

The idea of a more intense highland racism was widespread even in other parts of the South. In his recent memoir of his sharecropping childhood in middle Georgia, for example, black author Raymond Andrews wrote of a particular overseer: "Mister Brown and his family were mountain folks, or 'hillbillies,' but were considered unusual for the breed, as it was often said that folks from up in the hills had no use for lowlanders, particularly colored folks." William Styron made a similar point in *The Confessions of Nat Turner,* perhaps the most insightful portrait of the slaveholding South in modern fiction. In attempting to explain why Joseph Travis split a slave family by selling a mother and child south, he noted that Travis had moved to Southampton County from "the wild slopes of the Blue

Ridge mountains." Styron, in Nat's voice, speculates: "Maybe it was his mountain heritage, his lack of experience with Tidewater ways, that caused him to do something that no truly respectable slaveowner would do."[18]

But while there is evidence of intense negrophobia among southern highlanders, the diminished presence of slavery there led many to far different conclusions as to the reasons behind the institution's relative absence. The belief has long held sway that "Appalachians have not been saddled with the same prejudices about black people that people of the deep South have," as Loyal Jones, one of the region's most perceptive interpreters, has expressed it.[19] This idea of a moral superiority among highlanders in regard to their racial attitudes is deep rooted and is based in large part on the stereotypical "rugged individualism" credited to mountain men. That perception, along with the reality of comparatively fewer slaves in the region, led many to the conclusion that the rejection of slavery was a conscious choice.

The concept of Appalachia as a bastion of liberty was well developed by the time the Civil War broke out, largely because the area was seen as a refuge for escaped slaves. The region was considered part of the Underground Railroad route out of the South, where according to one contemporary source, "rugged mountaineers forfeited life for the furtherance of the means of justice, and mingled blood . . . with the blood of millions of slaves."[20] More recently, Boston social worker Leon Williams described the region as "settled to a substantial degree by slaves and indentured white servants fleeing from exploitation and angry with established colonial America." "The hills, in their exquisite isolation," he continued, "became havens for the disenchanted black and white . . . who needed to escape burdensome drudgery and slavery."[21]

Historian Barbara Fields has even suggested that the movement of yeomen into the backcountry can be viewed as a southern counterpart to the northern free-soil movement. They migrated into the hills, she maintains, "to escape the encirclement of the plantation and create a world after their own image." Highlanders themselves often extolled the slavelessness of their region in Calvinistic terms later adopted by the abolitionist movement. "We are more moral and religious and less absorbed . . . than the people of West Tennessee," noted East Tennessean David Deaderick in his journal in 1827, virtues he credited to the fact that "where slaves exist in large numbers and where all the work, or nearly all, is performed by slaves, a consequent inaction and idleness are characteristics of the whites."[22]

John Brown long saw the southern highlands as central to his abolitionist schemes. As early as 1847, in a meeting with Frederick Douglass, Brown pointed on a map to the "far-reaching Alleghenies" and declared that "these mountains are the basis of my plan," both as an escape route out of the South and a base of operations from which uprisings against the plantation South could be directed. Douglass quoted Brown as saying, "God has given the strength of the hills to freedom; they were placed here for the emancipation of the negro race; they are full of natural forts . . . [and] good hiding places, where large numbers of brave men could be concealed, baffle and elude pursuit for a long time."[23] When Brown finally enacted his attack on Harpers Ferry twelve years later, the highlands were still crucial to his aims. He hoped to move south through Virginia and the Carolinas, liberating the slaves of the plantation piedmont and sending them to a chain of fortresses established in the mountains to their west, from which they would hold their opponents at bay as reinforcements, black and white, gathered to form an army of liberation. "The mountains and swamps of the South," Brown reiterated to a fellow conspirator a year before his 1859 raid on that western Virginia arsenal, "were intended by the Almighty for a refuge for the slave and a defense against the oppressor."[24]

In the early months of the Civil War a Minnesota journalist suggested that the key to putting down the southern rebellion lay in the federal government embracing and utilizing that support it enjoyed within the South, particularly among southern Appalachians.

The reason, he maintained, was that "within this Switzerland of the South, Nature is at war with slavery." Bondage, he implied, was incompatible with high altitudes: "Freedom has always loved the air of mountains. Slavery, like malaria, desolates the low alluvials of the globe. The sky-piercing peaks of the continents are bulwarks against oppression; and from mountain valleys has often swept the most fearful retribution to tyrants," and thus the Appalachians remained loyal to the Union and a "golden opportunity . . . to strike for Liberty and Union in all the Highlands of the South."[25]

Such sentiments became even more prevalent after the war, as northerners acknowledged the Union loyalty of much of the region. In an 1872 sermon William Goodrich, a minister from Cleveland, Ohio, was among those who extolled the virtues of the highland South. "Explain it as we may," he preached, "there belongs to mountain regions a moral elevation of their own. They give birth to strong, free, pure and noble races. They lift the men who dwell among them, in thought and resolve. Slavery, falsehood, base compliance, luxury, belong to the plains. Freedom, truth, hardy sacrifice, simple honor, to the highlands."[26]

So the creation of "Holy Appalachia"—as Allen Batteau has termed it in his recent study of the region's "invention" by outside interests—was under way. It was a creation sometimes based on rather convoluted reasoning. The admiration for the Anglo-Saxon purity of mountaineers' identity carried with it the implication that a conscious rejection of slavery on ideological grounds played a major part in their lack of racial or ethnic contamination. Abraham Lincoln himself was worked into this increasingly idealized formula and became to a later generation of mountain residents a patron saint of Appalachia.[27]

Even Harry Caudill, whose haves-versus-have-nots analysis of Kentucky's Cumberlands extended to antebellum tensions between the area's few slaveholders and its vast majority of nonslaveholders, believed that the latter's Unionist stance during the Civil War stemmed not so much from class resentment as from the fact that in some vague way "these poorer mountaineers, fiercely independent as they were, found something abhorrent in the ownership of one person by another." John Fox's idealistic young hero in *The Little Shepherd of Kingdom Come* was not, Caudill maintained, "the only mountaineer to risk or endure death on the battlefields because of a sincere desire to see the shackles stricken from millions of men and women."[28]

Another major factor in the image of Appalachia as "holy" ground was the establishment of several abolitionist footholds in the region. The frequently touted claim that the abolitionist movement began in the mountains rests on early efforts in Wheeling, Virginia; in East Tennessee; and later at Berea, Kentucky. As early as 1797 a Knoxville newspaper advocated the forming of an abolition society, and the next decade saw Benjamin Lundy fulfilling that charge in Wheeling. Lundy later moved to northeastern Tennessee, where he joined a number of "New Light" Presbyterians and Quakers from Pennsylvania and Ohio, who established what were among the nation's first manumission societies and produced the earliest antislavery publications. By 1827, according to one claim, East Tennessee had one-fifth of the abolition societies in the United States and almost a fifth of the national membership.[29] But most organized efforts were phased out or moved elsewhere within a few years, so that Maryville College in Blount County remained the only substantial base of antislavery activity for the rest of the antebellum period.[30]

Other forms of highland antislavery were more sectional in nature. In 1847 Henry Ruffner, a Presbyterian minister and president of Virginia's Washington College with small slaveholdings in Rockbridge County, stirred debate over—and for a brief period, considerable support for—a proposal that slavery, while firmly entrenched in eastern Virginia, could be gradually abolished west of the Blue Ridge "without detriment to the rights or interests of slaveholders." He proposed that all slaves in the Shenandoah Valley and surrounding mountains be transported to Liberia and that future importation of blacks into the region be banned. But much of Ruffner's agenda and the basis for much of the initial enthusiasm for his proposal grew out of resentment of sectional inequities that benefited a Tidewater slaveholding elite at the expense of westerners. Once constitutional reforms in 1851 alleviated many of those perceived abuses, support for Ruffner's emancipation scheme evaporated.[31]

Though less explicitly abolitionist in purpose, Berea College stood as a model of interracial education from its origins in the 1850s until almost the end of the century, the product of Kentucky-born, Ohio-educated abolitionist John Fee's quest for "a practical recognition of the brotherhood of man." Ellen Semple cited Berea as an example of "the democratic spirit characteristic of all mountain people" and concluded that its location on the western margin of the Cumberland Plateau was "probably the only geographic location south of the Mason and Dixon line where such an institution could exist."[32] As unusual as this experiment was in the postbellum, much less the antebellum, South, one can hardly credit its existence to Appalachian liberality. The school's turn-of-the-century shift to an exclusive mission aimed at mountain whites and preservation of their folk arts bestowed on Berea a reputation as a cultural center of Appalachia. Fee himself never thought of it as even located in the mountains. "We are in the 'hill country,'" he wrote in 1867, "between the 'blue grass' & the mountains. From the former region we now draw our colored men, from the latter the young white men & ladies."[33]

Merely on the basis of these rather limited or regionally marginal efforts, however, the concept of Appalachia as a solid bastion of freedom and equality has been difficult to shake, as scholars from Carter Woodson in the 1910s to Don West in the 1970s have implied that Appalachia was thoroughly and deeply abolitionist. Yet they have all distorted the evidence to make such a case, and their treatments of the subject are deceptive. Woodson, himself a black Appalachian native, published his landmark 1916 essay, "Freedom and Slavery in Appalachia," in the very first issue of the *Journal of Negro History,* which he founded and edited. He maintained that the Scotch-Irish who settle the southern highlands, a "liberty-loving, and tyrant-hating race," exhibited "more prejudice against the slave holder than against the Negro," and he stressed their antislavery sentiment in the region as pervasive and ongoing. Woodson's geographic scope was deceptively broad, however, and encompassed far more than the southern highlands, so that as much of his essay deals with abolitionist activity in piedmont North Carolina and central Kentucky as it does with those short-lived efforts in East Tennessee.[34]

West, a northern Georgia native and cofounder of the Highlander Folk School, has used only scattered evidence—from the East Tennessee abolitionists to incidents of Confederate disaffection in northern Georgia—to draw even more generalized conclusions regarding mountain liberalism on racial matters. From these few examples he claimed to demonstrate that the mountain South "consistently opposed slavery" and "refused to go with the Confederacy." The southern mountaineer, West wrote, "may be said to have held the Lincoln attitude generally."[35]

There was more than a touch of presentism in both Woodson's and West's historical claims. Each maintained that the racial tolerance of the antebellum period was part of a legacy still very much in evidence in the Appalachia in which they were raised. Woodson concluded his essay claiming that "one can observe even day-to-day such a difference in the atmosphere of the two sections, and in passing from the tidewater to the mountains it seems like going from one country into another. . . . In Appalachian America the races still maintain a sort of social contact," working, eating, and worshipping together. West, too, drew on his own childhood memories to make the same case. He recalled that he never saw a black person until he was fifteen years old and his family had moved from Georgia's mountains to sharecrop in the cotton country of Cobb County. Unfamiliar with the racial mores of the lowland South, the Wests welcomed their black neighbors as guests in their home and at their dinner table, much to the chagrin of local whites. When asked about it, his mother replied that she had always been taught to treat people equally, an attitude West claimed "was indicative of the sentiment of many people in the Appalachian South."[36]

So what is one to make of these extreme contradictions regarding highland attitudes toward blacks? Both contain significant elements of truth and perhaps even accurately convey the sentiments of certain pockets of southern highland society. However, there is another body of evidence that, while by no means either comprehensive or systematic, can be mustered in support of the idea that southern mountaineers were first and foremost southerners and that they viewed slavery and race in terms not unlike those of their yeoman or even slaveholding counterparts elsewhere in the South.

Certainly the most useful contemporary source on the subject is Frederick Law Olmsted. As a New York journalist he spent fourteen months traveling through the South in 1853 and 1854, observing and reporting on the region and its peculiar institution. The final month or so of his "journey through the back country," as he called the latter part of his tour, was spent in the highlands of Georgia, Tennessee, North Carolina, and Virginia. Although Olmsted was not completely objective in what he sought and how he reported it, his account of highlanders' opinions on slavery and race are invaluable for two reasons: first, unlike numerous other travel accounts on the region, his alone focused specifically on the issues of slavery and race; and second, he moved through so remote a section of the mountains that he was able to give voice to the most obscure and yet probably typical segment of the Appalachian populace.

While Olmsted noted some differences in slavery as it existed in the mountains, the comments he evoked from residents in many ways reflected attitudes not unlike those of nonslaveholding yeomen or poor whites elsewhere in the South at the time. Most seemed to be equally contemptuous of slaves, their masters, and the system itself. But given the option of eliminating slavery and the privileged class it supported, they consistently deferred to what they saw as the lesser evil. Few advocated abolishing the institution, and most were blatant in demonstrating that racism dominated their rationales for tolerating its perpetuation. Olmsted said of one Tennessee mountaineer, "He'd always wished there had n't been any niggers here . . . but he would n't think there was any better way of getting along with them than that they had." A highland woman reacted with "disgust and indignation on her face" when Olmsted informed her that blacks in New York were free. "I would n't want to live where niggers are free," she said. "They are bad enough when they are slaves. . . . If they was to think themselves equal to we, I don't think white folks could abide it—they're such vile saucy things." An East Tennessee farmer found the mere presence of blacks to be the system's worst feature and refused to be a part of it. Slaves were "horrid things," he said, insisting that he "would not take one to keep if it should be given to him."[37]

Olmsted and others after him recognized the degree to which class resentment was also at the core of whatever opposition mountaineers felt toward slavery and its beneficiaries. In his 1888 paean to the "loyal mountaineers" of Tennessee, Thomas Humes echoed a major theme of Olmsted's by noting that slavery, "even in the modified, domestic garb it wore" among these highlanders, had "a depressing, degrading influence" on them.[38] Slave labor and the plantation system forced yeomen from their seaboard and piedmont homes up into the mountains, where they were somewhat insulated from the system's direct competition but were nevertheless denied the greater economic opportunity the outside world had to offer. Southern highlanders, according to a 1903 analysis, "were penned up in the mountains because slavery shut out white labor. . . . It denied those that looked down from their mountain crags upon the realm of King Cotton a chance to expand, circulate, and mingle with the progressive elements at work elsewhere in the republic."[39] As northern Georgia's Lillian Smith even more eloquently phrased it, "A separation began in minds that had already taken place in living: a chasm between rich and poor that washed deeper and deeper as the sweat of more and more slaves poured into it."[40]

At least some mountain masters sensed the potential for lower-class resentment to transform itself into antislavery sentiment. Former Virginia governor David Campbell, a Washington County slaveowner, cautioned fellow slaveowners in the state's southwestern corner about how tenuous the commitment to the institution was among their nonslaveholding neighbors. Most Virginians west of the Blue Ridge, he observed, "never expect or intend to own" slaves and were thus not susceptible to the fervent proslavery defenses to which they were subjected during the sectional debates of 1850. While he recognized the common bonds of white supremacy that bound whites of all classes, he urged owners to tone down their impassioned rhetoric to their yeoman constituencies, since "they are not at all interested—so far from it [that] many of them feel exactly like the men of Indiana and Illinois or any of the northwestern states."[41]

Yet whatever element of truth there was to these claims of yeoman indifference to slavery's survival—and Olmsted for one offers considerable first-hand verification—a part of the cultural baggage mountain settlers brought from the lowlands was an intense and deeply rooted racism. In that sense they were very much like their "plain folk" counterparts throughout the South. Even nonslaveholding whites living closer to slavery and feeling even more directly victimized by it kept their resentment of the institution in check by more dominant feelings of contempt, hostility, and social superiority toward all blacks, free or slave. Many, in fact, lumped "crackers" and "rednecks" together with "hillbillies" in describing these effects.[42] In short, antislavery sentiment among Appalachians did not mean that they, any more than other southerners, were what Carl Degler has labeled "enemies of slavery on behalf of blacks."[43]

The strong racial prejudices in areas without a black populace were not a phenomenon limited to the mountain South. Other Americans in nonslaveholding parts of the country were hostile to what little black presence, if any, they lived with and felt threatened by future prospects of a black influx. Alexis de Tocqueveille had observed this racism without tangible targets during his visit to America in 1831. "In no part of the Union in which negroes are no longer slaves," he wrote, "they have in nowise drawn nearer to the whites. On the contrary, the prejudice of the race appears to be stronger in the states which have abolished slavery, than in those where it still exists; and nowhere is it so intolerant as in those states where servitude has never been known."[44]

Eugene Berwanger, in his study of attitudes toward slavery in the Old Northwest and other western frontiers, demonstrated that antislavery sentiment there was fueled far more by residents' prejudice against blacks and a desire to keep them out of their region than by any moral qualms about the peculiar institution. It took Rodger Cunningham to point out perhaps the most obvious link between Appalachia and other slaveless areas of the country. Dismissing moral components as causal factors, he stated that "the mountains were largely free of slavery 'only' because their climate, terrain, and soil were mostly unsuited to crops and plantation sizes for which slave labor was profitable." But this, he continued, "was also the reason the North had no slaves."[45]

Just as resentment of slavery was rarely based on humanitarian impulses toward its black victims, so there was little correlation during the war years between loyalty to the Union and abolitionist sentiment. Nevertheless, the degrees to which mountain men were committed to slavery's preservation has been a point of contention. Two nineteenth-century historians of East Tennessee (both natives of the region) have argued that its commitment to slavery was so strong as to endanger its place in the Union. Just before the state voted on 8 June 1861 to secede, Knoxville lawyer Oliver Temple laid out his priorities: "If we had to choose between the government on one side without slavery, and a broken and dissevered government with slavery, I would say unhesitatingly, 'Let slavery perish and the Union survive.'"[46] Thomas Humes contended that most "loyal mountaineers" would have agreed with Temple's choice. "Generally they looked upon slavery as something foreign to their social life," he wrote. "They would have been displeased at its coming near their homes in the imperious majesty it wore in the cotton States. At the same time they were satisfied to let men of the South keep serfs at pleasure, but they counted it no business of theirs to help in the work." Thus, he concluded, they would have had no hesitation in choosing "perpetuity of the Union over that of slavery."[47]

Most mountain Unionists were sensitive to charges that they opposed black bondage, however, and emphatically asserted their full support of the institution. In fact, highland spokesmen such as Zebulon Vance, William Brownlow, and Andrew Johnson argued against secession to their highland constituencies and readerships on the grounds that slavery was safer in, rather than out of, the Union. Alexander J. Jones of Henderson County, one of western North Carolina's most vocal Unionists, asserted that "by throwing off those guarantees—the Constitution and the Union—southern states have done the cause of slavery more injury than anyone else could have done." Others warned of the devaluation of slave property and the difficulties of reclaiming fugitive slaves who went north into what would be foreign territory.[48]

"Parson" Brownlow, whose Knoxville newspaper made him among East Tennessee's most visible opponents of secession, was quick to state that his "contempt for the Abolitionists of the North is only equaled by my hatred of the Disunionists of the South." Nevertheless, he expressed what were likely the sentiments of large numbers of mountain residents: "The Union men of the border slave states are loyal to their Government and do not regard the election of Lincoln as any just cause for dissolving the Union. . . . But, if we were once convinced that the Administration in Washington and the people of the North contemplated the subjugation of the South or the abolishing of slavery, there would not be a Union man among us in twenty-four hours." Many mountain Unionists felt betrayed by Lincoln's Emancipation Proclamation, and some even abandoned their loyalist stance as a result. Former congressman Thomas A. R. Nelson, one of East Tennessee's most influential antisecessionist voices in 1861, declared two years later that he would have advocated secession if he "had believed it was the object of the North to subjugate the South and emancipate our slaves." "The Union men of East Tennessee," he declared emphatically, "are not now and never were Abolitionists."[49]

The very fact that mountain slaveholders were among the most ardent Unionists is indication enough that abolition was hardly the basis of their anti-Confederate tendencies. Both Zebulon Vance and Andrew Johnson had modest slaveholdings, and many who owned far more slaves were equally as resistant to secession. Analysis of election returns in western North Carolina on a referendum to hold a secession convention indicates a fairly even split between slaveholders and little or no correlation between a county's slave population and its vote on secession.[50]

Perhaps the most striking example of this pattern—or lack of pattern—was the situation in Kentucky's Tug Valley. In her masterful study of the Hatfield-McCoy feud, Altina Waller noted the paradoxical fact that Harmon McCoy, one of the valley's few slaveholders, was also among the few residents who remained loyal to the Union when the war broke out. But in that area he was not alone. Slaveholders in Pike County were as a rule less likely to support the Confederacy than were most of its nonslaveholding farmers.[51] Studies of northern Georgia's mountain counties also indicate that the few residents with substantial slaveholdings were actively Unionist and in several instances served in the Union rather than the Confederate army.[52]

Likewise in those parts of southern Appalachia where support for secession was strong, highlanders' concerns about slavery's future under a Republican regime was a vital factor in shaping that support. In 1944 historian Henry Shanks argued that the strong secessionist vote in Virginia's southwestern corner (85 percent of its delegates voted to withdraw from the Union in May) was due to substantial ownership of slaves by local farmers and their bitter hostility to "abolitionism, to the Republican party, and to the election of Lincoln."[53] While such sentiments were taken for granted in most other parts of the South, much of the explanation for highland support of the Confederacy has generally been the independence and individualism inherent in mountaineers. Even more vaguely, as a western Carolinian wrapped in the romance of the "lost cause" explained in 1905, the mountain South seceded not as a defense of slavery but, rather, over "the real issue . . . a lofty and patriotic sense of duty which animated the Southern people of all classes."[54]

Until recently such rationales were accepted with little acknowledgment of how central slavery's survival was as a motivating factor for much of Appalachia's support of secession, despite evidence of considerable rhetoric to that effect. The crisis raised even greater fears as to the impact of slavery's abolition on the southern highlands, fears that mountain secessionists were quick and effective in exploiting. Georgia governor Joseph E. Brown, himself a native of the state's mountain region, appealed to the racial fears of his fellow northern Georgians in urging them to support their state's separation from the Union. Within the Union, slavery was no longer safe, he reasoned, and "so soon as the slaves were at liberty, thousands of them would leave the cotton and rice fields in the lower part of our State, and make their way to the healthier climate in the mountain region. We should have them plundering and stealing, robbing, and killing in all the lovely vallies of the mountains."[55] Western North Carolina politicians were just as vocal in raising the specter of such an influx among their constituents as they described "the terrible calamity of having three hundred thousand idle, vagabond free negroes turned loose upon you with all the privileges of white men." By the same token, in seceding from Virginia, West Virginians were sharply divided as to the future status of slavery in their new state constitution, but they had no problem in agreeing to a Negro exclusion policy that would ban either slave importation or free black migration into the state.[56]

There are other indications that some sections of Appalachia could claim no exemptions from the evils of southern racial prejudice. Slave markets existed in a number of mountain communities, such as Wheeling, Winchester, and Abingdon in Virginia; Bristol, Jonesboro, Knoxville, and Chattanooga in Tennessee; and London and Pikeville in Kentucky. (Witnessing the cruelties of the slave trade in Wheeling, in fact, set Benjamin Lundy on his abolitionist course.)[57] Slave auctions elsewhere in the upper South were apparently dependent on slaves supplied from highland areas, and it was not an uncommon sight, according to British geologist George Featherstonaugh, to see slave coffles moving through southwest Virginia and East Tennessee headed for deep South markets. On an 1844 trip through the southern highlands, he expressed amazement at the sight of slave-drivers with over 300 men, women, and children in chains, which he encountered both along the New River valley and then again in Knoxville as they moved their human cargo toward Natchez, Mississippi.[58]

At least one observer saw the mere living conditions of mountain slaves to be intolerable and was skeptical of claims for their well-being. Joseph John Gurney, a British Quaker traveling through the Virginia mountains in 1841, encountered black workers at White Sulphur Springs and was distressed at the "miserable manner in which the slaves were clad." After chiding their master, a physician, on their appearance, Gurney reported, "he assured me that the slaves were among the happiest of human beings; but it was nearer the truth, when he afterwards observed that they were remarkably able to endure hardships." He concluded from this encounter that "certain it is, that the negroes here, as elsewhere, are an easy, placid, and long-suffering race."[59]

Former slaves themselves bore witness to the fact that bondage in the southern highlands was not necessarily any less abusive than elsewhere. Sarah Gudger recalled the visits of a "specalator" to a neighboring plantation near Old Fort, North Carolina. He and "Old Marse" would pick out a slave from the field, and then "dey slaps de han'cuffs on him and tak him away to de cotton country." Mary Barbour, from the same county, testified that her master sold almost all of his slaves, including at least twelve of her brothers and sisters, when they reached age three. Aunt Sophia, a former slave from eastern Kentucky, contended that though her master "wuzn't as mean as most," a nearby owner "wuz so mean to his slaves that I know two gals that kilt themselfs."[60]

After the war the racial violence that plagued so much of the South was evident in the mountains as well. The influx of blacks into such cities as Knoxville, Chattanooga, and Asheville led to open unrest not unlike that in other southern cities. In Ashville, the attempt by a black man to vote in 1868 led to a race riot that left one black dead and several blacks and whites wounded. In his study of this and other such incidents, Eric Olson noted that in terms of reactions expressed in the local newspaper, there was little to differentiate Asheville from Savannah.[61]

Several studies of the northern Georgia mountains make the case that racial violence was no less apparent there than in other parts of the state during the postwar decades. Edward Ayers has noted that although blacks in Whitfield and other mountain counties posed little political or economic threat to white residents during Reconstruction, the Ku Klux Klan in that area was notorious for the brutal treatment it and other mobs inflicted on the relatively few blacks in their midst. "Honor reigned," Ayers observed, "with as much volatility among the whites of the hills as among their low-country brethren."[62] Yet Ayers argued that the postemancipation abuse of highland blacks was distinguished from that elsewhere in the South by the fact that it was integral to a long tradition of group violence and extralegal retribution among mountaineers, the majority of which was inflicted by whites on other whites. In analyses of the whitecapping that plagued Georgia's mountain counties during the moonshine wars of the 1880s and 1890s, both Will Holmes and Fitzhugh Brundage confirm the biracial makeup of whitecappers' targets but note that blacks were whipped and murdered for offenses that included insolence or miscegenation as well as any threat they might have posed to moonshiners' security.[63]

In his statistical analysis of racial violence in late nineteenth-century Kentucky, George Wright noted that while mountain residents lynched fewer blacks than did other Kentuckians, they did so at a rate proportionate to the region's African American populace.[64] In a more broadly cast statistical study of racial violence in Appalachia, Robert Stuckert suggests that blacks were more often victimized by white mobs in mountain areas than elsewhere. Though only 6 percent of the black population of seven southern states lived in the highlands, over 10 percent of the blacks lynched in those states were Appalachian residents.[65] Brundage confirms these findings with his rather startling discovery that no area of Virginia saw more lynchings than did its mountain counties. Of a total of seventy blacks lynched in Virginia between 1880 and 1930, no less than twenty-four lost their lives in southwestern counties, a phenomenon Brundage credits to the "furious pace" of the region's postwar social and economic transformations, particularly the influx of itinerant black and foreign workers into mining and lumber camps. The fact that most occurred in towns, the centers of this change, rather than in the hills or countryside, confirms the economic roots of this particular expression of mountain racism.[66]

Although some Appalachians exhibited the same violent and abusive treatment toward blacks as other southerners, there are also indications of "kinder and gentler" race relations in the region. I have suggested elsewhere that slaveholders in the Carolina highlands exhibited more benevolent attitudes and lenient treatment toward their black property than was usual in the lowland South. Despite the conclusions of British Quaker Joseph John Gurney that slaves in southwestern Virginia were no better off than those in other parts of the South, other outside observers have provided among the most explicit testimony that there was indeed a qualitative difference in the treatment of highland bondsmen. Charles Lanman, for example, wrote in 1849 that "the slaves residing among the mountains are the happiest and most independent portion of the population." Olmsted noted that in the southern highlands, slavery's "moral evils . . . are less, even proportionately to the number of slaves." He detected that they were "less closely superintended. . . . They exercise more responsibility, and both in soul and intellect they are more elevated."[67] I also detected among mountain masters in North Carolina what seemed to be a preponderance of acts of goodwill, affectionate references to their slaves, unusual efforts—including on occasion financial sacrifice—to ensure their welfare and happiness, and even occasional pangs of conscience about the system.[68]

Other scholars have also noted greater moderation or leniency in highland race relations. In an analysis of political divisiveness in Virginia from 1790 to 1830, Van Beck Hall demonstrated the degree to which western legislators, while fully supportive of slavery itself, often differed from their eastern counterparts on more peripheral issues regarding blacks. On various occasions Appalachian delegates blocked proposals to toughen manumission procedures, to pass retaliatory measures against blacks after Gabriel Prosser's aborted 1800 rebellion, and to ban the distribution of abolitionist publications in the state. At the same time they supported measures to liberalize restrictions on the state's free black population, to end compensation for masters of slave criminals who were executed or banished, and to support Richmond free black efforts to establish their own church.[69]

Even during the intense racist repression of the Reconstruction era, some highlanders showed more restraint in dealing with the new freedman population than southerners elsewhere. In his comprehensive study of the Republican Party in the southern highlands, Gordon McKinney credited at least part of the explanation for its success there to "the relative lack of hostility between mountain whites and blacks," though he noted that it was an alliance based far more on political pragmatism than humanitarian ideals.[70] Despite John Eaton's observations regarding racism in Reconstruction Tennessee, a recent study has suggested that emancipation was accepted more quickly in East Tennessee than was true elsewhere in the occupied South.[71] Eric Olson concluded his study of racial postwar violence in Asheville with the suggestion that the incidents he described were more the exception than the rule; the disruptions remained more isolated and their effects more easily contained than was the case in similar incidents in Atlanta, for example.[72] J. Morgan Kousser, in documenting racial disfranchisement in the turn-of-the-century South, noted that hill country whites were among the few who opposed denying blacks the political rights they had gained a generation earlier, though such resistance had less to do with any benevolence toward blacks than with the realization that they were often the unacknowledged secondary victims of such measures as literacy tests, poll taxes, and understanding clauses.[73]

So where are we left in terms of characterizing the racism of nineteenth-century Appalachians? The reality seems almost as contradictory and confusing as the myths. If the evidence presented here does not span quite the extremes of the popular assumptions laid out in fictional form by Fox and Faulkner, it fills in much of the intervening space along that vast spectrum of opinion. The nature of the evidence on racism at the grassroots level of any populace is and must remain scattered, speculative, and circumstantial, so that any definitive or comprehensive statement on how mountain whites viewed blacks remains elusive. But the sheer range of experiences—lynchings and race riots occurring in areas where abolitionism had thrived; blacks moving quickly into some parts of the region when given the option, while deserting others just as rapidly; some highlanders willing to leave the Union to protect slavery while others proved relatively receptive to emancipation—all demonstrate the dangers of generalizing about highland attitudes and of drawing any hard and fast conclusions about a society that has been subjected to far more than its share of homogenization, stereotyping, and image-making.

Barbara Fields has warned us of the dangers of according race "a transhistorical, almost metaphysical, status," noting that "ideas about color, like ideas about anything else, derive their importance, indeed their very definition, from their context."[74] The variety of white responses to blacks in southern Appalachia serves as a vivid reminder of the fact that racial attitudes and actions are indeed functions of other social, economic, political, or even sectional forces. The power struggles between a state's mountain region and its state government or lowland elite; the politicalization of slavery, emancipation, and later disfranchisement and segregation; the demographic shifts, often dramatic, of populations black and white into or out of highland areas; the effects of poverty and other forms of material stagnation or deprivation; the new dynamics of community and class, and accompanying tensions, brought on by colonialism, industrialization, urbanization, and other forces of modernization—all of these were very real aspects of the Appalachian experience that could, and often did, affect racial attitudes. The actual contacts between mountain whites and blacks were of course a crucial—but far from consistent or predictable—factor in shaping race relations in the region. But these other factors were equally significant, if more subtle, determinants of highlanders' perceptions and treatment of blacks. The variations in pace and degree at which these changes were felt throughout the region may be the key to explaining the quiltlike character of highland racism.

Fields reminds us, too, that racism can be a slippery concept to pin down. "Attitudes," she maintains, "are promiscuous critters and do not mind cohabiting with their opposites."[75] Such was certainly true of racism's highland manifestations. The fluidity and often contradictory expressions of racial opinions among mountaineers reflect the diversity and complexity of experience rarely acknowledged about Appalachia and its historical development. Once that range of experience is recognized, it may be that the most that one can draw from this admittedly sketchy overview is that there was nothing truly unique about Appalachian racial attitudes. The region's residents were first and foremost southerners. Despite demographic deviations in their racial makeup and their political alienation from the South's dominant slaveocracy, white highlanders' views of African Americans in theory and treatment of them in practice were for the most part well within the mainstream of attitudes and behavior elsewhere in the South, a mainstream that was in itself by no means monolithic. Likewise those views manifested in the few areas of Appalachia without a significant black presence were not so different from those of Americans in other nonslaveholding parts of the country. On either side of the Mason-Dixon line, nineteenth-century white America was racist, varying only in degree and in form of expression. The same was true of Appalachia.

It is one thing simply to chronicle or to categorize the varieties of ways in which white mountaineers viewed or treated blacks, and that is all that has been attempted here. It is quite another to sort out, identify, and explain the more elusive causal factors behind such views. That formidable task still looms large as one of the more exciting challenges confronting Appalachian scholars and can perhaps proceed once the debris of myth and misconception that has for so long obstructed the route to such insights is at long last cleared away.

7

by Judith Ivy Fiene

Gender, Class and Self-Image

Little systematic attention has been given to the importance of gender in determining the individual life course in Appalachia (Tickamyer and Tickamyer 1987; Walls and Billings 1977). Little data is available on female-headed households and there is a paucity of statistical data regarding Appalachian women in general (Weeks 1980). Analyses of social structure in Appalachian communities frequently define women's lives solely in relation to their position or role functions within the traditional family group (Photiadis 1986; Stephenson 1968; Schwarzweller, Brown, and Mangalam 1971).

Low-status Appalachian women, in particular, have been typically represented by stereotypical images not only in the media but, at times, in the professional literature of the past fifty years. Images of this type are still prevalent in some programs serving the rural poor and can structure the quality of institutional interactions with the women themselves. Such images fail to communicate the diversity of interests, skills, and abilities among women in this segment of the society. Frequently overlooked is the flexibility women display in response to their stressful environment and the strength that some have gained through adversity.

This chapter examines the impact of both gender and social status on the mental health of low-status rural Appalachian women. It will review the images of low-status women presented in contemporary Appalachian studies literature and the sources of some common stereotypes. Descriptions of low-status women derived from the following four sources will be addressed: (1) sociological and anthropological studies that map social stratification and social structure in rural Appalachian communities, (2) studies of the psychological characteristics of Appalachian women and their families, (3) social science studies concerned with the impact of the political and economic dynamics of the region on its people, and (4) accounts of the lives of individual women contained in oral histories or biographies.

Whatever the source, descriptions of a group of people, such as low-status women, can become static, frozen in their spot in time. Considerable intellectual energy is then expended in attempting to determine how and why the women have developed as they have. Because it is not possible to see the people they will become, it is easy to overlook the fact that they may change, mature, learn from experience. Their own perspective on who they have become and how they define themselves, will be addressed using an analysis of the self-descriptions of some low-status women as contained in their life stories. The chapter will conclude with an assessment of the implications of these varied perspectives for the mental health of low-status women.

Social Status in Rural Communities

Discussions of women in the majority of ethnography and sociological studies focused on Appalachia are embedded in analyses and descriptions of the family. Recognizing the prevalence of familism in the region (Heller and Quesada 1977), these studies concentrate their attention on either the kinship network or the generative family: parents and minor children. Low-status women may be perceived in their rural communities in terms of the, often derogatory, labels placed on their kinship group or they may be categorized as members of families clinging to traditional mountain values.

Studies in isolated mountain communities with a high degree of kinship have found that the ideal of egalitarianism, merging with the need for cooperation, minimizes the stratification process while blunting intragroup aggression (Beaver 1976, 1986; Hicks 1976). Even these closely knit communities, however, are socially stratified, and women or men who are deemed to be lazy, unwilling to work, or prone to dependency on social agencies are at the bottom of the group socially and economically and are labeled worthless by the larger community (Beaver 1976). In such communities, where close scrutiny of behavior is inevitable due to the small size of the group, problematic behavior is tied to deviations from the group work ethic.

Closely associated with this perspective is another form of labeling applied to women identified as members of stigmatized families with a multigenerational history of "sorry" behavior. Female "sorry" behavior has been said to include promiscuity, social dependency, alcoholism, and inadequate mothering (Cavender 1981; Hicks 1976). The existence of expectations based on community experience with earlier generations of an individual's family creates the possibility of qualitative differences in interactions with these individuals across their life span: in school, church, etc. Labeling by family association can lead to the maintenance of the social status quo, influence the development of self-identity in low-status youth, and probably controls the nature of the resources made available to individuals in this group.

Other ethnographic studies in Appalachia have reported a clearer stratification system with some variation of high, middle- and low-strata (Keefe, Reck, and Reck 1985; Schwarzweller et al. 1971; Stephenson 1968). A common assumption has been that the critical demarcation between social strata is determined by each group's level of adaptation to the norms and life styles of the urban middle class. Low-status groups are seen as least assimilated to the new norms and women in this category are said to be more bound by traditional sex-role mores (Kaplan 1971; Photiadis 1970). Traditional female role behavior, restrictions in the choice of role models, and limited employment opportunities are all seen as factors affecting the occupational aspirations of women (Photiadis 1986).

A composite picture of the low-status woman, drawn from the types of studies just discussed, portrays a socially isolated woman whose role choices are limited to those of homemaker and mother except in the face of serious economic necessity. She is seldom self-assertive and chooses to avoid problematic situations. She may be content with her lot in life or fatalistic about God's will. There is a high probability that she is dependent, at some time, on community social services and has more children than the national average. At various times in her life, she may exhibit symptoms related to chronic stress and depression. She may become the victim of family violence and yet be unable to act decisively for herself. Her inexperience in the larger social world makes it difficult for her to deal with impersonal representatives of assisting agencies.

The multiple sources of stress in rural poverty families has been delineated by Fitchen (1981). Parents are portrayed as struggling through economic losses and unemployment, overcrowded and inadequate housing, acute disruptions in the marital relationship, and the myriad problems presented by illness to maintain the family unit at all costs. A similar scene was observed in southern Appalachia by Coles (1971). When the family unit remains the focus of attention, however, the specific position of women is often obscured. Given the socialization of American women as the guardians of the family's emotional welfare, women in poor families would seem to occupy a dangerously stressful position in our social world.

Psychological Perspectives

Specific personality traits have been associated with low-status women. Ball (1968) and Photiadis (n.d.) suggested that a lack of integration into mainstream cultural norms and perceptions of social and economic deprivation have created specific personality attributes and values in low-status individuals. In this model low-status women are said to evidence resignation, fatalism, apathy, and frustration while displaying social dependency, a present orientation with the seeking of immediate gratification, alcoholism, fecundity, and low levels of education. Attributions of this type are a mixture of concepts drawn from descriptions of regional personality characteristics thought to constitute an Appalachian subculture (Weller 1965), and studies of the characteristics of poverty families (Parenstedt 1965), typical of research using the culture of poverty model. This model has been criticized extensively and its deleterious applications to the Appalachian population have been reviewed by writers including Fisher (1977) and Walls and Billings (1977).

Two prominent studies, conducted in the early 1970s, touch on the socialization process in low-income or low-status rural Appalachian families. Although these studies are concerned with special populations, families with psychologically disturbed children (Looff 1971), and neglectful mothers (Polansky, Borgman, and De Saix 1972), their conclusions have influenced present-day images of low-status Appalachian women.

Looff (1971), a psychiatrist, concluded that the most common mental health problems in rural Appalachia are school-phobia, overly dependent personality disorders, conversion reactions and hysterical personality disorders, and elective mutism. Women, viewed in their maternal role, are described as so nurturing, warm, and indulgent (a personality strength) that many of them end up being overprotective, particularly of male children (potentially pathogenic). Other negative results of this strong orientation to feelings are said to be a lack of control of aggressive impulses and reduced verbal communication.

In addressing the special problems of the very poor, Looff warns against generalizations regarding poverty populations, pointing to the diversity of experience in differing environments. He also recognizes the role of insufficient economic opportunities and resources in creating stresses that are interactive with individual personality configurations.

Polasky et al. (1972) paint a negative picture of an intergenerational cycle of poverty and futility stemming from pervasive inadequacies in maternal personality, resulting in serious child neglect. Subscribing to subcultural theory, the authors identify four cultural themes said to be both regressive and distinctive of Appalachian culture. These are infantilization of males; separation anxiety, conformity, and fusion fantasies; inexpressiveness; and fatalism. Polansky et al.'s study is significant both because it labels Appalachian mothers and traditional family styles as pathogenic and also because the paucity of subsequent research has left these conclusions unchallenged in psychological literature. As such, it has contributed to the stereotype of low-status Appalachian women.

Economic Dynamics

The impact of economic exploitation and cultural imperialism on the welfare of Appalachian communities and families has been extensively described (Gaventa 1980; Lewis and Knipe 1978). These observers locate the economic problems of the Appalachian region in the usurping of the area's resources by outside moneyed interests and depict the region's women and men as powerless to control the nature or profits of their labor (Lewis and Knipe 1978).

Strategies for coping with their environment may place low-status women in conflict with the community representatives commissioned to assist them. The source of this conflict is seen to result from the historical incompatibility between traditional mountain women and their values (simplicity, cooperation, egalitarianism, and familism) and the values of the newcomers to the region at the end of the nineteenth century (hard work, education, cleanliness, and competitiveness). The unsophisticated mountain woman encountered a powerful new role model in the missionaries, teachers, and nurses who came to the area. What ensued, unfortunately, has been a continual denigration of the indigenous culture leaving the natives on the defensive.

From this perspective, local cultural patterns, such as passive behavior and fatalistic attitudes, are functional coping mechanisms developed in the face of external threats to existence and serve to preserve the family unit as a refuge for individuals powerless to change a hostile environment (Lewis, Kobak, and Johnson 1978). Families become resistant to change and encourage child behaviors that increase family harmony while rejecting outside social institutions. For example, maternal overprotection, which is defined as problematic by child development specialists, is not defined as such by many low-status families and can be viewed as their means of binding children to the haven of the family group, where they will be valued. Efforts to teach middle-class child rearing practices are often met with passive resistance. This would suggest that health and welfare personnel attempting to modify such behaviors are treating the symptom rather than the problem.

Regardless of the larger politico-cultural causal factors, however, disturbances in the families of the very poor are perceived as problems to be dealt with by a variety of community institutions. In the absence of any systemic reforms in the economic-social system, the available remedies (such as shelters for battered women, psychological counseling, foster care for children) entail the risk that families will be dissolved and individuals with little access to economic resources will be set adrift from the very family systems that have been their strength and protection.

It is in firsthand accounts of the ordinary lives of individuals, in oral histories and biographies, that one often encounters a more sympathetic treatment of Appalachian female character. In studies of this type, Appalachian women are likely to be portrayed as proud and decent with a natural dignity (Kahn 1972; Lewis, Selfridge et al. 1986). The realities of their uncompromising environment and the economic exploitation of their families may have led to feelings of frustration and anger but have also motivated efforts to resist future exploitation (Kahn 1972). The women are noted to show "courage, humor and strength in the face of formidable odds" (Smith 1986). Although it is the nature of this type of literature to feature the positive traits of the subjects, these reports also demonstrate that the central role for women is as the protector of the emotional well-being of the family (whether that be the nuclear family, the single-parent family, or the larger family of humankind). These women have been called upon to comfort and cater to men who have faced failure and humiliation in the larger world. They have attempted to defend their children in the larger world. They have attempted to defend their children against the slurs and prejudices of those who have superior economic positions. They have banded together to protest the industrial insults to their families and their environment. But the documents also make it clear that this role expectation—to be a strong, emotionally supportive women—has its own price, paid in fatigue, emotional depletion, depression, and frustrated anger that can result in periodic emotional dysfunction.

Self-Perceptions of Appalachian Women

The perspectives of low-status women discussed up to this point may seem, at times, contradictory. Are they unsophisticated hedonists and apathetic drudges or stoic protectors of the family? The wide variety of reported perceptions are probably attributable to the range of persons and behaviors encountered by the observers, the level of observation dictated by different professional disciplines, and the underlying ideological positions that structure the studies. It is certainly feasible that much of what has been reported is true for some part of the population under discussion. But, there is a further dimension that can be added to enhance an understanding of the social world of low-status women in Appalachia. This dimension can be derived from an analysis of the ways the women describe and explain themselves. For the women under discussion are more than products of their social context or the sum of their psychological characteristics; they are creative actors within their social sphere.

This approach differs methodologically from the more strictly narrative methods of oral histories. It entails the analysis of women's stories, using the grounded theory method developed by Glaser and Strauss (1967), to discover the embedded categories of meaning in their revealed social world. The possibilities of this approach for understanding low-status women will be demonstrated in the following illustrations taken from a series of informal interviews, conducted by the author, with eighteen rural women over a five-month period.

The study was conducted in an East Tennessee county, hereafter referred to by the pseudonym Clark County. Clark County is essentially rural; the majority (75%) of the population lives outside of its two small towns, and 87% are native Tennesseans. The county's largely unspoiled environment consists of scenic mountains, narrow river valleys, and rolling, rocky farmland. Although the county lacks major mineral deposits, it has a wealth of timber that is still being harvested. The industrial park in the county seat flourished during a brief boom in the early 1970s, but there has been a steady attrition of small industries out of the county. Unemployment is endemic, averaging over 20% in the winter months. The tourist industry in nearby areas provides temporary summer employment, usually consisting of minimum wage jobs in service occupations for women. Almost one quarter (23.68%) of the families in the county have incomes below the poverty level (U.S. Bureau of the Census 1982) and are receiving food stamps (Tennessee Advisory Commission on Intergovernmental Relations 1985). Only 40% of the residents graduated from high school.

The subjects of this study were participants in a local child development program, which serves children under four. The study participants were Appalachian born and raised. Excluded from the study were women experiencing current, severe family or legal problems.

The eighteen informants, all mothers, ranged in age from 21 to 67; slightly more than half of them were in their twenties. They represented fourteen different households. Only four women lived in traditional nuclear families, six households contained three generations of family members, and seven households were headed by women, representative of the varied family composition so seldom noted in Appalachian studies. Three women had never married, seven were divorced, two had separated, and one was widowed. This group of women had a fertility rate considerably higher than the national average of fewer than two pregnancies per woman. The women under 30 had averaged 3 pregnancies apiece while the older women had on the average 6.6 pregnancies. (These figures exclude the subject in her sixties who at 20 pregnancies had more than double the pregnancies of anyone else in the group.) Although the younger women had stayed in school a few years longer than the older women, only one had graduated from high school and one had a GED.

In Appalachia, as in the rest of the United States, female-headed households are over represented in poverty groups. In the southern Appalachian region, which includes all of Tennessee's Appalachian counties, 11% of the non-female-headed families live in poverty, compared to 36.8% of the female-headed families with children (Tickamyer and Tickamyer

1987). All the households in the study under discussion were below the rural poverty level. Nuclear family groups, however, were more likely to have earned income than female-headed households. The majority of the families existed on some combination of Aid to Dependent Children, Social Security, or VA benefits supplemented by food stamps. Few of the informants had ever worked outside the home and belonged to the class of women described by Petchesky (1983) as being "the high fertility, low-labor-force participation group . . . who never or hardly ever work outside the home and are married to working-class men or receiving welfare" (p. 231).

The following self-descriptions were not necessarily planned or deliberate statements about self. That is, the informants were not asked to describe themselves nor did they say, "This is what I'm like." Rather, the descriptions were embedded in the context of stories about life events and emerged during data analysis. A few contextual facts about each informant will be appended to their self-definitions to provide a context for the reader and to illustrate the ways in which the women also fit into descriptive categories developed through the use of alternative perspectives discussed earlier.

These women have experienced multiple stresses in their lives. Chronic economic hardships have affected their health, their marital relationships, and the life chances of the children they have nurtured. They had a high probability of being born into families that were fractured by divorce or the early death of a parent; some of them have been the victims of sexual abuse and physical violence. Yet their self-images display resiliency and resourcefulness.

One self-perception which emerges is that these are women who persevere. Perseverance is highlighted in stories about continuing to tackle a problem in the face of apparent failure or in doing what is needed despite multiple obstacles. Lorraine keeps trying to learn how to swim despite her fear of water. At age 56, she keeps going back to swimming class each summer and doesn't plan to give up trying. She is raising two grandchildren and her own children move in and out of her housing project apartment.

Ida persevered and is proud of it. She remembers her struggle after her husband left her with 15 children to raise and little income. Five of the children came down with pneumonia. She nursed them back to health at home and even the doctor complimented her efforts. Ida accomplished her child-rearing tasks in the early 1950s while receiving $91 a month from AFDC and before Medicaid benefits were available.

A second image which emerges is that of hard-working women. Hard work was defined by the informants as physical labor done outside of the house. It might entail physical upkeep of the house and property (fixing the roof, painting the house, mowing the large yard), or actually building a home. Women in female-headed households taking responsibility for the care and upkeep of their residences were likely to express this type of self-definition.

A less traditional way of defining themselves as workers was expressed by two of the women in their twenties. They felt the happiest when able to work outside the home. Here it isn't the nature of the work that is important (one subject has been a nurse's aide, another a motel maid) but the invigorating feeling that accompanies being employed away from home. The self-definition as a worker thus takes precedence over identification in homemaking roles. The informants believe working in the community enhances their performance in the home. These statements were made by Jane and Barbara (both married to men from outside of the area), who have three and four children, respectively. Both husbands have periodic difficulty finding employment. Barbara and her family had to camp out in a garage recently for several months after she had a new baby and they were down on their luck. Jane and her family spent the coldest winter in recent memory, four years ago, in an uninsulated, converted bus.

A third way in which these informants characterized themselves was as worldly women. The importance of access to experiences in developing positive self-concepts is demonstrated by the following two women.

Other informants had confided that they felt physically unwell when they left their county; however, when they were forced to do this over time (as when they had to take a handicapped child to repeated medical appointments in a nearby urban area) their anxiety abated. Low-status Appalachian women are not alone in harboring fears of the bigger world outside of the known perimeter of home and neighborhood.

Two women described their ability to have anxiety-free interactions in the larger social world outside of home and family and even outside of the local community. They credit this ability to the experience they gained through living and/or traveling to places outside of Tennessee. Ida attributes her superior knowledge of the world to living in a milltown in North Carolina during her childhood, 60 years ago, while Lorraine, after separating from her husband, has traveled on her own to visit relatives over 300 miles away.

In a fourth means of self-definition, some women perceived themselves as independent minded. This is defined by one woman as not taking orders from others. True to the Appalachian nonconfrontational style, this is not done in defiance. In Barbara's definition, an independent-minded woman knows how to bargain to gain her own way. Her husband, who is practically illiterate, had been against her reading so many books. Barbara told him she'd give up the books if he'd give up something of comparable value, but they could not decide on what that something would be. Her husband finally just gave up his demand, and recently he even bought her a whole box of books at the flea market. An independent-minded woman also knows when to compromise and when to keep her mouth shut, so she can continue to have her own way. Barbara is determined to discipline her children her way despite the criticism of her husband and father-in-law, so she just listens to what they say, smiles to herself and does as she pleases, since she spends most of her time alone with the children. Barbara contrasts this type of independent-minded women with "women libbers who want to be like a man." She is defining her style of being her own person, and regardless of feminist critiques of this style, Barbara perceives it as a way of controlling her social reality.

A fifth self-definition, in contrast to the description of women in this status group as present oriented, is that of planner. Present behaviors are justified by the women interviewed based on their projections of the behavior outcomes. They describe themselves as either being concerned with behavior outcomes or as convinced that certain outcomes are tied to specific behaviors.

Jane brought this up when she reflected on why she remained a virgin until she married (her own mother hadn't married the fathers of her several children). Jane said, at first, that she hadn't been much interested in boys and romance, but then added that she always was one to worry about the future and "what was down the road." Nora has a firm idea about how she should train her grandchildren to act when they are in autos, based on her assumptions of the possible consequences to children who are rowdy and disturb the driver. Nora is an illiterate grandmother, who protects her two young grandchildren by keeping them in their cribs much of the day (to the despair of her child development worker). Barbara chooses not to interfere in the disputes among her four children so the younger ones will learn not to allow older or larger children to bully them. An outside observer might assume that Barbara is a lazy or uncaring mother, or apathetic about the behavior of her children, unless enlightened by her view of her parenting priorities.

Finally, some of the informants considered themselves women with backbone. The ability to turn one's life around, to bring victory out of disaster, is an all-American story, featured regularly in our Sunday magazines. Such stories appear no more miraculous than the turn-around demonstrated by two women in this study. Both had spent years of their lives in desperate marriages filled with abuse and neglect. If interviewed during those years, each would have qualified for Polansky et al's (1972) study of the apathy-futility syndrome.

One of the women described the change in her life as the process of getting backbone.

Backbone, as she defines it, is the inner feeling that you can stand up to life and you won't let anyone beat you down. Lorraine said she used to "hump up to life," just taking the blows as they came but now she can stand up tall. For more than 15 years, she accepted her husband's opinion that she was dumb and, thus, no one would want to employ her. She credits her growing hatred of her philandering spouse as the means of her emancipation and new sense of selfhood.

Reena conveyed the same substantial feeling when she talked about her passage from a beaten, helpless wife to the confident, competent woman she is today. Backbone seems to be something one has to find within oneself and significantly both of these women suffered endless indignities before they initiated self-change. Reena had lived in abject poverty with her abusive husband and five children, begging for food because he had stolen the food stamps. When community agencies intervened and she faced the loss of her children, Reena began to change and, with the aid of a human service agency's homemaker, has made a new life for herself. Reena ultimately left her husband, although she continues to live in fear of him.

The positive self-images of women in this study often seem incongruent with some of the more visible aspects of their lives. Many of the older women appear lined and careworn beyond their years. Even the younger women show the beginnings of chronic dental problems that distract from their appearances. Their clothing is secondhand and their haircuts may be shapeless and unflattering. Yet, their self-definitions demonstrate that to evaluate them only in terms of these appearances or the roles they enact within their families and social strata does them an injustice.

Implications for Mental Health Planning

The prevalent images of low-status women in the social science literature and the contrast with women's own self-perceptions suggest the following implications for those concerned with mental health issues.

Pertinent to the lives of individual rural low-status women is the nature of change in their social world. More of them are finding themselves single parents with little expectation of economic assistance except from government programs. Faced with a life of poverty, some women search for alternatives, but their socialization and education have not prepared them to enter competitive job markets or even given them the skills of interacting with the world outside the circle of their immediate acquaintances. The question to be addressed is how to assist these women to broaden their horizons and opportunities while avoiding the "make them like us" approach of the nineteenth-century missionary women.

The social and economic dependency of low-status women leaves them few choices when they are faced with failing or violent marriages or separation and divorce. While individual or group counseling may help them weather the immediate emotional stress, it cannot prevent them from falling even deeper into poverty. The women would benefit from access to jobs (paying better than minimum wage and carrying health and retirement benefits) and the supportive systems necessary to their employment, affordable day care and reliable transportation. Job-training programs keyed to the available job markets could enhance their opportunities. In this respect, the resources valuable to women are little different in Appalachia than elsewhere in the United States. But to what degree is it practical to focus on the needs of individual women in light of the overall economic picture in the region? In this respect, as in many others, the well-being of low-status women is inexorably tied to planning that will affect the future economic development of Appalachia.

Low-status women are frequently sent as family representatives to negotiate with community agencies for resources needed to meet family needs. As such, they easily become the focus of services that attempt to intervene in the family and ensure its adherence to community norms in terms of health and child care and protection. Intervention programs then can become a source of stress for low-status women and can reinforce their isolation and burden of responsibility. Transportation and child care are often cited as the barriers that prevent agencies from developing the type of self-help groups that have proven beneficial to women in urban areas. Such barriers must be addressed in planning any program for rural women.

Finally, the continued stereotyping of low-status women must be challenged. Social scientists and mental health professionals can play a role in discrediting stereotyped images, in communicating to the larger community the complexity of the low-status woman's social world, and in ensuring that her voice will be heard.

8

by Kate Black and Marc A. Rhorer

Out in the Mountains: Exploring Lesbian and Gay Lives

This research focuses on the lives of gays and lesbians and their experiences growing up in the mountains. The idea for this project began when Marc wanted to do a research paper on lesbians and gays in Appalachia and asked Kate, curator of the University of Kentucky Appalachian Collection, about prior research on the subject. Kate said, "There isn't anything." A few months later, while returning from the 1993 Appalachian Studies conference, we decided to present something about lesbians and gays at the 1994 conference. Though neither one of us is from the mountains, we both grew up in the rural South. Being gay and lesbian, we both knew other lesbians and gays in Lexington who grew up in the mountains. We hope that this exploratory work-in-progress will stimulate other researchers to include gays and lesbians in the conversation of Appalachian Studies.

We talked with five lesbians and four gay men from Eastern Kentucky, West Virginia, East Tennessee, and Western North Carolina ranging in ages from twenty to forty-five, in focused interviews. Only one of the interviewees continues to live in the mountains; the other eight live in Lexington and Louisville, Kentucky. All are white. We plan to interview others who have remained in the mountains. Participants were asked to allow their recorded interviews to become part of the oral history collection at the University of Kentucky, and most agreed. Before the interviews, we agreed on areas to explore: coming out experiences, homophobia, AIDS-phobia, and community building. Using a grounded research approach, an inductive method, we found several common themes in the rich stories of the participants: feelings of isolation, the importance of community, fears from inside and outside the closet, various forms of oppression and discrimination, and identity.

Feeling of Isolation

When we asked people to talk about the differences between being gay in the mountains and in urban areas, every interviewee expressed feelings of isolation in the mountains. While growing up, participants said, they had no one to turn to for guidance, support, and information when they began realizing they were homosexual. People felt there were no others with same-sex attractions, even to the extreme that some did not know gays or lesbians existed. When some participants mentioned the possibility of moving back to the mountains, they noted that the most difficult part would be coping with the isolation from other gays and lesbians. One interviewee made contacts in Lexington before moving back home to insure some access to the gay community. Among a few participants there was a sense that mass-communication technology (particularly cable/satellite television) has the potential to reduce feelings of isolation by providing young lesbians and gays in the mountains access to non-heterosexist images.

The interviewees expressed feelings of isolation in a variety of ways. A lesbian put on academic probation her first year at Morehead State University in Morehead, Kentucky, said, "A lot of the problem was I discovered the gay community. I never knew one existed. It was unbelievable! Every other person was gay" (5 1993). A gay man, speaking of his high school friends whom he now knows are gay, said, "At the time I thought they were people I got along well with, but I didn't realize why . . . I didn't know people who were gay" (7 1993). One of the interviewees often gives talks on homophobia at Kentucky colleges. Once when she was at Morehead State, a young man came up to her afterwards and asked, "How old did you say you were?" She answered, "Forty-two." Then he said, "You're the same age as my Mama. I didn't know there were any gay or lesbian people as old as my mama!" (2 1993). Another lesbian said, "The saddest part to me about growing up in the mountains as a gay person is that . . . you end up feeling like an outsider; you've got no one to talk to about these strange feelings you have and you have to end up like lots of young people growing up gay, being isolated, and you think about killing yourself 'cause you're so strange" (6 1993). One lesbian who came out to herself when she was thirteen found out the definition of lesbian when she "went to the public library and looked up 'homosexuality'. . . . There was absolutely no one to talk to" (5 1993). One young gay man explained, "To be gay in Clay City [Kentucky], it's hard" but it is harder out in the county where there isn't access to cable TV. He said, "MTV is preaching 'Free Your Mind' [but] your mind is not going to be free if you don't live inside the city limits" (9 1993).

Finding a Community

This sense of isolation greatly diminished when people moved from the mountains to the city because in the urban setting they could meet and be with other gays and lesbians. While finding a community of other gays and lesbians was crucial, ironically, an increased feeling of anonymity in the city was equally important. Anonymity, which many could not obtain at home, allowed greater freedom from the scrutiny of those who might condemn them; most people expressed a much greater sense of comfort about being out in the city. In contrast, at home people felt as if they were under surveillance and subjects of the gossip networks, even after moving away to the city. However, several people mentioned a positive aspect of the tightly-knit nature of rural community: if a person came from an established family lineage in the mountains, she or he was less likely to be harassed for being lesbian or gay.

While discussing the differences between being gay in the mountains and in Lexington, one gay man said, "When you move to a bigger city, your reputation doesn't necessarily have that much weight. . . ." (3 1994). A lesbian summed it up this way: "Appalachian queers migrate out of there . . . the few that do live there are usually not totally rejected by the family but rejected by the community. They'll be real kind [to your face] but still say stuff behind your back" (5 1993). A woman who came out in the late 1960s and came often to the gay bar in Lexington said, "You had community [at The Bar], which gave you family, family of choice" (6 1993). A gay man made a similar assessment about his life in Lexington two decades later: "Living here, there's a lot more opportunities . . . to meet those of your kind—a lover, a boyfriend, a fuck buddy . . . to live in Clay City, I wouldn't want to do that . . . it's just not open enough"(9 1993). One interviewee sees himself as both insider and outsider, a perspective from which he can examine the tension between the two. When he was eight he and his mother moved back to her family's community after years of living in Ohio. He described both his parents as coming from old Eastern Kentucky families. He said, "If someone comes in from the outside—straight or gay—it doesn't make any difference. They are going to have a very difficult time fitting into the community. If, however, they are from this long lineage, they will find it much easier to be who they are, regardless if they're gay or straight" (3 1994).

All the interviewees were asked to talk about how they found other lesbians and gays, either in the mountains or in their city homes. We found a variety of creative responses: "You go to the gym, you find gym rats" (6 1993). "[I]t takes one to know one" (9 1993). "In Boone [North Carolina], there was a lesbian softball league. It wasn't an official lesbian softball league, it just happened that most people on it were probably lesbian. . . . There was a student group. A lot of people would go to a regional gay bar. . . . Recently, I know of people in Boone who get on e-mail and try to meet people that way" (7 1993). "Gaydar" (2 1993).[1] Finally, several people mentioned being invited to lesbian and gay parties, especially in mountain college towns.

Identity and Community

We believe that identity and community are intricately linked. Since they can sometimes be in opposition, we were curious about how people reconciled this. For instance, we wondered if people identified themselves as both gay and Appalachian. While everyone readily identified themselves as gay or lesbian, we found that may people seemed to avoid directly addressing their Appalachian identities. In addition, some of the interviewees had not resolved their sense of conflict over being from the mountains.

One man referred to his "trapped" life in the mountains, equating living in the mountains with cultural isolation: "If I was trapped in Clay City, I would be myself, just like I was when I *was* trapped there. . . . Information and exposure to different cultures and different people is what really changes minds. . . . That's what causes accents, when people are trapped up in the mountains" (9 1993). The youngest of the interviewees, who is twenty, proudly said, "People are surprised when they find out where I'm from. . . . [My friends] say, 'I can't believe you turned out the way you did'" (8 1993). The one participant who has continued to live in Eastern Kentucky readily identified herself as Appalachian: "It's home, this is where the roots are" (6 1993). Another lesbian, describing what being Appalachian means to her, said, "It's the family, the heritage" (5 1993). One man, who used to live in Boone, expressed conflict over wanting to move back to the mountains but was not sure it is possible for him. Yet, in Boone, he feels a certain freedom not found in Lexington. "I feel sometimes people [in Boone] know me more as a person than as a gay person" (7 1993).

Facing Fears

Since all the interviewees expressed an overwhelmingly greater sense of freedom and ability to be out in the city, we wanted to know how the dimensions of the "closet" change with a move to the city. We asked people to talk about what was scary or fearful about being out at home versus being out in the city. Though fear of being out was experienced in the city, the participants all noted that the situation was more hostile in the mountains for gays and lesbians. Males experienced much more physical aggression at home and seemed to have a limited definition of the term "fear," equating it with the treat of physical violence. We also found that males endured much verbal taunting in junior high and high school. Males and females both told stories of physical violence and verbal taunting directed toward gay males in the mountains.

For females fear included psychological as well as physical violence. Women seemed to sustain more social ostracism (i.e., from family, friends, and church) and/or were forced into psychiatric care for a "cure." None of the men reported being sent to a therapist. Men were tormented because those around them suspected they were gay, while women were more likely to face threatening conditions if they were caught being sexual with a woman. However, one interviewee contradicted this representation when she told of local police cruising places where teenagers parked. She said when she was caught making out with her girlfriend, the police would generally laugh and tell them to go home, but when her gay male friends were caught, they were likely to be brutalized.

When asked about fear, a man said, "I've been scared that people would find out. I've been scared that if people knew I was gay, I would lose my job, people would say something to me, that I wouldn't have any recourse, wouldn't have any place to go." He went on to say how he was scared to kiss his lover good-bye when he dropped him off for work. Also, he feared "they'd hear my partner and I and they would come and bust down the doors and get us," a fear grounded in the North Carolina sodomy law (7 1993). Another gay man said, "I've heard stories of incredible physical violence against [gay] people." Then he told the story of a man in Breathitt County, Kentucky, who was killed and dismembered by local people because he was thought to be gay (3 1993). A lesbian said that one of her gay male friends was stabbed twenty-seven times while shopping in a country store in West Virginia, solely because he was homosexual.

Several males noted they were persistently taunted with works like "fag" and "sissy" throughout their adolescent schooling. A lesbian, who left her truck overnight at a body shop, said, "While it was there someone painted on the tailgate [near the pink triangle and rainbow decals] 'die fag' and slashed the two back tires." She explained that the perpetrator probably thought the truck was owned by a man because of the reference to "fag" (4 1994).

While describing the social ostracism she experienced, one lesbian said, "When I was in the eighth grade . . . because I came out to a couple of my friends . . . that proceeded to get me ostracized from overnight parties and church. . . ." (4 1994). One of the participants had a relationship during high school that was discovered by her girlfriend's parents. The parents came to a motel room where the two young women were staying for a softball tournament and pulled their daughter out of the room at 4:00 A.M. Another lesbian, who had a relationship with her teacher at Berea College, said "It turned out to be pretty devastating for both of us. She lost her job over it. I became this crisis point in my family. They decided I needed psychiatric help." After Berea College officials exposed her to her parents, she was caught by her mother at her lover's house at 1:00 A.M. She ended with: "Here was this woman corrupting some poor little Appalachian girl who obviously didn't know what she was doing." At this point Kate and the interviewee started giggling and Kate said, "Yeah, you're supposed to be making brooms." Then she finished, "yeah, or spoon bread at the Tavern!" (6 1993).

Levels of Discrimination

Gays and lesbians face discrimination both in the mountains and in the city. We defined "discrimination" as the public/civil face of homophobia, as did interviewees. Not surprisingly, gays and lesbians who work with children or young adults appear very susceptible to discrimination. We heard the story of two teachers in the mountains who were fired because they were rumored to be homosexual. One participant, who is out in most parts of her life, says she would never come out at her job working with school children in Eastern Kentucky because she "would be fired in a heartbeat" (5 1993). Many people expressed fear of being out at their jobs in the city, even when they did not work with children, because they were afraid of being fired or passed over for raises or promotions. Two of the participants told stories about gay bars that involved discrimination or the threat of it. These incidents gain even more importance because bars as public meeting places are historically central to the gay and lesbian community. One woman told of police surveillance behind The Bar in Lexington to observe those who went in and out. A man spoke about a gay bar owner in Huntington, West Virginia who did not want to be associated with anything "political," in this case having an AIDS literature table in his bar. The interviewee said the bar owner felt too vulnerable to actions of the local authorities and, therefore, did not want to do anything to call attention to his bar or his clientele.

A gay man told the story of how a lesbian high school teacher in North Carolina lost her job. One of her students believed the teacher was a lesbian and "prayed for her" publicly at church. She was fired "on the pretext that she cussed in class . . . but it was well known that it was because she was a lesbian" (7 1993). Recently in Lexington, a woman noted, "I can't prove anything from this, but I would swear I'm being discriminated against at my job. After I'd been working there for three months, one of the people who was in middle management took me into his office and told me that I shouldn't be working there because of my sexual orientation and that there was no reason for me to come back . . . apparently he forgot to tell anyone else this and the next time my shift rolled around I got a call asking me where I was. So I went in, didn't say anything about it, and I've been working there ever since" (4 1994). Several of the interviewees told stories of discrimination at public meeting places. In Boone in the late 1980s, a group of gays who were not students wanted to start an off-campus gay organization and meeting place. Bomb and death threats were made. The police provided protection and "were pretty good about dealing with it . . . people would have to come in around the police when these meetings first went on" (7 1993). A lesbian who went frequently to the gay bar in Lexington during the early 1970s said, "it was frightening, going to The Bar. It was rough, tough. Police cars parked out back. People said, 'don't drive your car, they're taking down license plate numbers,' so there was all that harassment. So coming to the bar was not only an act of celebration, but an act of defiance" (6 1993).

AIDS-phobia

We also asked people to talk about AIDS. We included AIDS-phobia in the discussions about various forms of homophobia, since the two have been viciously linked ever since the early days of the epidemic when AIDS was called GRID—Gay-Related Immune Deficiency. Surprisingly, one of the gay men interviewed did not know anyone who is HIV positive or has AIDS. Everyone acknowledged that AIDS-phobia exists, but did not seem to think it was more rampant one place or the other, except for one man who said he'd experienced more AIDS-phobia in Lexington—by both the straight and gay community—than in the mountains. He correlated AIDS-phobia with a higher HIV incidence in Lexington. Two people said that because they stick closely to the lesbian and gay community, or are outspoken advocates for the lesbian/gay community and for people with AIDS, they are not as likely to hear AIDS-phobic remarks and discussions.

When asked if she heard AIDS-phobic statements at home, one woman said, "More that anything else. More than homophobia, more than racist things . . . it's not really [expressed] as trashing people with AIDS, it is just terror that they're gonna get it" (5 1993). There were a few who said they had experienced people relating AIDS directly with homosexuality. One man noted that when he told his grandmother he was gay, the first thing she said was, "You're gonna get AIDS!" He noted that she is an intelligent, politically aware woman, yet she immediately connected being gay with AIDS (8 1993). A lesbian said that when she comes out to people, they often respond with "Aren't you afraid of AIDS?" This same woman, who works at an urban YMCA, stated employees must take an AIDS awareness class. The Y's policy is to notify the supervisor if an HIV positive person is in a class or program. This information is passed up the ladder to the executive director. The interviewee pointed out to her co-workers at a post-class discussion that no one needed to know this information. The purpose of the AIDS awareness course was to treat *anyone* who is injured as if they were infected to prevent infecting anyone else. "[I] was . . . knocked down by everyone else in the room, saying that it didn't matter, they [YMCA employees] deserve to know because they work with these children and adults and if they were infected they [YMCA employees] were going to treat them differently," she said (4 1994).

Internalizing Homophobia

Like racism, homophobia is not only perpetrated by those who dominate, but is also internalized by those who are dominated. The internalized homophobia was sometimes acted out in religious proselytizing. One of our participants noted she knew a lesbian couple and used the Bible to try to convince them that their sexuality was a sin, prior to her own coming out in high school. Organized religion played an important part in most of the interviewees' lives—socially, morally, and spiritually. We found that many had deep inner struggles over their homosexuality, rooted in religious notions of sin and guilt. Two of the lesbians, however, resisted the oppression and repression of the church by questioning and railing against it. One woman, at a young age, was able to transform her questioning into a belief in social justice. For most of the interviewees, the extreme isolation contributed to their internalized homophobia. Many spoke movingly of the need to help lesbian and gay young people in the mountains know they are not abnormal or alone. Many suggested lesbian and gay visibility as a partial solution to this problem.

Here are some of the responses of the interviewees about these internalized conflicts: "[T]he church was the only social outlet in the town. So I wasn't going to church so much for religious/spiritual reasons as I was for social reasons. In fact, I learned quite early to keep my mouth shut when discussing the Bible and other issues because I asked too many questions that the answer was always 'pray about it and you'll see the truth'" (4 1994). "I really struggled with religion and going to hell . . . I really did not want to be gay. I've had a hard time accepting it . . . probably the last five years it has gotten easy" (5 1993). A gay man, one of the youngest interviewees, went to Mass every day when he was thirteen and prayed, "Why do I have to be different? Why can't I be like everyone else?" He concluded, "I would hate for another generation of gay people to have to grow up and feel alienated, to feel like they are outcasts. . . . I consider myself, in a way, one of the lucky people who have finally been able to draw themselves into another community and find other people like themselves, so that they don't end up being drug addicts, or jumping off a bridge, or hanging themselves just because they have no role models, have no other friends that they can come out to. . . . They need someone to show them that they're OK, that they're not bad, that they're not going to hell. . . ." (9 1993).

Some Last Words

Marc A. Rhorer: We have examined various aspects of the lives of gays and lesbians from the mountains. All of our participants addressed issues that revealed difficulties related to growing up homosexual in Appalachia. There are several areas which need further attention, specifically class differences and race. The differences in educational backgrounds of participants' families deserve further exploration. A few interviewees noted that their families were more racist than homophobic.

All of those who participated in this project have exhibited courage in many aspects of their lives. They have overcome a multitude of obstacles in their paths and have emerged to lead positive lives that are a reflection of their true selves. Though some participants were reluctant to identify themselves as Appalachian, they still expressed a sense of compassion for the gay and lesbian youth who inhabit the region. This expression of humanity came at the close of our interviews when we asked if there was any issue we had not covered that they would like to speak about. In some way, perhaps the sincerity of these people's stories can pave the way for a better understanding of what it is like to grow up gay or lesbian in the mountains, and foster the acceptance of future generations.

Kate Black: Several gaps and some problems emerged from our research methods. For example, class differences and perspectives appear in the interviews, yet we did not really probe our interviewees with questions about class. We did not address the subject of gender with the interviewees, but we did extract gender differences from the material. Several people brought up the categories of "butch" and "fem" for lesbians and "butch" and "queen" for gay men and these need to be explored further. For example, one gay man said, "People [he means gay men] in rural areas of Kentucky and North Carolina tend to be queenier. It is like they try to mesh with the stereotype of gay people more than people in larger cities who feel free to emulate other things" (7 1993). The statement possibly provides a window into class and gender differences, roles (both chosen and prescribed), internalized homophobia, varying notions about power and resistance, and, maybe, rural and urban dissonance.

Even with the additional voluminous work that this research requires, begs really, the stories of these lesbians and gay men growing up in Appalachia are important for their own sake. Each person we interviewed, in his or her own way, contributes to the spirit conveyed by that favorite Queer Nation chant, "We're here, we're queer, we're fabulous, get used to it."

Finally for me as a lesbian researcher, doing this work was often very emotional and, at times, painful. After all, the struggles of the lesbian and gay participants were not really any different from my own. But there was another potent theme in all the stories: desire. Together, the pain and the desire seemed to produce this incredible resistance to the ever-lurking and pressing homophobia and heterosexism. I think I finally understand, in a very rooted way, Foucault's statement, "Where there is power, there is resistance."

III

Migration and Urbanization

This section includes material on three distinct topics in Appalachian studies: migration, the status of migrants in cities outside the region, as well as in cities within the Appalachian region. Phillip Obermiller and Steven Howe use recent census data to update our knowledge of migration trends. The authors find that patterns of Appalachian migration vary greatly by sub-region, and have become localized around major metropolitan areas in and near the region. In "'We ain't agoin' back,'" the editors of this volume describe the status of three generations of urban Appalachians in greater Cincinnati. Using both census and survey data, they compare the socioeconomic status of Appalachians with other groups in the city. Emily Satterwhite's article, "Seeing Appalachian Cities," confronts those who think of Appalachia as an entirely rural area with a different perspective. She challenges readers to discard these old mental images in order to understand that cities are home to a majority of the region's population. She goes on to discuss the implications of this revised mental image for the Appalachian identity movement.

9

by Phillip J. Obermiller and Steven R. Howe

New Paths and Patterns of Appalachian Migration, 1975-1990

Appalachian migration has been a topic of interest and public policy debate for nearly a century. For the migrants themselves it has been a social reality for a much longer period. In the early twentieth century historian Carter G. Woodson (1916:4) noted: "It was during the period between 1826 and 1840 that Cincinnati had to grapple with the problem of the immigrating Negroes and the poor whites from the uplands of Virginia and Kentucky." For the most part, however, nineteenth century internal migration in the U.S.—Appalachian and otherwise—was considered a normal function of the country's westward expansion, and little note was taken of it. It was not until the twentieth century that perceptions of Appalachian population dynamics, and migration in particular, began to change.

Previous Migration Studies

The Depression era generated a nation-wide interest in migration flows. A federally-sponsored study conducted in the 1930s by Carter Goodrich and associates (1936) advocated that the population of farmers and miners in the eighty-four coal-producing counties of the Cumberland Plateau be reduced by twenty-five percent through outmigration. A similar recommendation appeared in a study sponsored by the federal Bureau of Agricultural Economics (1935). The bureau concluded that "encouragement of emigration" was the rational solution to the basic problem of overpopulation in the mountains (U.S. Dept. of Agriculture, 1935:6). By the early 1940s Congress was holding hearings on "the interstate migration of destitute citizens," including migration streams from the Appalachias (U.S. Congress, 1940).

In 1962 sociologists James S. Brown and George A. Hillery confirmed that many people did indeed leave the Southern Appalachian region between 1940 and 1960. Although a great deal of movement took place within the region, southern Appalachia experienced a net loss of 13% of its population between 1940 and 1950, and a net loss of 19% between 1950 and 1960 (Brown and Hillery, 1962:59). In a review of the 1970 census data, Brown notes that between 1960 and 1970 outmigration from southern Appalachia continued but at a considerably slower rate, resulting in a net loss by migration of 5% for the decade (Brown, 1972:138). During the 1960s the populations of metropolitan areas in southern Appalachia increased by nearly 8%, principally by inmigration because natural increase had declined significantly during this period. The rural areas did not fare as well. With the exception of those in Georgia, the nonmetropolitan counties in the Appalachian areas of ten states experienced an overall population loss due to net migration (Brown, 1972:135–138).

Paralleling national trends in rural-to-urban migration, the majority of Appalachian migrants moved to large, industrialized metropolitan areas. Clyde B. McCoy and James S. Brown (1981) documented in some detail the migration streams from southern Appalachia into major metropolitan areas of the country. Although the rates of outmigration decreased over the thirty-year period ending in 1970, McCoy and Brown found great consistency in the direction and proportions of Appalachian migration into the top thirty metropolitan receiving areas they identified.

A major finding of the Appalachian Regional Commission's *Report to Congress on Migration* (1979) was a turnaround in net Appalachian migration. An analysis of the Social Security Administration's work history sample for 1965, 1970, and 1975 indicated that Appalachian migration changed from a net loss to the region during the period from 1955 to 1970, to a net gain in the period 1970–1975.[1] The pattern of outmigration also changed: while northern states remained the destination of the largest number of Appalachian migrants, states in the South showed the greatest proportionate gains. The report concludes that most Appalachian migrants earned larger incomes than they did in the region, and quickly gained income parity with workers in the areas where they settled (Appalachian Regional Commission, 1979b).

The "migration turnaround" of net inmigration to Appalachia during the 1970s was a short-lived phenomenon; by the early 1980s the movement of people into Appalachia reversed itself and the well-established streams of net outmigration resumed their flow (Pickard 1981a; 1981b). But the rivers of Appalachian migrants had changed course. Phillip Obermiller and Robert Oldendick (1987) used IRS area-to-area population flow data to study Appalachian migration in the early 1980s. They found that the migration streams from Appalachia had clearly changed direction from cities in the Northeastern and Midwestern states to those in the South and the West. They also found internal migrants moving to metropolitan areas within the region at much higher rates than in the previous decade.

Richard Couto examined 1990 census data in his report on economic trends and social issues in Appalachia. While not dealing with migration specifically, his analysis provides useful insights on the recent dynamics of population change in the Appalachian region. Between 1980 and 1990 Couto (1994: 105) documents a net loss of population in both Northern Appalachia (–3.11%) and in Central Appalachia (–4.92%). However, the population of Southern Appalachia grew substantially (8.76%) during the same period, giving the Appalachian region a slim population gain (1.38%) for the decade. Much of this growth was realized in the metropolitan counties of Southern Appalachia.[2]

It is possible that the changes Couto noted could be attributed to variations in rates of natural increase and mortality, rather than migration. Graham Rowles and John Watkins (1995) addressed this issue in a demographic analysis conducted for the Appalachian Regional Commission. Although they had no county-to-county migration data to work with, they calculated inferred net migration using the annualized difference between the 1980 population of Appalachia, adjusted for births and deaths, and the 1990 census population. They found that:

> Between 1980 and 1990 the population of Appalachia recorded a natural increase of 84,236 persons, but experienced a net loss of 54,739 migrants . . . Northern Appalachia recorded a net loss of 61,580 migrants. Central Appa-

lachia also recorded a net loss of 18,725 migrants. In marked contrast, Southern Appalachia recorded a net gain of 25,725 migrants (Rowles and Watkins, 1995:12).

Using Public Use Microdata Samples from the U.S. Census, historian James Gregory has recently tracked the movement of southern-born whites into the Great Lakes states of Ohio, Indiana, Illinois, Michigan and Wisconsin as well as into California, comparing the southern migrants with other whites, Hispanics, and blacks in those states on a variety of socioeconomic characteristics.[3] He concludes that although the migrants in his study lag in educational attainment, they are doing quite well in terms of income and employment. They reside in suburban areas, have predominantly blue-collar jobs, and are no more likely to be poor than their northern-born white counterparts. Gregory (1995:130) notes that between 1975 and 1980 280,000 southern-born whites came to the Great Lakes states, while 340,000 left the area; in the period between 1985 and 1990 the ratio had changed: 294,609 came to the area while 262,795 left it. In California, southern-born newcomers just about equaled departees between 1975 to 1980, but between 1985 and 1990 southern newcomers (267,722) greatly outnumbered the departees (200,829).

Projecting from 1990 census data, the Appalachian Regional Commission has published estimates of population change for Appalachia between 1990 and 1998. The ARC projects a net gain of 830,553 migrants over the eight-year period, including federal movers (military and civilian employees and their families) and international migrants. These projections show a marked growth in the Appalachian counties of Georgia, Tennessee, and North Carolina from migration and net losses in Appalachian New York and Pennsylvania. For the period in question the ARC predicts that net migration will be a more salient feature of population change in Appalachia (4.0%) than in the U.S. as a whole (2.9%) (Appalachian Regional Commission, 1999).

Overall these studies indicate that migration still has a strong effect on the region and its people. It is clear that migration accounts for an important part of the population growth in Southern Appalachia; that Appalachians have been migrating to urbanized areas both inside and outside the region for decades; and that the direction of outmigration has generally shifted from northcentral and northeastern states to southern and western states. Among these studies, however, none has employed the census data on county-to-county migration available for the entire U.S., none has used the current ARC definition of Appalachia that includes 406 counties, and none has presented a recent socioeconomic profile of Appalachian migrants. Although we can make many informed assumptions about the nature of contemporary Appalachian migration from the previous studies, little in the way of geographically specific or recent migration research is currently available. In this article we use recent census data to describe in detail the changes that have appeared in Appalachian migration patterns.

The Current Study

This study presents a comprehensive examination of Appalachian migration in the periods 1975–80 and 1985–90. We begin by presenting statistics on the size and direction of inmigration, outmigration, and internal migration flows, along with changes that may have occurred during the intervening years. Using 1980 census data we provide limited comparisons of migrant characteristics, principally of a demographic nature. The questions we answer are: In what numbers and in what directions are people entering the region, leaving the region, and moving within the region? How do the earlier migrants (1975–80) compare with the later migrants (1985–1990) in terms of age, race, and sex? Is the trend toward urbanization in Appalachia continuing?

Because the 1990 data are more detailed in terms of migrant characteristics, we can ask specific questions about the more recent migrants. What are the sources of migration into Appalachia? Are the southward, westward, and cityward trends continuing? What are the socioeconomic characteristics of the migrants, and do these features correlate with specific migration patterns? Which areas of the region are internal migrants coming from and going to? Are the inmigrants an older cohort, hinting at return migration among retirees?[4] What are the racial and ethnic characteristics of the migrants?[5] Are the migrants settling in urban counties or in the suburban counties that ring cities?[6] Do the migrants seem to be moving in a "step-wise" fashion from smaller areas to those of intermediate population size, or are they taking the "total immersion" approach of moving from small towns directly into large metropolitan areas?[7]

Data and Methodology

The 1980 data come from the Bureau of the Census (U. S. Department of Commerce, 1986). The data set provides gross in- and outmigration statistics between 1975 and 1980 for each county (or county equivalent) in the United States. The migrant data are arrayed by age, race, and sex; included for each of these categories are statistics on college attendance, military status, group quarters status, and residence abroad in 1975. Data on country of birth are also provided by race and sex.[8]

The 1990 data also come from the Bureau of the Census (U.S. Department of Commerce, 1995). This data set provides statistics on non-movers, movers within counties, and all county-to-county migration streams between 1985 and 1990. In New England, flows between minor civil divisions are also given.[9] The 1990 migrant data include the following characteristics: age, college enrollment, educational attainment, Hispanic origin, household type, income in 1989, industry, occupation, place of birth and citizenship, poverty status in 1989, race, sex, and housing tenure.

Our analyses will be presented by type of migration stream: outmigration, inmigration, and internal migration. The geography of the analyses includes the three subregions as defined by the Appalachian Regional Commission (ARC)—Northern, Central, and Southern Appalachia; the thirteen states which have ARC-designated counties; and rural, urban, and metropolitan counties within the region. To make identification easier, we will often refer to counties by their principal city.

Migration Streams

Although the Appalachian region gained about a quarter of a million new residents from net migration between 1975 and 1980 and a slightly larger number between 1985 and 1990, the internal dynamics of the migration streams tell another story. Much of Appalachia's 1980 growth due to migration occurred in the central and southern portions of the region, while northern Appalachia lost population through net outmigration. In 1990 northern Appalachia's migration losses remained steady, but central Appalachia's earlier migration gains turned to a loss as well. It was only southern Appalachia's substantial growth in inmigration that gave the region a net gain from migration in 1990.

Overall, the data indicate that migration continues to be an important part of the Appalachian experience; between 1985 and 1990 the region's counties received 3.1 million new residents while losing 2.9 million former residents. This county-to-county migration indicates that a large portion of the region's population has been on the move. Although Appalachia had net gains in population in both census periods, these gains did not compare with those in the rest of the nation. Moreover, the figures for the region as a whole masked the fact that the populations of Northern and Central Appalachia were shrinking.

None of Appalachia's counties ranked in the top forty in the nation for attracting migrants in either census period, but in 1980 Pennsylvania's Allegheny County ranked twenty-sixth in the country for total outmigration, and thirty-third ten years later. Allegheny County, which encompasses the city of Pittsburgh, is representative of the region's revolving door counties—typically metropolitan counties with larger cities or college towns. This population churning occurred in urban areas located in the northern (17 counties) and southern (13 counties) subregions. There are no large population centers in central Appalachia, consequently none of its counties experienced this phenomenon. Very little had changed by 1990. Thirty-two counties had high numbers of both in- and out migration, and with only three exceptions (Douglas Co., GA, Washington Co., TN, and Anderson Co., SC) they were identical to the counties in the 1980 ranking.

County-to-county data are unavailable from the 1980 census. In 1990 the chief non-Appalachian sources of migrants to the region were in every case metropolitan areas located just outside the perimeter of the region. Montgomery, Atlanta, Marietta, and Greensboro all lie in close proximity to the southern and eastern borders of the region; similarly, Cincinnati and Buffalo lie along its western and northern borders. By 1990 the main sources of new residents in Appalachia were short-distance movers coming primarily from southern metropolitan areas that abut the region.

A similar phenomenon occurs among those leaving the region. In 1990 the chief Appalachian donor counties were located on the peripheries of major cities situated just outside of Appalachia. These counties abut Greensboro and Thomasville in North Carolina, Marietta and Atlanta in Georgia, and Cincinnati and Youngstown in Ohio. The only exception, Nashville, is located one county away from the region.

Most of the migration within the region took place between a metropolitan core and its suburban ring communities. For instance, over a quarter of the forty largest county-to-county migration streams in Appalachia were simply exchanges among Pittsburgh's core and periphery counties. Similar exchanges occurred in Alabama on the Birmingham-Tuscaloosa axis as well as in the Huntsville area, and in South Carolina along the Greenville-Spartansburg-Anderson corridor. Knoxville, Chattanooga, and Johnson City were the focal points for core-perimeter exchanges in Tennessee; the same dynamic occurred around Cincinnati, Ohio; Charleston, West Virginia; Winston-Salem, North Carolina; and Birmingham, New York.

Long-distance migrants from Appalachia have a much more diverse set of destinations than the short-range movers. Again using Pittsburgh's Allegheny County as an example, the migration flows were principally south to Florida and Georgia, west to Arizona and California, and southeast to Maryland, Virginia, and North Carolina.

Migration Demographics

Appalachians appeared to be aging in place because older migrants were not contributing significantly to the overall population or to the older cohort within it. Between 1985 and 1990 the region netted only 12,036 residents over the age of 65 through migration. By comparison, the region had a net gain of 115,887 school-aged migrants (5–19) and 116,339 migrants in their prime working years (20–64). The largest net flows of older migrants were into suburban Appalachian counties abutting Cincinnati, Atlanta, and Pittsburgh. Although western North Carolina is widely perceived as a retirement destination of choice, only Henderson County, NC appears among the top forty Appalachian destinations for older migrants in the 1990 data.

In terms of age, the important story lies in the subregional data. Northern and central Appalachia had small net losses of residents 65 and older through migration, and these areas experienced substantially larger net migration losses of people typically in the labor force. Moreover, central Appalachia lost nearly 10,000 school-aged children. Appalachia's success story as a migration magnet was in the southern portion of the region which netted well over a third of a million new residents, most of whom were of an age to be productively employed.

From 1975 to 1980 the sex ratios among both inmigrants and outmigrants were reasonably equal. Between 1985 and 1990 the migration streams brought slightly more men on net into the region than women, but the only population growth from migration was in the south where the sex ratios were fairly balanced. Central Appalachia gained slightly more men than women; in northern

Appalachia the exodus of women from the area was about equal to that of men. In 1990 women left Northern and Central Appalachia at higher rates than did men.[10]

Appalachia as a whole had a net loss of 6,444 African-American migrants in the 1975–80 period, and about two-thirds of this loss occurred in southern Appalachia. Outmigration from central Appalachia composed the other third. In 1990 some 200,000 black migrants took up residence in the region, and another 180,000 moved away from the region. The net gain of about 20,000 African-American migrants occurred predominantly in the south, reversing by a wide margin the losses seen in the 1980 census. Northern Appalachia again had a net gain in black residents from migration, while the central portion of the region had a small net loss of about the same size as it had in 1980.

The small Hispanic population in Appalachia grew between 1985 and 1990 with a net gain of 26,989 migrants, the majority of whom settled in the Southern subregion. While this number, on its face, appears small, it is proportionally large: the net gain from migrantion represents 34.3% of Appalachia's 1990 Hispanic population. Fully half of the top forty Hispanic migration streams into the Appalachian region had their sources outside of the United States; the destinations for these migrants were primarily urban and suburban counties in the Atlanta and Pittsburgh metropolitan areas.[11]

The issue of an Appalachian "brain drain" has been raised by many people concerned about the region's future. The migration data address at least a portion of this concern. In 1990 Appalachia gained approximately 100,000 more college students than it lost through migration, but there was extreme variation by subregion. Northern Appalachia gained a net of 37,566 college enrollees, southern Appalachia gained 66,684, while the central part of the region had a net loss of 3,988 college students. Clearly, many Appalachian college seats are occupied by students from outside the region.[12]

While many students came into the region to obtain an education, the question remains whether they stayed in the region after graduation. Between 1985 and 1990 Appalachia netted nearly as many migrants over age 25 without high school diplomas (63,604) as it did high school graduates (65,711) through migration. A net gain of migrants with associate's degrees (5,060) and graduate degrees (3,607) was more than offset by a net loss of 24,368 migrants holding bachelor's degrees. At the subregional level, the educational differences in net migration were quite distinct. Northern Appalachia gained over ten thousand migrants without a high school education, accompanied by net losses of migrants with higher educational attainment. Central Appalachia gained over 2,000 migrants with less than a ninth grade education while experiencing net losses in all higher educational categories. On a proportional basis, net migration cost Central Appalachia nine percent of its Bachelor degree holding population. Southern Appalachia had net gains in all educational categories including migrants without a high school diploma (50,234), high school graduates (71,815), migrants with some college or an associate's degree (74,361), and migrants with a bachelor's or graduate degree (47,902).

Regarding the occupational status of Appalachian migrants, the region as a whole had a net loss of 47,303 higher status workers while experiencing net gains of 8,469 service workers and 40,685 lower status workers. Northern and Central Appalachia lost workers in all employment categories with the heaviest net losses in the professional/managerial and technical/sales categories. Southern Appalachia had net gains across all categories, a slight majority being in the professional/managerial and technical/sales categories.

The Appalachian region lost a net 34,342 migrants with 1989 incomes of more than $20,000 while netting 209,407 migrants with incomes of less than $20,000 during that year. Northern Appalachia netted 69,562 new residents with incomes of less than $10,000 while losing migrants in each of the three higher income brackets. Central Appalachia had net losses in all income categories with the heaviest being in the two highest income brackets.

The southern subregion had gains through migration in all income categories with the majority by far being in the lowest two.[13]

Appalachia had a net gain of well over a quarter of a million homeowners between 1985 and 1990, with the vast majority of that gain realized in the southern subregion. Northern Appalachia lost both renters (–119,980) and homeowners (–8,624), Central Appalachia saw a slight net gain in homeowners (302) and a substantial loss of renters (–45,741), while homeowners entering the southern subregion (241,744) outnumbered renters (126,189) almost two to one.

The 1990 census data also give the poverty status of Appalachian migrants in 1989. Eighteen percent of those entering Appalachia were in poverty while 15% of those departing had the same economic status, giving the region a net gain of 111,687 persons in poverty. Both Northern and Central Appalachia showed net losses due to migration of persons not in poverty, while also showing net gains in persons below the poverty line. The southern subregion experienced an opposite phenomenon with impoverished inmigrants being outnumbered five to one by those above the poverty line. Large metropolitan donor areas like New York City, Los Angeles, Atlanta, Cleveland, and Cincinnati were net contributors to the top forty inflows of poor migrants into the Appalachian region.[14]

Migration Streams and Demographics by State

The Appalachian areas of twelve states and all of West Virginia vary greatly in population size; to adjust for this discrepancy the net proportionate gain or loss of population due to migration was calculated for each category. The following summary statistics are based on those net proportionate gains and losses. In terms of total migration flows, Georgia grew by 12.3% while at the other end of the spectrum West Virginia lost 4.1%. Maryland had the most uneven sex ratio among its migrants, gaining over two and a half times more men than women.[15] Georgia gained population in all age categories while West Virginia had the largest loss of migrants in the under-55 age cohorts, and New York lost the most residents over 55 to migration. The African American migration flows were stable in most states, but Maryland's black population grew by 25.6%, New York's grew by 12.5% and West Virginia's dropped by 5.4%. The Hispanic populations in each of the Appalachian states grew substantially, led by Georgia at 53.8%.

Migration contributed substantial numbers of people with incomes less than $10,000 to New York (11.3%), Virginia (8.8%), and Maryland (6.8%). Proportionately, Georgia gained the most migrants with incomes of $35,000 or more (17.1%) while Virginia, New York, and West Virginia had net losses in this income category of 9.3%, 7.7%, and 7.4% respectively. West Virginia lost 1.4% of its homeowners to migration, while in Georgia migration added 10.7% to the number of homeowners. In New York the number of people living in poverty grew by 12.3% due to migration, the largest gain of this kind among all the states.

Georgia posted the largest gain in migrants in the top occupational category (18.8%) while Kentucky, Ohio, Mississippi, Pennsylvania, New York, Virginia, and West Virginia lost migrants in this category in numbers ranging between five and ten percent. Migrants in service work grew by 13.4% in Georgia and 6.2% in South Carolina, while posting losses in West Virginia (5.6%), Ohio (4.3%), and Kentucky (4.2%). Migrant laborers contributed 13.4% to Georgia's workforce, and 5.1% to South Carolina's, while out-migration diminished this occupational category in West Virginia by 7.4% and in Kentucky by 4.5%.

West Virginia was the only state to have a net loss of population in all educational categories, followed by Kentucky with losses in the highest categories. Alabama, Georgia, North Carolina, and South Carolina each had net educational gains across the board. Georgia also had the highest proportional net gains from migration, and this growth came predominantly from migrants with higher educational attainment.

The state-level data support the general conclusions reached for the subregions. Southern Appalachia has been growing and prospering. The states in Northern and Central Appalachia have been losing migrants with skills, education and higher incomes while gaining migrants in poverty.

Migration Streams and Demographics by Type of County

Appalachian counties can also be categorized as rural, urban or metropolitan using a standard classification scheme.[16] In general, the rural counties of Northern and Central Appalachia lost population through migration while those in Southern Appalachia experienced net increases from migration. The urban counties of Northern and Southern Appalachia, for the most part, saw growth from migration while those in the Central Appalachian subregion had net outmigration. Overall, the metropolitan counties of Central and Southern Appalachia had net inmigration, while most metro counties in Northern Appalachia lost population through migration.

The demographic data indicate rural Appalachia lost both men and women under age fifty-five to migration. Rural and urban counties lost African American migrants, while all three types of counties gained Hispanic migrants. Rural counties had a net loss of migrants with incomes above $10,000 and urban counties had a similar loss of migrants with incomes above $20,000. Conversely, rural and urban Appalachian counties experienced a net gain of migrants living in poverty. Rural Appalachia lost workers in all employment classifications except farming while urban Appalachian counties lost migrants in the two most highly-skilled employment categories. Metropolitan counties in Appalachia gained migrants in all demographic categories. Rural Appalachian counties had a net loss of women and men with some college experience or more education. Urban Appalachian counties lost women and men with an associate's degree or more education. Metropolitan Appalachian counties had gains through migration in all categories for both women and men with the exception of women with bachelor's or higher degrees.

Conclusion

Migration is a key element in understanding of the Appalachian region. Between 1975 and 1980 and again between 1985 and 1990 there were large turnovers in the region's population, a trend that reinforces the current understanding of Appalachia as a socially and culturally heterogeneous region. This phenomenon affects the region internally as well; because of their radically different migration patterns, it is becoming increasingly difficult to think about portions of the Appalachian region in the same terms. For example, West Virginia and Appalachian Georgia have little in common from a demographic perspective.

Appalachian migration patterns have changed from long-range flows into Northern, Southern, and Western states outside the region, to short-range urban-suburban exchanges principally centered around cities in and immediately adjacent to the region. Rural counties, with some exceptions in southern Appalachia, continue to lose population through outmigration. With the largest migration flows concentrated between large cities and their surrounding suburban counties and 48% of the region's population living in urbanized counties, it is becoming increasingly difficult to characterize Appalachia as a demographically rural region.

Appalachians are, for the most part, aging in place and there is scant evidence to suggest that earlier Appalachian migrants are returning to the region in large numbers for retirement. Migration patterns are bringing about clear changes in the racial distribution of the region's population while Hispanic migrants in particular are changing its ethnic makeup. Moreover, colleges and universities in the Appalachian region have become popular destinations for students seeking higher education.

The migrants entering Appalachia had lower-status jobs, lower incomes, less education, and were more likely to be in poverty than the people migrating away from the region. The impact of these migration patterns, however, was not even across the region. Northern and Central Appalachia were losing population while at the same time becoming refuges for low income, blue-collar workers with little formal education. Southern Appalachia, on the other hand, was gaining population. Overall, the southern migrants were more ethnically and racially diverse, better paid, educated, and housed, and worked at higher status jobs than did migrants to the other two subregions.[17]

The demographic makeup of the Appalachian region is changing, and the principal component of that change is population movement. Tracing the various paths and patterns of Appalachian migration will continue to be an important element in regional studies during the twenty-first century.

10

by Phillip J. Obermiller and Michael E. Maloney

"We ain't agoin' back": A Retrospective Look at Urban Appalachians in Greater Cincinnati

The great African-American historian, Carter G. Woodson, identified one of the earliest Appalachian migration streams into Cincinnati when he wrote: "... during the period between 1826 and 1840 ... Cincinnati had to grapple with the problem of the immigrating Negroes and the poor whites from the uplands of Virginia and Kentucky." Woodson himself was a migrant from his birthplace on the edge of the Appalachian uplands in Virginia's Buckingham County. He worked as a miner in the Kentucky coalfields before attending Berea College, and later served as dean of West Virginia State College. His experiences piqued a scholarly interest in the social conditions of African Americans in Cincinnati and in the Appalachian mountains.

As a migrant himself, Woodson was fairly typical. He was born poor in a rural area, but pursued a successful career in several different urban locations. Like Woodson, many Appalachian migrants had experience in the coalfields and some were black. And like Woodson, although they moved away, most never forgot where they came from.[1]

Young and old, men and women, miners and farmers, white and black, people have been moving from the rural environs of the Appalachian mountains to urban and metropolitan areas for a very long time. Long enough, in fact, that they are no longer referred to as migrants but as urban Appalachians. As used in this chapter, the term 'urban Appalachian' includes both migrants to cities outside of the region and to their descendants. The original migrants are referred to as first-generation migrants, their children born outside the region as the second generation, and so on.[2]

Most urban Appalachians have now lived outside of the region for all or the greater portion of their lives. Because millions of Appalachians have made the transition from rural newcomers to long term residents of urban neighborhoods, several questions arise. Given the fact that it has been well over forty years since Appalachian outmigration peaked, how are these people and their descendants doing in the cities? How do they compare on key social indicators with other

This makes ppl from Appalacia seem like a different species

urban groups? Do they show signs of economic and social assimilation?

To begin answering these questions researchers at the Urban Appalachian Council in Cincinnati placed a series of questions on the Greater Cincinnati Survey (GCS) in 1980, repeated them in 1989, and repeated them again in 2001. The GCS is conducted by the Institute for Policy Research at the University of Cincinnati using random-digit-dialing techniques to contact approximately 1,100 residents of Hamilton County. As a consequence, the Urban Appalachian Council now has longitudinal information about the urban Appalachian residents of Cincinnati and its surrounding county. These are the data we will use in the first part of this chapter to address the questions asked above.[3]

There is another dimension of the urban Appalachian experience that large-scale surveys like the GCS cannot adequately assess—questions about urban Appalachian communities. For instance, what do we know about the social dynamics of the urban neighborhoods where many Appalachians reside? What are the social issues that challenge the central-city neighborhoods where some Appalachians live in poverty? We will address these questions in the second part of this chapter using ethnographic reports and another longitudinal study (1970–1990) that analyses census tract data from predominantly Appalachian neighborhoods in Cincinnati.[4]

Appalachians in Greater Cincinnati

The proportion of all first- and second-generation Appalachians in Hamilton County has remained fairly constant at just over 20% for the past twenty years. As might be expected, the percentage of first-generation migrants has declined from 52% in the 1980s to 40% at the end of the 1990s. This decline has been compensated for by the growth in the proportion of second-generation Appalachians from 48% to 60%, and by a slight gain (1%) in the proportion of black Appalachians over the last decade. Black Appalachians now constitute equal proportions (17%) of both the county's African Americans and of the urban Appalachian population. Clearly black and white Appalachians remain a substantial part of the county's population.[5]

Appalachian women outnumber Appalachian men by close to a three-to-two ratio (61% to 39%). Mortality rates among the first generation may account for a portion of this difference because women typically outlive men; another contributing factor may be the rising divorce rate among white Appalachian couples because divorced men may be more transient. At the end of the 1980s the white Appalachian divorce rate (8%) was comparable to that of non-Appalachian whites (8%), and was well under that of non-Appalachian blacks (26%). By the close of the 1990s this situation had changed significantly with the white Appalachian divorce rate rising to 16% and exceeding that of either the non-Appalachian white (12%) or black (12%) cohorts. Conversely, the proportion of white Appalachians who are married (60%) dropped to its lowest point in twenty years. After decades of stability, urban Appalachian nuclear families have begun to experience a substantial decline.

Because we are dealing with migrants, the first generation of whom came to the Cincinnati area at a specific age, over time the Appalachian cohort will artificially appear to be aging faster than the general population. The survey data reinforces this perception: in 1980 there was no significant difference in the average ages of Appalachian whites (41), non-Appalachian whites (41) and non-Appalachian blacks (42), but by 2001 the average age for the Appalachians was 49, for the other whites 43, and for the blacks 42. Nevertheless, the actual age distributions of white Appalachians in the surveys are skewed toward an older cohort in a way that differs significantly from the other two culture groups. Many of greater Cincinnati's Appalachians are among the area's older residents.

Over the two decades encompassed by the survey data, age has played an important role in Appalachian household composition relative to the comparison groups. Greater Cincinnati's Appalachians have generally lived in households of a size comparable with non-Appalachian whites and smaller that those of non-Appalachian blacks. Overall, urban Appalachians households have more adults and fewer children than do those of the comparison groups. To the extent that Appalachian households differ from the others, the variation can be attributed to age.

A different perspective comes from observing the number of years a respondent has lived in Hamilton County. Given that the peak years of Appalachian migration occurred in the late 1950s and that the non-Appalachian residents of greater Cincinnati have typical mobility rates, one would no longer expect to find important differences among the three culture groups for this variable. This is in fact the case—by 2001 all three cohorts had lived in the county for an average of about 33 years. Although the migration factor still affects Appalachian age distributions, it is no longer a significant influence on their time of residency. Appalachian migrants have truly become urban Appalachians.

The number of white Appalachians over 18 years of age with less than a high school education has declined from 1980 to 2001, yet nearly one in four (24%) still does not have a high school diploma. Appalachian high school graduation rates dropped by 10% from 1989 to 2001, but are almost identical to those of the non-Appalachian cohorts for the same period. In 2001 more Appalachians (28%) reported having taken some college courses than ever before, but only small gains have been made by white Appalachians in acquiring a college degree or some post-graduate education. In 1980 only 17% of Appalachians had this level of educational attainment, by 1989 the proportion had risen slightly to 20%, and by 2001 the rate was 21%. White Appalachians have improved their educational status over the last two decades, but still are not on a par with non-Appalachian whites in overall educational attainment.

Ninety-five percent of white Appalachians in the labor force were employed in 2001, either in full-time (80%) or part-time (15%) work. The work ethic among Appalachians that manifested itself in earlier surveys remained intact, but in this they were no different than members of the other two cohorts. White Appalachian, white non-Appalachian, and black non-Appalachian workers in greater Cincinnati all took advantage of the high-employment trends that swept the nation in the 1990s.

The high rates of employment resulted in substantial income gains for white Appalachian families in Hamilton County. In 2001 only 5% of the Appalachian families surveyed reported incomes of less than $20,000 as compared with 10% of non-Appalachian white families, and 31% of non-Appalachian black families. At the other end of the income spectrum 44% of Appalachian families reported incomes of over $50,000 while the same was true for 53% of non-Appalachian white families and 25% of non-Appalachian black families in the county. Just over half of all Appalachian families in the most recent survey (52%) are in the middle-income bracket with incomes ranging between $20,000 and $50,000, which is a proportion substantially higher than that for either non-Appalachian white families (37%) or non-Appalachian black families (44%). In the period 1989–2001 considerably more white non-Appalachian households were earning over $50,000 a year compared with white Appalachian households. Nevertheless, well over nine out of ten Appalachian families surveyed in Hamilton County are in the middle or upper income brackets.

Between 1980 and 1989 the population from each of the three culture groups grew in the city of Cincinnati. From 1989 to 2001, however, all three groups lost population within the Cincinnati city limits while gaining population in the Hamilton County jurisdictions outside of Cincinnati. Black non-Appalachians in Cincinnati had the greatest loss (–13%), followed by white Appalachian (–6%) and non-Appalachian white city residents (–6%). Members of all three culture groups appear to be participating in the national trend toward suburbanization.

Although they remain predominantly Protestant (66%) in 2001, white Appalachian religious affiliations have gradually changed in the past twenty years. While Catholic affiliation has decreased for non-Appalachian whites and blacks over this period, the Appalachian Catholic affiliation rate has risen from 15% in 1980 to 19% in 2001. Moreover, survey respondents could designate their affiliation as Protestant, Catholic, Jewish, or other/none; the proportions of all three groups opting for the other/none category rose substantially between 1989 and 2001. The proportion was greatest for non-Appalachian blacks (32%), followed by non-Appalachian whites (24%) and white Appalachians (15%). These gradual but definite changes in religious affiliation may indicate that the process of assimilation is in fact well underway among urban Appalachians.

Comparing the two generations adds little to our understanding of urban Appalachians. The first two generations of Appalachians in greater Cincinnati had achieved nearly equal educational backgrounds by 2001. Both have high rates of employment, although second-generation migrants are more likely to have part-time jobs. Well over a third of both generations are city dwellers with the balance living in the rest of the county. Second generation Appalachians are somewhat less likely than the first to be Protestant and more likely to respond "other/none" to questions about their religious affiliation. They are also less likely to be married and tend to live in larger households with more children than the first generation. Where these small differences do occur, nearly all of them can be explained by the age differentials between the two Appalachian groups. The average age of first generation Appalachians is 60 and only 12% of them are under 30; conversely the average age of second generation Appalachians is 43 and 20% of them are under 30.

A sample of third-generation Appalachian migrants was also studied in the 2001 survey.[6] Again, it is their relatively low average age (22) that determines much of their demographic profile; fifty-three percent are under the age of 18. Their sex ratios are about even, half are in school, and nearly two-fifths are working full time. The most distinctive finding about this cohort is that 62% live within the city limits of Cincinnati.

Appalachians in Cincinnati's Neighborhoods

Cincinnati, like many central cities in America's Midwest, has experienced major population loss and an increase in poverty during recent decades. Factors contributing to this pattern of decline are deindustrialization along with the related transition to lower paying service jobs, and the flight to the suburbs of the affluent. Cincinnati and other Midwestern cities have also experienced an increase in the percentage of minorities, African Americans in particular.

These same trends have impacted Cincinnati's Appalachian neighborhoods.[7] From 1970–1990 Cincinnati lost 100,000 people while its Appalachian neighborhoods experienced losses of anywhere between 6% and 51%. None experienced gains. The 2000 census reveals that these trends continued during the 1990s.[8] The city lost another 9% of its population and all but two Appalachian neighborhoods lost at a higher rate than the city as a whole at rates ranging from 3.3% to 29.9%. In nearly all cases, however, the rates of decline were down dramatically from the 1970–1990 period.

Population loss in key Appalachian neighborhoods does not necessarily mean that the city as a whole lost Appalachian population during the period. The population could have just become more dispersed. The total population of the ten neighborhoods where Appalachians are known to be concentrated is less than 50,000, although the total number of first- and second-generation white Appalachians in the city is approximately 67,300.

Racial change in Cincinnati's Appalachian neighborhoods was a mixed picture. Two of the ten neighborhoods experienced large increases in both the number and percent of African Americans. In the smaller neighborhoods some of the percentage changes were high but the numerical increases were small. One neighborhood lost both black and white population in almost equal numbers, while in another the African American population increased from 2 to 6 people. It should be noted that if the same picture holds true for the city as for the county, at least 17 percent of the new African Americans in Cincinnati's Appalachian neighborhoods are also Appalachian.[9] Neighborhoods on Cincinnati's west side saw significant increases in the Hispanic population in the nineties, but the Hispanic population changed little during the 1990s in three of the city's Appalachian neighborhoods.

Between 1970 and 1990, six of the Appalachian neighborhoods declined in socioeconomic status (SES) while three improved.[10] Where the SES index improved, the percentage of children under 18 who live in two parent homes remained high. The decline in SES in other Appalachian neighborhoods was partially a function of declines in family status. Why the Appalachian family is holding together better in two neighborhoods and not in the others is unknown.

Poverty rates doubled in four of the Appalachian neighborhoods between 1970 and 1990. In three neighborhoods the poverty rate was closer to tripling. The highest poverty rate among Cincinnati's Appalachian neighborhoods was 74% and the lowest was 13%. In 1970, two thirds or more of all children under 18 in these neighborhoods were in two parent families, but by 1990 only three neighborhoods fit this description. Yet in all neighborhoods except two at least half the children lived in two parent homes in 1990.

The failure of urban public schools to adapt to the needs of Appalachian students is perhaps the number one concern of Appalachian migrant advocates in all Midwestern cities. The measure of school dropouts used by the census is the percentage of 16–19 year olds not high school graduates and not enrolled in school.[11] Between 1970 and 1990, dropout rates fell in seven of the Appalachian neighborhoods. Appalachian advocates believe the dropout rates would have been much higher if thousands of families had not fled the city in response to forced busing and rapid decline in public schools. They expect the dropout rates in the 2000 census will be significantly higher than those reported in the 1990 Census.

Unemployment rates increased in each of the ten neighborhoods during the 1970–1990 period but remained below 20% in eight of them and were below 8% in two of them. Due to the economic prosperity of the 1990s, unemployment rates declined in that time period, even in the inner city. It should be noted that in the census tract with a 74% poverty rate, only 25% of the job seekers were recorded by the Census Bureau as unemployed in 1990. These data support the notion that failure to work is not the prime cause of poverty among urban Appalachians.

Community studies, and ethnographic studies in particular, offer deeper insight into what life is like in specific urban Appalachian neighborhoods. Using case studies of families Patricia Timm studied "school leavers" in Cincinnati's East End neighborhood.[12] The families Timm studied for the most part had lived in the neighborhood for more than a generation, and several had lived in the neighborhood four or more generations. A minority lived in extended families, but 88 percent of the families in the study had kin networks in the neighborhood. The study families were mostly employed, according to Timm: "33 percent are in low-paying jobs in the service sector; 29 percent have wage-based employment; and 31 percent participate in a complex informal economy that includes hauling, appliance repair, house painting and repair and flea market merchandising and 8 percent are unemployed. A large number of men and women assist their families by vigorous, inventive efforts to find economic resources."[13] Timm's study families were almost evenly divided between homeowners and renters, and the median value of their housing in 1990 was $36,000. With regard to schooling, Timm describes the impact of closing neighborhood schools and other neighborhood institutions as the East End population declined, concluding that school attainment was lower in the current generation than that of the students' parents.

Another study in the same neighborhood cosponsored by the Legal Aid Society and the Urban Appalachian Council found that some homeowners were reluctant to invest in their homes because they feared displacement by urban renewal.[14] Loss of their homes by "gentrification" is a fear East Enders expressed in both of the studies cited above. Much of the East End is also in the Ohio River flood plain, a fact that further depresses home values.

Anthropologist Rhoda Halperin conducted an ethnographic study of the East End which amplifies the description of family and community life in that neighborhood. Her study outlines the informal economy and the organized efforts of community residents in planning and neighborhood development.[15] The East End as characterized by Halperin is a diverse neighborhood with a strong sense of community among its Appalachian, African American, and European-heritage residents. She describes community as:

> . . . a dynamic and contentious and changing process that plays out as a series of everyday practices by people who have or have had some link to the East End. Many East Enders have been displaced and no longer live in the East End itself. At the extreme, people may live in Texas or Florida or, more commonly, in another neighborhood in Cincinnati, in a nearby town, in rural Ohio, or in Kentucky. Everyday practices—caring for children and the elderly, providing work, helping in times of crisis, granting favors, passing along information or lending support—represent the essence of East End life and culture. They are, however tenuously and fleetingly, embedded in specific East End structures that are old and enduring—the extended family, the church and the neighborhood as a place that confers working class identity. The practices involved in maintaining those structures take priority over all others. A real East Ender will take a lesser job, quit a job, or drop out of school before denying help or money to family or community members who need support.[16]

Conclusion

While urban Appalachians in greater Cincinnati overall seem to be well along in the process of social and economic assimilation, there are issues, particularly those revolving around education, that remain unresolved. There are also pockets of deep Appalachian poverty in Cincinnati's central-city neighborhoods; the residents of these neighborhoods, often third-generation white Appalachians, are beset with social problems similar to those affecting the local African-American community.

But the picture for low-income Appalachians is not bleak. Like other urban social groups, Appalachians in Cincinnati have created organizations to address their own political, cultural and educational concerns. Community-based educational programs are operating across the city; an annual Appalachian Festival is held in the city every spring; *The Appalachian Connection*, a neighborhood newspaper is published monthly; and an Appalachian political action committee actively backs candidates and issues of local importance. The Urban Appalachian Council supports summer programs for youth, educational and job training opportunities for adolescents and adults, and cultural events and community organizing in neighborhoods across the city.[17]

As Carter Woodson has pointed out, Appalachian people have been coming to Cincinnati to make their homes for well over 175 years. During the twentieth century urban Appalachians in many other American cities have also become a fixture of the urban landscape. And, in the words of one eastern Kentucky migrant who was threatened by strikebreakers at his new workplace in Ohio, they "ain't agoin' back."

11

by Emily Satterwhite

Seeing Appalachian Cities

Since at least the end of the nineteenth century, the people of the Appalachian mountains have been stereotyped as backwards, backwoods hillbillies. Even today, pop culture representations of Appalachia depict the region as uniformly consisting of near-wilderness hills and hollows where people live without access to the accoutrements of modern life. Appalachian people have been denigrated, and sometimes envied, for what is portrayed as their inability or refusal to participate in "progress."

In the 1960s and 70s, a number of Appalachian scholars and activists reacted against the assumption that "progress" and "development" are unequivocal blessings. They founded a pro-Appalachia political and academic movement that upheld prevalent views of the region as rural, isolated, and unmodernized but insisted upon the dignity and worth of rural mountain ways of life. They pointed to Appalachian people's propensity to love and live off of the land as an antidote to a destructive, wasteful, and exploitative stance toward the environment and to a materialistic, consumer capitalist mentality that they associated chiefly with wealthy, urban non-Appalachians. By accepting the premise that Appalachians are different from other Americans while reversing the negative value judgment placed upon them, these Appalachianists fashioned what sociologist Manuel Castells refers to as a "resistance identity." The formation of an Appalachian resistance identity has allowed numerous individuals to claim their Appalachian heritage with pride and has given them a means by which they can think critically about the presumed inferiority of rural people. Many Appalachian Studies scholars and activists continue to extol the virtues of rural mountain experiences and values today.

Yet hundreds of thousands of people living within Appalachia live what is clearly not a quintessentially rural "Appalachian" way of life: they live in cities. Some city residents are newcomers who have migrated from other parts of the country. Some have recently moved there from more rural Appalachian counties in search of employment or educational opportunities. Some belong to families that moved to the city a generation ago or more, and may share common traditions, common history, and continued ties with others from more rural parts of the region. Whatever their origins, few residents of Appalachian cities would willingly trade metropolitan residence for rural living, much less trade urban levels of consumption for a supposedly more "Appalachian" devotion to subsistence.

Appalachian Studies literature has seldom discussed what it means to be city *and* moun-

Source: From *Southern Changes,* 21:2, Summer 1999 by Emily Satterwhite.

tain, or what it feels like to inherit or embrace contradictory sets of values. Only in the past few years have some Appalachianists begun to address the need to better understand the presence of cities in the region. For the most part, scholarly representations of Appalachia, like pop culture representations, have rendered Appalachian cities wholly invisible.

Cities in Appalachia are made invisible despite the fact that even in 1965, when the federal government first labeled Appalachia an underdeveloped region deserving of aid, fully 47 percent of its residents fit the federal definition of "urban" (meaning they lived in an incorporated locale with a population of 2,500 or more). In 1990, the percentage of urban Appalachian residents of the federally-defined region had not changed significantly—it remained at approximately 47 percent of the population. What *had* changed was that a greater proportion of Appalachians lived in the region's *largest cities* than ever before. In 1960, 24 percent of "core" Appalachians lived in a county that is now part of a metropolitan statistical area (MSA).[1] In 1990, the number of people living in Appalachian MSAs had jumped to 40.5 percent. Over one-third of the region's population lived in one of the Appalachian counties of Knoxville, Tennessee; Johnson City-Kingsport-Bristol Tennessee-Virginia (the Tri-Cities); Chattanooga, Tennessee; Asheville, North Carolina, Atlanta, Georgia; Huntington West Virginia-Ashland Kentucky; Hickory-Morganton, North Carolina; Charleston, West Virginia; or Roanoke, Virginia.[2]

What does this 16.5 percent population increase in the region's metropolitan areas tell us about the Appalachian experience? The answer to this question may vary from city to city, but a couple of possibilities present themselves. The increase might be primarily the result of an influx of non-Appalachian middle and upper class Americans moving into suburbs around cities inhabited by proportionally fewer native Appalachians, potentially resulting in less retention of "Appalachian" characteristics as newcomers influence natives. On the other hand, the increase might point primarily to the continuation of a classic Appalachian trend: historically, rural mountain residents have moved close enough to urban or industrial areas to obtain employment while maintaining a foothold outside the city where cash income is more easily augmented by farming or gardening. There has been so little research on Appalachian cities within a regional framework that we can only speculate.

Scholars interested in the alternative values purportedly embraced by Appalachians have concentrated almost solely on rural Appalachia, and their work is vital to a complete understanding of the region. After all, while

Metropolitan Statistical Areas Partially or Completely Within Core Appalachia,[1] 1990

Metropolitan Statistical Areas for which at least one component county falls within core Appalachia (population)

Atlanta, Georgia (2,959,500)

Huntington West Virginia-Ashland Kentucky (312,529)

Hickory-Morganton, North Carolina (292,405)

Charleston, West Virginia (250,464)

Roanoke, Virginia (224,592)

Metropolitan Statistical Areas for which ALL component counties fall within core Appalachia (population)

Knoxville, Tennessee (585,960)

Johnson City-Kingsport-Bristol Tennessee-Virginia (436,047)

Chattanooga, Tennessee (424,347)

Asheville, North Carolina (191,772)

some portions of the region have a very large metropolitan population (East Tennessee was 66 percent metropolitan in 1990), huge tracts of the mountain region contain no metropolitan statistical areas whatsoever (including a 27-county-area in southeastern Kentucky). Expanding Appalachian scholarship to include Appalachian cities and urbanization can sharpen the tools already available for thinking about the region and any political movement centered on it in at least the following four ways.

First of all, throwing out our old mental maps of rural Appalachia in order to see cities may enable us to observe the region's entire geography more clearly. Many of the earliest analyses viewed Appalachia primarily in terms of mountains, mines, and towns, but these categories are not sufficient. Not only Appalachian cities, but also the region's industrial parks, strip developments along highways, and Walmarts—and even its century-old coal camps and tourist resorts—tell a different story of urbanization than often recognized.

Secondly, any careful understanding of urbanization recognizes it as an on-going process, one closely associated with capitalist accumulation, whose affects are not reserved solely for cities. Even the most rural of areas participates in and is affected by urbanization and capital accumulation. Natural resources are removed with the aid of locals for profit and growth in distant processing and financial centers and, more recently, local leaders welcome retail chains stores that funnel cash away from local economies. Differential development takes place *within* the region as well, with regional cities often profiting by serving as brokers between more rural areas and more urban areas in the movement of natural resources, goods, money, and tourists.

Thirdly, recognition of continued urbanization in the region forces us to realize that basing an Appalachian identity movement upon only those who live an unadulterated rural "Appalachian" way of life undercuts any chance of real success since an ever-decreasing number of people are capable of claiming and organizing based on any such identity. In fact, it may be the case that the majority of people drawn to the Appalachian identity movement are *not* rural. Many Appalachian scholar-activists were raised in, were educated in, or currently live in metropolitan areas within or adjoining the region. Preliminary discussions with some of today's leading Appalachianists indicate that growing up in cities often meant experiencing greater exposure to mainstream America's denigration of rural mountain customs and values. This suggests that residents of large mountain towns or cities have had as great a need for the affirmation offered by an Appalachian identity movement as those who grew up in more rural, and perhaps to some degree more sheltered, Appalachian places.

The final suggestion I would like to make is that grappling with the phenomenon of Appalachian cities, and perhaps the "Appalachian-ness" of some cities or the urbanity of some Appalachians, may help temper the tendency towards romanticization and impractical idealism. While some who claim an Appalachian identity may privilege back-to-the-land ideals over consumerist urbanism, we must recognize that the majority of Appalachians want access to the same consumer goods appreciated by other Americans. Not only does nostalgia about a mythical Appalachian past obscure harsh realities (such as the intolerance of difference evident in many small communities and the economic difficulties and insecurities inherent in family farming), it also prevents the formation of workable visions for the future by causing us to disregard the impracticality of a region-wide return to rural subsistence agriculture.

If it ever made sense to think of a premodern rural Appalachia entrenched against wealthy urban outsiders, we are quickly outgrowing the suitability of such a model. Appalachianists could continue to avoid inclusive geographic boundaries of the region and persist in pointing to the shrinking spaces of rurality and poverty as the "real" Appalachia. However, to do so would mean missing significant transformations in the dynamic economy and culture of the region. We need to understand how, in Appalachia, turn-of-the-century capitalism and mid-century industrialization have given way to a late-twentieth-century service economy and a continuing trend toward the concentration of people and wealth in cities. A more complete scholarly understanding of the history, political economy, and ongoing evolution of the region will require that we develop a new schema for understanding Appalachia—one capable of incorporating Appalachian cities.

IV

Appalachian Stereotypes

A major concern in Appalachian studies over the past three decades has been to challenge stereotypes of the region and its people. Although all nine sections of this volume have references to stereotyping, in this section we focus on negative labeling more explicitly. This section begins with an article by John Solomon Otto tracing the application of the term "hillbilly" to mountain people and their music. In the second article Jean Haskell Speer addresses the practical aspects of countering media stereotypes of Appalachians. She proposes six strategies "proven most effective for groups trying to influence the media."

In "Beyond Isolation and Heterogeneity" Ronald L. Lewis frames Appalachian history as a part of our nation's "new" social history. As his title implies, the region was never entirely isolated or homogeneous, nor were all of its residents rural and self-sufficient. Goods were manufactured and exported as Appalachian towns developed as centers of industry and trade. Two Appalachias existed side by side—town and "back country." The towns were racially diverse and hosted "a bewildering array of peoples and cultures" as immigrants poured into them. The belief in a distinct subculture encompassing the entire region is challenged by these historical insights. Lewis concludes that because such a subculture does not exist, it cannot be used to explain the "backward" economy of much of the region.

12

by John Solomon Otto

"Hillbilly Culture": The Appalachian Mountain Folk in History and Popular Culture

Even today, any mention of the Appalachian mountains conjures up images of "hillbillies," log cabins, "shootin' arns," "feudin'," "moonshine," "revenooers," and dueling banjos in the popular mind. The southern "hillbilly" has become a stock character of popular culture, appearing in comic strips, television, fiction and movies. Despite his popularity, the "hillbilly" has little basis in fact, and the hillbilly stereotype is bitterly resented by the contemporary inhabitants of the Southern Appalachian mountains—a region which includes West Virginia, eastern Kentucky, southwestern Virginia, eastern Tennessee, western North Carolina and northeastern Georgia.

The people of Southern Appalachia do not refer to themselves as "hillbillies." Nor do they call themselves "mountaineers," or, more politely, "highlanders" (Williams 49, 54). They simply refer to themselves as "just plain folks," which is precisely what most of them are—the descendants of the "plain folk" of the Old South.

Historian Frank Owsley first drew attention to the "plain folk"—the mass of southern white farmers who lived outside the plantation economy and who comprised the bulk of the Old South's population. The plain folk included the slaveholding farmers with fewer than twenty slaves as well as the more numerous slaveless farmers. Most plain folk farmers aspired "to acquire land and other property sufficient to give them and their children a sense of security and well-being" (Owsley 36).

To achieve this sense of security and well-being, plain folk practiced a "grazing and farm economy" (Owsley 37). They grazed cattle and hogs on the unfenced public lands, or open-range, at no charge, a practice that was safeguarded by law until after the Civil War. In addition, they practiced "patch" farming—clearing temporary fields, or "patches," from the forests, planting corn until yields declined, abandoning the old fields and then clearing new fields from the remaining forest. Open-range grazing furnished meat for family consumption as well as surplus livestock for sale. Patch-farming of corn, in turn, offered food for families, fodder for livestock, and even cash—if the corn was distilled into

Source: From *The Southern Quarterly: A Journal of the Arts in the South,* 24:3, Spring 1986 by John Solomon Otto.

liquor. Taken together, livestock-grazing and patch-farming allowed plain folk families to meet their subsistence and cash needs; and these agricultural practices provided the economic base for a distinctive lifestyle or folk culture, the outline of which one finds in travelogues, reminiscences and oral traditions. Plain folk lived in dispersed rural neighborhoods; occupied houses built of horizontal logs cut from surrounding forests; fashioned their own agricultural implements, household furnishings and even garments; patronized crossroad mills, stores and churches and periodically visited county seat towns to trade, vote and socialize (Otto, "Upland South" 74–76).

By 1860, the eve of the Civil War, the plain folk were found throughout the Old South from Delaware to Texas, but they were especially prominent in the Appalachian mountains, where they were the vast majority of the inhabitants. Before the Civil War, these Appalachian plain folk attracted little attention in the outside world. Their lifestyle differed little from that of the plain folk who lived elsewhere in the Old South (Otto, "Oral Traditional History" 26–27).

The Civil War and the postbellum cotton boom shattered the lifestyle of most southern plain folk. In an effort to protect cotton fields from wandering livestock, postbellum state legislatures enacted laws forcing plain folk to fence in their range cattle and hogs. Since these fence laws effectively ended the right to graze livestock on the open-range, the plain folk living in the cotton-producing regions turned to cotton-growing as a livelihood. They borrowed money for cotton seed and fertilizers as well as for food and clothing to last them until harvest and market. If cotton prices were high, they paid off their debts and made a small profit. If prices were low, they became debtors, often losing their farms in the process. Landless plain folk then joined the growing mass of tenant farmers and mill workers (McDonald and McWhiney 1115–18).

Although the postbellum cotton boom swept away many southern plain folk, cotton-growing proved unfeasible in the Appalachian mountains. The poor soils, rugged terrain and unpredictable frosts of the mountains limited the spread of cotton cultivation. The Appalachian mountains remained an enclave of plain folk farmers long after the Civil War (see U.S. Department of Agriculture, "Economic and Social Problems" 9–10; Newton 144).

But during the late nineteenth century, a series of family feuds, including the infamous Hatfield-McCoy vendetta, focused national attention on the previously little-known Appalachian mountains. The first "discoverers" of the mountains were journalists, but they were soon followed by missionaries, teachers and academics. These outsiders found a world of log cabins, split-rail fences, ox-drawn plows, homemade chairs, and spinning wheels—all the familiar attributes of plain folk life. Outside observers, nevertheless, believed they had entered a lost world, being transported back to the time of Daniel Boone, Davey Crockett and Abe Lincoln's boyhood. By the late 1890s, academic visitors were proclaiming the Appalachian mountains to be a "retarded frontier" still bearing the stamp of pioneer America. Entering the Appalachian mountains, one could hear traditional ballads, listen to folktales about witches and view "lost frontiersmen" plowing their corn fields and grazing their livestock on the open range (William Brown; Frost; Vincent).

The "lost frontiersman" stereotype of the 1890s gave way to a less favorable stereotype in the early twentieth century. Following the defeat of Spain in 1889, the United States became a minor colonial power, shouldering the "white man's burden" in Puerto Rico and the Philippines. Concern for "civilizing" the primitive people of the world, however, was not confined to the areas outside the continental United States. American reformers soon turned their attention to the mountain folk of Appalachia, believing them to be as lost in ignorance and poverty as any foreign "people of color." After all, mountain folk feuded with their neighbors, believed in witches, raised broods of uneducated children and avoided hard work—except to raise corn for illegal moonshine whiskey (May 192–230; Klotter 842). In short, they were "hillbillies."

The word "hillbilly" first appeared in print in 1900, when a *New York Journal* reported defined the term: "a Hill-Billie is a free and untrammeled white citizen who lives in the hills . . . has no means to speak of, dresses as he can, talks as he pleases, drinks whiskey when he gets it, and fires off his revolver as the fancy takes him" (qtd. in Green 204). The word "hillbilly" soon appeared in a spate of early twentieth-century mass media articles and novels, purportedly describing the lifestyle of the southern mountain folk (Green 204). And by the 1920s, the term "hillbilly" even circulated among the mountain folk themselves, serving as a jest or as an insult.

As an example, a mountain string band, journeying to New York City in 1925 to record fiddle dance tunes, was asked the name of their group by the record producer. In reply, one band member blurted out: "We're nothing but a bunch of hillbillies from North Carolina and Virginia. Call us anything." The record producer wrote down "The Hill-Billies" as the band's name. On their return trip from New York, the band members expressed misgivings about their new title. As one of the musicians later recalled: "Hillbilly was not only a funny word, it was a fighting word" (Green 213–14). The band's records, nonetheless, sold widely, and "The Hill-Billies" even toured the vaudeville circuit. Dressed in overalls and straw hats and playing mountain music before urban audiences, "The Hill-Billies" did much to popularize the "hillbilly" stereotype (Malone 43–44). In fact, "The Hill-Billies" achieved such success that mountain music and the word "hillbilly" became inextricably interlinked. The mixed lot of fiddle dance tunes, traditional ballads and tin pan alley songs which southern whites recorded during the interwar years were popularly known as "hillbilly music" (Malone 43–44).

"Hillbilly music" remained a disquieting term, however, and no one proudly proclaimed himself to be a "hillbilly." As portrayed in the printed media, "hillbillies" were ill-kempt, ill-educated, and poverty-stricken farmers-cum-moonshiners who lived a static and unchanging life in the isolated Appalachian mountains (Bradley; Smith 329–31). This "hillbilly" stereotype was not only demeaning, it was also inaccurate, since it ignored the profound changes that occurred in the lives of Appalachian mountain folk as a result of industrialization, overpopulation, migration and urbanization (Eller 37–38).

At the turn of the twentieth century, most Appalachian mountain folk were still rural agriculturalists. They grazed cattle and hogs in the unfenced forests and grew corn in fields cleared from hillside forests, as their plain folk ancestors had done (for example, see Semple 600–3; Kephart 42–45, Morton 53–54; Haney 85–87). Since every cow needed a minimum of fifteen acres of forest range in order to find sufficient forage during the year, a herd of only 100 cattle required as much as 1,500 acres of unfenced forest (Hilliard 136). And when the corn yields in a hillside field declined, farmers simply abandoned the old field and cleared new ground from the remaining forest (see U.S. Department of Agriculture, "Message" 25–26, 58). Thus, the continued success of mountain agriculture required an abundance of forest land.

After 1900, forest land was no longer abundant in the Appalachian mountains. Extractive industries such as coal mining and logging competed with farmers for the use of mountain land. During the first three decades of the twentieth century, private companies acquired vast tracts of public and private land. Whole valleys were given over to railways, coal mines and coal towns, while forested slopes were denuded to provide timbers for mines and lumber for coal towns (Eller 40–42; Caudill, *Night Comes* 98–88; 144–46; Shackelford and Weinberg 133–55). By 1930, only 60% of the land in the Appalachia mountains was still owned by farmers (Gray 9).

The loss of agricultural land was exacerbated by overpopulation. Southern Appalachia had one of the highest birth rates in the United States, for mountain families needed children to aid in farm work. Larger families, of course, increased the population pressure on the land (Barron 211–12). Traditional "patch" farming could no longer support the burgeoning rural population. During the early twentieth century, many mountain families migrated to Texas and Oklahoma, hoping to continue their agricultural way of life as cotton tenant farmers. Other abandoned farming altogether, settling in the coal towns and logging camps of Southern Appalachia (Combs 43–44; Caudill, *Night Comes* 193–209; Shackelford and Weinberg 193–209).

During the Great Depression of the 1930s, some migrants returned to the mountains to subsist on tiny hillside farms. Unemployed workers from the coal mines and saw mills also joined the ranks of mountain farmers. About 400,000 farms were to be found in the Appalachian mountains during the 1930s; half of them were less than fifty acres in size, and one-fourth were smaller than twenty acres. This meant that thousands of families were "trying to make a living on from three to 10 acres of poor land" (Taylor 13). During the depths of the Depression, much of Southern Appalachia was occupied by marginal farmers who made little money and whose working efforts were exerted in merely subsisting from year to year (Williams 49–50).

Depression-era newspapers rarely reported on the plight of marginal mountain farmers, but most papers featured the antics of cartoon "hillbillies" in daily comic strips. In 1934, Al Capp launched the "Li'l Abner" strip, which was set in the Kentucky mountains and which featured a comic "hillbilly" family—the Yokums. Though "Li'l Abner" proved so popular that it inspired an RKO movie in 1940, it was the "Barney Google" comic strip which introduced the archetypal cartoon "hillbilly"—"Snuffy Smith." In the same year that Al Capp began his "Li'l Abner" strip, cartoonist Billy De Beck led his comic hero, "Barney Google," deep into the Kentucky mountains. There Google met the disreputable "Snuffy Smith" and his wife, Lowizie. She did all the plowing and housework, while "Snuffy" stole chickens, made "moonshine" whiskey, tangled with "revenooers," and slept off the effect of too much "corn squeezins." By the late 1930s, "Snuffy Smith" was so well received by the American public that he crowded "Barney Google" out of his own strip (Horn 99–100, 450–51). In conjunction with "Li'l Abner," the "Snuffy Smith" comic strip portrayed "hillbilles" as the shiftless denizens of the Appalachian mountains. "Hillbillies" were poor, because they were lazy like "Snuffy Smith" and not because they were the victims of complex demographic and economic circumstances.

Before World War Two, the "hillbillies" had been safely ensconced in their Appalachian mountain homes. But during the war, a booming national economy precipitated a massive wave of out-migration from Southern Appalachia. Between 1940 and 1960, over two million people left Appalachia to seek jobs in the industrial cities of the North. Among the migrants were hundreds of thousands of marginal farmers who abandoned their tiny hillside farms in search of a better life (Brown and Hillery 54–78).

Arriving in northern cities, the mountain migrants received a cool welcome. Journalists warned of an "invasion of the hillbillies." Urban Americans, expecting an influx of "Snuffy Smiths," shunned the mountain folks who settled in slum neighborhoods that were dubbed "hillbilly ghettos." Living in an impersonal urban world, where one rarely knew one's neighbors, the mountain migrants turned to storefront Pentecostal churches and to the "hillbilly bars" for solace (Votaw; Flynt 136–40).

In their own taverns, the mountain migrants listened to musicians performing songs which outsiders dismissed as "hillbilly music." Aware of the negative connotations of "hillbilly music," mountain musicians began referring to their repertoire of dance tunes, ballads and topical songs as "country music." To escape the "Snuffy Smith-hillbilly" image, mountain musicians adopted the dress and style of Texas "honky-tonk" performers such as Ernest Tubb. Despite the incongruity, Kentucky and West Virginia musicians donned Stetson hats, western shirts and cowboy boots when performing before migrant audiences. And finally, mountain musicians incorporated the latest Nashville "country" hits into their repertoires, particularly the mournful ballad "Detroit City," which became an anthem for "urban hillbillies" working in northern factories (Wilgus 170–73; Malone 166, 216–17; Tribe 46–47):

Home folks think I'm big in Detroit
    City,
From the letters that I write they think
    I'm fine:
By day I make the cars and by night I
    make the bars,
If only they could read between the
    lines.

Refrain: I want to go home, I want to
        go home.
    Oh, how I want to go home.
(Bobby Bare)

Although some migrants returned to their mountain homes, most remained in the industrial cities, where they came under the scrutiny of social workers and reformers. Michael Harrington among others directed national attention to the "urban hillbillies" and their kinsmen in the Appalachian mountains. In 1962, Harrington published his influential book, *The Other America,* wherein he recommended massive federal aid to cure the poverty of Appalachia and thus stem the migration of mountain folk to the northern cities (Harrington 40–43, 96).

Thanks to the renewed interest in Southern Appalachia, Congress passed the Appalachian Development Act in 1965, authorizing expenditures of 840 million dollars for highway development but only 250 million dollars for human and environmental development. Although urban areas in the mountains benefited from federal highway construction, the Appalachian Development Act did little to alleviate rural poverty. The much publicized "war on poverty" slowed but failed to halt the out-migration from Southern Appalachia. Rural families continued to abandon their hillside farms and move to the urban North in search of jobs (Flynt 142–44; De Jong).

As American taxpayers were funding the "war on poverty" during the 1960s, they viewed Appalachian mountain folk in a long-running television comedy that was purportedly set in western North Carolina. The "Andy Griffith Show" (1960–68) featured such fictional Appalachian folks as Briscoe Darling and Ernest T. Bass (Terrace 1: 55–56). Briscoe Darling and his family were the personification of the positive "lost frontiersman" stereotype. The Darlings were superstitious but upright and honorable. They farmed, lived in a log house and played traditional dance tunes and ballads, as the "plain folk" had once done. Ernest T. Bass, on the other hand, was the very embodiment of the negative "hillbilly" stereotype. He was poor, lazy and filthy. Bass searched vainly for a woman to share his squalid life; and when frustrated, he howled in the streets, broke windows and disrupted the peaceful life of Mayberry.

"Hillbillies" also figured prominently in James Dickey's bestselling novel of 1970, *Deliverance,* which was released as a movie in 1972. In *Deliverance,* four suburban businessmen planned a canoe trip down the Cahulawassee River, a scenic Georgia mountain stream. Arriving at the headwaters of the Cahulawassee, one of the businessmen met a deformed "hillbilly" banjo-picker who bested him in the now-famous "dueling banjos" scene. During their canoe trip downriver, the suburban men ran afoul of two mountain men. Unlike Snuffy Smith and Ernest T. Bass, who were dissolute but harmless, these were "murderous hillbilly" sodomites who sexually abused two of the businessmen. Killing their depraved "hillbilly" assailants, three of the businessmen survived the harrowing canoe trip and were delivered back to their suburban homes. At novel's end, the Cahulawassee River is dammed, the valley is flooded, and the resultant lake is ringed with marinas and vacation homes (Dickey).

Despite its highly biased portrayal of mountain folk, *Deliverance* contained an element of truth: outsiders were transforming the Appalachian landscape to suit their own needs. Appalachian streams were dammed to generate electricity for urban centers; valleys were flooded to create lakes for suburban vacationers; and finally, hillside farms were incorporated into the growing public forests. In 1930, the U.S. Forest Service managed only two million acres of public forest in Southern Appalachia. By 1970, there were more than fourteen million acres of government forest in the Appalachian mountains (Caudill 49–50;

Gibbard 115; Carawan xi). Valleys and hillsides which had once supported thousands of agricultural families were now the homes of forest rangers and weekend tourists.

Today, the Appalachian mountains are dominated by public forests and tourist parks. Agriculture is largely confined to the broad valleys, where the terrain permits intensive commercial agriculture based on livestock, grains and tobacco. The traditional practices of open-range grazing and "patch" farming which date back to the days of the plain folk have virtually disappeared. Modern Appalachia scarcely resembles the rural, agricultural landscape that gave birth to the "hillbilly" stereotype in the early 1900s. But in spite of the great change Appalachia has undergone, the "hillbilly" stereotype lives on in the "Snuffy Smith" comic strip, the syndicated "Andy Griffith Show" and late-night showings of the movie "Deliverance." Appalachian mountain folk, who range from commercial farmers to blue-collar workers to white-collar businessmen, share one common attribute: they resent being called "hillbillies." They continue to regard themselves as "just plain folks."

13

by Jean Haskell Speer

From Stereotype to Regional Hype: Strategies for Changing Media Portrayals of Appalachia

When one or two are gathered in the name of Appalachian Studies, discussions of media images of the region ensue, and the conversation is generally punctuated by dismay or venom (*Deliverance,* for example, has become an Appalachian epithet). We cringe when we read something like a recent newspaper article about the ways U.S. culture "rocks the world"; author Pico Iver recalled growing up in Oxford, England, "that citadel of learning," and being raised on "The Beverly Hillbillies" (*Roanoke* [Va.] *Times and World News* 17 March 1992).

Because we in Appalachian Studies are so familiar with the problem of stereotypical media images, I will define the problem only briefly. My interest here is to offer an agenda for change, a set of strategies for revising media portrayals of Appalachia and Appalachian people. For too long, we have treated media stereotypes like the weather—everybody talks about them, but we have done little to change them.

From the earliest days of the Appalachian Studies movement, scholars and activists in the region have written about media perceptions and portrayals of Appalachia. As early as 1971, James Branscome, in "Annihilating the Hillbilly: The Appalachians' Struggle with America's Institutions," wrote:

> Each week millions of Americans gather around their sets to watch this combination ["The Beverly Hillbillies," "Green Acres," and "Hee Haw"] which has to be the most intensive effort ever exerted by a nation to belittle, demean, and otherwise destroy a minority people within its boundaries. Within the three shows on one night, hillbillies are shown being conned into buying the White House, coddling a talking pig, and rising from a cornpatch to crack the sickest jokes on TV. America is allowed to continue laughing at this minority group because on this, America agrees: hillbilly ain't beautiful. (p. 25)

Shortly thereafter, in 1973, David Whisnant observed:

Source: From *Journal of the Appalachian Studies Association*, 5, 1993 by Jean Haskell Speer.

> Networks which have long since discontinued "Amos n Andy" and other racist programs and which have shown some signs recently of reassessing their sexist images of women, continue to run shows such as "Hee Haw" and "Green Acres" and "The Beverly Hillbillies." Al Capp's "L'il Abner" appears in virtually every hometown newspaper. In their gross insensitivity to the feelings of Appalachian people, to their spiritual and material needs, and to the richness and variety of their culture, the media have been agents of a broader pattern of cultural imperialism. (p. 129)

In 1976, Curtis Seltzer, in "The Media vs. Appalachia: A Case Study," noted that women, racial minorities, ethnic groups, low-income people, and groups challenging powerful interests were routinely excluded from the unofficial news net on which journalists rely. And of all these groups, "hillbillies" received the worst media treatment. Seltzer wrote:

> . . . millions of ordinary people in Appalachia . . . are routinely thought of as hillbillies, creekers, rednecks, grits, and trash. Where people are in a society's pecking order is reflected in offhand images used in the national media. . . . A reporter's job is to describe a situation . . . with fairness, accuracy, and, when time and talent permit, truth. These simple guidelines disappear, however, when the national media covers an Appalachian story . . . No other minority is subject to such ridicule in the national media. (p. 10–11)

In 1977, I did a study (Speer 1977) of "The Beverly Hillbillies" in which I noted that the producers consulted out-of-print volumes on mountain customs, notions, and superstitions to get the "proper" background for the show. Out-of-print volumes means they were consulting old local color writing which never contained "proper" descriptions of the culture in the first place. In 1979, Horace Newcomb in "Appalachia on Television: Region as Symbol in American Popular Culture," wrote, "Appalachia is perhaps the only region of America to have been systematically represented in a fictional context on commercial television. . . . Only the increasing number of programs dealing with black American culture comes close to being a definable body of fiction comparable to that of Appalachia" (p. 155).

Sometimes the problem is not the treatment of Appalachia in the media, but the region's exclusion from media consideration. In a 1983 *Appalachian Journal* interview, Tom Rickman, director of *Coal Miner's Daughter,* talked about plans for a television series based on material from the film. He recalled:

> . . . I wrote the pilot script, which was set in Butcher Holler in 1959, and the family was back, and there was a great deal of family story in it as well as some local characters, Appalachian characters, I'd invented. . . . We were supposed to start filming in February, and we kept waiting for the call, and, finally, when it came, it was that an executive at CBS had read it and had decided that Appalachia was too depressing to be a TV series. Appalachia by definition was a depressing area; therefore, it had no place on network television, which, presumably is not depressing. [T]he feeling that an area of the country that [is] interesting and rich could be eliminated from network television by some man's feeling that it's too depressing was pretty hard to take. (p. 348)

Sometimes the problems go beyond media content to media policy. In a recent issue of *Now and Then* that focused on "The Media and Appalachia," Appalachian storyteller Anndrena Belcher recounted her fights with the movie industry. She quit the set of *The River* as Sissy Spacek's stand-in when she found out that she and other locals were being victimized by not being paid the union wages that all others on the set received. She stayed with the film, *Next of Kin,* with Patrick Swayze, to try to influence the director and cast to modify their stereotypes of Appalachia. She still was disappointed with the final result (Belcher 1991, 22, 25–26).

Examples of ill-informed and damaging media portrayals and polices are abundant. Such portrayals and policies are a continuing problem and one that has engaged scholars in Appalachian Studies for years. But too often we are speaking to ourselves (preaching to the choir, if you will). I would argue that we in Appalachian Studies need an agenda for systematic action to influence the media. We need first to understand how advocacy or pressure groups can affect the media, and then we need a plan to implement our own agenda.

Activism to influence the media has been more effective and visible in recent years than ever before, even though the media became targets of public pressure as early as the mid-1700s with the advent of novels. Most pre-World War II media criticism was concerned with protecting the lower classes from the corrupting influence of mass media and protecting the established social elites from being weakened by media messages. Today, criticism comes most from those on the margins of society, who believe that the media do not give them enough voice or portray them in denigrating ways (Montgomery 1989). These groups include minorities, women, gays, seniors, the disabled, social issue groups (such as abortion groups), anti-violence groups, and conservative religious groups. But, as Joseph Turow says in *Media Systems in Society,* "most people will not take the time or trouble to find out what further steps they might take toward successfully pursuing their demands" (1992, 130).

There are six strategies that have proven most effective for groups trying to influence media, especially the visible and powerful broadcast media (Montgomery 1989; Turow 1992). These strategies are:

- Putting pressure on authorities who regulate media—the courts at all levels and the Federal Communications Commission. Groups can complain to the FCC about media content and, because the FCC grants and renews licenses of broadcast stations, this media criticism does arouse concern in the industry. This kind of pressure is effective only if there has been some legal violation that allows judicial consideration or if the FCC complaints seem to represent some strong political constituency. Filing FCC complaints, however, may be useful for convincing legislators to put pressure on media producers.

- Approaching local affiliates of networks, and either appealing to their need to be sensitive to community interests, or threatening to file complaints if they do not do what your group wants (for example, preempting a program or airing your side of the issue). When groups can get a preemption, it sends a message to the national network because it affects ratings. These goals of preemption or representation are difficult to achieve, but they can happen. In 1972, two affiliate stations dropped episodes of *Maude* in which the title character was seeking an abortion; PBS aired the controversial documentary *Days of Rage: The Young Palestinians,* even after receiving pressure, but the network held a panel discussion after the broadcast that presented opposing positions.

- Targeting advertisers. Pressure groups may organize massive letter campaigns to advertisers in a given medium or threaten the advertiser with a boycott. Boycotts will be effective only if a pressure group can mobilize the numbers of people to have real impact on the advertiser. The issue around which the protest is organized has to be significant to the advertiser; for example, if a company tends to be conservative in policy, it may be a likely target for groups complaining about too much sex or violence in the media. Large companies that produce multiple consumer goods sometimes are skittish about getting on an advocacy movement's hit list.

- Focusing attention on the network, publisher, etc. Pressure groups usually take two approaches when using this strategy. They may (1) plan a radical protest, such as gay organizations "zapping" (stalling or shutting down) the day-to-day operation of a media organization, or (2) try to work with the media organization on a fairly regular basis to maintain the type of coverage they want. The National Organization for Women, for example, worked with NBC on *The Burning Bed* (with Farrah Fawcett) to assure sensitive treatment of abused women; the Harvard Alcohol Project worked with NBC and CBS to balance the presentation of the glamour of drinking with the responsibilities and dangers of drinking.
- Targeting production companies of broadcast programs. In addition to protesting negative coverage, some advocacy groups have had success by giving awards to those who create images they do like. Sending out press releases of praise or blame may be effective, as well as making personal contacts with production groups. For example, an episode of *M.A.S.H.* in which Hawkeye has a drinking problem was developed with help from an anti-drinking lobby.
- Using media against media. Advocacy groups can use media to campaign for their own stance when reacting to media portrayals they do not like, or to gain support for their own agenda. When NBC aired the miniseries *Beulah Land,* which some groups found demeaning to African Americans, one pressure group took out a full page ad in *Variety* attacking the program.

It is clear that advocacy groups can have an impact on media. The options seem to be either working with the media system, whereby groups have to play by system rules and run the danger of being co-opted by the very system they protest, or working against media systems, which offers no guarantee a group will be heard and little chance for long-term change.

What can the Appalachian Studies Association, as a major advocacy group for the Appalachian region, do to change the media portrayals of Appalachia we abhor? First, we can accept this responsibility as part of our mission as an organization. We need to establish a media watch committee to which information about positive and negative media portrayals may be funneled and which then has responsibility to respond. This assures that our response will be swift, sure, and not piecemeal as it is so often now. We can respond as an organization, with the force of numbers and expertise giving our positions more clout.

Turow says in his book, "When a social group does not have a strong advocacy body in its corner—as, for example, in the case of gypsies, and, until recently, Arabs—media creators feel no need to be subtle [in their stereotypes]. Using these groups as well as Nazis and extraterrestial creatures, producers can dip into a storehouse of unfavorable cultural images—foreign, secretive, alluring, dangerous, deceptive, [stupid]—to evoke certain moods and accomplish certain plot goals" (1992, 200). This certainly has been true of Appalachia, and it is because we are not on the national media agenda. The studies I reviewed about advocacy groups and the media pointed to such groups as the National Black Media Coalition, the Italian-American League to Combat Defamation, the Jewish Anti-Defamation League, the German-American Anti-Defamation League, the Media Office (which represents the disabled), the National Latino Coalition, the Gray Panthers Media Watch Task Force, NOW, and a host of others. There is no recognized Appalachian advocacy group, even though we argue that we are the most maligned group in the media!

We need to do more than simply react to negative portrayals about Appalachia in the media. We need to take a positive and active position in highly visible media, such as the *Washington Post, New York Times,* national magazines, and television. Then we need to funnel these same concerns and positions to local media in our own areas throughout the region, by writing opinion page pieces for newspapers, appearing on local public affairs programming, radio talk shows, and other venues.

Another useful strategy would be to involve the national media more in our activities as an organization and with the work of individual members (but always establishing our ties with the larger organization). We should establish an award for those in the media whose work we applaud and perhaps one for those we decry; this likely would help us attract national coverage for our activities. We may be able to work with the major media organizations, much like the Harvard Alcohol Project, to refine their portrayals of the region.

Establishing an agenda for change in the media and a committee to oversee our response will help promote systematic action throughout our organization. We can amass documentation of the work of individual members at local levels (letters to the editor, op-ed pieces, reviews of films, books, etc., and successful work with local media), and we can assist members and groups in learning strategies for developing media contacts, mobilizing media on our behalf, and providing praise and blame for the media when needed. To be effective, we will need to be programmatic and consistent.

John Shelton Reed in *Southern Folk, Plain and Fancy* noted that in media images and popular culture, "hillbillies appear to be the last acceptable ethnic fools" (1986, 43). The evidence of history shows us that media portrayals of groups can change. We bear responsibility for making that change occur.

14

by Ronald L. Lewis

Beyond Isolation and Homogeneity: Diversity and the History of Appalachia

Appalachia is a region without a formal history. Born in the fertile minds of late-nineteenth-century local color writers, "Appalachia" was invented in the caricatures and atmospheric landscapes of the escapist fiction they penned to entertain the emergent urban middle class. The accuracy of these stories and travelogues, the dominant idioms of this genre, generated little or no critical evaluation of their characterizations of either mountain people or the landscape itself.

If local color writing in the Appalachian motif must have a beginning, it would be with Will Wallace Harney's 1873 travelogue, "A Strange Land and Peculiar People," published in *Lippincott's Magazine*.[1] His emphasis on physical and cultural isolation was greatly magnified over the next two decades by subsequent writers. The publication in 1899 of Berea College president William Goodell Frost's famous article, "Our Contemporary Ancestors in the Southern Mountains," signified the maturity of the concept of Appalachia as a spatially and culturally remote remnant of a bygone day. From this essay, only one of Frost's storehouse of appeals for support to finance his missionary work in the mountains, came some of the most widely recognized phrases applied to Appalachian mountain dwellers. They were "our contemporary ancestors," our "eighteenth century neighbors" who had just awakened from a long "Rip Van Winkle sleep," pure Anglo-Saxons "beleaguered by nature" in "Appalachian America," one of "God's grand divisions."[2] Frost the publicist certainly knew how to turn a phrase.

"Local color" Appalachia reached its apogee in the novels of John Fox, Jr., undoubtedly the most popular author of the genre. Scholars recognize that Fox was a major figure in the creation of Appalachian "otherness," but Darlene Wilson has shown most emphatically how self-serving were Fox's creations. Declaring his writing "deliberate acts of self-creation and self-mythologizing," Wilson's research in family papers reveals the direct linkage between Fox's fictional images and his "role as a publicist for absentee mineral developers" who, along with their agent, Fox's older half-brother James, were involved in the development of the coal industry in central Appalachia. John Fox Jr. perpetrated and then perpetuated the myth of Appalachian otherness to facilitate absentee corporate hegemony by marginalizing indigenous residents economically and politically. In short, for Fox (and how many others?) "Appalachia" was a willful creation and not merely the product of literary imagination.[3]

This fictional representation became accepted and then reified as "history" by subsequent reporters, scholars, and policy makers into what Henry Shapiro has called the "myth of Appalachia." As Shapiro and Allen Batteau show in their work on the "invention" of Appalachia, the idea of Appalachia as a homogeneous region physically, culturally, and economically isolated from mainstream America has its genesis in fiction. In fact, "much of what is believed to be known about the life and people" of Appalachia actually is "knowledge about a complex intertextual reality" that treats the "diverse preindustrial localities in the southern mountains as if each were representative of a single, regionwide folk society."[4] This view has persisted in part because so little formal written history about preindustrial Appalachia exists to provide a measure of empirical authenticity. However, if we examine the region's economic evolution from the perspective of rural nineteenth-century America, without assuming prior knowledge of its fictional existence, or the industrial developments that were to come, it is clear that much of Appalachia was neither unusually isolated, physically or culturally, nor was its population uniformly more homogeneous than that of other sections of rural America.[5]

Acknowledging the risk of exaggeration, much recent scholarship either refutes or greatly revises the standard perspective of preindustrial Appalachia as an isolated frontier. This is particularly true if isolation is understood as the absence of commercial or cultural linkages with regional and/or national markets. Appalachians were not "precapitalist" either, strictly speaking, for even the earliest settlers emigrated from areas where capitalist terms of exchange were well understood. No one generalization holds true for the entire region or over time. Historically, writers have assumed that the conditions they found in the twentieth century were held over from earlier frontier days. In fact, geographer Gene Wilhelm rejects the notion that early Appalachia was a land without commercial or cultural communications with the world beyond the hollow. According to Wilhelm, "the Appalachian region has been an admixture of cultural contact and socioeconomic enterprise rather than a bastion of isolated individuals and a slow sequence of economic development" as numerous new writers have generally insisted. Wilhelm has argued that "the idea that the Appalachian Mountains acted as a physical barrier, either for the people living within the mountain region, or for those individuals trying to cross them, hardly stands up against the evidence at hand."[6] For example, the Blue Ridge Mountains between Front Royal and Waynesboro, Virginia, were marked out by a complex series of trails and trade routes, traversed by Indians for hundreds of years, even before the Europeans came. Before roads were built, horse and wagon trails crossed the mountains north and south, east and west. During the nineteenth century, innumerable public roads and private pikes connected the region internally and externally. Wilhelm correctly points out that animal drovers provide an excellent example of mountaineers who traveled the lines of trade and cultural transmission connecting the mountains with local and urban markets. Cattle dealers journeyed out to the markets and brought back goods, cash, and ideas. Lowland culture bearers, such as lawyers, doctors, seasonal teachers, tax collectors, circuit preachers, peddlers, salesmen, and mailmen, traveled the same avenues of transportation and trade into the mountains. One of the first backward linkages settlers fought for were postal roads to connect them with the lowland population centers. The high level of newspaper and periodical subscriptions, and later catalog circulation, in the mountains suggests an ongoing desire for knowledge of and goods from the broader world. Wilhelm insists that "geographical isolation for the mountain folk is a myth."[7]

Several major works which subsequently dealt with the topic presented variations on Wilhelm's theme. Ronald D Eller agreed with Wilhelm in general but concluded that travel was nonetheless always difficult and ensured a relative isolation.[8] Steven Hahn's study of up-country Georgia between 1850 and 1890 argues that during the antebellum era local farmers were isolated from the external markets and so they relied on community networks, but after the railroad penetrated the region they became increasingly dependent on the cotton export market.[9] Lacy Ford came to a different conclusion in his study of antebellum up-country South Carolina. While yeomen farmers produced a subsistence first, they also participated in the market economy after the arrival of the railroad in 1850.[10] Although Durwood Dunn generally infers that Cades Cove, which is located in the Tennessee Smokies, was isolated and self-reliant during the early years, he emphasizes that "this isolation was always relative" and shows that during the antebellum years Cove people had relatively ready access to regional markets.[11] Most recently, Wilma Dunaway argued that Appalachia was a peripheral region of an emergent world capitalist system and was linked to that system of exchange as a supplier of raw materials from its inception.[12]

Conversely, Altina Waller's Tug Fork, the borderland between Kentucky and West Virginia where the Hatfield-McCoy feud occurred, was isolated in every respect before the area was opened up in 1889 by the railroad. There were no towns, and county seats were physically isolated from even regional markets. Unlike the Blue Ridge, up-country Georgia, or Cades Cove, Tennessee, there was little migration into this section after 1840, and trade beyond the mountains was "almost non-existent."[13] Moreover, Dwight Billings, Kathleen Blee, and Louis Swanson found that Beech Creek residents of eastern Kentucky remained an isolated people "still living a relatively precapitalist life on the eve of World War II." In Beech Creek, "isolation permitted an independent economy to persist in the Appalachian mountains long after it had vanished elsewhere in the United States." Even here, however, national market forces made it increasingly difficult to sustain the local economy.[14]

David Hsiung's study of northeastern Tennessee called for a more critical examination of "isolation" as a conceptual construct and suggested that focusing on the early period between 1780 and 1835 may provide a broader context for measuring Appalachian isolation relative to the rest of backcountry America in the nineteenth century. Not surprisingly, he concluded that isolation was a relative concept both temporally and spatially. In the Revolutionary era residents used the elaborate trail system that fed into the Great Warrior Path and Boone's Trail in northeastern Tennessee. The crude roads made travel and trade difficult and also sparked the creation of new counties so that residents could be closer to the county seat. Residents in these counties were not cut off from the state capital, but clearly they believed themselves to be isolated by poor access to government and the markets. Hsiung noted that it was the "psychic power of physical separation" that motivated county building among the people. By 1820, however, the roads connecting county seats were carrying wagonloads of goods from Philadelphia and other eastern cities into these counties in a brisk interregional trade.[15]

Tracy McKenzie qualifies the development trajectory implied in Hsuing's characterization of northeastern Tennessee. Using 1860 census data, McKenzie has compared the economies of the three grand divisions of western, middle, and eastern Tennessee and found great economic variation among them. Only the mountain counties did not rely on slavery for agricultural production. Even within the three sample Appalachian Tennessee counties (Johnson, Greene, and Grainger) McKenzie found significant differences in their linkages to the regional market. Johnson County farmers "were probably as close to total isolation from the surrounding region as it was possible to be in the nineteenth century," for there were few roads and the railroad did not penetrate the area until the mid-1890s. Grainger and Greene Counties are located in the Valley of East Tennessee. There the land is fertile, and farmers practiced a productive, mixed agriculture.[16] Farmers of Grainger and Greene Counties also were limited by inadequate roads, but they could transport their produce to Knoxville by flatboats down the Tennessee River and its tributaries, or by rail over the East Tennessee Railroad, which was completed through Greene County in the late 1850s.[17]

Similarly, the idea that Appalachia was the land of subsistence farmers until recent times is under serious reevaluation. John Inscoe took direct aim at this notion in *Mountain Masters*, a study of slavery in western North Carolina. Inscoe quotes Olive Dame Campbell's observation in 1925 that "there is no fundamental reason for separating mountain people from lowland people, nor are mountain problems so different at bottom from those of other rural areas in the United States," an unusual insight for the time. Inscoe suggests that much the same could be said of antebellum society in the southern Appalachians generally.[18] On the eve of the Civil War, Inscoe argues, "western North Carolina was far from the backward, isolated area it was later seen to be." In fact, "the variety of situations and the diversity of its populace equaled if not surpassed those of any other rural section of the antebellum South." Furthermore, although the Carolina mountains retained some of the "crude aspects of its frontier origins," the area "constituted a thriving, productive, and even a progressive society."[19]

Scholars of the 1960s broke with the established school of historical approach which focused on universal themes that thread their way through American history, binding the nation together, and became much more interested in the diversity of the American experience. More recently, this shift in focus found expression in Appalachian history as well. The "new" social history, as it was called, has exerted more influence on Appalachian studies than any other branch of history by challenging many of the assumptions (and shibboleths) of American history. One of these challenges in particular, that individualism and capitalism provided the economic foundation of America from earliest colonial origins, is a debate that promises to rewrite what has passed for Appalachian history. Another debate involves the nature of community culture in early America: Was it essentially cooperative or competitive? Were colonial farmers a self-sufficient, precapitalist people who emphasized community harmony over personal self-interest, or were they commercially aggressive, market-oriented, profit-maximizers? In short, were communal farmers initially "modernized" by capitalism into competitive economic men and women, or was capitalism part of their culture from the beginning?[20] Ideology, of course, provided the motive power behind this debate.

Scholars who apply this approach to mountain life are rapidly changing our historical perspective on the relationship of community to market development in preindustrial Appalachia. Historical geographer Robert D. Mitchell's study of frontier Virginia rejects the self-sufficiency thesis. He argues instead that settlers moving west were motivated by economic profit from the beginning.[21]

Robert McKenzie's study of Tennessee directly refutes the oft-repeated view of Ronald D. Eller that in preindustrial Appalachia mountaineers owned their own farms, worked the land as a family unit, and employed a strategy of household self-sufficiency that allowed them to avoid reliance on the market economy. Until the industrial transition at the turn of the twentieth century, "few areas of the United States more closely exemplified Thomas Jefferson's vision of a democratic society."[22] McKenzie contends that the isolation of northeastern Tennessee farmers from the markets meant that they were indeed "self-sufficient," but self-sufficiency meant a "precarious" existence at best. He rejects the idea that hardship was offset by the benefits of communal support, strong kinship networks, and particularly, economic independence. While there were social and cultural costs associated with market involvement, he contends that "it is important also not to lose sight of the undeniable economic costs of persistent market isolation."[23] The income disparity among individual farming households in the mountain counties, McKenzie found, "stemmed not from difference in land tenure or slave ownership but in commercial orientation."[24] In any event, self-sufficiency was not inconsistent with production for exchange, and most farmers engaged in both modes of production. Indeed, only those with the smallest farms did not produce anything for exchange. It was neither an aversion to risk nor an indifference to wealth accumulation that discouraged a commercial orientation among them, but rather high transportation costs, low commodity prices, declining soil fertility, and above all, the declining size of farms. McKenzie concludes that agricultural historian Morton Rothstein is correct in observing that self-sufficiency is merely a "delightful euphemism for rural poverty."[25]

Certainly there were isolated sections of Appalachia, such as Beech Creek, Kentucky, where Brown and Schwarzweller, and Billings, Blee, and Swanson have shown that residents continued to rely on household production until well into the twentieth century.[26] Paul Salstrom turns the issue upside down in his book, *Appalachia's Path to Dependency,* contending that, instead of self-sufficiency losing ground to the entrepreneurial ideology, Appalachia followed the reverse pattern. According to Salstrom, declining agricultural production was the primary reason for Appalachia's shift from market production in the 1840s to a subsistence, producer-consumer system as a way to survive under increasingly marginalized economic circumstances—a reversal of the process as it is commonly understood.[27]

Studies of Appalachia that do not attack the self-sufficiency thesis directly have demonstrated by strong implication that a commercial orientation developed early in sections of the region suitable to market production. A wide variety of economic activities have been documented in Appalachia, taking us far beyond the marginal hard-scrabble hill farm stereotype. By far the most significant of these economically and historically was the livestock business. During the antebellum era, Appalachia was the livestock-raising center of the eastern United States. Most recently, Richard MacMaster examined the early cattle industry in western Virginia and found that from the colonial era forward backcountry stock raisers were "remarkable" in their receptivity to new methods, improved breeding stock, and scientific agriculture in a way that most planters were not. They originated the feeder-lot-system, were among the first to import pedigreed cattle, and played a major role in the diffusion of the beef cattle industry beyond the Appalachians into Kentucky and Ohio.[28]

Stock raising played a significant role in the upper Shenandoah Valley and Potomac highlands of western Virginia. The South Branch valley was known for its cattle as early as the 1750s, and by the 1780s was a major center for cattle raising and feeding for export to eastern markets. In fact, the modern feeder-lot system has its earliest developmental roots in western Virginia, having evolved in the South Branch of the Potomac River and the Greenbrier River valleys. Cattle from Ohio were sent here to be fattened up for the final leg of the drive to eastern cities. In the 1850s shipment by train took the place of driving, and feeders tracked market prices in order to time the arrival of their stock in the markets at the most advantageous moment. Towns and even small cities grew around the trade as gathering centers developed where local producers could sell their cattle to professional drovers. Lewisburg in Greenbrier County, West Virginia, for example, was one local node in a distribution network that pointed livestock toward the regional center of Covington, Virginia, from which they were shipped by rail to Richmond as early as the 1850s. Winchester, in the Shenandoah Valley, became the regional shipping center for stockmen of the South Branch.[29]

John Inscoe demonstrated that at the southern end of the Great Appalachian Valley in North Carolina "livestock production was the most substantial form of commercial agriculture practiced in the mountains and the primary means of exchange used by merchants and those they dealt with locally and out-of-state." As early as 1800 cattle and hogs were being driven from the Carolina mountains to markets in Charleston, Savannah, Norfolk, and Philadelphia. Although hogs were by far the preferred livestock, cattle, sheep, ducks, and turkeys also were driven over the roads to market. Asheville, located on the Buncombe Turnpike, was the regional center for the western Carolina stock trade, but the traffic significantly increased other related economic activity. Hog drives stimulated corn production among local farmers who also sold their stock to drovers passing on the road. Merchants, innkeepers, and feeding station operators also set up businesses along the pikes to rest and feed the herds and serve the drovers. Inscoe concludes that "most western North Carolinians were involved in this complex trade network" and that "dependence on southern markets was pervasive throughout the mountain counties."[30]

Prominent Appalachian cattlemen were the elites in their world, but most mountain farmers engaged in mixed farming and a range of diverse economic activities in addition to agriculture. Nineteenth-century mountain farmers in eastern Kentucky, for example, spent considerable time hunting and trapping for food and pelts for either the market or to pay taxes. Tyrel Moore found that farm exports from the region included small quantities of ginseng, furs, deer hams, chestnuts, honey, and beeswax. These items were exchanged locally but also exported downstream to the Ohio River valley. Poor roads hindered commercial farming, and many scarce items, such as butter, wool, flax, beeswax, and honey, were produced for home consumption. Cattle and hogs were the preferred livestock and corn the principal grain.[31] Gordon McKinney's study of antebellum western North Carolina leads him to conclude that "the geographic isolation of the North Carolina mountain population was not as great as usually portrayed, and many individuals had substantial dealings with people of the outside world." Even though western North Carolinians attempted to grow much of their own food, they had ceased to be truly self-sufficient by the Civil War at the latest. That they had become dependent on the markets to supply their needs is apparent by the strong demand for finished goods and the suffering that they endured from war-inflated prices.[32]

Economic diversification grew hand in hand with a much greater degree of social stratification than the myth of Appalachia would allow. New studies show that almost from the beginning mountain settlements spawned a commercial elite, and subsequent population growth and the adoption of slavery ensured that mountain society would not only be class-differentiated but heterogeneous as well. Also, it is becoming increasingly clear that different sections of the mountains followed different development patterns. In fact, even within the same county significant variations in social and economic relationships often coexisted. A small but influential middle class of doctors, lawyers, merchants, and politicians who served preindustrial mountain communities were directly linked to, and served as mediators with, the broader market economy.[33] Access to land, however, was the key ingredient to the formation of social stratification in preindustrial Appalachia. Scholarship on this issue has only just begun for Appalachia, but we have much to learn from studies of older settled regions, such as early New England and the Mid-Atlantic colonies. Studies of the western Virginia backcountry during the eighteenth century by McClesky, Hughes, Hofstra, and Rasmussen demonstrate that the best lands were engrossed by a small interrelated elite who either operated on their own or acted as agents for wealthy clients.[34] The acquisition of ever larger landholdings by small select groups continued during the nineteenth century. Mary Beth Pudup's study of antebellum southeastern Kentucky revealed the extent to which land-ownership was one of the key factors in the emergent social stratification in these counties as early as the 1820s. Kinship also was important in facilitating the acquisition of lands by providing another vital strand in the political and economic web that bound together local elites.[35] Robert McKenzie found similar evidence for social stratification in the mountains of Tennessee. On the eve of the Civil War, Tennessee's mountain counties were characterized by a great concentration of wealth, extensive landlessness (42.5 percent average), and great income disparity between a minority of farmers who produced for the market and a poor majority who did not.[36] A similar conclusion was reached by Ralph Mann in his work on four farm communities in Tazewell County, Virginia, between 1820 and 1850. The social structure of these communities confirms Pudup's thesis that the control of local resources and the ability to respond to changes maintained the dominant, and usually earliest, landowning native elite families in a position to retain economic control and political power.[37] The economic stratification suggested in the new studies underscores the dangers of facile generalizations about preindustrial mountain communities and challenges the notion of Appalachia as a Jeffersonian Eden.

It is easy to forget that manufactures related to agriculture served a vital function in the early mountain economy, particularly gristmills, wool-carding mills, sawmills, and tanyards, which grew in relationship to the density of settlement and social complexity that evolved over time. Natural resource industries, although secondary to farming as a means of securing a livelihood in preindustrial Appalachia, also employed an increasing number of people throughout the nineteenth century. It was natural for mountaineers to harvest the forest around them for profit. From the earliest settlement they had used the timber to construct dwellings, barns and outbuildings, mills, and other necessary structures. As demand for wood products increased with the population in the mountains and beyond, timber became a market commodity. From the antebellum era to the end of the nineteenth century, mountain rivers were choked in the spring with rafts of logs heading downstream to the mills. They sent more than raw sawlogs to downstream markets, however, as illustrated in the report of the chief engineer for just one lock and dam on the Little Kanawha River in West Virginia for the period between 1876 and 1877: 388 rafts of logs; 1,162,900 feet of sawed lumber; 3,406,200 oil-barrel staves; 57,749 railroad ties; 343,000 hoop-poles; 45,050 cubic feet of ship timber. Except for the staves, these products were exported to Ohio, New York, Pennsylvania, Maryland, and England.[38]

Salt and iron were among the first industries to develop in the mountains, and both contributed to the development of a nascent coal industry in central Appalachia. The Kanawha Valley of western Virginia became a major supplier of salt for the Ohio River cities and even farther downstream to New Orleans for export. For a half-century after its founding in the early nineteenth century, the salt industry grew and stimulated local development of coal to fire the salt brine boilers, and after the Civil War when the salt industry declined, a vital coal industry took its place as a major employer.[39] Throughout the mountains local blacksmiths plied their trade, but in areas where suitable iron ores were found, the iron industry thrived. During the earliest period charcoal provided the primary fuel for iron furnaces, and a plentiful supply of wood was readily available in the mountains. The charcoal iron industry grew to major proportions in western Maryland, western Virginia, and eastern Tennessee, but charcoal furnaces smelted iron for local markets throughout Appalachia. By the mid-nineteenth century, technology permitted the use of coal to fire iron furnaces. Consequently, the proximity of coal and iron deposits provided the points of concentration for the industry in the mountains, especially in the Cumberland River basin of Tennessee, southeastern Pennsylvania, and northwestern Virginia.[40]

Historians now find a much more politically diversified region as well. Gordon McKinney's study of Appalachian politics from the Civil War to 1900 demonstrates that a significant number of residents in certain sections of the mountains, such as eastern Tennessee, northwestern Virginia, and eastern Kentucky were Unionists in their sympathies.[41] By no means, however, did mountaineers represent a Unionist dagger pointed at the heart of the Confederacy. John Inscoe's study of western North Carolina revises the popular notion that Appalachia was a Union bastion filled with freedom-loving frontiersmen. Indeed, 90 percent of western North

Carolinians were not slave owners, and they had waged a protracted and sometimes bitter political struggle with eastern elites. But in the end they marched off in record numbers to join the Confederate armies because they identified themselves as southerners, and their economic interests, forged by the traditionally strong trade ties with Georgia and South Carolina, were tied to the South.[42]

It was the development of trade ties that prompted Southwest Virginia to follow Richmond out of the Union and into the Confederacy, a process that ultimately led to the rending of Virginia and the creation of loyal West Virginia. Kenneth Noe shows how the Virginia and Tennessee Railroad, completed between Richmond and Southwest Virginia in the 1850s, linked the economic fortunes of the mountain section with the eastern tidewater capital of Richmond. The creation of West Virginia, which abolished slavery and forged close commercial ties with the northern markets by trade over the Baltimore and Ohio Railroad as well as by river and road, demonstrates the divisiveness of secession politics in the mountain sections of the slave states.[43] The dismemberment of Virginia also reemphasizes the importance of understanding the history of economic development in the mountains, which often is assumed to have begun only with the industrial transition at the turn of the twentieth century.

The reason northwestern Virginia counties remained with the Union and the southwestern counties followed Richmond into the Confederacy is part of a much larger set of issues, but clearly secession sympathies were directly linked to economic dependencies. Noe states that the commercially-minded in Richmond "unloaded their ideology as well as their goods off the train. Not only did southern modernization and slavery go hand in hand, but the determination to defend slavery and the broader economic and social system it held on its back joined them. . . . The leading factor convincing most southwestern Virginians to don gray and most northwestern Virginians blue in 1861 was the divergence among western Virginians caused by their railroads; where they ran and what they carried, and how economic change caused by railroad building shaped ideology.".[44]

There were few slaveholders in western Virginia, but the southwestern and northwestern counties split over the issue of secession from the Union, demonstrating some fundamental differences in the political economy of the mountain districts. Van Beck Hall's study of politics in Appalachian Virginia between 1790 and 1830 documents just how early, vigorous, and universal the push for economic development was at least within some sections of the region. By analyzing voting patterns on key economic development issues in the Virginia Assembly and at state conventions, Hall found that settlers in Appalachian Virginia were more diversified, less fearful of change, and more inclined to use government to accomplish development than were "the more cosmopolitan, longer-settled residents of Virginia counties east of the Blue Ridge."[45]

A cursory examination of western Virginia even during this early period reveals the folly of thinking about the region in simplistic terms even for its early years. Most rural settlements had their own grain mills, tanneries, salt, and iron manufacture. Along with the settlements, numerous small towns and resorts along the Allegheny Front provided local markets for farmers throughout the nineteenth century. Larger towns dotted the western landscape. In fact, Wheeling, Martinsburg, Harpers Ferry, and Wellsburg in present West Virginia were among the fifteen largest towns in the state and represented an evolving urban-commercializing process that increased the political influence of merchants and professionals and the growth of social institutions associated with urban life.[46]

"The growth of these towns created two Appalachias," Hall contends, one composed of counties with growth centers and another made up of rural farm counties, often referred to as "back counties." The counties with growing towns spearheaded the economic diversification of Appalachian Virginia, while the counties without towns failed to develop much commercialization or diversity, according to

Hall. Significant differences existed within the western counties, of course, with the residents of towns and more developed counties leading the campaign for economic development and political reform. Westerners stood as one in demands for economic development measures, especially bank charters. But it was the battle over internal improvements that indicates most clearly the economic orientation of western Virginians. Westerners, both rural and urban, almost unanimously supported improvements in transportation. They supported improving navigation of the Potomac in 1795 and constructing a bridge over the Cheat River in 1805, and they backed the James River and Kanawha Canal improvements from 1816 on. Likewise, western support for the improvement and construction of existing roads and turnpikes was nearly unanimous, with little difference between rural and urban counties.[47]

According to Hall, historians have failed to recognize that supposedly backward Appalachian residents "actually backed democratization, the involvement of more individuals in the political process, banks, internal improvements, the protection of the flow of capital and credit, and education and occasionally challenged the institution of slavery." In fact, even the subsistence farmers of the underdeveloped counties voted for programs that many historians associated with progress and modernization. "These actions simply cannot be fitted into the usual portrayal of an Appalachia trapped in a sort of late eighteenth or early nineteenth-century 'time warp' or of a culture and society that was easily manipulated by powerful outside interests," Hall argues. What popular and scholarly writers alike have failed to appreciate, Hall concludes, is that in western Virginia,

> Two Appalachias existed side by side. The one with towns, newspapers, banks, and early industries already differed from the more rural, isolated, farming counties. These counties, much easier to identify with the traditional picture of Appalachia, were less interested in many of the programs backed by their more urbanized colleagues, but even those who lived in the second Appalachia worked much harder for reform and development than did the supposedly more commercial, involved, and aware residents of eastern Virginia. The traditional picture of isolated mountain folk uninterested or uninvolved in outside political questions did not yet exist by 1830.[48]

It is noteworthy that, at the height of local color writing and the reification of the myth of Appalachia, strategic sections of the region were in the throes of a wrenching industrial transition. No section of the mountains was affected by this process more dramatically than central Appalachia. Industrial society advanced into the mountains behind armies of resident and imported laborers who laid the tracks for three major railroad systems. The first to cut its way through the plateau was the Chesapeake and Ohio Railroad, fulfilling a dream dating back to the eighteenth century, when planners of the C and O Canal hoped to connect Virginia tidewater ports with the Ohio River. Armies of laborers invaded the formerly inaccessible New River Gorge country laying the iron rails that would bind Richmond and Huntington in 1873.[49]

The Pocahontas and Flat Top coalfields of West Virginia, southwest of the C and O line, were connected to the national markets by the Norfolk and Western Railroad. This company was organized in 1881 specifically to serve as a coal carrier linking the southern West Virginia and southwestern Virginia coal country with the port of Norfolk and eventually the Great Lakes. The N and W offered financial assistance to investors for the construction of mines and towns along its right-or-way, and in 1883 when the railroad reached Pocahontas, Virginia, on the West Virginia line, the town was already in full operation with large stockpiles of coal ready for immediate shipment. Eventually, the N and W built a major branch line to Big Stone Gap in Wise County, Virginia, and forged ahead with the main line along the Guyandotte River Valley to the Ohio River, and on to the Great Lakes.[50]

While the C and O and the N and W were developing central Appalachia from the east, the Louisville and Nashville Railroad began constructing lines into the Kentucky coalfields from the west. The main line passed along the edge of the plateau running from Louisville to Knoxville. Determined to dominate the eastern Kentucky fields, the L and N constructed a branch line from Corbin, Kentucky, to the Cumberland Gap in the 1880s, but the Kentucky River highlands were not reached by rail until the eve of World War I, when the L and N branch line was completed into Harlan, Letcher, and Perry Counties.[51] Eventually, the entire region was integrated into an elaborate network of main lines, branch lines, feeder lines, and spurs for transporting natural resources extracted from the central Appalachian countryside.

In the southern Appalachians the boom came to the western North Carolina and eastern Tennessee regions with the arrival of the Western North Carolina Railroad at Asheville in 1880 and at the Tennessee state line in 1882. Asheville became a boomtown, and the pioneer developers soon gave way to the large companies, often with operations in several states as the industry was consolidated during the first decade of the twentieth century.[52] Because of its strategic location within the southern mountain region, Knoxville had been an evolving commercial and transportation hub for nearly a century when the convergence of railroads and Cumberland coal and iron elevated the city to the status of regional development hub. From this growth center commercial and modernizing influences reached out into the surrounding mountains. Because Knoxville's coal and iron became locked into a supporting role to the Birmingham coal-steel complex by United States Steel Corporation, and because the city was a major railroad hub, Knoxville's primary industry became light manufacturing, which drew on the surrounding mountain population for its labor force, rather than the black "industrial reserve" of the Black Belt.[53]

The tri-cities of Elizabethtown, Bristol, and Johnson City, Tennessee, held a similar strategic position on the emerging railroad system in the mountains, and they, too, went through a period of development. The tri-cities' industrial expansion attracted immigrants and blacks, but most of them worked in construction and extractive industries. The subsequent development of the tri-cities as a textile manufacturing center provided work primarily for white people in the surrounding countryside, following the southern pattern of a "dual economy" whereby blacks worked in the cotton fields and poor whites worked in the mills.[54]

The enormous capital investment poured into central Appalachian railroads, timber, and coal mining completed the social and economic transition of the region. Trains carried away forest products, but they also returned with manufactured goods such as food, dry goods, household furnishings, farm supplies, and whatever else people ordered out of the mail-order catalogs that supplied the needs of town dwellers and farmers. The railroad connected local communities to the national markets and, as elsewhere in rural America, exerted a profound influence on the way people lived. They were the lines of communication that brought in intellectual and material culture in the form of city newspapers, the telegraph, and the telephone along with incoming manufactured goods.

With the circulation of cash and the virtual explosion in the population of wage earners in the mill and mine towns, merchants were increasingly attracted by the potential for trade beyond the towns in the surrounding countryside.[55] Because of the railroad, for example, the county seat town of Logan, West Virginia, had banks, a newspaper, running water, sidewalks, fire hydrants, and a fire department even before there were a single coal mine in the county. Logan was not urban, according to David Corbin, "but the people were neither isolated nor wholly ignorant of industrialization or capitalism. No longer was the area, as a journalist covering the Hatfield-McCoy feud a few years earlier sensationalized, 'as remote as central Africa.'"[56]

Coal operators entering central Appalachia found few of the supporting services required to sustain a workforce, and so the railroads also hauled in the equipment operators required to build their own. The unincorporated company town became one of the defining features of life in the region. Its very nature militated against the development of those civic ideas that became the catechism, if not the practice, of enlightened corporate capitalism elsewhere in America. The company constructed the town's physical plant, became the miners' landlord, provided the police force, built the churches and stores, and provided any other service that the towns required. Of course, there were great differences among company towns, ranging from crude coal camps erected on "gob piles" to model towns with all the modern conveniences and a benevolent owner-operator. All of them, however, were privately owned entities, not sovereign political jurisdictions.[57]

Pioneer industrialists not only had to build their own towns, but a scarcity of labor in the region also necessitated the importation of a workforce. The central Appalachian districts dominated by the coal industry experienced the greatest demand for labor and, therefore, the greatest importation of workers. Consequently, the population of the central Appalachian plateau grew dramatically between 1880 and 1920 from under two hundred thousand in 1870 to over 1.2 million in 1920. However, growth did not proceed uniformly, nor was it evenly distributed. The West Virginia plateau grew rapidly throughout the era, with the population of its southern counties nearly quintupling from 93,174 to 446,051. Kentucky's plateau counties, which already contained a sizable population on the eve of industrialization, grew sporadically from 216,883 to 538,350 during the same period. Virginia's central Appalachian counties, however, grew moderately but steadily from 55,349 to 155,405. The several plateau counties of northern Tennessee contained the smallest population, and over the course of this forty-year period they doubled their population from 45,375 to 96,063.[58]

The preindustrial African American population of central Appalachia was relatively small, totaling only 14,360 in 1870, but by 1890 that figure had more than doubled to 30,226 and quadrupled to 64,251 by 1910. During the decade of World War I, the number of blacks in the region continued to climb, reaching 88,076 by 1920 and 108,872 by 1930 when the immigration ended. Most of this increase was associated with the rise of the coal industry. In 1870 only 36 percent of the African American population of central Appalachia resided in the sixteen major coal-producing counties of the fifty-six-county region. By 1920, however, 96 percent of the blacks living in central Appalachia resided in those sixteen coal counties. By far the greatest increase in the black population came in southern West Virginia, where 69 percent of the region's African Americans (totaling 60,488) and 62 percent of the state's black miners (totaling 17,799) resided by 1920. Here the scope of industrial transformation was greatest and, correspondingly, the demand for labor was strongest as well.[59]

In the coalfields blacks met and mingled with a bewildering array of peoples and cultures. As the immigrants poured into industrializing America during the late nineteenth century, bureaus were established to help deploy (for a fee) the newly arrived laborers to states where employers sought their services. The number of immigrant miners in the region grew dramatically between 1880 and 1920. Although there are no precise estimates for central Appalachia, the number of immigrants must have reached at least one-quarter of the mine workforce, and in some locations, much higher. In West Virginia, the number of foreign miners among the mine labor force was less than one thousand in 1870. By 1907 their number had reached nearly sixteen thousand, and on the eve of World War I (1915), after the flow of new immigrants had stopped and at least half of the immigrants had returned to their native lands, immigrant coal miners in West Virginia still totaled almost thirty-two thousand. These immigrants, representing nearly all of the nations of Europe, came to the Appalachian coalfields in much the same manner that immigrants came to other areas of America during this period. Some were deployed from Ellis Island by labor agents who worked the port towns as

Table 1.	**African American Black Population of Central Appalachia, 1880–1990**				
Year	***Kentucky***	***Tennessee***	***Virginia***	***West Virginia***	***Totals***
1880	6,734	2,570	4,242	5,781	19,327
1890	7,444	3,653	6,552	12,577	30,226
1900	7,602	3,609	7,056	21,584	39,851
1910	10,222	4,415	7,669	41,945	64,251
1920	15,692	2,943	8,953	60,488	88,076
1930	18,286	2,129	7,616	80,841	108,872
1940	18,662	1,918	7,709	85,465	113,754
1950	14,284	2,941	6,659	86,421	110,305
1960	10,240	2,884	4,083	64,613	81,820
1970	7,232	2,718	2,585	44,956	57,491
1980	6,506	3,253	2,688	42,277	54,724
1990	5,602	3,413	2,446	35,004	46,465

Source: U.S. Bureau of the Census, Characteristics of the Population for the decennial censuses 1880 through and including 1990.

Note: Counties included within the central Appalachian subregion: (Kentucky) Bell, Breathitt, Carter, Clay, Elliott, Estill, Floyd, Harlan, Jackson, Johnson, Knott, Knox, Laurel, Lawrence, Lee, Leslie, Letcher, Magoffin, Martin, Menifee, Morgan, Owsley, Perry, Pike, Powell, Rockcastle, Rowan, Wayne, Wolfe, and Whitley; (Tennessee) Anderson, Campbell, Claiborne, Morgan, and Scott; (Virginia) Buchanan, Dickenson, Lee, Russell, Tazewell, and Wise; (West Virginia) Boone, Braxton, Clay, Fayette, Kanawha, Lincoln, Logan, McDowell, Mercer, Mingo, Nicholas, Raleigh, Summers, Webster, and Wyoming.

representatives of either states or companies. Many followed the typical chain migration pattern whereby family and friends established a "beachhead" for others from the region who joined them later.[60]

In the coalfields, native whites, African Americans, and foreign immigrants lived and worked in company towns where they usually were segregated into sections designated as "Colored Town," "Hunky Hollow," or "Little Italy." Generally, there was discrimination in the kinds of jobs available to each group in the mine as well, with natives or British immigrants serving as bosses or in the technical positions, and blacks and immigrants in the harder, more dangerous, and most unsteady jobs. Still, blacks and immigrants were attracted by relatively high wages. Underground the men worked together, but even on the surface the rigid segregation often became blurred in company towns, and without other employment opportunities, the workers came to focus on their common economic interests in the United Mine Workers of America, the one organization in the coalfields they could control.[61]

Industrializing Appalachia was a matrix of cultural interaction among very diverse races and cultures. Coal operators sought a "judicious mixture" of native whites, blacks, and foreign immigrants to balance the dissonant cultural traits that were seen as weaknesses by the operators. Like workers elsewhere in America before work was mechanized and control was shifted to the owners of production, mountaineers tended to take time off from work for hunting and fishing, planting, harvesting, family reunions, weddings, and

TABLE 2. **Race and Ethnic Origins of West Virginia Coal Miners by County, 1909**

	Fayette	*Raleigh*	*Mercer*	*McDowell*	*Totals*
Mines Reporting	96	24	17	70	207
Native/White	5,724	1,062	907	3,217	10,910
Black	2,949	455	927	4,419	8,750
Italian	978	137	398	1,648	3,161
Hungarian	392	83	227	1,056	1,758
Polish	319	67	42	179	607
Lithuanian	46	10	—	5	61
Swedish	9	2	—	20	31
English	122	26	7	21	176
Austrian	70	3	—	10	83
Russian	77	30	17	416	540
German	108	15	6	36	165
Scottish	93	15	—	4	112
Litvitch	24	12	—	4	40
Greek	5	61	—	130	196
Irish	14	—	—	15	29
Slavish	155	40	33	401	629
Syrian	15	—	—	—	15
Romanian	9	—	—	120	129
Unknown/Other	1,750	801	369	2,894	5,814
Totals	12,859	2,819	2,933	14,595	33,202

Source: West Virginia Department of Mines, Report of the Chief Inspector (Charleston, 1909), 94–95.
Note: The number of blacks and Hungarians would be considerably larger if figures for the Virginia portion of the Pocahontas field were available, because one of the largest employers of black and Hungarian miners in the field was located just across the state line.

other family affairs. Recognizing "blue Monday" by staying in bed after a weekend drinking bout was common throughout industrializing America.[62] Most immigrants in the coalfields were from southern and eastern Europe, and their Catholicism itself provided striking contrast to the austere Protestantism found among most of the indigenous residents. One Catholic priest observed of the southwestern Virginia coalfields around Norton in the 1920s: "As to the nationalities that make up the vast congregation at present . . . there are only four American born families in the whole section; Roda is all Hungarian, Inman half Hungarian and half Slavs, in the other camps the Catholics are about evenly divided between Poles and Slavs . . . and at occasions like First Communion, Confirmation or dedication of a new church, the outpouring of Catholics is quite a revelation and one would imagine to live for the time in a village of the former Austrian-Hungarian Empire."[63] The extent of cultural exchange and eventually intermarriage among this extremely heterogeneous population usually is unappreciated even by regional scholars. All of these groups carried their own cultural traditions with them into the mountains and influenced others by their presence.

The transition to industry in central Appalachia produced the most dramatic example of development of racial and ethnic diversity within the region, but we should not lose sight of the fact that African Americans and the racially mixed Melungeons had resided in southern Appalachia since the earliest settlement days, and Native Americans from time immemorial.[64]

Until recently, writers have accepted the longstanding assumption that, because of geographical isolation, rural Appalachia had functioned in the past as a subculture that was essentially autonomous from mainstream society. Accordingly, its culture was regulated by traditional values they associated with the frontier, such as traditionalism, individualism, familism, and fundamentalism. Many believed that Appalachia's traditional values, insulated by geographic and cultural isolation, were barriers that explained the "backward" economy found in the mountains and sustained by a "culture of poverty."

The belief in a distinct, regionwide Appalachian subculture resistant to economic development was shaped by a large body of literature that accepted uncritically a fictional Appalachia invented by local color writers of the late nineteenth century. A review of this literature, however, reveals remarkably little empirical evidence for the proposition that Appalachian culture was the product of continuing frontier isolation. Recent historical research challenges the fictional Appalachia by demonstrating that, when viewed from the perspective of the preindustrial era, Appalachia was not much different from other regions of nineteenth-century rural America. Therefore, the pervasive assumption that modern economic problems in the region somehow stem from Appalachia's long physical and cultural isolation must be reconsidered.

V

The New Appalachian Culture

In this section, we look at how Appalachia is both changing and staying the same. In "Diversity in the Mountains and Regional Cultural Identity" Gordon McKinney continues the process of taking apart the old stereotypes. McKinney puts the development of the Anglo-Saxon purity myth in the context of America's concern about being overwhelmed by waves of non-Protestant immigrants in the post-Civil War era. McKinney then discusses the presence of African Americans, Latinos, Cherokees, and mixed race groups in the region. Sexual orientation and gender identification now add further diversity and complexity in what was once considered a homogeneous region. McKinney says that a new Appalachian identity must include the diversity that actually exists, and that each self-identified group should join the common struggle for equity.

Bill C. Malone's article on Appalachian music describes how the idea of "Appalachian" music originated in the Anglo-Saxon myth. The reality of what Appalachian music (if such a term is even appropriate) really is, says Malone, is more fascinating than any fantasy. Patricia Smith Jones' article about dialect could just as well have been included in the section on "Resistance." It describes how Appalachian migrants use dialect as a means of preserving group cohesiveness. Next is a chapter from Loyal Jones' recent book on Appalachian religion. Jones shares with the reader his admiration of "the way Appalachian people have dealt with the complexities of theology and with their ability to use the Scriptures and lore from their culture to find meaning in life."

In "Appalachia's New Crisis: No Kids," Ron Crouch analyzes a trend revealed by the 1990 census showing that in some parts of Appalachia, there are fewer young people. Crouch goes on to examine the impact of this demographic trend on employment and education. Alan de Young uses the Braxton County, West Virginia school system to explore the notion of schools as cultural bridges between rural Appalachians and the broader world. At least some rural schools, de Young notes, serve as agents of the national culture and train Appalachian children to be successful migrants. David Sutton, who chronicles Appalachian election results in the *Appalachian Journal*, says George W. Bush won the presidency as a result of his support in Appalachia. Al Gore carried only 13 of the 50 counties in Appalachian Tennessee, and had similar problems in West Virginia. Gore's poor showing in Appalachia, says Sutton, was the result of a cultural referendum on the moral quality of the Clinton presidency. Results of the congressional and gubernatorial races were largely determined by the advantages incumbents had over their challengers.

15

by Gordon B. McKinney

Diversity in the Mountains and Regional and Cultural Identity

It is absolutely essential that we place the question of diversity in Appalachia in the proper perspective. It is clear from the earliest written records that human beings have differentiated themselves from each other throughout history. Language, religion, culture, skin color, social status, economic class, and many other variables have been used to distinguish one group from another. Part of this process has been positive. Loyalty to Athens, Yahweh, and Rome produced the basis for modern western thought and culture in all of its depth and vitality. At the same time, unimaginable cruelties have been perpetrated in the name of these same loyalties. The victims of these claims to uniqueness and purity were not always outsiders. Political and religious opponents and the lower classes often suffered substantial damages at the hands of their fellow group members.

The modern world has seen many of the same trends continue with the rise of the nation-state and accelerate as the technology for destruction has become more efficient. The Nazi attempt to destroy the Jewish community in Europe is just one of many examples of wholesale slaughter that can be found with unconscionable frequency around the globe since 1459 C.E. The Muslim-Hindu violence in India has been endemic for at least five centuries. From Martin Luther to Northern Ireland, Christians have been killing each other in Europe in wars between governments, in pogroms and security measures instituted by governments against their own citizens, and in attacks by neighbors against neighbors in cities and the countryside. European Americans have carried out an unsystematic—but deadly—campaign against American Indians in the Caribbean and North America. Political dictators in Cambodia and Uganda have added millions more to the enormous list of people killed because they belonged to the wrong ethnic group or belief system.

The United States has not been immune to this type of violence and discrimination even though it prides itself on being a "nation of nations."[1] In fact, this type of hostility and violence appears to almost certainly have preceded the coming of the Europeans. One of the reasons that the Spanish were able to destroy the mighty empire of the Incas was the latter's oppressive rule over other American Indian groups who were, therefore, willing to give aid to the "enemy of my enemy." In the United States, we have ample documentation of colonial European and American governments being able to use ancient hostilities to weaken the Indian groups opposing the European American claims on Indian territories. When the Indians proved to be unable to withstand European diseases or were resistant to commercial discipline, the Spanish, Portuguese, French, Dutch, and English transported millions of Africans to the Americas. Many of these transplanted people were people captured in Africa by their fellow Africans of different ethnic groups. When large numbers of Europeans reached the west coast of the United States in the nineteenth century, they resorted to the importation of Asian workers to fill labor needs. This experiment in diversity prompted the passage of the Chinese Exclusion Act in 1882 and the creation of concentration camps for Japanese Americans in World War II.[2] Of course, the animosities of Europe were transferred to the United States as well. In the 1850s, 1890s, and 1920s, Protestant Americans sought to make the United States safe from the supposed power of the Pope.[3] Jewish Americans suffered overt discrimination in much of the urban north, and acts of violence in the South.[4] Irish, Italian, German, Hungarian, Polish, Greek, and many other European Americans have been singled out for discrimination at different periods and in different places in American History.[5]

Post-Civil War

It was in the midst of the great influx of European Americans after the Civil War that Appalachia became a place of interest to Americans. As several scholars have clearly demonstrated, descendants of older European lineages in the urban north felt threatened by the massive influx of southern, central and eastern European immigrants. These newcomers did not speak English for the most part and were often Catholic, Orthodox, or Jewish in faith. Their presence exacerbated the problems created by the growth of large urban centers.[6] In addition, they provided the votes that challenged the elites' control of the political system. The old elite struck back by trying to purify the American scene. In politics, they passed civil service laws, introduced the Australian ballot, required poll taxes, and instituted primary elections.[7] In the South, these measures had the "virtue" of essentially eliminating the African American voter from the electoral process.[8] In private, many older Americans became obsessed with their British roots. The Daughters of the American Revolution and the United Daughters of the Confederacy flourished.[9] Genealogy became an enthusiasm among this group as they sought to connect themselves to some prominent English family.

It was in this rather frenzied atmosphere that the Appalachians were singled out as an ethnic group. As Henry Shapiro and others have demonstrated, novelists, home missionaries, newspaper reporters, movie producers, and educators provided the descriptions and rationales that differentiated people in the southern mountains from other Americans. [10] This separate identification was not an unalloyed benefit, however. While all observers conceded that the mountaineers were indeed English and had shown commendable loyalty to the Union during the Civil War, there were some obvious problems. These descendants of "good" stock were also obviously poor, ignorant, unchurched, violent, and uncouth. Since the prevailing ideology of the time required that good breeding would lead to cultured offspring, some sort of explanation was required.[11] One of the explanations was that the forebearers of the southern mountain people were the lower class of Englishmen who were outlaws in Virginia and escaped the law by entering the mountains.[12] Another and much more popular explanation was the negative impact of geography. The mountains had isolated these people and they had simply not advanced to the same exalted level as the other English groups in the United States.[13] While many were bemoaning the fate of these underachievers, William Goddell Frost and others were pointing out what they perceived as a significant benefit. The isolation of the mountain people had preserved a traditional culture that their more advanced cousins had left behind. This was the culture of Shakespeare and the great English Renaissance. In fact, ballad collector Cecil Sharp seemed to be able to demonstrate that these people were more English than the English.[14]

Others pointed out, however, that many of the European descendants in the mountains were actually the offspring of people whom the Americans had designated as Scotch-Irish. This observation was enthusiastically adopted by another strong heritage movement that sought to explain the origins of many other southerners of European descent. Claiming to be the ethnic base of many American presidents, these activists eagerly claimed the cultural high ground in the mountains. These assertions have been supported by proponents of the Ulster origin of Cracker culture in the broader South.[15] Interpreters of the Appalachian past as different of Cratis Williams and David Hackett Fischer have supported the importance of the Scotch-Irish cultural contribution.[16] While this perspective has been subject to some significant questioning, the Scotch-Irish are perceived as being an important component of the Appalachian population.[17]

Ironically, the great migration of unemployed mountaineers to the urban midwest, starting as early as the 1920s, has created another view of the claim for Appalachian uniqueness. Books by Harriet Arnow, Chad Berry, and Phillip Obermiller and Thomas Wagner have carefully documented this migration and its impact.[18] As the Civil Rights movement of the 1950s and 1960s raised the consciousness of African Americans, many other groups took note and began to make similar statements about their people and heritage. A concrete example of this process was the designation of Appalachian whites as an official minority group in Cincinnati.[19] Ironically back in Appalachia, many groups that had been overlooked in the rush to create an English or Scotch-Irish ethnic group began to claim the right to a separate cultural identity.

The most obvious of these other groups were the African Americans. They had been the most numerous "other" throughout the period of European American settlement. Enslaved African Americans had been brought into the mountains in pioneer days and had provided the essential labor for many agricultural, commercial and industrial enterprises in the southern mountains.[20] After emancipation, they faced lynching, segregation, and other forms of discrimination as part of their daily lives.[21] Even with the legal end of segregation in many parts of Appalachia in the 1950s, they led marginalized lives in their home communities.[22] Like many other blacks in the American South they sought to alleviate their condition through two strategies. The first was migration to urban centers—this exodus was also prompted by the economic dislocations in the mining industry.[23] The other option pursued by those African Americans who remained in Appalachia was to form groups to defend their rights under the law and others to celebrate their heritage. The best known of these groups is the John Henry Foundation that is directed by Ed Cabbell and is centered in the large black community in McDowell County, West Virginia. Several writers including Cabbell and Bill Turner, Henry Louis Gates, and Francis X. Walker have demonstrated beyond any doubt that African Americans have been a positive and continuing diverse presence in Appalachia.[24]

Many African Americans were brought to Appalachia in a deliberate attempt to create a diverse population. As large corporations tried to exploit the vast mineral wealth of the Appalachian coal fields they sought to secure a compliant labor force. On the positive side, many of the companies provided access to services usually not found in the rural mountain South. Recognizing the limitation of that strategy, the industrialists looked for ways to insure that workers would not rebel against the harsh discipline that the mine owners sought to impose. Starting in the 1870s, mine and factory owners rented state prison inmates from the states of Alabama and Tennessee. The vast majority of the prisoners were African Americans. Looking for experienced and skilled miners, the industrialists also hired European-born miners. To complete the roster of workers the companies also hired local mountaineers.[25] Not unexpectedly, these groups of workers shared little in common. The delighted mine owners recognized that this formula would work even if convict labor was not available. By the time that companies began to build entire communities in southwestern Virginia, eastern Kentucky, and West Virginia, they had perfected the diversity formula. African Americans, eastern and southern European immigrants, and impoverished Appalachians were brought together in a deliberate attempt to divide the workers along cultural, religious, and racial lines.[26]

Other economic imperatives have brought another group of "outsiders" in increasing numbers to the mountains. Before the coming of the timber, textile, and mining companies came to the mountains in the late nineteenth century, most people in Appalachia worked on the land. As late as the 1930s, perhaps a majority of the population of the mountain South continued to farm. But the great migration after 1940, the urbanization of the highland region, and the rise of the service economy have encouraged the vast majority of people in the region to stop farming. While the amount of land farmed has declined in the region, the reduction has not kept pace with the decrease in farm population. Many of the labor intensive jobs in row crops, fruit, and tobacco are no longer the preferred occupation of mountain men and women. Instead, most of the people actually working the land are women and—more particularly—men of Hispanic-Latino heritage.[27]

In Appalachia—as elsewhere in many parts of this country—the Hispanic-Latino group is viewed as an undifferentiated whole. That assumption is simply not accurate. While many of the field workers are Mexican natives, there are many other Latin Americans in the mountains from El Salvador, Guatemala, Honduras, Puerto Rico, and other nations and cultures.[28] These peoples share a common language and similar religious traditions, but in many other ways they are not alike. Perhaps the most important point is that they view themselves as different. There are also a growing number of persons of Asian heritage in many mountain counties as well. Ironically, persons from this group are often found at the other end of the economic scale. Particularly persons from the Indian subcontinent can be found in the new technology jobs found in the region and in the medical field. Despite their common geographical origin, they come from the numerous subgroups in their own countries.[29] Thus, they are part of a new identity created by the American need to classify.

These previously noted groups also have a viable identity outside of Appalachia, but there are also some claims of special identity within the existing populations. This would include the members of the Eastern Band of the Cherokee Indians. This largest group of Indians left in Appalachia is centered in western North Carolina, and these original Appalachians are experiencing a significant cultural and political revival after centuries of discrimination.[30] Another regional group is the tri-racial isolates including the Melungeons of Virginia and Kentucky and the Guineas of West Virginia. These individuals were encouraged to deny their ethnic diversity by the discriminatory segregation laws. As these legal proscriptions ended, a new leadership has emerged that has claimed the right to be recognized as a distinct group.[31] The same is true for the gay and lesbian community. Many of the members of this cohort hid their identity because of severe social, religious, and legal sanctions. The AIDS epidemic forced a broader reevaluation both within this community and the broader mountain society. One significant result of this reevaluation has been a growing openness on the part of the gay population and a resulting activism to seek greater civil and legal rights.[32]

Finally, some note should be taken of the significant role that gender has played in the region. While gender roles have been clearly articulated throughout human habitation of the highland region, these roles and peoples' perceptions of them have been in a constant state of change. From the best information available, scholars like Theda Perdue make a strong case for an approximate parity among women and men among the Cherokees.[33] African American slave women had few opportunities to claim a separate sphere and many of them worked in what the broader society thought of as male jobs.[34] In pre-industrial farm households, the role that women played was crucial to the success of the family and the broader community.[35] With the coming of industrialization, the separate roles for women in the integrated community in Appalachia came to an end and women's fate was increasingly one of isolation as the wives of miners, lumberjacks, and the middle class. Women's efforts to secure the right to vote, to gain reproductive rights, and to achieve equity before the law has created another definable group in Appalachia requiring identification as a distinct component of mountain society.[36]

Given the enormous diversity found in this region previously perceived as undifferentiated, how does one approach the question of cultural identity in the mountain South? First, obviously one must do so with care and humility. As this overview suggests, every statement that could be made about culture and diversity in the region could easily be contradicted by a well-documented counter example. Several things do appear to be clear, however. The first is that there has always been diversity in the mountains. Starting with the Indians to the present day, there have always been identifiable groups that resisted being classified as part of a larger group. A second point of some significance is that some observers have almost as consistently wanted to impose an artificial identity on the people of the region. Starting with the colonial powers who wanted to make treaties with the Cherokee "King" to popular culture entrepreneurs who try to capitalize on the "hillybilly" stereotype, these observers were willing to overlook the differences to find selected similarities.

What lessons can we learn from past developments? The first is that the people of Appalachia are quite diverse and many of them claim primary identity as a member of a minority or non-elite group. These self-identifications must be recognized and honored. Each of them has a contribution to make to the cultural, social, and economic life of the broader community. But those involved in education and community activism must also seek to act as mediators amongst these communities and attempt to educate all of them about each other. Only in this manner can the Appalachian region use all of the insights that these different people have to offer to the region. Equally important, we need to encourage members of these self-identified groups to address issues that threaten the well being of all of us who live in the mountains. For example, we have a responsibility to teach all of the peoples of the mountain South about the land itself. Without a living ecosystem, the human diversity of the mountains will perish. Finally, we have the responsibility to energetically seek equity for groups and individuals in the mountains. Historically, we know that all members of southern society—black and white, rich and poor—were intellectually enslaved by forced bondage and separated from a wonderful richness of life by segregation. If we fail to do this, diversity will simply be the mechanism that continues to divide creative people from each other and stifles all efforts to bring about greater opportunities for growth and understanding in the entire population.

16

by Bill C. Malone

Appalachian Music and American Popular Culture: The Romance That Will Not Die

A recent ad for a popular New Orleans-based rock band, the Subdudes, noted that, in addition to their contemporary qualities of musicianship, the group also projected an "Appalachian flavor." Though unexplained, the phrase was merely the most recent example of an uncountable number of scattered references to "Appalachian" or "Mountain" that have crept into descriptions of musicians, songs, styles, or quality of life over the last century or so.

Such usage is often merely lazy—a shorthand term to describe a quality that the writer, critic, musician or fan cannot explain or comprehend. But it also reflects an impulse often encountered in the attempts to define American folk music styles—the investing of music with descriptions or labels that connote or conjure up certain qualities of life that are appealing to listeners (as in Downhome Blues, Western Swing, Plantation Melodies).

The linking of "Appalachian" and "music" began approximately 100 years ago, as did the perception that such music was not only *different* from other music but that it was also *better* in certain aspects. These perceptions first took shape in the minds of a small cluster of academicians and professional musicians, in the period running roughly from the turn of the century up to the beginning of World War I, who had discovered that people were still singing very old British songs in some of the mountain counties of the South. The discovery of Appalachian balladry was both cause and effect of the larger discovery of the Southern Appalachians and the conception that they constituted a special place.[1]

Appalachian Music's reception as a unique and presumably homogeneous form of cultural expression was shaped by a variety of contradictory perceptions. While the music was presumed to be very old, and even of Elizabethan British origins, it could also be described in

Emma Bell Miles's suggestive phrase, as "real American music."[2] It was attractive to those who wanted to believe that a subculture still survived in the United States that was different from the racially heterogeneous and crassly materialistic society that prevailed elsewhere in America at the turn of the century. Although dramatically different from mainstream America, Appalachian society had nevertheless preserved a body of music and folklore that was reminiscent of the nation's cultural roots. Appalachia was, in short, both a museum of early British music and a source of American music. Appalachian music and dances, it was argued, were relatively uncontaminated by modern or commercial influences—Cecil Sharp, for example, described the "Kentucky Running Set" as a dance that pre-dated those collected by John Playford in 1651.[3]

The early assumptions that Appalachian Music was very old, relatively pure, and simultaneously British and American have never really died, nor has the corollary view that such music was inherently decent and moral. Although the songs spoke often of such topics as murder, violence, feuds, seduction, illicit love, and moonshining, the music nevertheless seemed to convey the image of a simple but decent people who lived in primal and direct relationship with the earth and nature.[4] Mountain music stood in strong contrast, it seemed, to such urban-born styles as Ragtime and Jazz which, like the city itself, exuded a tone of sinfulness and immorality.

Until the 1920s little awareness of Appalachian Music existed outside the circles of academicians or concert audiences who read Cecil Sharp's books, or who perused the small body of available songbooks, or who had access to the recitals given by such professional musicians as Howard Brockway and Elaine Wyman. While some songs of presumed Appalachian provenance had become available, almost nothing was known about the singers from whom the music was collected, and even less about the styles of performances indigenous to Appalachia. In the decades since the 1920s, however, two conceptions of Mountain Music have contested for legitimacy in American life, each supported basically by two very different audiences. Scholars, concert recitalists, folk festival promoters like Jean Thomas, John Powell, and Annabel Morris Buchanan, and the record labels that catered to a specialized, academic audience promoted one approach, while the other was popularized by the hillbilly musicians of radio and recording.

Hillbilly music provided a forum for the commercial dissemination of mountain songs and styles, and for the national exposure of mountain singers themselves. The music also provided a format through which new songs and styles could *continue* to enter the repertories of mountain people. The hillbilly business presented conflicting images of mountain life, images which reflected a similar confusion of attitudes held by both the American public and the mountain people. Lil Abner types appeared early and often (and may even have influenced Al Capp's creation of the comic strip).[5] The remarkably popular "Hee Haw" television show is only the most recent example of the media exploitation of mountain stereotypes that extended back to the beginnings of commercial country music when some entertainers performed under such names as "Moonshine Kate" or "The Beverly Hillbillies," or recorded "rural dramas" that portrayed feuding and moonshining.

More positive, though romantic, images also clung to the music at the moment of its commercial birth. It is difficult to know which of the images—negative or positive—was most influential in popularizing mountain music among potential listeners. If my own introduction to "mountain music" is in any sense representative, contending visions of laconic, hard-drinking, feuding, and yet gentle Christian ballad singers were easily absorbed and reconciled. From the time the little Philco battery radio entered our East Texas farm home in 1939, an overall perception of mountain life—an amalgam of John Fox, Jr., Sergeant York, Roy Acuff, and yes, Lil Abner—began to fill my mind. I gravitated especially toward the feelings projected in such songs as "Blue Ridge Mountain Blues" and Roy Acuff's sometime-theme song, "Carry Me Back to the Mountains." Like the message found in these songs, the Appalachian metaphor has always been used to describe or suggest those musicians, styles, or songs that call us back to a symbolic "home"—to purer styles, values, or lifestyles that are either real or imagined.

While the term "mountain music" was used often to describe certain styles of country music, the promotional material surrounding Bradley Kincaid offered the most explicit early assertion of the mountain image. When Kincaid began presenting his repertoire of old-time songs on the broadcasts of WLS in Chicago, neither he nor his program directors could have been unaware of or uninfluenced by the public perception that the Southern Appalachians were the repository of traditional people and traditional songs. Kincaid was from Kentucky, and, to many people, Kentucky meant mountains. Kincaid, on the other hand, carried to Chicago a cluster of perceptions concerning mountain balladry shaped by his education at Berea College. He sincerely believed that mountain music was not simply old; it was also deeply moral, just as its creators and preservators were. Performing as "The Kentucky Mountain Boy" on a variety of radio stations in the Midwest and Northeast, Kincaid contributed powerfully to the idea that mountain songs came from an undefiled Anglo-Saxon past, and that, unlike most commercial hillbilly songs, they were decent and moral.[6] In Kincaid's way of thinking, his music fulfilled the formulaic criteria associated with mountain music: it was old, pure, honest, and moral. In short, Kincaid tried to stake out within commercial country music the kind of moral high ground[7] that the academic folklorists, concert recitalists, and mountain settlement schools had already occupied in their treatment of Appalachian music.

Kincaid's employment of mountain metaphors can be easily understood, but it must be admitted in all candor that neither he nor his music really fell under the "mountain" rubric. He was not a mountain boy. His songs, while usually old—and probably moral—were not exclusive to the mountains, although they were undoubtedly loved by mountain people as they were by rural and working-class people everywhere. Kincaid succeeded in linking a basically Victorian, though rural, parlor style to the performance of a presumably mountain-derived repertoire. Most important, he succeeded—perhaps unintentionally—in convincing much of the American public that such performance was authentically "Appalachian" in style and content.

Although the idea of a distinctly recognizable entity known as "Appalachian Music" exerts a strong appeal, we should recognize by now that Appalachian people always have made music in a wide variety of styles. Variety was present, though ignored, when Cecil Sharp made his first forays into the mountains in 1916.[8] It was there when Ralph Peer brought his recording crew to Bristol, Tennessee in 1927, and when Jean Ritchie was growing up and singing her family's songs in Viper, Kentucky. Variety remains a defining trait of Appalachian music today even as festivals and workshops strive to preserve the older styles.

The myth of Anglo-Saxonism has been, for the most part, discarded, even though a preoccupation with Celticism still creeps into discussions of Appalachian music. Scholars such as David Whisnant, William Tallmadge, and Robert Winans[9] have noted increasingly the African-American presence in and contributions to Appalachian culture. Abundant evidence suggests that songs of popular, gospel, and commercial origin successfully competed with the older British ballads and lovesongs long before the hillbilly music business began disseminating its products in the Southern hills. Songs and song lists collected from students at Berea College before World War I, for example, display a large percentage of Tin Pan Alley songs.[10] Published folksong collections exhibit similar choices, as do the early commercial recordings of mountain musicians like Ernest Stoneman, Frank Hutchison, Fiddlin' John Carson, and Bradley Kincaid. Songs like "The Fatal Wedding," "Maple on the Hill," and "I'll Be All Smiles Tonight" were not foisted upon an unwilling public by the hillbilly musicians. Such songs were already present in the mountain consciousness well before the first hillbilly records were made. Among the many contributions made by Jean Ritchie in her delightful reminiscence, *Singing Family of the Cumberlands,* is the evidence she presents of the early penetration of the Kentucky hills by outside commercial influence. The songs included in her dad's songbook, produced on his own printing press, provide vivid evidence of the mountain folk's easy absorption of new material. "Sweet Kitty Wells," of blackface minstrel origin, lies in comfortable companionship with old ballads and spirituals. Even more revealing is the information about the talking machine, and its supply of such records as the vaudeville coon songs, "Whistling Rufus," which entered the Ritchie household in 1905.[11]

Despite the growing recognition of ethnic and cultural diversity in Appalachia, as well as the knowledge that many types of songs, both British and American, have long competed for the affections of mountain folk, the "idea" of a special entity known as Appalachian Music, with certain enduring but hard to define traits, has clearly preserved its force in American culture. One often encounters the assertion that country music began in the Southern hills, and that its purest and perhaps most moral expressions still reside in those hills, or in those performers (like Ricky Skaggs) whose styles seem closest to the Appalachian source.

Still another oft-encountered assumption is the belief that musical purity and tradition can most easily be found off the commercial beaten track and within the Appalachians themselves. The Appalachians as a geographical entity, as well as Appalachian music, have continued to be retreats for musicians and others who seek alternatives to mainstream culture or a return to the roots of American culture. Most Americans have found such retreat only in the lyrics or rhythms of a song (such as "Rocky Top, Tennessee" or "Country Roads"), in attendance at a mountain folk festival, or in the occasional visit to a folk museum or theme park. John Lair, though, demonstrated almost sixty years ago that fantasy can become reality. While working for WLS in Chicago, this homesick Kentuckian wrote a song called "Take Me Back to Renfro Valley," which expressed his nostalgic recollections about a community that had never really existed. He later built a big barn near his old Kentucky homeplace, christened it the Renfro Valley Barn Dance, and eventually saw a real community and post office emerge around the very popular radio show.

No one has duplicated John Lair's feat, but, beginning with Bascom Lamar Lunsford's establishment of the Asheville Folk Festival in 1928, and extending on through the consummation of John Rice Irwin's personal vision, the Museum of Appalachia near Knoxville, and Dolly Parton's theme park, Dollywood, near Sevierville, Tennessee, several enterprising individuals have presented us with alternative ways of viewing and appreciating Appalachian culture at least for a day. The Folk Music Revival of the 1960s drew much of its inspiration from the idealization of Appalachian culture, or from the borrowings made from musicians of that culture. The folk boom began, of course, with the Kingston Trio's immensely popular recording in 1959 of the North Carolina murder ballad, "Tom Dooley." Many young musicians, however, were not content to perform in such a watered-down style, and they sought sustenance in other presumed Appalachian forms, drawing songs and styles from such earlier protest singers as Aunt Molly Jackson and Jim Garland, or from the traditional balladry of Jean Ritchie or Texas Gladden, or from the hillbilly recordings of people like the Carter Family, or Clarence Ashley. Led by the New Lost City Ramblers, a growing number of mostly Northern-born musicians began experimenting with old-time string band styles or with bluegrass, a newer style that was presumed to be a modern adaptation of mountain music.

The Folk Revival enjoyed its brief moment of glory in mainstream American popular culture and then faded from the limelight. Before it departed, however, the Revival provided a forum for the rediscovery of such pioneer hillbilly musicians, and genuine mountaineers, as Dock Boggs, Buell Kazee, and Clarence Ashley, and it introduced new musicians like Doc Watson to the American public. The Revival also left behind a thriving culture composed of string bands, ballad singers, clog dancers, annual workshops (like the one at Augusta, West Virginia), and dedicated journals such as Alice Gerrard's *Old Time Herald*.

Meanwhile, bluegrass music left its base in the Upper South and reached out to an increasingly larger audience that now extends around the world. While superb musicianship clearly marks the driving force behind bluegrass's world-wide expansion, the music's identification with the Folk Revival was also a major factor in its winning a youthful audience outside the South. It would be impossible to determine the extent to which visions of Appalachian purity, tradition, and virtue contributed to bluegrass music's acceptance, but early accounts of its expansion routinely linked the music to mountain beginnings. The first recorded anthology of the music was entitled *Mountain Music: Bluegrass Style.*[12] And Robert Cantwell, in his provocative study of the form, *Bluegrass Breakdown: The Making of the Old Southern Sound,* spoke for many fans and commentators when he described bluegrass as "*the* music of the Appalachian people.[13] Bluegrass music *is* popular among many Appalachian people, both within the region and in such cities as Detroit, Dayton, Cincinnati, and Washington, D.C., where Southern hill people have thronged. Many pioneer bluegrass musicians were born in the Appalachians, and many younger musicians still come from the region. The founding "father" of bluegrass, however, Bill Monroe, whose "high, lonesome" style of singing originally set the standard by which singers were judged, came instead from Western Kentucky and looked toward singers like Jimmie Rodgers, the Mississippi Blue Yodeler, as his personal mentor. Indeed, no Appalachian musicians played in the seminal Monroe band, the Blue Grass Boys, which made the first bluegrass records in the period from 1945 to 1948. Earl Scruggs, the popularizer of the sensational three-finger style of banjo playing, came from the Southern Piedmont region (near Shelby, North Carolina), as did Don Reno (from Spartanburg, South Carolina) whose banjo style was even more eclectic than that of Scruggs. These musicians' styles represented not the purity nor archaicism of Appalachia, but instead the dynamic fusion of folk and commercial pop styles born in a cotton mill region inhabited by rural people.

The linking of bluegrass music to mountain images again represents the powerful persistence of the Appalachian idea in American popular culture—the preference of imagination over reality. Bluegrass means many things to many people, but it has also been a refuge for those who would preserve older country styles, and for those who resent the seaminess and tawdriness of mainstream country music. Similar quests for tradition, purity, and basic morality had helped to inspire the search for "the lonesome tunes" of Appalachia early in the twentieth century; they had accompanied Bradley Kincaid's career as a "mountain singer" in the 1920s and 1930s; and their association with Roy Acuff's style during the W.W. II era makes that entertainer's great success more understandable. Revisionist academicians might wish for greater clarity in the conception of "Appalachian Music" and for a more precise historical understanding of the ways in which the concept developed, but no one should really despair about the consequences of the romantic preoccupation with mountain songs and styles. If the Appalachian idea has inspired a search for the preservation of old songs and styles, as it clearly has, then that idea has wrought beneficial consequences for a society that is too much wedded to progress and change. Numerous "outsiders" who have made Appalachia their special music province—from Olive Dame Campbell and Cecil Sharp to Mike Seeger, Ralph Rinzler, Si Kahn, John McCutcheon, Alice Gerrard, and Jeff Titon—have worked mightily to make the world aware of the region's musical wealth. But their contributions are in no way diminished by the reminder that our main emphasis should be on the music of the Appalachian people themselves. When we assay the music of the region today, in the Old Regular Baptist and Pentecostal Churches, in the honky tonks of any city, on radio stations throughout the region, at VFW jam sessions, at fiddle contests, folk festivals, or rock concerts, we find that music is as important in the lives of Appalachian people today as it was when Cecil Sharp collected his songs almost eighty years ago. But when we make our investigation, we will find that the music's strength and vitality comes from its diversity. Above all, I believe that we will find that the *reality* of Appalachian Music is even more fascinating than any fantasy that yet lingers.

17

by Patricia Smith Jones

Dialect as a Deterrent to Cultural Stripping: Why Appalachian Migrants Continue to Talk That Talk

Many complex factors combine to strip the cultural identity from people who belong to low-prestige ethnic or cultural groups. Language is a primary symbol of group identity. It is also a powerful automatic signaling device second only to race to identify targets for possible privilege or discrimination. Despite prejudicial treatment by the dominant status group, members of low-status groups such as urban Appalachians often consciously use stigmatized, non-standard dialects in an attempt to foster group distinctiveness and to preserve their cultural identity.

This essay will examine some of the ways in which culture and dialect are intertwined and how group cohesiveness serves to prevent cultural stripping. The discussion will focus on speakers of Appalachian English who relocated from eastern Kentucky to Dayton, Ohio, during the Great Migration of the mid-twentieth century. It is my intent to present a personal perspective of the collision of culture and language varieties based on an investigation of non-standard language and group solidarity in members of a Morgan County, Kentucky, family wherein four adult children migrated to urban Ohio areas in the 1940s and three remained in the mountains. On a recurring basis over the past eight years, sixteen extended family members comprising first, second, and third generation migrants and non-migrants were interviewed as part of an oral history project. The personal experiences and linguistic features of the families members were compared.

Numerous studies show that speakers of non-standard dialects or varieties are generally held in low esteem (Ryan and Carranza 1977; d'Anglejan and Tucker 1973; Labov 1966, 1972). In the judgment of mainstream society, such dialects often serve as markers which are assumed to reveal personal traits such as morality, integrity, and intelligence. Linguist Walt Wolfram writes that "attitudes about language trigger a whole set of stereotypes and prejudices based on underlying social and ethnic differences" (Wolfram and Christian 1989, 18). Moreover, ample documentation exists that speakers of non-standard dialects are aware that Standard English has a prestige which their variety lacks. Indeed, many low-status speakers themselves accept as valid the biases against their own dialect (Edwards 1989, 88; Wolfram and Christian 1989, 9).

Given that low-prestige speakers are aware of the negative stereotypes surrounding their dialect, assimilation or language leveling would seem predictable. Research supports the opposite view, however. Despite the increased status associated with prestige varieties, vernacular dialects are held in high regard by members of many ethnic and cultural communities (Labov 1966, 477). Social scientists have suggested many reasons for this phenomenon; cultural solidarity is one of the strongest.

Non-standard language has consistently been linked to group solidarity. Research on populations such as Mexican Americans (Ryan 1979), African Americans (Labov 1972, 250), Jews (Dillard 1985, 61, 105), and Cajuns (Dillard 1985, 61, 107) supports the contention that speakers choose from a "linguistic repertoire" available to them, in part, as a way of signaling loyalty to their group. Linda Blanton reports that Appalachians, too, use speech to demonstrate group solidarity. Blanton studied residents of Breathitt County, Kentucky, to determine whether or not the speech of Southern Appalachians can be accurately labeled non-standard language. She also noted the link between language and cultural bonds (Blanton 1985, 83).

The power that comes from social networks and group inclusion is derived from the strong distinction between outsiders and insiders (Blanton 1985; Milroy and Milroy 1985). Ellen Ryan (1979) reports that language difference can serve two functions with respect to maintaining solidarity and group identity: it strengthens insider unity by heightening group differences; and increases outsider distance by acting to restrict communication between the two groups. Linguists assert that language and ethnic or cultural authenticity are highly interdependent in many American ethnic groups (Dillard 1985, 124). Sociolinguist J.A. Fishman defines ethnic-related authenticity as a continuity of being, of doing, and of knowing. And language, he says, triggers this self-identity within the context of the group (1989, 217). In the framework of the in-group, remarks such as insults, criticisms, and obscenities constitute a threat not just to the individual but to the group as well.

Dialect, then, is used as a medium to affirm community ties, maintain loyalty to the in-group, and lessen cultural stripping. George Philipsen concludes that dialect serves, "by its use or disuse, or by the particular manner of its use, to signal that one knows one's place in the world" (1991, 42). Through the use of distinctive language varieties, speakers can "flag" themselves appropriately to both insiders and outsiders.

Failure to conform to the linguistic norms of the dominant group usually proves costly in both economic and social terms. Many dialect speakers, however, willingly pay the price. Despite the contemptuous perceptions of the dominant group, a desire by members of low-status groups to maintain their cultural identity remains an important sociolinguistic concept. Ronald Wardhaugh writes that many children who speak a non-standard dialect find much to be gained from hanging onto their language. Therefore, they frequently resist attempts by others to change their speech patterns. He contends that the prestige of the non-standard dialect within the in-group may be covert, but that it is, nevertheless, prestige. Moreover, Wardhaugh says that these children may be fully aware of what it means to change their language code: "almost certain alienation from their peers without necessarily gaining acceptance by social superiors" (1992, 342).

Studies have shown that children and adults, too, to a lesser extent, often incur ill will at home and among in-group friends if they speak Standard English in order to escape denigration by the out-group. Social scientist John Walton expresses this paradox succinctly in describing his British grammar school education during which teachers tried to teach Received Pronunciation instead of the dialect spoken in the English Midland coal mining region where he grew up. He writes, "The recipients of the attempted indoctrination in 'proper' speech were already only too aware of the significance of how they talked, and of the potentially disastrous consequences of 'talking posh' in playground or street, where using accents beyond one's station and the consensus of the neighbourhood invited ostracism or worse" (1996, 284).

The same conflict occurs for speakers of Appalachian English who migrated to urban areas such as Dayton, Ohio—and for the second and third generation migrants who choose to continue speaking Appalachian English. Urban Appalachians often struggle to avoid derision and disdain at home when they use Standard English and ridicule in the urban world when they do not. Powerful culture-language incongruities such as these make language changes perilous and complex for speakers who desire social and economic mobility and, at the same time, want to avoid cultural stripping. For example, one second generation informant in my study reported being ridiculed by urban schoolmates when she used eastern Kentucky vocabulary and pronunciation ("poke" for "bag" or "sack," "reckon" for "guess," "far" for "fire"). Conversely, the same informant was censured by friends in her urban Appalachian neighborhood for using "buckeye" markers such as "tire" for "tar" and "once" for "onct."

Appalachian language varieties furnish a graphic example of a phenomenon studied in other contexts by Dell Hymes: the bonding of culture, place, and voice (Hymes 1991, 340). Whether the "place" is a current residence or, in the case of urban Appalachians, an idealized home place in the hills, the connection between culture, sense of place, and language endures. Blanton writes that the variety of Southern Appalachian speech spoken in Breathitt County provides social and regional identity and cultural cohesion that binds the people as a group. She maintains that ethnicity, not geography, keeps language intact (1985, 83). Migrant status, therefore, does not necessarily lead to cultural stripping in the new environment.

Estimates are that as many as seven million people migrated from Appalachia to northern urban areas in the 1940s to 1960s when restructuring in the coal industry caused massive economic dislocation. Many migrants lived in substandard housing or decaying areas of cities, worked in defense plants and automotive factories, and generally separated themselves from mainstream life in the North (Kahn 1973, 86). In Dayton, transplanted Appalachians clustered in blue-collar enclaves in urban neighborhoods and surrounding small towns. The continuous influx of migrants often resulted in the Appalachians outnumbering the indigenous population in the neighborhoods in which they settled. Urban Appalachians lived with or near relatives and other acquaintances of Appalachian descent. They worked with fellow migrants in the factories. They associated primarily with their own group in city schools, labor unions, neighborhood grocery stores, and churches (Obermiller 1994, 9).

In so doing, they preserved their "mountain" dialects and were successful in avoiding assimilation and language leveling. Because many urban Appalachians chose to limit interaction with the other groups, opportunities for developing diverse language contacts (should the contacts have been desired) were limited. The result of these strong cultural-language ties is that English is spoken by urban Appalachians in Dayton in much the same way it is spoken in the backwoods and mountainous regions of Central Appalachia.

My extended family—the Bentons and the Smiths—provides a real-life laboratory wherein the scholarly theories presented in this paper can be examined. The first contacts my Morgan County, Kentucky, foreparents had with speakers other than native Appalachians probably did not occur until coal companies imported "outsider" labor to the region in the late nineteenth century. My grandparents' speech reflected the language patterns of their social group within the mountain community. They passed these forms on to their children.

The Bentons and Smiths, along a host of other relatives and friends, were part of the migration from eastern Kentucky to the Dayton area. Many of them settled in Wright View. This lower socioeconomic section of Fairborn, Ohio, attracted hundreds of migrant families because of its proximity to Dayton's labor-hungry factories and Wright-Patterson Air Force Base. It became a virtual Appalachian ghetto and remained so until the 1970s, when the opening of a state university nearby attracted a more diverse population to the neighborhood's inexpensive housing. Many first and second generation urban Appalachians still live in this neighborhood—and they still speak varying forms of the "mountain" speech they brought with them when their families migrated decades before.

Of the sixteen subjects I interviewed, six remained residents of Morgan County when the other family members migrated to the Dayton area. With the exception of typical innovative markers, many of the migrants I recorded exhibit pronunciation, morphology-syntax, and vocabulary which is remarkably similar to the variety of Appalachian English spoken in their home county in eastern Kentucky. One informant who migrated to the Dayton area in 1939 from Morgan County told me the story of her children's initial experiences in an urban school system. Analysis of her spontaneous conversation recorded in a 1994 interview reveals that she speaks a variety of Appalachian English typical of that spoken in Morgan County.

> Well, my childern [*sic*], some of 'em wouldn't say it, that they lived in Wright View. They went to school up thar in Fairborn. They wouldn't tell 'em they lived down hur because they hear'd some of 'em a-talkin' about the people that lived hur. They wouldn't even tell 'em whur they lived. They was kindly embarrassed to tell 'em, the kids was. That's the truth. They was afraid they'd say somethin' to 'em. But they never did say nothin' to me.

Among the informants in my study, all but one first generation migrant exhibits pronunciation and vocabulary characteristic of eastern Kentucky speech. They use morphology and syntax considered to be markers of Appalachian English. Some but not all of the second and third generation informants who migrated to Ohio have exhibited language change. The study reveals that some members of the family exhibit relatively fewer markers of assimilation than other family migrants. The less assimilated appear to be those who have had less formal education and fewer interactions with outsiders.

Because an eastern Kentucky variety of Appalachian English was spoken in my family, I had already learned these forms when I was forced to transfer from a small rural Appalachian school to an urban Ohio school. Pronunciation and vocabulary set me apart from the other students in my new fourth grade class. Classmates taunted me, and I subsequently dropped words and phrases from my vocabulary that provoked embarrassment and adopted the urban language of my peers. I valued the higher level of education offered at the new, three-story brick school, and I tried hard to be one of them. At home and in the neighborhood, however, I knew better than to talk like a "buckeye." I took on what J.K. Chambers (1993, 139) has labeled the "patina of acceptability" at school without relinquishing my inner core of cultural identity.

Forty years after my fourth grade experiences, prejudice against speakers of Appalachian English is still widespread in the Dayton area. A recent interview with a former administrator of a highly-regarded suburban school district in the Dayton area—and a West Virginia emigrant—illustrates this point. The administrator was talking with a teacher in an elementary school hallway when a small girl stopped to ask for directions to the cafeteria. Noting the Appalachian English spoken by the child, the teacher snapped, "How am I supposed to teach that [her]!" Informal interviews with teachers and employers in the Dayton area disclose similar, albeit more subtle, biases against "mountain" speech.

Insider-outsider tensions such as those described above have serious implications for urban Appalachians. Educators in the Dayton

City Schools and other area school districts have struggled to address the extremely high dropout rate of urban Appalachian students. An understanding of how cultural identity, dialect, prejudice, and learning are conjoined should help educators meet the current and future needs of the Appalachian population.

Wolfram and Christian have posited that language prejudice seems more resistant to change than most other kinds of prejudice (1989, 19). Sol Adler notes that disrespect and nonrecognition of dialects and home languages can lead to the development of negative self-concepts, poor morale, and low motivation for students (1993, 178). His description fits many of the urban Appalachian students who are enrolled in Dayton and nearby suburban school districts. Data from Dayton Public Schools (1995, 15) highlights very high dropout rates among urban Appalachian students, and teachers interviewed cited poor attendance and lack of motivation.

Research supports the contention that though non-standard language varieties may change somewhat, varieties of Appalachian English show no sign of total assimilation with the mainstream varieties spoken by the dominant status group (Montgomery 1992, 637). Many first, second, and even some third generation migrants walk the line between two cultures and two language varieties. Neither exposure to mass media, upward mobility, nor education has eliminated this culture-rooted dialect. Indeed, Appalachian English is alive and well in Wright View and throughout the Dayton area.

18

by Loyal Jones

Some Observations

Over the past thirty-some years, in gathering material for this book, I have looked for evidence of positive and enduring values in the people of the Southern Uplands. Along the way, of course, I have seen many negative and disturbing things—poverty, violence, degradation, ignorance, exploitation—partially a legacy of the region's industrial activity, which over many years has pillaged both people and natural resources in pursuit of capital gain. I have seen people corrupted or left unprepared and vulnerable by bad politics and poor schools, although I have met many fine leaders, public educators, and teachers. We have had more than our share of venality in the mountains, both imported and homegrown, and some people have suffered from it, not only economically, but morally and socially as well. Many Upland natives have not reacted well to the problems they faced or to the opportunities that others have taken.

Yet most people have prevailed in spite of their problems, and there are those who have been ennobled by them. Some are poor in cash and property but rich in values and faith, finding a deeper meaning in life than that which was presented to them by circumstance. These are the people I sought and whose words appear in this volume.

I grew up among such people in the mountains of western North Carolina. My grandfather, Francis Marion Morgan, and his brother William were Baptist preachers, but I must also report that my other grandfather, William Jones, was "churched" by the Baptists for an altercation with his son-in-law and was too proud ever to ask for reinstatement, although I doubt that this unpleasant affair affected his basic religious life. My father, George Alec Jones, was a Baptist deacon, and my remaining brother, Garnett Jones, is also a Baptist deacon. My three departed brothers, Troy, Elmer, and Willis, were all faithful to the Baptist church. My sisters, Vertie Mintz, Wilma Ciber, and Nina Cotton, are also devoted Baptists. My mother, Cora Morgan Jones, did better than the Baptist tithe by giving to the church the income from eggs her hens laid on Sundays. We children were brought up in a loving family, although we had very little in the way of cash and the world's goods. Most of our neighbors were poor also, but they were decent and honorable folk, supportive of their families and considerate of others. (I include here one neighbor who made a little moonshine on a kitchen-stove still to get by in the Great Depression. His wife, to keep me away from their secret when I was a boy, gave me a ceramic Noah's Ark that I played with then and still treasure.)

I saw courage, integrity, resiliency, and flinty values among alumni brothers and sisters and later my students at Berea College, an institution that seeks eighty percent of its students from Kentucky and elsewhere in Appalachia, all from relatively low-income families. Some came to Berea from meager economic backgrounds or real hardship to take advantage of Berea's offerings and to go on to do extraordinary work.

I admire the intensity of faith and the simplicity and richness of language in describing it that I found among the people whom I interviewed and observed or whose writing or statements I collected. I am impressed at how well ordinary people have dealt with the complexities of theology and with their ability to use the Scriptures and lore from their culture to find meaning in life.

I have concluded that Calvinism is still strong here in the Uplands. This does not mean that Arminianism is weak. It is just that in the early days, especially in the back country, Calvinist teaching created an outlook that persists. Several scholars have written that the main characteristic of Appalachians is fatalism. Fatalism does not mean that those it inhabits always believe in predestination. They may, however, believe in some kind of fate that influences their lives, as most of us do secretly. This can be attributed as much to economic circumstances and the number of choices available as to Calvinist teaching. Sociologist Helen Lewis has written that many mainstream Americans believe that Appalachians have created a "culture of poverty" and thus that their poverty and outlook are somehow their own fault. She suggests instead a different model, that of parts of the region being used as a colony by exploitive national or international industries. What appears to be fatalism is thus a response to absentee ownership and the limitations of a resource-extraction economy, a feeling of powerlessness. Religion has been both a source of personal strength for those who were colonized and a means of resistance. However, many see this resistance as passive at best and fatalistic at worst.

This lingering Calvinism, along with social and economic circumstances, has influenced other values or characteristics, some of which have been mentioned previously:

Humility and Modesty I have already dealt with humility and modesty in chapter 2. The Apostle Paul's frequent advocacy of the modest mien has certainly taken hold in the Uplands. The normal stance is to downplay one's own talents or qualities and to defer to others. It needs to be emphasized that although this humility is a profound religious stance, it is also part of the manners system, a way to negotiate matters. Mountain people fear more than anything being called "forward," that is, egotistic or pushy, of thinking too highly of themselves and their abilities. Thus every effort is made to downplay one's ability. It is for others to judge. Church workers, teachers, and social workers from outside the region need to know about this value, for otherwise they may take mountain people at their self-deprecating word and thus undervalue them.

Independence The other side of the coin, however, is independence, which bespeaks a strong determination underneath the manners system. One story is of a country Baptist invited by a county-seat Presbyterian to preach in his church. When he got there, the Presbyterian asked, "Will you wear a robe?"

The Baptist, who never used such trappings, asked, "Do I have to wear a robe?"

"Well, no, you don't *have* to wear a robe," answered the city preacher.

"All right then," said the Baptist, "I'll wear one."

Appalachia has often been described as the "Lingering Frontier," with people capable of fending for themselves. Coming out of the religious Reformation, they also were imbued with a strong sense of spiritual independence in terms of discerning the Word and finding out about God on their own, without ecclesiastical hierarchy, clergy, seminaries, and other institutions that previously were thought to be necessary for religious life. It is not accidental that the Old Baptists call their ministers "moderators" rather than another title that might suggest authority over the flock.

Personalism Both Jesus and St. Paul dealt with others in personal ways, and Upland people talk of Jesus as a personal Savior. In relations with one another, they are more personal than abstract, and they are usually careful to be scrupulously egalitarian. As levelers, they resent any hint of condescension. Their religion has taught them to respect the sometimes fragile egos of others.

Familism The letters of St. Paul have had a strong influence on the people of Upland churches. Paul's comparison of the hierarchy of the family to the hierarchy of the church has seemed reasonable to them, although many women do not submit to Paul's scheme of things. The children generally are taught to be respectful of adults and to keep a modest demeanor. Most churches limit the role of women to teaching, church work, singing, and sometimes praying, although others allow or encourage women to take a leadership role or even to preach. Beverly Bush Patterson writes perceptively of the role of women among the patriarchal Primitive Baptists in *The Sound of the Dove.* More liberated outsiders have difficulty with these traditions, but many Baptist women have supported this hierarchy. In fact, however, I know that the women of Appalachia are far more influential in family matters than one might expect from the patriarchal system. They tend also to be more progressive than the men in education and health care, and they usually are the leaders in these matters. I have noted that young women from the traditional churches, after graduating from colleges such as Berea, tend to join more liberal churches in later life as a means of dealing with changing ideas about gender roles. Many, however, speak fondly of the churches of their childhood.

The strong sense of family values includes the extended family of grandparents, aunts, uncles, nephews, nieces, and the many denominations of cousins. However, forces that have wrought havoc with the family nationwide have also taken a toll in the Uplands. One-parent families with children in poverty are common now in Appalachia. In fact, because of family breakups and the lack of jobs, one out of four children lives below the poverty line in parts of the Uplands. Despite divorce and parental abandonment, however, familism as a value is strong, and frequently grandparents or other relatives care for children of broken homes.

Reluctance to Confront Others The sense of independence, the modesty, and the leveling tendency growing out of Calvinism encourage the toleration of the weaknesses of others. They also discourage the judging of others. The teachings of Paul are important: "But why dost thou judge thy brother? or why dost thou set at naught thy brother? for we shall all stand before the judgment seat of Christ. . . . Let us not therefore judge one another any more" (Romans 14:10, 13). Another reason for a lack of confrontation is kinship. People are reluctant publicly to criticize those who are related by blood or marriage. Yet another reason is that many Uplanders have limited skills at talking things out. They know that confrontation might lead to temper and violence. Nonetheless, we must remember the history of trade unions in Appalachia and the involvement of poor people in the 1960s War on Poverty, which show that when the issues are clear and important, mountain people will confront others.

The Calvinistic and Arminian polarities in mountain religion separate folks whose outlook suits each pole, and there are those in between who seek modification of extreme views. The region's social makeup has required many kinds of churches. Not all of us have the same outlook and temperament, and we seek the theology that best suits our personality, our needs, and our longings. But let me try to assess the consequence of religious choice and the efficacy of each of the polarities in helping believers to get along and find meaning in life. There are also some possible problems.

First the Calvinists. Their religion has made them independent but tolerant of others' independence. They usually don't proselytize or question the validity of the faith of others. They have a reputation for being good, moral people, although they may see themselves as corruptible and having many shortcomings. They are always aware of their imperfect condition in contrast to the magnificence of God. This has created a profound sense of humility but also a tolerance of others who fail. They have a degree of fatalism in regard to the human condition, but they are not daily disillusioned.

Their shortcomings may be that they tend to believe it is not possible to improve the basic human condition on earth, and thus they may not always work rigorously to modify the behavior of others and to solve social problems. They may also see church solely as a place of worship and thus reject any organization within the church to deal with social problems. Surely, too, the emphasis on limited atonement and reliance solely on God's grace for salvation leaves some with feelings of powerlessness and anxiety about their condition on earth and their fate in the hereafter.

The benefits of Arminian theology are obvious. Arminians teach that all who heed and repent may be saved. They teach also that saving grace makes a new person of us and that it is possible to rise above fleshly sin. If we can become better persons, then we can also make better institutions and a better world. Arminians believe that they need to work to bring others to salvation and that it is possible to work on social problems within the framework of the church.

On the debit side, Arminianism spawns missionaries who feel called to proselytize. By their very presence in the Uplands, missionaries seem to be saying that we are lacking in important ways, and they have at times convinced us that we are not only inadequate but somehow un-American. Arminians teach that salvation will transform our lives and that we can avoid sin. The failure of such a transformation can breed disillusionment and sometimes a heavy load of guilt. Arminians are perfectionists, and as such they look for things that may be a hindrance to attaining a state of holiness. Thus they are sometimes judgmental. They may preach against traditional ways that are dear to the people, such as singing and playing secular music, dancing, going to festivals, and the like. This may put some people in a serious bind.

Each spread of belief, then, has attracted those whose outlook fits it, and they have found comfort and hope therein. But religion has not done all things for all Upland people. Some have not chosen to become involved in religion, although studies have shown that almost all believe in some concept of God. The different denominations of the Uplands have attracted adherents, and their teachings, with responding commitments, have profoundly affected their members. The teachings of the churches, moreover, have extended far beyond church members. The philosophy and outlook of the whole population has been influenced. The Bible and the Christian faith are the main sources of meaning in life throughout the culture.

But religion is not the sole cause of the way Upland people are or of their economic and social problems. Isolation; subsistence farming; an exploitive economy, whether in mining or in the renter and sharecropping farming systems; and poor schools and government service have molded us also. Yet some writers have put heavy blame on religious fundamentalism for the region's psychological, social, and economic problems.

As conditions change in the Uplands, the churches and the people's relationship to them will also change. This is not to say that the churches will be better or that the people will be better Christians, but there will be change. The study by John Photiadis and B. B. Maurer, "Religion in an Appalachian State," shows us how religious belief may change if the educational, social, and economic lives of the people continue to improve in the mountains or if people continue to migrate to areas that offer better opportunities for economic security. Alas, the study concludes that as people became better educated, more financially secure, and more urban, their degree of religiosity lessens; that is, they began to seek security in things other than religion, such as education, a good job, income, and assets. The authors raise interesting questions in their conclusions:

> From the historical perspective, it has been the experience of organized Christianity that "man's extremity is God's opportunity." These data tend to confirm that observation. The hypothesis that the dispossessed, deprived, and alienated resulting from the upheaval of social and technological change in Appalachia would be those

> exhibiting the greatest need for the support of religion is substantiated in the data. The aged, poor, less educated, alienated and infirm all rank significantly higher in religiosity than do the socially well-adjusted. . . .
>
> The basic question appears to be: Can the Institutional church develop programs which are capable of meeting the multiple religious needs of people who want, (a) something of life to hold on to and give meaning, (b) to enhance and stabilize their social position and (c) to live a spiritual life in accord with their value orientation—under the same roof—in the same Denomination? Or should the existing pattern of diversification be accepted, understood, and legitimized as the total ministry to the religious needs of man?[1]

Most of the people quoted in this book were by no means the "dispossessed, deprived, and alienated" people to whom Photiadis and Maurer refer. Yet most of them came from modest economic means, and some were indeed poor. Whatever their economic status, however, they rank high in religiosity. Regardless of their social status in life, they make meaning of it through religion. Assuming that the region will continue to improve but will also continue to trail the country as a whole in education, employment, income, and other social factors, let me try to answer Photiadis and Maurer's questions from the experience of doing this book.

Yes, the institutional church can develop programs to meet the needs of *some* of the people who want to find something to give their lives meaning, to improve and stabilize their social positions, and to live spiritual lives in ways consonant with their values. The mainline churches are there—and should be there—for those whose needs they meet, offering a choice to people who are overcoming poverty, lack of education, and opportunity, but these churches will not meet the needs of all. They do not promote or even condone the intensity of faith that is meaningful and necessary for a lot of people. Administrators and ministers in the mainline denominations should therefore develop and keep a proper humility in terms of their own effectiveness and that of their churches in reaching and serving the needs of all in the Uplands. Such humility will help them immeasurably in their relationship with the so-called sect churches—and they should have a relationship with those churches, but one built on respect for these fellow Christians.

The answer to the second big question posed by Photiadis and Maurer is, yes, the religious diversity of the Southern Uplands should be accepted. Before acceptance, however, we need understanding. The several new books on Appalachian religion show that there is a strong scholarly effort to understand the religious nature of the people.

There have been several attempts by mainline churches, as well as other organizations, to relate in some way to religion in the region, beginning with the Conference of Southern Mountain Workers, which was formed in 1913 (later the Council of the Southern Mountains, now defunct, for which I worked for twelve years) mainly as an organization of mainline denominations and other agencies that were working to alleviate the many religious, social, and economic problems of the region. The Commission on Religion in Appalachia (CORA), founded in 1965 during the heyday of the War on Poverty, is perhaps the best known, continuing today with headquarters in Knoxville, Tennessee. It has energized churches of mainline denominations to look for opportunities to serve in the region and has directed denominational and foundation money to many grassroots organizations that are working on social problems. CORA was also in the forefront in securing money for a land-ownership study that has been important in such issues as fair-rate taxation of land and unmined minerals.

Other groups are the Coalition for Appalachian Ministry (CAM), made up of Reformed churches, which runs workshops and conferences to orient their ministers to Appalachian people and culture; the Appalachian People's Service Organization (APSO), representing some fifteen Episcopal dioceses, which provides funding for studies and for grassroots programs; and the Christian Appalachian Project (CAP), growing out of the Catholic Church's Covington, Kentucky, diocese, which raises a significant amount of money for schools, economic enterprises, housing programs, shelters, and counseling for the neglected and abused and also for grants to other regional organizations.

However, most of the efforts of these organizations and of their member denominations are concerned with the social gospel or, as Deborah McCauley has pointed out, promoting a liberation theology. The people of local sect churches are often seen as oppressed victims of absentee owners and ineffectual or corrupted government. I do not say that some are not, but I do say that well-educated, compassionate people from mainline churches (and other organizations, such as colleges) have trouble in seeing ordinary Upland people as legitimate in their culture and faith in their time and place, regardless of the problems they face. The organizations just mentioned have been far more effective in promoting social and cultural uplift—important to be sure—than they have been in relating in a mutually respectful way to fellow Christians in the nonmainline Upland churches.

A good sign is the Appalachian Ministries Education Resource Center (AMERC) in Berea, Kentucky. This is a consortium of seminaries and Bible schools from throughout the country that accepts seminarians for workshops, field trips, and church visitation to help any who choose to work in Appalachia or other rural areas to understand the people of Appalachia and their economic, social, and religious lives. This is important, for the needs of the rural churches get shorter shrift at the urban-oriented seminaries. AMERC now has the potential to offer workshops to a variety of people within and outside the region. However, AMERC must constantly guard against pressure from the mainline denominations and seminaries to use the consortium as a how-to-do-successful-mission-in-Appalachia program. It needs to ensure also that it employs teachers because they truly understand Appalachia and its religious life and not just because they represent seminary, denomination, idealogical, or other balance.

Mainline Christians could learn a great deal about faith from members of Upland churches. These churches, despite what some have written, serve the needs of their members very well. Many of the people I have met are as faithful to God and as reliable and honorable as human beings as any Christian I have known. For one thing, they teach that each person must be treated with respect. Mainline Americans sometimes do not respect those who are different from themselves, and when they launch programs to change them, their efforts are wasted and are sometimes harmful. Effective programs, whether religious or secular, require mutual respect between helper and helped. Respect grows out of interaction and real knowledge and understanding, not from stereotype, hearsay, hasty impressions, and cultural bias. Unfortunately, people who are reared and educated to believe that all good people should strive for the high culture that the elite admire are at some disadvantage in understanding expressions that they feel to be uncultured.

I have long felt that schools should try to teach everyone observation and appreciation skills, such as are taught in anthropology or folklore classes. That is, we should all be helped to see that what any group of people do as worship, as art, or as work is meaningful to them and therefore should be of interest to all of us. As the late folklorist Richard Dorson pointed out years ago, one thing lacking in the revered liberal arts canon of colleges and universities is the oral tradition, the major part of human communication. General academic disinterest in the lives of ordinary people, indeed, calls into question just how "liberal" those who embrace the liberal arts really are.

19

by Ron Crouch

Appalachia's New Crisis: No Kids

As it approaches the twenty-first century, the Southern Appalachian region is experiencing major changes in its population structure. These changes will affect all institutions in Appalachia—families, education, health, social services, employment, and business/industry. Southern Appalachia includes all or parts of nine Southern states: Alabama, Georgia, Kentucky, Maryland, North Carolina, South Carolina, Tennessee, Virginia, and West Virginia. This article will primarily utilize data from the 1980 and 1990 censuses for the fourteen Appalachian counties in Eastern Kentucky and all counties in West Virginia (West Virginia's fifty-six counties are all considered Appalachia). In a future issue, we will present a broader study of the larger Southern Appalachian region, which will show how representative the trends occurring in Eastern Kentucky and West Virginia are to the larger region.

Birth Rates

The Appalachian region and, particularly, Kentucky and West Virginia, are often referred to as the region where women are "barefoot and pregnant." Though in past decades this may often have been true, data from the Vital Statistics section of the *Statistical Abstract of the United States* now reveal dramatic changes in the birth rates of states in the Southern Appalachian region between 1960 and 1989 (Table, p. 162). In addition to a low birth rate, the fertility rate, which measures the number of births per 1,000 women ages 15–44 per year, was 67.2 for the United States in 1988. West Virginia ranked 50th with a fertility rate of 50.3 and Kentucky ranked 49th with a fertility rate of 57.7. So much for the barefoot and pregnant stereotype. Data just released by the Census Bureau for the period April 1990 to July 1991 show the trend continuing into the 1990s.

In 1960, seven of the nine Southern Appalachian states had birth rates above the national birth rate. In 1970, seven of the nine Southern Appalachian states again had birth rates at or above the national birth rate. In 1980, only three Southern Appalachian states had birth rates at the national birth rate. In 1989, only one Southern Appalachian state had a birth rate above the national rate. The past is not the future in Southern Appalachian states. These data are only for states with Appalachian counties and apply to the entire state. Analysis of the data for the Appalachian

POPULATION TABLE	**Birth Rate for Southern Appalachian States***						
State	***1960***	***1965***	***1970***	***1975***	***1980***	***1985***	***1989***
Un. States	23.7	19.4	18.4	14.8	15.9	15.8	16.2
Alabama	24.7	20.4	19.4	16.1	16.3	14.9	14.2
Georgia	25.3	21.7	21.1	16.2	16.9	16.1	17.1
Kentucky	23.8	19.4	18.7	16.1	16.3	14.2	14.1
Maryland	24.9	21.0	17.6	12.9	14.2	15.5	14.4
No. Carolina	24.1	19.9	19.3	14.6	14.4	14.3	15.6
So. Carolina	25.1	20.8	20.1	16.6	15.6	15.3	15.7
Tennessee	23.0	19.0	18.4	14.9	15.1	14.0	15.5
Virginia	24.1	20.0	18.6	14.1	14.7	15.1	15.3
West Virginia	21.2	17.7	17.8	15.6	15.1	12.5	12.4

*Birth rate is the number of births per 1,000 population of the state.

counties in each state would be useful; such analysis will be a part of our future study.

An Aging Society

Analysis of 1980 and 1990 census data for the forty-one Appalachian counties of Kentucky's 120 counties and all fifty-six counties of West Virginia reveals some dramatic birth trends. The United States is getting older. I recently realized this when I turned forty, and realized that at forty I was closer to age sixty, old, than I am to being a teenager, age nineteen, young—a discovery that many of us are making. Between 1980 and 1990 the median age of Americans rose from 30.0 years to 32.9 years. For Kentucky the median age increased from 29.1 years to 33.0 years, from well below the national median age in 1980 to slightly above the national median age in 1990. For West Virginia, the median age rose from 30.4 years to 35.4 years, an increase of five years in median age in the last ten years. This median age is second only to Florida's 36.4 years. So if West Virginians look older to you, you are correct. They *are* older.

The period between the 1980 and 1990 censuses saw the total population of the United States grow by 9.8 percent. This compares with an 8.0 percent decline in the population of West Virginia and a 3.9 percent decline in the population of Kentucky's forty-one Appalachian counties. These numbers are much more revealing when broken down by age segments. The population 65+ grew 22.3 percent in the decade for the United States, while the 65+ population grew much more slowly in West Virginia, 13.0 percent, and Appalachian Kentucky, 13.9 percent. Therefore, contrary to belief, the 65+ population in West Virginia and Appalachian Kentucky is not growing faster than that of the United States as a whole but is increasing at a much slower rate.

How can the median ages of West Virginia and Kentucky be growing faster than the national median age if their 65+ population is growing more slowly? West Virginia and Kentucky are not "growing more old, they are growing less young." This raises questions about the migration of retirees back to Appalachia from manufacturing centers like Detroit, Chicago, and Cincinnati that I frequently hear about. The reasoning has been that the people who had left Appalachia to find employment in urban areas would be coming back to retire in the counties where they were raised and where relatives still live. In fact, the majority (twenty-six) of Kentucky's forty-one Appalachian counties lost population in the age 65–74 segment, while the state registered a 7.7 percent increase in the age 65–74 segment. Are retirees moving back while other seniors leave the area? Or are seniors not moving back into Appalachia as some have expected?

One factor that may make the growth in seniors appear more dramatic than it is would be the increase in the old old vs. the young old. In West Virginia the senior population age 65+ grew by 13.0 percent over the decade while the population 85+ grew by 31.1 percent. This would mean that the age structure of seniors would be getting older with more seniors living longer. An age segment that includes more old old increases the visibility of an aging population. The West Virginia growth of the old old is much closer to the national growth, 37.5 percent, than is the case for the age 65+ population.

Growing Less Young

During the same time West Virginia and Appalachian Kentucky had some growth in their senior population, the population of young declined dramatically. Nationally, the population of youth ages 0 to 17 did not grow during the 1980s, with only seventeen of the fifty states having increases in their young population. There was actually a loss of two-tenths (–0.2%) percent nationally in the young population. However, in West Virginia the population ages 0 to 17 fell by 20.7 percent and in the forty-one Appalachian Kentucky counties the population ages 0 to 17 fell by 18.9 percent. Kentucky's young population overall fell by 11.9 percent, with the forty-one Appalachian counties with 25 percent of total population accounting for 43 percent of the loss in the population of young, 27,055 of the state's 96,776 loss of school-age population.

Youngest of the Young

This trend becomes even more dramatic when the population of young is segmented into the very young, ages 0 to 4, and school age, ages 5 to 17. For the decade, the Unites States experienced a drop of 4.5 percent in its population of school-age children. West Virginia and the forty-one Appalachian Kentucky counties experienced a significantly greater loss in their school-age population with a loss of 18.6 percent in West Virginia and a loss of 16.9 percent in Appalachian Kentucky. The forty-one Appalachian Kentucky counties with 25 percent of Kentucky's total population accounted for 38 percent of Kentucky's drop in the school-age population. These numbers are not uniformly spread across the forty-one Appalachian counties, and further analysis at the county level or other geographic regions like Northeastern or Southeastern Kentucky shows substantial variation. An article in the *Lexington Herald* of May 12, 1991, quoted a figure from the school superintendent of Pike County, Kentucky, who said that school enrollment went from 23,000 students at the height of the coal boom in 1976 to 13,652 students in 1991.

When comparing the youngest of the young, ages 0 to 4, the decade of the 1980s found West Virginia and the forty-one Appalachian Kentucky counties on a very different path from the United States as a whole. The population of the youngest young, ages 0 to 4, increased by 12.3 percent nationally. Yet West Virginia experienced an additional drop of 26.7 percent in their population ages 0 to 4 and the forty-one Appalachian Kentucky counties experienced a similar drop of 24.7 percent in their population of the youngest young.

Appalachian areas already experiencing a loss of their school-age population will see a furthering of that trend with the accelerated loss of the youngest of the young in their population. The Pike County superintendent stated that his system's kindergarten enrollment had slipped from 1,200 five years ago to 850 in 1991. This has led the school system to project enrollment to decline further to 10,000, as the youngest of the young move into the higher grades. The forty-one Appalachian Kentucky counties with 25 percent of Kentucky's total population accounted for 59 percent of the loss in the Kentucky's population of the youngest young—18,839 of the state's loss of 31,860 of the youngest young, ages 0–4.

Consequences

What are the consequences of a state's or a region's "not growing more old, but growing less young"? As someone has said, "predictions are difficult, especially about the future." The fact of a society's aging because it is losing its young population and because we are living much longer is something we in the United States have never had to deal with in our history. We have always been a pyramid-shaped society with lots of young and very few old. If you looked at age segments, our age structure resembled a pyramid, with the base of young being larger than the base of those in their early work-age years, and the latter being larger than the mature work-age population, and so forth. That is not the case anymore in this nation. We are squaring the pyramid, as our youth population does not grow as fast and the baby-boom generation, born between 1946 and 1964, moves into the mature work-age population, and we all live longer.

Mark Twain said when the end of the world came he wanted to live in Appalachia, because everything there happens ten years later. But the truth is West Virginia and the forty-one Appalachian Kentucky counties are experiencing an inverted pyramid, with our population of young being smaller than the young work-age population and the young work-age population moving toward being smaller than the mature work-age population. West Virginia and the forty-one Appalachian Kentucky counties are leading a national trend, with the population structure moving to a form we have never experienced before. They are bellwether areas, as we move toward a future society that is older with larger population segments at the older age segments than ever before. This inverted pyramid will require us to invent new rules for a new ball game, because the demographic ball game that will shape our future is different and challenging.

Realities

Thus West Virginia and the forty-one Appalachian Kentucky counties, as well as the Appalachian counties in the other seven Southern Appalachian states, will have to confront a number of new realities. The following section briefly raises some of the issues the new demographics will challenge us with in the areas of education and employment. Readers can see that there are many more issues and areas that also come to mind as they review the preliminary list below.

Education

As enrollments in schools go down, fewer schools may be needed. Students may have to be transported farther to ensure adequate class size. Fewer students are now resulting in teacher layoffs in Appalachian counties of Kentucky. The need for new teachers and the desire of college students to return to Appalachia to teach will be in conflict as new teachers may be unable to find openings. Programs to prevent students from dropping out may receive more priority. Funding for education may decline as there are fewer students. More of a state's education dollars will be spent elsewhere, in areas where the population of students has not declined as dramatically as in the Appalachian counties.

Employment

Appalachia, with a disproportionate population of disadvantaged young receiving food stamps and Medicaid, will with fewer young see a decline in demand for health care, groceries, and other goods or services for the young. This may be offset slightly by the small growth in the senior population, who will need more health care and other goods and services. A decline in the young also means a shrinking entry-level workforce and greater need to ensure that Appalachia does a better job of educating its young. With a limited workforce, there will be no room for throwaways. Additionally, the need to better educate the adult population will be increasingly critical. Women appear to be more willing in Appalachia to go back to school to upgrade their education and to train for new jobs; Appalachian men are having a rude awakening to employment opportunities that require more brain power than muscle power. The need for older workers will increase. Lifelong learning will be required for jobs that continually require new skills.

The Future

"Appalachian's New Crisis: No Kids" is an overview of the demographic trends occurring in West Virginia and the forty-one Appalachian Kentucky counties. It raises issues not just about kids, but about adults and seniors. The changing demographics will require the development of new rules, a process that will not be easy. Here I have only touched the tip of the iceberg. But this article is a beginning that I hope will help others to think about and address the implications that underlie a changing Appalachia.

20

by Alan J. DeYoung

Constructing and Staffing the Cultural Bridge: The School as Change Agent in Rural Appalachia

In many rural places subcultures remain that operate in a different fashion than metropolitan America, and it is often the local public school that mediates between them. Small schools can be found, for instance, that serve only handfuls of extended families; where teachers and students often know each other intimately through formal and informal networks outside of the school; where the separation of church and state may be openly contested; where expectations for the utility of a high school (rather than college) education often persist; and where the "schoolhouse" itself is highly valued as a link to earlier generations of relatives who attended the same school.

Once under the primary control of local communities, state and national school reform efforts this century have placed increasing emphasis upon making rural schools outposts of the national culture. Locally operated rural schools have typically been portrayed as unsystematic, unscientific, and inefficient since the 19th century (Katz 1971; Tyack 1974). Most professional educators who believed in the future of metropolitan America assumed (and hoped) that such places would succumb to the advances of "progress" without intervention, for cities and city schools were the wave of the future (Cubberley 1914). For rural schools that persisted, state departments of education often took up the task of centralizing, bureaucratizing, and professionalizing them in an effort to make them more like city schools (Sher 1977; Tyack 1974). The transfer of governance and control from local communities to state and national boards and agencies is perhaps the easiest school-reform movement to document this century (Spring 1993; Wirt and Kirst 1982).

Mainstream social scientists, too, proclaimed the public schools as central agents in American 20th-century progress (Dreeben 1968; Parsons 1959). Dreeben, for example, argued that the success of American schooling lay in its ability as an organizational form

Source: Reproduced by permission of the American Anthropological Association from *Anthropology & Education Quarterly* 26(2). Not for sale or further reproduction.

to transform the normative behaviors of American children away from the ascriptive, dependent, particularist, and diffuse norms of families. Such norms, of course, were and remain frequently used to describe rural communities and rural school cultures, cultures that rural school reformers hoped to transform via their bureaucratic, professionalization, and centralization efforts (Haas 1991).

Literatures Focusing on Rural Communities and Their Schools

Recognizing how modernity and industrialism threatened the social stability of most rural communities, some educational historians have focused upon how state centralization and bureaucratization interests were accommodated and/or resisted by remaining rural communities (e.g., Fuller 1982; Link 1986). Such historical accounts have provided perhaps the best view of rural-school and rural-community dynamics. Another primary source for viewing rural schools has been provided by rural sociology. Researchers within this tradition have paid moderate attention to the changing nature of schooling in some of their rural community studies (e.g., Hollingshead 1975; Schwarzweller and Brown 1962; West 1945). Unfortunately, the only educational anthropologist who has written particularly on rural American schools and their cultural dynamics has been Alan Peshkin (1978, 1982). There have been other important ethnographically informed or interested studies involving rural schools, yet "ruralness" *per se* has not been their focus. We have additional historiography on rural ethnic groups and their ability (or lack of ability) to utilize the school to improve life chances. Struggles of rural African Americans to form and use schools as avenues of upward social mobility in the Deep South are illustrative (Anderson 1988; Theobald 1991). Similarly, there are several excellent studies of rurally based ethnic groups who attend school in the South, the Southeast, and Alaska (e.g., Heath 1983; Kleinfeld 1979; Wax et al. 1964).

Available research on contemporary rural schools remains glaringly sparse, however. This is all the more curious since 28 percent of all American schools are still rural, and almost seven million children in the United States attend educational institutions in the countryside (Stern 1994). While most of these schools and school districts are in fact populated by Anglo-Protestant students, the fact that both historically and contemporarily they have been targets of state and federal school-reform efforts suggests that their dynamics ought to be of interest to sociologists and anthropologists of education far more than they seem to be. This essay continues with a brief description of rural schooling issues and rural school reform. Following this I attempt to illustrate several critical rural school issues and dynamics using data collected in one central-Appalachian county school system that I have been involved with during the past five years.

Images of the Rural Schoolhouse

Few states had mandatory school attendance laws prior to industrialization, although some sort of educational opportunities were provided by most rural communities for some portion of the year. Rural schools were typically small one- or two-room frame structures on the prairie or in the woods built upon less-desirable farm land, where "scholars" undifferentiated by age frequented the schoolhouse as directed by parents who may or may not have had a great love of learning for its own sake.

Rural teachers were reputably an unpredictable lot. Some were itinerant surveyors or disabled veterans without property or prospects. Others were the daughters of local trustees who had not yet married, or perhaps did not want to. Such places were usually lay controlled; depended heavily upon local subscription to operate; were often on the brink of closure for lack of funds or a teacher; were difficult for many children to walk to; and often had little or no equipment or books (Fuller 1989; Link 1986; Theobald 1991).

By the 1870s, industrial development and attendant emigration from rural areas and overseas swelled North American cities to the point where formal institutions became a primary focus of American civic and cultural leaders (Katz 1971; Tyack 1974). As the "social problem" of crime led to police departments and the "social problem" of refuse led to sanitation departments, the "social problem" of ostensibly unruly and "normless" city children led urban reformers to create education departments and compulsory schools (Perkinson 1991).

Rural schools, the experts said, could not provide a model for urban education. Immigrants without North American cultural or political experience who were likely non-English speakers and without the training perceived necessary for an emerging industrial order required a new educational institution. Americans migrating from the countryside into the city, too, were deemed to require a formal organization that not only reinforced Protestant "character training," but would also transform second-, third-, and fourth-generation American rural residents into city dwellers, industrial workers, and consumers (Spring 1980; Tyack 1974).

As America became metropolitan, norms of extended families engaged in household economies directed by family heads were greatly diminished. Rather, industrial work habits demanded attention to time and workplace efficiency; careers within growing mercantile and bureaucratic organizations; workplace operations that were clearly divided by specialized labor; the exclusion of distracting kin from the shop floor (particularly after the establishment of child-labor laws); and new systems of authority based upon norms of expertise and efficiency rather than of the family, clan, or tradition. And metropolitan public schools were increasingly dedicated to turning out human resources to these ends (Kliebard 1986).

Progressive educators of the 1910s and 1920s did advocate the importance of community schools and hearkened back to rural communities in their efforts to reform increasingly regimented and bureaucratized schooling (Perkinson 1991). In many rural places, of course, instructional aims of the school were but one reason that they were supported by the local community—not the sole or perhaps even the primary reason (Fuller 1982, Hartford 1977). But even the staunchest supporters of community schools conceded defeat to advocates of administrative efficiency in the mid-20th century, as even city schools became perceived as mechanisms to escape rather than rebuild urban (or rural) communities. City schools today have much less significance as community centers than they once did, just as geographical communities themselves are today seen as secondary to communities of "interests" (or networks). Today most Americans equate good *schools* as places of good *schooling;* good schools are the place where learner outcomes are measured to exist and where students are well disciplined.

Many objectives of early-20th-century school reformers have thus become the contemporary norm. Schools have become "rational," in that "what an education is good for" is often today defined with respect to expanded occupational possibilities and living standards made possible by "obtaining a good education" (Spring 1980). At the same time, schools teach individuals that they are free from the constraints of local communities and families, since desirable economic and geographic mobility is theirs via the careers that good schooling has opened up to them (Perkinson 1991).

Contemporary Rural Typologies

Even after massive movements of the American population into metropolitan areas and after decades of concerted efforts to merge and consolidate rural schools, there remained 22,400 rural community schools in the United States in 1992 (Stern 1994). Tom Gjelten classifies five different U.S. rural community types today, based primarily upon economy and demography (1982). He further suggests that school cultures in each community type are significantly different and that at least two of them have social dynamics and norms very different than those found in metropolitan areas.

Two of these five rural types are actually enmeshed in rapid social and/or economic change due to their proximity to metropolitan places. *High growth* locales are those immediately adjacent to expanding metropolitan areas, and *reborn* rural communities are those currently inundated by city "refugees" attempting to escape urban congestion, crime, and so forth. A third type of rural community is the sort of place studied by Peshkin (1978). Gjelten describes such places as *stable rural* communities, places still involved with market agriculture and able to maintain important local school traditions, as well as adjust to national schooling demands due to a stable local tax base and meaningful engagement with the national economy.

Gjelten's remaining two rural community types include *depressed rural,* where the local economy is underdeveloped and outmigration is high, and *isolated rural,* those typically far removed from the transportation and commerce centers of the nation. Unfortunately, the number of *stable* agricultural counties continues to decline in the United States, while the number of persistently impoverished, mining-independent, and retirement-income-dependent countries continues to grow. There remain, in other words, many communities of the last two types even in late-20th-century America (Bender et al. 1985; Children's Defense Fund 1992).

Isolated and Depressed Rural Communities in Appalachia

Although schools are powerful enculturative sites, they are but one of several sorts of institutions that teach or model values, aspirations, expectations, and motives of the national culture. Historically, Cremin notes (1977), American metropolitan schools typically have had powerful collateral educative institutions that have underscored their values and utility. Inkeles and Smith (1974), too, argue that employment in large-scale industries, engagement in the daily interactions of metropolitan life, and access to mass communication and information sources are critical agents involved in creating "modern" individuals and "modern" societies internationally. But while mass-communication and mass-consumer markets are visible to most rural Americans, not all rural communities or rural schools are witness to nearby structures of economic opportunities that cement the ostensible connection between schooling and work.

The situation of perhaps thousands of rural Appalachian schools and communities could be utilized to illustrate contemporary versions of the earlier discussion. Many Appalachian counties and communities remain among those described by Gjelten as isolated and depressed, and by Bender et al. as mining-based, persistently impoverished, and/or retirement-income-dependent. Since public schools often exist in such places as the primary local formal organization linked to the outside world, some believe that rural schools in eastern Kentucky, East Tennessee, western Virginia, western North Carolina, and West Virginia bear a particularly central role in educating the young for participation in the national culture (CEDaR 1987).

Although isolation and economic depression are obviously relative terms, both of these adjectives have been used to describe rural Appalachia for almost one hundred years. The upland South had few plantations, few slaves, and little tenant farming. Neither did commercial farming and agribusiness ever gain prominence in the mountains since there was little expanse of flat land nor adequate transportation systems to move agricultural products out of the region (Billings 1988).

Appalachia was also never more than a satellite of modern American industry. The region was drawn into the sphere of national industrial development in the late 19th and early 20th centuries, but it was primarily tapped for its natural resources, which were harvested locally but sent to the Northeast and Midwest for manufacture (Eller 1982; Lewis et al. 1978). Major industries in lumber, oil, gas, and coal developed, but jobs created in these industries were primarily labor intensive and low wage. And as in most boom-and-bust natural-resource economies, the mid-20th-century legacy of industrialization here has been poverty and environmental degradation (Gaventa 1980). In point of fact, the poverty and unemployment associated with isolation and lack of economic possibilities in Appalachia was a primary impetus of the War on Poverty programs of the 1960s and 1970s, and led to (or reinforced) major "social engineering" programs of the national government like the Appalachian Regional Commission. As Whisnant argues, programs like those of the ARC (and the earlier TVA) were explicitly designed to help "modernize the mountaineer," as cultural deficiencies in the region were often believed to be the cause of regional underdevelopment (1980).

The Public School as "Cultural Bridge"

Isolated by several different mountain ranges and dependent upon subsistence and barter economies, pioneers on the Appalachian frontier developed a social organization of production by the mid–19th century which depended upon a strong kinship system and small-community stability (Eller 1982). This isolation further enabled the refinement and persistence of a regionally distinct subculture well into the 20th century. Prior to industrialism, families that were engaged in subsistence and local-market farming moved up the hillside or further up creekbeds as the population grew. Communities were often organized around lay-ministered churches, and transportation into or out of the region was an ever-present difficulty due to mountainous terrain and hazards involved with navigating flood-prone creeks and rivers.

Regional social scientists earlier this century accepted the notion that an Appalachian "subculture" persisted into the mid–20th century and that a number of personal values and traditions to be found within isolated mountain communities approximated an earlier agrarian era (Shapiro 1978, 1983). Ergood and Kuhre summarized several decades of scholarship upon this topic thusly:

> [W]e find the mountain people described as independent, kin-involved people whose lives are closely bound to their physical environment, whose activities are traditional, and whose beliefs are both fatalistic and religiously fundamentalist. This description has slowly emerged and expanded from the earliest attempts by social scientists to the most recent. [1991:47]

More important from the perspective of this essay was the effort by rural sociologists Schwarzeller and Brown to articulate key differences between Appalachian subculture(s) of eastern Kentucky and "the great society" (1962). A critical component of their theoretical essay was to focus upon the region's public schools as a critical link between rural Appalachian communities and the national culture. Much of their articulation illuminates the historical and conceptual discussion presented earlier in this essay.

In Appalachia, Schwarzeller and Brown claim, the school is the primary or only cultural bridge between regional subcultures and the national culture. Unlike other formal institutions that either do not exist in the mountains or whose impact can be minimized, pubic schools are local sites of the national culture that pervade in one way or another virtually every family in the region: they are paid for by public taxes, they compel families to send their children, and often they are the largest employer in rural counties without industry.

Schwarzeller and Brown, too, claim that eastern Kentucky (and arguably most of rural Appalachia) is dominated by "familism, traditionalism, and puritanism" (1962:359). And with the exception of public schools, most other regional institutions continue to help reproduce the regional subculture. They argue that:

> structurally, from the viewpoint of the community, the family institution is decentralized or multicentered. Each kinship unit is a more or less closed social system with membership ascriptively assigned. Interfamily linkage through linkage of family members with other subsystems in the community is limited and weak. For example, formal organizations occupy a very small part of the social life in (Appalachian) com-

munities, and any change-promoting program, such as that offered by the Extension Service (USDA) has a difficult, almost impossible, task of implementing that program if it relies only on communication through formal organizations. [Schwarzeller and Brown 1962:360–361]

In the national culture, Schwarzeller and Brown assert, work organizations and the church are typical participatory institutions that model social roles and institutional norms similar to those detailed by Dreeben (1968): independence, achievement, universalism, and specificity. In much of rural Appalachia, on the contrary, extractive and seasonal work involving rules and norms beyond physical endurance—when work is available at all—is often all that is available. Life in boom-and-bust economies, too, suggests that upward occupational and social mobility is more likely to occur somewhere else rather than locally. Since many residents continue to desire "place," securing employment in mining, timbering, and the oil and gas fields has historically been obtained and is carried out within and among family and friends.

Schwarzeller and Brown contend that it is primarily the few out-migrants returning home for a visit who display very briefly the instrumental norms of individuals engaged in careers rather than those tied more intimately to place. But these individuals return to work in the cities and are thus not present to sufficiently reinforce the national cultural norms that Schwarzeller and Brown view as positive. In their place remain more "traditional" norms: patterns of economic and political life that have changed little since earlier in the century when allegiances between families and political parties were first made and that continue into the present, and where male dominance in family and community matters remains strong.

A final primary institutional setting (not counting the school) whereby national norms might be modeled, according to Schwarzeller and Brown, could be the church. But here, too, there are few organizational norms in mountain churches consistent with mainstream American culture (or at least the culture of the 1960s):

> The dominant mountain (Protestant) religious traditions emphasize congregational autonomy, which weakens ties with the outside and reinforces the localistic orientation common to much of the region's institutional structure. Furthermore, the general religious orientation strongly emphasizes direct personal relationships between the individual and his [*sic*] God to such an extent that great social pressure is put upon each individual to establish such a relationship. This stress, coupled with the low educational levels always characteristic of the region, has tended to make (Appalachian) religion more emotional, more fundamentalistic, more personal, and more familistic than the Great Society's religion. [Schwarzeller and Brown 1962:362–363]

Without the ostensible benefit of stable white-collar employment; controlled by families tied to traditional politics, opposed to public expense due to declining economies, suspicious of "do-gooder" programs sponsored by outside formal organizations, and without the civic infrastructure of more metropolitan places, schools have virtually by default become the single best source of change in the mountains, according to Schwarzeller and Brown. Schools, they argue, are typically staffed by teachers who are from local families but who are trained outside; who teach courses dealing with the national culture and the subjects instrumental to working there; who reward on-the-job performance by evaluation rather than patronage; and who operate in a rational and efficient manner as they are subject to state and federal guidelines and funding imperatives.

It is important to contrast Schwarzeller and Brown's view of public schools in isolated and impoverished Appalachia with schools like those of Peshkin's Mansfield (1978). In the former, schools as "change agents" is the focus; in the latter, schools as bearers of tradition is the critical theme. But again, Mansfield is a comparatively stable Midwest agricultural community, while it has probably been at least forty years since any Appalachian mountain community could be described thusly.

Researching Educational Dynamics in Braxton County, West Virginia

School battles and school dynamics in Braxton County, West Virginia, display much of the earlier discussed rural education legacy *and* contemporary cultural dynamics involving rural schools, their local communities, and state reform mandates. Historical struggles over means and ends of schooling within Braxton County are easy to find, as are contemporary schooling dynamics and issues surrounding the workings of the "cultural bridge." The case of Braxton County, in other words, provides a window both on rurality and schooling in the past as well as the present. Eschewing the opportunity to suggest that the Appalachian "experience" is somehow idiosyncratic, I will argue that contemporary community and school interactions and relationships with the national culture remain as examples of the larger history of rural-metropolitan education and school reform. A number of dynamics in the county illustrate state and national imperatives for Braxton County schools to conform to extralocal mandates in ways very similar to the historical record. My fieldwork also underscores the efforts of local educators to compel students to use their education as a cultural bridge from central West Virginia to the national culture.

My research efforts in Braxton County covered a period of almost five years between 1988 and 1993, and I employed a variety of qualitative methods as outlined in such standard texts as Bogdan and Biklen 1982, Merriam 1988, and Stake 1978. Between 1988 and 1991, Braxton County High School and its high dropout rate was the focus of both the state department of education and a federal school-improvement project that I helped to evaluate as participant observer (DeYoung 1991). Braxton County being a rural county far from any metropolitan area, the farming and extractive economy there allegedly drew most able-bodied boys to work long before they might have graduated from high school. Investigating teacher narratives, completing oral histories, and investigating old school records at the central office thus were incorporated as research tools in my work. Not surprisingly perhaps, they revealed that most rural families expected few children to proceed beyond the eighth grade, until perhaps the 1950s (Walters 1986). In my research I interpreted part of the "battle" at the high school over dropout rates to be between a school administration charged to improve such statistics by the state versus subject-matter high school teachers who believed that high school was not for everyone anyway (DeYoung 1991).

Most recently, I spent a two-year period as participant observer in Burnsville School, one of the three county middle schools that was consolidated under administrative and fiscal imperatives and "opportunities" provided by the state. This school consolidation was hotly contested by the affected community, much as rural school consolidations have been in the United States for over one hundred years. Consolidations of the type that took place at Burnsville, however, have rarely been studied in-process, and thus I decided to continue my fieldwork in the county. Results of this research are in DeYoung 1995.

Structured and unstructured interviews with parents, teachers, and local citizens were employed as part of this research, as were document analyses and additional oral histories. Having simultaneously "served" the county system as evaluator and consultant and also having written favorably about the plight of rural and isolated schools nationally, I was simultaneously viewed as sympathetic to both the organizational difficulties of the central office *and* to the problems of a small community about to lose its school. Entrée and access to the perspectives and issues involved were freely provided by school officials and by community leaders (DeYoung 1995).

Braxton County and Its Appalachian Context

Braxton County's economic history clearly falls within the parameters of Appalachian historiography, with several important exceptions. Hillside farming along creeks and hollows there throughout the 19th century gave way by the early 20th century to timbering, coal mining, and gas- and oil-drilling activities. And as resources in the county were extracted and harvested (often by absentee owners), local economies began to wither, and people began to move away. Braxton had a population of 24,000 in 1920, but only 13,000 in 1970. By mid–20th century standards, Braxton was considered isolated, and by Gjelten's 1982 standards, both depressed and isolated. Like most typologies, though, such categories can be misleading. For instance, there were small but important professional and skilled working-class families in Braxton during the early 20th century, for the county had two navigable rivers and later a thriving railroad industry that enabled moderate commercial and manufacturing industries to develop alongside those involved with extraction into the 1930s. Perhaps the most significant modernizing influence in Braxton County, in terms suggested by Schwarzeller and Brown, may have been the railroad industry. The switchyard and repair shops near Gassaway employed hundreds of semiskilled and skilled craftsmen between 1910 and 1950. Importantly, many school teachers and administrators in Braxton County today—those who staff the cultural bridge—are the children of former railroad employees. Town boosters in booming Gassaway, Sutton, and Burnsville from the turn of the 20th century until at least the Great Depression would likely have described their neighbors in outlying areas as isolated, but not themselves. And residents of these towns continued to struggle for their small-town way of life and the promises of America at least until the 1960s, when Presidents Kennedy and Johnson came to Kentucky and West Virginia to tell them as Appalachians that they were chronically depressed and needed federal help.

Rural Schooling for a National Culture

Approximately 70 percent of the Braxton County's 3000 students, who are almost all Anglo-Protestant in background, receive free or reduced-price lunches. In addition to being primarily poor, most county students ride the bus to school. There are a number of hollows where students must walk out to the paved road since buses cannot navigate the hills and muddy roads; and when the rains come, several schools must let out early or open late since overflowing rivers and creeks make some roads impassable.

Much of what I observed in several of Braxton's eight public schools between 1988 and 1993 was explicitly "cultural" and often appreciated by parents. Other efforts of local educators were less explicit and sometimes contested. With regard to culturally explicit undertakings, teachers and administrators carried out many instructional and extracurricular activities explained and understood as compensatory, that is, designed to offset what they perceived as the cultural disadvantage associated with poverty and isolation.

Participant observation at Burnsville School revealed that teachers and staff understood that part of their mission was to compensate for disadvantages that children allegedly had at home. Winter clothes, for example, were frequently channeled discreetly through the principal's office to the families of poorer schoolchildren throughout the year. Field trips to local shopping malls and movie theaters were also almost routine rewards for good school attendance, and monthly award ceremonies for good attendance, successful academic performance, and good citizenship were prominent features of the school. Many teachers and the principal believed that parents were not always supportive of school civic and academic goals, and that it thus became their responsibility to particularly reinforce acceptable behavior and performance by "at-risk" children.

The line between official school practices and extraschool community/compensatory involvement is alleged to have been a major feature of rural community schools in the past, and this certainly was the case during my fieldwork at Burnsville School. Many teachers and the principal there were involved heavily in the after- and before-school activities of many children, particularly the ones whom they considered most disadvantaged. The principal was a church elder, taught Sunday School, and was involved in both Boy and Cub Scouts. He used his position as school principal to inform and entice students whom he considered in need of positive influences into one or more church or civic youth groups. As a schoolteacher and principal at Burnsville for over twenty years, he believed he knew enough about almost every family in his community to be able to judge who needed extraschool social support and who did not.

A popular teacher at Burnsville was also heavily involved in regional Girl Scout activities. One corner of her classroom, in fact, was given over to a huge pile of boxed Girl Scout cookies during the spring of 1992. Burnsville School in essence served as a distribution point for cookies, just as it did for clothes. Burnsville School was the only K–8 school in the county between 1969 and 1992. Before that it had been a 1–12 school; afterwards a K–4 school. Opponents of school consolidation both times argued that the small and nurturing features of Burnsville School specifically facilitated the social and cultural needs of a school population with many disadvantaged students. One teacher put it this way:

> I [think] it is a good place for kids. I think the teachers are caring; I think this is the only social activity that a lot of these kids get. Since we're so rural, there aren't a lot of places where kids can get together and do things together, and school is mainly their social outlet. And I do think it's a good place for kids. We do have activities after school for the kids, you know, the sports activities, the dances for the kids. We have the Brownies and the Girl Scouts, and now we're doing Boy Scouts. And it is mainly through the school.

Some of the compensatory efforts of the school, of course, I found personally ironic. For example, the same sorts of commercial activities that led me to eschew the study of suburban and urban school-community relations were ones held out as positive by many teachers in Braxton. I was sometimes disappointed, for example, to arrive at school after a long road trip past hundreds of fast-food restaurants and strip malls along the interstate to find that a third or a half of the school had just left on a field trip to visit such places as part of some culturally enriching activity planned by the school. Unlike field trips in metropolitan America, however, trips to the mall, the (only) county movie theater, or to the (only) county skating rink were seen as very important. There just was not much else in the region for students to do that even approximated what teachers in metropolitan America would think culturally enriching—like museums, government buildings, or a TV or radio station.

And then there were culturally compensatory schooling practices that must have seemed ironic even in the eyes of Braxton County teachers. Braxton schools, for example, pride themselves on providing a highly nutritious breakfast and lunch program at school in an effort to improve the diets of students who some administrators believe rarely eat anything but candy bars and high-sugar soft drinks at home—if they eat anything. And state and district policy is that only real fruit drinks, milk, and low-fat snacks can be sold in school buildings during the school day. But this is still America, and the fast-food industry makes its advertising pitch even into the prettiest and most remote hollows of Appalachia. Enabling students to participate in the fast-food culture of America is thus facilitated in Braxton County as part of the routine away-game athletic trips undertaken by many students in the middle and high schools. The out-of-county bus trips that I took as participant-observer almost always involved a stop at some fast-food restaurant along the interstate. Such stops invariably enabled students to spend considerable amounts of money upon commercial high-fat foods (cheeseburgers, french fries, and milkshakes). And the bus drivers usually got a free meal as reward for choosing the restaurant that they did.

Resisting "Opportunities" to Cross the Cultural Bridge

Few of the above practices were contested or opposed by Burnsville or Braxton County parents. Active parents in the life of the school typically appreciated the "enrichment" activities schools sponsored. Yet, there were very few active parents at the schools that I visited in Braxton, with the exception of booster groups of parents supporting athletic programs. On several occasions the county superintendent confided to me that satisfying athletic booster groups in the county was among the most difficult policy areas in the district. Committed to improved instructional programs, he often shook his head in mock disbelief at the heat generated over who coached the football and basketball teams, while rarely did any citizens ask questions or push for reforms in courses or curricula.

Burnsville School, with a student body of almost 300 in 1992, had fewer than two dozen PTO members, and teachers by default comprised half of the elected officers of this organization. School officials often complained that significant numbers of students came from families where any extraschool efforts were appreciated because parents worked or were unable or unwilling to spend much time with their children on a day-to-day basis. As in the other schools, active athletic boosters far outnumbered attendees at school PTO meetings.

Cultural enrichment or compensatory activities, however, were important but arguably less critical activities in school leaders' hopes for enculturating students. Although there appears to be a national movement to transform schools into more complete service providers, the state department of education in West Virginia and the central office in Braxton County remained focused upon academic program accountability. As elsewhere, the development of human resources for gainful employment and economic growth was a primary aim. In contemporary Appalachia, however, *providing* a "cultural bridge" is no longer considered enough: schools are specifically rewarded or punished in West Virginia and surrounding states based upon their success in graduating students from high school and moving them to postsecondary "opportunities" that invariably lie somewhere else in the state or nation. Getting local parents and communities to support such aims is not always easy in isolated and economically depressed areas. Familism, place, tradition, and religious fundamentalism, for example, were all important components of Braxton County communities, as Schwarzweller and Brown described. At the same time, Braxton County schools are clearly tied to national objectives and concerned with systematic school reform (DeYoung 1991). This being the case, struggles over educational means and ends in a real place—rather than in a theoretical argument—might have been anticipated. And they often were.

Trying to get parents and community groups in Braxton County to view the schools as important and essential to the success of their children beyond the county was a consistent concern and struggle by school leaders there throughout my fieldwork. A persistent annoyance of the central office in Braxton, for example, was fights between parents and the transportation director over the timing of bus routes and the placement of bus sheds along the way. To administrators these were trivial pursuits, for busing was merely a means to an end. For parents, however, efforts to control bus schedules and where children could wait for their rides was one of the few remaining school matters not dictated by state education policy. In other words, they could (and sometimes did) have the ability to "control" the schools rather than be controlled by them.

Struggling over means and ends of schooling was also a primary interpretation of my high-school and school-consolidation studies. Disagreements between the schools and many local families over definitions of work and careers were part of each of the above narratives. Many locals (who have not migrated) still adhere to the dignity of skilled labor and the value of physical work. Their values are confronted by a state department of education that emphasizes postindustrial skills and the mythical "information highway." Braxton County High School sits in between such interests, according to the school's vocational director:

> *AD:* [The county superintendent] once told me that over 90 percent of the kids in the high school took vocational classes.
> *Vocational director:* Oh, yeah. I [may have told you] that. They almost all do. Now, however, that's not as noble as it sounds. That's because sometimes there is nothing else to fill out their schedule. . . . But to have a salable skill is a value to most of our families here. That's a value. For example, here in vocational section we have almost no problems with parents. None. They love what we do because that fits their norm. A boy is learning carpentry. He's learning to weld. Now, understand that I said, "a boy." If you walk up and down the hall, you don't see too many girls in our classes. We do our best. We have a few, few boys in home ec[onomics]. And we have an occasional tough girl that takes welding or something. . . . So our parents are very—they can relate to what we're doing. We're teaching skills. And they like that. And they love to see their daughters going through our secretarial branch. That all fits very well. So we have almost no parental problems whatsoever to worry with, [whereas] in academia they just have problem after problem because of the parents. . . . [In academia] it's much more difficult for their parents to relate to the need for academic skills as far as there is to earn a living, because most of them don't have them either. We have sort of a trap in this area geographically. I have [many] young ladies and young married people and young adults up in these hollows that have great skills as far as working IBM typewriters and word processors and those types of things. But for what? Where are they going to go? You can't go to Charleston or Clarksburg for minimum wage. What are you going to do? Then, plus the fact that most Appalachians are not mobile anyway. They want to live here. They want to stay here. There is a sort of security in the mountains.

Rural Appalachian subcultures, then, often define the nature of work and of gender in ways somewhat different than national school-reform leaders of the late 20th century. Many Braxton County families continue to believe that wage labor is valuable, but not important enough to leave family, friends, and home to pursue for any extended period of time. Many men who obtain city work leave their families behind and return weekly or monthly to visit and perform household maintenance. Such patterns and beliefs about work have been inherited from an earlier (which is not to be confused with inferior) era.

In the early 20th century, outside representatives of the national culture complained about many mountain men in much the same way that today's teachers complain about students who are absent in pursuit of outdoor interests. When timbering and mining industries were booming, mill and mine owners were concerned that the men who came to work one day might take off and go hunting or to their homeplace to see their family the next day; that is, they appeared to have no long-term commitment to the companies for which they worked. Eller (1982) and Lee (1968) argued that miners and millworkers back then often viewed wage labor as supplemental to hillside farming and hunting, not a replacement. Employers then sometimes attempted to solve their unsteady labor supply by constructing company towns where only the most dedicated workers could obtain housing and shopping privileges for their families as a function of their dedication.

Getting today's students, particularly male students, to define their lives in ways congruent with the objective of teachers is alleged to be a major objective of Braxton County educators, thus approximating a long-term cultural battle in the mountains. As the vocational director suggests, physical work remains more often understood as real work, while book learning and academic pursuits are less frequently valued as suitable for able-bodied boys. Appeals for academic success and high-school completion have not always been as highly valued in Braxton County as school officials would like, for success in an academic curriculum implies college attendance and careers away from home and family and thus is often viewed with mixed local emotions. Braxton County schools have attacked their low graduation rate (as defined by the state) with aggressive drop-out prevention programs and field trips to state institutions of higher learning in efforts to get students to think about careers and futures somewhere else.

Coming of age in rural Appalachian places like Braxton County also often involves firearms and all-terrain vehicles, especially for boys. Many school leaders believe that hunting pursuits and the allure of riding back trails is okay on the weekend or after school but suggest that students most in need of school services are often the ones who skip school altogether to undertake these activities. Middle and high schools in the county attempt to accommodate and even serve aspects of the local outdoor subculture by holding hunter-safety courses as part of the curriculum, and by recessing school the entire first week of deer (rifle) hunting season every November. They begrudgingly acknowledge that attendance at school would be very low among boys then, no matter what the sanctions. So they no longer make the effort to hold classes during this week.

Maleness itself is thus associated in central West Virginia with cultural values different from if not oppositional to the public school. "Macho" cultural values certainly exist, as they do in the larger national culture, but they are perhaps not as dominant there as they remain in Braxton. Outdoor interests and blue-collar occupations are clearly symbolized throughout central West Virginia in the types of vehicles that people drive and the types of clothing that men wear. The vehicle I drove throughout my fieldwork in Braxton County was at the time the nation's number-one selling domestic sedan. Sedans, however, did not appear to be the vehicle of choice in Braxton, and many people were surprised to find out that Ford Motors made a car like mine. As well, shirts, ties, and sportscoats were apparel rarely seen in Braxton away from the courthouse or the school. With the exception of a few bankers and businessmen, the only other males in Braxton's towns not sporting denim jeans or insulated jump suits and boots are usually teachers. Not infrequently they are verbally accosted for dress unbecoming of their gender.

Differing notions of the value of "place," too, pit many residents of Appalachia and rural America against the interests of geographic mobility inherent in the national culture. In a nation that invented the form and justification for such things as "bedroom communities," school teachings enabling students to jump from one place to another in search of career mobility are commonly accepted. Some argue that it is a major reason the (urban) public continues to support common schooling (Perkinson 1991). And schools in Braxton County have "career days" and guidance counselors to help young adults plan for their futures outside the county, much as any other school system. Traditionally, however, sense of place has been important to central West Virginians, and youngsters are not sure under what circumstances they want to leave and how far they may be willing to go. Many prefer to live close to the place of their birth and to their families, and allegedly would prefer to live on some sort of government assistance instead of looking for work that is uncertain.

As Schwarzeller and Brown outlined, local role models who demonstrate the value of persistence and career-orientation are not plentiful in more isolated parts of Appalachia. Most

Braxtonians who have successful careers, for example, have them somewhere else. The most popular type of celebrations to be found in Braxton seemingly occur on three-day national holidays like Memorial Day and the Fourth of July. Family and school reunions are plentiful then, and they are usually announced weeks ahead of time in the local newspapers.[1]

Meanwhile, those who are retired and living on fixed incomes and/or those who would rather work seasonally and spend time in the woods hunting and fishing are easily found in Braxton, and according to some educators, this gives kids the wrong message about life. The principal of Burnsville School cited an example of this situation within his own family, a situation that he found troublesome. Braxton became an economically depressed area between 1940 and 1960, as the boom years of 1900–30 faded into memory. In the late 1960s and 1970s, however, dam construction and highway building came briefly into the county. From the principal's perspective, these cyclical events and seasonal work in general harmed the modeling of acceptable work habits required for a good education and a good career:

> In the late 1950s and early 1960s [we had] a pretty low-key lifestyle. [Then] the interstate [and the dam] construction came in here. People were all of a sudden given jobs . . . that paid enormous salaries. I mean, people who were used to living on 300 dollars a month were all of a sudden making 300 dollars a week. . . . A lot of people were able to deal with it; a lot weren't. They had become used to the opulent lifestyle that these jobs allowed them to have, and I can still see many of them doing that, many of them my relatives who had jobs that paid 10, 12 14 dollars an hour. But now those jobs are no longer available in this area, but they still live here and they complain that they'll never take another job unless they can get 10, 12, 14 dollars an hour. So some of them [remain] unemployed. . . . [Today] the union calls my cousin out for work every spring, and he works six or eight weeks and makes good money as a laborer, but then he's laid off for long periods of time and he draws his unemployment. He would be probably a whole lot better off to take a 4.50 to 5.00 dollars an hour job that worked eight hours a day consistently year round and stick with it. He probably could come up with some retirement system for himself. As it is now, he'll probably live that way and for the rest of his life until he's ready to retire, and when he retires will he have anything? Who knows? I hope he will have, but I see a lot of people doing that.

Schools as Employers

Schwarzweller and Brown were probably correct in arguing for the centrality of public schools as change agents in Appalachia, but they certainly underplayed the local conflicts over the means and ends of schooling such as the ones I mentioned above. They also assumed, perhaps too easily, that local schools could remain clear of the patronage and nepotism of which rural (and city) schools were historically accused. Braxton County, for the most part, was able to avoid such charges in the years of my research, but surrounding counties were often accused of these practices, and the history of Braxton County schools suggested such dynamics in the past (DeYoung 1995).[2]

The "cultural bridge" metaphor is probably too simplistic with regard to teacher careers. Since the school board here is the largest employer in the county—like all adjacent counties—many Braxton citizens seek teaching careers in an effort to obtain careers that are secure and personally satisfying—both values of the national culture. On the other hand, obtaining a job in the school system has, for decades, been a strategy for well-connected and/or high-achieving students (usually women) to obtain work and stay in the community.

The county school superintendent, himself a native with nearly twenty years in the school system, believes that a critical purpose of his schools is to expose students to worlds outside of central West Virginia. On the other hand, positions in the school system are highly valued, for they are more lucrative and stable than almost any other skilled occupations. While he is pleased to be able to provide employment for local families and while he sits on an advisory board at the local teachers college, he is at the same time an active recruiter of out-of-state candidates for teaching positions.

Teachers from local communities have typically been trained very close to home and often go to great lengths to stay teaching in the county, even if the pay is substandard and staff reductions change the nature of their work. One teacher summarized her equivocal belief in teaching as a career in the passage below. I asked her why she stayed in Braxton even though she earned substantially less than the national average for teachers and she had little job security in a system that continued to downsize. She responded:

> I stay in West Virginia because I choose to. I like West Virginia; I like being near my family. That is very important to me. I have a friend that lives in Florida and is all-the-time saying, "Come down, move down here with me. I have a job for you in the room next door. You can make twice your salary." But I told her it was too far away from my mom. That's very important to me. I want my daughters to grow up around their grandparents. I don't want them to be 18 hours away, where they get to see their grandparents only twice a year. Family is very important to me. Plus I like the area. I like the rural area. I don't want my kids to live in a big, large city. I don't like the statistics I see coming out of cities. I like the fact that, if my kids stay (after school) for a Brownie or Girl Scout meeting, . . . they can walk to their grandmother's without worrying that something is going to happen between the school and the house.

Dodging Fundamentalism

The above-quoted teacher's commitment to place and family, as well as career, does not weaken the argument that rural public schools are or can be a bridge to the national culture, but it does suggests that the schools themselves are affected by both the national culture that they seek to serve and the subcultures in which they must operate. It is also somewhat ironic that Braxton teachers who are hired and rewarded at least partly for their ability to teach skills and values enabling students to graduate and leave have themselves been able to escape this predicament by becoming teachers.

In addition to those who use the school as a bridge to leave or to secure local employment that pays well, there are also those who publically criticize what many view as the decay of the national culture (Dorgan 1993; Page and Clelland 1978). They, too, view the school as a cultural bridge; but they literally see it as a cultural bridge to hell. "Fatalist" interpretations of life emphasize the lack of control that individuals have over income, life, illness, and death. In Appalachia, fatalism is typically a worldview attached to religious fundamentalism, and both conflict with the aims of many public school officials to transmit norms of personal efficacy and instrumentality.

A number of fundamentalist churches remain in Braxton County, and leaders of these churches are often open critics of modern American schooling and the schools of Braxton County. Passionate appeals to children and adults are audible every Sunday over the radio here, as they are weekly and on Sunday at dozens of county church services. Preachers invariably urge local sinners to be born again, urging them to let go of their earthly pursuits, like wealth and fame. And it takes no formal schooling to be saved, only a personal experience with Jesus and commitment to follow his teachings.

Churches, of course, have often been keenly involved with rural schools and rural school life. Burnsville School has always had a close working relationship with the town

Methodist and Baptist churches. The conservative and independent churches, however, appear not to have appreciated the evolution of our more secular national culture. Ironically, the small and usually poor church groups who today assemble to hear sermons preached against the schools system often congregate in former one- and two-room schools in the countryside, schools that were abandoned by the school district in previous rounds of consolidation.

For religious conservatives, the tolerance of perceived misbehavior in school represents and adds to the decline of morality in the United States. Students with a behavior problems in Braxton today are invariably considered "at-risk" and/or "culturally disadvantaged" by the school. When this occurs, students often receive special attention in order to keep them from failing and dropping out. These categories and "treatments," of course, are all very "modern" and "professional." "Traditionally," however, misbehaving children were encouraged to leave school in rural America, and there are those in Braxton today who continue to believe that this is desirable. Repositories of such beliefs are often to be found within conservative and fundamentalist church congregations. One pastor of a small independent church—which held services in a former two-room school—was one of those highly critical of national and local public education. Among his congregation were several dozen Burnsville students who lived in another small community to the west of town, which is why I visited the church several times. He used the following terms to describe the national culture and the misguided direction of the cultural bridge:

> *Pastor:* I remember when I went to the one-room school and God was part of the curriculum and in the morning you would have prayer and you would have "pledge of allegiance to the flag" and, you know, you reverenced God and the country. And, too, you know, the teachers were somebody that you looked up to as a role model. And you respected them because they were who they were. . . . [Today] our school system is [in trouble] because they took prayer out of the schools, Bible reading out of the schools, and don't have any rules about anything anymore. . . . One of my girls talks about teaching even the small children, fourth graders, and they are so rowdy you can't teach them . . . but if you can't make them mind, you can't teach them. . . . And I believe [there are] other reasons for the problems we are having in the public schools right now. [There is] the dope situation, and they teach premarital sex and extramartial sex in school, and it hasn't helped the pregnancy situation one bit—adding wildfire. And it seems the more we try to teach it and talk about it, the worst it gets. Our nation is sin crazy.
>
> *AD:* The people, though, that run the Braxton County school system [are] all native Braxton Countians. Why does the school system not teach the things that you think are important, when it is your own people that are in the school system?
>
> *Pastor:* Well, because the biggest majority aren't in church. The biggest majority of them aren't saved. Some of them are saved, but the biggest majority of them are not saved, and therefore they and the ones that—you know—run this country (like the news networks) are unsaved. . . . They're ungodly people and the same way in our school system. People running the school systems and different things are not saved. They have gotten away from God. . . .
>
> *AD:* You've got a bunch of kids in your congregation that go down to [Burnsville] school. Are you worried about them? Do you worry about what happens to them when they're not here?
>
> *Pastor:* Yeah. I do worry about that they're taught and this, that, and the other. That's why we try to instill in them while we've got them here, so

> that when they do go out, you know, that they can sort out what's right and what is wrong. Because they're being taught some things wrong.

Today's school leaders would likely face intense organized opposition except for several facts. For instance, suspicion of formal organizations as a rule carries over to collective action in Braxton County. There is little *organized* opposition to much school policy because, as Schwarzeller and Brown suggest, there appears little faith in formal organizations at all. Perhaps realizing this, the county superintendent—who is a strong advocate for separation between church and state—continually reminds those who would use the schools for religious purposes that this is against the law. Furthermore, the school system is the county's largest employer, and many self-ordained ministers work (or have close relatives who work) somewhere in the school system. At Burnsville School both janitors pastored their own congregations and had their own ministries on the side. Such dynamics have the potential—if not the demonstrated effect—of making direct frontal attacks on public school policy in Braxton County a matter to approach with some care.

Summary: The School as an Agent and Target of Social Change

Braxton County school practices and controversies obviously cannot represent the universe of rural school dynamics to be found today in the United States, but I believe that they are quite suggestive. They illustrate how at least some rural schools in isolated and economically depressed locales can explicitly and implicitly act as agents of the national culture. Disputes over the nature of work, the importance of family, and the significance of place, among others, has played heavily in rural school dynamics for over one hundred years. They certainly did and do in central Appalachia. And rural schools remain the target of state education policy: policy usually aimed at making such places even more cost-effective and more outcome-driven. I have not been able to develop such themes here, but they are central in any discussion of school consolidation (DeYoung 1995; DeYoung and Howley 1992; Peshkin 1982).

If evidence of the former claim still appears inconclusive, I will conclude this essay with part of the educational philosophy offered by the Braxton County school superintendent on such matters. Notice that these are not the words of a novice or inexperienced superintendent out of touch with his community. His 18-year tenure in Braxton makes him the second-longest-sitting county superintendent in the state, and he has won numerous civic (i.e., local) and professional (i.e., state) awards. As well, Braxton County was one of the only school systems statewide to always make its payroll during turbulent economic times of the 1980s. He is thus also celebrated as a shrewd businessman, since he has helped the local school board from having to ask for a property tax increase *and* at the same time kept the board from fiscal review by the state.

During the course of my research I had occasion to share with him the writings of various sociologists like Schwarzeller and Brown. I also passed along to him various writings extolling Appalachian virtues and culture. He was somewhat impressed with the former, but less than enthusiastic with the latter. His views of the purpose of public schooling clearly represented instrumentalist, as well as civic and nationally inspired, hopes for the educated person. They have virtually nothing to do with celebrating contemporary Appalachian culture or living in what he considers to be the past. Rather, they portray a pragmatic approach to functions of the gatekeeper on the cultural bridge of (at least) isolated and economically depressed rural schools. Although I remain torn on such issues, those who champion the function of rural schools to act as such a bridge to the national culture would likely applaud. There can be little debate that this remains a function in Braxton County, West Virginia. The county school superintendent has one grandfather critically injured in a coal-mining accident, and his father lost his job with the railroad in the 1950s. Today he both owns the "home-place" of his parents and has a doctorate. He believes mightily in the imperative of the cultural bridge, and he is not shy in proclaiming it. He shares the view of many in the county that most students must find their futures somewhere else but also that they should be prepared by the school and not abandoned to the vicissitudes of the city as some of his own relatives were:

> A school system must always try to lift hopes and dreams and raise the level of expectation of persons who are in a nonproductive mode and content with the present. Schools provide the path to new horizons and new ways of viewing [one's] surroundings. Appalachians are prone to accept their circumstances as inevitable and think they have no control over events and the future. Such a fatalistic attitude pervades many communities and families and creates dysfunctional units in modern society. . . . Education is the catalyst or the empowering elixir that allows options to be available to the "good old boy" that can free him of caretakers and transfer payments.

21

by David Sutton

There Ain't No Starbucks in Appalachia: The Election of 2000

Al Gore won the nation's popular vote by more than 500,000 votes in the 2000 election, but he fell three votes short of a majority in the Electoral College.[1] If Ralph Nader, the Green Party nominee, had not been on the ballot in Florida, it is reasonable to infer based on exit polls that Gore would have carried the Sunshine State and its 25 electoral votes, giving him a comfortable electoral college margin. But a strong case can also be made that George Bush won and Gore lost the presidency in the Appalachian region. If Gore had won the 11 electoral votes of his home state, Tennessee, or the 5 votes of traditionally Democratic West Virginia, he would have realized his long ambition of becoming president. Yet he lost both states to Bush—Tennessee by 51 to 47 percent and West Virginia by 52 to 46 percent.

Prior to November 2000, Gore had never lost an election in Tennessee. For eight years he had represented in the U.S. House a Tennessee Congressional district which included several Appalachian counties. In his last house election in 1982 in Tennessee's 6th District, Gore won without opposition. In his re-election bid for the Senate in 1990, he not only captured 70 percent of the state's votes but won in all 95 counties. As Bill Clinton's running mate in 1992 and 1996, he helped deliver Tennessee's 11 electoral college votes. Election 2000 was a different story—stunningly so. Although Gore carried 9 of the 17 counties which made up his old 6th District, he lost its overall vote by more than 25,000. He carried only 13 of the 50 Appalachian counties in Tennessee. Twelve of the 13 counties, including Smith where he spent summers as a child and still owns a house, are located in Middle Tennessee. Gore lost Tennessee by about 80,000 votes but it was the Appalachian counties which cost him his home state. An analysis of election returns in the 17 Appalachian counties which make up the 1st and 2nd congressional districts in the state's eastern end shows Bush winning by a landslide—over 100,000 votes. Gore acknowledged in his concession speech he needed to spend time in Tennessee and "mend some fences, literally and figuratively".

Gore had good reason to assume a victory in West Virginia too. For several generations, the state has been one of the Democratic Party's most solid bastions. Registered Democrats outnumber Republicans two-to-one. Prior to the 2000 election, Democrats had carried the state in three consecutive presidential elections, five of the past six, and eight of the past ten. In 1996, the Clinton-Gore ticket won 43 of the state's 55 counties. Bob Dole, the Republican nominee, won just 37% of the vote. Yet in 2000 Bush won, becoming the first Republican presidential candidate to carry the state as a non-incumbent since Herbert Hoover. He captured 41 of the counties to 14 for Gore. Nine of Gore's counties were in the 3rd Congressional District which includes most of the coal country in the southern part of West Virginia. He won these counties, however, by smaller percentages than Clinton had four years earlier, and even lost two coal counties, Raleigh and Mercer. A decline in voter turnout in the coalfields also hurt him: voter participation in West Virginia's 3rd District dropped from 62 percent in 1996 to 54 percent in 2000.

Gore's problems in Tennessee and West Virginia were mirrored throughout Appalachia. Bush swept North Carolina's 29 Appalachian counties, Georgia's 37, and Maryland's 3. He took 40 of 49 Appalachian counties in Kentucky, 25 of Ohio's 29, 32 of Alabama's 37, 12 of New York's 14, 40 of Pennsylvania's 52, and 19 of Virginia's 23 (losing only the mining counties of Buchanan, Dickenson, Russell, and Norton/Wise). An examination of a sampling of voting returns in Appalachian counties, grouped in four different categories (Democratic mining, "distressed" counties, urban areas and traditional mountain Republican counties) shows again the significant drop in Gore's percent of the vote in 2000 versus Clinton's in 1996 (see Table 1). Three "distressed" counties (Wolfe, Swain, and Pike) and two urban areas (Buncombe and Cabell) switched from the Democratic standard-bearer in 1996 to the Republican in 2000. The table also shows the Green Party Presidential candidate Ralph Nader failed to emerge as a factor in the sample counties. Indeed, the Nader impact was very small statewide in Kentucky, Virginia, Tennessee, and West Virginia. If Gore had received all the Nader vote in these states, the outcome would have been the same. In North Carolina and Georgia, Nader failed to qualify for the ballot, demonstrating how the electoral process remains far less open to minor-party or independent candidates than to those of the major parties.

Why did Gore lose in Appalachia, especially in Tennessee and West Virginia? Shouldn't voters in areas which lag behind the U.S. average in per capita income vote for the Democratic nominee? Aren't our elections and politics really fights over questions of economic distribution? In his book, *Our Country,* Michael Barone examines five decades of U.S. political history and concludes that American politics more often divides our people along cultural rather than economic lines. Barone sees politics revolving more around questions of region, race, ethnicity, religion, or personal values than about the distribution of wealth and income.[2] Some political observers viewed the 2000 election as basically a cultural struggle between the liberal city and the conservative country. As a Democratic media consultant put when assessing the prospects of Democratic candidates, "If you didn't have a Starbucks in your district, you were hurtin."[3] Clearly, lifestyle differences had a powerful impact on the way Americans voted in 2000. The largest metropolitan areas voted heavily for Gore and rural America for Bush. Frequent churchgoers blessed Bush while those who never or seldom attended religious services favored Gore. Gun owners came out for Bush and the unarmed for Gore. The exit polls left little doubt that in this election voting was a cultural act. Burt Soloman of the *National Journal* wrote that "Karl Marx, perusing the exit polls, would have gagged at the specter of self-described upper-class voters who preferred left-of-center Gore (by 56 percent to 39 percent) and working class voters who backed Gore tepidly (50 percent to 46 percent)."[4]

The 1982 Appalshop film, *The Big Lever, Party Politics in Leslie, Kentucky* portrays beautifully the cultural dimensions of voting in Appalachia. In the film, James Mosley, a member of the school board in Leslie, explains why he and his county always vote Republican:

> A lot of our people have been taught to be Republicans. The majority of our

> forefathers were Republicans. Therefore, they've told son and daughter this is their party and this has gone very much so in our churches as well. I myself am a Baptist Republican and I'm proud of it. And my folks in front of me were Baptist Republicans.
>
> Down through the years, the Republican party—and this hasn't been true in Leslie County—has always been thought of as made up of a lot of rich people and the Democratic Party has always claimed to be the working man's party. But most of us are not Republicans because we are rich because there are no rich people here.[5]

The 2000 election turned out to be a cultural referendum in Appalachia with President Clinton as the moral backdrop. Exit polls show Bush benefitted among some voters from a general dislike of President Clinton's personal misconduct. In West Virginia exit polling showed 63 percent of the voters having an unfavorable opinion of Clinton as a person and these voters broke 2 to 1 for Bush. In Kentucky 66 percent of the voters had an unfavorable opinion of Clinton as a person and Bush captured 77 percent of these voters. Gore's support for gun control also hurt him in a region where hunting is part of the culture. Legislators from the region typically earn the National Rifle Association's highest ratings. The NRA made a major push to win Tennessee and West Virginia for Bush. The organization's television ads showed Gore as an implacable enemy of gun owners and it put Charleton Heston on a gun-rights road show in these states. A few days before the election Jack Germond, a veteran columnist, said "If you turn on the car radio in West Virginia, you cannot escape those commercials of Charlton Heston sounding like God speaking for the National Rifle Association."[6] Exit polls showed residents of gun-owning households voted strongly for Bush. The pro-life movement was also active in the region. West Virginians for Life conducted their own campaign to help Bush, distributing thousands of fliers describing Bush's pro-life stance. In addition, the 31 percent of West Virginia voters who identified themselves as "white religious right" in exit polling decisively (69 percent to 29 percent) favored Bush.

Differences in environmental values too played a part in the election. Exit polls in the Mountain State showed 35 percent of voters ranked environment more important than economic growth. Gore won 60 percent of these voters. Fifty-seven percent of the respondents picked economic growth over environment and as eagerly voted for Bush (61 percent). A major controversy in the state centers on mountaintop removal and what it could mean in terms of jobs. Gore's identification with environmental issues made it easy to depict him as an environmental extremist whose agenda would devastate coal mining and power generation. Campaign fliers implied the state would lose 42,000 jobs if he won. During a campaign foray into the state, Bush was introduced by an unemployed miners' union official wearing a miner's helmet. In his comments, the union official said, "The Democratic Administration shut my mine down and I lost my job." He called Gore "an extreme environmentalist" and said if he won "he'd shut down the whole state."[7] Gore received the endorsement of the United Mine Workers of America, but observers described the union's support as tepid. In the Northern Panhandle of West Virginia, some voters viewed the Clinton-Gore administration as failing to fulfill promises to protect the steel industry against imports.

In addition to the presidential contest, there were House races, a few Senate seats, and a couple of governorships at stake in the region. In the second part of this article, I will look at some of these races to see if the electoral process in the region offers voters the opportunity on Election Day to express their concerns by choosing between at least two viable candidates representing different interests. How do elections in Appalachia measure up? To answer this question, I first examined election races in sixteen House districts in central and southern Appalachia and collected campaign spending data for the races in the 1999–2000 election cycle. The sixteen

TABLE 1 Sample County Voting Patterns

	Bush	*Gore*	*Nader*	*1996 Winner*	*Democratic Change, 1996–2000 (points)*
National Vote	48%	48%	3%	Clinton (49%)	–1
Democratic Mining					
Harlan Co., Ky.	47	51	1	Clinton (58%)	–7
Pike Co., Ky.	44	55	1	Clinton (60%)	–5
Monroe Co., Ohio	44	51	2	Clinton (56%)	–5
Buchanan Co., Va.	39	58	1	Clinton (64%)	–6
Dickenson Co., Va.	43	55	1	Clinton (57%)	–2
McDowell Co., W. Va.	32	66	1	Clinton (73%)	–7
Mingo Co., W. Va.	38	60	1	Clinton (70%)	–10
Distressed Counties					
Wolfe Co., Ky.	52	47	+	Clinton (57%)	–10
Swain Co., NC	51	48	*	Clinton (50%)	–2
Pike Co., Ohio	51	47	2	Clinton (52%)	–5
Campbell Co., Tenn.	47	52	1	Clinton (54%)	–2
Russell Co., Va.	47	50	1	Clinton (54%)	–4
Webster Co., W. Va.	46	53	1	Clinton (69%)	–16
Urban Areas					
Boyd Co. (Ashland) Ky.	48	50	1	Clinton (51%)	–1
Buncombe Co. (Asheville) N.C.	54	45	*	Clinton (46%)	–1
Hamilton Co. (Chattanooga) Tenn.	55	43	1	Dole (50%)	0
Knox Co. (Knoxville) Tenn.	58	41	1	Dole (51%)	–3
Roanoke City, Va.	44	54	2	Clinton (54%)	0
Cabell Co. (Huntington) W. Va.	51	46	2	Clinton (50%)	–4
Kanawha Co. (Charleston) W. Va.	48	50	1	Clinton (53%)	–3
Mountain Republicans					
Fannin Co., Ga.	68	30	*	Dole (49%)	–10
Jackson Co., Ky.	84	14	1	Dole (71%)	–8
Garrett Co., Md.	71	27	2	Dole (55%)	–2
Mitchell Co., N.C.	76	24	*	Dole (66%)	–1
Johnson Co., Tenn.	66	32	+	Dole (59%)	0
Floyd Co., Va.	60	34	4	Dole (48%)	–5
Grant Co., W. Va.	79	20	1	Dole (61%)	–8

Notes
*Nader was not listed on the ballot in Georgia and North Carolina.
+Nader received less than one percent of vote.

congressional districts are in West Virginia and in the Appalachian areas of Kentucky, Tennessee, Virginia, North Carolina and Georgia. The campaign spending data are compiled by the Center for Responsive Politics based on reports filed with the Federal Election Commission by candidates for congressional office. Table 2 summarizes the campaign spending data and shows the significant edge of winning House and Senate incumbents who sought re-election over their top vote-getting opponent in the 2000 election.

Fifteen of the sixteen incumbents sought re-election to the House in 2000. Only Bob Wise of West Virginia's 2nd Congressional District chose to leave the House and run for another office. Two of the incumbents seeking re-election had no opponents—Bill Jenkins in Tennessee's 1st District and Bob Goodlatte of Virginia's 6th. Tennessee's 1st is so Republican it has not elected a Democrat to the House for more than 100 years. In four congressional districts, incumbents faced only a minor-party opponent—West Virginia's 1st and 3rd Districts, Tennessee's 2nd, and North Carolina's 5th. All four incumbents won with more than 85 percent of the vote. Six of the 15 incumbents (40 percent) thus ran with no opponent or only minor party opposition. Incumbents in North Carolina's 10th and Kentucky's 5th faced only token major party opponents with basically no campaign money to spend. The challengers in the two races filed no reports with the Federal Election Commission because their campaign activity never exceeded $5,000 in either contributions or expenditures. In still two more races, the major party challengers spent so little money they could not be taken seriously—Virginia's 9th and Georgia's 9th. Congressman Rick Boucher of Virginia's 9th outspent his opponent—$676,000 to $34,000—and won 70 percent to 30 percent. Incumbent Nathan Deal in Georgia's 9th spent about $430,000 to his opponent's $70,000 and captured 75 percent of the vote. Challengers in Tennessee's 3rd, 4th and 6th Districts spent enough to make a credible campaign but were outspent by the incumbents 4 to 1 in the 3rd and 4th Districts and by more than 6 to 1 in the 6th. The three incumbents won in order of their district 64 to 35, 66 to 33 and 62 to 36.

The remaining two congressional districts —North Carolina's 11th and Georgia's 7th— demonstrate the difficulty of defeating an incumbent even when the challenger is financially competitive and the incumbent is carrying some personal baggage. Five-term Republican Charles Taylor of North Carolina's 11th found himself not only locked in battle with a well-financed quality opponent, but also plagued by a series of negative news reports. Officials in two counties in his district accused him of failing to pay property taxes and threatened garnishment of his congressional paycheck. Other controversies included questions about his business dealings in Russia and his association with a local bank being investigated by a federal grand jury for making fraudulent loans. Democrat Sam Neill, a wealthy attorney and former Chair of the University of North Carolina Board of Governors, put together a campaign which spent over $850,000. Taylor spent almost $1.6 million, making the race the most expensive congressional contest ever in western North Carolina. Neill aired ads highlighting Taylor's tax troubles and attacking the millionaire tree farmer's environmental record. Clean air became one of the campaign's hottest issues. Neill said the polluted air in the area affected the health of residents as well as the viability of the region's tourism and recreational economy. Taylor blamed air pollution from TVA plants as being responsible for most of the pollution in the mountains and noted he had submitted legislation designed to force the TVA to lessen its emissions. The Sierra Club endorsed Neill in the contest and ran a series of TV ads and distributed "voter guides" which showed the differing environmental positions of the two candidates. In the end, Taylor won 55 percent to 42 percent and carried all but one county in the district.

In only one House contest did the challenger outspend the incumbent. Georgia's 7th District featured a wealthy Democratic challenger, Roger Kahn, taking on Republican incumbent Bob Barr, one of the House's most

TABLE 2 Incumbent Advantage in Appalachia in 2000

State	*Congressional Race*	*Re-elected Incumbent Spent*	*Top Vote-getting Opponent Spent*
West Virginia	Senate	$1,045,993	$ 0[a]
	District 1	$ 335,864	$ 16,469
	District 3	$ 354,164	$ 0[a]
Kentucky	District 5	$ 459,993	$ 0[a]
Virginia	District 6	$ 395,342	$ 0[b]
	District 9	$ 676,127	$ 33,501
North Carolina	District 5	$ 421,060	$ 0[a]
	District 10	$ 266,557	$ 0[a]
	District 11	$1,555,039	$ 851,434
Tennessee	Senate	$4,628,637	$ 176,105
	District 1	$ 92,463	$ 0[b]
	District 2	$ 327,629	$ 0[a]
	District 3	$ 737,216	$ 160,076
	District 4	$1,320,669	$ 339,539
	District 6	$1,135,811	$ 174,937
Georgia	Senate	$2,533,450	$1,093,408
	District 7	$3,575,020	$3,859,860
	District 9	$ 429,979	$ 69,884

[a] A candidate triggers reporting requirements under the Federal Election Campaign Act when campaign activity exceeds $5,000 in either contributions or expenditures. The candidate filed no reports with the Federal Election Commission.
[b] Incumbent had no opposition.
Source: All the numbers in the table for the 1999–2000 election cycle are based on Federal Election Commission data released on August 6, 2001 and made available by the Center for Responsive Politics.

polarizing figures. A colleague described Barr as "never throwing a grenade when a nuclear bomb will work." Democrats had targeted Barr for defeat in 2000 for a variety of sins, including his role as a House manager in the Senate impeachment of President Clinton. Kahn, a former Atlanta liquor distributor, more than matched the financial resources of Barr by contributing $3 million of his own money to his campaign. He outspent Barr by more than $250,000 and criticized the congressman for his inattention to local problems and jobs. In his first television spot, Barr mocked Kahn who had purchased a ranch in the district but retained a residency in Buckhead, a wealthy section of Atlanta. The ad depicted a Kahn look-alike falling off a horse and a tractor and landing painfully bestride a fence while an announcer alleged the Atlanta businessman was just a "millionaire carpetbagger from Buckhead" while a parody of the song "The Great Pretender" played in the background. As in the other cases, the incumbent fought off the challenge, defeating his opponent 55 percent to 45 percent.

One of the few opportunities for a non-incumbent comes when an incumbent office-holder elects to retire or seek higher office. Open seat congressional races are especially rare in West Virginia since incumbents usually win easily and stay for decades. Rarer still is a Republican winning one of West Virginia's three House seats. The last two Republicans to represent the state in the House were each elected to a single term 20 years ago. But these unusual occurrences came about in the state's 2nd District, the least Democratic of the three. Last year nine-term incumbent Bob Wise announced for governor, providing an open seat and setting off a wild scramble to fill it. Republicans had the right candidate to make the race highly competitive—Shelley Moore Capito, a state representative and daughter of Arch Moore, a three-term governor and multi-term congressman. Although Moore was convicted in 1990 for five corruption-related felonies, he still enjoys support in the state and campaigned on behalf of his daughter. Capito's Democratic opponent, Jim Humphreys, was a state senator and a lawyer who had amassed a fortune by suing asbestos manufacturers. Humphreys' campaign spent almost $7 million in an effort to win the House seat—more than five times the $1.3 million Capito spent in the overall campaign. He contributed $6.1 million of his own money to the fight or 87.5 percent of his total campaign expenditures. While Capito spent $11.84 for each of her votes, Humphreys ended up spending $67.62 for each vote. The nonpartisan Center for Responsive Politics called the House race the third most expensive in the country in both money raised and spent. Capito edged out Humphreys 48 to 46 with a Libertarian candidate collecting 6 percent. The 2nd District contest shows that the candidate with a dollar advantage does not always win (just 95 percent of the time).

The sad fact about congressional elections today is that most are over before they start. Increasingly, the only competition in House races is for open seats. The campaign spending edge has tended to produce a permanent incumbency in most of the districts. In early August 2001, or fifteen months before the 2002 election, many House incumbents had already accumulated enormous campaign war chests to scare off potential challengers. According to reports filed by the incumbents with the Federal Election Commission, many of them finished their 2000 campaigns with a big surplus. Nick Rahall in West Virginia's 3rd District had over $1.4 million on hand; Richard Burr in North Carolina's 5th and Jimmy Duncan in Tennessee's 2nd had $900,000; Hal Rogers in Kentucky's 5th had $800,000; and Boucher in Virginia's 9th reported cash reserves of almost $600,000.

Senate races pretty much followed the House pattern. Only one incumbent senator in the region, Virginia's Charles Robb, was defeated. George Allen, a popular former Virginia governor, outspent Robb by more than $3 million and emerged the winner by a narrow margin, 52 to 48 percent. Other incumbents in the region won easily. In Tennessee's Senate contest, Senator Bill Frist, the first physician to serve in the Senate for fifty years, spent $4.6 million to his opponent's less than $200,000. Frist won 65 percent to 32 percent, losing only five of Tennessee's 95 counties. In Georgia's election contest, Senator Zell Miller, another popular former governor, outspent his opponent by almost $1.5 million. He easily defeated his opponent, 58 to 38 percent, winning all but 10 of Georgia's 159 counties.

In West Virginia, Democratic Senator Robert Byrd coasted to re-election. Even the chairman of the state's Republican Party acknowledged early in the election year, the impossibility of denying the 82-year-old Byrd his quest for an eighth Senate term. Byrd spent over $1 million while his Republican opponent David Gallaher failed to spend enough to trigger federal requirements for filing a report on expenditures. Byrd crushed his politically unknown opponent 78 percent to 20 percent. For the third time he carried all 55 of the state's counties. During the campaign, Gallaher argued that Byrd had brought nothing to West Virginia but "pork-barrel politics". Unfortunately for Gallaher, West Virginians over the years have rewarded politicians who can show them the money and Byrd, the Chair of the Senate Appropriations Committee, long ago mastered the fine art of channeling federal dollars, projects, and jobs to his state. Thus, with the exception of the Virginia contest, incumbents in Appalachia's Senate races faced weak opposition with little financial backing, leaving the senators virtually impregnable to electoral threat.

With one exception, the nation's 11 gubernatorial races ended with the same party holding power. Only West Virginia produced a change—Democratic Representative Bob Wise edged out Republican incumbent Cecil Underwood, 50 to 47 percent. Underwood, the nation's oldest governor at age 78, ran what one newspaper called "a textbook campaign—albeit out of a circa 1950's textbook."[8] Throughout the campaign, he moved from town to town bestowing more than $16 million in state largess and spending millions more on a road-paving spree. Wise called it the largest publicly financed campaign in state history. The state of the state's economy was the campaign's dominant issue. Wise argued West Virginia's economy had not advanced far or fast enough under the governor's stewardship. Underwood pointed to an overall improving state economy but said it could be even healthier if not for the uncertainty surrounding the future of the state's coal mining. He blamed the Charleston legislator for a decline in federal permitting for mountaintop removal mining, citing Wise's call in 1998 for a temporary moratorium on permitting. Wise countered that Underwood's lax regulation of the industry and his support of a bill that nearly doubles the permissible size of the mountaintop removal mine sites had ignited the fierce opposition in the state to mountaintop removal. In his television campaign, Wise aired an ad suggesting the governor, a one-time coal executive, was in the mining industry's pocket. The ad featured the governor's appearance earlier in the year on "60 Minutes", in which he stammered at length when Mike Wallace asked why coal companies had given so generously to his campaign and inauguration.

An interesting feature of the close race was the presence of a third gubernatorial candidate-Denise Giardina of the new Mountain Party. Giardina, a community activist and author whose works include "Storming Heaven" and "The Unquiet Earth", said she ran for the governorship because the coal companies are chopping down the mountains she loves. In her platform, Giardina promised to end the state's economic dependence on coal and pledged to ban mountaintop removal strip mining. She also called for taxing coal royalties and imposing an excess acreage tax on landowners with more than 10,000 acres. In a televised debate with her major party opponents, Giardina listened as Underwood and Wise paid homage to the coal industry. When her turn came, Giardina said, "If the Statue of Liberty was in West Virginia, they'd be tearing it up for scrap iron if it would create jobs."[9] Although Giardina did not carry a single county, she received over 10,000 votes statewide or two percent of the votes cast for governor. It was enough to assure the fledgling Mountain Party ballot access in the next election. The new party pledged to become the alternative to "politics as usual" in the state.

A review of the 2000 House and Senate elections in Appalachia provide support for the notion of a decline in the significance of the electoral arena as a principal means by which voters in the region may act upon their concerns or generate change. For the most part, the elections were characterized by an absence of genuine competition with the incumbents facing only token electoral challenge. Finally, the presidential contest in the nation and Appalachia reminds us that politics is not just economics. The 2000 election was more about cultural than economic factors in determining why we voted the way we did.

VI

Health and the Environment

Important work has been done toward creating an ideal of what Appalachia could be in terms of protecting both the physical environment and the spiritual, physical, and cultural quality of life for the region's people. The *Appalachian Bishops Pastoral Letter* acknowledges that, in many parts of the region, environmental destruction is a threat to the mountains as home to Appalachian people and other living creatures. Publications of the Mountain Institute describe strategies being used around the world to aid mountain people in carrying out their role as custodians of the mountain environment. Others have written on various aspects of the Appalachian environment: for example, deforestation is the theme of Ronald L. Lewis' *Transforming the Appalachian Countryside*; sustainable economic development is explored in *Appalachia, A Regional Geography: Land, People, and Development* by Karl B. Raitz and Richard Ulack; and the environmental dilemmas facing African Americans are explored in *Communities and Economic Crisis: Appalachia and the South*, edited by John Gaventa and colleagues.

There is clearly enough happening in health studies and environmental issues to deserve a separate volume. We offer only a small sampling of that literature here. Sandra Barney's article explores the introduction of modern medicine to the mountains at the turn of the twentieth century. She shows how the emerging medical profession used its relationships with capitalists and the government to gain the upper hand over practitioners of traditional medicine, "untrained" local medical doctors and chiropractors. In "Family Health in Rural Appalachian Ohio," Sharon Denham describes current perceptions and practices regarding the health of rural Appalachian families. She concludes that there is a cultural component to rural Appalachian family health, but it does not consist of sole reliance on traditional folk medicine.

Those interested in environmental activism will find information available from such groups as the Ohio Valley Environmental Coalition (OVEC) or Save Our Cumberland Mountains (SOCM). These and other groups monitor mountain top removal and other forms of surface mining, stream pollution, and air quality. An excellent resource on air pollution and tree death is the Sierra Book Club's *An Appalachian Tragedy*. It includes a chapter on the environment, "Rape of the Appalachians" by Jedidiah S. Purdy, which we have included in this section.

22

by Sandra Barney

Bringing Modern Medicine to the Mountains: Scientific Medicine and the Transformation of Health Care in Southern West Virginia, 1880–1910

The transformation of West Virginia during the industrial boom of the late nineteenth century was a complex process that affected mountain society on myriad levels. While traditional evaluations of the period focus on the invasion of outside capital and portray indigenous people as unwilling victims of powerful processes beyond their control, recent scholarship by such historians as Ronald L. Lewis, Altina Waller, and Mary Beth Pudup remind us that the introduction of modern industry and the involvement of the state in the national marketplace was a phenomenon as enthusiastically supported by some mountain residents as it was vigorously rejected by others.[1]

The diverse reactions exhibited by West Virginia residents to the introduction of modern institutions may, in part, be explained by acknowledging the competing interests of the mountain residents. For commercially ambitious mountaineers, increased involvement in the national market promised new wealth and the possibility of expanding their social and economic status. More rural residents, entrenched in traditional customs, were suspicious of the metamorphosis of the region, seeing it as an invasion of new philosophies and expectations that threatened to supplant, and eventually destroy, their way of life.[2]

The struggle between proponents of these two views was played out on a number of stages. For example, in *The Americanization of West Virginia,* John Hennen studies the confrontation that developed as new industrial interests fought to create an educational system that produced complacent workers.[3] In some public venues, like education and health care, the contest between the old way and the new was complicated by the extensive benefits modern skills and knowledge offered. The transformation of medical practice in the southern mountains of West Virginia during the late nineteenth and early twentieth centuries demonstrates that modernization promised mountain people significant fundamental improvements if they accepted their roles as patients in the new order. When these benefits alone were insufficient to convince West Virginians of the advantages of modern life, ambitious physicians turned to other institutions in an effort to induce the state's residents to embrace new methods of health care.

Medical care in rural West Virginia during much of the nineteenth century was frequently primitive and often entirely absent. Claude Frazier, a physician who was raised in the state's southern coal camps where his father was employed as a company doctor, wrote in *Miners and Medicine* that "hardy mountain people had to rely entirely on themselves in sickness and in health." Faced with little outside assistance, they trusted herbal remedies administered by family members or "mountain grannies" who were, according to Frazier, "more often than not on solid ground with their home remedies."[4]

While rural West Virginians found it difficult to secure sophisticated medical assistance before industrialization, they sought the best health care they believed possible for themselves and their families. Once convinced that a product or a procedure was efficient, many embraced it enthusiastically. In the late nineteenth century, for example, mountaineers came to share the attachment of other Americans to patent medicines, and panaceas like oil for earaches and salves for chest ailments became increasingly popular in Appalachia.[5]

Recognizing the rising reputation of these tonics and believing that the state was obligated to regulate such trade, West Virginia initiated court cases against itinerant vendors who sold "drugs or nostrums" without paying the appropriate tax. When, in 1887, J. B. Ragland arrived in Boone County selling "Ragland's Lightening Relief" at fifty cents per bottle, he found a receptive market. The local sheriff, however, arrested Ragland for failing to pay "the special tax" levied on this type of commercial activity. Ragland's arrest and conviction eventually were upheld by the West Virginia Court of Appeals and he was forced to pay the assessed penalties and taxes.[6]

West Virginians relied on tonics, home remedies, and folk healers because they had little familiarity with formally educated physicians. With minimal information about scientific medicine and limited access to trained physicians, many mountain people did not consider medical science an option.[7] In part, West Virginians distrusted educated physicians because their state government did not support a public institution to train medical doctors. Unlike its neighbors, West Virginia did not establish a state-supported medical school until well into the twentieth century. Although a "College of Medicine" functioned at West Virginia University in Morgantown from 1902 until 1911, it was never a fully accredited program and did not confer its own terminal degree. The university did not grant M.D. degrees until 1962.[8]

The state was also unable to provide vigorous supervision of medical practice in the nineteenth century. Without state supervision, legitimacy was based on personal experience and local custom and was only occasionally authenticated by formal education or training. Before the State Board of Health initiated formal procedures to license physicians in the 1880s, self-proclaimed medical practitioners often lacked even the most rudimentary knowledge and skills. The 1870 census recorded only two self-identified physicians in Logan County, for example, and neither of them was literate.[9] These early, sometimes poorly trained, practitioners continued to practice after the state government stepped in to standardize the licensing of physicians because many of them were grandfathered into the new system.[10]

The lack of formal academic education does not mean that all nineteenth-century practitioners were completely without training. Many mountain physicians gained their education through apprenticeships with older, experienced physicians, a standard practice across rural America in the nineteenth century. Emmanual Church, who practiced in

McDowell County after the Civil War, was "a typical mountaineer, uneducated—hardly able to read or write." Church studied medicine with a Dr. Crockett in Graham, Virginia, and received a county license to practice before the West Virginia State Board of Health began examining prospective doctors. Hiram Christian, who also apprenticed with Dr. Crockett, eventually set up a medical service at Sandlick in the Tug River Valley.[11] These men certainly gained significant knowledge through their empirical training, but the care they provided was sometimes inferior to that offered by their better-educated colleagues. In 1881, when a self-taught physician named Hess diagnosed smallpox as chicken pox and failed to observe the appropriate precautions, he allowed a deadly epidemic to spread through the villages of eastern Mercer County and adjacent Pocahontas, Virginia.[12]

While rural mountain residents of preindustrial West Virginia did not generally enjoy the services of formally educated physicians, their health was, in fact, remarkably well preserved by the relatively unpolluted environment in which they resided. According to Claude Frazier, rural West Virginians were generally well because "they escaped many of the big epidemics of cholera and typhoid that swept" through urban America.[13] A comparison of infant deaths in Logan County in 1872 and 1910 supports his claim. Infant mortality from contagious diseases was actually lower before the region was transformed by industrialization than it was almost fifty years later.[14]

Involvement in the national economy through the mass production of coal created new challenges to the well-being of the state's citizens whose lives and health care customs were intrinsically transformed by the industrial order. In particular, mountain residents saw their landscapes recast as new towns were formed and previously existing villages dramatically increased in size.[15] Bluefield, for example, contained 1,775 residents in 1890, but it grew to accommodate a citizenry of over 11,000 by 1910. Beckley developed from a village of 158 in 1890 to a community of over 2,000 just twenty years later. Williamson and Scarbro, unincorporated settlements in 1890, grew into towns with populations of over 1,000 residents by 1910.[16]

The workers who flocked to these towns engaged in dangerous work in the coal mines. In 1909–10, accidents killed more than one hundred miners in McDowell county, sixty in Fayette County, and nineteen in Raleigh County.[17] Non-fatal injuries were even more prevalent. McDowell County operations, clearly the most dangerous in southern West Virginia, lost 246 men in non-fatal accidents, while Fayette County followed closely with 213 during the same period.[18] To treat the injured miners and to care for their families in the newly established coal camps, companies hired physicians, who began to transform medical practice in the mountains.

Company operators employed doctors because many of the coal camps were simply too remote to attract independent physicians. According to coal archivist Stuart McGehee, "labor was scarce, and trained doctors were an incentive to attract good miners."[19] These physicians generally possessed more formal training than the empirically educated practitioners who had previously provided care to the region's inhabitants. Trained to use anesthesia, aware of the germ theory of disease, and possessing prophylaxis to prevent infection, these newly arrived physicians were well equipped to compete with the empirically trained healers who traditionally served the region.[20]

When formally educated physicians entered a community, traditional practitioners often moved to less settled areas where the competition was not so fierce. Emmanual Church withdrew from McDowell County when the coal companies arrived to the mountains of Greenbrier and Pocahontas counties where he continued his practice. Hiram Christian also left his practice when competition for patients became too intense. Rather than relocate to a more isolated area, he switched careers and set himself up as an attorney in Welch. Finding the legal profession too crowded in the McDowell County seat, he eventually moved to War, where he was the only lawyer and became the community's justice of the peace.[21]

During the late nineteenth century, the numbers of educated physicians practicing in central Appalachia increased considerably as railroads, lumber companies, and coal mines brought in well-trained doctors to care for employees and their families. The increased number of physicians in the coal regions did not reflect a rise in the aggregate number of doctors so much as a redistribution of physicians. Educated practitioners determined that mining regions were potentially lucrative locations in which to practice.

There were 1,046 licensed practitioners in West Virginia in 1890.[22] By 1900, that number had risen to 1,385, and by 1910, 1,755 individuals were licensed to practice medicine in the state.[23] In relation to its population and geographical size, however, there were relatively few physicians across the still primarily rural state. In 1890, there was on average only one licensed doctor for every 729 West Virginians. By 1900, that ratio had dropped to one per 629 citizens; in 1910, it had climbed slightly so that, theoretically, an individual physician would serve 695 patients.[24]

The coal mining counties of southern West Virginia were especially underserved by licensed physicians before the industrial boom. While Fayette and Raleigh counties in 1890 boasted a doctor-patient ratio that was only slightly higher than the state average, few other mining counties could report the same conditions.[25] In the same year, residents would have found it difficult to secure the services of a licensed doctor in Logan or McDowell counties. There was only one doctor for every 1,216 residents of Logan County and one per 1,387 inhabitants in McDowell County. Licensed physicians were true oddities in Mercer County in 1890, where the ratio was 2,000 residents per physician.[26]

However, southern West Virginia's coal mining regions experienced a dramatic rise in the number of educated physicians practicing in their communities during the years of industrial growth. In Fayette County, for example, the doctor-patient ratio decreased from 733 citizens per doctor in 1890 to 564 in 1910. In McDowell County, the patients-per-doctor statistic declined accordingly from 1,216 to 839. The most dramatic transformation of medical service occurred in Mercer County, where an influx of new physicians halved the patient-physician average in twenty years.[28]

Number of Physicians in Southern West Virginia Counties, 1881–1909

County	***1881***	***1890***	***1909***
Fayette	16	28	92
Logan	1	8	32*
Mercer	7	8	48
McDowell	1	6	57
Raleigh	12	11	28

*Includes physicians practicing in Mingo County, which was formed from Logan County in 1895.[27]

Many of these doctors worked for industrial concerns, but others were private physicians drawn by the region's economic prosperity. In the early years of the boom, however, independent physicians were often frustrated by the opposition they met from native people. Some locals, unwilling to pay scarce currency for services they distrusted, remained loyal to their traditional healers. The lack of cash also meant doctors often had to accept compensation in produce or in manual labor. Without the financial security guaranteed by company employment, some physicians gave up their practices and moved from the region, as did Dr. W. R. Iaeger, the lone physician in McDowell County before the coal boom.[29]

Even with the support of industrial interests, physicians faced resistance from workers. Company employees sometimes rejected the requirement that they contribute a portion of their salary to retain a physician when they were not actually ill. To protest this policy, they occasionally feigned illness in order to acquire medicine. After securing a desired drug, one miner examined it and declared it to be useless, protesting that the doctor offered only "soda and flour."[30]

Considering the frontier-like conditions under which doctors labored and the opposition they encountered from those they sought to cure, it is surprising that educated doctors agreed to venture into West Virginia's coalfields at all. Those doctors who did hazard the coal camps undertook the mission for a variety of reasons. For some, the mountains were home and they welcomed the opportunity to pursue their chosen profession at a time when the region's economy was booming and its growing population legitimized the establishment of medical practices in rural communities.

Dr. Wade St. Clair did not venture far from home when he opened his practice in the growing town of Bluefield in 1902. A native of neighboring Tazewell County, Virginia, he attended the University of Virginia's Medical College and completed postgraduate training at New York's renowned Polytechnic Clinic. He also pursued additional training in the hospitals of Vienna, Austria, enjoying the benefits of an outstanding education that qualified him to set up practice in any community in the United States. By selecting the Bluefield area, he maintained family connections and positioned himself to take advantage of the financial benefits offered by the expansion of the coal economy.[31]

To pursue his ambitions, St. Clair joined with an outsider, Francke Fox, to set up the Bluefield Sanitarium. Fox, who hailed from North Carolina, was the son of a physician. A graduate of the University of Virginia who completed his medical degree at New York University, Fox established his first practice in Waynesboro, Virginia, in the Shenandoah Valley. This enterprise failed to prosper, however, and in 1892, he accepted a contract with the Norfolk and Western Railroad to care for its employees in the Pocahontas Coalfield.[32]

Fox and St. Clair combined to establish Bluefield' first hospital in 1902, an institution that eventually developed into one of the most modern and progressive in the region.[33] When they expanded the facility in 1914, the doctors took advantage of the financial success achieved by St. Clair's father, a native industrialist who had profited from the region's development. Alexander St. Clair, who continued to reside on the family farm in Tazewell County, became a partner in the corporation established to fund the new facility.[34] Through their partnership, St. Clair and Fox achieved the prosperity available to those physicians, whether local or newly arrived, who exhibited a willingness to treat medicine as a commercial enterprise and to pursue financial success aggressively. The Bluefield Sanitarium grew into a thriving business that offered miners and their families unique opportunities for medical and hospital care and illustrated the creativity and vigor of educated physicians' new medical ideas.

St. Clair and Fox were only two of the hundreds of doctors who set up practices in the West Virginia coalfields during the economic upswing of the Progressive Era. An examination of the West Virginia State Board of Health's reports demonstrates that, in addition to the significant increase in the number of educated physicians who settled in the state, the geographic origins and experience of these new physicians was quite different from that of the doctors who cared for the region's inhabitants before the coal boom.

Prior to industrialization and the drive to professionalize medicine, local mountaineers pursued empirical training and used their community status to earn legitimacy as medical practitioners. With the introduction of new professional standards, state residents were disadvantaged by the lack of formal medical education in the state. As professional credentials became increasingly critical, and eventually necessary, for licensure, West Virginians were either forced to go elsewhere for their medical training or see medical positions within the state filled by outsiders.[35]

In 1883, for example, only 6 physicians who had been educated in Illinois were practicing in West Virginia; by 1903, that number had increased to 304. Only 45 doctors trained in New York practiced in West Virginia in 1883, but more than 500 of their colleagues were licensed by the state in the succeeding twenty years.[36] By 1903, in fact, medical colleges from thirty-three states and the District of Columbia were represented by graduates licensed to practice in West Virginia, reflecting the national recognition of the economic opportunity available in the coalfields.[37]

In spite of increased representation by physicians educated in other regions, the doctors who set up practices in the coalfields were most often trained in surrounding states. From July 1898 to July 1900, nearly 50 percent of those who passed the West Virginia licensing board graduated from schools in Maryland, Ohio, Kentucky, or Virginia.[38] Of the 141 who applied for licensure in 1902, 87 were from the neighboring states.[39]

Many of the physicians who moved into the coalfields were still relatively new to the practice of medicine, Dr. J. S. Malory, an 1898 graduate of the Medical College of Virginia, opened his practice in McDowell County in the same year he completed his education. His classmate, Dr. A. Irvine, set up an office in 1899 in the nearby community of Bramwell, where he soon found himself competing with Dr. W. V. Clyde, an 1899 graduate of the Maryland Medical College. Dr. W. C. Hall, who completed his training at the University of Virginia in 1897, opened an office in Welch in 1898.[40]

The careers of these young men were quite varied; some of them spent only a few years in the area, but others committed themselves and their families to the region. Many of the physicians who entered the mountains as employees of coal companies moved on rather quickly. Dr. Woods, the company doctor for the Ritter Lumber Company, served the Dry Fork and Panther Creek regions of southern West Virginia from 1900 until 1907. When the company completed its cutting in the region, he departed with the rest of the workers. Dr. Kell, an independent physician in Welch, signed on to serve as the company physician for the Lathrop Coal Company in 1913. After supervising the health of the residents of Lathrop's four mine camps, Kell eventually left the area around 1926. Dr. S. D. Hatfield, the son of feudist Anderson "Devil Anse" Hatfield, opened a medical practice in Iaeger in 1907 and remained in the community until 1920. He was the only physician in the area after outside timber companies abandoned their activities, but he too soon departed because the roads were so primitive and the people had so little money with which to pay him.[41]

Hatfield's concern about financial compensation was shared by other doctors. Traditionally, folk and herbal healers had accepted non-cash payment for their services. Educated physicians, who embraced the ideals of the market economy and ignored the mountaineers' cultural practices, dismissed these traditions and demanded that their patients recognize medical attention as a service acquired through a cash exchange rather than barter.[42]

Accustomed to relating to their healers as members of their own communities, mountain residents often failed to comprehend fully the physicians' desire for immediate compensation. Some doctors resorted to harsh tactics to teach patients their proper role in the economic relationship that supported modern medicine. A physician in southern West Virginia was called to inspect the children of an isolated mountain family. Upon arrival, he discovered they had been exposed to diphtheria and one of the children was already exhibiting symptoms. The physician, who carried with him the appropriate antitoxin, "refused to administer the medicine unless he was paid $60 in advance."[43] In his book *Coal Towns,* Crandall Shifflet related the story of a mountain family who lost their farm to a doctor who foreclosed on their home when they were unable to pay the $300 medical bill accrued by a dying grandparent.[44]

Since medicine was frequently an uncertain enterprise, some physicians pursued alternative or related endeavors to augment their incomes. Like Drs. Fox and St. Clair in Bluefield, a number of physicians opened hospitals that both supplemented their incomes while also providing their communities with in-patient facilities.[45] Other physicians scrambled to acquire government positions in state institutions or as county public health administrators, a reflection of government's increasing reliance on educated physicians as well as the doctors' own desire for a secure income.[46]

Finally, many physicians invested in industrial enterprises. A significant number of the investors in the Williamson-Thacker Coalfield were physicians. An assembly that included the future governor of West Virginia,

Dr. Henry D. Hatfield, these men resided in communities such as Bramwell and Bluefield and used their profits as physicians to finance their business ambitions.[47]

Some physicians invested in industrial ventures as a way to diversify their earnings, but the vast majority of state doctors relied upon the revenue they generated through their professional activities. To protect that income, educated physicians agitated for the increased regulation of the practice of medicine and the elevation of their professional ideals. For many, if not most, physicians, the desire to heighten their professional status was a complicated one founded on both philanthropic concern and economic ambition. While they genuinely believed the care they provided was the standard against which all others failed, they also stood to profit by eliminating competition from traditional healers, empirically trained physicians, and various medical sects who gained prominence in the late nineteenth century. In order to protect the public and to better their social and economic conditions, West Virginia doctors followed the lead of the American Medical Association, a professional alliance founded in New York state in 1846, and organized coalitions to improve their status and protect the public health by elevating their principles of practice above traditional healers and sectarian competitors.[48]

The American Medical Association, and its state and local components, was founded to protect the precepts of clinically educated physicians who embraced allopathy, the principle that illness must be treated by medicines or procedures intended to terminate the symptoms of a disease. Physicians who embraced this axiom sought to uncover treatments through medical research and clinical inquiry and, over time, discovered the nucleus of information that now supports contemporary medicine.[49] While allopaths were recognized as "regular" physicians who set the standard of medical practice, they were frequently challenged in the late nineteenth and early twentieth centuries by competitors such as homeopaths, osteopaths, and chiropractors.[50] To combat those rivals and to elevate the principles of scientific medicine, allopaths around the United States joined county and state affiliates of the American Medical Association.[51]

West Virginia physicians formed a state medical organization in Wheeling in 1867. The Medical Society of West Virginia was the last state medical association to be instituted in the nation at that time. Like their colleagues elsewhere, state physicians adopted the American Medical Association's code of ethics and formally allied themselves with the national association.[52] As recent converts to the drive for medical organization, state physicians were quite vociferous in proclaiming the sanctity of their profession. According to the booklet they published to celebrate their society's organization, "the true physician . . . stands upon a lofty eminence, clothed with the authority of science to interpret nature." The author of the pamphlet proclaimed that "no calling represents more fully or more honorably than ours, the intellectual tendency of the times in which we live," and finally declared that "a pervading sense of progress is everywhere at work in the medical world."[53]

In spite of its declarations, West Virginia's medical society was inferior to its neighbors both inside and outside the region. When Dr. C. H. Maxwell, a Morgantown physician, was appointed to represent the West Virginia society at the Pennsylvania Medical Association's meeting in 1907, he was more than a bit chagrined by the distinct differences he noted between his home society and that of the Pennsylvania physicians.

According to his calculations, the Pennsylvania Medical Association had enrolled more than 50 percent of the state's physicians, while West Virginia had recruited only 37 percent of those practicing within its borders. Local chapters were active in sixty-five of Pennsylvania's sixty-seven counties, but twenty of West Virginia's fifty-five counties contained no organized medical association.[54] These comparisons embarrassed Maxwell, who recognized their detrimental consequences for the advancement of allopathic ambitions in the state. Without a strong medical association, allopathic physicians were stymied in their attempts to regulate the practice of medicine. He asserted that the inability of the state's physicians to seize control of the definition and regulation of medicine had adverse consequences for the profession as well as for the population of the state. Maxwell warned that West Virginians had not "been trained," and that they had not been "taught" that communicable disease was a "shame." Having failed to "create the proper public sentiment," doctors had not yet achieved full control of the public's expectations about the practice of medicine.[55]

Maxwell's evaluation reveals that, while formally educated physicians had acquired significant prominence in the medical marketplace, they had not yet acquired the ability to define medical care or to secure a monopoly over its delivery. These ambitions had to be achieved to support their claim to sole professional legitimacy and scientific knowledge. To that end, doctors pursued continued patronage and support for fledgling county medical societies and the creation of a closer alliance with the government.

Educated, allopathic physicians needed government support because they faced strong competition from other practitioners. Still new to their role in the modern medical system, many citizens persisted in their reliance upon traditional medicine as well as on the promises of such sectarian practitioners as homeopaths and chiropractors. Physicians looked to the government to aid them in their battle against the popularity of these alternative sources for health care.

Sectarian healers vehemently challenged the state association's campaign for the passage of laws regulating medical practice. In addition to rejecting the allopaths' insistence upon a monopoly over legitimate medical knowledge, sectarians also disputed the state government's right to interfere in their pursuit of a medical career. Legal challenges to West Virginia's medical practice law were pursued all the way to the United States Supreme Court which, in *Dent* v. *West Virginia,* upheld the state's right to regulate and control the practice of medicine.[56]

Although the Supreme Court affirmed the government's prerogative to license medical practitioners, sectarians also challenged the composition of the state's medical examining boards. The West Virginia Public Health Council, also known as the Board of Public Health, promulgated public health policy as well as examining and licensing fledgling physicians. The multiple duties demanded of the board were quite exhausting, but the state's recognition that regulating the practice of medicine was a component of its mandate to protect the public good significantly boosted allopathic physicians. Since allopaths dominated the board, they gained significant prestige and reinforcement for their claim that they alone were capable of dispensing medical care. Members of the state society actively opposed efforts to separate medical examination from public health supervision. They feared that defining these duties separately would reduce allopathy to just another school of medical practice and might proscribe their attempts to achieve a monopoly over the public definition of legitimate medical care.[57]

With the *Dent* decision and their ability to maintain control over the State Board of Health, educated, allopathic physicians celebrated a critical victory in the struggle to protect and elevate their status. The allopaths who controlled the medical society and the Board of Public Health were secure in their ability to deny legitimacy to traditional and sectarian competitors. This success, made possible by the alliance of private physicians, organized medicine, and the government, completed the process begun during the late nineteenth century when educated physicians began streaming into West Virginia seeking to profit from the economic boom.

The arrival of large-scale industrializing forces in West Virginia in the late nineteenth century prompted a transformation of the state's medical system. Physicians, educated in clinical programs and trained in allopathic procedures, moved into Appalachia as investors opened the region to development. Like many of the capitalists who invaded the mountains seeking marketable resources, these physicians believed that they were bringing progress to a retarded region too long isolated from the modern world.[58]

To protect their professional standards and to prevent unqualified practitioners from preying upon the community, West Virginia's doctors emulated their colleagues at the national level and organized state and, eventually, local medical societies. In the early stages, these associations were quite fragile and doctors were challenged to recruit and maintain membership from the often isolated physicians who served the coal camps.[59]

While the medical associations struggled to gain legitimacy, doctors also reached out to form an important alliance with government. At both local and state government levels, academically trained physicians encouraged the state to take an active role in the regulation of medicine. They insisted that the government satisfy its duties as protector of the public good and prevent substandard healers from endangering the health of the state's citizens.

Through their association with the capitalists who acquired control of many of the region's resources, the promotion of their own professional societies, and their affiliation with the government, allopaths succeeded in creating powerful networks that elevated their professional model while denigrating other medical philosophies. These nascent alliances did not mature until the first decades of the twentieth century, but nineteenth-century physicians laid important groundwork for the creation of institutions and associations that shaped both the definition as well as the delivery of medical care in West Virginia throughout the twentieth century.

23

by Sharon A. Denham

Family Health in a Rural Appalachian Ohio County

A broad body of literature supports the need to better understand: (a) the ways families define their health, (b) the manner in which health practices are incorporated into family life, and (c) the effect of larger systems on family health. While strong evidence exists that health is mostly learned and experienced within a family context (Bomar 1990; Harkness and Super 1994; Keltner 1992), few family-focused investigations of family health have been completed (Backett 1992; Gillis 1991; Thomas 1990). The contextually embedded patterns of family health have also rarely been examined (Backett 1992; Duffy 1988; Gillis 1991; Ransom 1986; Thomas 1990). Contextual embeddedness is a term used in this study to describe the family's nested status within the larger community and the effects of larger systems on family health. The embedded context, which includes peer relationships, institutional settings such as work and school, familial support systems, social, political, and economic environment, and cultural perspectives, has a dynamic influence upon the family (Bronfenbrenner 1979; Garbarino 1992) and is assumed to influence family health.

Family health though often discussed, is a poorly understood phenomenon. It has seldom been studied in the Appalachian population, and cultural and/or ecological determinants have rarely been investigated. The purpose of this study was to describe how rural Appalachian families with preschool children define and practice their health within their contextually embedded households. An investigator modification of Bronfenbrenner's (1979) ecological framework was used to conceptualize family health and guide the study.

The literature has strongly linked close kin networks and culture as influencing factors for individual lifeways. Previously, stereotypical themes about the Appalachian subculture have been discussed as if they definitively characterize regional persons. The findings in this study identified some themes relevant to family health that seem to refute previously reported cultural notions about Appalachians. Differences in the sociodemographic factors of parental age, employment and family economics, education, and availability of resources were not found especially influential in the ways family health was defined and practiced within the community families. Unique personal and family characteristics appeared to be more explanatory of differences found than the sociodemographic factors. However, the

Source: From *Journal of Appalachian Studies,* 2:2, Fall 1996 by Sharon Denham.

abiding presence of extended family, a common cultural and historical experience, and living in a shared contextual environment evoked similarity in health concerns.

The Ethnographic Family Health Study

Meigs County is a rural Appalachian community located in the southeastern region of Ohio and is considered a distressed area by the Appalachian Region Commission. In 1990, the population of the county was 22,987 with a 1989 per capita income of $10,787, considerably less than the state per capita income of $16,462. The county's poverty rate in 1970 was 23.8 percent, declined to 17.1 percent in 1980, and increased to 26.9 percent in 1994. During the 1995–96 school year, one school district had a 48.3 percent eligibility for the free lunch program while two other school districts reported 78.3 percent and 72.3 percent eligibility. Poverty in this region resulting from diminished employment opportunities has been considered worse than it was two decades ago.

Eight Meigs County families (n=39) participated in the study. Key informants helped in selecting families who showed diversity in economic status, employment type, neighborhood locations, and marital and sanguineous relationships. A criterion for selection of family participants was their inter-generational roots in the community. At least one parent in each family was identified as a third generation community resident and several parents traced their ancestry back five generations.

A series of four taped and transcribed semi-structured interviews lasting from one to two hours was conducted over several weeks with multiple members from each family participating in their homes. Additionally, community informant interviews (n=15) provided information about the community and the embedded context of family health. Additional data was gained through field experiences in the community and use of local source materials. Field notes were kept to describe the observed experiences and a journal kept to record the research experience. Qualitative software was used to thematically code the complex family data with continuous comparative methods used during the cross-case analysis (Spradley 1980; Yin 1994).

Family Health Definition

Ideas about family health were initially identified in terms of personal meaning for individual family members. When asked to describe family health, parents were not immediately able to identify their beliefs and values in a definitional sense, but readily recalled behaviors and routines. Parents identified themes related to individual health that they learned in their family of origin and were now intentionally and unintentionally teaching their own children.

In this study, individual health had five defining characteristics. First and foremost, it was explained as the absence of illness and disease. One father explained: "Health to me is . . . is your body doing what it's always done ever since you were born . . . performing the way it should and not being sick all of the time." A second characteristic of health was identified as an active engagement with life. A father explained: "Ya gotta basically just stay fairly active. You're not going to be a healthy person if you just lay around and don't do anything." Thus, keeping active and able to perform usual life activities was a defining health characteristic.

Next, individuals talked about the importance of maintaining a life balance, keeping things in check, and not being swayed too quickly to try everything heard through the media. For these families there was an openness to new ideas, but conservatism in making changes. Individuals talked about the need to sustain their personal resilience or to take care of themselves. Finally, they felt personally accountable for their health, but often identified an inability and/or inconsistency in matching actual health practices with their ideals.

A final characteristic of individual health in these families was a holistic view that health extended beyond the physical and included relationships, emotional stressors, and spiritual dimensions. Parents believed these dimensions were interconnected, but had difficulty explaining these connections. For study participants, health was viewed as a means to an end and not a goal in itself. Only one parent alluded to the concept of optimal health as part of his personal health paradigm. Participants mostly described individual health as staying free from illness in order to work and actively engage in usual daily lifeways.

Family health was described contextually by the combined health status of the individual members, their relationships with one another, and recurrent family themes about health related beliefs, knowledge, and behaviors. Questions about family health were initially answered with responses about illness conditions of individual members. However, families with members who had chronic illnesses or children with developmental disabilities did not perceive themselves as unhealthy families. In addition to member health status, family health was largely defined through cooperation, communication, and caregiving.

Cooperation was described as the relational interactions of family members to achieve what is agreed to be the desired and achievable health status for the individual members of the family. It should be noted that this may not be universally agreed upon within the family and the dissenting person may be the one other members are cooperatively attempting to help or change. These families rarely pre-planned their cooperative family health efforts. The dynamic interactions evolved as part of a social construction of family health that included their revered health beliefs, health knowledge, and health behaviors.

Communication was another concept found vital to the family health construct in these families. Communication was the means for: (a) teaching children values and beliefs about health, (b) developing member and family behaviors that provided structure for family health, and (c) establishing familial coping patterns for handling health related information and experiences confronting the family. Communication was affected by the family's relational interactions and was difficult to separate from cooperation.

Caregiving was the final concept identified and was mostly perceived as a female role. The mother was the primary health care decision maker, director, provider, and coordinator of health. The caregiving role had three separate implications for family health. First, it entailed managing the health concerns relevant to the family's heritage and biological concerns. Second, it included nurturing the routine health behaviors that formed the family health construction. The third caregiving area involved the negotiation of the boundary permeability between the family and its context. Media consumerism by participants meant continual bombardment by information that both strengthened and threatened the enculturated family views. An important caregiving task for the families was making sense of this multi-modal affront. The family health paradigm of the encultured family was affected by its embedded context and resulted in a dynamic, but contiguous, construction of family health.

Cultural Components of Family Health

In many respects, identifying the cultural themes related to family health may have been the most difficult part of the analysis. Separating the assumptions of a subculture from those shared with the larger culture is difficult when the ideological views are not necessarily distinctly different.

A number of cultural themes, related to family health were identified in this study. For years, people have associated the term "fatalistic" with the Appalachian culture and used it to imply a sense of life predetermination. Although fatalism may be evidenced in some Appalachian populations, it was not identified in this study related to family health. Families demonstrated a strong sense of living in the present as praxis, an instrumental means for coping with their health needs, which often meant contentment and thankfulness for their context. This reality held true even when family experiences were less than desirable or when faced with multiple health problems.

For instance, one family had three children with special health care needs that presented daily demands and frequent crises, but the family has learned to live within the present context of their dilemma. The mother explained:

> You never know what's gonna happen. In any life . . . when you have three special need kids . . . you never know! I think we're always wondering what we could have done . . . or what we didn't do. . . . But it's just part of everyday life now. We ain't got time really to sit and wonder what we could of done. I've learned to live with it a lot easier.

Some might describe this as fatalistic, but this mother and family were proactively responding to their children's needs and earnestly seeking the best medical and health care available. She later said: "Yeah, today's a healthy day. I think every day that goes by and we don't have to run to the doctor [is a healthy day]." For this family, living in the present meant treasuring the good days, but did not imply accepting life as predetermined or unchangeable. This mother frequently negotiated with health care providers to identify and obtain optimal health services for her children and seldom accepted information without ascertaining its validity.

A mother in another family said: "I've always been somebody that whatever will be will be. I try not to worry about it much!" Again, the words may sound as if she were reactive to life, but in reality this pregnant mother was taking charge of her circumstances, aware of current health issues and risks, and obtaining timely prenatal care. A father in another family said, "You just got to live your life . . . can't worry about everything. You just gotta live day by day, 'cause you just can't look into a crystal ball and see where you're go'en." The words may sound fatalistic, but a contextual view of the dialogue identified a family who demonstrated a life contentment while using a practical daily caregiving approach to increasing members' health and coping with life's unexpected stressors. Family health for these families was taken care of on an as needed basis and was not viewed as a distant goal to achieve.

Living in the present for these families described an optimism and hopefulness in living with the unpredictability of life and coping with its randomness. Their lifeways demonstrated a peaceful acceptance, caring for the troubles of today, but not prematurely fretting over tomorrow's woes. However, this acceptance was not identified as an inability to determine or control their lifeways. Living in the present sometimes meant caution and slower movement toward making changes, but these families were neither tied to folkways and home remedies nor resistant to modern health care practices.

Sense of place and extended family were closely aligned for these families. Several families lived on land previously owned by their family and two of the families lived within extended households. Of the fifteen parents in this study, six always lived in Meigs County, six lived away for a brief time, and one grew up across the river in West Virginia. All but two parental figures in the study had extended family members within twenty minutes of their homes. Families were ambivalent about close kin networks because they provided both support and stress. Having family close meant strong connections with the past, but exposure to the popular media and availability of transportation meant they were keenly aware of beliefs, knowledge, and experiences different from those of their families of origin.

Living in the midst of a continuing past and an evolving future meant sometimes feeling conflicted when alternative ideas and experiences were encountered. Families were exposed to the same news and messages as those in the rest of the nation, but choosing differently from their kin patterns sometimes meant rebuff from extended family members and accompanying stress. Families were not stuck in a time warp. Grandparents, siblings, and other kin informed the families about health information learned through the media or care providers. All families had complied with child immunization, taken their preschool children for well baby checks, and used car seats for their younger children. Health care was sought from a variety of practitioners and participants had a broad base of health knowledge similar to the mainstream culture. One family recently obtained the chicken pox vaccine for their preschool son, a vaccine only made available in the nation during the previous six months. For some participants, close kin networks implied a need to check with extended family before making nonemergency choices, slowness in taking action when situations were not perceived as life threatening, and a preference for seeking care close to home. However, some traveled distances for specialists or to receive health care from other practitioners when they were dissatisfied with local providers.

Individualism and a sense of self-sufficiency came through clearly in family conversations; some community informants referred to this as "Appalachian pride." Parents strongly validated a need to take care of themselves and their families. Self-reliance often resulted in the use of over-the-counter medications, sharing of prescription drugs ordered for other family members, and a "wait and see" attitude prior to seeking expert consultation about health needs. Family members varied in their degree of individualism; while some were reserved about seeking care, others readily sought services.

Male dominance was frequently discussed by community informants as characteristic of family relationships, but less frequently suggested by the study families. The presence of a stranger may have altered family behaviors and the interview content about family health may not have aroused discussion of issues where male dominance might be identified. However, when the concern was family health, the female in all families had the dominating role.

Clearly, mothers were dominant when it came to making health decisions, assuming responsibilities for family health matters and teaching children about health behaviors. In some families, the mother also encouraged and arranged for the father's needs. Although males contributed to health beliefs and practices in their families, it was largely the female who established the patterned health behaviors for the family. Many of the females checked with their partners, but this was most apt to take place when health needs meant going outside the home for services, involved nonemergency situations, and involved dietary patterns. Meeting the daily caregiving health needs of the family members was dominated by female roles and fathers strongly relied upon their wives' decision making and skills.

Several community informants discussed the stereotype that persons in these communities are mostly non-confrontational. The data did not fully support this idea, but suggested rather that this behavior may be found within certain individuals and families without necessarily being a subculture characteristic. Mothers in this study appeared to reflect others in the nation who have been exposed to the same feminist ideas. All mothers in the study demonstrated behaviors and discussed events where they confronted family members and health care providers when they were concerned about family health needs. It would be wrong to consider these mothers as submissive, subservient or non-confrontational when it comes to individual or family health. Instead, the data identified them as advocates and risk takers.

Cleanliness may seem to be a strange way to describe family culture, but this value came through so clearly in the data that it was viewed within the cultural context. All of the families, without exception, when asked to describe what was essential in making their families healthy identified cleanliness or personal hygiene. They remembered this as an important area of childhood learning and emphasized teaching hygiene to their own children. Perhaps the importance here is related to a reverse ethic which identified being dirty as less healthy, illness producing, and something to avoid. These findings may reflect a national bent toward sexual attractiveness linked to personal hygiene and concerns with communicable social diseases. However, an emphasis on cleanliness within this community may also imply revulsion against the unkempt appearance of some area welfare recipients.

The final area related to culture that emerged from the data was related to faith, religion, or spirituality. Many residents in the community evidence a history of religious roots, but attendance and membership may be minimal. In this study, only two families regularly attended church, in three families the mother regularly took the children, one family had fairly consistent church attendance but not necessarily as a unit, one mother rarely attended because of the difficulty in readying children, one mother never attended but thought it would be a good idea, and three fathers never attended. However, family members who neither considered themselves religious nor church attenders talked about God and faith being related to health. Participants ascribed both health and illness to God, and faith was perceived as beneficial for overcoming health concerns. Participants stated that they questioned God when health dilemmas occurred, but also recognized God as a source of good health. Faith, God, and church members were viewed as supports and often relied upon as sources for health related questions.

Although these families may be different from other community families, the findings have implications for those interested in family health. First, family health has defining characteristics unique to individual families, but commonalities among families can be identified and could be used for family health assessment and intervention. Second, family health has multiple determinants and practitioners need to use holistic and ecological models to identify and address its complex context, function, and structure. Third, families' embedded context has important effects upon children's health learning, family health practices, and health/illness of the members. However, care should be taken to not prematurely ascribe stereotypical cultural views to family health. For instance, five families in the study either fell below or near the poverty level and four families received entitlements based upon the presence of preschool children in the home, but family health was found to be similar to those families with higher incomes and extensive health insurance. Assumptions about individual and family health based upon Appalachian stereotypes need to be re-examined.

Implications for Future Research

This study has implications for family health research. Additional studies about embedded families are needed to more clearly identify which determinants most clearly predict family health. Second, research about family health in Appalachian populations should be founded in an agenda based upon cultural strengths rather than unconfirmed stereotypes. Third, longitudinal studies need to examine familial patterns of health over time to identify outcomes when members are exposed to new values, information, and experiences. Finally, family health in other subcultures should be examined to identify if cultural stereotypes are tenuous when family health is so closely linked to the embedded context (e.g., media, policy, politics) and mainstream society.

24

by Jedediah S. Purdy

Rape of the Appalachians

Driving his battered sedan through Blair, West Virginia, a cigarette dangling between thin fingers, James Weekley passes among ghosts. "There stood three houses," he says, gesturing at a flat, grassy area below the narrow, two-lane road, "and across the creek were two more. They sold a year back, then they burned." Five years ago, this small town, strung along a creek bottom between two mountains, had stores, an elementary school, and twice the 80 families who now live here. Then the Dal-Tex coal company began strip-mining Blair Mountain. Since then, the community has been darkened by dust storms, battered by flying rock, and shaken by dynamite blasts. Every month more residents sell their homes to the company and move out. When the job is done, not much will be left of the town or the mountain.

Coal mining is an old story in Appalachia, but Blair has been claimed by a new kind of boom. Today's mining is driven by mountaintop removal, a method of strip-mining that does just what the name suggests. On a mountaintop mine, a company blasts and bulldozes hundreds of vertical feet from a cluster of connected peaks, turning them into a single field of pulverized rock. The bulldozers push millions of tons of earth and stone into the surrounding valleys, filling them hundreds of feet deep. These "valley fills" sometimes run for several miles. Mountains here are small and valleys narrow, and in the wake of a mountaintop mine they blend into a uniform, stony terrain utterly unlike the lush, rugged West Virginian slopes. The hardwood forests of the region do not return to the mine sites. The land mainly supports tough grasses and scrub trees.

Coal companies have strip-mined 500 square miles of West Virginia since 1981, and the pace has increased rapidly. In the past three years, the state's Division of Environmental Protection (DEP) has authorized 27,000 acres of new mountaintop mining, after permitting only 9,800 acres throughout the 1980s. The largest existing mine will cover perhaps 20,000 acres before it closes early in the next century, and mines on the same scale are becoming more common. Valley fills have buried 469 miles of streams in five southwestern watersheds and covered an estimated 700 miles of streams across the state.

Most of West Virginia's mountaintop mines are probably illegal. But the DEP has continued to authorize them, with the support of the federal Office of Surface Mining (OSM). Since Congress passed strip-mining legislation in 1977, state and federal regulation has presented a Rake's Progress of good law gone bad under hostile or indifferent administrations. Meanwhile, no one knows the

Source: Reprinted with permission from *The American Prospect,* Volume 9, Number 41, November 1–December 1, 1998. The American Prospect, 5 Broad Street, Boston, MA 02109.

ecological consequences of pushing tens of thousands of acres of mountains into hundreds of miles of streams. And the strip-miners are not waiting to find out.

The Stripping Boom

Although almost invisible to the public eye, the coal industry is booming as never before. Coal produces 56 percent of American electricity, and its cost per unit of energy is lower than that of any other fossil fuel. U.S. coal production went over a billion tons for the first time in 1990 and has stayed there in each year since 1994. The average coal miner has tripled his productivity in the past decade.

Those gains come at the cost of wholesale changes in the coal industry. Although dust-coated miners in headlamps still emerge every evening from mines in West Virginia, Kentucky, and Pennsylvania, their numbers have been dwindling for decades. Increasingly they are replaced by bulldozers, explosives, and the Goliaths of the coalfields, earth-moving machines that stand 20 stories high and can pick up 130 tons of dirt and rock with one bite of their shovels. The numbers are striking. Coal employment has declined from 163,000 to 85,000 nationwide in the past decade, and from 29,000 to under 20,000 in West Virginia—down from almost 60,000 20 years ago. In 1948, before the advent of strip-mining, West Virginia alone had more miners than work in the entire nation today.

The heart of the new coal industry is strip-mining and the most efficient form of stripping is mountaintop removal. Strip-mining now accounts for 62 percent of U.S. coal production and one-third of West Virginia's. Nationally, the average stripminer produces three times as much coal as his underground counterpart.

Dropping prices and mounting competition have pushed Appalachia's coal operators toward stripping. The price of coal has fallen steadily from over $30 per ton in 1981 to just over $20 today, thus intensifying the pressure to increase productivity. Western miners have increased their share of national production by more than 10 percent since 1987, benefiting from thick, easily accessible coal seams, and increasing the squeeze on the thin seams and steep mountains of the East. New federal regulations have also increased the value of West Virginia's hard to access coal deposits. The 1990 Clean Air Act mandates that power plants use coal low in sulfur, because high-sulfur coal is the chief cause of acid rain. Southern West Virginia is rich in low-sulfur coal, which is often distributed in thin horizontal veins, like icing in a layer cake, through hundreds of vertical feet of sandstone, earth, and shale. These thin deposits are difficult to mine by traditional methods, but they are ready-made for mountaintop removal.

Law and Outlaws

Strip-mining in the United States is governed by a 1977 federal law, the Surface Mining Control and Reclamation Act (SMCRA), called "SMACK-ra" by those who work with it. The act was passed after six years of congressional battles and vetoes by President Ford in 1975 and 1976. Its real origins, though, lie in eastern Kentucky, where strip-mining exploded in the 1960s without meaningful regulation, and people whose property lay over coal owned by mining companies found their fields, woods, and family cemeteries destroyed without recompense. (Ownership divided between minerals and surface land has been common in Appalachia since a wave of speculators visited the region at the beginning of this century, buying mineral rights from often illiterate landholders for a tiny fraction of their value.)

In incidents that became folk legends, elderly mountaineers threw themselves to the ground in front of approaching bulldozers, sometimes shaming the strippers into withdrawing. Others broke into the dynamite sheds at stripping sites and used the stolen explosives to sabotage bulldozers and backhoes. At the same time, Kentucky lawyer Harry M. Caudill won national attention with powerful histories of the coal industry's presence in his state, including the bleak, elegiac masterpiece *Night Comes to the Cumberlands.*

By 1972, coalitions of local residents, VISTA staffers fresh from college, and members of the region's nascent environmental movement were agitating across Appalachia for an end to stripping. Then a dam built of mining detritus burst, sending a wall of black water down Buffalo Creek, in Logan County, West Virginia. One hundred and twenty-four people died in the flood. Now no serious person could any longer pretend that a scarred landscape was the only price of stripping.

Strip-mining legislation had already been introduced in Congress by Ken Heckler, a flamboyant, idealistic representative from southern West Virginia. From the beginning, Heckler wanted to ban stripping outright and grant enforcement responsibility to the Environmental Protection Agency (EPA). After the Buffalo Creek disaster, the Nixon administration introduced a weaker bill that would have given states chief responsibility for regulation, overseen by the Bureau of Mines—then widely considered a political arm of the mining industry. Representative Morris Udall of Arizona engineered a compromise that included strong federal standards, allowed strip-mining under restricted conditions, and placed the law in the hands of the new Office of Surface Mining in the Department of Interior. The legislation passed.

Heckler opposed the compromise, warning his colleagues, "You know the economic and political history of this nation. You know the realities of economic and political pressure. You know that neither a State legislature nor any administrative authority can stand up against the wealth and power of a dominant economic group."

Indeed, "King Coal" had long ruled West Virginia politics, with coal companies on the right and the equally imperial United Mine Workers of America (UMWA) on the left. The coal industry owns half of the land in the Appalachian coalfields and as much as 75 percent in West Virginia's top coal-producing counties. In the early 1970s, a study found that every governor and president of the state senate in the previous 20 years had worked in the coal industry before taking office, afterward, or both. Current Governor Cecil Underwood, who had long worked in the coal industry, received more than 20 percent of his campaign contributions and 30 percent of the cost of his million-dollar inauguration from coal.

An Outlaw Industry

Hechler predicted that as long as the coal industry dominated Appalachia, an inch of regulatory leeway would rapidly become miles of stripped land. From the beginning, West Virginia's regulations were peppered with omissions and innovative interpretations. Newly hired field inspectors were introduced to this "local version" of the law and in some cases did their work unaware that they were in violation of actual law. Patrick McGinley, a West Virginia University law professor and environmental litigator, recalls challenging illegally issued permits during the 1980s: "Virtually everything the law required was not being done. I had the agent who had issued the permits read the relevant section of SMCRA aloud to me. He said 'I've never seen that before.'"

Under a corrupt governor who would later land in federal prison, coal companies went on a binge in the 1980s, ignoring basic environmental standards and then ducking reclamation requirements by declaring bankruptcy and reconstituting themselves under different names. Investigative reporters, who did much of the enforcement agencies' job in this period, found multiple "companies" working in single underground mines and parent corporations spawning scores of short-lived offspring.

West Virginia's environmental regulators have shaped up considerably since then, but the DEP has kept the habit of collaborating with the coal industry, producing a tangled map of discrepancies between state practices and the language and intent of federal law. Most dramatically, SMCRA requires that after stripping, a company must restore the disturbed land to its "approximate original contour"—that is, put it back more or less the way it was. According to the original federal act, companies can be exempted from this requirement only when the leveled land is put to a new, productive, and valuable "commercial or recreational" use. The thrust of the law is that mountaintop removal might be an acceptable shortcut along the road to certain forms of economic development, but that otherwise mountains should be left as they are.

Yet most mountaintop jobs leave landscapes undeveloped and isolated. State agencies in Virginia and Kentucky permit mountaintop removal for "wildlife and forest management," a category broad enough to catch any swath of land where trees might someday grow or deer browse. West Virginia counts a company's promise to open exhausted mining sites to hunters and fishermen as sufficient to make the land a "recreational facility." But neither approach is more than a dodge since hardwood forests refuse to grow on strip-mined land: eliminating forests and streams does not improve wildlife habitat.

Even so, enforcement has been as lax as the state regulations are dubious. Ken Ward, Jr., a reporter with the Charleston Gazette, examined 81 permits for mountaintop removal operations and found that 61 did not include exemptions from the approximate original contour requirement. That is, 75 percent of the operations were illegal on their face. The DEP countered by arguing that since "contour" means shape, a change in altitude is irrelevant. That is to say, a company that drops a mountain 550 feet but leaves the bottom somewhat rugged has restored the site's approximate original contour. Removing a mountaintop, then, does not constitute mountaintop removal.

A suit now being prepared for the Highlands Conservancy, a West Virginia environmental group, requests that the state's regulation of mountaintop removal be brought back into sync with federal law. Beyond the approximate original contour question, the suit reminds the court that SMCRA requires a comprehensive study of how strip-mining affects water systems, which has not been conducted. The suit also asserts that the federal Clean Water Act bars the burial of steams with waste from mine sites. If upheld, this objection will mean that valley fills are simply illegal. Moreover, while SMCRA requires that a company post sufficient insurance or collateral to clean up the site should it go bankrupt or simply abscond, low-ball estimates and lax enforcement have left bond amounts well below the sums required to clean up abandoned sites. The OSM estimates the deficit at $60 million. Patrick McGinley puts it at ten times that amount.

Looking for the Feds

All of this takes place under the oversight of the Office of Surface Mining, the agency charged with ensuring that federal law is strictly enforced through a combination of field inspections and annual reviews of state programs. It's a demanding charge. SMCRA was an unusual piece of legislation. It contained elaborate requirements rather than broad guidelines for state programs, and mandatory citations and punishments for any violation. These stipulations were an acknowledgment that corrupt collaboration between government and industry was the rule in the coalfields, and that only strong national standards could end that pattern.

The program began auspiciously. President Jimmy Carter's OSM hired administrators and field inspectors who were known for their commitment to enforcement. Inspectors shut down illegal mines and brought irresponsible operators to heel, over sometimes violent resistance. A few inspectors were taken hostage by entire crews of angry miners.

Then, after Ronald Reagan's election in 1980, things began to fall apart. Interior Secretary James Watt appointed OSM administrators who had fought SMCRA in the courts. They promptly approved state programs that, according to an OSM official who was with the agency then, "did not in any way, shape, or form meet the federal standards." For much of the 1980s, the agency was strained by low-level warfare between would-be enforcers and Reagan appointees, with the latter slowly gaining ground. The program reached its nadir under George Bush's first OSM director, Harry Snider, who cut deals with companies to weaken enforcement, then imposed his arrangements in haranguing, late-night telephone calls to his underlings' homes. Bill Clinton's 1992 victory raised hopes among the remnants of the original OSM staff, who by then had become a corps of toughened dissidents. They have mostly been disappointed. President Clinton's first OSM director, Robert Uram, developed a reputation for indecisive leadership. Uram was widely perceived as caving in when the 1995 Republican Congress passed a 25 percent cut in the agency's program budget. The subsequent firings fell heavily on the corps of field inspectors, many of whom were precisely the same ones who had spent years resisting Reagan/Bush administrators.

Since then, OSM inspections of mining sites have fallen by as much as 50 percent in some states. People within the OSM describe the agency as isolated and nervous. Lacking active support from the Clinton administration, resented for its mere existence by industry, and scorned by disappointed environmentalists, the OSM is at constant risk of further cuts or complete elimination. From director Kathy Karpan to field inspectors, OSM agents tread carefully. Inspectors describe working to bury citizen complaints in communities where house foundations are cracked and water wells ruined by blasting. They know that the complaints are valid, but know also that they cannot uphold them without jeopardizing themselves or drawing fresh political attacks on the agency.

In recent months, citizen pressure and expressions of concern from two of West Virginia's congressional representatives have sparked the beginnings of federal action. The OSM has announced that West Virginia needs a clear definition of mountaintop removal. The Army Corps of Engineers has suggested that no new permits should be issued while the legal disputes surrounding the practice are settled. The EPA, which oversees the water-quality portions of strip-mining regulation, has warned against further relaxation of state law. However, permitting continues, and there has been no serious discussion of stopping ongoing mining.

Though the OSM now has almost no defenders, the agency remains the best hope for sound coal policy. Unless Democrats control both houses of Congress by a substantial margin, revisiting SMCRA could be disastrous. Although the OSM has permitted coal regulation to become a mockery of federal law, the agency remains better positioned than any other body to reinvigorate enforcement. Observers and OSM members agree that a few tactical appointments and a mandate from the secretary of the interior and the White House would be enough to revive the remaining inspectors and point the agency in the right direction. A push to restore the OSM's funding and rehire inspectors could also spur renewal. So far, the OSM remains a political orphan, and the land and people of the coalfields pay a stiff price for its abandonment.

Coal's True Cost

The deterioration of mining regulation covers over a deeper set of questions. What are the longterm effects of removing mountaintops and filling valleys? Should mountaintop removal and other forms of strip-mining be legal? And should we rely as heavily as we do on coal?

No one knows what the legacy of mountaintop removal will be a century from now. Even the basic question of whether the valley fills will remain stable—a question inevitably posed in the shadow of the Buffalo Creek disaster—is uncertain: the West Virginia Division of Environmental Protection's Ed Griffith declares briskly, "I have complete confidence in the stability of those fills." In contrast, a former OSM employee who received a national award for his engineering work before leaving the agency says, "I'm very concerned. As time goes by, and these fills become saturated with water, they're going to begin to fail. I am convinced of that." There have been landslides reported at the feet of valley fills in Kentucky, but there is no consensus on whether those fills were representative or just exceptionally ill-engineered.

Another unanswered question is how stripping will affect Appalachia's waterways. River life depends on decaying leaves and other organic matter that small streams carry. But these delicate processes are diminished with every mile of valley fill. Moreover, no one knows how churning together complex layers of porous and nonporous rock will affect drainage patterns and water tables. Appalachia's water already carries a grim legacy of coal mining. Both strip-mining and traditional deep-mining disturb sulfur, which reacts with oxygen to produce acid water that can kill a creek. Roger Calhoun, director of the West Virginia OSM office, estimates that 2,000 miles of the state's rivers and streams are "severely impacted" by acid runoff and other mine pollutants, and that many of those waterways are dead. He also acknowledges that as hundreds of mines in the state's high-sulfur coalfields close and the operators cease treating nearby water, thousands more miles will be endangered.

All this means that while coal is the world's cheapest source of energy it is also the most laden with hidden costs—the dead lakes of Russia and corroded statues of Eastern Europe, for example, began with draglines and dynamite. Coal is the number one culprit in producing acid rain, causing 70 percent of the United States's sulfur dioxide emissions and much greater amounts in places that still depend heavily on high-sulfur coal. Burning coal produces twice as much carbon dioxide as natural gas and 50 percent more than oil and gasoline, making coal a leading cause of global warming. With the arguable exception of nuclear power, no other energy source displays such a dramatic gap between its immediate price tag and its true long-term costs.

These costs will not go down as long as mountaintop removal fits so readily into the logic of the country's energy economy. Berating the coal industry for destroying mountains and communities evades the reality that mining companies simply answer the country's every-expanding appetite for cheap energy. West Virginia lawyer Tom Rodd, who won a landmark case in the early 1990s curbing some of the coal industry's worst excesses, judges that "West Virginia is the latest of the country's energy sacrifice zones, surrendered to keep power cheap. It isn't the first, and it may not be the last."

The best response to the disparity between coal's immediate and actual costs would be to change the terms of the fuel economy by erasing coal's artificial cheapness. Sound regulation and tax policy could build the environmental and social cost of mining and burning coal into its market price. Making coal more costly, in turn, would shift incentives throughout the economy, giving companies reason to invest in fuel-efficient technology and even nonpolluting energy sources. Simply enforcing SMCRA and the Clean Water Act also would have this effect, since responsible mining and restoration is more expensive than mountaintop removal. A bolder approach would revive the idea of a "carbon tax" on fossil fuel emissions, taxing energy use in proportion to the amount of greenhouse gas that it produces. By using carbon tax revenue to finance, say, a cut in the regressive and economically dampening payroll tax, lawmakers could re-orient the economy toward both high employment and clean technology.

The near demise of SMCRA also holds lessons for the conduct of public policy. One concerns the hazards of administrative law. Agencies like the OSM and DEP blend the functions of the executive, legislative, and judicial branches. They write regulations, sometimes departing significantly from the original intent of legislation, and establish interpretations of those regulations in their own administrative law courts. Administrative agencies have no direct, democratic accountability. Although citizen suits and political pressure sometimes affect agencies, regulatory law operates mainly beyond citizen's view. It is, however, subject to constant legal challenge and lobbying by industry's lawyers. Sometimes, as with SMCRA, it becomes nearly unrecognizable. Making administrative agencies more democratically accountable will hardly be a straightforward task, but it is an urgent one.

The fate of SMCRA also highlights the poverty of the current enthusiasm for state control of programs of every sort. The new federalism aims to let states work as laboratories for innovative policies and to permit state governments to respond to local conditions—social, economic, and ecological—that uniform national programs dough over. The history of mining regulation in West Virginia reminds us that those local conditions may include great disparities in political power, and sometimes even endemic corruption. Those problems occasioned the drive for federal standards in the first place, and they have not disappeared as federal policy has become less popular. Often, the challenge of effective government is not to unload federal programs but to make them work.

Although the coal industry is no longer the sole engine of Appalachia's economy, it has retained its political impunity. Musing on the days when he worked as a stripminer, Blair resident Carlos Gore observes wryly, "I reckon what goes around comes around." Asked if, by that principle, the coal bosses will get their comeuppance, he shakes his grizzled head: "The Lord don't seem to look on them that way." So far, the coal companies have been largely exempt from recompense and retribution even as their product has helped exempt the rest of the nation from environmental responsibility.

Any good resolution of the mountaintop removal struggle will have to break this vicious circle. And in so doing, it will necessarily address questions that run beyond stripmining. Political commitment will have to overcome almost two decades of administrative neglect to revive the Office of Surface Mining. Political and ecological responsibility will have to take precedence over economic recklessness. Citizens will have to insist that market prices and profit margins should not alone determine the shape of the country's landscapes and communities. We will have to decide whether to maintain our comfort at the price of more sacrifice zones, with their dead towns and leveled mountains. In Appalachia, the time for a decision is running out.

VII

The Political Economy of Appalachia

Political economy, as the name implies, refers to the economy in reference to the political setting with which it interacts. The economy of a region is partially determined by the interactions of laws, regulations, and political institutions. The writers in this section take this view of the causes of poverty in Appalachia; none blame poverty on cultural factors alone. Some contemporary analyses do, however, acknowledge the role of local elites in the creation of poverty in sections of Appalachia.

We begin this section with a selection from Richard Couto's *An American Challenge.* His article deals with the impact of economic trends on family life and children. This is followed by Roger A. Lohman's "Four Perspectives on Appalachian Culture and Poverty." Sally Ward Maggard's article looks at the impact of gender relations and gender ideology in the transition from agriculture to mining and service work. She points out that the lack of industrial diversification in Appalachia influenced the sex segregation of the labor force. Consequently, outcomes of development strategies may be different for women and men. Mary Beth Pudup provides a new interpretation of life in preindustrial Appalachia. She documents the early evolution of a social class structure in which middle class "boosters" promoted outside capital investment. Carl G. Kilbourne proposes tree farming as a sustainable cash crop for Southern Appalachia that would replace tobacco farming. Garry Barker defends craft production and sales as an economic development strategy. Steven Paul Whitaker offers a thought-provoking critique of the travel and tourism industry. The history of the United Mine Workers, once one of the largest labor unions in the world, is reviewed by Maier B. Fox in an essay addressing current issues faced by the miners' union.

The transition from agriculture to coal to a service economy is a thread that ties this section together. Readers should be aware, however, that even before the Civil War manufacturing was important in many mountain communities. The role of local elites and outside capital during various phases of development is another important thread, as is the role of labor unions, churches, and the media. The role of government is addressed more directly in the following section on policy issues.

25

by Richard A. Couto

Poverty

Changes in work and income have meant significant changes for families in Appalachia. The family, the first means of social capital, has the primary responsibility for the creation and sustenance of people in community. Yet, the changes in work and income have meant more families in poverty and families with fewer resources. These families have diminished capacity to accumulate and provide social capital. This has had a severe impact on children in many parts of Appalachia.

New and Old Poverty in Appalachia

The Appalachian region did better than the nation in reducing poverty from 1970 to 1990. During that time, the percentage of people in poverty nationally dropped modestly from 13.3 percent to 13.1 percent. Within the region, however, as Table 25.1 reports, the percentage of people in poverty declined from 17.7 percent to 14.9 percent. Despite this larger decline, the Appalachian region continues to have a higher rate of poverty than the nation. In addition, the rate of Appalachian poverty declined more sharply than poverty nationally in the 1970s but increased more sharply in the 1980s, as Figure 25.2 indicates.

As with every other measure, the rate of poverty in Appalachia requires extensive scrutiny and eludes simple generalizations. Central and Southern Appalachia had higher rates of decline in poverty than the nation, from 1970 to 1990. Of course, Central and Southern Appalachia had much higher rates of poverty in 1970. Northern Appalachia had increases in the people living in poverty. Southern Appalachia had two decades of growth in per capita personal income while Northern Appalachia had two decades of decline in per capita personal income. These income changes explain, in part, the decrease of poverty in Southern Appalachia and the increase in the North, from 1970 to 1990.

The poverty of Central Appalachia remains the highest in the region, almost twice the national rate, despite the substantial decline from 1970 to 1990. The decline in Central Appalachia marks the passing of exceedingly high rates of poverty, 40 to 60 percent in some Eastern Kentucky counties in the 1960s. The declines in those rates occurred primarily in the 1970s. The 1980s brought increased poverty in these counties. In some cases, the southern coal counties of West Virginia in particular, poverty rates are returning to pre-1970 levels. Figure 25.2 indicates the dramatic decline in poverty in the region from 1970 to 1980 and the increase in poverty

TABLE 25.1 Percent of Population Below Poverty Income Level in Appalachia, 1970 to 1990

	1970	*1980*	*1990*	*Rate of Change 1980–90*	*Rate of Change 1970–90*
United States	13.31%	12.40%	13.10%	2.93%	–4.14%
Appalachia	17.65%	13.68%	14.88%	8.74%	–15.69%
Northern	12.99%	10.97%	13.60%	23.97%	4.75%
Central	34.04%	22.34%	25.34%	13.43%	–25.55%
Southern	20.20%	14.85%	13.90%	–6.42%	–31.19%
Metro Counties	13.50%	11.21%	12.28%	9.54%	–9.02%
Northern	10.68%	9.36%	12.01%	28.25%	12.45%
Central	17.18%	14.04%	15.83%	12.79%	–7.83%
Southern	17.07%	13.49%	12.44%	–7.84%	–29.72%
Rural Counties	21.69%	15.93%	17.28%	8.47%	–20.34%
Northern	15.80%	12.77%	15.32%	19.97%	–3.06%
Central	35.86%	23.16%	26.30%	13.55%	–26.66%
Southern	22.85%	16.28%	15.53%	–4.62%	–32.03%

Source: U.S. Bureau of the Census.

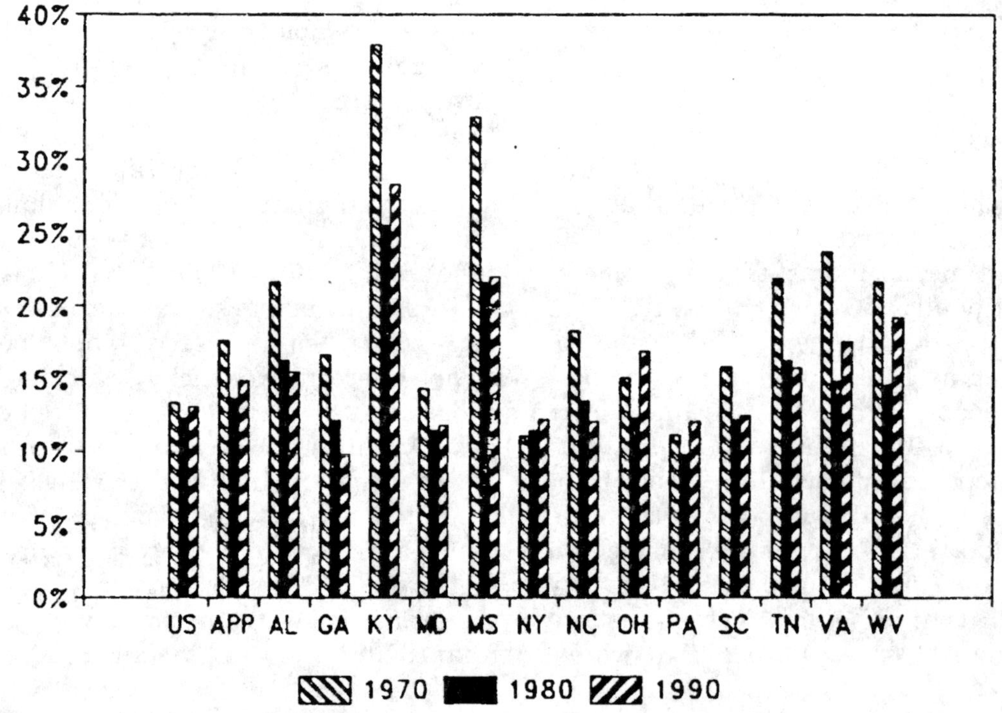

Figure 25.2. Percent of Population Below Poverty Income Level in Appalachia, 1970 to 1990

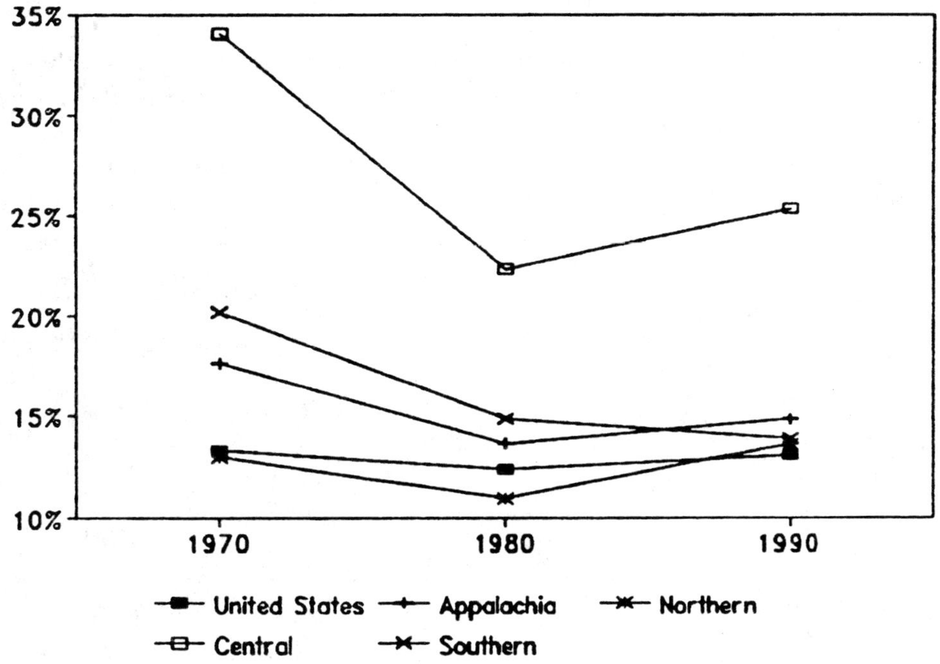

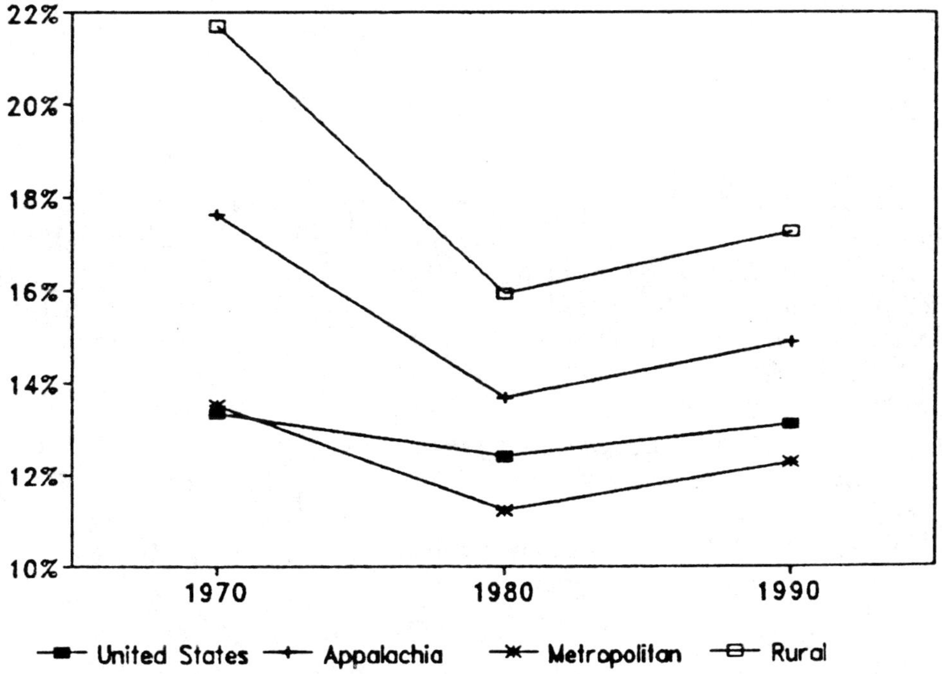

Figure 25.2. (Continued)

from 1980 to 1990, except for a continuing modest decline in Southern Appalachia. Despite the improvements, one in four people in Central Appalachia lived in poverty in 1990.

Although the rate of poverty in Southern Appalachia continued to decline in the 1980s, the number of poor people in Southern Appalachia actually increased by about 21,700. The total population increased at a high rate and the rate of poverty population dropped, accounting for an increase in the number of persons in poverty but a decrease in the percent of the population in poverty. On the other hand, the number of poor people in Southern Appalachia declined by 152,000 from 1970 to 1980. Only the 1970s brought a decline in the total number of people in poverty in Southern Appalachia. Maps 25.4 and 25.5 indicate that most of Northern Appalachia had a much higher increase in poverty than the rest of the region.

The 1980s were particularly severe from Western Pennsylvania down through West Virginia and Appalachian Ohio and into the coal countries of Eastern Kentucky. As Map 25.3 illustrates, Central Appalachia has a concentration of counties with high levels of poverty. Mississippi has another concentration of counties with high levels of poverty and remains the Southern Appalachian state with the greatest resemblance to Central Appalachian income and poverty.

Most counties in Appalachian Pennsylvania and New York reached the range of the national and regional poverty in 1990. However, the new poverty has brought rates much higher than the nation's to already low-income counties in Appalachian Ohio and West Virginia.

Despite the improvements of two decades in Southern Appalachia, a solid core of counties in Tennessee, Alabama, Georgia, and Mississippi still have very high rates of poverty. Appalachian Mississippi had a slight increase in poverty rates from 21.7 to 22.0 percent from 1980 to 1990.

The map of poverty in 1990 suggests how poverty is distributed in Appalachia. In general, those counties showing poverty rates less than 10 percent, which is lower than the national rate of 13.1 percent, are on the periphery of the region and are urban or suburban counties and close to large urban areas. Appalachian Ohio offers a striking example. Clermont County adjoins Cincinnati. It reported a poverty rate of 8.6 percent in 1990. The county marks a margin of affluence between the city and its adjoining, more rural counties. Rates of poverty decrease immediately upon leaving Cincinnati and then increase as one travels into Appalachian Ohio. Similarly, Jefferson County, Alabama and the city of Birmingham with its rate of poverty of 15.7 percent are next to Shelby County with a poverty rate of 9 percent. Shelby almost doubled its population between 1970 and 1990 and cut its poverty rate in half as people with high incomes chose this county over Birmingham for their residence. This pattern of enclaves of relative affluence next to a city is apparent in Appalachian New York, Pennsylvania, Maryland, Virginia, North Carolina, and especially Appalachian Georgia where five counties with low rates of poverty literally encircle Atlanta. Drawing from the cities for employment and wealth, these surrounding counties concentrate the benefits of income and wealth between their neighboring cities and rural counties. In general, counties immediately surrounding a large city have higher levels of income and lower rates of poverty.

Of course, some urban areas have concentrations of poverty, low incomes, and declining economic activity. The term "inner city" conjures up images of decline, unemployment, and poverty as strong as the term "Appalachia." In these places we find concentrations of poverty and need. Despite the affluence of Atlanta and its surrounding counties, 47.3 percent of the children in Atlanta under 6 years of age were in poverty in 1990. Cincinnati had a rate of child poverty of 41.2 percent; Pittsburgh had 56.9 percent of its African-American children under 6, more than 15,000 children, in poverty despite its average per capita income that exceeded the nation's (Children's Defense Fund 1992).

Family Income

From 1970 to 1990, median family income in Appalachia stayed at approximately 83 per-

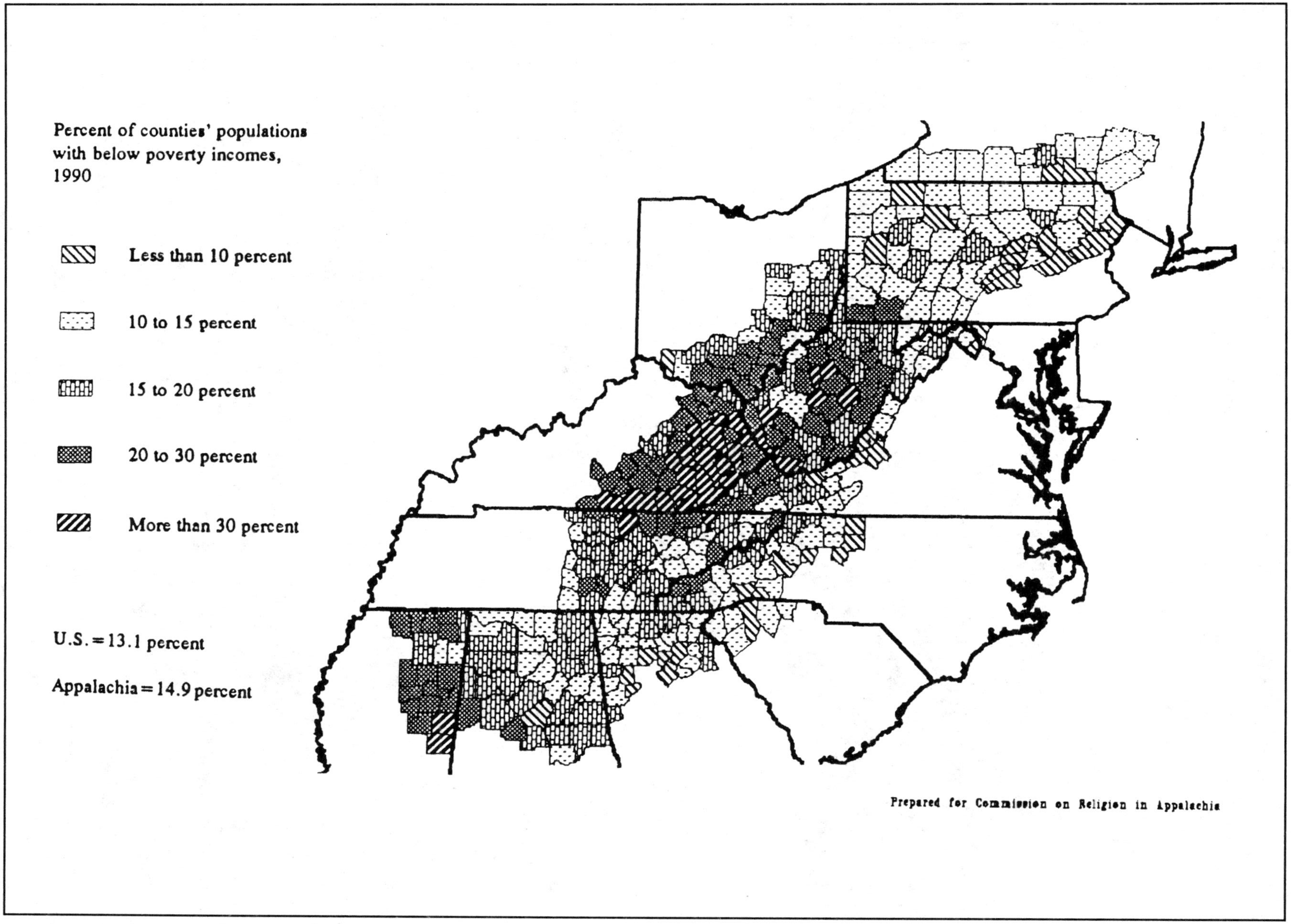

Map 25.3. Poverty Population of Appalachian counties, 1990

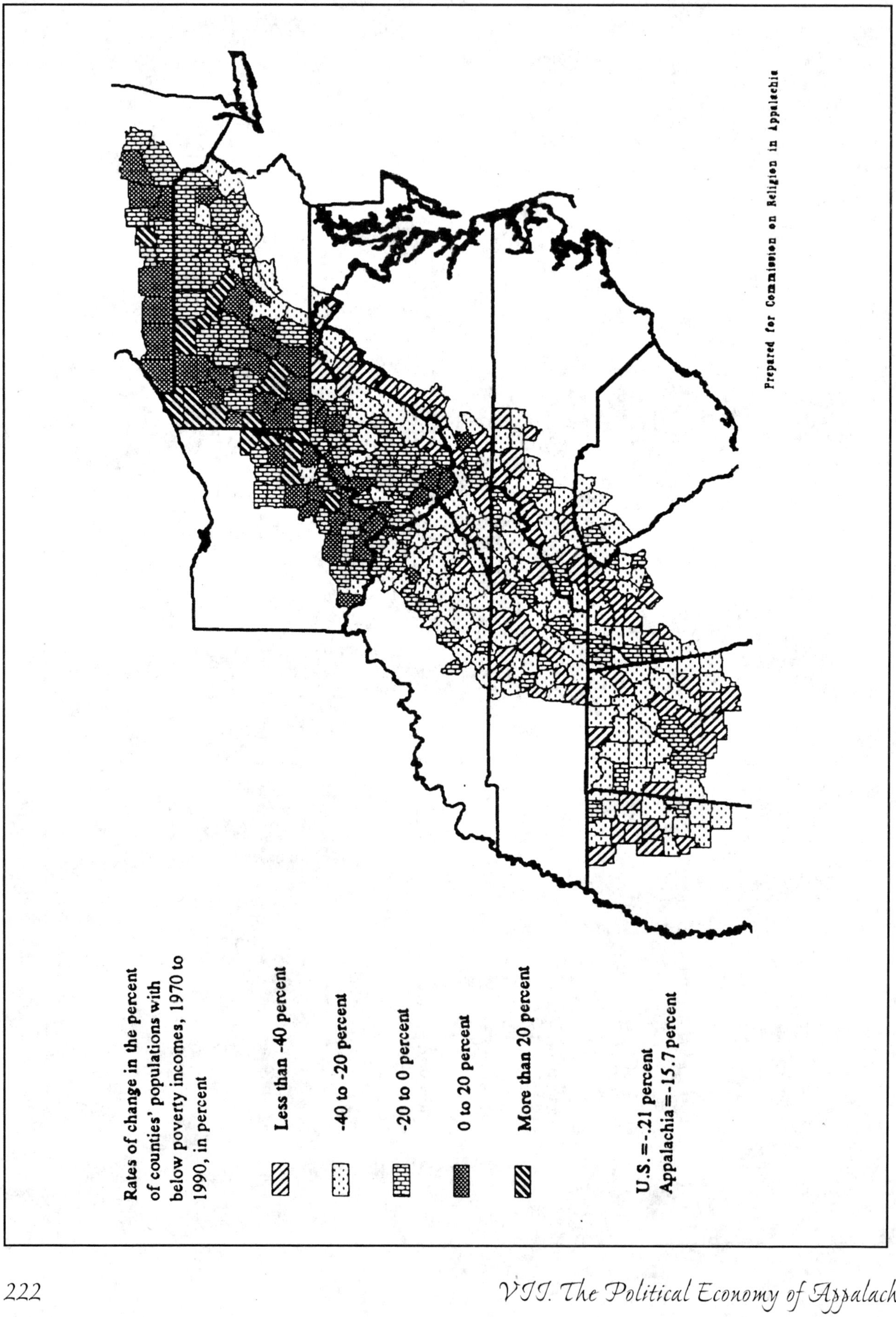

Map 25.4. Rates of Change of Poverty Population of Appalachian counties, 1970 to 1990

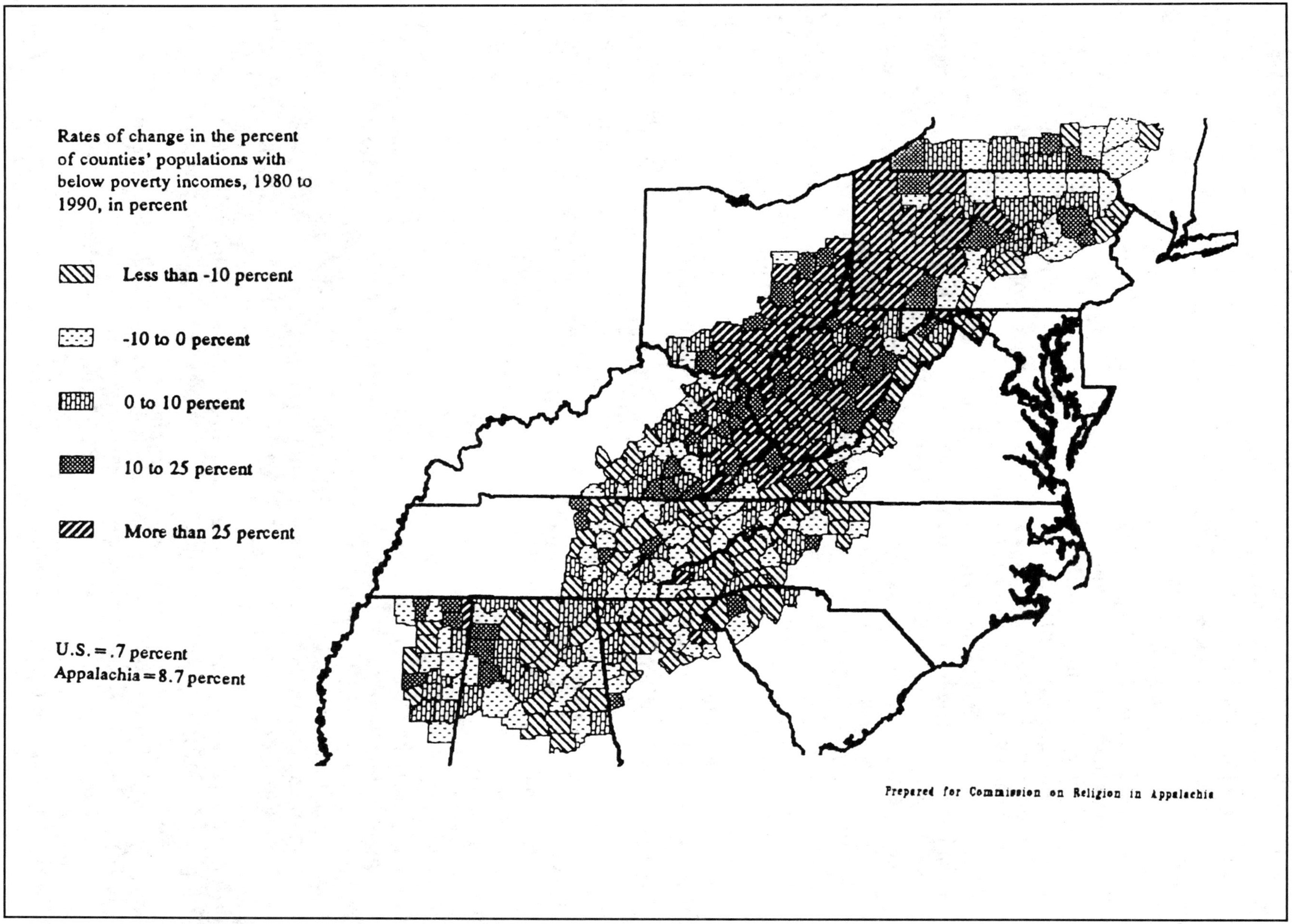

Map 25.5. Rates of Change of Poverty Population of Appalachian Counties, 1980 to 1990

cent of median family income in the nation. It increased and decreased in each decade by roughly the same rate. The family incomes of subregions varied. Family incomes in Northern Appalachia fell by 5.7 percent from 1970 to 1990, indicating the decline of the working middle class, especially in the 1980s. The decline then was even higher, 9.3 percent. The median family income in Central Appalachia plummeted in the 1980s by 13.4 percent, which wiped out most of the gain of the 1970s. From 1970 to 1990 family income in Central Appalachia increased 4.8 percent. Southern Appalachia had two decades of increased family income. In these two decades family income in Southern Appalachia increased from a place far lower than Northern Appalachia to a level slightly higher. Only the Appalachian portions of Georgia, North Carolina, and South Carolina had two decades of improved family income. Only Appalachian New York lost ground in the 1970s. All the other Appalachian states' portions lost ground in the 1980s. Table 25.6 and Figure 25.7 provide measures for family income in Appalachia for 1970, 1980, and 1990.

As the fortunes of Northern and Southern Appalachia switched, the relation of urban and rural areas changed as well. The gap of rural and metropolitan counties in Northern Appalachia narrowed. Metropolitan and rural counties approached equality at lower levels of income for both. The gap between metropolitan and rural counties in Southern Appalachia grew. Increases in metropolitan counties were greater than those in rural counties. Urban and rural counties grew further apart at higher levels of median family income.

The high-wage and heavily unionized states of Ohio, Pennsylvania and West Virginia were worse off in family income in 1990 than they were in 1970. The drop was particularly precipitous in Appalachian Ohio, which went from a much higher than regional level to a much lower level. Maps 25.8 and 25.9 illustrate family income in 1990 and changes from 1980 to 1990. Obviously, Northern Appalachia has lost the most. Its losses, however, dropped it to a level to which Southern Appalachia rose. Central Appalachia and contiguous counties have the concentration of counties with the very lowest family incomes, especially Eastern Kentucky.

Families and Poverty

While it stands to reason that family income will change with the changes in the amount and nature of work, the extent of those changes are not apparent. The drop in family income has meant more families in poverty. In Northern Appalachia, with the most severe decline in wages and manufacturing employment in the region, we also find the largest increase in families in poverty, especially in the 1980s. By 1990, 10.7 percent of the families in Northern Appalachia were in poverty, a rate that exceeded the national rate for the first time for this set of counties. Table 25.10 reports on these changes. Other measures of family poverty appear in Figure 25.11, Map 25.12, and Map 25.13.

In Southern Appalachia, with the greatest increase in wages and retention of manufacturing employment, families in poverty declined for both decades and reached their lowest point in 1990. Despite this improvement, the urban counties of Southern Appalachia have rates of families in poverty almost equal to those of Northern Appalachia. Similarly, the large discrepancy of families in poverty between the rural counties of Northern and Southern Appalachia in 1970 had almost disappeared by 1990. Improvements in Southern Appalachia and increased family poverty in the 1980s in Northern Appalachia have brought the two subregions much closer together. The gap between the metropolitan and rural counties in Appalachia has narrowed but the rural counties still have about 50 percent more families in poverty than the metropolitan counties. Rural counties had 14.1 percent of their families in poverty in 1990.

In Central Appalachia, family poverty rates are more than double those of the nation. The rate has declined since 1970 but that change entailed a decrease in the 1970s followed by an increase in the 1980s. One in four

TABLE 25.6 Median Family Income in Appalachia as a Percentage of National Median Family Income 1970 to 1990

	1970	*1980*	*1990*	*Rate of Change 1980–90*	*Rate of Change 1970–90*
Appalachia	82.79%	87.50%	83.49%	–4.58%	0.86%
Northern	90.15%	93.75%	85.00%	–9.34%	–5.72%
Central	58.34%	70.61%	61.12%	–13.44%	4.76%
Southern	78.55%	84.18%	87.08%	3.44%	10.85%
Metro Counties	92.07%	96.32%	92.92%	–3.53%	0.92%
Northern	96.28%	100.02%	90.54%	–9.48%	–5.96%
Central	87.29%	95.44%	86.18%	–9.70%	–1.27%
Southern	85.85%	91.55%	95.80%	4.65%	11.60%
Rural Counties	73.70%	79.44%	74.85%	–5.77%	1.56%
Northern	82.55%	86.56%	78.93%	–8.82%	–4.39%
Central	55.09%	68.09%	58.53%	–14.03%	6.24%
Southern	70.94%	76.56%	77.63%	1.40%	9.43%

Source: U.S. Bureau of the Census.

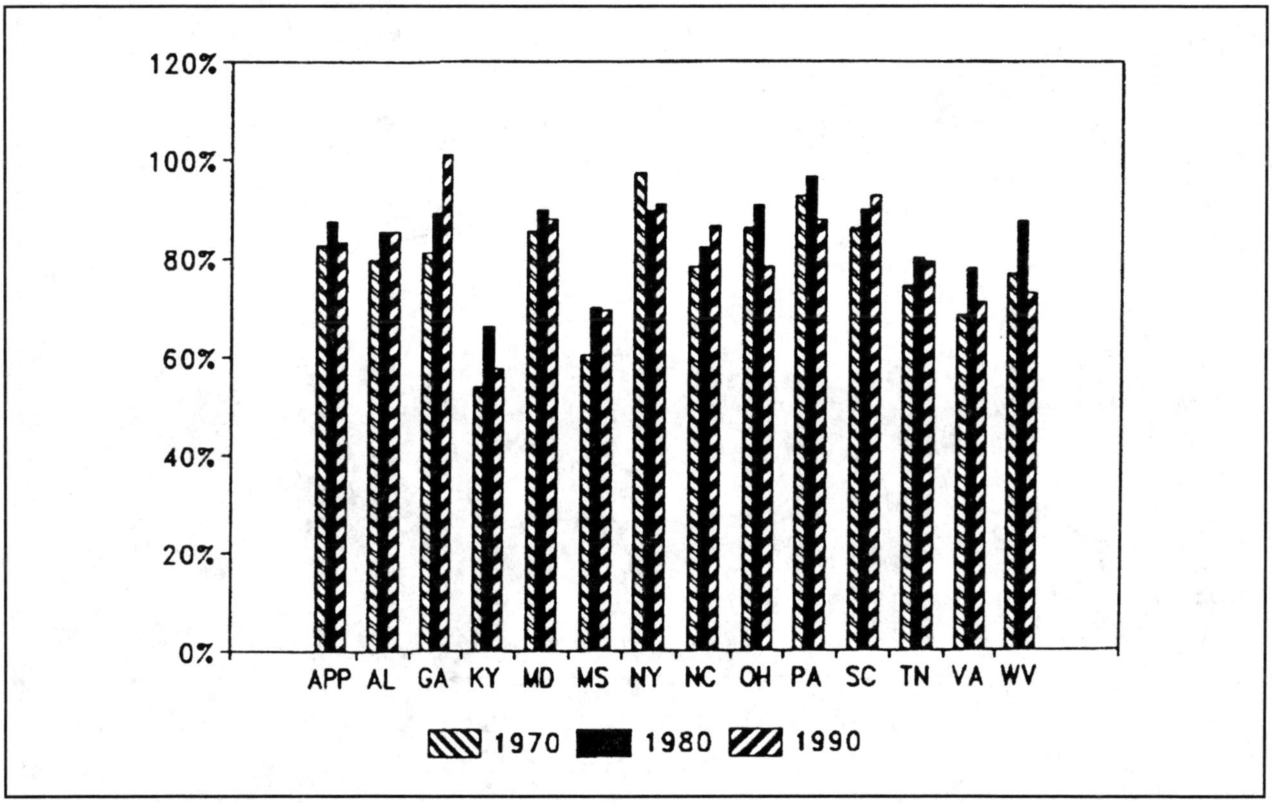

Figure 25.7. Median Family Income in Appalachia as a Percentage of National Median Family Income, 1970 to 1990

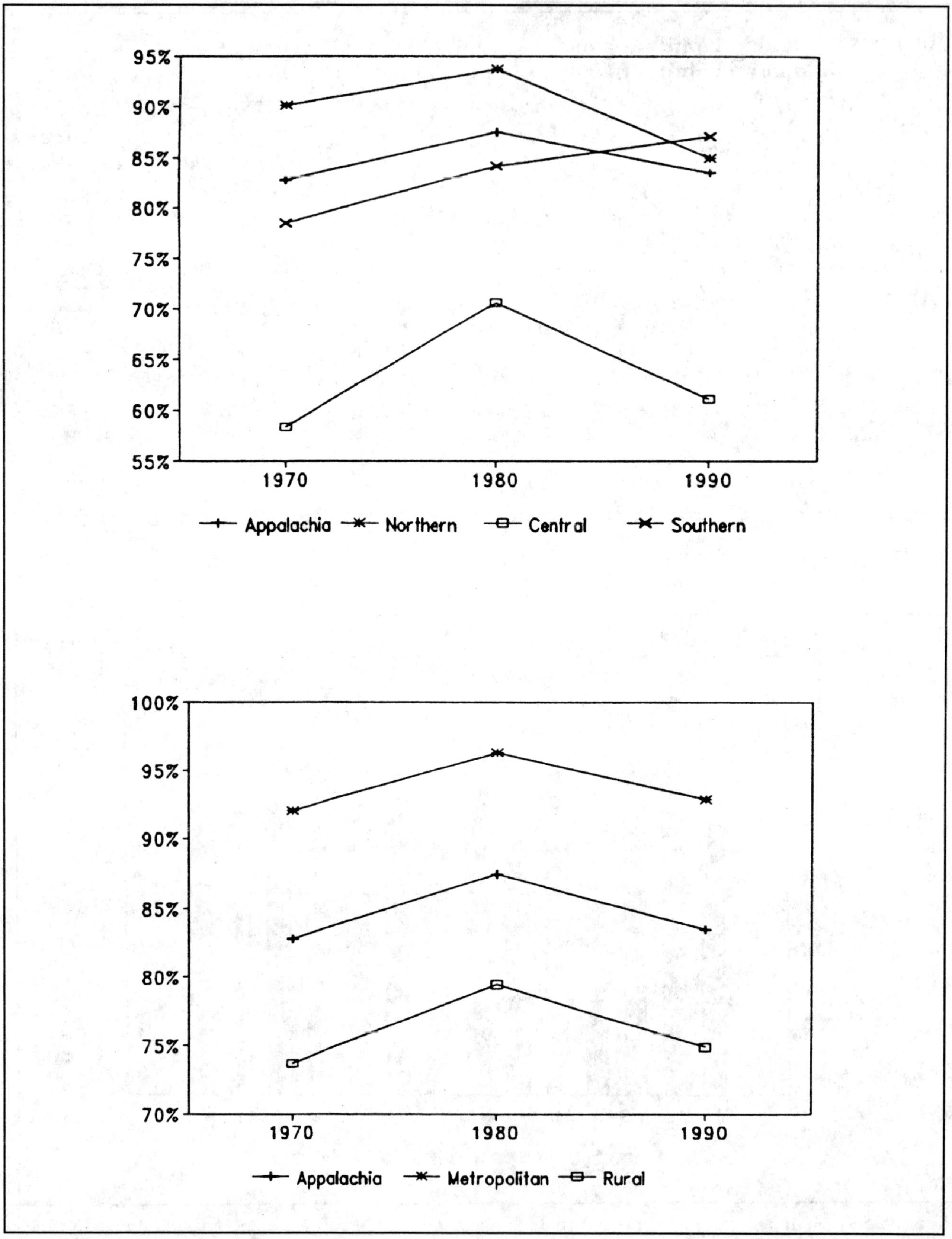

Figure 25.7. Median Family Income in Appalachia as a Percentage of National Median Family Income, 1970 to 1990 (Continued)

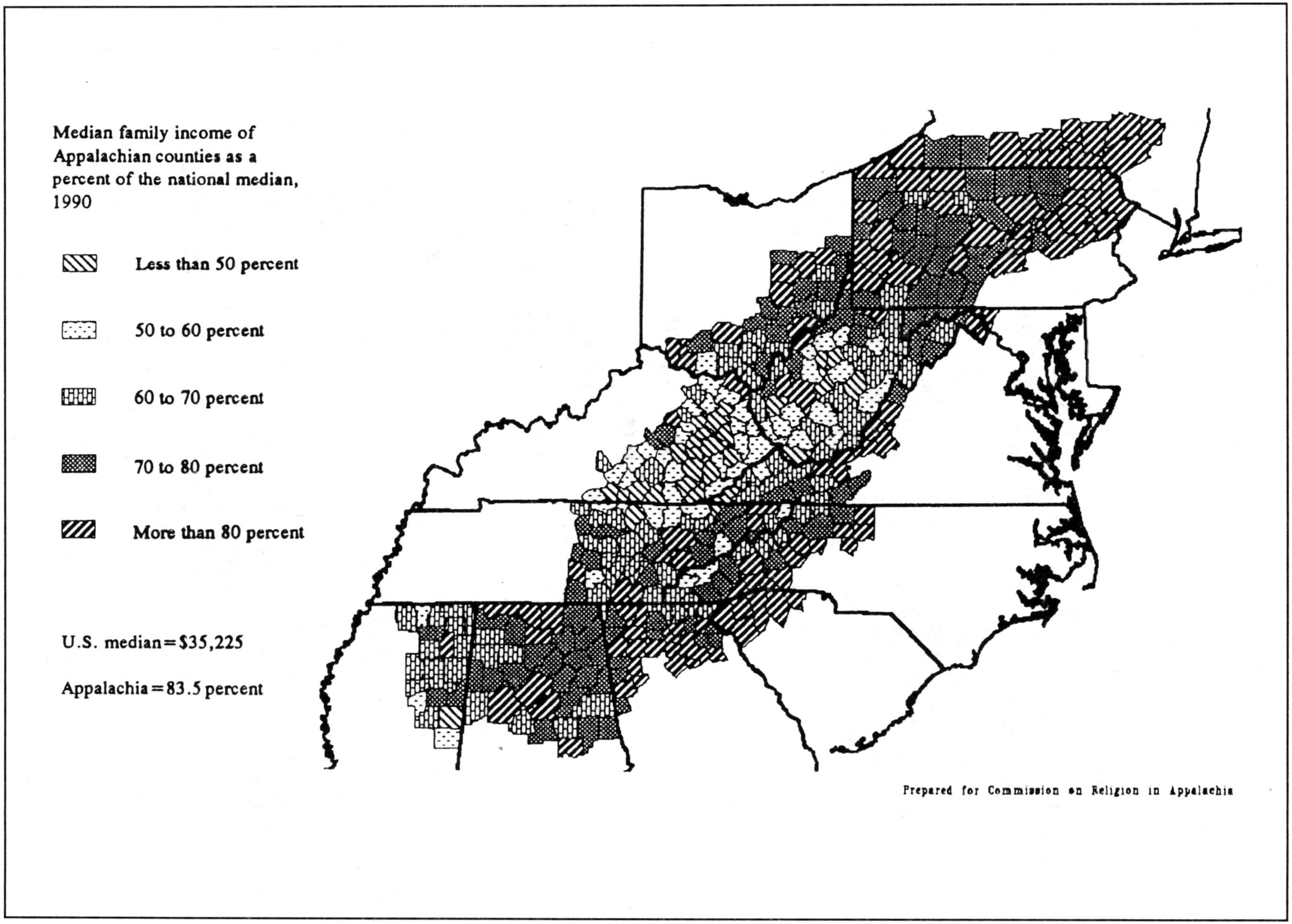

Map 25.8. Median Family Income of Appalachian Counties, 1990

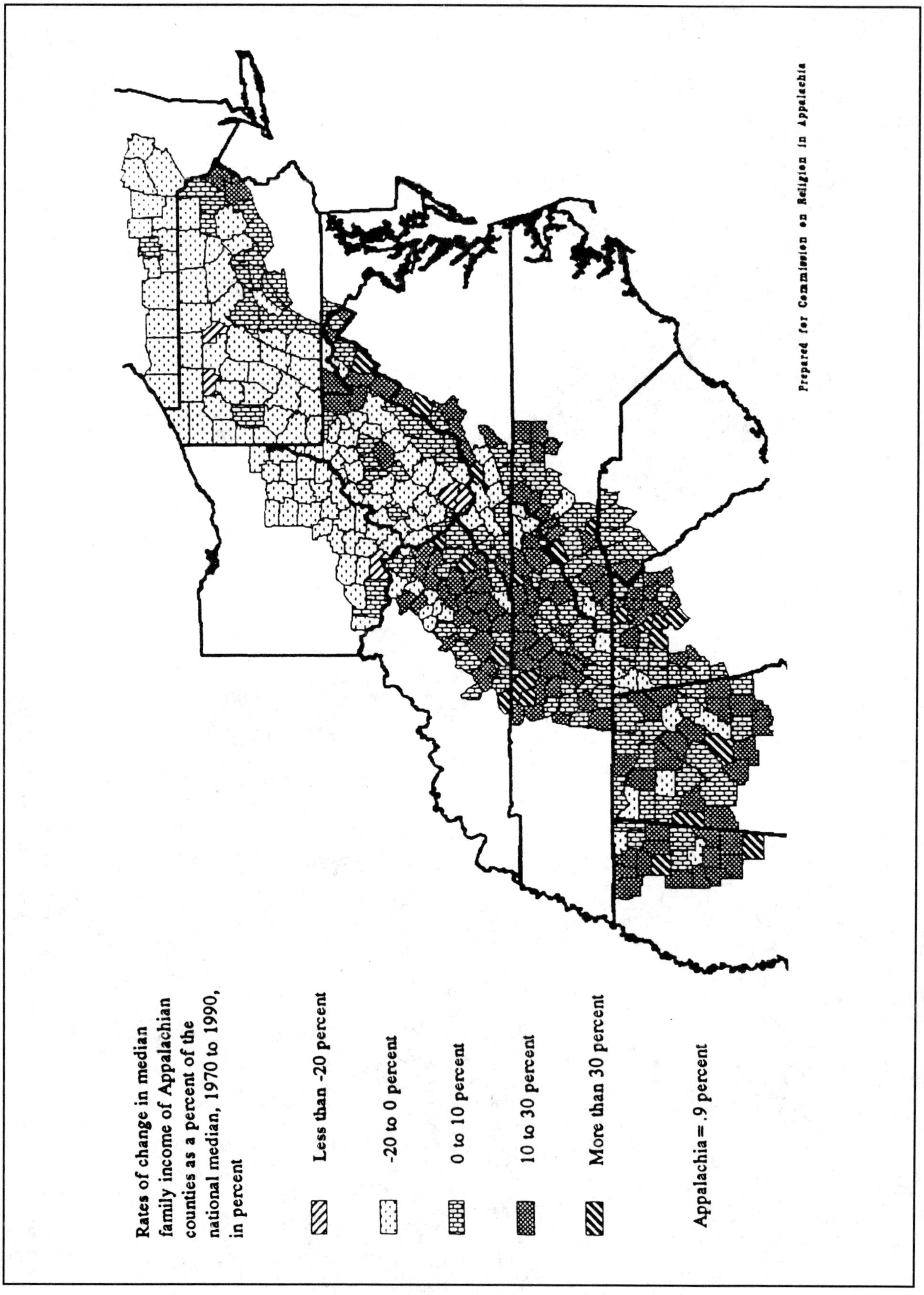

Map 25.9. Rates of Change of Median Family Income of Appalachian Counties, 1970 to 1990

TABLE 25.10 Families in Poverty in Appalachia, 1970 to 1990

	1970	*1980*	*1990*	*Rate of Change 1980–90*	*Rate of Change 1970–90*
United States	10.70%	9.60%	9.97%	3.85%	–6.82%
Appalachia	14.89%	10.98%	11.94%	8.69%	–19.80%
Northern	10.38%	8.41%	10.73%	27.59%	3.40%
Central	30.19%	19.21%	22.18%	15.43%	–26.54%
Southern	17.39%	12.02%	10.87%	–9.60%	–37.51%
Metro Counties	10.97%	8.82%	9.59%	8.78%	–12.61%
Northern	8.35%	7.21%	9.49%	31.59%	13.64%
Central	14.15%	11.41%	13.35%	17.02%	–5.65%
Southern	14.85%	10.79%	9.54%	–11.51%	–35.71%
Rural Counties	18.71%	12.97%	14.09%	8.68%	–24.68%
Northern	12.90%	9.79%	12.09%	23.56%	–6.23%
Central	31.98%	20.01%	23.09%	15.40%	–27.82%
Southern	20.04%	13.30%	12.30%	–7.52%	–38.64%

Source: U.S. Bureau of the Census.

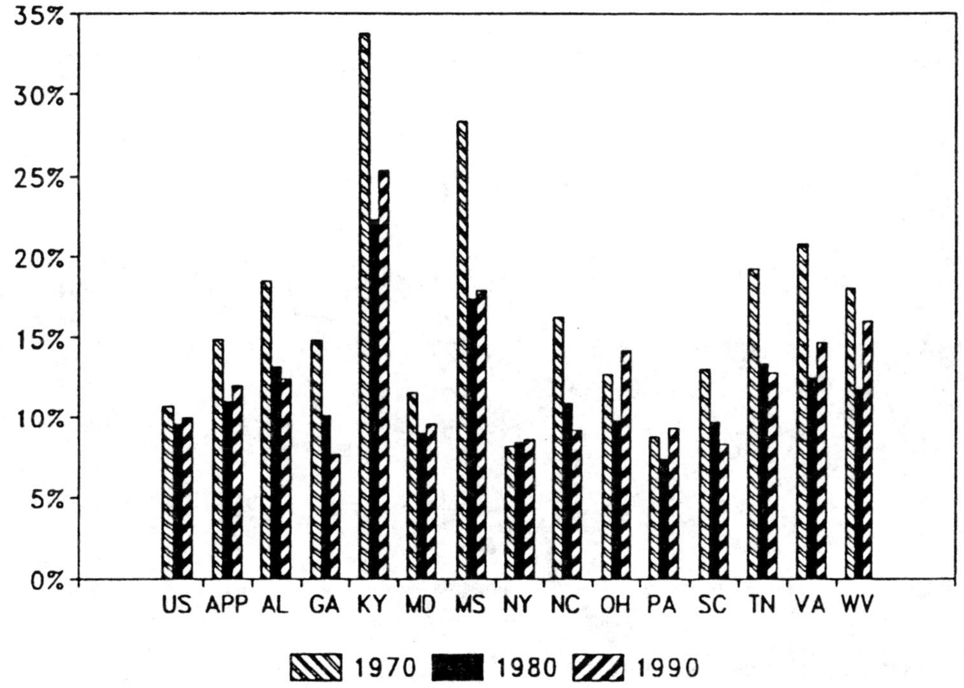

Figure 25.11. Families in Poverty in Appalachia, 1970 to 1990

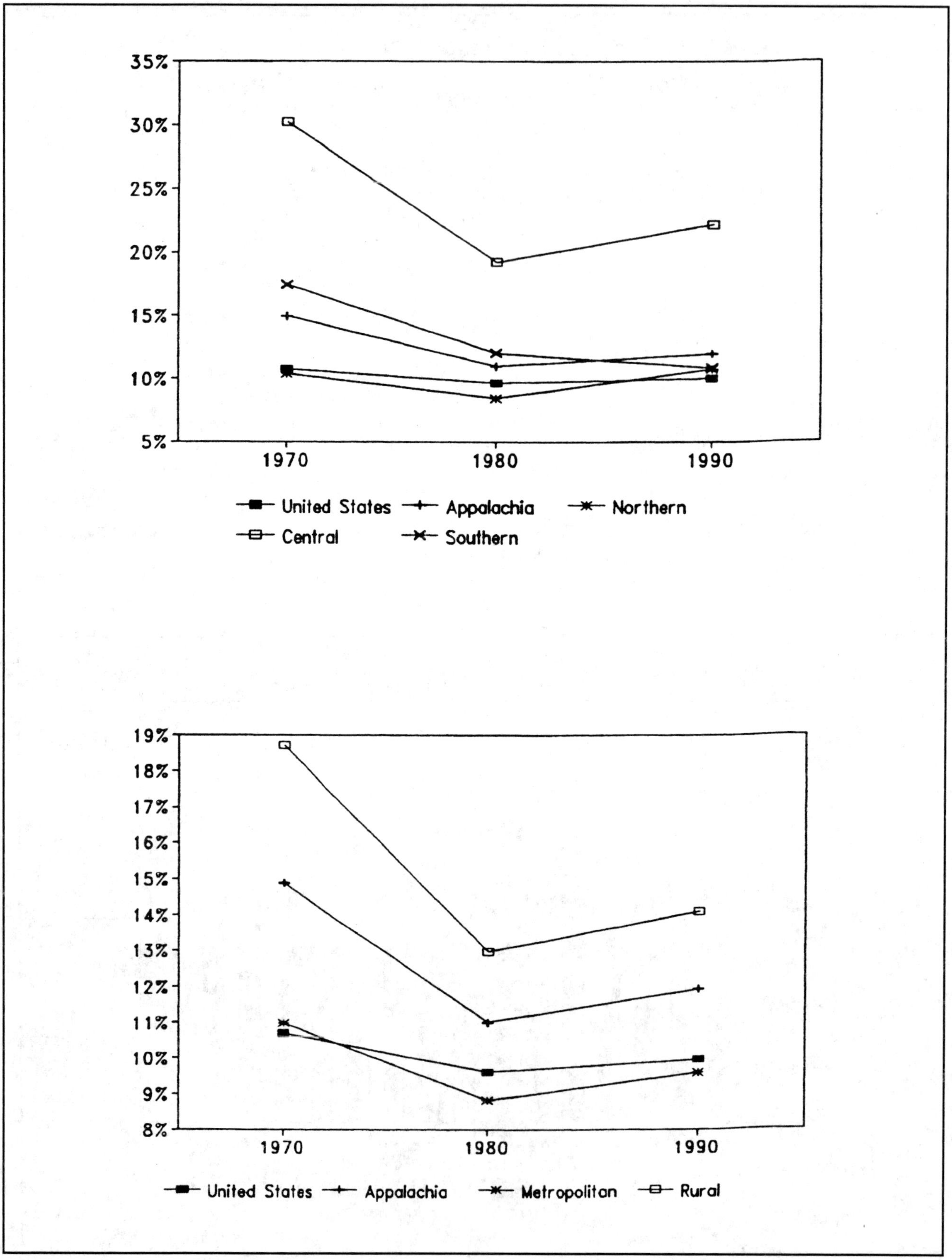

Figure 25.11. Families in Poverty in Appalachia, 1970 to 1990 (Continued)

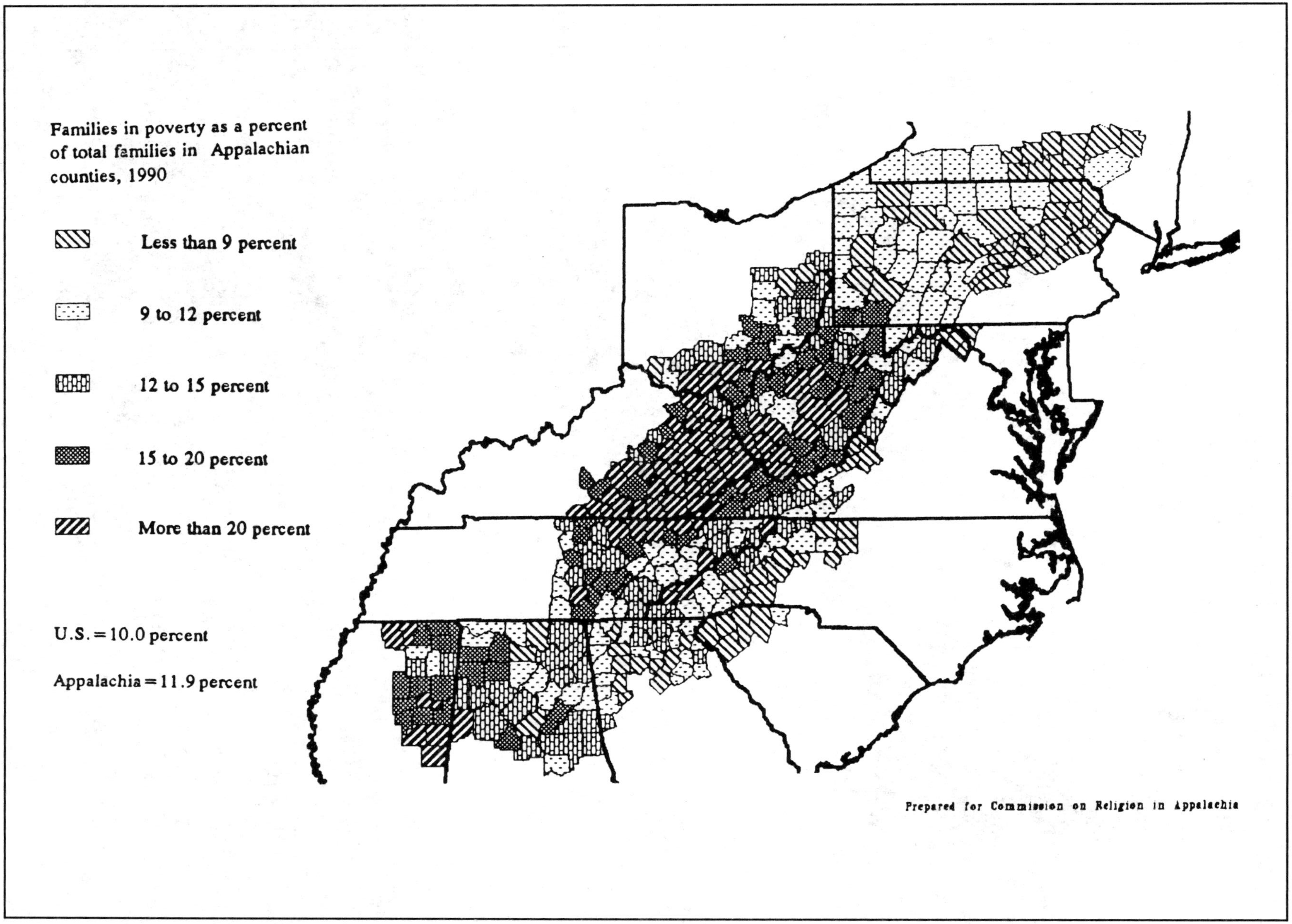

Map 25.12. Families in Poverty in Appalachian Counties, 1990

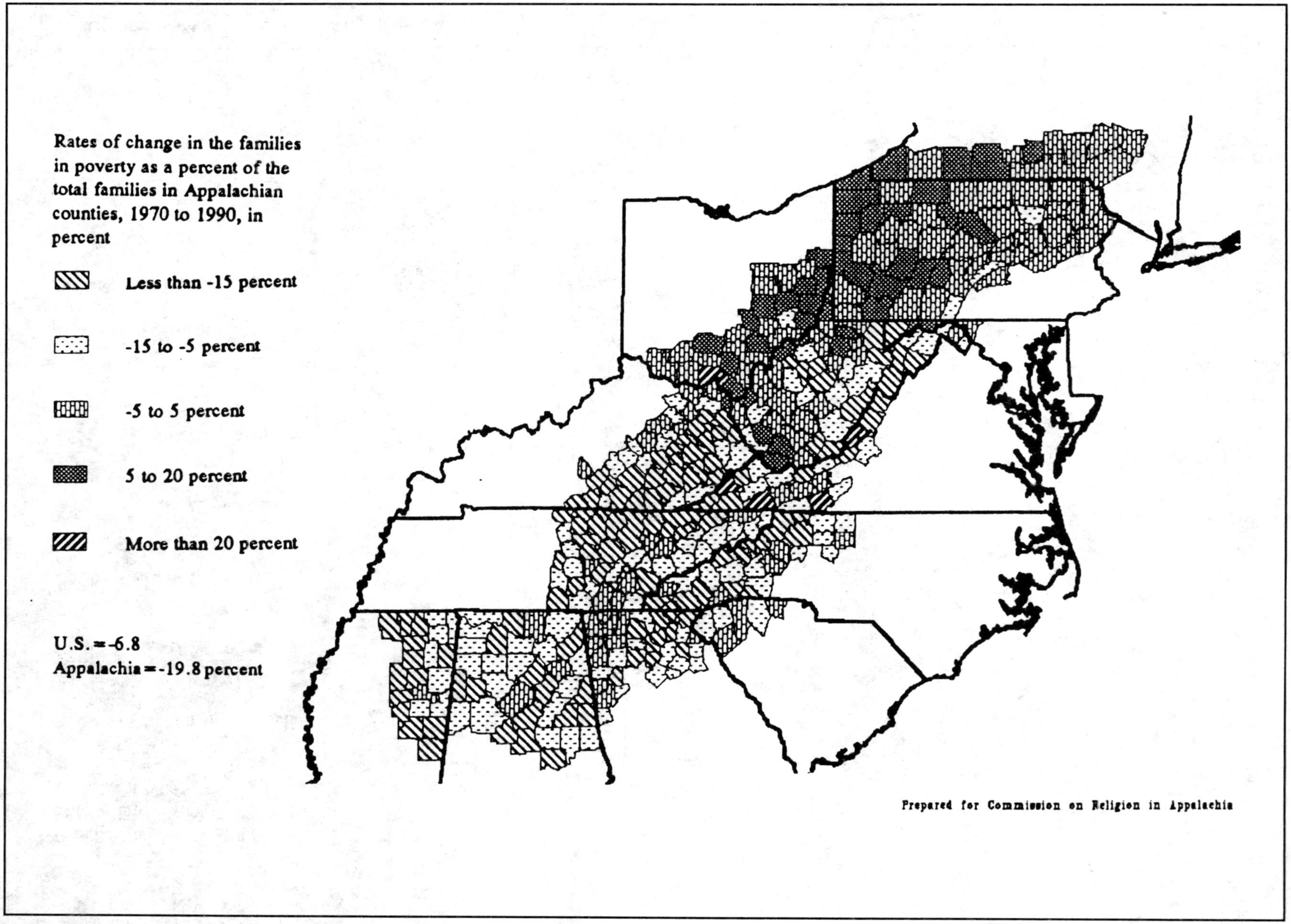

Map 25.13. Rates of Change of Families in Poverty in Appalachian Counties, 1970 to 1990

families in Eastern Kentucky in 1990 had incomes below the poverty level. Map 25.12 shows that the largest cluster of counties in Appalachia with incomes less than one-half of the national median family income figure are in Eastern Kentucky.

Appalachian Ohio and West Virginia had the region's highest rates of increase of families in poverty, 44 and 36 percent, respectively, to reach levels of 14.2 and 16.0 percent. Some families in the working middle class, predominantly white, not only saw their income decline but drop below the poverty level. Figure 25.11 provides a bar graph illustrating the levels of family poverty in each of the states.

The core of severe family poverty appears in Eastern Kentucky, West Virginia, and contiguous counties of Appalachia Ohio, Virginia, and Tennessee. A smaller concentration is in Appalachian Mississippi. Despite improvement from 1970 to 1990, most counties there, especially those with African-American populations over 20 percent of the total population, have very high rates of family poverty. Counties in Alabama report high rates of family poverty as well. Georgia, South Carolina, and North Carolina have clusters of counties with low levels of family poverty and two decades of reduction in the percentage of families in poverty. Appalachian New York and Pennsylvania still had low rates of family poverty in 1990 despite increases in Pennsylvania.

Children

High rates of family poverty translate into very high rates of poverty for children. In Appalachia, 33 percent of all individuals below the poverty level in 1990 were under 18 years of age. Put differently, 20.3 percent of all the children of Appalachia were in poverty in 1990 compared with 17.5 percent of all American children. The national figures represent a rate increase of 18.1 percent since 1970. Childhood poverty in Appalachia increased 7.5 percent in those twenty years. The 1970s actually saw the percentage of children in poverty decline, but the increase in the 1980s was almost 20 percent.

The measures of child poverty vary widely among states and subregions in the Appalachian region, as Table 25.14 and Figure 25.15 report. Central Appalachia's children experience more poverty than children of other subregions. This is lower than the rate of poverty among children in 1970 but much higher than the rate of poverty among children in 1970 but much higher than the rate in 1980. Eastern Kentucky had the highest percentage of children in poverty, 37.1 percent, which was approximately midway between the rates of 1970 and 1980. As we would expect, Northern Appalachia had increased rates of childhood poverty. In 1990, for the first time, this subregion's rate, 19.7 percent, exceeded the national rate of 17.6 and Southern Appalachia's rate, 18.6 percent. Northern Appalachia had two decades of increases in childhood poverty rates. Child poverty increased by almost 50 percent in Northern Appalachia from 1970 to 1990. Northern Ohio, Pennsylvania, and West Virginia in particular had large increases in the 1980s. Appalachian New York, despite improved economic measures had an increase in the portion of children in poverty in the 1980s. Southern Appalachia had a major decline in the 1970s and a modest increase in the 1980s. Only Appalachian Georgia among the Southern Appalachian states had a decline in the rate of childhood poverty in the 1980s. Appalachian Mississippi's rate, although far lower than 1970, remains second only to Eastern Kentucky. The economic growth of North and South Carolina was not enough to push down rates of children's poverty in the 1980s. Appalachian metropolitan counties had higher rates of increases from 1970 to 1990 than the nation. Rural counties had a decrease from 1970 to 1990, but the percent of childhood poverty remains higher in rural counties of the region.

Maps 25.16 and 25.17 portray rates of childhood poverty in the 1980s and changes from 1970 to 1990. More children in Northern Appalachia are poor in 1990 than before. Central Appalachia's poverty rates for children are the worst in the region despite some improvement since 1970. Once again, improvements in the 1970s were more than offset by the losses

TABLE 25.14 Children In Poverty In Appalachia, 1970 to 1990

	1970	*1980*	*1990*	*Rate of Change 1980–90*	*Rate of Change 1970–90*
United States	14.86%	16.00%	17.55%	9.68%	18.07%
Appalachia	18.91%	17.02%	20.33%	19.44%	7.52%
Northern	13.31%	14.20%	19.65%	38.35%	47.62%
Central	34.98%	25.68%	30.10%	17.20%	–13.95%
Southern	22.60%	18.00%	18.63%	3.51%	–17.58%
Metro Counties	14.41%	14.36%	17.53%	22.13%	21.64%
Northern	10.65%	12.38%	17.69%	42.90%	66.08%
Central	20.63%	17.67%	22.87%	29.47%	10.85%
Southern	19.71%	16.61%	17.18%	3.42%	–12.82%
Rural Counties	23.19%	19.29%	22.80%	18.21%	–1.69%
Northern	16.42%	16.06%	21.60%	34.46%	31.53%
Central	36.25%	26.33%	30.67%	16.48%	–15.38%
Southern	25.77%	19.46%	20.29%	4.27%	–21.29%

Source: U.S. Bureau of the Census.

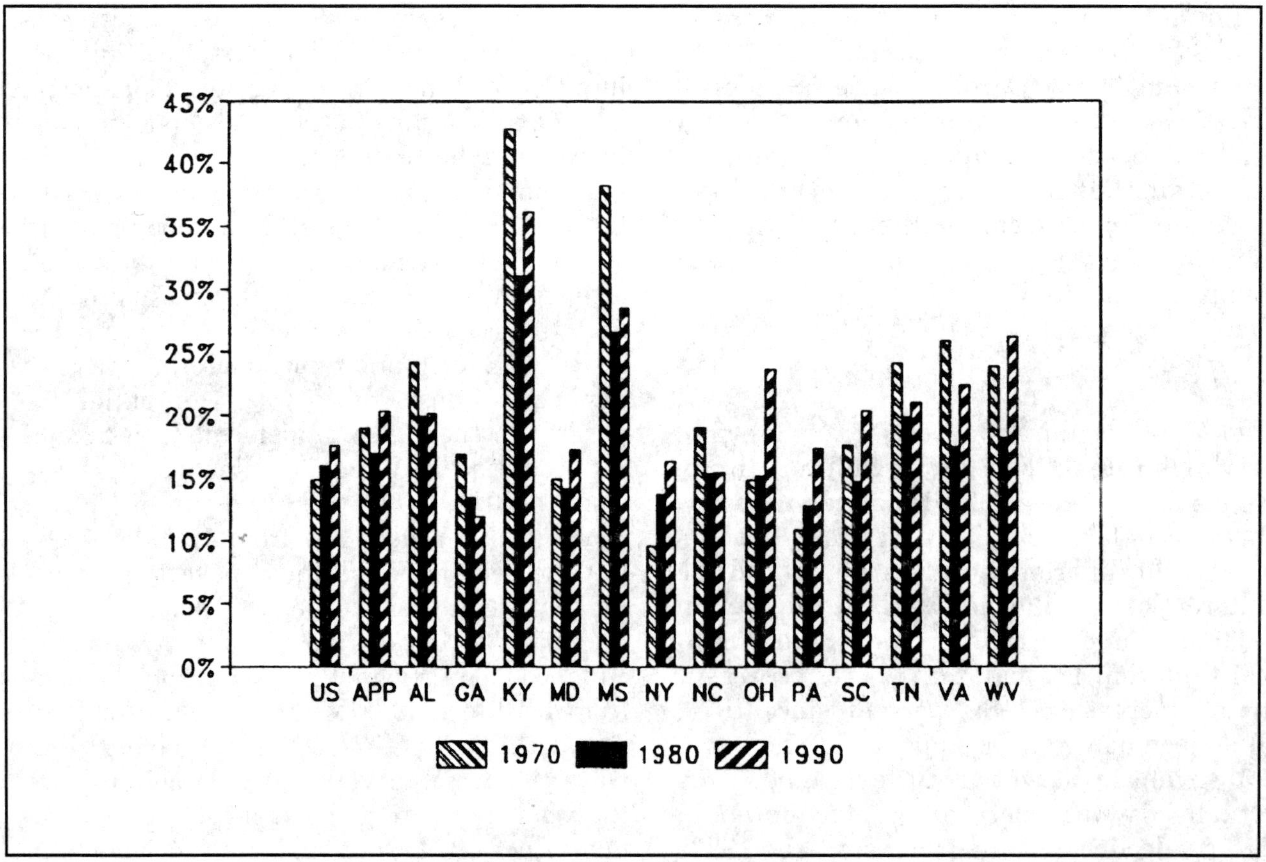

Figure 25.15. Children in Poverty in Appalachia, 1970 to 1990

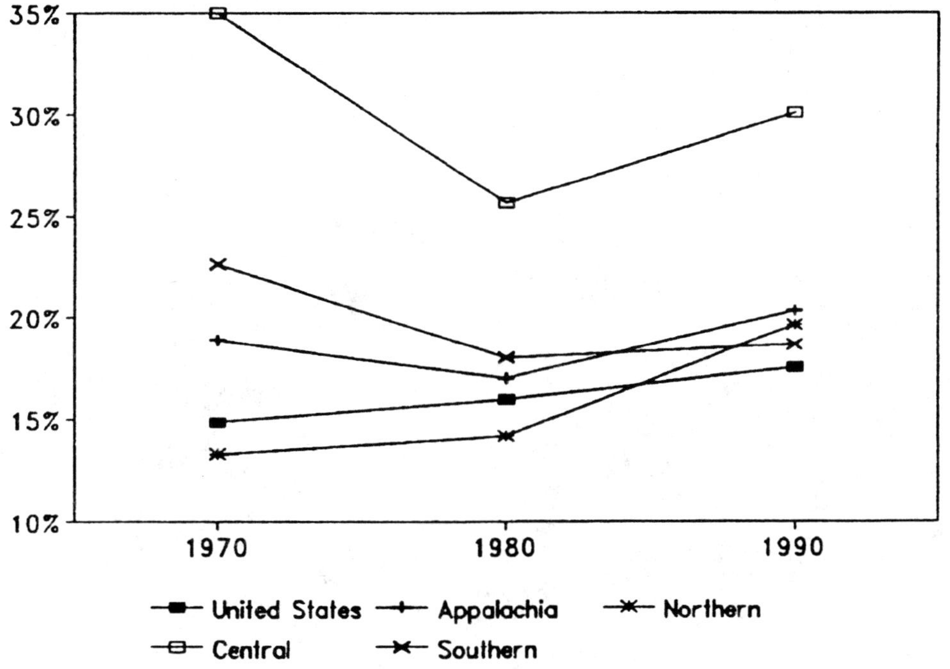

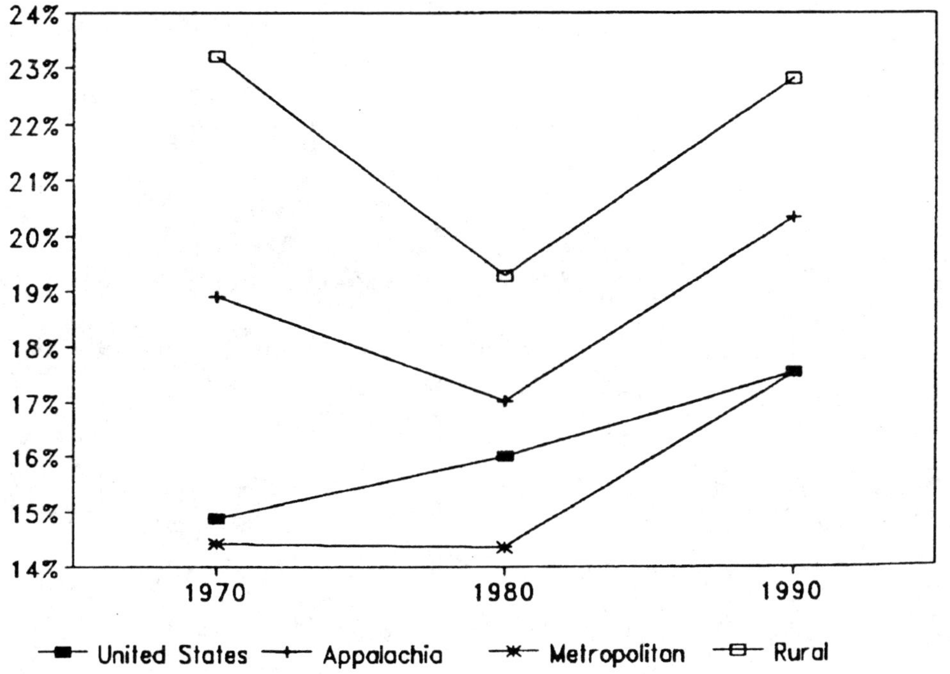

Figure 25.15. (Continued)

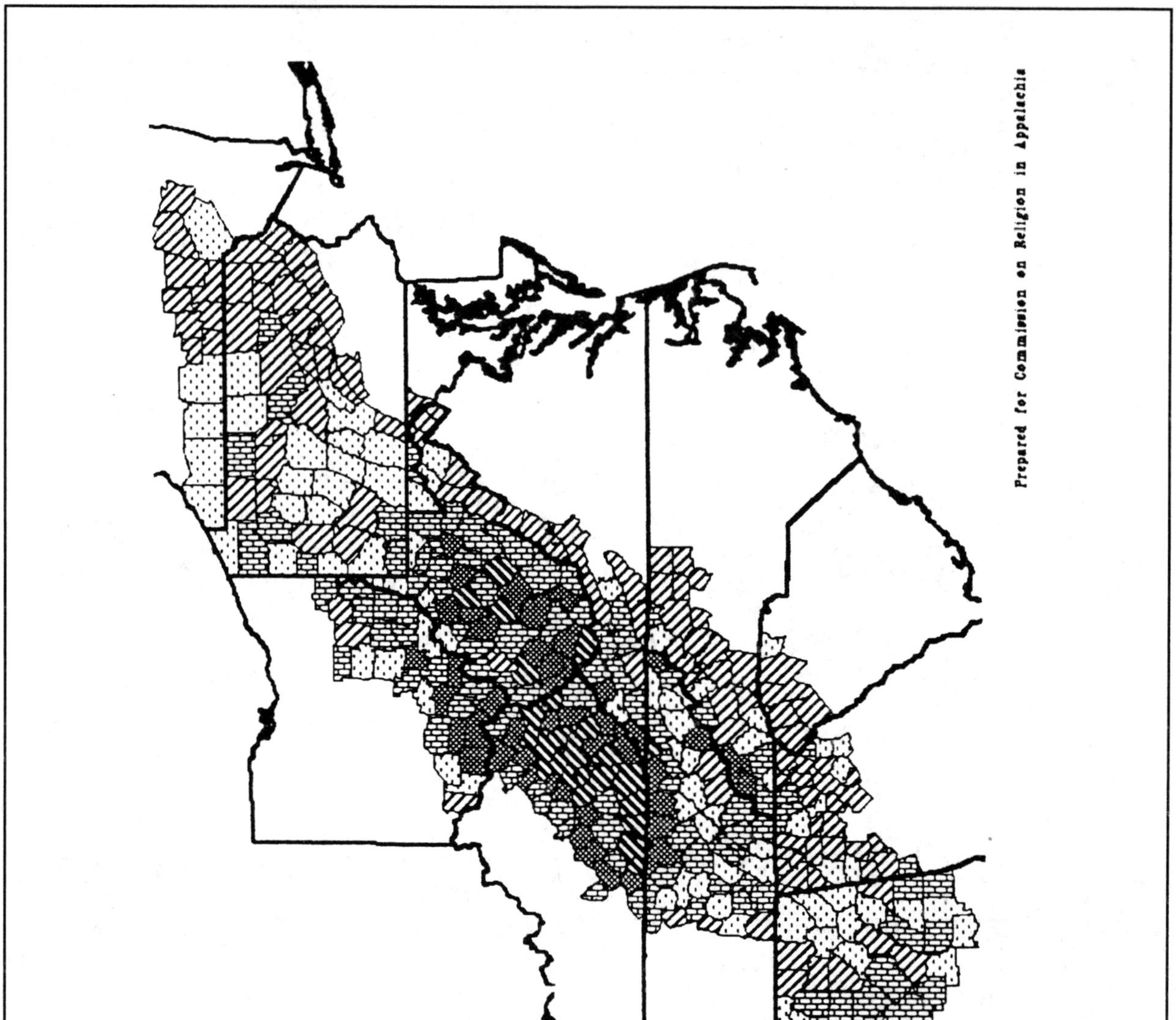

Map 25.16. Children in Poverty in Appalachian Counties, 1990

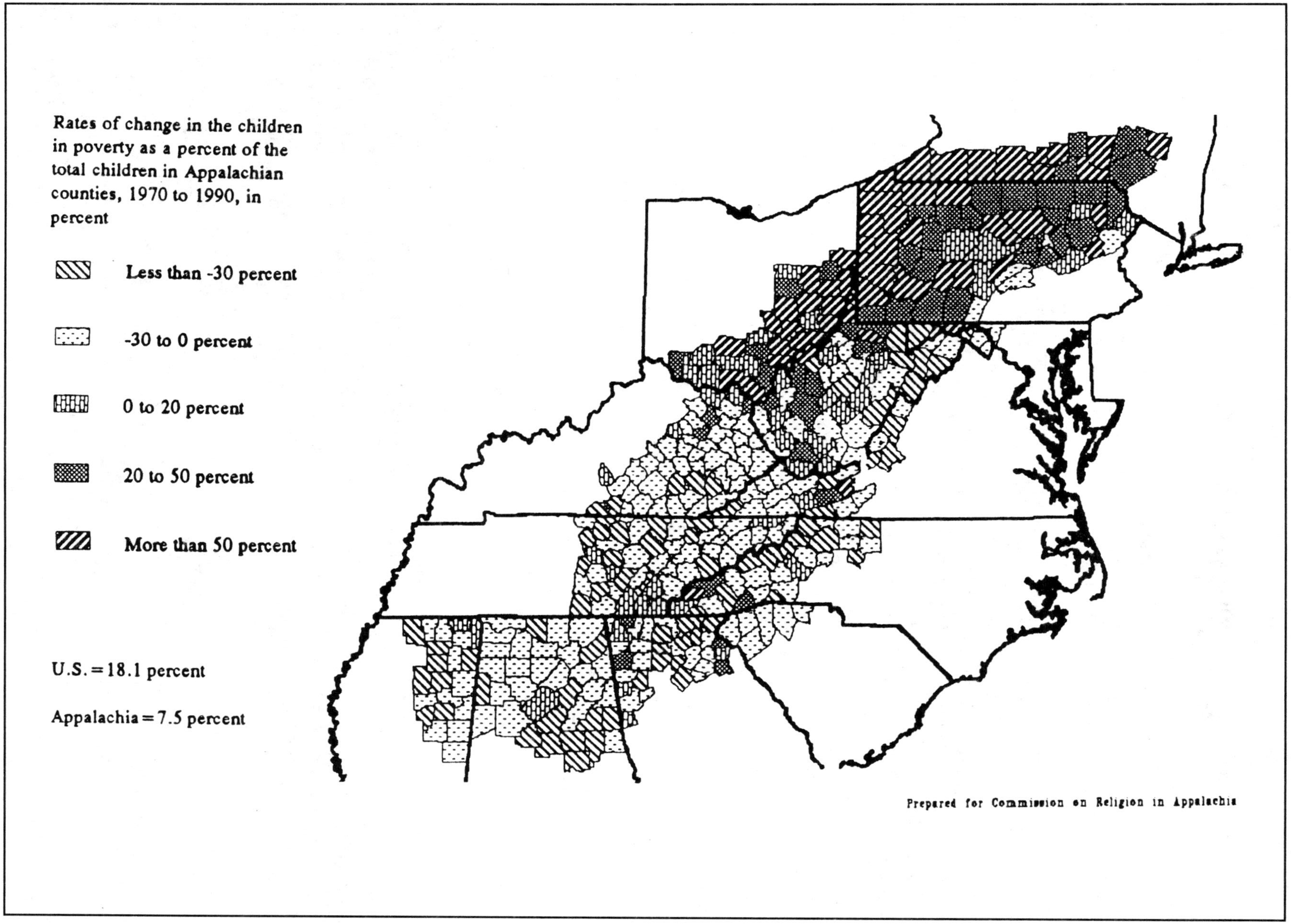

Map 25.17. Rates of Change of Children in Poverty in Appalachian Counties, 1970 to 1990

of the 1980s. Southern Appalachia's children have lower rates of poverty than before. That progress came in the 1970s. The 1980s brought a small increase. Shockingly high rates of childhood poverty continue among some counties of Southern Appalachian states, especially Tennessee, Alabama, Mississippi, and Virginia.

In addition to concentrations of childhood poverty already described, Map 25.16 also indicates very low rates of childhood poverty in counties surrounding urban areas. The eastern tier of Appalachian Pennsylvania, counties outside of Pittsburgh, Cincinnati, Winston-Salem, Birmingham, and especially Atlanta have the region's lowest rates of childhood poverty. Further, the rates have almost all declined, especially where the population has increased. This spatial concentration of childhood well-being indicates movement of relatively affluent families to areas of increased social capital—schools, housing, and recreation in particular. This map does not show higher rates of childhood poverty in the cities left behind. In 1990, in Pittsburgh, 32.5 percent of all children were in poverty; Cincinnati 20.6; Winston-Salem 23.4 percent; Birmingham 35.9 percent; and Atlanta 42.9 percent (Children's Defense Fund 1992). Some of the rates approximate those Central Appalachian counties and all of them exceed the regional average. This map suggests that the polarization of income has a spatial component with higher and increasing concentrations of childhood poverty in large urban areas and dramatically lower rates in some counties immediately surrounding them.

In addition, to the spatial concentration of children's poverty, there is a racial component as well. The counties with the largest portion of African Americans, the southernmost counties of Appalachian Alabama and Mississippi, also have higher rates of childhood poverty. Similarly, the percentage of African-American children in poverty in the cities we examined approximate the worst rates of Appalachian counties: Pittsburgh 56.9 percent; Cincinnati 53.9 percent; Winston-Salem 37.1 percent; Birmingham 42.4 percent; and Atlanta 48.8 percent. Even Chattanooga and Knoxville display this racial component. While 28.1 and 29.8 percent of all children in these cities are in poverty, the rates for African-American children reach 44.3 and 50.6 percent, respectively (Children's Defense Fund 1992).

Conclusion

There is not one poverty in Appalachia, there are several. In Central Appalachia, there is chronic poverty greatly reduced in the 1970s, primarily by a boom in coal, and greatly increased in the 1980s by a simultaneous decline in the economy and in public programs. In Northern Appalachia, there is new poverty brought about by the decline of work and wages for the working middle class. In Southern Appalachia, there remains higher than national rates of poverty despite increases in income. The increased poverty in Appalachia in a time of economic recovery suggests challenges to the equitable distribution of benefits and wealth in a postindustrial and deindustrializing America. The increased poverty among children during an economic recovery sends a particularly loud challenge about the extent to which we will permit American children to be impoverished by the economic misfortunes of their families.

26

by Roger A. Lohmann

Four Perspectives on Appalachian Culture and Poverty

Poverty in The Appalachian Context

Poverty is as closely associated with the Appalachian region as coal mining and the hammer dulcimer. Appalachian poverty has seldom been portrayed simply as poverty, but as the expression and symbol of something larger. Images of poverty—poorly dressed, sooty, emaciated, barefooted, mostly white, rural children and adults beside cabin porches—are as closely associated with Appalachia as cowboy hats with the West or moss-covered trees and white-columned mansions with the Old South.

Buried deeply beneath the images and stereotypes, the realities of poverty in the Appalachian region have changed greatly in the past 25 years. Yet our views of poverty have remained remarkably stagnant during that period. Such a situation might be tolerable if there were evidence of the continuing decline—and eventual disappearance of poverty as a major fact of life in the region. Current data suggest a quite different picture, however. Poverty rates in Central Appalachia remain nearly twice the national average (Tickamyer and Tickamyer, 1987). The collapse of employment in the steel industry has been added to the earlier decline of mining employment to make the problem of structural unemployment a region-wide phenomenon. Further, recent indications are that the situation for poor children in Appalachia may have gotten significantly worse during the 1980s, after nearly two decades of gradual improvement (West Virginia Human Resources Assn., 1988).

An electronic media wag on one of the all-news channels suggested (in 1988) that nobody believed theories of poverty anymore—not even the theorists who had developed them. This statement may represent a slight exaggeration—academic theorists are generally quite reluctant to give up on their favorite theories. It does not, however, adequately convey the present overall lack of enthusiasm with theories and explanations of poverty.

While we have recently been subjected to a number of laser-like penetrating insights into contemporary poverty, summed up by terms such as "new poor," "near poor," "feminization," "urban underclass," "rural ghetto" and "deindustrialization," nothing like the sustained interest of two decades ago in theorizing about (or, even thinking about) poverty appears to be evident at present. And no single theoretical approach or perspective seems capable of provoking much reaction. Even the seemingly heretical view that federal programs are the ultimate causes of poverty draws largely a yawn from most of the academic community.

Such lack of interest is particularly true with respect to poverty in Appalachia. With the notable exception of poverty among the elderly, most of the poverty-related problems which attracted significant attention in the 1960s are more or less as serious in the 1980s, while some new forms of poverty have emerged alongside the older forms. Yet, nothing like the sustained interest of that earlier time can be found today. Two decades of energy crisis, federal deficits, social program cutbacks, accountability, and privatization has had remarkably little impact on the remaining poverty problems in Appalachia. Mine and factory closings have made problems worse; inadequate public benefits, occasional new industries, and outmigration have, each in its own way, acted to lessen the severity of problems without ever offering a realistic hope to completely eliminate them.

One of the things which is most needed, at present, is renewed discussion and debate over the nature and circumstances of poverty in Appalachia. First and foremost, researchers and scholars with interests in the Appalachian region need to recognize the continued existence of poverty as an important economic, political, and social fact of life. One way to begin refocusing our attention on the phenomenon of poverty in the region, is to begin where we left off: to reexamine some of the thrusts and foci of previous research and writing on Appalachian poverty.

In the most general terms, there are probably four identifiable positions on poverty in Appalachia which have impacted most directly upon issues of public policy and community life in the region. These four positions, outlined in Table 1, can be termed: Bureaucratic Realism, Appalachian Culturalism, Predatory Capitalism, and Domestic Colonialism. It is possible to begin with any of these four dramatically different world-views on Appalachia and to reach startlingly different conclusions regarding the problem of poverty in the region. Like the television commentator cited above, however, each of these perspectives rings somewhat hollow in the world of the 1990s.

TABLE 1 Four Perspectives on Appalachian Culture and Poverty

	Appalachian People Are	
	Typically American	Culturally Unique
The Poor Are:		
Disadvantaged	Administrative Realism	Appalachian Culturalism
Oppressed/ Exploited	Predatory Capitalism	Domestic Colonialism

We shall briefly examine each of them in turn:

Bureaucratic Realism

This is a view of the Appalachian region shared by most federal and state public agencies, including the Appalachian Regional Commission and the state government departments which administer the categorical aid programs for the eligible poor. From this vantage point, the Appalachian Region is a congressionally defined, 13 state, multi-jurisdictional, administrative district characterized chiefly by a number of inter-related social and economic problems, the solutions of which are important objects of public policy concern. The region as a whole is the administrative domain of a federal agency, the Appalachian Regional Commission, which has ultimate responsibility for the problems of the region.

The lack of employment opportunities for residents of the region is a high priority consideration in any list of such problems (Zeller and Miller, 1968). Economic development, heavily concentrated upon capture of new industries for the jobs and tax revenues they bring, is perhaps the most important proximate objective of recent public policy in the Appalachian region. In bureaucratic realism, the problem of poverty has dissolved into the more general problem of economic underdevelopment.

The sources of this dissolution are not hard to trace. Shortly after its creation in 1965, the Appalachian Region Commission embarked upon its imaginative, but controversial, regional development strategy, which stressed highway construction and health care facilities as the key elements in the improvement of the economic infrastructure of the region. This strategy still tends to enrage many in the region who see it as a strategy of bringing a distinctive cultural minority into the homogenized middle-class mass, or who feared that "highways in are also highways out" and will contribute further to the depopulation of the region.

To administrative realists, poor people are fairly normal people—clients of public assistance, perhaps distinguishable by their eligibility or "ineligibility." Poverty is an economic condition whose principal characteristic is lack of money. Work is what people must do in order to enjoy a satisfactory quality of life. Unemployment, or underemployment therefore, are the principal proximate causes of poverty.

Above all else, stress upon national public policy and economic development tends to discount most of the unique or distinguishing characteristics of poverty in Appalachia. Poverty is defined in largely statistical terms following standard methods. Orshansky (1966, 1968), Perry (1979), and Tickamyer and Tickamyer (1987) are among the many statistical studies of poverty in the region. Poverty may exist in the region in greater numbers and proportions, but the essential characteristics of Appalachian poverty are not seen as fundamentally different from poverty elsewhere.

Traditionally, bureaucratic realism has been built for the past two decades upon a two-fold strategy against poverty in the region: On the one hand, reliance upon the same programs and services found elsewhere in the U.S., and, on the other hand, the Appalachian Regional Commission "growth centers" strategy in which health and other services are concentrated in areas with high growth potential while highway development provide egress to these areas from more isolated pockets of poverty. (U.S. News and World Report, September 27, 1965; WVGOECD, 1980; WVGOECD, 1983). Largely because of this continuing Appalachian Regional Commission strategy, community-level economic development remains as the preferred anti-poverty strategy of bureaucratic realism in the 1970s and 1980s. (Whitman, 1986; Trent, Weigand and Smith, 1985; Blair, 1973; McNeill and Miller, 1971). Grave doubts continue, however, about the efficacy of bureaucratic realism as an anti-poverty strategy.

Appalachian Culturalism

One of the sources of those doubts is a view of poverty which is grounded in a social outlook on the region which can be termed "Appalachian Culturalism," and which tends to stress the uniqueness of beliefs, attitudes, and folkways in the region as important factors in understanding poverty. At least since the time of the local color writers of the 19th Century, and probably well before, there has been a conception of the Appalachian region as a place apart in which ways of life unique and distinct from those known by most Americans existed. Whether in the form of popculture stereotypes like Lil Abner and Snuffy Smith, or in serious scholarly studies of Appalachian values, or Appalachian arts and crafts, the sense of a unique and cherished cultural heritage has been encouraged and promoted. One of the defining characteristics of this strange place is the acceptance of subsistence life styles and high levels of poverty as normal or characteristic.

From this vantage point, Appalachia as a cultural unity is not in any fundamental sense the large region associated with the federal administrative district served by the Appalachian Regional Commission, but a much smaller area composed of parts of western North and South Carolina, eastern Tennessee and Kentucky and most of southern West Virginia. (Approximately this same area is known in the Appalachian Regional Commission argot as "Central Appalachia.")

Weller (1965) identified a long list of traits which he says define Appalachian culture. Probably the most important for an understanding of the Appalachian poor is the sense of resignation and fatalism. Irelan (1966) summarized studies of social attitudes, family patterns, education levels, health, and consumer practices among the poor in Appalachia and other "subcultures." Dial (undated) has discussed the uniqueness of Appalachian language, and Coles (1971) has discussed distinctive Appalachian child-rearing practices.

In its more romantic strains, Appalachian culturalism is prone to view work as passé in the world of the hollows, where people survive by hunting, fishing, gardening, and collecting welfare. As with other cases of romantic poverty in distant, remote and picturesque places, poverty may not be viewed as quite so negative because it is part of a traditional way of life.

As one source puts it:

> Thus, the mountaineer appears to be at variance with the standardized image of the American in everyday life. Consequently, he is accused of possessing negative attitudes, of being a defeatist, of having an inferiority complex, and of lacking appreciation for education. His lack of social skills in modern social situations is dubbed by some as having a "backwoods flavor." His inability to follow expected behavior patterns in group situations is assigned to what some call "rural values." (Zeller and Miller, 1968.)

Appalachia, it is often said, was a region settled by rugged individualists, more interested in their own private little worlds" than in any large-scale plans for society or the state (Zeller and Miller, 1968).

This view of Appalachian uniqueness as an indigenous cultural product has not been entirely unchallenged. While others have viewed the region as a distinct subculture within contemporary American life, Shapiro (1980) views "the myth of Appalachia" as largely a fabrication of journalists and intellectuals which began in the colonial era, when the region was the "wild west." It was substantially supplemented by the missionaries and local color writers, who among other things, fostered the arts and crafts movement in the region—thus originating mountain music, quilting, and clogging—some of the more colorful cultural artifacts found in the region.

This view has often been associated with other culture of poverty arguments, for obvious reasons. It is even quite likely that such culture of poverty explanations have been largely discounted as general explanations of poverty in Appalachia. For example, Billings (1974) casts doubt upon the theories of Ford, Weller, Photiadis, et al, that traditional Appalachian culture is a cause of continuing poverty in the region, and suggested that fuller understanding of the causes of poverty in the region would "require a comprehensive social history." It seems likely that Appalachia might better be viewed as a culture of subsistence than a culture of poverty. It is also reasonable that poverty is not an individual, but a family and community concern. Everywhere in the region, localism prevails, with relative indifference to the outside world.

Appalachian culturalism accounts for a large portion of the total research output on poverty-related phenomena in the region. Rebow, Berkman and Kessler (1983) isolated "learned helplessness" as a component of the culture of poverty in Appalachia. Lowndes (1972) examined the impact of mass communications on modernization among the Appalachian poor. Ball (1968) examined Southern Appalachians in what he termed an "analgesic subculture." Peterson, Stivers, and Peters (1986) studied the role of family members and others in the career decisions of low-income Appalachian youth.

Gender is one of the most examined issues in this literature. Thus, Philliber (1982) examines the phenomenon of working wives in relation to low-income status of low-income Appalachian migrants. Kenkel (1980) examines the occupational and marriage plans of low-income high school girls in Appalachia and the Southeast. Hennon and Photiadis (1979) investigated the changing role of rural Appalachian males in low-income family structures.

Predatory Capitalism

Bureaucratic realism and Appalachian culturalism generally fail to capture the sense of frustration and anger among the Appalachian poor and those who speak for them. Others have sought in various ways to get at these questions.

One of these views is the "social control" thesis which posits that the function of public assistance in capitalist society is to regulate the poor and keep them underemployed for the benefit of corporate profits. The most extensive general statement of this view of poverty is by Richard Cloward and Frances Fox Piven in the book *Regulating the Poor* (1971), and a paper presented by them at a conference on public welfare held at West Virginia University in 1971.

Although the paper discusses the Anglo-American public welfare tradition, and makes numerous references to contemporary national issues, it contains no unique or distinct references to the Appalachian region. Piven and Cloward (1972), and Walls (1976), however, applied a similar perspective to the region.

From the vantage point of predatory capitalism, poverty is a necessary precondition of the effective functioning of labor markets in capitalist economies. Succinctly stated, in Appalachia, profits of outside corporations are dependent upon a large, enduring class of workers who are kept unemployed and/or underemployed. Walls (1976), for example, speaks of this as "cultural hegemony and capitalist domination."

Two issues have been particularly important to an understanding of poverty from the viewpoint of predatory capitalism: The declining importance of mining (and more recently, manufacturing) as a source of employment in the region, has resulted in a growing "surplus population" of workers. In addition, ownership of a large percentage of the land in Appalachia is by outside interests (Miller, 1972; Gaventa and Horton, 1982). One of the most persistently heard criticisms of the Appalachian Regional Commission development strategy from this perspective is the view that the principal effect of economic development will be for the natives to become the servants of middle-class retirees and vacationing second-home owners (Whisnant, 1974).

In large measure, predatory capitalism has served the historic mission of giving voice to the alienation and sense of powerlessness often shared by poor and nonpoor alike in the region. At the same time, from this perspective poverty is often reduced to a mere background or preamble concept serving only to introduce other questions. Alas, the essentially sound insight that an understanding of poverty also requires an understanding of the wealthy and powerful, has proven to be the pretext for a generalized loss of interest in the problem of poverty in the region.

Domestic Colonialism

A fourth model is based on an implicit comparison of Appalachia with "underdeveloped" regions in Africa and Asia formerly colonized by European nations. Although this view overlaps to some degree with that of predatory capitalism (e.g., Walls, 1976), the primary emphasis here is generally more political than economic.

In one of the earliest statements of the domestic colonialism view, Friedmann (1966) suggests that comparisons of characteristics common to poor regions and poor nations suggest the existence of a syndrome of collective poverty, but do not support a hypothesis of structural similarities. Kahn (1970) blends aspects of the culturalism and colonialism views in his comparison of rural Appalachian and urban poverty. Appalachia, he says, is an economic colony, drained of important resources by absentee ownership and political control. Parsons (1969) raised questions about the appropriateness of the comparison with underdeveloped countries as a basis for issues of public policy. Lewis (1978) brings together a variety of perspectives on this issue.

The colonialism model appears to be largely an outgrowth of the experiences of local community organizers in the War on Poverty. Much literature from that period is approached from that standpoint. For example, Bould (1977) argues that rural poverty is a political, as well as an economic, problem.

The domestic colonialism perspective often shares much of the anger and stridency of poverty in the context of an unbroken history of Anglo-American class domination; adherents of this view tend to set issues within a unique regional history of exploitation.

The basic view of domestic colonialism is that Appalachia represents a domestic colony within the United States—with a largely surplus population stockpiled for national emergency purposes, and rich mineral resources exported by outside sources with maximum cost and minimum gain to the state. Unlike any of the other three positions, the domestic colonial view typically links public welfare issues directly with environmental issues (strip mining, air, and water pollution), land ownership, housing, and other issues.

The following excerpt summarizes important aspects of this view:

> Appalachia is America's Third World. The absolute control the coal companies had over people's lives in the old company towns is no more, but the power of absentee corporate owners to affect the economic future of local communities is still massive. The situation is most severe in the coal counties, where half the land surface is corporately owned and 72 percent is absentee-owned. In Logan County, West Virginia, 11 corporations own nearly everything . . . (*Southern Exposure,* Jan–Feb, 1982, 41).

One of the most basic issues raised by the domestic colonialism model is a definitional one: What exactly is that that is being referred to as poor? The region itself, or a portion of the population within it? Simon, for example, focuses on the region in his contrast of domestic colonialism with what he calls the "uneven development" model (1981). The question, then, which is begged by domestic colonialism is one very comparable to that raised by Appalachian cultures: Is the experience of poor persons in Appalachia in any way different than that of being poor elsewhere in American society?

Universes of Discourse and Poverty

The essential differences between these four perspectives are less a matter of rival hypotheses about the nature and causes of poverty than a matter of the different universes of discourse with which they are anchored. Without remarking at all on the truth or values of the statements produced in these perspectives, we can make some observations about each perspective solely as a system of terms. For example, the language of bureaucratic realism is primarily the language of policy analysis, with heavy accents of political and economic utilitarianism and individualism. In general, the language of bureaucratic realism tends to rationalize poverty into a series of negative strategic choices that tend to infuriate Appalachian culturalists in particular. "Unemployed? Then move where the jobs are!" and so forth. Statements of Appalachian culturalism are often spoken in local dialects of the region, with heavy reliance upon metaphorical or archaic localisms. Appalachian culturalism often tends to romanticize Appalachian poverty into a developmental experience, moral challenge, or personal and family struggle. The words "poor but happy" come easily in this language. Predatory capitalism, and to a lesser extent, domestic colonialism tend to be built on a substructure of Marxian sociology and critical theory, relying heavily on terms like "alienation," "class," and "exploitation." Such language seems, to many, particularly apt to describe aspects of the localism, Jacksonian populist politics, and tradition of exploitive business practices of the region. At the present time, speakers of these dialects are finding it easy to adopt the term "underclass" as a suitable descriptor of the Appalachian poor.

It is almost as though we were faced with theoretical statements about poverty in English, Swahili, Farsi and Korean. So long as the purpose of statements in these various languages is (as it often may be) to support the general world views of their respective communities, one need feel little discomfort with this state of affairs.

If the problem is defined as one of constructing a coherent general theory of poverty in Appalachia, however, quite a different problem arises. Before we can possibly compare or evaluate these four perspectives on Appalachian poverty in any great depth, it would be desirable to translate them into a single language. Except that, in this case, there is no apparently neutral fifth language into which to translate statements about Appalachian poverty. Thus, the challenge of furthering general understanding of Appalachian poverty at present may well boil down to translation of the key insights of each perspective into the theoretical languages of the other perspectives. Some of this translation happens already on a more or less ad hoc basis. One commonly hears references to "empowerment" scattered among statements of bureaucratic realism and Appalachian culturalism, for example. And, at least for a time, the term "underclass" may well permeate all four perspectives.

Conclusions

What is needed at the present time is yet another "rediscovery" of poverty in Appalachia. A contemporary rediscovery of Appalachian poverty has not one, but four, rich traditions of research and inquiry with which to work. Each of these perspectives has its strengths and weaknesses. These perspectives are, however, as a group somewhat dated and out of touch with the realities of poverty in the region in the late 1980s. The simplistic division of the region into Northern, Central, and Southern Appalachia by the bureaucratic realists of Appalachian Regional Commission, for example, fails to deal adequately with the essential social, economic, and political boundaries within the region. However, the tendency of the Appalachian culturalists to deal only with the Central subregion as *the* real Appalachia is similarly limited. Both might well benefit from the much more refined subregions offered by the Economic Research Service Population Section in the U.S. Department of Agriculture which divides the counties of Appalachia into at least five separate subregions.

The rediscovery of poverty in Appalachia should seek a more balanced view of the continuing political, economic, and social phenomena of poverty in the region and in the nation than that offered by any of the four past perspectives. Future studies of Appalachian poverty should take into account such factors as regional urbanization and deindustrialization, and the impact of recent national trends such as rural poverty, deinstitutionalization, growing homelessness, and the feminization and racialization of poverty. Such approaches are likely, of necessity, to touch upon many of the themes most central to each of the four perspectives.

One of the most important themes for contemporary research on poverty is likely to be the convergence of the Appalachian poor into the mainstreams of poverty in the U.S. In the past twenty years, the Appalachian Regional Commission growth centers strategy appears to have brought a clustering of populations—poor and nonpoor alike—into the cities of the region. As a result, it is quite likely that both the urban Appalachian poor and the rural poor left behind are much more like urban and rural poor of the rest of the country than they were twenty years ago. In this context, family breakup may be as important a factor in Appalachian poverty as in mainstream America (Pierce, 1978). Similarly, deinstitutionalization, deindustrialization, urbanization, and an increasingly ancient housing stock have all contributed to the phenomenon of homelessness in the region as they have elsewhere.

This convergence thesis is likely to be closely associated with the perspectives of bureaucratic realism. Acceptance of such convergence arguments should not necessarily be equated with rejection of culture of poverty explanations of the causes of poverty. There is still a role for studies of the family structure and other subcultural characteristics of the

Appalachian poor. Such foci need not dwell exclusively on the poor, however. There is probably still merit in Weller's (1967) question asked in the title of an article in Volume 1 of *Appalachian Review:* "Who is the Target Group?" (of research and intervention)? His recommendation in that article was to concentrate upon studying wealthy industrialists and economically secure residents of the region to gain a more complete picture of the problem of poverty in Appalachia. In many cases, studies of small town businessmen, politicians, social welfare professionals and other "middlemen" would prove equally rewarding.

Nor should one ignore or reject the insights possible with the Predatory Capitalist and Domestic Colonial approaches. The Appalachian land ownership study (Gaventa and Horton, 1982), as well as recent indictments of local officials in a southern West Virginia county, shows that there is still merit in such approaches in a region where economic exploitation and political corruption remain important realities bearing upon the condition of the poor.

The cleavages in ideology, politics, and world views which are behind the four viewpoints on Appalachian poverty identified in this paper, remain strong within the region and the scholarly community today. Thus, it is probably naive to argue for any theoretical or research convergence among them. It is not naive, however, to suggest that each of these perspectives is a bit dated and showing signs of age due to the general neglect of any research interest in Appalachian poverty in recent years. Yet, each points to important research questions which have gone uninvestigated and to hypotheses which have gone untested. At the same time, none deals adequately with the "new poverty" which has arisen in the region and the nation. All things considered, therefore, the time has come to reopen serious study of Appalachian poverty.

27

by Sally Ward Maggard

From Farm to Coal Camp to Back Office and McDonald's: Living in the Midst of Appalachia's Latest Transformation

Introduction

As the principal fuel of industrialization throughout the twentieth century, coal is one of the world's most valued natural resources. The industrial development of the world's coal reserves involved social transformations of enormous scale. A substantial body of literature addresses these social changes, including research on the concentrated control and ownership of natural resources and land; the social transformation of pre-industrial economies and creation of coal communities; the creation of an industrial labor force; class divisions and conflict; regulation and management of the industry; workplace safety and health; the distribution of income, jobs and resources; and relationships between the state and capital in coal development.[1]

What is not well understood in the history and organization of coal mining is the importance of gender relations and gender ideology. This paper examines ways that gender shaped the mining of coal, the nature of local labor markets, and the structure and operation of households in the coalfields. Further, it argues that a particular mix of industrial heritage, culture, and gender shapes current economic restructuring in the coalfields, as well as policy initiatives promoted in the name of regional development.

Appalachian Coal: a Fact of Industrial Life

One of the most important coal basins in the United States is in Central Appalachia, the source of more than half of the bituminous coal mined in the country and almost all U.S. coal exports (Harvey 1986). For over two hundred years miners have dug this coal from the ground, initially supplying fuel for blacksmiths and home heating, and then, as the nation industrialized, providing fuel for factories, steel mills, railroad boilers, and power plants (United Mine Workers of America 1976; Harvey 1986; Seltzer 1985). As early as 1914 the famous labor agitator, "Mother" Mary Harris Jones passionately extolled the importance of this labor:

> ". . . in the last fifty years in the history of this nation look and see what the miners, and the miners alone, have done. Look at the thousands and hundreds of thousands of miles of railroads that you have built. Look at the liners that are plying the oceans, connecting nation with nation. Look at the telegraph lines, look at the streets, the subways, the elevated ways. Who has built them? The miners. You move the nation!" (quoted in Steel 1988, 143)

Since World War II, mechanization in mining has increased productivity but decreased the demand for human labor. This is illustrated by changes in mining employment in West Virginia, one of the most important Appalachian coal states. From 1950 to 1970 the state's mine work force fell by 70 percent, while productivity rose as the "continuous miner" replaced labor intensive pick and shovel mining methods. In 1967, the average coal miner produced 3,567 tons a year, up from a 1950 average of 1,217 tons (U.S. Bureau of Labor Statistics 1961). Over the next two decades an additional 30,000 mining jobs were lost (Nyden 1989) while productivity continued to climb with the introduction of long-wall technology. By 1988 the average West Virginia miner was producing 5,921 tons a year (Lewis 1992). These trends mean that while Appalachian coal remains viable in world coal trade, the industrial labor force and communities which have traditionally supported the development and growth of the industry are in crisis. To understand the crisis and the nature of its impact, it is important to review industrial history and consider the structure of local coal economies as the region entered its current era of transformation.

Gender and Industrial History in Coal Mining

In the initial phases of coal development, an industrial infrastructure was carved from rural, independent agricultural economies in Central Appalachia (Billings, Blee, Swanson 1986). This involved purchasing and clearing timber, buying coal rights and land, brokering financial packages between investors and producers, extending rail transport into coal regions, constructing the industrial sites themselves, constructing coal camps and towns, and recruiting an industrial labor force (Lewis 1992; Eller 1982; Maggard 1981).

In general, women were not in positions to direct this industrial development. Most of the necessary productive assets were and continue to be owned and managed by men: land, capital, geological survey capability, technology, and labor. Decisions to sell agricultural land and/or rights to minerals underneath the land were usually made by male members of households (Weise 1993). Similarly, decisions to relocate families to the new coal camps were usually made by men (Coles and Coles 1978; Kahn 1972; see also González 1991; Flynt 1986). Women were largely on the sidelines as ownership and control over natural resources were negotiated, and again as the necessary infrastructure was constructed. Corporate decisions about the composition of the labor force, efficient ways to support and reproduce that labor force, and tolerable degrees of economic diversity resulted in a rigid division and valuing of labor by sex in the coalfields. Production jobs in the mines were reserved for men, recruited to constitute a "judicious mix" of mountain farmers, foreign immigrants, and southern blacks (Lewis 1987; Bailey 1973). Women were assigned to the "auxiliary" work of managing households and caring for dependents and the disabled.

A family settlement pattern in the coal camps served to "discipline" miners, provide unpaid domestic service to support the mine labor force, and increase profits for owners and stockholders. The thousands of men recruited to mine coal were housed near mine sites with the family members who fed them, cleaned their clothes, and cared for them when injured or sick. Miners' wages were recycled in company owned stores and rents. The presence of wives and children acted as a stabilizing force, discouraging absenteeism and high employee turnover (Pudup 1990; Simon and Justice 1981; U.S. Department of Labor 1925).[2]

For men, leaving agriculture for coal mining meant working inside the coal mines in exchanges for wages. Men lost control over the means of economic production, but their labor was understood as central to the economy. Women, too, lost control over the means of production. Now their economic survival depended on their connections to the men in their households who earned miners' wages.[3]

Women had been directly involved in all phases of rural production in farm economies (Pudup 1990; Verhoeff 1917). In the coal camps, women found that many of their agricultural skills were necessary for survival. Gardening and livestock raising were widespread, and small-scale home production of goods stretched miners' wages (Pudup 1990; Trotter 1990; Lewis 1989). In addition, some women in mining camps earned income by taking in boarders and doing laundry.

Although almost all women worked without pay inside their households, some women found employment in and around the Central Appalachian coal camps (Pudup 1990). Mining increased the need for rural hospitals, and some women learned nursing through a system of apprenticeships (Maggard 1988). As domestic servants and seamstresses, some women provided goods and services for middle and upper income residents of coal towns. Others worked as teachers in company towns.

Overall, there were few opportunities for waged work in mining regions for women or for men. Economic activity centered on a single industry. Competition among many coal producers and from other fuels intensified pressures to keep production costs low, resulting in severe measures to control the work force (Dix 1988; Seltzer 1985). Owners opposed a diversified local economy that could create competition for labor and could inflate wages above levels set by the industry. As a result, most men worked in mining, some in forestry and agriculture. Others worked in construction, building coal camps, mines, rail lines, and new buildings in the expanding county seat towns (Maggard 1981). Most women did the less visible, unpaid work required in social reproduction and household management.[4]

A two-pronged, gendered ideology emerged to justify this division and unequal valuing of labor. The ideology of the "male breadwinner" first of all assigned women's "proper" place to domestic labor inside coal camps.[5] Second, it assigned men's "proper" place to the dangerous work of mining coal. Ideas of femininity and masculinity came to be tied up with this allocation of labor and reinforced economic arrangements, as the issue of coal mine safety and health illustrates.

The coal industry in the United States has a dismal health and safety record (Curran 1993; National Research Council 1982; McAteer 1973), and mining is consistently ranked as the most or second most dangerous industry in the country. Industry representatives have been quick to argue that little can be done to change this, that fate, nature, and carelessness of miners themselves are to be blamed for the death, injury, and disease that plagues coal mining. Comparative research on mine safety and health, however, demonstrates tremendous variation among industrialized nations and challenges such explanations (McAteer and Galloway 1980; Drury 1965). The position that mining is "naturally" dangerous excuses unsafe working conditions and mining practices and appalling rates of injury and death. Reserving mining jobs for men and then equating masculinity with the daily risk of death and disability makes men the principle victims. Both notions work to keep production costs low in mining.

The belief that coal mining should be reserved for men has kept women out of mining jobs throughout most of the history of the industry. In the United States women were able to break through this cultural barrier and force their way into these industrial jobs only in the 1970s (Hall 1980; Scott 1977).[6] "Women's work" has always involved heavy physical labor and long hours. Furthermore, women have suffered terrible rates of injury and death in other industrial labor (Groneman and Norton 1987; Milkman 1985; Conway 1979). In an economy dominated by a single industry, the argument that women should not work in that industry because it is dangerous reserved the highest paid employment in the local economy for men.

In the Appalachian coalfields, cultural norms segregating "men's work" and "women's work" and identifying males as the sole providers of the "family wage" functioned as powerful ideological supports for the economic system that developed in coal. They defined men as expendable, left women dependent on these men, and assigned women to perform unpaid domestic labor. The situation left working class women and men extremely vulnerable.

This mix of industrial history and culture structured occupational opportunity and the quality of work life throughout much of this century. Men's work has been higher waged and more highly valued, but dependent on changing technologies in the production process and on fluctuating demand in the world coal market. Women's work has consistently been understood as secondary to men's work, as supplementing income earned by a male "breadwinner." Much of women's work has been highly productive and located within households, but it remained unwaged and, in effect, invisible.

From the earliest period of industrialization in coal, then, local economies were sharply segregated by sex in terms of work and income. This segregation was overlain with and supported by gendered ideology. Patterns of economic opportunity, earning capacity, market and household divisions of labor, and gendered self-identities which characterize the coalfields today can be traced to this period of industrial history.

Local Labor Markets, Gender, and Restructuring

One indication of the legacy of this economic history is the pattern of men's and women's participation in the formal labor force. Table 1 compares labor force participation rates in the United States with West Virginia for selected periods from 1900 to 1990. Two patterns are evident. First, both men's and

TABLE 1 **Civilian Labor Force Participation Rates* for United States and West Virginia by Sex, 1900–1990**

	Male		*Female*	
	United States	***West Virginia***	***United States***	***West Virginia***
1900	88.0%	80.0%	18.0%	90.0%
1930	84.1%	72.4%	21.9%	13.1%
1950	78.9%	74.6%	27.8%	19.6%
1960	83.3%	67.8%	37.7%	24.3%
1970	79.7%	66.0%	43.3%	29.4%
1980	77.4%	68.4%	51.5%	36.5%
1990	76.1%	64.6%	57.5%	42.6%

*Rates are calculated for persons gainfully employed according to age thresholds which change over time. The Census counted persons 10 years of age and above through 1930; persons 14 and above in 1940 and 1950; persons 16 and above since 1960.

Source: U.S. Census of Population, U.S. Bureau of Labor Statistics, and Statistical Abstract of the U.S. for selected years.

women's labor participation has been consistently lower in West Virginia than the national average. Second, women's participation rates in West Virginia have been dramatically lower than men's, the lowest of any state in the nation throughout most of this century. These patterns are related to the structure of occupational opportunity and to the rigidly sex segregated roles that have characterized West Virginia's economy.[7]

A second legacy of West Virginia's economic history is the pattern of employment across industrial sectors. As late as 1970, the economy of Central Appalachia was less diversified than the nation as a whole in terms of population employed in different industries (Appalachian Regional Commission 1979). Fewer people in the region worked in retail and wholesale trade, professional services, manufacturing, domestic and entertainment services, finance, insurance and real estate, business and repair services and construction than in the nation as a whole. Far more people, however, worked in mining, forestry, and educational services.

Table 2 illustrates the lack of industrial diversification in West Virginia in 1980 and 1990, and its relationship to the sex segregation of the labor force. In 1980 and 1990, men's employment was concentrated in four industrial sectors: mining, manufacturing, construction, and retail trade. Women's employment was concentrated in three sectors: retail trade, health services, and education, but with some concentration in manufacturing.

Within those industrial sectors in which women work, their jobs are often clustered at the low-waged end of an industry. For instance, in 1990 of all people employed in manufacturing in West Virginia, men (83.4 percent) were far more likely than women (16.6 percent) to be producing chemicals and allied products. Women (87.1 percent) were far more likely than men (12.9 percent) to be working in apparel and other finished textile products. The average wage in chemical manufacturing in 1990 was $804.13 a week. In contrast, the average weekly wage in apparel and textile manufacturing was $191.01 a week (WVBEIS 1991). Overall, this means that women are at a disadvantage relative to men in terms of earning power. In 1990 employed women earned only fifty cents for every dollar men earned. West Virginia men with high school degrees had incomes greater than women with seven years or more of college (U.S. Bureau of Census 1990; West Virginia Women's Commission 1993).

Taken together, these data describe an undiversified and sex-segregated economy with particularly severe consequences for women. Women's participation in the labor force has been low, the range of opportunity for participation has been narrow, and the wages women have earned have been low. While men have traditionally had more options and worked in higher waged jobs than women, they, too have been constrained by a limited range of job choices. These patterns trace back to the industrial order created with industrialization in coal. Today, these patterns are dramatically changing, and women and men are experiencing the changes in very different ways.

During the 1980s, the economy in West Virginia moved from its traditional base in extractive and manufacturing industries toward an economy based in the production of services (Table 3). In 1979, mining was the largest industry in West Virginia in terms of earnings. By 1989, the largest industries in the state in terms of earnings were in services, accounting for 21.2 percent of all earnings. These developments represent an important shift in the structure of the economy in just one decade.

From 1977 to 1987, the state lost almost 70,000 mining and manufacturing jobs. In mining, 27,332 jobs were lost at the same time that coal production rose. Over this period, mining jobs averaged $36,400 in annual wages. Manufacturing, averaging $20,000 a year, declined by 41,823 jobs, primarily in metal and chemical industries. Other high waged sectors that decreased dramatically include construction (down by 13,056 jobs, average wages $20,000 a year) and transportation and utilities (down by 16,030 jobs, average wages $30,000 a year). Employment in mining has continued to plummet, dropping by 21.7 percent from 1985 to 1990 (Center for Economic Research 1991a).

TABLE 2 Industry of Employed Persons for West Virginia by Sex: 1980–1990

[Denominators = Total Employed Persons 16 Years and Over in 1980 (689,461) and 1990 (671,085)]

Industry	*Males* 1980 Number	%	1990 Number	%	% Change	*Females* 1980 Number	%	1990 Number	%	% Change
Total Employed Persons	430,240	100.0	381,984	100.0		259,221	100.0	289,101	100.0	
Agriculture, forestry, fishing	8,924	1.3	10,197	1.5	+0.2	2,311	0.3	2,307	0.3	0.0
Mining (coal, oil, gas)	65,983	9.6	34,488	5.1	–4.5	3,265	0.5	1,924	0.3	–0.2
Construction	48,437	7.0	43,262	6.4	–0.6	3,742	0.5	3,593	0.5	0.0
Manufacturing	8,139	14.2	75,462	11.2	–3.0	28,443	4.1	24,279	3.5	–0.6
-Apparel, textiles	709	0.1	586	0.1	0.0	4,586	0.7	3,961	0.6	–0.1
-Printing, publishing	3,494	0.5	3,970	0.6	+0.1	2,353	0.3	2,969	0.4	+0.1
-Chemicals and allied products	23,304	3.4	15,377	2.3	–1.1	3,471	0.5	3,066	0.4	–0.1
Transportation	26,118	3.8	24,182	3.6	–0.2	4,575	0.7	5,583	0.8	+0.1
Communication and other public utilities	18,555	2.7	17,434	2.6	–0.1	6,785	1.0	6,139	0.9	–0.1
Wholesale trade	19,207	2.8	17,399	2.6	–0.2	5,158	0.7	5,142	0.7	0.0
Retail trade	51,783	7.5	56,083	8.4	+0.9	56,917	8.3	66,739	9.7	+1.4
-General merchandise stores	3,869	0.6	3,913	0.6	0.0	11,164	1.6	10,806	1.6	0.0
-Food, bakery, dairy stores	11,015	1.6	11,515	1.7	+0.1	9,888	1.4	12,824	1.9	+0.5
-Eating, drinking places	7,522	1.1	11,386	1.7	+0.6	15,989	2.3	20,403	3.0	+0.7
-Auto dealers, auto supply	9,364	1.4	6,972	1.0	–0.4	1,865	0.3	1,525	0.2	–0.1
Finance, business related services	22,042	3.2	26,974	4.0	+0.8	19,232	2.8	25,830	3.9	+1.1
Personal services, including household	5,510	0.8	5,963	1.6	+0.8	15,214	2.2	14,722	2.1	–0.1
Entertainment recreation services	2,889	0.4	4,308	0.6	+0.2	2,216	0.3	2,982	0.4	+0.1
Health services, including hospitals	12,132	1.8	13,876	2.1	+0.3	41,533	6.0	52,871	7.7	+1.7
Other professional, related services	9,843	1.4	13,523	2.0	+0.6	10,006	1.5	19,844	3.0	+1.5
Education	22,862	3.3	23,080	3.4	+0.1	42,306	6.1	43,213	6.3	+0.2
Public administration	17,816	2.3	15,753	2.4	+0.1	17,518	2.5	13,933	2.0	–0.5

Source: Detailed Population Characteristics. Part 50. West Virginia. 1980 Census of Population. November 1983. STF4 1990 Census of the Population. June 1993.

TABLE 3 **Largest Industries and Percent of Earnings of Employed Persons for West Virginia: 1989 and 1979**

Industry	*Percent Earnings*
1989	
Services	21.2
State, local government	13.3
Manufacturing, durable goods	10.8
Mining	10.5
1979	
Mining	14.9
Manufacturing	14.6
Services	12.7
State, local government	11.0

Source: Center for Economic Research (1991a).

Overall, during the past decade the economy created relatively few new jobs in West Virginia and these were concentrated in lower waged industrial sectors, especially in services.[8] Between 1977 and 1987 there were 31,988 new service sector jobs, but they averaged only $15,000 a year in wages. The dominant service industry in West Virginia is now health services, but 62 percent of that employment is in the lower waged non-profit sector (Center for Economic Research 1991b). Other new jobs (over 9,000) were created in retail trade, but they averaged only $13,000 a year in wages. The 4,784 new jobs in finance, insurance, and real estate during this period averaged $14,500 a year in wages (Center for Economic Research 1991a).

The consequences of this economic restructuring for West Virginia are staggering. Many people have simply left the state. The population declined by 8 percent from 1980 to 1990. Forty four of the state's fifty five counties lost population over the decade (U.S. Bureau of Census 1990). After the 1990 Census, West Virginia lost one of its four U.S. House of Representative seats.

Earnings fell substantially. West Virginia ranked 50th in the nation in per capita income in 1989, dropping down from 47th in 1979. In the same period, median household income fell 14.8 percent (adjusting for inflation in consumer prices). The poverty rate for families rose from 11.7 percent in 1979 to 16 percent in 1989, and almost one quarter of the population now lives in poverty (Center for Economic Research 1991a).

Since the mid-1970s, the unemployment rate in West Virginia has been higher than the average national rate, and in 1992 it reached 11.4 percent. In coal counties like McDowell, Wyoming, Boone, Logan, and Marion, unemployment that year ranged from 13 to 22.7 percent higher than the state average (Yoder 1993). Two thirds of the 64,000 West Virginians who were out of work in 1990 had "fresh" work experience. That is, 66.5 percent of West Virginia's unemployed people in 1990 had just lost their jobs and were looking for work (Pitcher 1992).

Restructuring is felt in different ways by women and by men. Female-headed households are particularly vulnerable and represent the fastest growing group among the poverty population. A stunning 55 percent of West Virginia families with a female head and related children under the age of eighteen (no husband present) were below poverty level in 1989. The comparable figure in 1979 was 43.4 percent (U.S. Bureau of Census 1990, 1983).

The changing economic structure creates new opportunities and new disadvantages for women and men to earn income. Most of the industrial sectors that are shrinking are those which have traditionally employed men. Most of those that are growing have traditionally employed women (Table 4). This mismatch between new jobs and the skills of the unemployed means that unemployed coal miners and manufacturing workers are unlikely to fill new jobs in services and retail trade. Differences in male and female labor force participation rates from 1980 to 1990 reflect this problem. The female rate increased by 6.1 percent, while the male rate fell by 3.8 percent.[9] As a result, state economic forecasts do not project a drop in unemployment with current job creation (Center for Economic Research 1993).

Growth and decline trends of the late 1980s are expected to continue in West Virginia. Occupation projections to the year 2000 show most job openings in retail and services and the fewest in manufacturing related occupations (Culp et.al. 1991). Since new jobs in services and retail employment are in low-waged industries, these changes promise to impoverish households. Further, they may translate into realignments of gender relations inside families. Males, the predominant household "breadwinners" in the coalfields since early in the century, are losing their positions in the region's economy. Women, on the other hand, are moving into the paid labor force in ever larger numbers, even if they still participate at lower than national rates.

There is evidence that restructuring creates tremendous strains inside households. Layoffs in coal mines tend to be followed by spikes in the incidence of domestic violence. The Women's Shelter in Charleston, West Virginia, was able to map a pattern during 1980–1982, a period of severe mine layoffs. Within two days of each announced layoff the number of calls received on domestic violence doubled (Ewen 1989).

Against the current economic insecurity, even jobs that pay only $4.50 an hour look good to many West Virginians. Chronically high and worsening unemployment, high underemployment (when skills far outstrip demands of current jobs), and a large reserve of women poised to enter the labor force mean West Virginia has a plentiful—and needy—supply of labor. As the state's industrial structure shifts and service industries and retail trade expand, employers expecting to fill jobs with low paid (but highly productive) workers find West Virginia attractive.

TABLE 4 Performance of West Virginia Industry: Percentage Change in Employment 1985–1990

Industry	*% Change*
Top Ten Performers	
Social Services	50.0
Special Trade Contractors	25.3
Lumber, Wood Products	24.2
Health Services	24.1
Eating and Drinking Places	22.9
Apparel and Accessory Stores	20.8
Amusement Services	20.4
Hotels, Other Lodging	16.4
Miscellaneous Retail	16.3
Food Stores	14.8
Bottom Ten Performers	
Apparel and Other Textile Products	–4.4
Food and Kindred Products	–6.7
General Merchandise Stores	–11.4
Chemicals and Allied Products	–11.5
Fabricated Metal Products	–13.9
Electronic, Electrical Equipment	–16.1
Oil and Gas Extraction	–19.3
Stone, Clay and Glass Products	–21.2
Coal Mining	–21.7
Textile Mill Products	–76.9

Source: West Virginia Bureau of Employment Programs; prepared by Center for Economic Research (Culp et.al. 1991).

Economic Revitalization and Reindustrialization

Local and state development officials have outlined several economic revitalization priorities for West Virginia. Two that have been successful in creating new jobs include a program to attract "back offices" to the state, and efforts to expand tourism. Both represent economic growth strategies that rest on a low waged, heavily female labor force.

Back offices are decentralized production sites housing operations of service and manufacturing companies. Employees may work at data entry and processing, market research, telemarketing, medical transcription, publishing, customer service, financial services, and piece-rate assembly. Companies dividing up and reorganizing labor into dispersed operations look for a dependable, hard working but inexpensive labor force, along with cheap office space and a business climate which supports the externalization of production costs. Wages tend to be low, and work is often part-time (Dickstein 1992).

To tempt these and other companies to relocate operations to West Virginia, the state government offers an array of financial incentives including tax credits, pre-hiring screening, training subsidies, and loan programs (Fladung 1992). West Virginia's Super Tax Credit, for example, allows recovery of up to 90 percent of capital investment through state tax credits.

A joint project with Bell Atlantic and state government called "Office of the Future" markets the state to the information services industry, while simultaneously promoting West Virginia's state of the art fiber optic and digital telecommunications system.[10] Bell Atlantic researched the suitability of West Virginia as a location site for such back offices and concluded that one of the state's most important assets is its labor force (Pitcher 1992).

Comments from executives interviewed for the study expose the painful twists economic restructuring has created for workers. Executives of five companies now operating in the state talked about the ease with which they staff their offices. Chilton Research, for instance, closed two Pennsylvania offices and moved to Charleston. According to Andy Lohan of Chilton, ". . . in Charleston we can fill them [jobs] and fill them *when* we need to fill them. Labor is so much more available in Charleston" (Pitcher 1992, p. 7). By word of mouth and few, if any, advertisements, Chilton keeps its part-time work force of between 50 and 250 employees at capacity, paying $4.25 a hour to start. Other companies report word-of-mouth hiring. Roberta Fowlkes of Bell Atlantic commented, "We've never had to advertise, and there were just hundreds of applicants just from the announcement. . . . We have no problem getting the people" (Pitcher 1992, p. 8).

Who are these people flocking to low paid, often part-time, back office jobs? According to Bell Atlantic's research, three groups of people make up a pool of workers ripe for these jobs. First, an estimated 350,000 underemployed people in West Virginia represent "an experienced, enthusiastic pool of potential office workers" ready to work for low hourly wages (Pitcher 1992, p. 7). Second, a large pool of "voluntary nonparticipants" exists in West Virginia's "hidden" labor force. These are people the federal government defines as "discouraged workers," out of work so long that they have given up looking for new jobs. According to Bell Atlantic, such "experienced people will quickly put themselves back into the job market when they see that there are jobs available" (Pitcher 1992, p. 12).

Women constitute the third group in the hidden labor pool Bell Atlantic discovered in West Virginia. According to the study, the very presence of service sector employment acts as "a driver of higher female participation" (Pitcher 1992, p. 12). Of course, the very absence of other alternatives may be a more likely "driver" of women who move into the new back office jobs. The dramatic decline in mining, manufacturing, and construction jobs, the decline in per capita and household income, and the lack of other employment options combine to make such service jobs attractive to women, not just the lure of keypunching and data entry in a job processing medical insurance claims.

Tourism is a second industrial sector that experienced job growth in the 1980s in West Virginia. Three of the top ten job growth industries in the state—eating and drinking places, amusement services, and hotels and other lodging—are clearly related to growth in tourism, as is growth in miscellaneous retail trade and food stores (Table 4). Women are heavily represented in the labor force of all of these expanding industries, earning low wages and few, if any, benefits and often working on a seasonal and part-time basis. For example, women's employment in eating and drinking places grew over the decade, but wages in 1990 averaged only $130.61 per week, making this one of the lowest paid sectors in retail trade (WVBEIS 1991).

Michal Smith has produced a blistering critique of promoting tourism as an economic development savior. By analyzing an array of social and economic indicators, Smith found that the quality of life did *not* improve in eighty-four rural counties in twelve southeastern states where the tourist industry grew from 1970 to 1984. Tourist dependent counties had higher unemployment and higher rates of poverty than counties with a more diverse economic base. "Prosperity," Smith concluded, "simply failed to 'trickle down'" from this boom in tourist industry development (1989, v).

Smith's research demonstrates that the impact of development strategies is felt unevenly in an economy. In particular, Smith found that patterns of economic benefit and loss associated with tourism expansion follow sex and race divisions in local economies. Poverty rates, for instance, were especially high in households headed by women.

Tourism, it turns out, provides jobs for women, but these jobs are marginal, seasonal, low-waged jobs in food service, retail sales, and hotel service. Construction work generated by tourism expansion is dominated by males, as is the small pool of managerial jobs which results. African Americans fare so terribly in the tourist industry that, according to Smith, they leave the region. This research indicates that growth in tourism, like the growth of "back office" employment, may offer the good news of "new jobs," but does not guarantee a recovering state economy or renewed economic security for West Virginia households and communities.

Conclusions

For well over a century, business investment and industrial development in Appalachia has been closely aligned with a system of gender relations and gender ideology. Mixing cultural norms and beliefs about men's work and women's work made good business sense in coal mining. The production costs of labor and work site preparation were kept low by equating masculinity with a willingness to work in dangerous conditions and by defining men as expendable, easy to replace after injury and death or through investment in highly productive new technologies.

Other production costs—those associated with the social reproduction of the labor force and management of households—were written off and devalued by defining them as "proper" nonwaged, work for women. Women in paid labor earned low wages since their work was considered auxiliary to the family wage that men earned at the mines.

The economic system that took form around industrial development in coal is now being pulled apart. The cultural ideal of a male breadwinner who is sole supporter of spouse and dependent children is not achievable in the emerging economy. Women are moving into paid labor, even if much of it is low waged, and men are being displaced from those jobs that drove a single-industry and sex-segregated economy. This promises a social transformation as profound as the one that carved out the coalfields at the beginning of this century.

New strategies to make profits in the region seize on the patterns in this economic change. A desperate, skilled, willing to work, and inexpensive labor force promises a supply of cheap labor. State governments struggling to "create jobs" provide investment incentives to companies eager to find cheap labor. These new investment patterns do not necessarily promise widespread well being or economic health in the region.

Scholars and government planners alike need to raise careful questions about the development strategies they study or embrace. Some policies have the effect of carving up the labor force into especially vulnerable sections and treating these vulnerabilities as state or regional "assets." Because of the economic history of the coalfields and its integral gender differences, different outcomes of development initiatives for women and men are expected.

The Appalachian coalfield region is witnessing the disassembling of a nearly century old economic and domestic arrangement. Development that merely exploits these changes for profit is not likely to move the Appalachians coalfields out of crisis. Instead, it is likely to leave residents of the region mired in the very persistent poverty that has been its mark throughout much of this century.

28

by Mary Beth Pudup

Social Class and Economic Development in Southeast Kentucky, 1820–1880

Writing in the *American Journal of Sociology* in 1898, George Vincent gave voice to the emerging interpretation of *fin-de-siècle* Appalachia as an American region unscathed by the vicissitudes of history. "American history, he wrote, "has been described as very largely a record of the westward movement of a frontier, not a geographical boundary, but a type of social life which has reacted upon and modified the ideals and political institutions of the nation. . . . But this on-rushing tide left quiet pools in the mountains of Virginia, North Carolina, Kentucky, and Tennessee. There the frontier has survived in practical isolation until this very day."[1] Vincent was among a large number of incredulous academics and professional writers who at the turn of the century after hearing about peculiar conditions there, traveled through Appalachia "from a desire to see something of this old frontier life." Vincent well represents this intrepid group, furthermore, because his travels took him through southeastern Kentucky, perhaps the most favored venue of what another commentator immortalized as the "land where time stood still."[2]

Vincent and his contemporaries were fascinated by the supposedly arrested social and economic development of Appalachia. Sheltered by the mountains, it seemed that a homespun standard of living had survived in southeast Kentucky reminiscent of the primitive existence eked out by the likes of Daniel Boone. The people of Appalachia, according to one observer, were "our contemporary ancestors."[3]

During the 1890s, it was said, Appalachia was largely peopled by subsistence farmers living in log houses, producing corn, beans, and some livestock (mainly hogs), and tending household gardens and orchards. Local trade was based on barter, and surplus eggs and feathers were traded for such goods as coffee and sugar—in short, for those few goods outside the purview of household production. Because households made their own clothes, tools, and furnishings, commercial industry was limited to combination grist- and sawmills, and even these engaged chiefly in custom work. Transportation was by foot and horseback along meandering creek beds. Finally, material conditions of life in southeast Kentucky were sustained by a cultural ethic of self-reliance and a social fabric in which kinship bonds were both warp and woof.

For the student of American social history, the survival of these conditions made Appalachia a living museum of frontier life, "useful as furnishing a fixed point . . . to measure the progress of a moving world."[4] It was in this spirit that Vincent encouraged sociology students to abandon the classroom for the mountains, "and at first hand in the Cumberlands deal with the phenomena of a social order arrested at a relatively early stage of evolution."[5] Vincent also urged economists, anthropologists, linguists, and historians to join in a coordinated effort to study preindustrial Appalachia. His call was urgent, for precisely as it was being made, the development of the bituminous coal industry was bringing irreversible changes in the constitution of the region's social and economic life.

Yet few contemporary scholars responded with detailed studies of Appalachia during the nineteenth century, and with few exceptions, Vincent's call has remained unheeded to this day.[6] The curious mix of academics, activists, and professional writers continually drawn to Appalachia during the twentieth century has instead, and quite understandably, devoted attention to the special plight of the region's bituminous coal miners. Conditions of life and work in the characteristically dangerous and cyclically unstable industry have been carefully chronicled and repeatedly scrutinized.[7]

The tragic dimensions of Appalachian industrialization have been greatly enhanced by being staged against a historical backdrop portraying preindustrial Appalachia as a land of egalitarian self-sufficiency. This juxtaposition of the modern coal-dependent society to the premodern subsistence society has become part of the standard interpretation of Appalachian history. Using the past as background to the present, however, has illuminated the latter at the expense of a detailed understanding of the former. As a result, the epithet "retarded frontier" has taken on a double meaning, referring not only to the conditions of arrested development described by Vincent at the turn of the century but also to the study of the historical processes that engendered those conditions.

In this essay I seek a deeper social historical understanding of preindustrial Appalachia by going beyond notions of arrested development to examining social class formation in nineteenth-century southeast Kentucky, part of the more isolated Appalachians. Rather than compare the region to some normative path of social development, I make a close reading of Appalachian historical geography in the empirical case studies of three southeast Kentucky counties. I begin by appraising contemporary Appalachian studies, demonstrating continuity between recent claims about preindustrial society with turn-of-the century studies like Vincent's: namely, that preindustrial Appalachia was egalitarian, static, and therefore an example of arrested development. I suggest this portrayal is based on romantic mythology more than empirical evidence. Nor do notions of arrested development account for the emergence of the indigenous landholding and commercial elite, who performed a vital role in capitalist development.

From Retarded Frontier to Traditional Mountain Subculture

In the antimodernist spirit of the day, turn-of-the-century observers saw in the Appalachian subsistence economy the rugged individualism and earthy survival "instinct" being eroded elsewhere by the twin evils of industrialization and urbanization.[8] Yet these commentators, true also to their classically American ambivalence, tempered their fascination with the primitive with a celebration of the "progress" that would guarantee its demise. Recent Appalachian studies, too, have drawn comparisons, but from a rather different perspective. Reflecting on deepening poverty amid the height of American postwar prosperity, observers have asked why the region did not benefit from industrialization in the way other regions had. The wholesale integration of Appalachia into the larger national economy and society that accompanied development of the coal industry—integration once heralded as progress—has seemed to some a step backward, for it eliminated the bases for regional self-sufficiency.

This shift in the interpretive wind has had two related implications for the study of Appalachian social history. First, it has established that the axes of social differentiation most relevant to understanding Appalachia are those separating the region from the outside world. This proposition is rooted in a rejection of "culture of poverty" theories, which ascribe economic and social problems to the persistent isolation of the region.[9] Recent regional studies have sought to eliminate the historical misconception of isolation and to demonstrate that the contemporary maladies resulted from precisely the opposite condition. Guided by a variety of theoretical frameworks, most notably the internal colonialism model, Appalachian studies have agreed on an essentially geographical conception of social relations that depicts Appalachia as the colony and victim of industrialization and outsiders —speculators, investors, and missionaries— as the colonizers.[10] This sympathetic reading of Appalachian history substitutes spatial relations for social relations and transforms Appalachia into a social class *tout court*— economically, socially, and culturally exploited by outsiders.

The second and related implication of the interpretive shift had been a reassessment of preindustrial Appalachian history. Once caricatured, the social and economic practices of that era have been reclaimed in recent studies as elements of a traditional mountain subculture, characterized by a set of material practices surrounding the subsistence production and reproduction of individual households and a related *mentalité* emphasizing individualism, traditionalism, and familism.[11] Typical of this view is Ronald Eller's book *Miners, Millhands, and Mountaineers,* which begins: "Few areas of the United States in the late nineteenth century more closely exemplified Thomas Jefferson's vision of a democratic society than did the agricultural communities of the southern Appalachians. Long after the death of Jefferson and long after the nation as a whole had turned down the Hamiltonian path towards industrialism, the Appalachian Mountains remained a land of small farms and scattered open-country villages . . . nowhere did the self-sufficient family farm so dominate the culture and social system as it did in the Appalachian South."[12] A fundamental tenet of the traditional mountain subculture is the absence or unimportance of social class differentiation during the preindustrial era. Oral histories testifying "we're all kin" are taken as proof of a largely undifferentiated population and that kinship, rather than class, was the organizing principle of mountain society.

Yet egalitarian descriptions like the one just quoted usually come with the caveat that class distinctions did exist in the mountains during the nineteenth century and eventually became very important. Eller, too, juggles his depiction of social egalitarianism with the necessity to concede to stratification: "The dominance of a democratic ethos, however, did not mean the absence of a class structure in nineteenth-century Appalachia . . . class distinctions did exist in the larger community, county, and region. . . . The southern mountain country contained a minority of wealthier, landed families whose economic power and political influence set them off as an elite group. . . . These wealthier families provided the local political leadership in the mountains and often controlled local commercial enterprises . . . their political influence, access to resources, and contacts with the outside placed mountain elites in a strategic position to benefit from economic change."[13]

The existence of a preindustrial elite would seem to contradict an egalitarian interpretation of the traditional mountain subculture, especially if, as is often hinted, members of the elite benefited from capitalist development at the expense of their neighbors. The contradiction is avoided, however, by depicting the elite as supporters rather than initiators of development, who merely rode the development bandwagon drawn by outsiders. For example, Douglas Arnett cites evidence from local newspaper editorials to support his contention that "many of the citizens of the area—especially merchants, professionals, and real estate agents—welcomed capitalists, whatever their nationality, with open arms."[14] Eller echoes this sentiment: "Native middle-class entrepreneurs served as effective brokers for absentee investors and as energetic missionaries of the new industrial faith."[15] Eugene Conti suggests that "this local leadership pursued essentially a modernizing role, diffusing change from the American metropolis to the Appalachian hollers."[16] Only Allen Batteau has cast the local elite more provocatively, asserting that "in every form of major development . . . the pioneering entrepreneurs were not outsiders, but locally born and raised entrepreneurs from such towns as Hazard and Paintsville" in Kentucky.[17] Batteau's assertion notwithstanding, even the bandwagon consensus allows for a few extraordinary local individuals, such as John C.C. Mayo of Paintsville and T.J. Asher of Pineville, who became regional investment tycoons in their own right. This allowance is possible because their careers are considered "strange"—exceptions to the rule in an otherwise colonized region.[18]

Neither the recognition of preindustrial class distinctions nor the reputed activities of a local elite, therefore, vitiates an interpretation of Appalachian social history as chiefly a story of insiders and outsiders. Underlying this interpretation is a romantic vision of a preindustrial society presided over by the traditional mountain subculture, which has effectively restricted analysis of social history during the nineteenth century. Many assertions about egalitarianism, the social origins of the local elite, and the elite's role in capitalist development actually rest on limited social historical data.

The absence of concrete historical studies has left many vital questions unasked, let alone unanswered. For example, quite possibly the stellar careers of Mayo and Asher were more typical than has been previously assumed, and therefore local elites may really have been "pioneering entrepreneurs," leaders rather than followers. In any case, a pivotal question is how and to what extent their activities at the turn of the century were rooted in earlier decades of social and economic practice. The local elite could not have emerged *sui generis* in 1880. One might also ask whether each county had its own local elite or whether the elite was really only a handful of truly uncommon individuals scattered through the region. Finally, to what extent did class and kinship constitute mutually supportive rather than exclusive social relations in preindustrial Appalachia?

Drawing Class Boundaries

These questions surrounding social historical process in preindustrial Appalachia strike at two related dimensions of class formation: first, how the local population became *internally* differentiated; and second, how these axes of local differentiation meshed with patterns and processes of differentiation *externally,* in the wider society. Both dimensions are necessary in explicating the historical paths of Appalachian social and economic development. Figure 28.1 presents a framework depicting these two dimensions of class formation in terms of the historical geography of preindustrial Appalachia. Conceptually, the framework draws heavily on the work of historian Robert Brenner, whose studies of agrarian class structure and economic development in preindustrial Europe show how variations among the class structures of different European nations set each on a rather distinctive long-term trajectory of economic development. According to Brenner's theoretical argument:

> Class structure, . . . has two analytically distinct, but historically unified aspects. First, the relations of the direct producers to one another, to their tools and to the land in the immediate process of production—what has been called the "labour process" or the "social forces of production." Secondly, the inherently conflictive relations of property —always guaranteed directly or indirectly, in the last analysis, by force—by which an unpaid-for part of the product

> is extracted from the direct producers by a class of non-producers—which might be called the "property relationship" or the "surplus extraction relationship." It is around the property or surplus extraction relationship that one defines the fundamental classes in a society—the class(es) of direct producers on the one hand and the surplus-extracting, or ruling class(es) on the other . . . different class structures, specifically "property relations" or "surplus extraction relations," once established, tend to impose rather strict limits and possibilities, indeed, rather specific long-term patterns, on a society's economic development.[19]

Social relations surrounding the organization of direct material production and reproduction establish the boundaries within which a local class structure forms. Throughout southeast Kentucky these social relations constituted wide-spread household access to means of subsistence outside the spheres of commodity production and exchange. That is, households were able to reproduce themselves without producing for a commercial market. Noncommercial relations of production and reproduction became entrenched in southeast Kentucky during the middle decades of the nineteenth century as the regional economy became progressively isolated from the deepening commercialization and sectoral specialization of the national economy.[20] The isolation itself had tangled roots, but chief among them was a wholesale lack of investment in mountain resources and infrastructure.[21] Industrial demand did not yet exist for southeast Kentucky coal, and therefore the region remained agricultural. Yet the absence of investment in farm and transportation improvement kept agriculture entrenched in subsistence production. In sum, a cumulative lack of investment prevented effective competition with other agricultural regions.

Various forms of subsistence production, including farming and home manufacturing, prevailed until demand for coal penetrated the region at the turn of the century.

Over the course of the nineteenth century these material processes translated into a social formation chiefly composed of subsistence producers and a small number of merchants and professionals. Subsistence production and barter terms of trade did not permit local accumulation of money capital. Both direct producers and nonproducers, therefore, lacked the financial means to become a vanguard class and to finance regional capitalist development. Effective barriers to local capital formation render moot the question of whether local elites were leaders or followers. Whatever its aspirations, the local elite simply lacked the financial resources to become capitalists unassisted. This barrier was raised over the course of the nineteenth century as industrial capital investment requirements escalated. Absentee capitalists eventually occupied the vacancy at the top of the regional social structure, a position to which local elites could not ascend.

The local class structure associated with the subsistence economy was also sustained by social relations binding the local area to the larger political economy. These external relations constituted the second dimension of class formation. Although these relations included those that tied Appalachia into the national and even international political economy, perhaps the most important relations were geographically proximate to the mountain region. Appalachia has been referred to as the "backyard" of various southern and border states. The analogy is useful in recalling how during the nineteenth century, before the nation became fully integrated, individual states were critical arenas of local social and economic development.[22] The relationship between the locale and the nation was typically mediated through the particular historical geography of whatever state to which the locality belonged.

In this way, historical geography enters into the process of class formation by drawing boundaries in a different but no less fundamental way. The experience of southeast Kentucky provides a case in point. Kentucky is renowned for its internal social, economic, and political differentiation, which has divided the state like Gaul, into three parts. Most relevant

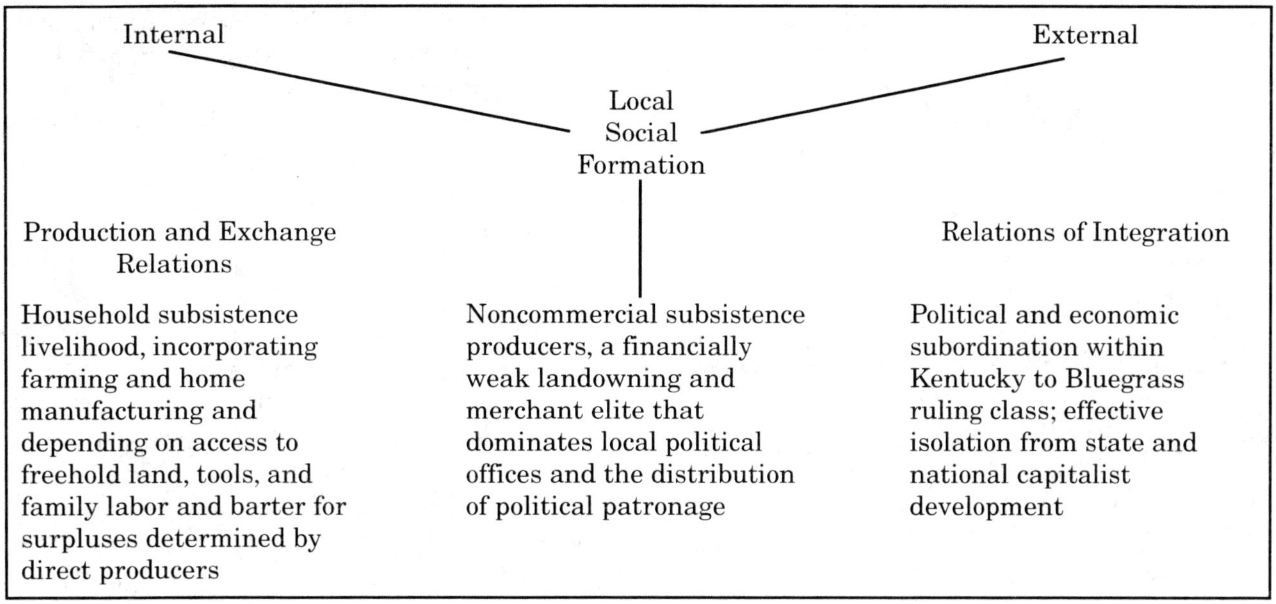

Figure 28.1. Class Formation in Southeast Kentucky, 1820–1880

here are the lines of differentiation between the southeastern mountain region and the central Bluegrass region. Drawn sharply at an early date, these lines eventually became more than physiographic divides.

Although farther west than the mountains, the Bluegrass region was settled earlier and quickly developed an economy based on commercial agriculture. Moreover, the Bluegrass became the principal locus of political and economic power within the state throughout the nineteenth century. One legacy of early ties between Kentucky and Virginia, developed when the former was part of the latter, is the quasi-aristocratic class of slave-owning planters and lawyers who came to dominate the Bluegrass and, through it, the state as a whole.

Between the upper class in the Bluegrass and the predominantly yeoman mountain area "was renewed the old conflict that had characterized the struggle between the back-country and the tidewater in the older seaboard states."[23] The heart of the struggle during the antebellum era involved issues of slavery, taxation, property qualifications for voting, and the basis for legislative representation.[24] Each section's predominant class made competing claims on the statehouse; their contest cannot be detailed here, but historical accounts report neither side lost entirely. One immediate and enduring result was the regionally Janus-faced politics of the state, witnessed most clearly in its position as a border state during the Civil War. As Merton Coulter has shown, however, that position was very much a token, since Janus usually smiled more warmly and more frequently in the direction of the Bluegrass.[25] For example, the state policies governing public investment in the critical sectors of transportation and farm improvement always favored the Bluegrass to the exclusion of the mountain region.[26] This historical political geography is a necessary context for understanding the formation and relative position of the elite in the three southeast Kentucky counties studied here. Whatever power the mountain middle class enjoyed was always limited by the subordinate political and economic position of the mountain region, which very early bore the label "pauper counties." The local power of the mountain middle class was exactly that, local power.

Yet the local arena afforded this class considerable room in which to maneuver. One enduring southern legacy was intense political localism in Kentucky, bred partly by the inheritance of the Virginia tradition of county government. Kentucky assumed the county tradition while it was itself a county of Virginia and, as historian Robert Ireland has shown, took it to unparalleled heights: "Early in her statehood, Kentucky displayed a particular predilection for the art of county-making which did not abate as the decades passed. By the end of the nineteenth century Kentuckians had created 119 counties, adding still another in the early twentieth century."[27] Although originally intended and officially mandated as only administrative subdivisions, Kentucky's counties became "little kingdoms." They "took on characteristics of semisovereignties. Once created, they refused to be abolished, fought with neighbors over boundaries, resisted encroachment on their territories, engaged in internecine struggles over county seats, and besieged the legislature with requests that their own particular problems be ameliorated by special legislation. Such activity not only tended to distract the attention of legislators from the more general needs of the Commonwealth, but also contributed to its prevailing localism."[28]

The centrality of the county to Kentucky history lends credence to the present endeavor of tracking the elite in three such entities. Political boundaries can often be dismissed as artificial, but not so in Kentucky. County lines in the state, as throughout the South, were and are very real social boundaries. Each was a crucible within which a middle class formed. County seats were not just administrative centers but commercial and social centers as well. In fact, Ireland claims, "the closeness of a rural resident to these communities often bore a direct relationship to his economic and social standing."[29] County seat residence became a most telling geographical characteristic of the mountain middle class.

Thus, the model of class formation put forth here accepts that southeast Kentucky became relatively isolated from changes taking place during the nineteenth century. But isolation did not so much "retard" or "arrest" development as establish a particular path of social and economic development for the mountain region. That development path was constituted through social relations both within and outside the region, especially through political and economic relations linking the mountains with the remainder of Kentucky.

Case Study Methodology

Had the preindustrial era in southeast Kentucky been different, documenting middle-class formation might be rather straightforward. For example, local newspapers would identify community "movers and shakers" and report their activities. Farmers' and merchants' account books would sketch patterns of business transactions, and mercantile and financial institution records would reveal who was lending to and otherwise making deals with whom. Finally, diaries and family archives would permit an intimate portrayal of how members of a rising middle class perceived their own position and its relation to others throughout the locality.

In most counties throughout the western Appalachians, however, newspapers were not published regularly until the twentieth century. Banks were not established until the turn of the century and commerce, such as it was, was conducted in small country storefronts without a predilection for record keeping. Family traditions among the middle class, as among the overwhelming majority of Appalachian families, were largely oral traditions. As a result, the set of qualitative sources commonly relied upon in social histories is largely unavailable for case studies of preindustrial Appalachia.

More than a methodological drawback, the dearth of primary documents limits what may ever be known about the social history of the southern mountain region. The prevalence of oral over written tradition clearly raises obstacles to the historical study of class formation in the mountains. At the very least, such obstacles necessitate more reliance on public records. Gaps in the historical record also force a certain creativity—commensurate with spinning gold from straw—in the gathering and use of the scattered written records that have survived.

I have met the problems of historical recovery here by casting a wide net to recover documentary sources for three Kentucky counties: Floyd, Harlan, and Perry (Figure 28.2). Together, the counties make up a "development cohort," for their economic bases were similarly transformed from subsistence agriculture to industrial coal production at the turn of the century. Identical public records, including tax and census schedules, were maintained in all three counties, providing baseline data on property ownership and occupation. Beyond these basic public records, however, the counties vary greatly in both the quality and kind of surviving written sources. Each county thus contributes somewhat different primary documentation. No single county or its sources is typical, but taken together, they paint a representative portrait of the preindustrial social history of southeastern Kentucky.

The representativeness of the case studies is further supported by their geographical differences. The counties are not fully contiguous. More important, each lies within a separate drainage basin, and the particular position of each county within its basin shaped its accessibility and the direction and pattern of its economic interaction within and outside the mountains. Floyd County straddles the Big Sandy River, a stream exceptional in southeast Kentucky because it was navigable inland by small steamboats almost to its mountain headwaters in neighboring Pike County. Social and economic ties link Floyd closely with its neighbors in the Big Sandy Valley. By contrast, Harlan County straddles the headwaters of the Cumberland River, which did not permit inland navigation, rendering Harlan largely inaccessible except by

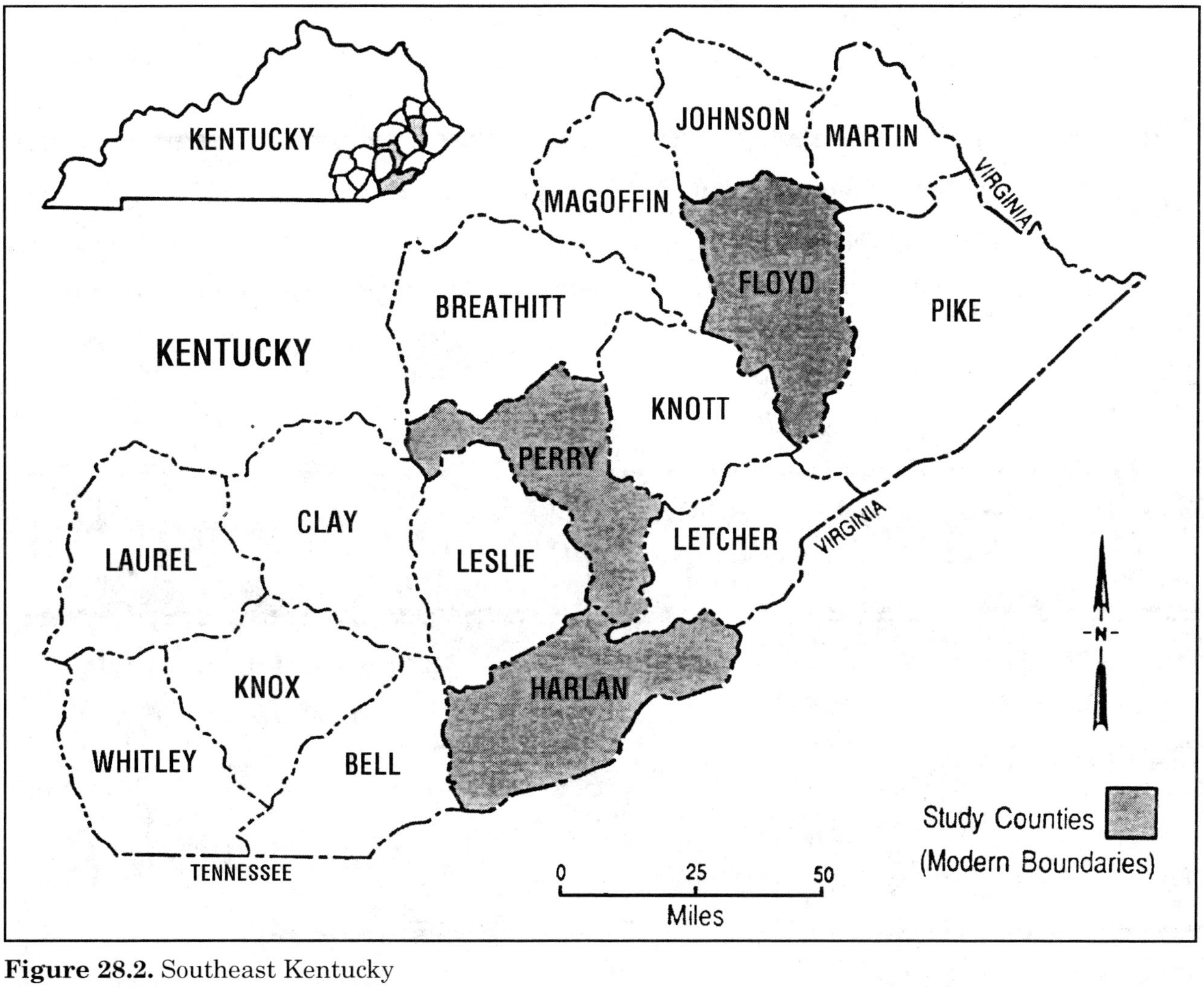

Figure 28.2. Southeast Kentucky

overland travel. Much of the county's economic interaction took place with and through the downstream counties of Bell and Knox. Perry County extends along the North Fork of the Kentucky River, and its accessibility was similar to Harlan's. Perry County's closest ties were with neighboring Letcher, Clay, and Leslie counties. The three case studies capture experience from each of the three major mountain drainage divisions. Important natural differences disclose themselves in their comparative historical geographies.

Property Ownership and Occupation

Individual ownership of property typically denotes social class membership when specified in amount, kind, and value within a particular historical and geographical context. In a preindustrial, rural society the most vital property relations involve land. But in such a society located in a mountain region, like southeast Kentucky during the nineteenth century, landownership takes on added specificity: who owns what land. Scarce alluvial bottomlands claimed by the earliest settlers carried a high premium.

Local tax assessor books are the chief sources of information about local landownership, recording names of landowners, amount and value of acreage, and, up to the 1870s, along what stream the property was located. The analysis here uses decennial data on land ownership for data years (1860, 1870, 1880) corresponding to those of the federal census before capital investment in mountain resources.

Since my goal is drawing the boundaries of a preindustrial elite, I focus on the extent and degree of landownership concentration. Table 28.1 makes an initial approximation by defining a "large landowner" as one possessing five hundred or more acres. As Table 28.2 makes clear, the small percentage of landowners in

TABLE 28.1. Local Owners of Five Hundred or More Acres

	1860		*1870*		*1880*	
County	***Number***	***Percentage***	***Number***	***Percentage***	***Number***	***Percentage***
Floyd	106	10.4	139	10.4	143	8.4
Harlan	140	16.0	112	15.8	110	11.3
Perry	170	27.1	139	18.0	115	12.4

Source: Floyd, Harlan, and Perry County Tax Assessor books, 1860, 1870, and 1880.

TABLE 28.2. Percentage of Assessed Acreage in Locally Owned Holdings of Five Hundred or More Acres

County	***1860***	***1870***	***1880***
Floyd	56.8	62.0	57.0
Harlan	83.4	43.0	56.2
Perry	79.5	59.4	42.2

Source: County Tax Assessor books.

this category controlled a large percentage of assessed county acreage. Yet the more revealing data on landownership concentration during the preindustrial era are contained in Tables 28.3 and 28.4. These considerably raise the stakes by limiting data to the largest landowners, those owning a thousand acres or more. At this threshold the percentage of acreage controlled is consistently and, in the case of Harlan County in 1860, vastly disproportionate to the percentage of owners in the category.[30]

These aggregate numbers suggest that if land was wealth, then both were significantly concentrated in each county long before absentee capital began investing in the resources. Moreover, the figures mask the huge size of some individual holdings. In Harlan County, for example, where landownership concentration was greatest in 1860, the largest individual holding was William Turner's 38,550 acres. Nor was Turner an anomaly; during the same year Noble Smith was assessed for 32,875 acres, and Henry Skidmore for 25,600. The average size of individual holdings within the thousand-acre-plus category did decline over the period. But even as late as 1880 in Perry County twelve local individuals were taxed for ownership of more than two thousand acres.

The membership of the largest ownership category did not change markedly among the three assessment years. Even more decennial persistence is evident for local family surnames. Surname tabulation reveals concentrated ownership in Harlan County is largely attributable to five families—Farmer, Howard, Lewis, Smith, and Turner—whose members together accounted for 41 percent of the assessed acreage in 1860. A similar pattern exists in the other two counties, though not as pronounced in Floyd County (Table 28.5).

A vital issue raised by the degree of concentration is the nature of the social relationships surrounding landownership. Simply

TABLE 28.3. Local Owners of a Thousand or More Acres

	1860		*1870*		*1880*	
County	***Number***	***Percentage***	***Number***	***Percentage***	***Number***	***Percentage***
Floyd	29	2.8	46	3.4	54	3.2
Harlan	71	8.1	51	7.2	41	4.2
Perry	82	13.1	58	7.5	49	5.2

Source: County Tax Assessor books.

TABLE 28.4. Percentage of Assessed Acreage in Locally Owned Holdings of a Thousand or More Acres

County	***1860***	***1870***	***1880***
Floyd	28.5	37.3	40.2
Harlan	67.5	33.0	31.6
Perry	57.5	38.2	33.0

Source: County Tax Assessor books.

TABLE 28.5. Large Landowning Families by Acreage

County	*1860*	*1870*	*1880*
		Floyd County	
Clark	4,760	7,115	6,110
Layne	7,880	5,255	7,545
Martin	11,200	12,785	9,220
Total acreage	23,840	25,155	22,875
Percentage of assessed county acreage	13.5	10.2	7.5
		Harlan County	
Farmer	27,983	3,000	15,565
Howard	26,283	16,396	11,695
Lewis	14,491	4,800	5,050
Smith	38,950	41,050	13,691
Turner	48,400	23,800	3,750
Total acreage	156,107	89,046	49,751
Percentage of assessed county acreage	41.0	21.7	19.0
		Perry County	
Begley	6,358	5,550	8,500
Brashears	15,580	3,000	3,850
Campbell	8,785	4,100	3,200
Combs	38,455	27,750	20,543
Duff	4,575	2,425	19,025
Eversole	9,274	5,700	5,400
Godsey	10,674	—	6,550
Total acreage	93,701	48,525	67,068
Percentage of assessed county acreage	34.0	19.0	21.6

Source: County Tax Assessor books.

put, how did large owners use their land? Did they constitute a landlord class, or were they subsistence farm operators, although on a grand scale? Gaps in the historical record permit only some tentative answers. The federal agricultural census began collecting farm tenure data in 1880, late for the period considered here and doubly unfortunate because the census enumerated tenants but not landlords. During this year, nonetheless, tenants made up from one-quarter to one-third of all farm operators in each county (Table 28.6). Very likely these tenants rented from local landowners, for absentee capital investments had not yet superseded local landownership.[31] Moreover, most were share-tenants rather than cash tenants, further suggesting largely local rental agreements.

TABLE 28.6. Farm Tenancy, 1880

	Number of Farms	*Owner Operated*	*Tenant Operated*	*Tenancy Rate*
Floyd	1,529	1,022	507	33.1%
Harlan	847	623	224	26.4%
Perry	816	617	199	24.3%

Source: Census of Agriculture, 1880, table V: Number and Size of Farms by Tenure.

TABLE 28.7. Owner-Operated Farms of a Thousand or More Acres, 1880

	Land Owners	*Farm Operators*	*Owners and Operators*
Floyd	54	41	26
Harlan	41	49	29
Perry	49	37	22

Source: U.S. Census of Agriculture, 1880, table V; County Tax Assessor books.

Yet it would be incorrect to conclude that all large landowners were landlords or, for that matter, that renting land to others precluded operating a farm oneself. Many large owners were farm operators, as becomes clear when tax records for 1880 are linked even partially with manuscript census schedules. For the three counties combined, the 1880 census of agriculture reported a total of 127 farms in its largest farm size class of a thousand or more acres. A majority (60 percent) of farm operators whose names appear in this census category were also landowners in the top acreage assessment category defined here (Table 28.7).

Data on slave ownership indicate a potentially different set of social relationships between landowning and farming at a slightly earlier date. Although not common, slavery did exist in the mountain region.[32] Because slaves were taxable property, their numbers and owners are listed in assessment records and cast additional light on landownership concentration. While slave owners and large landowners do not correspond perfectly, some patterns are evident. The largest individual slave owners in each county also tended to be the largest landowners (Table 28.8). The most obvious case in William Turner, who owned forty-two slaves in 1860, together with 38,550 acres of land in Harlan County. Furthermore, although the same individuals do not always appear in both categories, the same family surnames certainly do. This is especially the case in Harlan County, where landownership had reached a high degree of concentration among five families, who also owned 48 percent of all slaves in the county.

A second common measure of social differentiation and the formation of a middle class in an agricultural area is the incidence of nonfarm occupations. The southeast Kentucky economy was dominated late into the nineteenth century by subsistence farming and home manufacturing, and this lack of commer-

TABLE 28.8. Large Slave Owners and Landowners, 1860

Name	*Number of Slaves*	*Acres of Land*
	Floyd County	
James S. Layne	25	2,880
John Martin, Sr.	20	1,100
Samuel P. Davidson estate	19	—
James A. Lackey	18	—
	Harlan County	
William Turner	58	38,550
James F. Renfro	25	—
Aley Ledford	18	2,325
John Lewis, Sr.	17	5,033
Samuel Howard, Sr.	13	1,571
	Perry County	
John Walker, Sr.	12	1,950
Robert S. Brashears	11	4,000
Nicholas Combs, Sr.	11	1,650

Source: County Tax Assessor books.

cialization is evident in the small numbers of nonfarming occupations listed on manuscript schedules in the population censuses of 1860, 1870, and 1880; in no county did as much as 1 percent of the population have such occupations (Table 28.9). When nonfarm occupations are specified, moreover, the stunted commercialization and specialization of the preindustrial economy become even more evident (Table 28.10). Manuscript schedules show that as late as 1880 nonfarm occupations were limited to artisans, mechanics, and general merchants. These occupations were scattered throughout the county, with the last category usually located at the mouth of a large creek. By contrast, professionals, such as lawyers and political officeholders, typically resided in the county seats of Prestonsburg (Floyd), Mount Pleasant (Harlan), and Hazard (Perry). This tendency became more pronounced during the last two decades of the nineteenth century, but by 1880, it was already clear that the county seats were headquarters of a nascent middle class.

This tendency surfaced earliest in Floyd County. Prestonsburg was incorporated in 1867, the first town (county seat or otherwise) founded in the three counties.[33] Prestonsburg boasted the largest resident class of lawyers, merchants, and political officials during the 1860s, 1870s, and 1880s. The professional population was very stable, in fact, because the three professional groups were to a certain extent interchangeable: lawyers and merchant moved in and out of political office. The extraordinary circumstances of Floyd County helped an urban middle class to coalesce there earliest. Like other counties in the Big Sandy Valley, Floyd had relatively greater internal commercial development and sustained external interactions than other mountain divisions.

Lineages of the Middle Class

The early emergence of a commercial and professional middle class in the seat of Floyd County presaged what would take place elsewhere in the mountains. The intersection of

Table 28.9. Occupation Distribution

	1860	*1870*	*1880*
		Floyd County	
Aggregate population	6,388	7,877	10,176
Farmers	6,322	7,839	10,121
All nonfarm occupations	66	38	55
		Harlan County	
Aggregate population	5,494	4,415	5,278
Farmers	5,462	4,389	5,266
All nonfarm occupations	32	26	12
		Perry County	
Aggregate population	3,950	4,274	5,607
Farmers	3,931	4,269	5,590
All nonfarm occupations	19	5	17

Source: U.S. Census, Population Manuscript Schedules, 1860, 1870, 1880.

professional occupation, political office, county-seat residence, and property ownership—all within the compass of a certain few families—was the rule, not the exception, governing middle-class formation in southeast Kentucky. The following discussion imposes an inescapable linearity on reinforcing elements of a social historical process, but taken together, they suggest middle-class formation was supported by the twin pillars of longevity and kinship and shored up by the internal political geography of Kentucky. This argument accords with sociologist James Brown's findings about social organization in the "Beech Creek" neighborhoods in the Kentucky mountains during the mid–twentieth century. Writing about social class in the mountains nearly a century after the period considered here, Brown's study characterized "the high-class families in the Beech Creek neighborhood as being long-resident families of good background, moral athletes, hard workers, and good livers, less isolated and more modern than other families in the area and as people who emphasized self-improvement and who participated more widely in neighborhood affairs."[34]

The social origins of the mountain middle class extend back to settlement days. Earliest settlers, it is widely agreed, were fortunate in having their choice of the best lands, the relatively scarce alluvial bottoms. But it is also evident that the first-generation settlers could claim as much land as they wanted. Even in the absence of definitive land acquisition documentation, the large size of individual holdings and familial concentration of landownership is apparent from the 1860 assessment records. Furthermore, county histories make no secret that "first families" claimed huge boundaries of land, upwards of several thousand acres. These large acquisitions by the first families of settlers are, in fact, a common point of local historical pride.[35]

Apparently one common route of land acquisition among the largest owner families in each county was through the Kentucky land disposal laws. This series of laws, passed during the first half of the nineteenth century, gradually devolved control over the sale of

TABLE 28.10. Nonfarm Occupation Stratification

	Floyd County			*Harlan County*			*Perry County*		
	1860	*1870*	*1880*	*1860*	*1870*	*1880*	*1860*	*1870*	*1880*
Merchants	18	9	14	4	5	6	6	1	7
Lawyers	4	6	7	2	1	5	1	1	3
Political officials	2	3	7	1	3	1	1	2	2
Doctors	4	2	9	1	1	2	1	1	2
Clergy	3		2	10					
Teachers	4	1	2	1	1	2			
Tavern keepers	1								
Miners	4								
Tanners	2								
Shoemakers	5	2	1			1			
Clerks	6	4							1
Mechanics	7			1			2		
Saddlers	1								
Millers	1	2			1		1		
Carpenters	2		1			5			1
Sawyers	1		1						
Engineers	1								
Hotel keepers		3	3						
Blacksmiths		6	1	3	1	3	2		
Surveyors	1								
Wagonmakers				1					
Hat makers				1		1			
Basket weavers				1					
Tailors							1		
Stonemasons							1		
Boatmen							1		
Millwrights				1					

Source: U.S. Census, Population Manuscript Schedules, 1860, 1870, 1880.

land to individual county jurisdictions, ostensibly to assist local revenue raising.[36] By 1835 the law permitted individuals to claim, survey, and purchase two-hundred-acre parcels of "uninhabited" land for a minimum price of twenty cents an acre.

Evidence from tax assessment books for the nineteenth century suggests that after the initial wave of settlement in the mountains many first families took advantage of land laws to acquire thousands of acres of land. Figure 28.3 show size distributions of landownership in Harlan and Perry counties at earliest tax assessment, that is, shortly after the legal establishment of Harlan and Perry counties (Floyd is omitted because early assessment records do not survive). Very few holdings of more than two hundred acres were recorded. The size distributions of holdings thirty years later reveal a very different pattern, however; a significant number are holdings of a thousand acres or more. The assessment records suggest that first settlers usually established themselves on a hundred acres or less. Acquisition of large acreages was largely a postsettlement phenomenon. During ensuing decades

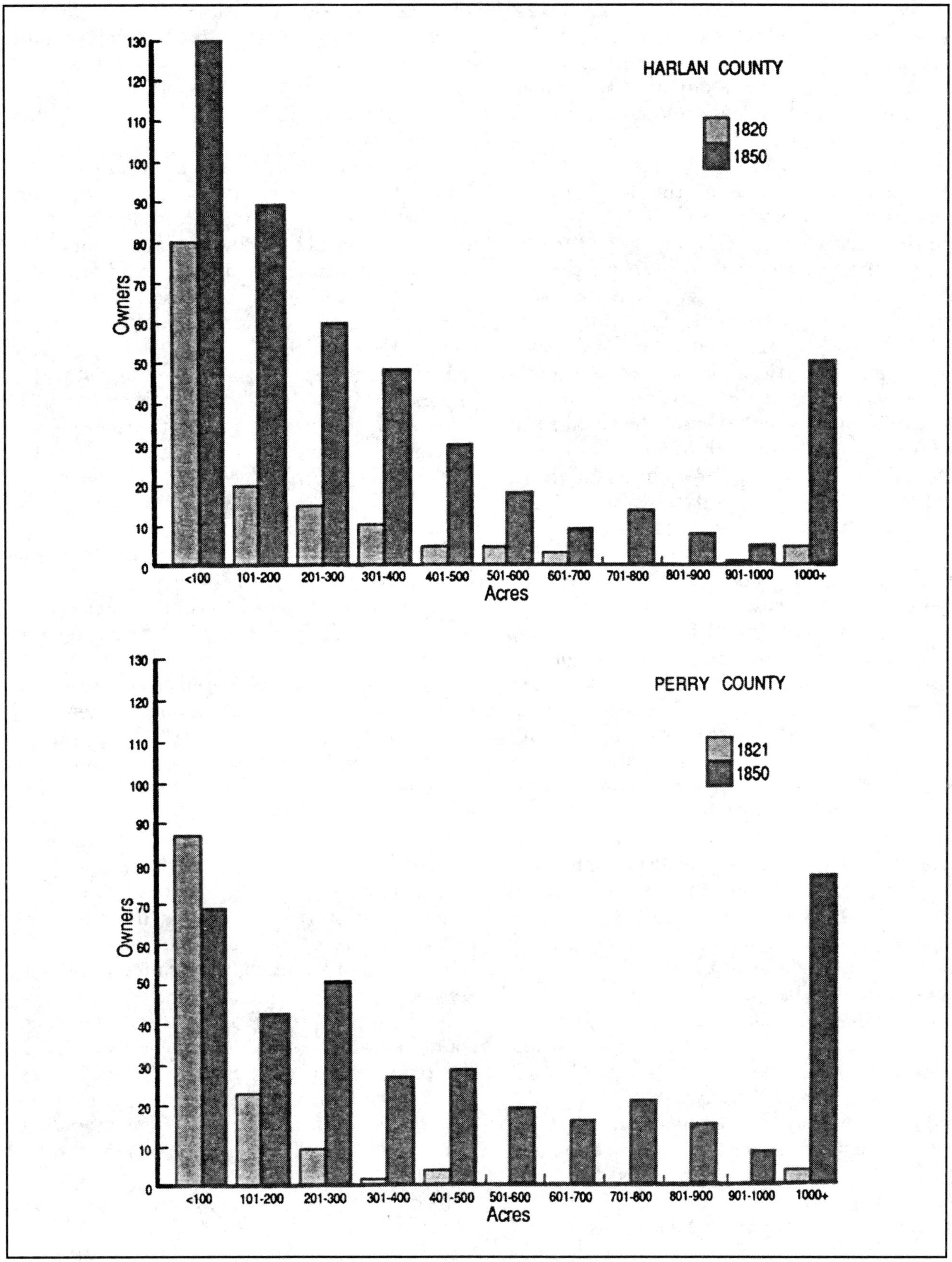

Figure 28.3. Landownership, Harlan and Perry Counties

inheritance practices kept land (and most likely the best lands) within first-family lineages. By the late nineteenth century owners of the best land in each county, therefore, could be counted among the descendants of the early claimants of large holdings.

Political activism among early mountain settlers followed closely on the heels of their arrival and initial land acquisition. In fact, the three activities were often closely linked. During the early decades of the nineteenth century, "most of Kentucky's counties were created because settlers found it difficult to reach county seats not within a day's travel from home."[37] Petitioning the state legislature to designate their newly settled area a separate county quickly established a political agenda among early settlers. These individuals surveyed the land, drew the boundaries, and when the new county became official, filled its first political posts. County creation provided an early nexus of local elite formation and from the outset tied political power to property ownership.

A case in point is the formation of Perry County. Elijah Combs had been one of the first settlers along the North Fork of the Kentucky River during the late 1810s and, along with his neighbors, agitated for separation into a new county. When the petition was granted in 1821, Combs was named one of three commissioners charged with locating and surveying a county seat. Combs's own large landholdings embraced an especially wide bend of the river and it was here that Hazard was located. Elijah and his wife Sally deeded ten acres to the county for the town in 1826. A town failed to materialize immediately, and so for over two decades their home served as the courthouse. Their eldest son, Jesse, was the first clerk of court, holding the position continuously until 1874.[38] In Harlan County, George Brittain, an early large landowner and member of the state legislature, is credited with using his political influence to have Harlan designated a separate county in 1819. As a reward for his efforts, Brittain became the first county clerk.[39] The county seat Harlan, initially named Mount Pleasant, was located at the confluence of the three forks of the Cumberland River, land claimed by the previously mentioned William Turner. Small wonder that in 1860 Turner owned sixteen of the total twenty-five town lots in Mount Pleasant or that he occupied many local political posts over the years.

State political practice, mingled with longevity and kinship, fostered the formation of an elite by permitting local political office to remain within landholding first families. The second state constitution, in effect until 1850, made the governor responsible for appointing all county officers. Despite this mandate, as Ireland has shown: "Normally [the governor] abided by the recommendation of the county court justices themselves. . . . If a justice of the peace sat on the court long enough to become a senior justice, he usually became the sheriff, since the county court controlled nominations to this office as well. . . . Before 1850, county courts appointed most of the other officers of the county directly without outside approval."[40]

During the nineteenth century local political officeholding in the mountains, despite the meager salaries, conveyed a premium commensurate in value to that carried by scarce alluvial land. Oral histories repeatedly testify that holding political office was one of the few paying jobs in the mountains. Tax commissioners, for example, earned a percentage on the amount of real and personal property they assessed.[41] Oral histories also clearly signal that along with employment and income, political office conferred considerable local status and power, not least because the conduct of county government centered on dispensing patronage, which frequently took the form of paying jobs. The distribution of teaching positions in each county became one of the most closely guarded patronage preserves: "Every little school in the county had one trustee . . . whoever he recommended that [county] superintendent had to hire. . . . This school election [for superintendent] was a special time of year [and] hotter than the President's because there were so many people that didn't have jobs. The ones that had the largest number of votes and relatives that could vote in their behalf [would] get the school . . . it was about the only paying job there was in this county."[42]

Election superseded appointment to county government with ratification of the third Kentucky constitution in 1850. This modification did little to change patterns of family dominance in officeholding. Before the twentieth century few county offices had any educational or professional requirements. In their stead, what may loosely be referred to as "family reputation," coupled with kinship alliances forged by marriage, became standard qualifications for election to county office. As late as 1970, for example, the *Harlan Enterprise* suggested that among the qualifications of incumbent county judge Hamp Howard was his relationship to the first man to settle in the area, Hamp's grandfather Samuel C. Howard.[43] During the middle decades of the nineteenth century Samuel Howard had filled many county offices, including county court justice, sheriff, and coroner.

Longevity and kinship also help to explain the conduct of local commerce during the nineteenth century. An economy that became increasingly dominated by subsistence production did not create many opportunities for merchant capital accumulation. Credit reports filed with R.G. Dun and Company, for example, frequently imply (and occasionally state outright) that local merchants were continually on the brink of failure during the century. In the face of such barriers to capital accumulation, the conduct of commerce was often supported by extraeconomic means, as evidenced by Dun and Company records.

Two critical factors determining Dun and Company's credit assessments were property ownership and "reputation." Obviously the two factors were interrelated, but longevity and kinship affiliations seemed equally solid, if intangible, ground on which merchants' reputation could be staked. For example, after listing the value of his real estate, the initial report (dated 18 December 1871) on Harlan general store merchant D.H. Smith noted that he was the son of the current county judge, Noble Smith, *and* the son-in-law of the "wealthiest man in the county," William Turner. The report urged: "Sell him all you can. He will always be good. They will back him."[44] This proved an accurate prediction when D.H. Smith was out of business five years later. His debts and assets had been assigned to his father, Noble Smith, "who has since been paying up debts on par." In Hazard, dry goods merchant Shadrack Duff possessed similarly sterling kin credentials. Dun and Company reported that "his father owns a good farm. I think Shadrack Duff is good particularly so if John A. Duff his father endorses for him." Duff had been among those securing numerous warrants for county land; in 1860 he listed thirty-three separate parcels amounting to 3,075 acres.[45] Also in Perry County, D.S. Vermillion earned a declaration in 1879 that he was "good for anything he undertakes" on the basis of mercantile experience beginning before the Civil War.[46] These sorts of judgments could and did cut both ways, of course, as when W.R. Richmond commenced business in Prestonsburg during the early 1870s. Dun employees warned wholesalers to "do cash business" with Richmond; his means were unknown, his reputation was not fully established, and he "had not been long in the county."[47]

Despite suggestive remarks filling Dun and Company's ledgers, merchants in southeast Kentucky are difficult to trace over the course of the nineteenth century. An absolute dearth of historical records notwithstanding, wounds inflicted during the Civil War cut deeply in the mountains, no doubt prematurely halting many promising commercial careers. One Dun and Company report, dated 8 July 1863, noted that "there is no person selling goods in Perry County now and has not been since the War broke out. The citizens of the Co. got into a war amongst themselves, and the M[er]chants have all left the Co. It would not be safe to trust any with a small capital to take them to Perry Co. at this time however honest he might be." Supporting the assertion about the cessation of mountain commerce during the war is a separate entry, dated 4 February 1863, which reported that merchant Austin Godsey "took his slaves and has gone to Va." and another for Robert S. Brashears, dated 9 July 1863, stating that "he took his negroes and went ab[ou]t the time the War commenced to the South where he died."[48]

Just as fundamental, however, was that merchants regularly, or rather irregularly, moved in and out of trade. Tracing merchants as a nucleus of a "commercial class" in the mountains is thus difficult, not simply because individual merchants "fall between cracks" in the historical record—listed in the *Kentucky Gazetteer* one year but absent from tax rolls the next—but because before the 1880s southeast Kentucky merchants did not resemble a coherent commercial class. Farmers and farmers' sons, individually and in partnerships, became merchants for a while and then, after a few years, resumed farming. Ensuing years might see the same individuals or a close relative resume trade in the family name. Clearly, many individuals considered themselves farmers first and merchants second. Even drawing a class boundary around those who claimed trading as their chief occupation is fraught with difficulties. Tax records show that many merchants (especially the most prominent) owned large amounts of land, which they rented to others for a share of the produce.[49]

In another pattern common to the southern mountains before 1860, merchants were also slave owners.[50] During his travels through the southern backcountry in the late antebellum era, Frederick Law Olmsted observed that to the extent that slavery existed in the mountains, it was most common among the middle class: "Of the people who get their living entirely by agriculture, few own negroes; the slaveholders being chiefly professional men, shopkeepers, and men in office, who are also landowners, and give a divided attention to farming."[51] The situation of Prestonsburg merchant John P. Martin during 1860 is illustrative. Aside from his commercial establishment, in that year Martin also was assessed for ownership of four thousand acres of land and ten slaves.[52] Likewise, Robert S. Brashears, prominent Perry County merchant, was also the largest slave owner in the county and owned four thousand acres of land.[53]

Much the same can be said for the practice of law in the mountains, again especially before the 1880s. Lawyers were required to gain admittance to the Kentucky bar but were not required to attend law school or, for that matter, to obtain a bachelor's degree. Some lawyers in the mountains did have formal legal education. But more commonly, individuals wishing to become lawyers simply apprenticed themselves to a local lawyer, judge, or justice, and "read law" under his tutelage. Like mercantile trade, law practice was often combined with farming, and frequently also with trading. A case in point was Hugh Harkins of Prestonsburg, a lawyer who was also a tanner and tavern keeper during the 1840s and 1850s.[54]

Certainly some merchants and lawyers in the mountains during the preindustrial era made their professional occupations their sole livelihoods. The greater commercial development of the Big Sandy Valley exhibits itself again in this regard, for among the three counties, Floyd possessed the largest and most continuously active professional class. Outside the Big Sandy, however, these professions did not usually become specialized until the turn of the century, when capitalist development created new local mercantile, legal, and other professional opportunities. By then each county possessed a closely knit group of merchants, lawyers, and politicians whose roots had been planted early and deep in the land. Although they often followed disparate paths to their collective destination, they formed the nucleus of the mountain middle class.

The Eversole family of Perry County represents the path of one middle-class lineage. John C. Eversole and his brother Joseph opened a general store near the family homestead on Grapevine Creek during 1855. Both were sons of Jacob, the first Eversole to settle in Perry County. Because of their family landholdings, which in 1860s totaled more than ten thousand acres, they were credited by Dun and Company as "perfectly good & prompt." During the war the brothers quit business, and Union army Major John C. Eversole was killed in a local ambush. In the following decade the next generation of Eversoles entered local commerce. Joseph C., son of the deceased John, opened a dry goods and grocery store in Hazard in 1875. Four years later he had taken his cousin Abner into partnership, no longer having sufficient time himself to devote to his trade, for along with being a merchant, Joseph C. was studying to be an attorney. In fact, he had married Susan Combs, and was reading law with his father-in-law, Josiah H. Combs, then Perry County clerk of court. Joseph C. Eversole was elected county school commissioner in 1875 and served two terms.

Joseph C. Eversole's life and career ended abruptly, however, when he was murdered in 1888 in an episode of the French-Eversole feud. His children and other kin followed his path into the middle class, however. Two sons took up law. One, John B., practicing in Lexington, became "actively identified with coal mining interests." The other, William C., was elected county attorney in 1897, and four years later county judge. By this time new professional opportunities were appearing in Perry County, and fittingly, two other sons took up practices as a doctor and a civil engineer.[55]

What the future might have harbored for Joseph C. Eversole can never be known, but considering the career of Arthur Blankenship Cornett in Harlan County permits some speculation.

Cornett was born on family land, son of farmer William L. and grandson of William, Sr., who had been a farmer, blacksmith, and in 1860, owner of nine slaves. A.B. Cornett called himself a "farmer" in the 1880 census even though he supplemented his farming income at Poor Fork by trading in livestock and teaching school. Already a large landowner by inheritance, of late he had begun investing in real estate. He abandoned farming and trading in 1883 to serve a one-year stint as superintendent of schools and then returned to trading, but this time setting up business in the county seat. In 1890 Cornett again stopped trading to assume duties as newly elected county clerk of court. Reelected in 1894, he held the position until 1898, when he was elected county judge. His path through farming, trading, and political office extended in other, new directions only then taking shape in Harlan County. He cofounded the First State Bank of Harlan in 1902 and became its first vice-president. Along with his son-in-law, W.W. Lewis, scion of another venerable Harlan lineage, he organized the Cornett-Lewis Coal Company and made his son D.B. Cornett its president.[56]

Some of the differences between Floyd and adjacent counties can be seen in the experience of the Davidson family. Joseph M. Davidson was a Prestonsburg merchant whose father, Samuel P., also a merchant, had arrived in Floyd during the early 1800s. Joseph M. was born in 1837. He formed an early commercial alliance by marrying into the Hatcher family, the most prominent merchants in the Big Sandy Valley. During various years he is recorded as trading with his cousin Green Witten, as well as with members of other mercantile families including the Steels, Mayos, and Martins. Like other merchants he had cash debts owed him, some of which were paid (because real property was often the only currency in circulation) in mortgaged land, livestock, and occasional crop liens. These mortgages were at least one basis for his substantial landholdings, taxed in 1870 as ten separate tracts amounting to 2,290 acres. Davidson also acquired land through the state disposal laws and by that means within ten years had more than doubled his acreage. In a firm styled "Davidson, May, and Hatcher" Davidson added to his Prestonsburg store a saw- and gristmill during the early 1870s, thanks to the investors' "high standing" among their creditors. In addition, Joseph M. Davidson was actively engaged in politics. Locally he served as a county court justice and sheriff, and served two terms in Frankfort as Floyd County representative in the state legislature.

Because of the activities of the brothers, the Davidson family name remained prominent in Prestonsburg economic and political affairs. But Joseph M. Davidson's patrilineage ended with him, since his children were all daughters. Their marriages, however, provide compelling evidence of the kinds of ties binding the middle class. As one source delicately put it, by family position and individual qualifications his daughters were "in every way fitted to share in the important destiny" of their husbands.[57] Mary Sallie Davidson married H.H. Fitzpatrick, a merchant and descendant of a Prestonsburg mercantile family dating to the early 1800s. Alice G. Davidson married Frank A. Hopkins, a lawyer and relatively late arrival in Prestonsburg (1874) from across the Virginia divide of the Big Sandy. Along with investing widely in local commercial and industrial development, Hopkins also enjoyed a stellar career in politics that began as superintendent of schools and led to the United States House of Representatives. The third daughter, Josephine B. Davidson, found a suitable match in Walter S. Harkins; indeed, she made perhaps the most prized match of all. Harkins was descended from a family of Prestonsburg lawyers. His grandfather Hugh had migrated to Floyd County in 1835, passed the bar two years later, and after that date the town was "not without a Harkins in its bar."[58] Walter S. Harkins did more than have a "role" in local development. On some occasions he sat in the director's chair. One early instance was spearheading the first bank in Floyd County in 1887, which he named The Bank Josephine in honor of his wife.

The Developing Middle Class

Although the preindustrial era has long been considered a period of arrested social development in Appalachia, the histories of these middle-class lineages suggest that the area was anything but a "retarded frontier." In the decades following 1880, the local middle class in southeast Kentucky became actively involved in developing the coalfields, and through these involvements, the middle class made itself.

Despite the often vast acreages owned by members of the nascent middle class during the preindustrial era, and despite their claim on local trade and politics, this class did not become a vanguard, financing capitalist development in the mountains. Local wealth and power remained bounded by political and physical geography and, within those boundaries, lacked the currency to underwrite a capitalist transformation. The preindustrial subsistence economy limited the ability of the middle class to carry out this potential role.

Many local individuals clearly understood these limitations. Harlan County judge George B. Turner, son of the much-vaunted William Turner, implicitly recognized them in an article published in the *Lexington Herald* during the 1880s. But rather than lament what he and his local counterparts could not achieve, Turner called on his Bluegrass neighbors to share his developmental vision:

> I have often marveled at the dormancy of the populous and wealthy portion of the enterprising people of Kentucky that they would for so long permit undevelopment of the vast resources lying within her borders, almost in sight of their very doors. Not only is this coal and timber needed for home consumption, but would prove a source of great advantage financially as a revenue paying section of the state. The development of the vast resources of the mountains of Kentucky would make an impoverished and pauper section of the otherwise grand old commonwealth rich, prosperous and happy, beneficial to consumers throughout the state and redound to the interest of our common country.[59]

Like town-based "boosters" across the nation, the mountain middle class actively and eagerly encouraged capital investment from the outside. In the process this class settled itself in the county seats of Prestonsburg, Harlan, and Hazard, building stores and hotels, founding banks and newspapers, and financing construction of streets and public utilities. Many individuals inherited or made farsighted and shrewd investments in mountain resources. Among these, some maintained their holdings to become coal mine owners and operators on their own account, others sold out at great profits, and still others traded their land for equity positions in new coal and land firms. Lawyers took on capitalist clients and handled property transactions, searched titles, abstracted deeds, and paid taxes for absentee owners. Furthermore, in this passage to a capitalist economy the local middle class tightened its rein on county government. Clearly the sum of these activities did not cast the middle class as follower or leader of capitalist investors outside the region. Rather, its role was that of a local commercial and service class, a role its history had prepared it for well.

29

by Carl G. Kilbourne

A New Sustainable Cash Crop for Mountain Farmers

Chris Bolgiano's *The Appalachian Forests* (1998) tells the fascinating story of how Alwin Schenck, a forester from Dorstadt, near Germany's Black Forest, came to North Carolina in 1898 to manage George Vanderbilt's estate of more than 100,000 acres—consisting primarily of abandoned farms and tracts of logged-over woods. Schenck, with whom the profession of forestry management originated here in America, was a century ahead of his times.

> Schenck taught selective tree cutting and thinning aimed at improving the growth of remaining trees. He clear-cut pines to favor hardwoods where possible, but he also planted pines to cover eroded fields. He taught how to monitor pests and diseases and to make harvesting decisions that saved as much timber as possible. He taught erosion control, measurement of lumber and, most emphatically of all, the economics of harvesting. He believed in a system of privately owned forests and educated his students in a forestry designed to yield private profits.

Today, owners of timberland in Southern Appalachia seem reluctant to harvest their trees, perhaps because of the bad logging practices of the past or because they are unaware of the present value of hardwood lumber. As a tree farmer and fifth-generation native of Eastern Kentucky and Southwestern Virginia, I believe now is the time for those small timberland owners to learn how to grow, harvest, kiln-dry and market their own hardwood lumber.

As a ten-year-old boy in Appalachia, Virginia, I helped my eighty-year-old Grandpa cut hickory saplings to get inner bark with which to bottom kitchen chairs. One day when I scolded him for cutting the young trees, he pointed to the mountains and said, "Son, the gold in them thar hills is black gold—coal."

Coal was king then. Appalachia was the busy trading center for hundreds of miners and families living up the hollows at the Inmar, Linden, Laura and Derby coal camps. We dug coal for heating from a five-foot seam on our own land, just behind our house. During the years of the Great Depression, our neighbors dug coal further up the mountain, from a four-foot seam on Grandpa's land, then hauled it home at night in burlap sacks to heat their pot-belly stoves for the winter.

The last coal mine in Appalachia, Virginia, shut down about two years ago, after the big eight-inch underground seam played out. The mine was so highly mechanized, a slow-moving railroad car could be loaded in less than one minute. Now the coal is gone—except for the foolish strip mining of two-foot seams on the mountain tops. The tobacco is going, too, but the great hardwood forests in the Southern Appalachian Mountains have rebounded in spite of the neglect and poor forest management of past decades. Now the gold in those hills is not coal. It is not tobacco. The gold is in hardwood trees that can last for centuries, if we are wise enough to learn sustainable tree farming and harvesting.

An excellent article by researcher LeeAnn Farrar, "Trees Fall at Record Rate" (Lexington *Herald-Leader*, February 21, 2000), discusses the present logging boom in Kentucky within the contexts of conservation concerns for the future and the poor forest-management practices of the past:

> Despite being recklessly leveled a century ago and neglected since then, Kentucky's vast forests have rebounded and are producing more than one billion board feet a year.

According to Farrar, future conservation concerns indicate that Kentucky will soon require better "management practices—mainly methods to prevent erosion and protect streams from becoming clogged with silt."

The article also reports on the bad forest management practice in called "high-grading":

> More than ninety percent of Kentucky's timber is privately owned. The average woodland is thirty acres. It is estimated that 200,000 people own ten acres or more of timber. The experts say the forests are, on the whole, badly managed. The common method of cutting is called high-grading. That means taking out the best trees and leaving the rest. Over a number of decades, it creates a forest full of poor quality trees of species no one wants.

Private ownership of woodlands and the "high-grading" method of cutting hardwood trees prevail in most of the region, especially in West Virginia, Tennessee, Western North Carolina and Southwest Virginia. In fact, there may be a million or more people in the region owning ten-acre stands or more of hardwood trees, who do not realize the long-term value of what they own.

The Kentucky Forestry Timber Improvement plan could correct most of the high-grading problems, as this tree farmer learned in the early 1970s. Kentucky foresters will cruise over scattered hardwood stands of ten acres or more. Unwanted species such as gum, cedar and pine, as well as such undesirable trees as those with double trunks and other defects, are marked with bright-colored paint. These low-grade trees are then girdled by their owners with a chain saw and left to decay so that they might return harmlessly to nature. If desired by the owners, some of the cull trees might be harvested for solar lumber kilns, storage sheds, or even for firewood. The desired high-quality species of hardwoods will then get the sunlight needed to thrive and later provide a sustainable crop to be harvested as each tree matures. Foresters will also mark with a different color of paint the remaining high-quality trees when they are mature and ready to cut.

On a trip to Germany, I saw tree farming at its best. Miles of new trees spaced in rows ten feet apart were growing up the ridges and mountains to stop erosion and to provide a renewable supply of lumber. The cardinal rule in Europe is to replace each mature tree cut with two new plantings. Of course, Germany is a venerable country. An English friend who visited me in Kentucky, assured me that, "You folks in America are still pioneers, and you will learn how to conserve trees in another hundred years."

On a fishing trip to New Zealand's South Island, I saw tree farming at its worst—as could also happen here in our region. The rolling hills of New Zealand reminded me of

Kentucky, except there were no trees. Over the past hundred years or so, all of the trees on the ridges and mountains were cut to provide pasture for over 350 million sheep. The 1986 flood, that nation's worst in over a century, almost washed the land away. Now New Zealanders are frantically planting trees, hoping to stop the erosion and save their land. One innovative conservation technique I observed involved small airplanes spreading fertilizer on the trees and pastures, especially where the terrain was rough and mountainous (incidentally, I caught two salmon about three feet long in the flooded rivers).

Southern Appalachia has the most hardwood trees in the world. About one third of them are oaks. Most hardwood species grow naturally here because of the ideal soil, adequate rainfall and the moderate climate. However, soon after the Civil War and during the early years of the twentieth century, most of the virgin timber was cut by large logging companies. In 1873, my great-grandfather sold his boundary of virgin hardwood trees near New Appalachia, Virginia, as well as the mineral rights under them *for two dollars an acre.*

As a young boy I lived in Lynch, Kentucky, and then moved over Big Black Mountain on a dirt road to Appalachia, Virginia. After the terrible Derby, Virginia, coal mine explosion that killed thirty-two of the thirty-four miners in his crew, my dad moved his family away from the coal fields—forever. We settled on an old family farm at the head of a hollow in Scott County, Virginia. The only people living further up our hollow were moonshiners.

The best crop Dad and Mom raised on that mountain farm were nine children. Later, all attended college, and with financial assistance from the G.I. Education Bill and much sweat equity, they earned a total of eleven college degrees.

Most of my life has been involved with hardwood trees. During my early years, I witnessed family members and friends sell their hardwood timber for a pittance. In 1937, one of my grandmothers sold about thirty large, wild cherry trees for five dollars a tree. In 1950, my dad sold fifteen huge walnut trees for 500 dollars, which even then were worth 2500 dollars or more.

For thirty-two years, I taught shop. But during successive summer vacations I built about thirty houses, so I could afford to teach. For some of that time I also owned and operated a lumber yard, and I conducted research for the federal government concerning how to build better and less expensive houses for low-income families in the Appalachian Region. For most of my life, my hobbies have been building hardwood furniture and tree farming.

During the 1970s and 1980s, I very successfully harvested hardwoods on my own property, but I was frustrated that there seemed no effective way for the small-time owner to harvest, kiln-dry and market the valuable hardwood trees. However, just as Eli Whitney's cotton gin revolutionized cotton production and spawned a vigorous textile industry, three inventions of the past few decades have the potential to help mountain farmers who own ten acres or more of timber increase their profits dramatically. These inventions are the portable chain saw, the portable horizontal bandsaw mill and the efficient and inexpensive solar lumber-drying kiln.

A friend once mused that, "If our early pioneers had possessed chain saws there would not be a tree left standing in Eastern Kentucky." Indeed, chain saws are very efficient and make cutting hardwood trees far easier than the old two-man saws.

Now for the first time in our history, the portable, one-man horizontal bandsaw mill makes it technologically feasible for mountain farmers to harvest effectively their own hardwood trees. The bandsaw mill can be pulled by pickup truck or tractor to the trees. In turn, the sawed green lumber can be hauled back to the farm for drying in the solar kiln.

The solar lumber kiln, which can be built for anywhere from 500 to two thousand dollars, may be the major technological breakthrough which now makes it economically feasible for farmers to kiln-dry their own hardwood timber after it is sawed on a bandsaw mill. It is very important to remember that *kiln drying hardwood lumber at least doubles its value,* because it can then be used for making oak flooring, kitchen cabinets, paneling, furniture and other valuable hardwood products, rather than for tobacco barns, construction, horse fences and firewood.

Most lumber used for house framing is dried from fifty-percent or more moisture content, cut green from the log, down to about twenty-percent moisture when used in construction. Lumber to be used for more valuable hardwood products must be further dried, down to between six and eight-percent moisture content, which prevents warping and cracking of the lumber. Now, with their chain saws, bandsaw mills and solar kilns—along with the practice of sustainable forestry—mountain farmers with woodland can grow, cut, mill and kiln-dry lumber to be brought to market as valuable hardwood.

A mature hardwood tree that will saw-out a two-foot by eight and a half-foot log should have about 200 board feet of lumber, currently worth 400 dollars or more. For the traditional mountain farmer, a dozen or more logs per year could replace the already-doomed tobacco base as a dependable source of cash money. If properly farmed, one acre of timberland can produce approximately 2,000 board feet of lumber per year. After several years of careful forestry practice, ten or more acres of privately-owned mountain timber can become a family's sustaining economic engine.

Marketing the high-quality, kiln-dried lumber may be the most formidable challenge, but there are successful farming precedents to consider. Think about regional warehouses where farmers can take their graded, kiln-dried, hardwood lumber to sell and where buyers come to purchase the many species of kiln-dried lumber, instead of tobacco. Bring the buyers to the graded hardwoods. The method used to market tobacco seems feasible for marketing kiln-dried hardwood lumber. Perhaps the farmers' cooperative model will serve the needs of these mountain foresters.

In any case, mountain farmers will need to learn more about growing, harvesting, sawing, kiln-drying and marketing hardwoods. For one thing, the dimensions preferred by manufacturers of valuable hardwood products are quite different from the conventional dimensions for construction framing lumber. However, for over two-hundred years, American farmers have proven to be very successful entrepreneurs. Hardwood farming and marketing should not be any more difficult than most other farm crops. In my lifetime, I have seen corn production increase from twenty-five gallons an acre to over 125 bushels per acre.

There must be a new mind-set about the value of the plentiful and renewable hardwood trees in Southern Appalachia. Imagine elegant oak floors in every living room, hallway and bedroom in America. Think of homes with poplar, maple or hickory paneling on at least one wall to break the monotony of drywall. Think of cooking meals in a modern kitchen, with hardwood cabinets to enhance the counter tops and ceramic-tiled floors. Imagine simple, beautiful Shaker-style furniture gracing every room.

Mountain farmers with hardwood trees can grow, harvest, saw, kiln-dry and market their renewable resource, which in turn can spawn local manufacturers of finished hardwood products here in Southern Appalachia. Clearly this is a much better idea than shipping the rough logs to Europe or Japan, where most of the value is added.

There are some practical sources available to interested farmers, such as the U.S. Forest Service, the Kentucky Division of Forestry, and manufacturers of portable sawmills, Wood-Mizer, for instance. The Sustainable Mountain Agriculture Center, based in Berea, Kentucky, can provide information and demonstrations regarding the total process of tree farming, harvesting and marketing hardwood lumber. Dr. Michael Best and Dr. Charles Haywood, marketing experts, are researching new methods to market kiln-dried, hardwood lumber. This young group of homefolk are way out in front of most research hounds and are plowing "new ground' to improve the economic quality of life for mountain farmers.

Young folks, if possible, buy your parents', grandparents' or older friend's woodlands of ten to thirty acres and become a tree farmer. The hobby will soothe your soul, and later the mature renewable hardwood trees could pay for your children's college educations.

One last request—tell your friends up the hollows and over the ridges the news. The coal is gone, and the tobacco is going. Now the "gold in them thar hills" is hardwood trees.

30

by Garry Barker

The Mountain Crafts: Romancing the Marketplace

Almost exactly 100 years ago, mountain "missionaries" were discovering the Appalachian treasure trove of crafts, that highly visible and marketable aspect of the culture which held appeal for the "outsiders" whose influence and money were needed to make things happen. Berea College President William G. Frost was making preparations for his horseback ride through Eastern Kentucky, West Virginia, East Tennessee, and Western North Carolina, a summer-long journey which would result in the formation of Berea's "Fireside Industries" crafts production and marketing program. In Madison County, North Carolina, Frances Louisa Goodrich was beginning the work which would create the living legend of Allanstand Cottage Industries.

The two unconnected efforts would later come together, join with forces from Penland, Brasstown, Gatlinburg, and the other more remote mountain pockets where settlement schools were preserving an almost artificial culture, and the lasting result was a regional phenomenon of craft training and marketing, promotion and publicity, and plenty of what David Whisnant would later term "cultural intervention."

So successful was this marketing of Appalachia's "culture" that Whisnant was to write, in 1983, "To this day there a thousand people who 'know' that mountaineers weave coverlets and sing ballads for every one who knows that millions of them have been industrial workers for a hundred years, have organized unions and picketed state and national capitols in pursuit of their constitutional rights. . . . Or that, today, they shop at K Mart and Radio Shack, drive Camaros, and watch as much television as people anywhere" (p. 33).

That conditioned, much-manipulated image of the quaint, crafts-making mountaineer has, for a century, been the cornerstone of a highly profitable Appalachian crafts marketing effort which continues today but now sells mostly the work of college trained designer-craftspeople.

Allen Eaton concluded his famed 1937 study *Handicrafts of the Southern Highlands* with these words: "To bring these people our civilization and yet save their culture is the task in which we should all have some part. There is but one approach to this task: that is the ethical approach which seeks, before imposing its own ideals on any person or group, to draw from them the best they have to give" (p. 333).

To draw from them their best, then use that "best" as a marketing tool for products and a culture which bear but faint resemblance to the crafts and lifestyle of a century ago is truly our task, a jaundiced 1990s observer might conclude.

Perhaps the best example of the successful crafts marketing myth is the crooked-seamed brown Double Bowknot coverlet now owned by the Southern Highland Handicraft Guild and labeled, according to Jan Davidson in his introduction to the recently reprinted *Mountain Homespun,* as "the coverlet that started the Allanstand Industries."

> Before it was a museum piece, it [the coverlet] was used by Frances Goodrich to personify the continuity of her handcraft revival; to raise funds for craft programs, schools, and hospitals; to star in the most dramatic moment of Goodrich's *Mountain Homespun;* and to launch a business that . . . survives to this writing. . . . Before Goodrich got it in 1895, it was a bedspread, probably greatly loved by an old mountain family because one of them made it completely herself. It is a crooked-seam coverlet made about 1850. (1990, p. 1)

The gift of the brown coverlet supposedly inspired Goodrich's work of reviving the weaving industry of Madison County, North Carolina, of building Allanstand into a craft business which became the foundation of the Southern Highland Handicraft Guild's sales success, and of the writing of *Mountain Homespun* and subsequent creation of the legend.

> "*Mountain Homespun*'s central dramatic incident, the gift of the Double Bowknot, caught the attention of the feature writers, who retold it frequently and compared that gift to the gift of Allanstand [Miss Goodrich donated her business to the Guild in 1931] thus making the Guild the final step in conferring the management of mountain handcrafts from the family, to the saintly woman, to a corporation directed by northerners, to a coalition with other production centers." (Davidson 1990, p. 34)

Well before 1931, though, Berea College's subtle production and marketing influence had reached Goodrich, who brought Berea's Swedish looms to North Carolina and did away with the "crooked-seam" assembly method. The crooked seams were both practical (so the coverlet could be taken apart for cold water creek washing) and inevitable; early mountain looms were home-made, cumbersome affairs incapable of the precision weaving demanded by Goodrich and by the Northern marketplace. "The irony of the old brown Double Bowknot that started Allanstand—the grand icon of the Appalachian handcraft revival—is that it could not have been sold as an Allanstand coverlet, because, like most old mountain coverlets, it has crooked seams . . ." (Davidson 1990, p. 5). But the old Double Bowknot survives, and dramatic stage interpretations of Frances Goodrich's words from *Mountain Homespun* are used to perpetuate the myth which mothered a modern marketplace.

David Whisnant's scathing description of today's market must be considered:

> Cultural objects, styles, and practices introduced by intervenors sometimes prove remarkably durable, regardless of how little prior basis they had in the culture. The tens of thousands of tourists who visit the publicly funded Folk Art Center at the entrance to the Blue Ridge Parkway or troop through the craft shops of Gatlinburg or Asheville, and the millions who listen to folk-revival musicians on National Public Radio, are "seeing" and "hearing" continuity which is partial at best: they are buying the fruits of hybrid cultures that were long ago severely pruned and grafted. What they

> have in their shopping bags as they climb back into the station wagons and onto the tour buses is, to use a term familiar to cultural anthropologists, "airport culture." (1983, p. 262)

Whisnant does not deeply explore whether the native mountaineers were *willing* collaborators in the "cultural intervention" of the early twentieth century. I suspect they were, for financial gain.

Some economic truths heavily influenced the early work and established the pattern which still exists—the basic premise of crafts as an economic development tool. To succeed in the business world, crafts producers must make what the market will buy. "Bread and butter" production lines pay the bills for the craftspeople who depend upon sales for a livelihood. Early customers for coverlets from Berea College and Allanstand wanted handcrafted perfection, straight seams, and precise weaving, *done by the quaint and colorful mountaineers whom their purchases were helping to become more civilized.* The purchase was a multi-purpose transaction, then, part sentiment and missionary zeal, part insistence upon first-class quality and, as Allen Eaton once suggested, bargain prices (p. 287).

In regards to making what the market wants, little has changed. Like so many other native Appalachians who have learned to perform for pay—the Cherokees who pose in Comanche warbonnets for tourist dollars, the local musicians who learn to play the dulcimer and sing folksongs to have a chance at the contest cash prize, or Garry Barker slipping in and out of the East Kentucky dialect to earn his fee as after-dinner entertainment—the craftspeople have learned to give 'em what they want and laugh all the way to the bank.

The contemporary products most similar to the early coverlets are the quilts which now sell for $300 to $3,000 each, which seldom if ever are actually used on a working bed. The traditional everyday Appalachian quilt was a hodge-podge of fabric and color, made to be used, meant to keep people warm in unheated houses. There were, of course, "show-off" quilts, the "company quilts," fancy and tightly stitched artworks to impress the neighbors and the mother-in-law, and it is these special quilts which are the objects now of the collectors' lust. The modern marketplace quilts are made of new materials, in designer hues, as mass produced as the technique will permit, artful wall hangings meant for the interior designer trade. Machine-pieced quilts are becoming more commonplace and more accepted, and a spin-off industry of printed quilt patterns has evolved to fill the market demand.

It is the reality of the craft world to use technology and shortcuts to lessen the burden of production drudgery—to use electric potters' wheels, bandsaws and sanders, fly-shuttle looms, gas-fired forges and pneumatic hammers, and even electric carving tools—but the concurrent reality is that customers must continue to believe the myth about quaint mountain craftspeople. Allen Eaton even subtly endorsed such an approach when he wrote:

> There is, however, no work so good but what some knowledge of the person who is doing it and the attendant circumstances will help make it more significant. . . . To appreciate it [the mountain craft] fully one must know something of the maker, his environment and his opportunities, or lack of opportunities. . . . The deep interest that many people feel in the Highlanders clusters about the true and quaint stories of them which have been captured by social workers, writers, and visitors to the region. To discard this element of appeal would be to throw away what is often a strong bond relating the possessor of an example of Highland handicraft to some mountain character, family, or group of neighbors. (1937, pp. 282–3)

We in the modern Appalachian craft world certainly have not discarded that "element of appeal," even though we have largely discarded the actual crafts and the "true and quaint" lifestyle of which Eaton wrote. Today in the newly-renovated Allanstand gallery in the Southern Highland Folk Art Center, you will find little or no "folk" art. You will find today's derivatives of the early crafts—nonfunctional baskets, art pottery, decorator quilts, brooms which cannot be used for sweeping, and cornshuck sculptures—plus the highly contemporary glass, wood, fiber, and clay works done by the skilled craftspeople who have moved to Appalachia to take advantage of the ready marketplace. You will also find the work of the hundreds of Appalachian craftspeople who carefully maintain and perpetuate the "quaint" image and prefer that the buying public never become aware that they (the quaint craftspeople) drive $18,000 vans, live in brick three-bedroom homes, watch cable television, and drink bottled water.

We all *are* willing participants in the marketing myth of quaint Appalachia, perfectly willing to swap image for cash-in-hand. Sometimes a perceptive observer can see the situation more clearly than can those of us whose daily lives are entwined with the marketplace, and Jim Wayne Miller perhaps described it best with his poem "The Brier Losing Touch With His Traditions":

> Once he was a chairmaker.
> People up north discovered him.
> They said he was "an authentic
>   mountain craftsman."
> People came and made pictures of him
>   working.
> wrote him up in the newspapers.
> He got famous.
> Got a lot of orders for his chairs.
> When he moved up to Cincinnati
> so he could be closer to his market
> (besides, a lot of his people lived there
>   now)
> he found out he was a Brier.
>
> And when customers found out
> he was using an electric lathe and
>   power drill
> just to keep up with all the orders,
> they said he was losing touch with his
>   traditions.
> His orders fell off something awful.
> He figured it had been a bad mistake
> to let the magazine people take those
>   pictures
> of him with his power tools, clean-
>   shaven,
> wearing a flowered sports shirt and
>   drip-dry pants.
>
> So he moved back down to east
>   Kentucky.
> Had himself a brochure printed up
> with a picture of him using his hand
>   lathe.
> Then when folks would come from the
>   magazines,
> he'd get rid of them before suppertime
> so he could put on his shoes, his
>   flowered sport shirt
> and double-knit pants, and open a can
>   of beer
> and watch the six-thirty news on tv
> out of New York and Washington.
>
> He had to have some time to be
>   himself. (1980, p. 44)

31

by Stephen Paul Whitaker

A New Wave of Colonization: The Economics of the Tourism and Travel Industry in Appalachian Kentucky

The tourism and travel industry increasingly is offered as a way to strengthen Kentucky's economic viability and diversity. However, contemporary state initiatives promote tourism and travel development in at least three ways that adversely affect Kentucky's Appalachian counties. First, controlling images that were historically integral to the domination of the Central Appalachian region are utilized by the state to capitalize on the "character" of the region. Secondly, instead of promoting small-scale local development, the state perpetuates and in some instances increases the possibility for the outside control of property and/or economic resources through tax break incentives. Finally, an economically questionable core-periphery arrangement is strengthened through a bureaucratic organization that recreates the pattern regionally. Considering each of these weaknesses in relation to Kentucky's current tourism development policies permits a critical look at the industry as well as invites a reconsideration of the role of the eastern part of the state, the Appalachian counties, in current marketing strategies.

Selling the Appalachian

Controlling images of Appalachians can be linked directly to at least two stereotypes: that of poverty and individualism. The historical links between the production of these stereotypes and the colonization of the region can be directly associated with the economic and cultural intrusion heralded by the tourism/travel industry of the mid 1800s. The "forced entry" of the Appalachian region was accomplished in part by the most powerful and effective device of mass dissemination of the day—the print media. Romanticization of Appalachia as the forgotten frontier became a staple of widely published nineteenth-century local color writers (Shapiro 1983). These writers portrayed the area as possessing the pre-industrial "quintessentially American" way of life which industrialism and urbanism were destroying. Between 1870 and 1890, at the very beginning of the literary exploitation of the region, at least one hundred twenty-five short stories and more than 90 sketches dealing with the nature of mountain life were published" (p. 75). The local color literature that appeared after the Civil War was aimed primarily at and appealed to readers from an emerging middle class in the industrial north which did not yet have the financial resources to travel abroad, but sought diversion instead inside America's borders (Eller 1982). This burgeoning seasonal tourist trade strengthened the images already widely disseminated, particularly since the tourists had preconceived notions of what they would find in the mountains: "These newly rich tourists and traveling journalists supported a seasonal tourist industry in the region, but they developed only marginal contacts with the local mountain people. More often than not, they ended by viewing 'the natives,' as they called the mountaineers, as quaint and primitive, if not degenerate, and they usually returned to the North with accounts of a beautiful and fabulously rich landscape inhabited by a race who lacked an appreciation of its potential" (p. 42). In fact, the material of one of the most prolific writers to use the Appalachian area as a foil for her work, Mary Noailles Murfree, was based solely on her memories of family summer vacations at a mountain resort "of wealth, of fashion, of beauty" (Hsiung 1997, p. 179). Murfree's writing in particular engaged in the transmission of the stereotypes of the dense, quiescent, and ignorant mountaineer while extolling the virtues of the region's beauty as a travel destination (pp. 175–182).

Along with the tourist-fueled transmission of a less-than-romantic view of mountain people, the "hillbillies" and "poor whites" of Appalachia became "the subjects of a massive missionary movement" to bring them "into the mainstream of American life" (Eller 1982, p. 42). Not surprisingly, then, one of Murfree's books became an instruction manual of sorts used by missionaries headed to the region (Hsiung 1997, p. 177). Much of this color literature established as conventional a "literary vision" of the southern mountains as a "strange land inhabited by a peculiar people" that eventually became accepted as fact. "In the literature of Appalachia, as a consequence, metaphor characteristically did the work of exposition. Because it was more interesting, the 'as if' was preferred to the 'is,' and came eventually to be identified as reality" (Shapiro 1983, p. 75). In an era when industrialization was under way in metropolitan parts of the country, then, Appalachia came to be viewed as a frontier haven: a curiosity for wealthy tourists, an undertaking for missionaries, a land of exploitable wealth for capitalists.

By 1870, the advent of the color-writer movement and its accompanying tourist trade coupled with the missionary migration culminated in a push for Appalachian modernization and progress. Ultimately, the dominant cultural values resulted in a concerted effort from within and outside Appalachia's borders to bring the region into the mainstream economic system. During the 1870s and 1880s campaigns were launched in every southern Appalachian state aimed at attracting foreign immigration and commercial investment. State authorities established immigration bureaus and dispatched agents to New York and Europe to spread the word of potentially profitable opportunities. Exhibitions of state resources were creatively displayed at conventions throughout America and Europe, much the same way the region's beauty is "showcased" at modern-day tourism and travel shows in northern cities: as an exploitable, consumable commodity (Whitaker 1994). By the turn of the century geological surveys were being commissioned to detail the extent of the state's mineral wealth for the benefit of potential buyers who were courted at these events (Eller 1982, p. 46). An important concept here relates to the states' role in "selling" the region. Robert Wood (1980) notes that the same tactics are involved in tourism promotion in Southeast Asia: "the role of the state as the self-appointed arbiter of culture which is to be preserved and presented to tourists" (p. 570).

A substantial critique should be undertaken of the way Kentucky has constructed—or reconstructed—its heritage to participate in the commodity imperative by devising or manipulating history to be most appealing and marketable to tourists. "The expanded cultural role of the state which results from the growth of tourism is one of the significant ways tourism promotes cultural change. This expanded role results both from the way tourism involves new forms of integration into the world economy and from the particular importance of cultural attractions in Southeast Asian tourism" (Wood 1980, p. 569). The costuming of "historical characters" at state parks, the funding of events like *The Stephen Foster Story,* the marketing of the Hatfield-McCoy feud, or the restoration of coal-mining towns like that at McCreary County's Blue Heron, all represent a complex commodification of stereotypes that are perpetuated by the state and a way for Kentucky to present itself to the world as it grapples for participation in the world economy. The situation represents both the construction and transmission of ideology that not only provides an image that is sold but a viable controlling image that establishes as normal a set of behaviors that are generated specifically by the state for marketing purposes. It also represents a dilemma:

> People who criticize the marketing of Appalachia tend to have a hate/love relationship with regional tourism. On the one hand they resent selling Appalachia as a tourist attraction. It is insulting. In places like Sevier County [Tennessee], Appalachian people—male, female, Native American, African American (not mutually exclusive categories)—actually dress themselves up and turn themselves into unrealistic, ridiculous distortions of their ancestors in order to entertain and please their visitors. According to Richard Blaustein, the region's past is 'deliberately reshaped, like a Japanese bonsai tree and vistas of the Blue Ridge Parkway, to evoke a state of nature that is purer than nature itself.' On the other hand, this business produces cash. (Maggard 1994, p. 138).

It is important to note, however, that not only does this business produce cash and construct a saleable image for the rest of the world, but it also has direct implications for the construction of the Kentucky resident's reality in which history becomes defined by the state and internalized by the local populace: "In addition to being an arbiter of living culture, the state also organizes cultural reproductions. The national museums which all Southeast Asian countries support make a cultural statement directed both to international tourists and to their own citizens. The swarms of local schoolchildren being shepherded through them testify to the authorities' belief that they contain something to be learned about the national culture" (Wood 1980, p. 571). The implication is fairly clear here despite the fact that Wood is discussing the impact of tourism on a country rather than a region. In deciding what is marketable to the tourist industry, the state becomes involved in setting an identity agenda in which history becomes a present-day performative act tailored to the market. "Official" history is redesigned to be pleasing to tourists and officially sanctioned by the state as such. An alternate view is provided again in research involving the international tourist trade. "[S]uch activities, which in the end convert culture into artistic performance, are highly regarded since it is believed that they should enable the tourist-receiving societies to safeguard or even recover, their cultural identify, while at the same time contributing their own special treasures to the common fund of universal culture" (Lanfant 1980, 34). Clearly, neither viewpoint is entirely accurate. The marketable images are not solely inventions of the state nor are they necessarily completely representative of dying cultures. Certainly the tensions represented by the dichotomy of the two perspectives point to a need for deep consideration of how, when, where, and which images will be presented. The debate also presents a fairly strong indication of the need for a critique of the expanded role of the state in cultural development because tourism represents the advent of a cultural "unique export" (Wood 1980, p. 580).

Selling the Region

In addition to examining the cultural implications of tourism on Kentucky, it is important to carefully analyze the industry's economic ramifications, especially in light of the historical commodification of the Appalachian region as a travel destination and the way tourism has been historically linked to the outside control of the region's resources. The highly dominated economic system can be viewed today in terms of tourism development in Appalachia as an induced system, a system in which the roles of the local population and government are impeded by both outside control and local elites. There is little research available regarding the commodification and exploitation of rural America within and by the tourism/travel industry. Again relying on international tourist market research, this time from Spain, an induced tourism system can be defined as one in which foreign control is overt and "the entrance of local people and institutions [into the system] may be difficult and accompanied by no little conflict" (Oliver-Smith et al. 1989, p. 345). This induced system of tourism, then, becomes another way for local resources to become exploited with little or no benefit to the region's people. A case in point in Kentucky is the passage of the 1996 Kentucky Tourism Development Act. "For the first time, Kentucky is now able to offer a major economic incentive for tourism development projects," touts the state's Tourism Development Cabinet web page (Commonwealth of Kentucky, 1999, http://www.state.ky.us/tour/latta.htm).

> This innovative new program is designed to spur development of major tourism attractions. The Kentucky Tourism Development Act provides incentives for qualified new or expanded tourist projects. This new program applies to cultural, historic, recreational, or entertainment projects. To qualify, a project: must cost a minimum of $1 million, must draw 25 percent of its visitors from out-of-state within four years, must operate at least 100 days a year, and must be a destination attraction. (1999)

Businesses that meet the qualifications are eligible to recover 25 percent of their initial investments through "a tax credit against state sales taxes collected from visitors to the attraction" (Commonwealth of Kentucky 1999). Under these terms, the areas of Kentucky which experience the greatest economic deprivation are those least likely to possess a population that would include individuals with the kind of capital required to benefit from the incentives. The state, in this instance, is actively fostering and rewarding outside ownership despite the known historical ramifications of such policies. In other words, the areas of the state already victimized by the outside ownership that accompanied the coal industry are those most likely to experience further foreign domination via the tourist industry. A governmental tendency to actively participate in and aid the development of exploitative *conditions* to promote tourism has been noted in international market research: "At the minimum, the state must cooperate with tourist development, for example, with visa policy, foreign exchange requirements, and import regulations. But usually the state plays an active role in opening up new areas to mass tourism, because either government expenditures or resources from international agencies are required for the provision of infrastructure (roads, airports, electricity, etc.) and often for tourist facilities themselves" (Wood 1980, p. 569). The result, in Kentucky at least, is that the tourism/travel industry is actually replaying the economic story of the Appalachian region and follows the classic core-periphery model (Walls 1978) that explains the relationships among countries in the modern economic arrangement. Core countries or highly developed and industrialized nations exploit the resources of semi-peripheral countries which in turn exploit peripheral countries. In reformulating the model to Appalachia, David

Walls offers the application of the term "peripheral" to regions like Appalachia because they "share many of the characteristics of underdevelopment, poverty, and dependency found in the peripheral countries of the Third World," and because the term represents a "more appropriate analogy than internal colony" (p. 338). He cautions, however, that the core-periphery analogy "should not be pushed too far?" (p. 338) for a variety of reasons: "[T]here are important differences between poor countries and poor regions in rich countries. The most important difference is that countries have a relatively greater degree of closure in their boundaries. Through the use of the tariff boundaries, control over investments, and other means, countries can achieve a greater degree of insulation from the world economy" (p. 338). In other words, peripheral countries are actually *more* autonomous than are peripheral regions because they avoid "constitutional and political limitations on the restraint of commerce" (p. 338).

This core-periphery arrangement is reflected in the amount of "travel expenditures" recorded in the state. These figures are calculated by the Kentucky Department of Travel Development using the 1993 "State Input-Output Models for Transportation Impact Analysis." They represent the calculated impact of money spent on tourism-related activities such as lodging, food, and entertainment by tourists to Kentucky. The figures show a sharp difference between the Kentucky regions containing the urban centers of Louisville-Lincoln (Louisville-Jefferson County) and Bluegrass (Lexington-Fayette County), and the other regions (see Table 2). Not surprisingly, the regions that experienced the least impact from tourism are those dominated by Appalachian counties (see Table 1). Moreover, the regions that are experiencing the greatest consistent impact from tourism expenditures are in western Kentucky—an area outside Appalachia that could be considered a semi-peripheral region (see Table 3). Clearly, eastern Kentucky is not reaping the labor benefits of other areas either (see Table 4) because the region consistently possesses the fewest tourism-related jobs. Ironically, but not surprisingly, it is often the eastern Kentucky region's beauty that is used to sell Kentucky as a travel destination location. Regional marketing strategies often include pushing the "day trip" notion of travelling to Appalachia during the day, but staying in the urban centers at night for lodging and food. So Appalachia becomes the periphery which benefits the core urban areas in Kentucky.

Tourism and travel represent Kentucky's third largest legal industry (Commonwealth of Kentucky 1999, http://www.state.ky.us/tour/latta.htm) and the second largest employer. Because of declines in the industrial, mining, and farming sectors, the tourism/travel industry has often been pointed to as the answer to economic development concerns. However, "the generation of income and development is not, in itself, a guarantee of development" (Hoivik and Heiberg 1980, p. 89) and the core-periphery arrangement of Kentucky's tourism/travel industry has fairly serious implications for long-term economic viability. Again, there is a paucity of research regarding rural tourism in the United States. However, a study considering the implications of "centre-periphery tourism" at the international level indicates that the market is "basically" weighted in favor of the central nations, their travel operators, and consumers" at the expense of the peripheral regions.

> Over time the position of the receiving countries is adaptive rather than innovative. They can provide facilities, but not customers. To invest in international standard tourism, therefore, is to invest in dependency. Tourism may generate enough income to help the country develop towards economic independence and equality. But its inherent characteristics do not facilitate this process. Only a strong government policy can channel the economic flows in the opposite direction: toward basic needs and local self-reliance. Tourism is but an indirect road to development, a road that can easily be blocked by the structures established to promote it. (p. 91)

TABLE 1. State-Designated Travel Development Regions (by county)

Bluegrass	Anderson, Bourbon, Boyle, Clark*, Fayette, Franklin, Garrard*, Harrison, Jessamine, Lincoln*, Madison*, Mercer, Nicholas, Scott, Woodford
Cave	Allen, Barren, Butler, Edmonson, Hart, Logan, Metcalfe, Monroe*, Simpson, Warren
Eastern Highlands-North	Bath*, Boyd*, Carter*, Elliott*, Floyd*, Greenup*, Johnson*, Lawrence*, Magoffin*, Martin*, Menifee*, Montgomery*, Morgan*, Pike*, Rowan*
Eastern Highlands-South	Bell*, Breathitt*, Clay*, Estill*, Harlan*, Jackson*, Knott*, Knox*, Laurel*, Lee*, Leslie*, Letcher*, Owsley*, Perry*, Powell*, Rockcastle*, Whitley*, Wolfe*
Green River	Daviess, Hancock, Henderson, Hopkins, McLean, Muhlenberg, Ohio, Union, Webster
Louisville-Lincoln	Breckenridge, Bullitt, Grayson, Hardin, Henry, Jefferson, Larue, Marion, Meade, Nelson, Oldham, Shelby, Spencer, Trimble, Washington
Northern Kentucky	Boone, Bracken, Campbell, Carroll, Fleming*, Gallatin, Grant, Kenton, Lewis*, Mason, Owen, Pendleton, Robertson
Southern Kentucky Lakes & Rivers	Adair*, Casey*, Clinton*, Cumberland*, Green*, McCreary*, Pulaski*, Russell*, Taylor, Wayne*
Western Lakes	Ballard, Caldwell, Calloway, Carlisle, Christian, Crittenden, Fulton, Graves, Hickman, Livingston, Lyon, Marshall, McCracken, Todd, Trigg

TABLE 2. Travel Expenditures by Region, 1991 to 1995 (in millions)

	1991	*1992*	*1993*	*1994*	*1995*
Statewide	$3,324	$3,579	$3,998	$4,235	$4,401
Bluegrass	792	849	903	950	954
Cave	206	233	247	275	300
Eastern Highlands-North	138	151	181	198	195
Eastern Highlands-South	170	197	224	235	253
Green River	141	155	185	199	191
Louisville-Lincoln	995	1,083	1,225	1,271	1,332
Northern Kentucky	417	436	460	492	492
Southern Kentucky Lakes & Rivers	995	201	234	247	277
Western Lakes	257	280	338	368	397

Source: "Tourism Research Series: Economic Impact of Kentucky's Tourism and Travel Industry," Kentucky Department of Travel, Commonwealth of Kentucky. Figures rounded to nearest million.
* Federally-designated Appalachian county.

TABLE 3. Percent Change in Annual Kentucky Tourism & Travel Industry Expenditures, 1991 to 1995 (adjusted for inflation)

	1991	*1992–1993*	*1993–1994*	*1994–1995*
Statewide	+4.3	+4.3	+2.9	+1.8
Bluegrass	+3.8	+4.1	+4.7	–0.6
Cave	+9.3	+7.5	+7.7	+5.3
Eastern Highlands-North	+6.2	+17.8	+6.8	–0.6
Eastern Highlands-South	+10.0	+6.8	+1.9	–3.6
Green River	+5.0	+16.7	+3.9	+5.3
Louisville-Lincoln	+5.4	+10.5	+0.8	+2.1
Northern Kentucky	+1.1	+3.1	+4.7	–1.3
Southern Kentucky Lakes & Rivers	–0.3	+6.8	+2.7	+6.3
Western Lakes	+2.6	+23.3	+4.9	+5.0

TABLE 4. Full-Time-Equivalent Jobs Resulting from Tourism & Travel Industry by Region, 1991 to 1995

	1991	*1992*	*1993*	*1994*	*1995*
Statewide	147,996	139,059	142,518	144,691	146,005
Bluegrass	24,460	23,502	23,797	23,777	24,006
Cave	7,353	27,804	7,287	7,990	8,588
Eastern Highlands-North	4,844	4,755	4,955	5,223	5,130
Eastern Highlands-South	6,048	6,158	6,510	6,260	6,711
Green River	5,111	4,958	5,187	5,280	5,678
Louisville-Lincoln	28,606	27,804	28,796	28,444	29,740
Northern Kentucky	13,012	12,156	12,244	12,528	12,543
Southern Kentucky Lakes & Rivers	7,004	6,453	6,686	6,711	7,315
Western lakes	8,599	8,142	8,548	8,946	9,581

Source: "Tourism Research Series: Economic Impact of Kentucky's Tourism and Travel Industry," Kentucky Department of Travel, Commonwealth of Kentucky.

Obviously there are distinct differences between the international tourism market and the system in Appalachia. First of all, the international market relies heavily on air transport. Secondly, it is countries with established borders that comprise this core-periphery arrangement. With these limitations in mind, however, it is important to consider some of their conclusions for the future of a core-periphery model of tourism and its implications for economic development in Appalachia. For example, they suggest that consumption in peripheral areas "is directed toward goods and services that can be provided cheaply by cheap labor" (p. 94). If this is the case, then Appalachia might represent a cheaper and more attractive destination location for some tourists. But do cheap products produced by cheap labor necessarily benefit the region economically, or do they represent an exploitative, dead-end situation for the worker? Certainly, the available research indicates that the tourism industry, particularly in peripheral areas, exploits the labor of marginalized groups, particularly women. "Tourism, as it turns out, provides seasonal, low-wage jobs in food service, retail sales, and hotel service with limited benefits for women" (Maggard, 1994, p. 140). In addition, there is evidence to indicate that "economic development" linked to the tourism industry is unstable and suspect.

> [W]hile the industry is fairly labor intensive in operation the expansion of productive capacity is rather capital intensive. Thus, tourism is not a very efficient means of creating employment. Further, not only does tourism require types of labor in short supply, but the work tends to be seasonal and low paid and creates social tensions. Apart from supply problems, certain features of tourism demand may cause some concern to underdeveloped countries; specifically, allowance must be made for its seasonality, its sensitivity to extraneous events [like weather fluctuations], and its composition. In sum, while it cannot be denied that for some underdeveloped countries tourism has been a great help, one should not be led to view tourism promotion as a general panacea. Turkish experience suggests a need for greater caution when assessing tourism's contribution to solving the economic problems of developing countries. (Diamond 1977, p. 548)

The price of fostering this type of shortsighted development policy is dependency on a national economy that brutalizes the local systems (Salstrom and Hollenhorst 1994) and perpetuates conditions which prompted state intervention in development planning to begin with.

The concept of "back-stage areas" is useful to this analysis as well: those areas that are used to "warehouse tourists and funnel them to target locations" (Salstrom and Hollenhorst 1994, p. 418). Appalachia also possesses "economic backstage areas" where workers in the tourism industry live and supplement their meager incomes. "Southern Appalachia's back-stage subsistence farming used to allow timber and coal industries to pay their workers low wages, at least until the United Mine Workers got a foothold in 1933. Prior to that, Appalachia's coal companies often paid their miners below the cost of feeding and housing an average family" (p. 418). In other words, the tourism industry represents not only a recreation of the economic status quo that victimized Appalachia to begin with, but also recreates the very conditions that result in the highly publicized poverty of the region.

Discussion

Rural Kentucky counties, particularly those with potential recreation attractions like rivers and lakes, are increasingly looking to tourism as a viable economic alternative to mining, manufacturing, and farming, particularly with the decline of the mining and tobacco industries. However, available research indicates that reliance on tourism ultimately means a continuation of crippling dependence and perpetuation of exploitative conditions that accompanied the coal industry into Kentucky. "Kentucky Open for Business," the motto of former Governor Wallace Wilkinson, has often meant "Kentucky Open for Exploitation." Certainly the Kentucky Tourism Cabinet's current slogan "Kentucky . . . Always in Season!" carries the same implications. The policies related to tourism development developed in the last ten years indicate that the same economic power dynamic that is indicative of the domination of Appalachia is being recreated. The analogy between Appalachia and marginalized/colonized countries may not be entirely accurate, but is certainly a close enough fit to warrant considering tourism research from those countries while the region conducts its own. A second way to avoid the mistakes of the past is to consider the implications of an induced system of tourism. The Appalachian Regional Commission advocates in its 1996 strategic plan an effort to "support leadership, marketing, and planning efforts to enhance local strategies for tourism development" (ARC 1999, http://www.arc.gov/). Such an effort could, if properly orchestrated, lead to the type of organic development that results in "local recognition and development of tourism as an exploitable community resource" that can "result in centers of control moving farther and farther away from the host area," and tends to promote local participation rather than impede it (Oliver-Smith et al. 1989, p. 345).

It is clear that the potential benefits and the potential detriments of the tourism/travel industry have not been thoroughly analyzed in Kentucky. Unfortunately, policy has been made and is being revised in a haphazard manner and at the whim of whomever happens to be in office. Despite the love-hate relationship that exists with the industry, the fact is that tourism-related business is here and that cannot be changed. What can be altered, however, is the way Kentucky does its business. The tourism/travel industry may not be able to answer Kentucky's economic problems, but intensive planning can at least prevent the industry from contributing to them.

32

by Maier B. Fox

Prospects for the UMWA

For 105 years, the United Mine Workers of America has been at the center of the country's industrial system. For that reason alone, it has received more attention than is normally accorded a labor union. But the UMWA has been of even greater importance than that simple fact suggests.

The UMWA, after the turn of the twentieth century and again in the 1930s and 1940s was one of the largest labor unions in the world. Nearly a half-million men (and all were men in those days) were covered by UMWA agreements with coal-mine operators at the union's peak. Because the existence of coal deposits is geographically restricted, the relative size of the union varied tremendously. Where mining was a mainstay of the local economy—as in much of Pennsylvania, West Virginia, and Kentucky—coal miners and their families often *were* the people.

And conditions in those geographical areas were among the worst in the country. As has often been the case in areas where the economy is based on extractive industry, wealth was also extracted from coal-mining communities. For generations, the American image of the coalfields was dominated by ramshackle housing, malnourished children, a devastated environment, crippled and short-breathed workers. The image reflected reality far too closely. Because the UMWA accepted this reality as its challenge, the union had extraordinary influence among people in the communities where miners worked, and then in the country as a whole.

The union used its strength in negotiations to modify and then eliminate the company town. When miners' families were allowed to live where they wished, and when miners' incomes rose to allow them to take advantages of options, mining communities started to improve.[1]

When government studies[2] confirmed the lack of quality health care available in many coalfield communities, the UMWA took it upon itself to solve the problem. With the government in control of the mines—an outgrowth of the inability of miners and operators to reach agreement during World War II—the union insisted on the creation of an employer-financed fund to aid injured and ill or retired coal miners. The funds that were created were extraordinarily influential. Under the control of union trustees, the program expanded to provide rehabilitation programs, build hospitals, and develop a fee-for-service medical care coverage system that was opposed by much of the traditional med-

Source: Laslett, John; *The United Mine Workers of America,* (University Park, The Pennsylvania State University Press, 1996), pages 545–554.

ical care community but succeeded in attracting idealistic young practitioners who made a long-term difference in the coalfields.

This UMWA creation set the standard for negotiated benefit programs in other industries, at least for a limited period. And its multiemployer, "portable" approach continues to be at the center of our debate over the appropriate system of health care coverage a half-century later.

But it was not unusual for the UMWA to set the pace for the American labor movement, either by devising new approaches to workers' problems or by setting a standard that other unions sought to meet. For example, even before the creation of the UMWA, organized miners fought to organize the operators and develop regional collective bargaining systems. These were well established in the 1890s and became identified with the first great UMWA president, John Mitchell.[3] Fully national multi-employer negotiations were not quickly gained even in coal mining, but the concept was fully accepted by about 1950 and the importance of large-scale bargaining became something of an article of faith in much of the labor movement.

A repudiation of racial discrimination was among the actions of the founding UMWA convention of 1890.[4] The union was also quick to admit Asian workers,[5] but its progressive attitude was not adopted by most American institutions for many years. The UMWA's repudiation of racial discrimination was for practical as well as ideological reasons. So was its decision to adopt a structure of "industrial" organization rather than the more common "craft" approach dominant in early American unionism. This also made it easy for the union to adopt a leading position in the creation of the Congress of Industrial Organizations in the 1930s.[6]

The UMWA also played a central role in some of the most important federal labor legislation ever passed in the United States. The New Deal's repeated guarantee to workers of the right to bargain collectively (as in the National Labor Relations Act) was drawn from wording originally prepared by Henry Warrum and W. Jett Lauck of the UMWA.[7] And the Taft-Hartley Act, restricting union rights, was probably passed in reaction to the UMWA's post–World War II strikes.

Finally, the UMWA's acceptance of mechanization, which began even before the turn of the century (and the "downsizing" that accompanied it) seems to have set a pattern for other industrial unions, though none seems to have fully accepted it and changes are still sought.[8]

One factor in the UMWA's willingness to set precedents was its militant self-image. Members believed they were willing to put themselves on the line whenever necessary—and often gave substance to this belief. Multiemployer strikes in the anti-union 1890s and the 1919 nationwide coal strike in the face of a government ban were proof of this militancy. Another factor in the UMWA's tendency to go in unexpected directions was recognized by longtime labor activist Len DeCaux when he described John L. Lewis as "an irreverent pragmatist."[9] Lewis may have been particularly irreverent, but the pragmatism was already traditional in the UMWA.

The miners and their union have often been militant and confrontational, though the periodic differences between the approach of the members and the institution they have built have often been documented and sometimes stressed.[10] The tendency toward pragmatism has been noted less often—and continues to be less appreciated. . . .

The UMWA has completed the first five years of its second century. It is not now the huge organization of 1905 or 1935, but it is as large or larger than it was in 1895 and 1930. What does the future hold for an organization that has affected America more than any other labor union—and is increasingly unknown outside of the coalfields today?

Two predictions seem particularly likely to be valuable. First, the UMWA's approach will be practical. Second, the members' militancy will be the key to success. Just as in the union's early years, practicality has been a hallmark of recent UMWA efforts. A willingness to take new approaches, to break from tradition, has been central to the union's attitude for more than a decade. It clearly surfaced in a series of decisions made in the early to mid-1980s. These included the selective-strike concept and the strike fund created to make it effective, the sale of the National Bank of Washington (NBW) and the decision to affiliate with the American Federation of Labor–Congress of Industrial Organizations.

Each of these was a practical decision that struck at tradition. The insistence on nationwide strikes had earlier been one of the keys to the miners' sense of solidarity. The NBW had been an innovation of the revered John L. Lewis, a guarantee that the union would be able to borrow money even when in a contest with employers who were allied with bankers. And Lewis's disdain for the unwillingness of the "House of Labor" to challenge government edicts was widely shared in the coalfields, making the decision to become part of labor's mainstream somewhat problematic.

Nevertheless, many of the union's present and probable future priories represent a continuation of traditional policies. First and foremost will be the need to negotiate agreements that provide miners the opportunity to make a living. Improved health and safety is a second continuing commitment, currently focusing on the dangers presented by the introduction of diesel equipment into the underground environment.

Clean air legislation that does not destroy the coal industry and maintenance of a health and retirement program that protects both current and past miners and their families are also basic. Along with the rest of the labor movement, the UMWA will—to the extent the political situation permits—fight for labor law reform that would place it on "a level playing field" with the coal operators when it comes to organizing new members and to protecting the jobs of strikers from replacement. The Coal Miners Political Action Committee, a modern version of UMWA and CIO pioneering efforts, has proven quite successful in making the case for miners on Capitol Hill.

In the long run, however, new programs, perhaps most important the future role of the Office of Allied Workers (OAW), will determine the future of the UMWA. In the late 1980s, OAW was designed to represent a group that had shrinking work opportunity in the coalfields. Coal-mine construction workers had little work opportunity because new coal mines were seldom being opened. But these union members had abilities that could be used outside of the mining industry, and OAW sought to find those opportunities for the construction workers.

By the early 1990s, people in the coalfields knew that the UMWA was representing these nonminers. Some called upon the UMWA to provide representation to a wider spectrum of workers. The union, new to the AFL–CIO and hesitant to become embroiled in jurisdictional disputes, was slow to respond. But the administration of Richard Trumka quickly found an approach that proved satisfactory. The UMWA would organize outside of its original coal-mining jurisdiction, but restrict itself to coal-mining areas where its reputation was a built-in advantage and other unions had little or no presence.

In the strictest sense, OAW was not a new departure but hearkened back to "District 50," a John L. Lewis creation in 1936. As with District 50, OAW was designed to provide representation within the UMWA to workers who were not coal miners. District 50 had been a challenge to other labor organizations and a potential challenge to both the AF of L and the CIO. The impetus behind OAW was different. In many coal-mining communities, there were few other employment options. Perhaps for that reason, other unions seldom appeared to try to organize the small number of workers with other occupations. But those workers often needed and wanted union protection—and the union with which they were most familiar was the UMWA.

The UMWA was slow to expand outside of coal mining. The decision to welcome nonminers into the union may prove to be one of the most important ones made by the union under Trumka. While usage of coal has been expanding consistently, the number of miners has been shrinking. At present, total nonsupervisory employment in coal mining is less than 100,000. That number is likely to decline further, as mechanization continues to lead to productivity increases in surface as well as underground mining.

Moreover, clean air concerns threaten to destroy the industry. Coal's primary market is the utility industry. Utilities, in recent decades, extended the life of coal-burning plants rather than build new ones. Increasingly, these will need to be replaced. Primarily because of concern over air pollution, current law discourages the use of coal, largely because of the expense involved in burning coal cleanly, and the popular perception that it can't be done. Meanwhile, evidence of abundant supplies of clean-burning natural gas suggest that utilities will turn more to that fuel.

The shrinking of the coal-mining population will be gradual, but it seems inevitable. If the UMWA is to remain an independent force in the American labor movement, the workers who have joined the union through the OAW—still a small proportion of the membership—will play an increasingly important role. In its second century, a successful UMWA will include, among others, the members who worked on Hoover Dam, the hospital workers in Dickenson County (Virginia), the public employees of Walker County (Alabama) and Sheridan (Wyoming), and the people in the Housing Authority of Evansville (Indiana), along with the country's coal miners.

The OAW may also prove to be important because of the difficulty the UMWA has had in finding other unions with which to merge. In the late 1980s, the UMWA and the Oil, Chemical, and Atomic Workers Union nearly consummated a merger agreement. It made sense for these unions to join forces because both were relatively small, both were in the energy field, and they negotiated with some of the same employers. On the other hand, their geographic strengths differed, and a merger would have created a union with greater national influence. The failure of those discussions leaves no such "natural" partner and the UMWA's growth is likely to be circumscribed.

Pragmatism has also proved to be the key to the bargaining goals in recent negotiations. The UMWA continues to make health care the centerpiece of negotiations, and is likely to do so until such time as the nation's health care system ensures proper care to all. This is a particularly important issue for miners because of the multigenerational tendency among coal miners. Miners will brook no system other than lifetime health care because the retirees in the industry are the parents and grandparents of the current workforce. But other leading goals have grown from the decline of the industry.

The Employment and Economic Security pacts that date from the late 1980s recognize that employment opportunity is declining and are designed to ensure that future opportunities will be given to UMWA members. The promise of first opportunity to unemployed union coal miners has been central to UMWA bargaining strategy and will likely continue to be in the near future. Still, the declining number of available jobs will continue to cost some UMWA members their livelihoods. The union's current answer to this problem is a second innovation in contracts, the Training and Education Fund, which provides college (or technical school) tuition and some expenses for laid-off members and, since 1993, for the dependents of active miners.[11]

For a job protection/job training strategy to bear fruit, it is important that employees and employers recognize a reciprocal commitment. Miners need to work toward greater productivity while employers provide increased security and opportunity. History makes the trust implied in this cooperative approach difficult for miners. Often, greater productivity has meant fewer miners or longer hours, and the union continues to react strongly to the mandatory overtime that has come to the industry.[12] Other efforts at cooperation collapsed because the operator approach was seen as divisive—as a new attempt in the old effort to "bust" the union.[13] Modern efforts have been successful when both sides have accepted the goodwill of the other.

Some years ago, for example, a Canadian UMWA local and mine management had established a cooperative relationship called "Relationship by Objective." It differed from traditional worker-involvement programs in that it was not mandated by the company and that changes had to be accepted by both parties. The program did not spread quickly, probably because of management dislike for modifying its prerogatives and miner distrust of management's objectives.[14]

However, the concept received a new lease on life at a western Pennsylvania mine in 1992. The miners got a new safety program, tuition payments, increased job security, and an end to mandatory overtime. The operators got better productivity, fewer conflicts needing resolution through the arbitration procedure and ten more years added to the life of the mine.

UMWA President Trumka indicates the union's desire to blend pragmatism with militancy in his approval of such programs and by his insistence that there are prerequisites. These are that the operators must be serious about their willingness to cooperate, and show it by putting an end to mandatory overtime. He feels that the industry is sometimes held back by an outmoded tradition of paternalism and by an insistence on centralized control that may not be useful in a given situation.[15]

Trumka's comments bring into question the commitment to better labor-management relations that has been displayed to date; in broad outline, however, the UMWA and the Bituminous Coal Operators Association (BCOA) accepted the need to cooperate in the National Bituminous Coal Wage Agreement of 1993.[16] Included in that pact was an updated cooperation program, the Labor Management Positive Change Process.

This program was based on the agreement that both the operators and the union "must discard old ways of dealing with each other in mistrust, and foster a new environment of mutual trust and good faith acceptance. In order to achieve these objectives, the parties recognize the need for new and creative approaches to labor-management cooperation." Labor-management committees, aided by expert consultants, work to improve productivity, protect job security, and otherwise encourage cooperation without encroaching on grievance procedures or other contractual dispute-settlement procedures. Similar provisions were included in agreements signed with non-BCOA members. Such a provision was successfully invoked at the Kellerman mine in Alabama but there has not been a strong indication that labor-management relations in the coalfields have changed fundamentally.[17]

Although the NBCWA of 1993 encompasses the union's willingness to be pragmatic and innovative, the events that led to that agreement underscore the continued militancy of America's coal miners. After a series of long and bitter contract strikes, the union and the BCOA reached agreement without a work stoppage in both 1984 and 1988. This did not herald a new cooperative era in the relations of coal miners and operators. In fact, there was a new threat to cooperation: the decline of the BCOA. The decline of the BCOA was central to the two large strikes that took place in the last half of the decade. With the splintering of the employers' association, individual operators with deep pockets thought they would be better off negotiating independent agreements with the union (or working nonunion) than by following the association's lead.

The union engaged in long and bitter strikes, first with A. T. Massey (a company particularly active in Virginia that had both union and nonunion mines), then with Pittston. In both instances, attempts to eliminate the union were beaten back. Complete victory was delayed nearly a decade in the Massey strike, but sale of the mines brought even nonunion former Massey miners into the UMWA fold in the 1990s. Extraordinary fines imposed in the Pittston strike hung over the union long after it was ended, until finally cancelled by action of the U.S. Supreme Court in 1994.[18]

Victory in these two strikes was not so important as the union's demonstration that it would stand by member militancy in the face of judicial threats to incarcerate the UMWA's officers and destroy the union economically. A threat that extreme had not faced the union since the days of John L. Lewis, and it was accepted as the price of doing business.

The union proved in both the Massey and Pittston strikes that it still had the will to avoid "give-backs." But Trumka's willingness to pit the union against the united employers may not have been recognized until 1993. In that year, the UMWA engaged in its first strike with the BCOA companies in more than a decade. It was a long and difficult confrontation. Still, membership—and leadership—militancy in the Massey and Pittston contests may well have moderated the 1993 contract strike, lengthy and difficult as it was. And that strike may have been less destructive to long-term harmony between the union and the operators, for the operators did not make the error of assuming they could eliminate the union as a force in the industry.

Militancy has always been ingrained in American and Canadian miners.[19] There are probably many different reasons that miners see themselves—and other see miners—as militant. Trumka refers to the danger that has always been inherent in mining and the resultant closeness among those who share the danger. Miners have faced the real possibility of accidental death on a daily basis. The dangers of confrontation with management pale in comparison. The forms that the miners' militancy will take in coming years are likely to be based on their history. Trumka recognizes this in statements that reflect his own familiarity with UMWA history. He speaks of the union rejecting the traditional paternalism of the operators and of the union's role as champion of the "working class," a term largely out of favor today.

Even the "innovations" in recent UMWA activity seem grounded in the union's history. The "Office of Allied Workers," for example, is not a carbon copy of the District 50 created more than a half-century ago. But it does recall the origins of that departure, organizing among gas and coke by-product workers who were considered part of an allied (or competing) industry, natural constituents of the UMWA. And the approach to the conflict with the Pittston Company, while it was a change from "normal" union procedure, also would have been recognized by earlier generations of UMWA miners.

As far back as the 1920s, the UMWA pioneered aspects of the "comprehensive campaign," picketing the New York City offices of Berwind-White and Consolidation Coal (along with the office of John D. Rockefeller Jr., principal stockholder of "Consol") during an organizing strike. Again in the 1970s' "Brookside" strike, the UMWA broadened the target from the Harlan County mine to the owners, Duke Power. There has been increasing sophistication in the tactics used by the union, but the basis for this kind of union action has clear precedents.[20]

Even the UMWA's role in the recent dispute over the future leadership of the AFL-CIO has historical precedent. The union has provided both leadership to the labor movement as a whole and challengers to that leadership. Samuel Gompers's leadership of the AFL was challenged successfully by the UMWA's John McBride and unsuccessfully by John L. Lewis. William Green of the AFL came out of the UMWA—and Lewis's antipathy for Green was repeatedly evident in the formation of the CIO. Both Lewis and Phil Murray headed the CIO. Trumka's recent election as secretary-treasurer of the AFL-CIO suggests that a larger role for the UMWA in the labor movement is again likely.

The UMWA is a proud institution, proud of its past and proud of the image of militant leadership it has maintained within the labor movement. It will likely maintain the same role.

VIII

Policy Issues

This section on public policy is integrally related to the previous section on political economy. Government programs and policies shape and are shaped by, to some degree, contemporary economic forces and institutions. Our first chapter is one excerpted from Richard Couto's book, *An American Challenge*. In it, Couto outlines the concept and elements of social capital and proposes a program of public expenditures to develop education, health care, art and culture, and housing resources. Michael Bradshaw evaluates the role and work of the Appalachian Regional Commission. After examining regional development theory, Bradshaw concludes that the impact of public investment in depressed areas has been modest. In the final article on policy, Michael Miskowiec takes an early look at the 1996 welfare reform legislation. Now that the law has been in effect for some years, readers may want to obtain additional data on the impact of welfare reform in Appalachian communities. Public policy is a broad area and various aspects of it are also covered in the previous sections on the economy, and health and the environment.

33

by Richard A. Couto

Policies and Programs

The vagaries of recent economic change work themselves into unimagined contortions in Appalachia. While we may discuss the "garrison economy" and deplore the paucity of social capital for education, in many areas, Appalachia is one place that portrays how the garrison and the school are related. Hancock County, Tennessee financed a portion of its school budget with fees collected from the District of Columbia for incarcerating an average of 85 of its inmates for $45 a day (Anderson and Binstein 1993). The social problems of a metropolitan area became the industry of a rural, impoverished county and a source of scarce social capital. To crown the improbable with irony, Whittle Communications Corporation in Knoxville, just 70 miles from Hancock County, plans sweeping, for-profit educational reform for the nation (Passall 1994; Toch 1993). Within the Appalachian region, social capital is borrowed from the garrison economy while others plan for private profit in face of the failure to provide sufficient social capital. Challenges and contradictions like these are writ large in Appalachia but with lines borrowed from American economic trends. These trends and the social consequences that ensue have stimulated considerable thought about solutions. This chapter reviews solutions involving the federal government and suggests national policies that are especially pertinent to Appalachia.

A Policy Agenda for Work, Income, and Families

Reactions to the excesses of accumulation and redistribution of wealth of the 1980s coupled with a political change from the conservative Republican administrations of the 1980s have prodded some social analysts to suggest new policies in different issue areas. Several policy centers have outlined reforms, including the liberal, progressive Citizens Transition Project (Green 1992). Its report provides an agenda of policy reforms to achieve more equity in the distribution of wealth and a higher level of basic services to those in need. It envisions economic growth with fairness; provision of family security; increased racial harmony; and the reinvention of government or at least the restoration of public faith in public action. In summary, the report proposed

> a public-investment-led economic recovery; affordable, accessible, universal health care; bold campaign finance reform; prenatal care for all pregnant women and a fully funded Head Start program for all eligible children; a 1993 version of Food for Peace for the former Soviet Union to generate exports here and democracy there; scholarships for all in need, paid back over

time via payroll deductions or national service; a technology extension service to help convert advanced technology into commercial uses; and the Freedom of Choice Act. One way to bundle several of these ideas together is to state the early goal will be "*health*—how to improve both the personal and economic health of all Americans by universal care and reinvestment in America" (Green 1993: pp. 11–12).

The extensive reach of this statement measures not so much a utopian approach to reform but the backlog of needs we have acquired during the time we were content to pursue the public good through the individual accumulation of wealth.

The components of the Citizens Transition Project report discuss policies in detail. Robert Kuttner (1992), for example, provides principles of reform of work that range from increased wages to improving the bargaining position of labor unions. He identifies the following policies to provide more training and security for workers and more flexibility and productivity for management:

- a comprehensive system of lifetime learning and retraining should replace unemployment compensation as the principal public subsidy of the labor market;
- labor law reform enacted to allow unions to contest representation elections without reprisal, to bargain collectively when they win such elections, and to prohibit the permanent replacement of striking workers;
- government policies should establish a new social contract between labor and management that ties wage increases to productivity as part of a commitment to full employment without inflation;
- government should encourage labor participation in corporate governance to improve the efficiency of corporations and to develop a more effective and durable form of trade unionism;
- public policy should promote new forms of employee ownership and participation in management; and
- participation in management should extend to work and safety on the job (Seminario 1992: pp. 578–588).

Kuttner makes three other recommendations of special relevance to Appalachia. He urges immunity of pension funds from management raids. Pensions are an important source of income to retired workers, who are increasing in number in Northern Appalachia especially. Their pensions are particularly vulnerable because they are based on social contracts of yesterday with steel, coal, and textile firms (Drape 1991). Firms of this declining industrial sector may disappear into merger, bankruptcy, or reorganization tomorrow. Coal miners, their widows, and their dependents have seen first-hand how the razzle-dazzle of corporate reorganization can leave retired workers and their families bereft of benefits. Kuttner laments especially the use of pension funds to leverage buyouts that put workers out of jobs or the attraction a generous pool of pension assets provides to corporate raiders (1992: pp. 164–65).

Kuttner also urges efforts to convert and upgrade low-wage, dead-end and contingent jobs. Such jobs abound in the service sector. Contingent jobs, part-time and temporary work, carry with them no social capital other than the wage. They are without fringe benefits most times and provide the worker no security. They shelter employers from abrupt shifts in a company's position and require workers to subsidize this protection. Some of these jobs, especially in the human service sector such as home health care, could provide paraprofessional jobs with career ladders. Head Start provides a good example of how this can be done. This form of person-to-person service work will expand in the American economy. In addition to the employment they provide, these services add social capital in areas, such as portions of Appalachia, where it is lacking.

Finally, Kuttner urges that low wages be supplemented or subsidized to assure any full-time worker sufficient income to maintain a family above poverty. Government funds would provide a wage subsidy and a set of benefits to assure that families with full-time workers reached an income level above poverty and received supporting benefits such as child care, health insurance, and training opportunities for advancement in current or new employment.

Kuttner is one of several analysts who tie work and income together. He describes government's role as assuring enough income from work to keep a family out of poverty and providing enough income and benefits to assure that work offers more rewards than welfare does. The means to do this, within our reach, include expanding the earned income tax credit (EITC), according to Robert Greenstein (1992), executive director of the Center on Budget and Public Priorities. The EITC returns income tax paid by low-income families and provides payments to families that have earned too little to pay income tax. The EITC, unlike welfare payments, rises with earnings and is targeted to wage earners living in families with children. Child and family advocates (Edelman 1992: p. 439; Kamarck 1992: p. 449–50) join Greenstein in suggesting the expansion of the EITC to provide higher benefits as the number of children in a family increases. Expansion would more likely assure that working wages are living wages.

Increasing the minimum wage is another means of assuring that work eliminates poverty. Full-time work at minimum wage left a family of three above the poverty level up until the 1970s. By 1992, inflation and no minimum wage increases in the 1980s meant income that was $2,000 less than the poverty level for a family of three with one full-time worker at minimum age. Most minimum wage workers are not poor only because there are generally other wage earners in the household. The low level of the minimum wage and only recent, modest efforts to bring it up to pre-1980 levels are a large part of the story of declining family incomes (Greenstein 1992: p. 421).

Work and income offer direct avenues to welfare reform. The Family Support Act of 1988 provided for the Job Opportunities and Basic Skills (JOBS) program, a welfare-to-work program for AFDC recipients. Preliminary studies show that such programs eventually mean more income and less welfare payments for participants. The program requires state matching funds, which many states do not have. Consequently, in fiscal year 1991 only nine states drew full federal allotments for the JOBS program (Greenstein 1992: p. 424). Programs like JOBS depend on the creation of new jobs for their success, especially in places of concentrated poverty, unemployment, and low levels of labor force participation, like Eastern Kentucky. Consequently, government should play the role of employer of last resort in these areas where job readiness simply means frustration because the labor force expands but employment does not.

Similarly, AFDC payments should not be terminated or reduced on the assumption that job-training means work and increased income. Under pressure to reduce spending, states take aim at AFDC, which makes an easy target because of the American disdain for welfare. Cutting already low AFDC payments will only mean increased child poverty and greater need among the poor. Ironically, budget-cutters invoke family values as partial justification for reducing AFDC payments to some women. Advocates suggest eligibility reforms that would continue some support for AFDC recipients despite work or marriage.

Poverty and family policies intersect around a set of policies for children that include:

- providing refunds to working poor and low-income families for child care expenses in the manner of EITC;
- increasing state and federal regulation to assure child support from absent parents;
- establishing a federal child tax credit of $1,000, in place of personal exemption, which would assist middle class working families as well;

- expanding Head Start to include more than the 30 percent of eligible children participating in 1992 (Greenstein 1992; Edelman 1992; and Kamarck 1992).

The Elements of Social Capital

In addition to general principles of work and income, some proposals address specific elements of social capital.

Education

Education, for example, has exemplary models for reform of school-based decision making; higher standards of academic achievement without segregation of students into tracks; school-based teacher renewal; smaller classes; more flexible and longer school days and years; links to family and children's needs for health care and social services; and performance-based assessment. Carrying out these reforms in new and broad replication efforts requires political leadership and public commitment (Littlefield 1992: pp. 457–71). College tuition and fees have increased by more than twice the cost of living between 1980 and 1992. Inflation, and states hard pressed to meet budgets in declining economic times, have pushed up college costs and restricted access to students with low and moderate incomes who stand to benefit most from their education and to contribute most to increasing the skills of the work force. While college costs increased by 110 percent, the maximum Pell grant, federal assistance with college tuition costs based on financial need, increased by about one-third. Abandoned dreams or heavy debt result. For students not going to college, including those students who do not finish high school, America needs a better system to help them acquire proficiencies for employment and to make the transition to work (Littlefield 1992: p. 467).

Several Appalachian states, including Kentucky, Tennessee, Virginia, and West Virginia, have addressed school finance equity. Funding for schools based on property taxes has aggravated differences among sections of the region so that school districts vary widely, and in some cases unconstitutionally, in their ability to provide all students a reasonably equal education. Establishing common and higher standards for all schools compounds the problems of poorly financed school districts if their resources are adversely affected by failure to reach those standards. Minimal standards such as staying open for an entire school year and providing transportation for school students have been beyond the financial means of some of the poorest counties in Appalachian Tennessee. Obviously state and national efforts are needed to achieve a greater degree of equality among school districts that will permit some reasonable prospects of achieving standards to which they should then be held accountable.

Health Care

The Appalachian region provides many lessons about health care for the nation. Work-related health care from company doctors to innovative union-initiated health plans have been major innovations. Community health centers continue to be a mainstay for the regions in greatest need of health services. This history instructs us about the limits of work-related health care, including recent efforts to cut back health benefits as part of the new competitiveness of American industry and companies such as Pittston. Managed competition reform efforts in health care are likely to fail in Appalachia. Trusting competition to provide more effective services in areas will not create services in areas where they cannot exist without subsidy and considerable community effort.

Principles of fundamental reform for health care include:

- universal insurance coverage for all Americans, with no significant deductibles or co-payment obligations on patients;
- comprehensive, broad coverage of all medically necessary medical care, comprehensively formulated and described;

- public administration and finance to promote accountability and control costs;
- freedom to choose providers and provider-patient autonomy in medical treatment and decision making; and
- portable medical insurance coverage, not tied to a specific job or geographic location (Marmor and Barr 1992: pp. 399–414).

In addition to these principles, Appalachia has special health care achievements and traditions to keep in mind. First, an extensive network of community health centers came from exemplary community responses to need. Policies of reimbursement and provider training, including health providers other than physicians, need to be in tune with the cost and staffing needs of community health centers and other community-based health programs. Second, the region has exemplary prenatal and child care programs that have demonstrated the utility of employing people in paraprofessional roles that increase the well-being of residents.

These programs tie work and welfare reform together with increased investment in social capital. Health care reform needs to be flexible enough to recognize successful innovation, provide adequate support for it, and to permit new community groups and others to initiate replications.

Art and Culture

Social capital extends to the cultural expression of people in community. Some measures to provide increased support to art and culture include:

- a box on income tax returns similar to that for presidential campaign funds that would permit taxpayers to specify up to $10 of their tax payment to state and national artistic and cultural programs;
- increased support for international exchanges of artists and of cultural heritages;
- increased support of artistic and cultural expression of and about women and racial and ethnic minorities; and
- new and higher levels of support for the arts and culture to make up for the lack of real growth in spending of the past twelve years (Gund 1992: pp. 472–79).

Increased support for local artists, like support for human service paraprofessionals, could come through programs of national service and citizen participation. Efforts to encourage college students and other youth in these programs should be supplemented with efforts to support local people in local efforts.

Housing

Perhaps only health exceeds housing as a social capital dilemma. The housing problem combines a lack of affordable housing and new levels of homeless and near homeless people. Despite the need for more affordable housing, market forces have not provided supply. Five general principles should drive specific housing policies:

- expand home ownership opportunities, particularly among young families;
- eliminate homelessness by providing direct rental assistance to Americans in poverty;
- restore the nation's inventory of public and subsidized housing by expanding resident participation and ownership;
- increase the supply of affordable housing, primarily by expanding the capacity of community-based nonprofit developers; and
- rebuild and stabilize the economies and social fabric of urban neighborhoods [and rural communities] by expanding job and home ownership opportunities and reinvigorating community self-help efforts (Dreier and Atlas 1992: pp. 383–98).

These last two principles have particular application in Appalachia. Numerous community-based nonprofit developers have addressed the housing needs of the region. In some cases, they have come together in state and regional organizations, such as the Federation of Appalachian Housing Enterprises, to assist one another and to affect public policy in the manner we described earlier in this chapter. Second, the concentration of poverty is related to accessibility of housing. Inner-city residents need programs, including housing, to get close to the jobs in the areas surrounding the cities. Rural residents need jobs that higher demand for home construction and improvement could supply. The context of community of which housing is a part also needs attention. Technical assistance to community-based, nonprofit organizations in planning, coalition building, research, and leadership development should be provided in housing and other programs.

Part of the costs for this and other housing reforms could come from a new graduated tax credit for homeowners. In 1991, tax deductions for mortgage interest and property taxes totalled $47 billion. Of that, 12 percent went to the wealthiest 1 percent of taxpayers with incomes in excess of $200,000 and 80 percent went to taxpayers with incomes in excess of $50,000. Permitting full deductions for the portion of mortgage interest equal to the national median and partial deductions for increments until capped at some point, such as twice the national median, would not only recover tax revenues from the wealthiest homeowners, it would also provide financial incentives for the construction and purchase of affordable housing (Dreier and Atlas 1992: p. 397).

Part of the housing problem, especially the shortage of capital for home purchase, stems from the savings and loan debacle of the 1980s. Paying for these failures will cost taxpayers between $.5 and $1.4 trillion over 40 years. The roots of those problems extend past the 1980s, but that decade watered and nourished speculation and profit-taking with a "greed is good" nutrient. Perhaps nothing demonstrates the manner in which American public policy socializes capital risk and privatizes profits than the failures of the savings and loans. Related problems of the banking industry and some pension funds may place additional burdens on the taxpayers. Taxpayers' exposure to the liabilities of speculators should be limited. In addition, channels to encourage the flow of capital into productive economy rather than renewed speculation should be constructed. Specific, though limited, steps to accomplish this include increased public accountability, such as that provided in the Community Reinvestment Act, and the creation of community development banks (Gilbert and Goodman 1992: pp. 589–603.)

Public Revenues for Social Capital

Finding revenues for an ambitious, expanded program of social capital investment means new taxes and perhaps some increases in current ones. At the very least, tax breaks for the wealthiest Americans need to be reversed. Placing more wealth in the hands of the wealthy has not produced the economic stimulation predicted by supply-side Reaganomics. It has produced a redistribution of wealth from the lowest to the highest income brackets, increased tax burdens on middle income groups, and the most skewed distribution of wealth in America since World War II. The richest 1 percent of Americans almost doubled their income to $576,000, in constant dollars, from 1977 to 1992. Assessing higher taxes on these and other high income brackets is not a punitive soak the rich policy. It simply recognizes that a nation with an annual budget deficit, and a national debt that escalated as high income earners accumulated wealth, cannot continue to forego the $71 billion gap in tax revenues from this top 1 percent income bracket that developed between 1977 and 1992. Even Adam Smith understood that taxation should "remedy inequality of riches as much as possible by relieving the poor and burdening the rich" (McIntyre 1992: p. 31).

Increased taxes on the most wealthy is one of three principles of progressive tax reform. The second principle protects middle and low-income families from increased taxes. The third principle would plug tax loopholes and increase the top corporate and personal tax rates. Current tax breaks for business and investment are expected to cost $291 billion in corporate taxes and $285 billion in personal taxes from fiscal 1992 to 1996 (McIntyre 1992: p. 37). Investments related to continued or increased employment should enjoy public reward through tax laws.

These principles lead to specific policy suggestions with estimated revenues over the next five years. Some of the major provisions related to the political economic changes we have discussed include:

- increasing tax rates to 36 percent for the wealthiest 1 percent, which would yield $53 billion dollars;
- levying a millionaires' surtax of 10 percent on taxable income above $500,000 and another 10 percent starting at $1 million, which would yield $25 billion;
- increasing corporate tax rates to 36 percent with a surtax of 10 percent on taxable income over $1 million, which would yield $66 billion;
- taxing capital gains as other income rather than capping it at 28 percent, which would yield an addition $22 billion dollars;
- scaling back depreciation write-offs to reflect the actual value of wear and tear, which would yield $24 billion;
- ending tax breaks associated with mergers and acquisitions, which would yield $9 billion;
- collecting taxes from multinational corporations on profits earned in the United States and overhauling the rules by which we determine what income is taxable, which would protect jobs in the United States and yield $23 billion; and
- reforming in the Alternative Minimum Tax, designed to assure that wealthy individuals and corporations pay taxes on some minimum, which would yield $76 billion (McIntyre 1992: pp. 37–42).

This tax reform would implicitly reduce subsidies to special interest groups and the wealthiest individuals. It is part of a major change in government fiscal policy to promote economic growth. Robert J. Shapiro, executive director of the Progressive Policy Institute, provided the ground upon which the Clinton administration campaigned and took its first policy steps. He described some assumptions about government within the Clinton administration:

> In the old economy, government proliferated tax, spending, and credit subsidies for selected industries, as government's way of promoting U.S. competitiveness by helping firms to cut certain costs. In a globalized economy, most of these subsidies undermine innovation and efficiency by making many corporations too comfortable to change. National economic success in the 1990s will require that government turn away from industry subsidies and protection of almost every kind, and toward national investments in the common economic resources that help promote innovation and flexibility, principally education and training, research and development, and advanced communications and transportation systems among our markets (R. Shapiro 1992: pp. 80–81).

Based on the economic development of Appalachia, Shapiro probably overestimates how new the global economy is. He also overlooks how much the old and new global economy resemble each other. International capital developed steel and coal in Appalachia in the 19th century. Lower labor costs still attract international capital to Appalachia to manufacture automobiles or to leave the mountains for the maquiladoras, and factories on the Mexican-American border. Consequently, Shapiro's emphasis on infrastructure investment without social capital investment overstates one need and ignores another.

Shapiro (1992: pp. 81–83) also suggests reducing entitlement transfer payments, such as social security, to the wealthy. Entitlement programs make enticing targets for budget cutters. Medicaid costs have driven many state budget increases as it and Medicare have done for the federal budget. There is certainly a fiscal case for introducing some means testing to reduce entitlement programs' payments and benefits to the very rich. Politically, however, means-tested programs lend themselves to interpretation as wealth-redistributive programs. Such programs lose political support quickly. Social security has avoided stigma, criticism, and cutbacks, unlike AFDC, precisely because its universal eligibility means widespread support. The dependence of many sections of Appalachia on transfer payments increased in the 1980s. This dependence provides substantial reason for concern about any efforts to change entitlement programs. Changes might reduce political support for these programs initially and diminished political support might later encourage reduced payments and more stringent eligibility requirements.

Shapiro (1992: p. 84) and other analysts of the Citizens Transition Project (Steinbruner 1992; Marlin 1992; Gray 1992) agree that funds for defense spending might and should be redirected to other forms of public investment. Such a change will cause economic dislocation for workers currently employed in the defense industry. Consequently, federal funds now spent on defense might be better and more productively spent on the social issues related to current economic dislocation. However, that shift will produce its own dislocations, social issues, and need for the investment of federal funds. The peace dividend will not come without some payback provisions.

Mediating Structures and Democratic Renewal

Policies alone are not the answer. Democratically controlled interventions provide the best hope of remedy for the problems this report has discussed. Political conservatives and liberals agree on that. The conservative policy center, the American Enterprise Institute, sponsored work on mediating structures, e.g., family, church, civic and neighborhood associations, and voluntary agencies, as mechanisms of social policy. Mediating structures are those organizations that stand between individuals and large social and economic forces and have received a great deal of attention from policy analysts and advocates. Mediating structures fall within the broader spectrum of the non-profit sector and incorporate their public role that the liberal Urban Institute developed (Salamon 1982: pp. 73–78). The conservative approach actually intends to substitute local, non-governmental interventions in social problems for government programs (Berger and Neuhaus 1977). Curiously, the model of the conservative's mediating structures can be found in the community action programs of the liberals' War on Poverty (Berger and Neuhaus 1977: pp. 39–40), which conservatives otherwise disparage.

Liberals look to social movements of the 1960s for examples of mediating structures' capacity to transform social policy (Bellah et al. 1985). Federal agencies within radical reform efforts of Reconstruction, the New Deal, and the War on Poverty included the formation of mediating structures as a key component of their work (Couto 1991). Recent calls for new policy directions invoke mediating structures explicitly (Osborne and Gaebler 1992) or implicitly (Schorr 1988).

The emerging credo of mediating structures, with appropriate references to "community" and "empowerment," influenced the Progressive Policy Institute, fittingly enough a radically centrist think-tank for the moderate Democratic Leadership Council:

> Unwilling to frame every public question in terms of a choice between government provision and market competition, progressives place new emphasis on the voluntary associations and institutions of community—America's "third sector." Government's role is to empower families, voluntary organizations, and institutions to solve their

> own problems, not to try to replace them with public programs or institutions. Community also means taking care of citizens in need and affirming the common civic values that unite us as Americans (Marshall and Schram 1993: p. xvii).

Liberal and conservative proponents of mediating structures differ about their role and makeup. Some proponents suggest a minimalist role for mediating structures, the participation of voluntary organizations in the design of public policy, for example. Other proponents suggest a maximalist role for mediating structures, conducting public policy through them as service deliverers, for example (Price 1980). Within the maximalists are those who would provide public resources for the public policy role of mediating structures. Minimalists are more inclined to leave to the mediating structures, such as homeless shelters, the matter of fund raising.

Proponents also differ about the organizations that are mediating structures. At a minimum, community groups, voluntary associations, religious groups, and the family make the list of mediating structures (Berger and Neuhaus 1977). Some lists go further and include labor unions and advocacy organizations (Greider 1992). As the list expands, so does the complexity of the role of mediating structures. Maximalists generally temper their faith in mediating structures with analysis of the complexity of their role in implementing public policy (Green 1992; Salamon 1981) and in achieving social change (*Social Policy* 1989; Fisher 1993).

However one defines them, one can find a plethora of "mediating structures" in the Appalachian region. Whether community health centers, media centers, domestic violence shelters, or citizens' environmental groups, the response to the region's needs has been extensive and exemplary to the nation (Greider 1992). This is one field in which the region has led the nation (Fisher 1993; Horton 1989).

Labor unions have played significant roles as mediating structures in the region as well. Organizations of textile workers have improved wages and safety and health in some plants and have counterpoised the unregulated business environment of the 1980s. Steel workers have organized alternative economic development in some areas and attempted worker run plants in Weirton, West Virginia. Coal miners have addressed changed conditions at work, from job security to the provision of health and retirement benefits to former workers, earlier than other American workers. In this regard, the Massey and Pittston coalminers' strikes of the 1980s signify the potential and limits of alliances of community organizations, advocacy efforts, and labor unions as mediating structures (Couto 1993). The community support of the Pittston strike testified to the role of the UMWA as a mediating structure. The Massey strike suggested the power of companies and courts to press labor unions to their limits. The range of mediating structures within the Appalachian region indicates a vibrancy that sustains their valued place in American political traditions and the opportunity for solid partnerships in change efforts.

One finds hope as well as challenge within the Appalachian region. In the unions, the community organizations, the school reforms, the economic development efforts, the community health centers, and similar services and organizations one finds the creativity and vitality of American institutional life. It is here in "the importance of individual and social responsibility within and for institutions" that some analysts find the means to "transform the great society into the good society" (Bellah et al. 1992: p. 17). William Greider finds hope within Appalachia to build "mediating mechanisms that enable people to connect with the higher realms of decision making" (Greider 1992: p. 19). Among such mechanisms, Greider mentions the community-based work of the Highlander Center on the environment. Implicitly, Greider includes labor unions and community organizations, such as those in Appalachia, as the forms of mediating mechanisms that give substantive meaning to self-government and provide shared civic values for democratic process.

Moving beyond rugged individualism to an American public philosophy of social responsibility requires the form of community institutions that flourish in Appalachia and which current economic trends imperil.

Programs That Work

Moving the invisible hand for democratic renewal requires community-based efforts, many of which can be found in Appalachia. Lessons abound about providing services well in order to prevent rotten outcomes. Lisbeth Schorr surveyed a set of programs designed to break a "cycle of disadvantage" related to poverty, such as poor health, family breakdown, poor schools, and low educational attainment. Many programs, like those she examined, function in an exemplary manner in the Appalachian region. She found that interventions that work have the following characteristics:

- a broad spectrum of services;
- more open professional and bureaucratic boundaries;
- flexibility;
- a contextual understanding of the problem;
- care and respect for those served, trust in those serving;
- coherent and easy to use services;
- an emphasis on needs of clients rather than traditional bureaucratic and professional roles; and,
- new self-defined, more effective roles for professionals.

Schorr found also that ineffective interventions, which are prevalent, have common characteristics as well. Among them, she lists:

- emphasis on efficiency and not effectiveness;
- fragmented services; and
- meager resources.

To move beyond models of successful interventions into full-scale programs, Schorr suggests that we need to evaluate programs for qualitative, long-term results and institute new methods of training and retaining skilled and committed personnel. Successful efforts do not come cheap and cannot be replicated with diluted resources. Likewise, flexibility is key and thus centralized, bureaucratic models need to be adapted to local circumstances. Replication can happen in a wide variety of circumstances also because of flexibility. Finally, Schorr makes a cost argument. Namely, the costs of the interventions, though expensive, save money. Prenatal care, for example, reduces risk for low birth weights and ensuing problems. Good family support reduces the need for more expensive out-of-home placement of children. In addition, there are costs of leaving social problems unattended and value, beyond dollar estimates, "of living in a fair and just society with a shared sense of civility and community" (Schorr, 1988: pp. 256–83). Citing Isabel Sawhill, Schorr concludes,

> Large deficits make it difficult to argue for new social spending [because they] lower the rate of economic growth and threaten future standards of living. Unfortunately, a failure to invest in the next generation has precisely these same effects (Sawhill in Schorr 1988: p. 294).

Schorr's work offers an inventory of successful interventions. It also offers hope that our social problems are manageable given care, compassion, and public commitment to economic justice and social equity.

Conclusion

Joblessness and poverty are increasingly concentrated in places like the inner city, portions of the rural South, and portions of Appalachia; among groups of minorities; and members of female-headed households. Reducing poverty where we find it means increasing incomes of poor people. This should be done primarily by providing employment. But employment is scarce where social capital is low, i.e., areas of concentrated poverty. Human capital investment, education, job training, and health care, are necessary increases of social capital but they fall short of jobs in terms of reducing poverty. This investment can, however, create jobs in places like Central Appalachia where both the services and the jobs are needed. Community organizations are crucial elements of addressing poverty and providing employment through increased social capital investment such as housing, environmental quality, and health care. To raise incomes without providing employment requires income transfer, a redistribution of wealth, the most unpopular form of public policy in America. Yet we know that it works in some instances. The poverty of Americans over 65 years of age has dropped dramatically thanks to increases in social security and the inception of Medicare.

34

by Michael Bradshaw

A Political Approach to Regional Development

Three separate but overlapping approaches evaluating the role and work of the Appalachian Regional Commission since its establishment in 1965 can be summarized in three questions:

Did the ARC fulfill its legislated charge?

Has the ARC been able to change the human geography of Appalachia?

What lessons has the ARC provided for regional development theory?

These three questions can be viewed as three circles of increasing generality. It is first necessary to assess how the Commission has matched up to the task set by the U.S. Congress. The language of the legislation and specific hopes expressed at the outset may be examined in relation to what has actually happened in Appalachia; however, to leave the assessment at that point would disappoint readers who are looking for a broader evaluation of the ARC's work. Second, then, there is an attempt to determine whether this agency has been able to change the human geography of Appalachia. Third, and depending on the answers to the first two questions, there is an inquiry as to whether the ARC experience has advanced ideas of regional development. If it has, then its contribution will be expected to provide a basis for approaching future cases in other parts of the United States and elsewhere.

Basic Facilities for Growth. One strand that can be followed throughout the language of the act involves economic growth to increase the productive capacity of the region. Appalachia would be assisted through the provision of "basic facilities." The expectation was that the provision of physical and transport facilities, together with the development of human resources, would give rise to a diversified industry.

"Basic facilities" are often known as infrastructure, the installations and building that provide a fundamental framework within which an economy may develop. They include transport links, communications, power supplies, and other public utilities. One of the major emphases of the Appalachian legislation from the start was the provision of roads to overcome the isolation of the region. The original plan was to build 2,350 miles of highways to link the rather sparse network of interstate highways that crossed Appalachia.

As additional states came under the ARC umbrella, the total was increased to 3,025 miles. Initially, the ARC was to provide 70 percent of the funds and the states 30 percent, but the federal portion was increased to 80 percent in 1978. By September 1980, 1,565 miles of the projected system had been completed. The linked program to build access roads from major highways to industrial plants had been expanded from its initial mileage. The highway construction was scaled back to the finish-up program to a total of 2,471 miles, and priorities for sections to be completed were set in relation to traffic volume and development potential. By 1985, 1,831 miles had been completed, and progress had slowed as funds were cut back. The new mood of 1989, however, led to further efforts to complete the more than 3,000 miles of the envisaged program (see Map 1).

Much has been written about the pros and cons of this emphasis on highways. It has become clear from studies in the 1980s (e.g., ARC 1982b) that the new highways have assisted greatly in individual mobility, providing access both to a wider range of jobs and also to social services, health care, schooling, and tourist attractions. At the same time they made Appalachian locations more attractive to firms looking for sites. New industrial estates were established along the roads, with a preponderance of manufacturing units but also some wholesale warehouses and business services. Yet not everyone using the Appalachian Development Highway System roads realizes that the ARC has been instrumental in planning and funding their construction: the roads have been given national route numbers instead of being identified as "Appalachian Highway Corridors."

The road program was such a major plank of the ARC's charge that its efforts in relation to other types of transport have been much smaller by comparison. The Commission has assisted with some branch-line rail rehabilitation to help industries in more isolated places, but of greater magnitude for the region as a whole are railroad companies' investments on the main lines, particularly on those that haul large tonnages of coal. Waterways are important in some parts of Appalachia, but again the Tennessee Valley Authority and the Army Corps of Engineers have been responsible for building and maintaining those; the ARC has merely supported such developments in wider ways. Air transport services in Appalachia have deteriorated since deregulation in 1978. The ARC has campaigned for retaining these services, even though air facilities were not part of its responsibility for major action.

Transport problems continue to be very real in all rural areas and not least in rural Appalachia. Although the ARC has funded management studies for rural transport systems and has helped some projects obtain assistance from other federal agencies, the Commission sees transportation as an unsolved set of problems. ARC may be criticized for not generating an integrated transport policy for its region, but it was not authorized to do so; nor does the rest of the United States have such policies.

Other aspects of infrastructure were also assisted by the ARC, especially after 1970, when national environmental legislation provided grant aid for improved water and sewer systems. The LDDs put EPA grants together with supplemental ARC funds and low-interest FHA loans to help poor rural districts obtain good utility services. Together with the new roads and other services, improvements in these utilities made it possible for many places in Appalachia to begin to think about attracting new employment opportunities or modern residential facilities. A large portion of LDD funding was devoted to projects for improving water and sewer systems.

Housing is another aspect of infrastructure where the figures for Appalachia had depressed the PARC reporters. The ARC had no authorization to get involved in housing provision until 1967, and then it was limited to planning grants; in 1971 it was allowed to provide site development grants and technical assistance; after 1975 it was enabled to help states set up their own housing funds and to assist any federal program for low- or moderate-cost housing. From 1976 to 1982 the states allocated $46.5 million ARC dollars

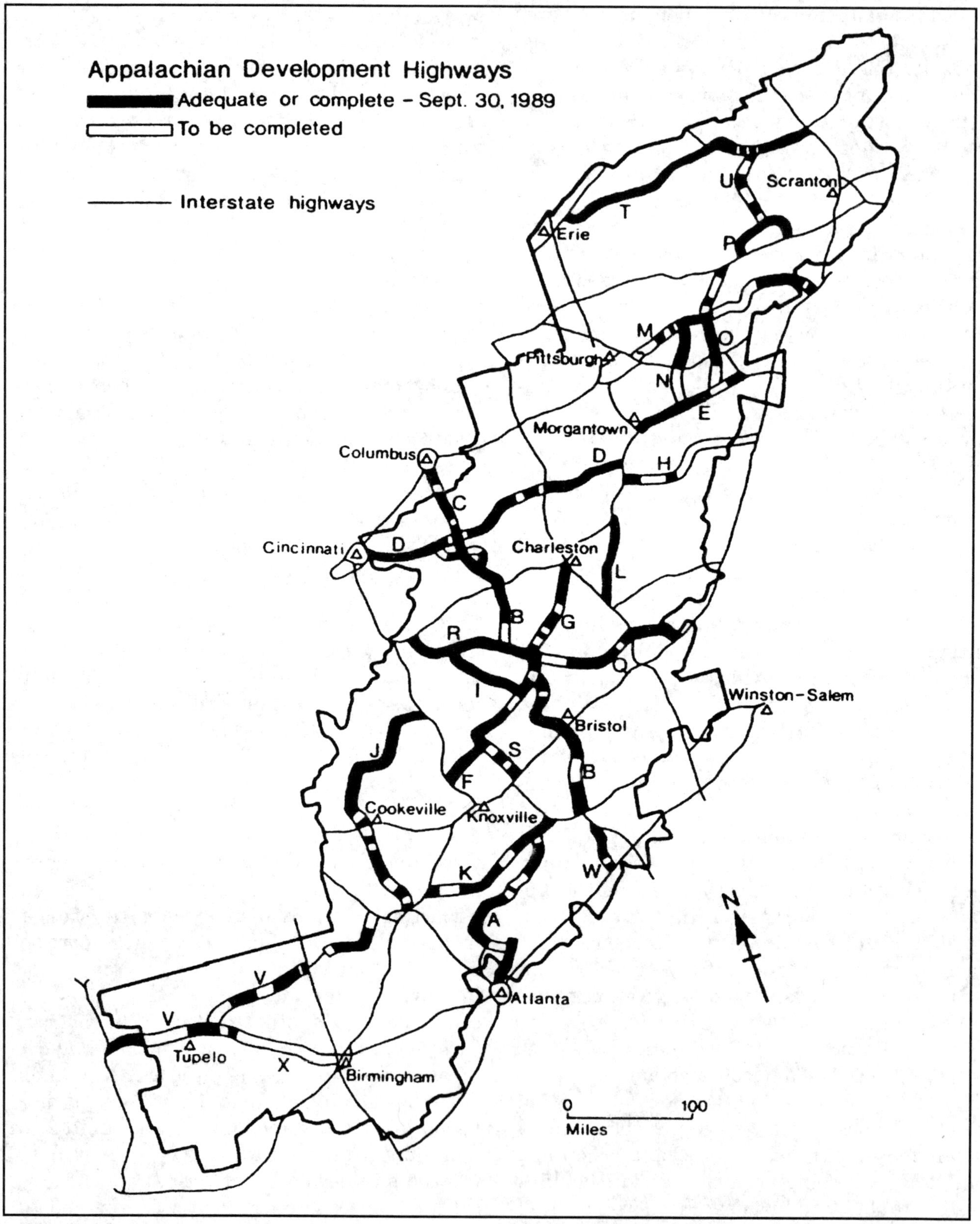

Map 1. The Appalachian Development Highway System to 1989. This system was envisaged as a series of linking roads to open up areas between the interstate highways in Appalachia. After twenty-five years of construction, some two-thirds of the total was complete; work is continuing. Each of the links is referred to as a corridor and identified by letter.

to housing, which leveraged over $400 million in public and private funds toward some 17,000 housing units. The Kentucky Appalachian Housing Program grew out of the ARC program and helped to bring nearly 5,000 new housing units to eastern Kentucky (ARC 1985a).

It can be seen that with regard to "basic facilities" the ARC has been somewhat selective, putting its major investments in roads and water and sewer projects, with housing as a more recent area of concern. There has been much less involvement with other aspects of transport and infrastructure, partly because these were covered by other federal and state programs. The ARC assisted increasing linkage between agencies, often being particularly successful at the LDD level, and sometimes made it possible for states to do what a federal agency such as HUD was not doing. Thus, though the ARC did not itself have the full range of programs to give it a preeminent position within Appalachia to accomplish major changes, its specific contributions complemented the work of other agencies, and at times it was able to initiate new approaches.

It is somewhat difficult to determine where physical infrastructure and human resource categories begin and end, since bricks-and-mortar projects supply buildings and facilities that are necessary to human well-being. If human resources are defined as the capabilities of the population of a region, they will at least include the educational and health status of that population: this means schools, primary-care centers and hospitals, and trained personnel. "Human resources" may also be extended to the demographic profile: whether the population is increasing or decreasing, and whether there is a preponderance of "dependent" age groups. Since U.S. government programs have seldom intervened to the extent of forcing people to migrate or alter their demographic habits, however, this section focuses on the ARC contribution to education and health facilities and programs.

In the climate of concern that Appalachians were not getting jobs because they were not trained for them, one of the most popular local developments from the ARC's early days was funding for vocational technical schools. Extending throughout Appalachia, a network of such schools was built by the states with the ARC's cooperation, and it became involved also in skills development and wider aspects of education. Once the schools were built, ARC funding was used for new developments, including equipment for specific courses, and this program was expanded after only a few years. Overall, some $350 million was spent in 700 facilities throughout Appalachia. In a similar way the provision of primary health care led not only to the building of clinics but to the funding of their running costs. A network of such centers was planned and implemented throughout the region. By 1981 primary health care was within reach of people in all but 65 of the 397 counties, despite great difficulties in recruiting adequate staff to work in the most isolated parts of the region. The finish-up program targeted these 65 counties, with the result that primary health care and prenatal care were extended to over half of them by 1985. ARC funding was also used to expand hospital facilities in critical parts of the region, and to develop aspects of higher education and libraries. An innovative experiment in education was the Appalachian Education Satellite Project, designed to beam educational programs into the narrow valleys of Appalachia. This was so successful that it became independent in 1980 and developed into the national Learning Channel.

Although road, water, and sewer projects always loomed large in the ARC balance books, then, human resources projects grew in significance, linked to community needs through the LDDs and the inability of local districts to obtain them from other sources. One of the major project areas opened by 1969 amendments to the ARDA legislation was child development. At the time less than 5 percent of Appalachian children under six had access to Head Start programs. Using its facilities for partnership with different levels of government and other federal agencies, the ARC developed a variety of local projects aimed mainly at preschool age groups. As the first five-year series of projects wound down, Congress gave the ARC powers to start new ones, and many continued after the end of the initial funding period. From 1970 to 1982, when the support ended, these programs reached 200,000 children per year in over 220 counties —more than 85 percent of the funds going to rural counties and small communities. ARC investment in the program was $173.4 million, but once again this was combined with funds from other agencies and the states. The finish-up program changed the rules and limited child-care grants to specific industries and employees, and for only one year.

Similar infrastructure and human resource funds have been available to local jurisdictions across the United States through other federal agencies. What the ARC was able to do was to assist poor Appalachian jurisdictions to obtain such funding and to enhance it so that the facilities basic to economic development and a better life could be afforded. The supplemental funds were a vital part for this process, since they made it possible for poor rural districts to plan infrastructure projects. Each project became less an entity in itself than part of a development plan for each locality. Single entities are in danger of becoming pork-barrel operations in which political influence is exerted to obtain facilities for a politician's constituency. ARC projects were not totally devoid of such involvement, but the fact that they had to be obtained through the process of local district prioritization and state selection meant that federal politicians had less impact on decisions to award them.

As the ARC developed in the 1970s, it began to emphasize the overall needs of specific communities for basic infrastructure. The communities with the greatest needs for overall development were those that had a long history of mining and were expanding again in the 1970s, remote rural areas without the resources to improve local facilities, and also older industrial towns where jobs were being lost. ARC community grants emphasized the physical infrastructure needs of these places: housing, sewerage, water, waste disposal, parks and recreation, and industrial site development. Such grants increased greatly after 1975, as LDDs worked in partnership with other federal agencies to bring in the necessary changes. The finish-up program focused on new job provision and on the most distressed counties.

The ARC's use of the term "community" is different from that of Appalachian activist groups. The latter emphasize the internal, self-generating properties of a group of people at the local level rather than the acquisition of government funding assistance from outside. The activists feel strongly that the positive contributions Appalachians can make to their own destiny have been underestimated, and that government programs (such as the ARC) have not involved a sufficiently wide group in decision-making.

In the annual report for 1989, ARC expenditures are divided into those for administrative functions (including LDD staffing), highways, and area development; the last category includes all the nonhighway programs. Chart 1 shows that the overall proportion of nonhighway funds—which leveraged several times their value in grant aid from other agencies—increased from 1965 to 1980 but was reduced during the Reagan years.

Federal-State Cooperation. A second major strand in the ARC's charge was the establishment of a framework for political cooperation between federal and state governments. The states were given responsibility for recommending local and state projects; in short, they were given the ability to spend federal money. The intention was to provide a basis for attacking common problems and meeting common needs on a coordinated and concerted regional basis.

This aspect of the ARDA grew out of the fact that the state governors had been instrumental in bringing forward the need for legislation to tackle the problems of the Appalachian sections of their states. Their continuing involvement led to the establishment of a unique federal-state agency. The federal co-chairman votes on the project package of the state governors and then repre-

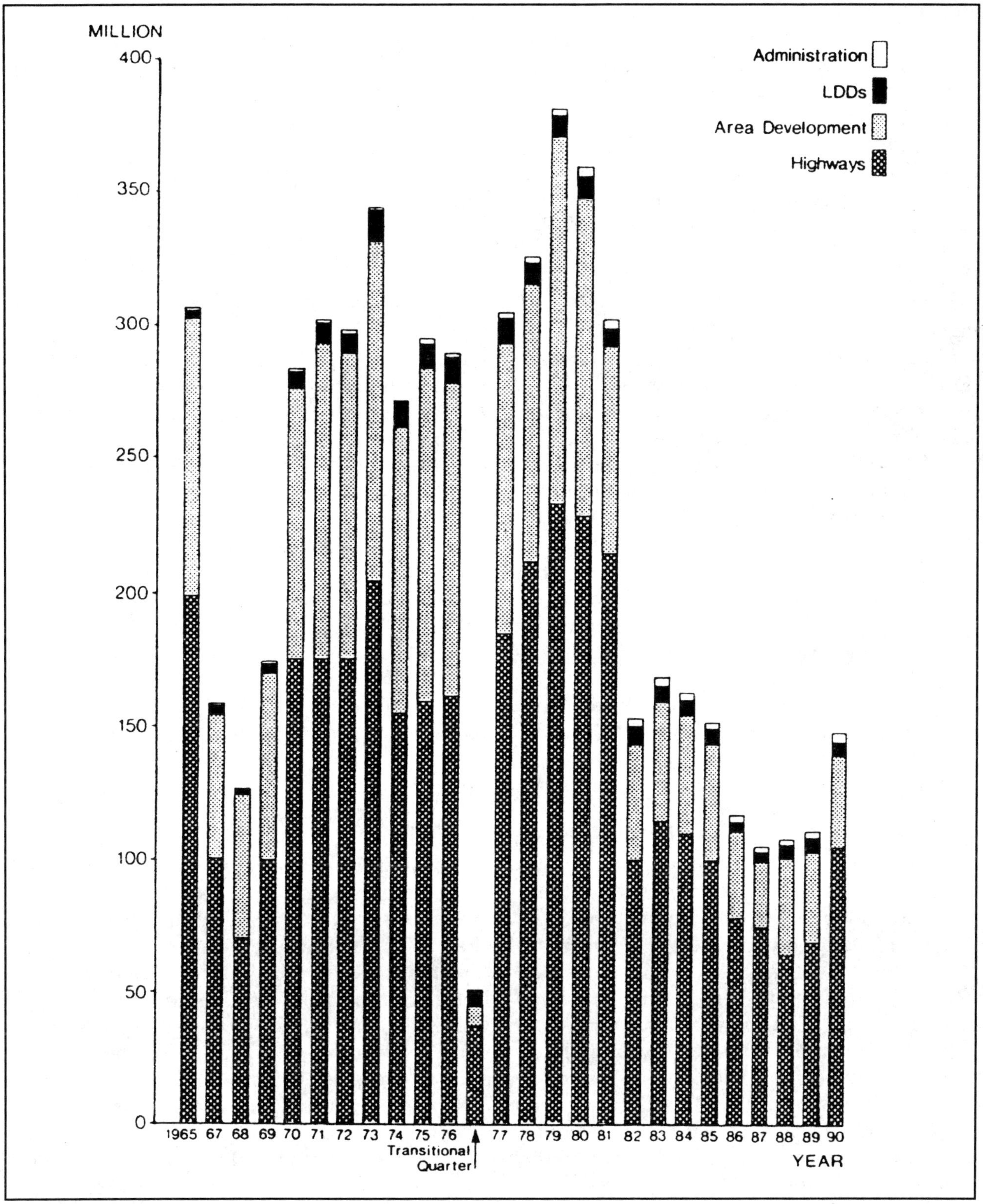

Chart 1. The division of ARC funds by category, 1965–90. The ARC has provided the bulk of the highway funds, which make up over half of the total, with smaller contributions from the states. ARC area development input has leveraged several times its total from other federal and state sources. It is notable that the administrative funds are such a small proportion and that those designated for local use are so much greater than those for the Commission's Washington headquarters.

sents the whole commission in discussions with Congress over appropriations. Even when the administration wished to do something as drastic as closing down the ARC, the president's appointee had to continue to work with the governors and to hold the partnership together. The federal role in providing funds was safeguarded by the fact that the federal co-chairman had powers of veto and shared the chair with state governors who served in rotation. This balance of power between federal and state elements could have resulted in stalemates, but it did not. The governors (always a mixture of Democrats and Republicans) appreciated the necessity of devising a combined package that the federal co-chairman could not refuse. The federal co-chairman knew that the state governors wanted action and used this fact to make sure that the pet projects of particular governors were not the only ones to be approved.

The state governors have continued to be centrally involved in the work of the Commission. Although they had a tendency to rely on alternates in the early 1970s, the 1975 amendments stated clearly that the governors themselves should be personally involved. This proved particularly significant in the difficult period of the Reagan presidency, when the bipartisan group of state governors stood firm and insisted on the survival of the ARC. It was significant that in one day the governor of Virginia went to a meeting at which the Title V commissions were closed and then joined with other governors to petition the president for the continuation of the ARC.

One important outcome of this federal-state process occurred when the Nixon administration began to allocate funds directly to states through the process of revenue sharing, placing a new responsibility on state governments. Many of the Appalachian states, however, had already experienced a similar process with the ARC, and they found such experience valuable in handling the new sources of revenues. Their links with the ARC had also been responsible for the initiation and development of much state planning expertise from the late 1960s on.

One development that helped to make the federal-state partnership work was the 1967 congressional decision to free the ARC from the need to deal with a wide range of other federal agencies for its funding and to make it report directly to the president. Previously, planning with thirteen states and several major federal agencies had been made extremely cumbersome by the federal bureaucracies. After 1967 the federal-state relationship flourished.

A number of coordinated and concerted regional efforts demonstrate that the Appalachian state governors did work together as well as furthering the wellbeing of their state. For instance, they devised ARC policies with regard to energy usage and tourism in the region during the 1970s. Nevertheless, the effort to develop an overall regional plan in the mid-1970s demonstrated that many of the governors were more concerned with conditions in their own states than with those of Appalachia as a whole; there was room for some overriding interstate issues that did not come within the scope of specific state responsibilities. Individual governors voiced their fears that an all-embracing plan would be weak in content and might cause difficulties between the Appalachian and non-Appalachian portions of their states.

The most significant aspect of the federal-state links has been the work of the local development districts, designated by each state. Although there was initial reluctance by some states to give local jurisdictions more say in the processes of federal grant aid, all thirteen states had fallen into line by 1973. The combination of cooperative planning by local jurisdictions, bolstered by the A-95 process and supplemental funds, made it possible for the ARC to overcome the problems that all previous programs had found in delivering grant aid projects to the most needy parts of Appalachia. It was not merely that the Commission was able to provide access to the basic facilities essential to growth through grant aid but that there was a mechanism for local contact and involvement in generating and managing the projects.

The LDD process was effective in reducing the time necessary to obtain federal grant money and to implement a project. An annual process was initiated in many LDDs in which the early months of the calendar year would be taken up by district meetings; in some, these were linked to consultation with communities throughout the district. After discussion with ARC staff and the state governor's staff, an order of priorities for projects was submitted to the state governor's office. An order of state priorities would then be established, and these became proposals to the Commission. By the end of the year, work could be starting on projects proposed at the beginning of that same year. The incorporation of the areawide action plan into the LDD process after 1975 extended the sequence of processes from needs assessment, goal setting, and choice of priorities to the evaluation of results and general progress. Occasionally, interstate projects were generated, but these were always a small minority.

The ARC also encouraged increasing coordination in another sense. The use of supplemental funds meant that the Commission and the LDDs had to come into frequent contact with other federal agencies, many of which came to work more closely at the local level with the LDDs. In particular, there were early links with HUD, EPA, and FHA, and at a later stage with TVA. Most TVA territory lies within ARC Appalachia, and by the late 1970s the TVA came to realize that the ARC was doing what the TVA had not been able to do in bringing in federal grant aid for infrastructure and industrial park facilities.

One important outcome of the establishment of this ARC framework for joint federal-state efforts has been the continuation of political support at several levels. The governors provided state-level support at crucial stages; the LDD work generated considerable support at the local level, particularly in the business communities; and this was turned into political support in Washington. Congressmen with Appalachian constituencies were impressed by the pleas for the ARC that they received from local elected representatives, and many with constituencies outside Appalachia viewed the ARC as a model for extending regional development. With such support, appropriations were voted through the House of Representatives with large majorities throughout the 1980s, despite the opposition of a popular president and the lack of authorization for ARC.

Concentrating on Growth Centers. A third major tenet of the ARDA legislation, that public investment should be concentrated in areas with significant potential for future growth and where the expected return would be greatest, arose partly from contemporary planning ideas based on the concept of "growth centers" and partly from the political need to concentrate the use of scarce public funds. The latter was a reaction to the ARA experience of the early 1960s, when too little money had been spread to thin across the United States to made any difference.

At first the ARC was conscious of this requirement of the legislation, and Widner's 1968 report made much of the moves to fulfill it. Over the years, however, the concept was found to be less than relevant to the needs of Appalachia, and eventually the finish-up program mandated that a reverse process should operate by designating a set of "distressed" counties to receive the remaining benefits of the ARC program. In fact, the manner of operation of the LDDs had much to do with the demise of this concept so far as the ARC was concerned, and it is significant that discussion with LDD staffs made it clear that they considered the idea of little practical use, chiefly because their board members bargained for a spread of project funding to each of the jurisdictions represented. Thus, all counties received funding for specific projects, whether they had major urban centers or not; this was clear from the 1981 study of the distribution of project funds by local jurisdictions within a group of LDDs. The local districts operated in a decentralizing rather than a centralizing fashion. Whatever the merits of such an outcome, the growth-center policy was an initial feature of ARC policy which did not survive the LDD process and was completely buried by the finish-up program with its focus on distressed counties. In short, although the ARC has often been criticized for adopting the growth-center policy as a means of changing an essentially rural Appalachia into an urban-industrial complex, the Commission's program, if anything, deflected developmental energies away from major growth centers. This view contradicts (and corrects) a perception repeated in recent writing about Appalachia (e.g., White 1989), that the ARC continued its emphasis on growth-center investment despite a clear indication of residents' wishes to retain a decentralized mode of life in such areas as eastern Kentucky.

Yet it is also clear that the major urban areas of Appalachia have seen the most economic growth. This fact emphasizes the point that the ARC and all major government programs can make only small differences to the dominant economic trends within society. Government programs may act as catalysts for some kinds of change, however, or may provide a respite from a particular trend that is causing social distress.

Diversified and Self-Supporting? It is clear that the ARC has fulfilled much of its charge. It has provided many basic facilities and has encouraged the development of human resources. It has been based on a federal-state relationship that has both assisted in getting federal grant aid to many of the most needy parts of Appalachia and has also helped to maintain the ARC's existence. It has not followed through on the demand to concentrate investment in growth centers but has increasingly spread such grant aid to places with the greatest needs. In carrying out these functions, the ARC has been economical in the allocation of funds to administrative functions, including those of the LDDs as well as of its own Washington headquarters.

Most difficult to evaluate is the extent to which the congressional expectations have been fulfilled: that the region generate a diversified industry and become able to support itself. It is evident that the economy of southern Appalachia is much more diversified than it was in 1960, when it was just beginning to emerge from its rural heritage; a wide range of manufacturing has been paralleled by growth in the number of jobs in the tertiary sector of the economy, from retailing to the professions. In northern Appalachia, too, there is a continuing diversification of industry from the dominance of heavy metals manufacturing to a wide range of manufactured products, together with the expansion of the tertiary sector. Diversification in central Appalachia has involved manufacturing less than the tertiary sector; the economy here remains problematic because it is still so centered on the fortunes of coal mining. While many parts of northern and southern Appalachia might be said to be in less need of federal support (and so "self-supporting"?), there are continuing needs within central Appalachia, as the distribution of distressed counties testifies.

These are generalizations, and there are still distressed counties in the northern and southern parts of Appalachia as well. Nevertheless, there have been changes, and the point in question is the extent to which the ARC and its programs have been responsible for them. The ARDA legislation wisely used the term "assist" in describing what the new federal agency would be doing; the ARC was not expected to do it all by itself, and even if it had tried, it would have been criticized for making Appalachians too dependent on federal handouts.

The Changing Human Geography of Appalachia

Since 1960, Appalachia has been subject to many forces that have affected not only the rest of the nation but also the wider world. Global economic trends have had an increasing impact on this region as mobility and trade have increased. In the early part of the century Appalachia was subject to economic forces affecting the rest of the United States; after 1950 the influence of global forces increased. The fluctuations in world energy markets have been of particular significance to Appalachia and its coal industry. In the 1950s and 1960s, cheap oil from the Middle East depressed U.S. energy markets and pushed the price of coal to such a low point that poverty was intensified in the coal-mining areas of central Appalachia. In the late 1960s and early 1970s, environmental legislation reduced coal mining further in those parts of Appalachia that produce high-sulfur coals. During the 1970s, however, the sharp rise in the world oil prices led to a revival of coal mining, aided by new technology that made it cost-effective to get at the coal by taking off an entire hilltop, using earth-moving machinery. Money and people flowed back into central Appalachia. But then the recession of the early 1980s, followed by the fall in oil prices in the mid-1980s, changed the scene once more, putting miners out of work.

Another set of major economic changes during the period since 1960 involved a shift in the job markets: there had already been a relative drop in the numbers of people employed in farming; now there was a similar drop in heavy manufacturing, while employment in light manufacturing and in the tertiary sector grew in importance. Parts of southern Appalachia had witnessed a fall in farm and mine employment from 50–75 percent in 1930 to 10–50 percent in 1950 and 2–10 percent in 1980. At the same time manufacturing employment had gone from 5–10 percent to 15–25 percent and 30–50 percent, while the tertiary sector had grown from 10–15 percent to 20–30 percent and 40–50 percent of total employment. In central Appalachia the farm and mine employment had also declined, but more slowly, from 70–80 percent in 1930 to 50–70 percent in 1970 and 20–30 percent in 1980. By the last date the primary sector was dominated by mine employment. Manufacturing had hardly developed at all, remaining at 5–15 percent in 1980; but the tertiary sector had compensated, rising from 20–30 to 30–40 and 40–55 percent. In the heavy manufacturing districts of northern Appalachia, farming and mining decreased from 10–20 percent in 1930 to under 10 percent by 1950 and only 2 or 3 percent in 1980. Manufacturing, already established, increased from 30–40 to 40–50 percent and then decreased somewhat to 30–35 percent. The tertiary sector increased from 20–30 to 30–40 and 45–55 percent of employment.

These were large shifts affecting all parts of Appalachia, taking the emphasis away from the primary sector and the contribution of local natural resources in all but the central portion. Manufacturing remained important in northern Appalachia and grew to even greater significance as a proportion of total employment in southern Appalachia, but it has not yet made great inroads in central Appalachia. The tertiary sector has become the major sector of employment in all parts of the region—as it has in the rest of the United States.

Yet another massive change in economy and social habits involved the growing significance of leisure and recreations, given the increasing leisure time, the greater personal mobility, and the affluence of many Americans. The eastern margins of Appalachia had been the playground of the rich from the eastern seaboard cities since the late nineteenth century: the Poconos (in Pennsylvania), White Sulphur Springs (West Virginia), and Asheville (North Carolina) had been major centers. After 1960 a new army of families came in increasing numbers to Appalachia to enjoy the wooded hills, the winter sports facilities, and the water surfaces being created behind dams built by the TVA and the Army Corps of Engineers. Great Smoky Mountains National Park on the border between North Carolina and Tennessee is the most visited in the United States. The tourist industry built a range of mainly seasonal facilities throughout the region, states created systems of state parks, and there was a second-home boom in some areas. Retirement homes and centers also became a feature of southern Appalachia.

These three major aspects of change have had significant impact on Appalachia. They illustrate the fact that the main ebb and flow of fortunes and people in the region since 1960 have been due to national and global market economic forces. Clearly, none was instigated by the ARC. Although the PARC report suggested that the Commission should be capable of initiating changes within the region to take advantage of its natural resources, those aspects were never incorporated in the legislation. Perhaps that was just as well, since subsequent events caused a shift away from industries based on natural resource extraction. The ARC has found itself dealing with a range of different conditions—from the upwardly mobile cores of southern Appalachia, to the urban-industrial districts in transition from heavy industry to a more diversified economy in the north, to the resource-rich but poverty-stricken central region.

What these changes did do was to present the ARC with a moving target as it aimed to fulfill its charge in Appalachia. The legislation passed in 1965 was based on conditions in the preceding years. Appalachian prospects improved generally in the 1970s but declined again in the 1980s. A positive view of the role of the ARC in these circumstances is that it has provided some assistance in making it possible for the region to take advantage of opportunities arising in better times, and in ameliorating the outcomes of the bad times. Some evidence for this view is that the new roads and other infrastructure facilities made it easier for the coal companies to expand production rapidly during the mid-1970s in response to world markets; they were able to compete with the new coalfields of Montana and Wyoming at this time and also to enter export markets. The growth in skills and health of the Appalachia population also made the region more attractive to potential employers, alongside the growing influence of rural and recreational amenities on the location of industry. When unemployment came to the mining areas in eastern Kentucky and West Virginia in the 1980s, poverty did not return on the scale experienced in the 1960s, because there were some alternatives (though poorly paid) for at least some members of the family.

One point that worries both critics and supporters of the ARC is that even though the most money per capita has been invested in central Appalachia, this area remains one of the poorest parts of the United States. Massive changes can be seen in the human geography of southern Appalachia, where ARC investments were a small part of the total investment but assisted in the growth processes. Shifts to maintain a position of moderate well-being can also be shown to have occurred in northern Appalachia, where, once again, ARC investment formed a small proportion of the total. But central Appalachia appears from the relative statistics to have experienced little change for the better. In fact, much change *has* occurred in eastern Kentucky and southern West Virginia, often in absolute rather than relative terms, but the improvements in conditions have not been sufficient to bring these districts closer to the advancing United States norms. And yet the ARC has probably had as much or more influence in central Appalachia as in the rest of the region: elsewhere its funds were a tiny part of the total invested, but in central Appalachia they formed a much larger proportion of the funds available for improving infrastructure and human resources. The amounts of money were far less than could have been spent—or were really needed to make an impression. But it is impossible to imagine what the condition of central Appalachia would have been today without these injections of federal funds, and it is impossible to know what threshold is necessary to create major changes. Clearly, the amount invested has not reached such a threshold. Nevertheless, it is likely that far fewer people would have living in central Appalachia today, and those at a lower standard, if the ARC (and other agencies) had not invested as much as they did.

One factor affecting the human geography of Appalachia is the way in which the land is owned. In central Appalachia in particular, large portions of land remain in the hands of the coal companies, and this often provides a barrier to development. Yet it would be an unheard-of step for U.S. public policy to intervene in such ownership and redistribute land to individuals or communities. The ARC funded a major independent study covering eighty counties to assess the full extent of external land ownership (Appalachian Land Ownership Task Force, 1983) and found that an average of 28 percent of the land or its mineral rights were owned outside the region; in twenty-one counties the average was over 50 percent. The study concluded that there was urgent necessity for public action on local land-use planning procedures—which at present are nonexistent in many rural counties—but little has been done to follow up this study with action by local, state or federal government.

In sum, the influence of the ARC on geographical change must be far less than the effect of the major economic forces that give rise to such change. It might have been easier to demonstrate a link between ARC investment and economic development if all ARC funds had targeted growth centers, but such funds would probably have formed a minor part of total investment in such centers. On the other hand, so much investment was needed to bring about major changes in places such as eastern Kentucky that twenty-five years of limited public-policy investment have not yet made a striking difference in their effort to catch up with national norms. Yet people living in these parts of Appalachia will point to major changes for the better in their wellbeing since the 1960s.

Regional Development Theory

The third question to be addressed in evaluating the role and experience of the ARC is whether it has contributed anything to our understanding of what development in a relatively underprivileged region involves and how it is generated. In particular, the experience of this Commission enables us to draw some conclusions concerning the role of public policy in regional development.

Most attempts by public-policy regionalism to engineer changes in underprivileged regions have been based on the provision of facilities for creating more jobs. Thus, they focus largely on economic conditions. The ARC has done its share with road programs and the funding of infrastructure, and some critics have felt that it has concentrated on economic development to too great an extent. More modern views of regional development emphasize the wider aspects of the needs of the people living in an area; social, environmental, and political changes assume greater prominence. In the middle to late 1970s the ARC tried to create a more balanced approach to development by encouraging human resource programs, but it was again limited to the more economic objectives during the restrictive 1980s. Socioeconomic change and the reactions of people to it are complex matters even for a small area, let alone a region the size of Appalachia with its great variety of places, economies, and cultural and environmental conditions. Appalachia has been divided into three subregions, but there are variations within these as well—for instance, in nearness to metropolitan centers. Each of the thirteen states involved in the ARC has its own political culture, which may vary in emphasis over time. Apart from these factors contributing to the complexity within Appalachia, others that impinge on regional change include the responses of individuals and groups to the strains imposed, and the causes of particular responses are still poorly understood. In the light of this growing realization of the complexity of understanding, and therefore of motivating, socioeconomic development in a lagging region, the objectives of the ARC appear to have been realistic and pragmatic in relation to what was politically possible in 1965 and since.

Alongside the recognition of complexity in regional change, there has been a growing influence of federal government in the United States. This should have shifted the focus of regional development theory from the economic toward the political realm. If public funds, voted by elected representatives, are made available for public-policy regionalism, it becomes important that the political processes be attuned to such needs. For a period during the 1980s the United States chose to be blinded by the political stance that "more government is bad for you." But some studies (e.g., Schwarz 1983 and 1987) have demonstrated the fallacy of this assertion by showing that the federal programs of the 1960s had a great deal to do with getting the United States through the "baby boom" era with less strain than other nations experienced. Schwarz (1987) concluded that the "wreckage of Reaganomics" had made coping with inequalities of opportunity more difficult in the immediate future, since the Reagan administration had dismantled some major programs that had contributed to the nation's and individuals' ability to deal with change in the 1970s without worse outcomes.

One of the main contributions of the ARC experience has been to emphasize the importance of political structures in the functioning and maintenance of such an agency (Bradshaw 1985). It has linked the "top-down" approach of many federal agencies with a "bottom-up" involvement of local districts. It has linked federal, state, and local governments and has brought about cooperation among a range of federal agencies.

Another contribution, one that takes this study beyond the normal parameters of regional development theory, is the major part played by individuals in the generation of the ARDA legislation and the running of the ARC: in particular, those involved in lobbying for and preparing the 1965 legislation; those in staff positions at local and federal levels; the series of state governors who helped take the work of the Commission forward and defended it; and the U.S. senators and congressmen who continued to support the ARC. Many more names could have been included and much more written about the influence of individuals. That might have been invidious. But it is important to record that any contribution the ARC has made to Appalachia has been dependent on the caliber of staff involved and on the crucial decisions taken and supported at each stage of the Commission's development.

A final point to be emphasized in this context is that although public policy is becoming a necessary part of regional development theory, evaluation of its involvement should be tempered by the fact that it remains limited in scope. The money available from government sources in countries with market economies will always be less than what is needed to make massive change possible; the involvement of politicians will always lead to a focus on short-term solutions to long-term problems. Public-policy regionalism is inevitably at most a catalyst: it may provide the structures and processes that assist change and improvement, but taking advantage of such provision much be done by individuals and groups at the local level.

This leads to the conclusion that in view of the ARC experience, public-policy regionalism should be seen as distinct from, and should be kept separate from, the factors that generate economic growth through the operation of the "free market" system. Thus, metropolitan centers have continued to act as a focus for economic growth, acting as growth centers, but public policy could not begin to compete with or even mimic such forces by setting up rural growth centers; they would not be of sufficient size. The best strategy for public-policy regionalism is to provide processes and structures that channel the limited funds available to places where it is seen to be needed—be they "distressed," in transition between one phase of economic growth and another, beginning to experience modernization for the first time. Much of the United States today would be included in such categories.

Conclusion

This chapter began by asking three questions concerning the charge legislated to ARC, the role of the ARC in socioeconomic change in Appalachia, and the contribution made by the ARC experience to an understanding of regional development.

Under the Appalachian Regional Development Act, the Commission has taken a major part in bringing improved physical infrastructure and support for human resources to the region. Even so, given the scale of its total contribution, it can be regarded only as a catalyst for economic development and social improvements; as such, it was most successful in the southern parts of Appalachia, where major economic growth took place between 1960 and 1990, fueled by private investment. In central Appalachia, where there was much less support from private capital investment, the results were not so obvious, especially in relation to U.S. norms. Alongside investment in physical infrastructure and human resources through specific funding programs, however, the establishment of a framework for federal-state cooperation provided a means of delivering federal grant aid to rural districts of Appalachia in a manner that had not previously been possible. These twin prongs have been the special contribution of the ARC. Because much of its work was carried out in association with other federal funding agencies, however, the Commission often had a low profile in the region, and its achievements were not fully understood or appreciated.

The changes that have taken place since 1960 have produced massive alterations in the human geography of southern Appalachia—the landscape, the employment patterns, and the general lives of the people. Farther north, the legacy of the past and its redundant infrastructure is still much in evidence, but both central and northern Appalachia have also experienced some major improvements in conditions for attracting new sources of employment and for living. These changes have had more to do with external economic factors than with the influence of the ARC, but the Commission's provision of local infrastructure and human resource investments have often made it possible for local areas to take advantage of the changes.

The position of the ARC relative to ideas on regional development shows that public policy can have at least a limited impact. The great paradox of Appalachian development since 1960 is that although relatively greater sums of money have been invested in central Appalachia, this part of the region has shown the lowest ability to increase its economic and social indicators relative to the rest of the United States. This is not necessarily a proof that regional policies are totally ineffective, but it does highlight their limitations. Questions concerning the precise level of funding required for the take-off and generation of self-sufficiency in such lagging regions remain largely unanswered, however. The complexity and scale of the problems, and the changes that have affected central Appalachia since 1965, further emphasize the fact that the ARC has been able to make only a modest contribution to improving conditions there. The ARC's role has been made more difficult by the rapid changes and unexpected swings experienced in a country with no national planning goals and no national industrial, transport, land ownership, or energy policies. Such policies would be opposed by most Americans, and so the role of a regional development commission in the United States must remain reactive and pragmatic.

And yet the ARC has sought to broaden the nature of regional assistance from a mere bricks-and-mortar approach to the development of human resources and to the general consideration of a community's needs. It moved in this direction in the 1970s but in the 1980s was forced to limit its interest to a narrower field of projects that might result directly in the creation of jobs. This vicissitude further emphasized the significance of the political dimension in regional policy in the United States.

35

by Michael Miskowiec

New Federal Welfare Law: No Hands For Picking Beans?

Appalachia is likely to feel the adverse effects of the new welfare law more acutely than any other region of the country. Southern Appalachian states are already facing changes that will impact people of all ages and poverty levels.

On August 22, 1996, President Clinton signed into law the Personal Responsibility and Work Opportunity Reconciliation Act of 1996, P.L. 104–193. This law shifts responsibility for the nation's poor families to the states. Furthermore, despite the rhetoric surrounding the bill's passage about granting states flexibility to move people from welfare to work, several provisions of the law tie the hands of the states to create effective programs to achieve an end to welfare dependency.

The most striking change made by enactment of this welfare reform bill is the repeal of the Aid to Families with Dependent Children program, a public assistance program in existence over sixty years that paid cash benefits to families with children who have been deprived of parental support. In place of the AFDC program, the law creates a block grant program called the Temporary Assistance to Needy Families program. Federal funding for the TANF program is fixed at a level below projected spending levels under prior law. The law specifically ends a family's entitlement to the assistance as a matter of federal law.

Under the terms of the TANF program, states may not use federal funds to pay assistance to families that have received benefits for a total of sixty prior months. The law also requires the states to meet annual percentage targets for family members to be involved in work activity.

The law also makes changes in the Supplemental Security Income program. The Supplemental Security Income provides cash assistance to needy disabled, aged, and blind individuals. The standard for disability for children has been tightened. The requirement that claims be decided based on an individual assessment of the child's ability to function, which was first mandated by the Supreme Court in 1990, has been eliminated. The law also increases the number and type of disability cases that will be reviewed for continued benefits.

Finally changes in the Food Stamp program will cause benefit levels to be reduced. In addition the law limits Food Stamp assistance to childless, non-working adults to a total of three months. The law also prohibits provision of a separate Food Stamp allotment to a parent under the age of twenty-one if the parent is residing with her parents.

The most obvious impact on Appalachia from the new federal block grants is an almost certain reduction in assistance to low income families. According to the Urban Institute, one in four families in America depends to some extent on programs modified by P.L. 104–193. Given the high level of poverty in many areas of Appalachia, the financial impact on families in this region is likely to be even more widespread.

The termination of entitlement status and a provision which allows states to implement different assistance programs in different locales within the state could lead to a return of the politicization of assistance programs in Appalachia. Before the U.S. Supreme Court in *Goldberg v. Kelly* established that families had a right to notice and a hearing before welfare assistance could be terminated, local politicos used welfare assistance to keep poor families allied with their respective factions. In many areas of Appalachia, families were required to obtain a letter or certification from the county executive before they could apply for welfare. These certifications were granted more often based on party affiliation and promises of future voting support than on any showing of need.

Without the protection afforded by a federal entitlement to the assistance payment, poor families may have no way to enforce the terms of the block grant or to prevent abuses. The remedy in the statute for violation of the block grant terms is not effective to protect poor families. The sanctions provided in the statute call for a fixed reduction in the block grant payment as a penalty. For example, if the secretary finds that a state is not exempting families with children under age six from the work requirement due to a demonstrated lack of available child care, the secretary may reduce the block grant for the following year by up to 5 percent. The state is required to make up that penalty out of state money. It is unlikely that this sanction will be imposed for any but the most wholesale violations of the block grant conditions.

Although the new federal law terminates the entitlement under federal law, the language of the statue may provide some rights to recipient families. The state is required to set forth objective criteria for the delivery of benefits and determination of eligibility and for fair and equitable treatment of recipients. While the statue makes clear that Congress did not intend that recipient families would have any vested rights to assistance, a violation of the eligibility and fairness provisions of the block grant document could lead to a finding that the state's program, at least as administered if not as described, is fundamentally unfair. Courts have held that state government is required to treat individuals reasonably and with fundamental fairness under the federal Constitution, without regard to the existence of an entitlement.

The proponents of the law claim that the law grants states greater flexibility to design programs to better assist families to move from welfare to work. Funding levels and program restrictions may prevent states from establishing effective programs to end welfare dependency.

Although the federal payment is capped at a level below projected expenditures under prior law, states are required to spend at least 75 percent of their FY (fiscal year) 1994 expenditures. In order to be eligible for loans from the Contingent Fund for State Welfare Programs, a state must expend 100 percent of its FY 1994 expenditure.

The states are required, as a condition of receipt of the federal block grant payment, to ensure that at least 25 percent of all families receiving welfare assistance work at least twenty hours per week in FY 1997. The percentage targets increase to 50 percent by FY 2002.

The percentage target for two-parent families is even higher: 75 percent engaged in work activity in FY 1997. To be considered engaged in work activity, a two-parent family must have one parent engaged in work activity thirty-five hours per week and the second parent twenty hours per week. The percentage target for two-parent families increases to 90 percent in FY 1999.

In order to increase work activity to meet these standards, states will be required to increase spending on employment and job training programs and to create public jobs where private employment is not available.

Given that federal funds for the TANF program are capped, states will have to choose whether to commit additional state money to expand their job programs or to reduce benefits across the board in order to shift limited federal funds to employment programs.

The law greatly limits the states' ability to use the one tool that is most likely to assist families out of poverty: education. This is crucial to Appalachian states seeking to create high technology jobs that are less sensitive to market cycles and less demanding of the area's natural resources.

The law does have several provisions that mandate high school attendance or equivalency. States may sanction a family if the parent is not ensuring that a child is attending school or if an adult in the family does not acquire a General Equivalency Diploma. The states are prohibited from providing benefits to teenage parents who do not attend high school or an alternative training program approved by the state.

The law does not encourage state funding of education beyond the high school level. Post-secondary education is not a permissible work activity for purposes of the percentage targets. It is unlikely that states will allow recipients to participate in post-secondary education unless they can do so in addition to work of twenty to thirty-five hours per week. While the TANF program does permit the creation of Individual Development Accounts into which recipients can contribute earned income for financing post-secondary education, it is unlikely that states will spend funds to assist recipients in obtaining post-secondary education.

Another example of the obstacles to education in the federal law is the amount of countable hours that can be devoted to training and education. In the first two fiscal years of the TANF program, single parents over age twenty who have achieved a high school degree may not count any hours of education toward their work activity requirements. A parent in a two-parent household can only count five hours per week of education toward the thirty-five hour per week requirement.

States will be limited in their flexibility to design appropriate means to terminate welfare dependency owing to limited funding and restrictions in the use of post-secondary education as a work activity. In addition, the new law limits states institutionally by mandating dramatically increased disability reviews in the SSI programs.

The new law requires that SSI claims for children who reach the age of eighteen be reviewed within one year of their eighteenth birthday. In addition, low-birth-weight babies who have been awarded SSI benefits must have their claims reviewed within twelve months of birth.

These reviews will be initiated by state disability determination agencies under contract with the federal Social Security Administration. At this time, these agencies are already laboring under the highest caseloads in the history of the disability programs. These reviews will necessarily add to the existing backlog. This will impact Appalachia significantly. Appalachian states have historically had some of the highest incidence of disability claims in the nation. This trend has been explained variously as a result of lack of access to health care, a cyclical economy in the region, weak educational infrastructure, and high concentration of high risk jobs such as mining and timbering.

The federal law changes dramatically the primary responsibility for alleviating poverty in this country. Financial responsibility for poor people is shifted to state government. States are handcuffed, however, in their ability to design effective programs to move people from welfare to work by limited funding and program restrictions.

One provision of the new law is most illustrative of the new federal-state relationship. In the event a state finds that the changes mandated by the federal law increase child poverty in the state 5 percent of more in a given year, the state must come forward with a corrective action plan. Having provided the states with less money to move more people off welfare in a race against a sixty-month "drop dead" limit, Congress demands that the states explain why they fail. One long-time advocate for the poor has analogized this provision to tying a person's hands behind his back and then asking him to explain why he can't pick beans.

IX

Resistance and Community Organizing

Author and activist Steven Fisher has noted that "The Appalachian region has never lacked a politics of change and alternative development." This section addresses a widespread misperception of Appalachians as passive victims. Contemporary Appalachian research focuses on the development of social capital, or in the words of Maxine Waller and Helen Lewis, "It has to come from the people."

During the last decade regional scholars have developed a growing interest in the various forms resistance has taken in Appalachia. We have included a chapter from Stephen Fisher's volume, *Fighting Back in Appalachia* in which Joe Szackos describes the work of the citizen's group, Kentuckians for the Commonwealth. In their article, Maxine Waller, Helen Lewis, Clare McBrien, and Carroll Wessinger write about efforts to revitalize Ivanhoe, a struggling town in southwestern Virginia.

Even where conscious efforts at economic development are not taking place, Appalachians have established their own economic microsystems. Rhoda Halperin conducted a six-year ethnographic field study in northeastern Kentucky in which she focused on the underground economy as a form of resistance to capitalism. "The Kentucky Way" is her shorthand description of the complex relationships among economy, culture, and kinship.

Almost forty years have passed since author Harry Caudill called for massive federal assistance to Appalachia modeled after the Tennessee Valley Authority. Perhaps the most dramatic development in Appalachian studies in the past decade is the broader understanding of the ways in which Appalachians have been active participants in changing regional conditions of poverty, depression, and environmental depredation.

36

by Stephen L. Fisher

The Grass Roots Speak Back

Contrary to popular images of Appalachians as passive victims, there exists throughout the Appalachian Mountains a tradition of individual and organized citizen efforts to establish community services and preserve community values. This essay describes the variety and extent of local and regional efforts for change in Appalachia since 1960 and examines the lessons to be learned from these efforts.[1]

The Appalachian region has never lacked a politics of change and alternative development. But what stands out in the literature describing life in Appalachia before 1960 is not the extent of change efforts but rather the obstacles to change, the conditions leading to quiescence.[2] The industrialization of Appalachia was characterized by single-industry economies, the control of land and resources by large absentee companies, high levels of poverty and unemployment, the frequent use of red baiting, intimidation, and physical force to squelch dissent, political corruption, and a highly stratified and oppressive class system. Collective struggles for change were further undermined by cultural traditions that stressed individualism, by the strength of capitalist ideology, by racism and sexism, by the lack of strong local organizations, by high illiteracy rates, and by poor transportation and communication systems.

During this period, one could find throughout Appalachia examples of the starkest political and economic oppression in American society. In recent years, anthropologists and social and feminist historians have taught us that, when faced with such repressive conditions, people find ways to resist. This was certainly true in Appalachia. The organized efforts of workers in the coal, textile, and steel industries to improve their working and living conditions are well documented. But in other parts of the Appalachian Mountains, responses to these conditions often assumed forms far less visible than picket lines and organized movements and included such individual acts of behavior as gossip, back talk, holding on to one's dialect, refusal to cooperate with outside authority figures, and migration. This type of protest is part of what James Scott refers to as the "hidden transcript" of the oppressed.[3]

Increasingly, Appalachian scholars are coming to recognize the existence and importance of such protest in Appalachia's history and to understand that it has most frequently occurred in struggles to preserve traditional values and ways of life against the forces of modernization. For example, Helen Lewis, Sue Kobak, and Linda Johnson describe the various ways in which mountain families and churches became defensive and inward in

Source: From *Confronting Appalachian Stereotypes: Back Talk from an American Region* by Billings, Norman & Ledford, ed.

order to protect their members from some of the harmful impacts of industrialization and the actions of outside change agents.[4] Kathleen Blee and Dwight Billings reinterpret early ethnographic studies of the region to show that work attitudes and other practices previously viewed as traits of a culture of poverty could better be understood as forms of resistance to the capitalist separation of work and control.[5] Altina Waller argues that the legendary Hatfield-McCoy feud can be seen as a battle between local defenders of community autonomy and outside industrial interests.[6] These and similar studies broaden our understandings of the nature and extent of resistance by rural working-class and poor people in Appalachia 1960.

Many of the obstacles that made collective struggles so difficult throughout Appalachia's history are still present today, and individual protests continue on a number of fronts. But new conditions after 1960 provided impetus and support to organized resistance efforts throughout Appalachia. The civil rights movement helped legitimize the notion of dissent in general and the strategy of nonviolent civil disobedience in particular throughout the region and the nation. The environmental and women's movements offered models and resources for local groups in the mountains. Moreover, these movements provided the impetus for national legislation that created opportunities for local organizations fighting to save their land and communities from environmental destruction or working to create alternative economic opportunities for women. The antiwar and student movements called into question the notions of progress, modernization, and national interest that had been used for so long to justify the destruction of traditional ways of life in Appalachia.

The War on Poverty spawned the Appalachian Volunteers and community action agencies throughout the mountains. While these programs had many weaknesses, they did bring young organizers into the region and provided opportunities for local leadership development. Mainstream churches, reflecting a new social consciousness, sent to Appalachia clergy and other church workers who were committed to working for social and economic justice. The construction of more and better roads, the availability of video recording equipment, open meeting and record laws, and increased church and foundation funding of Appalachian citizen groups also contributed to local organizing efforts.

These and other factors led to an outburst of grassroots community organizing across Appalachia in the late 1960s and early 1970s. Local residents fought to prevent the destruction of their land and homes by strip miners, dam and highway builders, the U.S. Forest Service, toxic waste dumpers, and recreation and second-home developers. People organized to secure welfare benefits, to enact tax reform, to build rural community centers and health clinics, to fight for better schools for their children, and to establish programs in literacy and child care. Community groups pursued a wide variety of alternative economic development strategies that resulted in agricultural and craft cooperatives, worker-owned factories, and new job opportunities for women. Efforts to preserve and celebrate local culture flourished in the mountains, as people began to develop a consciousness of and pride in being Appalachian.

In the 1990s people across Appalachia are still fighting back, often around similar issues.[7] The battle over strip mining continues as local groups challenge the Office of Surface Mining's nonenforcement of the federal strip mining law and join with other groups to lobby Washington for better water protection laws. Communities throughout rural Appalachia struggle to prevent their landfills from becoming the dumping grounds for the nation's trash, sludge, and toxic waste. The Yellow Creek Concerned Citizens and the Dayhoit Concerned Citizens in east Kentucky, the Dead Pigeon River Council and the Oak Ridge Environmental Peace Alliance in East Tennessee, and the Dickenson County Citizens Committee in Southwest Virginia are just a few of the groups across the region fighting the poisoning of their land, air, and water. The Ohio Valley Environmental Coalition organizes around industrial pollution where Ohio,

Kentucky, and West Virginia meet. The Ivanhoe Civic League and the Dungannon Development Commission in Southwest Virginia and the Appalachian Center for Economic Networks in Athens, Ohio, pursue innovative grassroots alternative economic development plans. The Mountain Women's Exchange in East Tennessee and Women and Employment in West Virginia work to improve the economic position of women in the region.

In sum, since the 1960s, hundreds of new citizen groups have been organized throughout Appalachia. Most arose in response to a particular issue. These single-issue groups have worked together from time to time, helped create local leadership, and won important victories. But because they have focused on a single issue, many of these groups have been short-lived, disappearing once their issue has been resolved. Thus, one of the most exciting and hopeful developments in community organizing in Appalachia in recent years has been the establishment and success of thriving and influential multi-issue, membership-driven organizations such as Save Our Cumberland Mountains (SOCM), Kentuckians for the Commonwealth (KFTC), and the Community Farm Alliance (CFA).

SOCM, organized in 1972 to fight strip mining in a five-county area in the northern coalfields of Tennessee, changed from a single-issue, staff-run group to a multi-issue, grassroots organization able to exercise power and influence at the state and national levels.[8] KFTC, started in mid-1981 by a small group of eastern Kentucky residents who wanted to address community problems that crossed county lines, has grown into a statewide, multi-issue, social justice organization of more than twenty-three hundred members in ninety counties.[9] CFA was transformed from a handful of people who were replicating the mistakes of the national farm movement of the 1980s to a growing and successful membership-based organization with over a dozen chapters across Kentucky.[10]

These organizations stress the significance of local indigenous leadership recruitment and training, shared and long-term consciousness raising, the development of internal democratic social relations, ideological patience, and the willingness to connect with people as they are. Their success illustrates the importance of using county chapters to build statewide organizations and of connecting local issues to state, national, and global patterns and concerns.

Since the 1960s, activist have attempted to organize citizen organizations in the Appalachian Mountains into a regionwide grassroots social movement. The most important attempts were by the Council of the Southern Mountains, the Peoples Appalachia Research Collective, the Congress for Appalachian Development, the Highlander Research and Education Center, and the Appalachian Alliance.[11] These attempts to build a unified movement failed for a variety of reasons, but primarily because, unlike class, race, and gender, region in the United States does not provide an adequate political and economic focus for social movements.

This failure to create a social movement in Appalachia similar to the civil rights or women's movements does not mean that change efforts in the region have occurred in isolation. While many of these struggles have been local and concerned with a single issue, they have often been assisted by and associated with other groups and individuals within a loose alliance or network of Appalachian organizations. At times the network has had a name; at other times, it has been little more than an informal chain of individuals and groups. Organizations and activists come and go and financial support is rarely stable; but the network persists, and there may be no other like it in the United States.[12] Key players in this network today include the Highlander Research and Education Center, an adult education center in eastern Tennessee that has served as a meeting place, training center, and catalyst for social action throughout Appalachia and the South; the Southern Empowerment Project, an organizer training program established and controlled by grassroots community groups; and the Appalachian Community Fund, a community-controlled foundation that provides seed money and small grants to groups in the Appalachian region.

As Bill Horton points out, this loose, informal network "is the form that the Appalachian social movement has taken—slowly winning victories, working together, laying the groundwork, building or trying to build democratic organizations. Perhaps this is the way the movement will be built, piece by piece like a patchwork quilt until it comes together to rid the region of oppressive structures and practices, in turn becoming a piece of a much larger quilt that must be created to rid the nation of those same structures and practices."[13]

Over the past three decades, activists and academics have learned a number of important lessons about the politics of change in Appalachia. Successful change efforts in the Appalachian mountains have centered more often around the concept of community than around the centralized workplace of the mine, mill, or factory. In addition, historical memory and a reliance on and defense of traditional values—a strong commitment to land, kin, and religious beliefs, an emphasis on self-rule and social equality, and patriotism—have fueled many of the popular struggles in the region. Indeed, the fact that so many of the protests in Appalachia have been the result of defensive behavior—action to prevent the destruction of a way of life and a set of values that could be labeled traditional or conservative —has led one observer to refer to Appalachians as "reactionary rebels."[14]

While it is important to understand that grassroots resistance in Appalachian history has most frequently occurred in single-issue battles to preserve traditional values and ways of life, it is also necessary to recognize that there are limits to community-based organizing strategies that focus on single issues and rely heavily on localism and traditional values and institutions.[15] Community in our history entails exclusion as well as inclusion. Tradition and local values include racism, sexism, homophobia, and isolationism. In addition, while localism offers a number of advantages, few significant problems can be solved at the local level. Local resources have been depleted and local economies gutted by national and global market forces and the actions of the federal government and multinational corporations. Those organizing in Appalachia must find ways to make clear the connections that exist between local work and national and international institutions if local citizens are to understand the importance of national and international forces as determinants of what happens locally and to see themselves as actors at the national level.

Without attention to the larger questions of power in society, local community groups are often not prepared for the legal, political, and cultural forces that established powers bring against them. This results in a politics of gradualism—a strategy of adaptation and retrenchment—and a suspicion of outsiders and their programs. Further, it does not create the conditions necessary for coalition work with potential allies—be they health professionals, church workers, or environmentalists. Many local revolts throughout Appalachia turn out to be "flashes of independent anger" rather than sustained efforts at effective movement building precisely because they lack an analysis and understanding of power beyond the local levels.[16]

In sum, single-issue, defensive, localized work, which has characterized much of the organizing in Appalachia, can win occasional victories but cannot by itself lead to substantive change at an individual or structural level.[17] Tackling issues as complex as poverty, strip mining, or inadequate health care requires ongoing, multi-issue, reflective, democratic organizations, the type of organizing being conducted by SOCM, KFTC, and CFA—the multi-issue, membership-run organizations described above. These groups pursue an organizing approach that is flexible, pragmatic, and grounded in the past and present of members' lives. But unlike the narrow single-issue organizing of the past, these groups' primary concern is to empower their members for the long haul—to provide a schooling in politics and personal empowerment. They do so by offering a self-conscious leadership training program designed to develop democratic skills and build a sense of ownership and community. These organizations provide the space where participants can begin to see the connection between their concerns and those of other exploited people, where members can come to confront issues of racism and sexism, and where people can start to envision new alternatives to the world in which they live. As Connie White, a past SOCM president, puts it, "We don't care just about winning issues; we care more about helping people get stronger. In the long run, that is how you win issues and make real changes."[18]

In the past, many organizers have arrived in Appalachia with pejorative, romanticized, or contrived notions of the cultural forces and values present in the Appalachian mountains. Appalachian culture is "a web of both resistance and complicity,"[19] and it is important for those organizing in the region to develop an understanding of the ways in which regional culture informs the construction of class consciousness, race and gender relations, regional identity, and community life.

Several points need to be emphasized in this regard. First, regional identity and cultural pride are not naturally part of community life. Regional identity is not a geographical or cultural given in Appalachia, but must be understood as an outgrowth of political dynamics and social change. Similarly, local cultural traditions are selective and fluid in nature; they are "historically formed, situated, and altered by people interacting with each other and with social and economic forces."[20] These cultural traditions are at the heart of the community networks necessary to sustain people during protracted struggles and enable them to foster change on their own terms. But cultural expression does not always arise spontaneously in struggles to challenge oppression and inequality. The seeds for such expression exist; but these seeds must often be deliberately cultivated and nourished by organizers and institutions that recognize the value of cultural forms to resistance efforts.[21]

Second, neither class nor culture alone is a sufficient tool for understanding political action in Appalachia. Although classes are shaped by economic concerns, they are cultural configurations. Indeed, the United States is one of the few places where class and culture are thought of separately. Lived experience is different—our lives are a messy amalgam of identities out of which social relations are conducted.[22] The difficult but crucial task is not to decide between culture and class, but to discover how class, race, and gender conflicts express themselves today in cultural and political formations in Appalachia.

In Appalachian research, some of the most important work in this regard is being done by Mary Anglin and Sally Maggard. Using different approaches and studying protest in different locales and industries, Anglin and Maggard probe the ways in which gender, kinship, and social class interact to specify women's political experience, action, and consciousness. They demonstrate convincingly how and why change efforts, to be successful, must be situated in a web of work, family, and community needs and histories.[23] Other significant contributions include Michael Yarrow's investigation of the ways in which Appalachian coal miners' gender consciousness affects their class consciousness;[24] Richard Couto's discussion of community-based approaches to environmental risks;[25] and Dwight Billings's use of Antonio Gramsci's approach to religion to explain activism and quiescence among textile workers and coal miners.[26]

Third, racism is a major barrier to successful grassroots organizing and coalition-building in Appalachia, as it is throughout the nation. Don Manning-Miller charges that many of the community organizations in Appalachia, while committed either explicitly or implicitly to combating racism and to building a multiracial people's coalition for progressive social change, in practice pursue a process of organizing and struggle that fails to challenge the cultural conservatism and racism of their constituency. Manning-Miller urges organizers and activists to use all available media and organizational forms to confront people's racism and offers a number of valuable tactical measures and suggestions for developing a systematic program to confront racism in Appalachia.[27]

Finally, to be successful over the long haul, those engaged in cultural, educational, and political work must search through the regional culture to locate its most humane, progressive, and transformative elements and then look for ways to link these transformative elements to a larger human agenda for change.[28]

This brief consideration of organized grassroots change efforts in Appalachia should dispel the stereotypical notion of Appalachians as apathetic and dependent. Activists and scholars have made major advances since the 1960s in terms of building effective community organizations and in intellectual efforts to grapple with some of the tough issues involved in mounting effective resistance.

What is currently needed in the region is a critical discourse and practice "rooted in an awareness of popular traditions and resistance, but not blind to the wider contours of power within national and international capital." This requires a knowledge of a "people's" history and a history of capitalism.[29] It involves the creation of resistance organizations that take culture and community seriously as places for political action while encouraging their members to discover the ways their grievances are a result of "structural processes occurring at an economic, geographic, and political level far beyond the particular locale where the grievance is experienced."[30] It requires creating an alternative radicalism that chooses to complicate rather than simplify by incorporating themes from the many movements and traditions present in Appalachia and the United States.[31]

This critical discourse and practice require courage, commitment, struggle, and patience, and at times it is difficult to imagine that they are even possible. But occasionally an event occurs that helps us focus, that provides us with a glimpse of what could be. The United Mine Workers of America's occupation of the Moss 3 coal preparation plant during the 1989–90 Pittston strike was one such occasion.

The resistance leading up to the takeover was fueled by family, community, and union loyalties that had instilled in generation after generation a deeply felt class awareness and anger. Camp Solidarity, local community centers, and weekly rallies provided free spaces where striking miners, relatives, and supporters from all over the country shared life stories and experiences that reinforced bonds of community and class solidarity. Old labor and gospel songs rang out along the picket lines. American flags and yellow ribbons became the symbols of resistance to uncaring corporate and governmental leaders and structures. The miners and their supporters drew upon their religious beliefs to strengthen their resolve and justify their dissent. Strike leaders worked hard to educate the miners about he issues of the strike, to forge links with other social movements nationally and abroad, and to involve African Americans and women in a wide variety of strike activities. Mistakes were made, and much still remains unresolved. But for those few days those who were there were able to "feel the possibilities that reside within us, and in the groups of which we are or can be a part."[32]

37

by Rhoda H. Halperin

The Kentucky Way: Resistance to Dependency Upon Capitalism in an Appalachian Region

Introduction

This essay focuses on "the Kentucky way" and resistance to dependency upon capitalism in an unstudied region of Appalachian America. The analysis derives from a six year ethnographic field study in a 10 county region of northeastern Kentucky (Halperin 1990). The region does not fit the conventional stereotypes of Appalachia, however. It is not presently, nor historically has it ever been a coal mining region; it is not mountainous; neither is it geographically isolated. Rather, it is somewhere in between the core and the periphery of economic life in the United States. The basic livelihood strategies operating in this region are generalizable to many other parts of the world where state systems undergo simultaneous industrialization, deindustrialization, urbanization and resistance to urbanization. The rural parts of Europe, areas of the Texas border, even Vermont's Appalachia might be cases in point.

The fieldwork began several years ago when, a very bright student, early in her graduate career one day in my office adopted the tone of a confessional and announced that she spoke two dialects of English: "country" and "city." She paused, and with some tension in her voice, told me how much she feared lapsing into "country" English while concentrating so hard to speak "city" (standard) English to her university professors. After I assured her that I would think no less of her if she used either dialect, she volunteered that she used "country" English at her parents' home in rural of Kentucky. There she experienced another sort of anxiety. If she slipped into "city" English, her Mom and Dad would consider her snobbish and uppity. The tensions evident in that anecdote—tensions between country and city, urban educational institutions and subsistence farm families, are only some of the many strains people feel as they resist dependency upon capitalism.

All of the key elements of the Kentucky way must be understood in the context of regionally based, three generation extended families. I will begin by describing the activities of one typical extended family in this Northeastern Kentucky region. The family is

Source: This article was prepared specifically for the third edition of *Appalachia: Social Context Past and Present.* Used by permission of the author.

typical because it is three generational in structure, it is involved in a multicentric economy of small family farms and subsistence gardens, factory based wage labor, and an informal periodic marketplace system. Family imperatives dominate people's choices of work tasks, places of residence and overall patterns of life and livelihood. All of the important clues to understanding the relationships between the Kentucky way and resistance to dependency upon capitalism are contained in the following brief scenario:

Harry, a former employee of Coca Cola and Ilene Smith, now retired from her job in the city as a dentist's receptionist, along with their daughter Sue, and son-in-law Nathan, are planning their economic activities for a fall weekend. Harry and Ilene were born and raised in the same county in the country where his family owned a sheep farm and hers were tenant farmers. They now live in one household in a hamlet in an area between the country and the city that I have called the "shallow rural." Shallow rural contrasts with deep rural ("the country") and with urban, "the city." Sue and Nathan (both temporary wage laborers in a nearby factory) live with their two children, a son, four years old, and a daughter, six years old, in another household in a mobile home park six miles from Sue's parents. The following activities must be coordinated. Harry has two housepainting jobs to finish before the weather turns cold; he also has several indoor house-renovating jobs. He and Ilene are regular vendors in the rotating periodic marketplace system (an organized system of "flea markets"), and they are eager to sell off the goods they have accumulated over the summer by attending garage sales and auctions. Harry specializes in selling (illegal) guns, Ilene in quilts and antiques. It is not unusual for Harry and Ilene to clear $400 to $1200 per weekend in market sales. Ilene has a talent for picking up bargains at garage sales. She will then clean her goods, repair them, or combine them with other items to produce highly saleable goods. She can transform old things worth a few dollars into items that sell for $35 or more. Harry has an extensive network of clients for his guns since he is a trustworthy dealer. Harry and Ilene do not report their income.

The best day to sell at the Roadside market, a major marketplace in the system, is Saturday or Sunday. Ilene is also very concerned about "putting up" her beans and cucumbers for the winter; if she does not process them in time, both beans and cucumbers will grow too large and tough to be eaten. Ilene's sister is ill, and Ilene must take her some cooked food sometime during the weekend. As temporary wage laborers, Sue and Nathan work six days each week; sometimes they work double shifts.

Ilene and Harry decide to set up their booth at the Roadside market on Saturday, the busiest day. They take their grandchildren with them. Sue and Nathan will harvest the beans and cucumbers and prepare food to take to Ilene's sister after work on Saturday. On Sunday they will all go to Sue's aunt's farm in the country for their Sunday dinner.

In the first part of this essay, I will discuss the Kentucky way as a cultural idiom and livelihood strategy for maintaining identity and autonomy in a rapidly changing post industrial economy. I will then illustrate how the strategy works by elaborating upon Nathan's experience as a rural person, carpenter, wage laborer, member of a three generation extended family and, most importantly, as someone who sees himself as a practitioner of the Kentucky way. There are female counterparts to Nathan in this regional system; there are also younger and older people who either have experienced or will experience his work patterns (Halperin 1990). The economic activities of all of these people are firmly embedded in regionally based extended families with ties to land.

The Regional Context of the Kentucky Way

The region is predominantly agrarian with small holdings. The landholdings in this region are, and have always been small, privately owned, subsistence-oriented units that use the labor of three-generation extended families (Precourt 1983). Only 2% of the farms in the region are larger than 500 acres. The average farm size in the region is 121 acres, and this is considered by most to be a large farm.

The agrarian holdings are themselves diverse, however. Some are small family farms with a few acres devoted to cash crops (primarily burley tobacco) and one or two acres planted in feed for livestock. Other agrarian holdings are homesteads, that is households located on small holdings with subsistence gardens. Still others are combinations of small farms, gardens, and workshops (welding, crafts, furniture, repairs, etc.). The agrarian holdings provide the baselines from which people negotiate their relationships to factory-based wage labor and to the informal economy of a rotating periodic marketplace system.

The "shallow rural" is the most problematic, as well as the most interesting and complex part of the region. It is an unstudied, unnamed, and uncategorized grey area between country and city. Small holdings with substantial kitchen gardens and plots of tobacco sit next to shopping malls, tract housing developments and mobile home parks. The rotating periodic marketplace system is located in the shallow rural along with the factories that employ temporary wage laborers. Thus, in the shallow rural we find the institutional representations of the formal economy of industrial capitalism coexisting alongside the informal economy of periodic marketplaces.

In contrast to the shallow rural, the deep rural is solidly agrarian. In one typical deep rural county, ninety six percent of the 206 square miles of land is farm land. People who live in the shallow rural are migrants from the deep rural parts of the region. A person who speaks "country English" is not at all conspicuous in the shallow rural; in the city, he or she will be labelled a "hillbilly." By the same token, speakers of "city English" are conspicuous as outsiders in the factories and marketplaces of the shallow rural. A complex infrastructure of superhighways and county roads weave their way through the shallow rural, linking it easily to cities in the north and south.

The Kentucky way is not unique to Kentucky or to Appalachia. The economic strategies of the Kentucky way are peasant-like in the sense that they are subsistence oriented and driven by ties to kin and to homeplace. The economic strategies are rural and agrarian. Indeed the same kinds of strategies operate with variations and transformations in many rural parts of the world, for example, what Daniella Weinberg calls, peasant wisdom in Europe (Switzerland) and what James Scott calls "everyday forms of peasant resistance" (1985) in Malaya. The implications of these common peasant strategies have for accomplishing identity, autonomy and a sense of control over life and livelihood are also similar, or at least comparable in many rural cultures. What makes the Kentucky case so compelling is its immediacy and its proximity to urban industrial cities in the U.S.; the Kentucky way is intensifying and transforming on a daily basis.

The practitioners of the Kentucky way are difficult to classify: They work constantly but officially they appear as unemployed, retired, or both. They live in rural areas and many work in factories or commute to jobs in the city, but they are not counted, nor do they define themselves as factory workers. They plant gardens and cash crops, but they are not farmers in the conventional sense of that term. They buy and sell goods in colorful, bustling marketplaces that form a full blown rotating periodic marketplace system of the sort found in many third world countries—Mexico and China—to name two, but they are not traders or merchants. Their work tasks are varied, numerous and constant, however, and these tasks change weekly, seasonally and generationally. These facts about the multiple livelihood strategies of rural working class people provide some of the clues to "the Kentucky way" and to understanding resistance to dependency upon capitalism.

I want to emphasize at the outset that it is not capitalism per se that people resist in rural Kentucky; rather people resist *dependency* upon capitalism. Resistance here is positive, energizing, and it has the effect of denying claims made by superordinate classes and by the state (resistance to proletarianization and to taxation). (1) If anything, it is seen as a revitalization of rural culture. Kin networks and a mosaic of economic processes provide the keys to understanding resistance to capitalist dependency. People use capitalism and its products in ingenious ways and their livelihood strategies combine elements of both capitalist and noncapitalist systems.

"The Kentucky Way"

What is "the Kentucky way" and how does it enable people to resist dependency upon capitalism? The Kentucky way is a cultural idiom that refers to the complex relationships between economy, culture and kinship. The Kentucky way refers to a broad spectrum of practical skills and of knowledge of local resources. People repeat the expression "the Kentucky way" often, sometimes with nostalgia, sometimes with regret, but always with affection and respect. The idiom evokes immediate associations—sympathies between people, common lifestyles, beliefs and sentiments. It identifies people with one another. "You must record" the Kentucky way "before it disappears," said a young country woman. I was flattered by her willingness to give me such a responsibility; I was also taken aback by the task she had assigned to me—namely to salvage something so essential to the culture before it changes or disappears. The Kentucky way provides the template for making a living and for living itself. Often people speak of the Kentucky way in a religious idiom, especially when they are talking about work. People say such things as "The idle body is a sin," or "I am working for the Lord," or "God sits above the government." As a system of local knowledge and practices, doing things "the Kentucky way" allows people to exercise control over their livelihood and provides them with a sense of autonomy that would not be possible were they to confine their economic and social relationships to an urban-based, cash economy.

At its core, "the Kentucky way" is about maintaining livelihood and maintaining rural culture. It includes commitments to kin, to hard work and self-sufficiency, to freedom and to the land, to generosity and reciprocity, and to certain kinds of practical knowledge. Economic knowledge itself is based on rural skills—knowing something about everything within the appropriate male and female domains. Maintaining a general, rather than a specialized repertoire of skills is extremely important. People resist becoming specialists for specialists must rely on others to perform tasks for them (Hicks 1973). Being a generalist is a strategy of self-reliance, a mark of one's versatility and flexibility, and one's ingenuity and cleverness. In this region, self-reliance does not serve to isolate people. It is not individualistic or self-serving. Rather it is a form of outreach to kin and to neighbors in the context of offering multiple goods and services in multiple arenas. The fact that people are so versatile creates great flexibility for livelihood strategies. Not only can people choose easily between various work tasks, they can switch from one task to another in accordance with the needs of family members and with the opportunities made available through kinship ties.

For both men and women, knowledge of the local ecology is essential for knowing when and how to hunt, fish and gather, as well as for knowing when and how to clear, plant, and harvest. Hunting and fishing are not mere sport in this area; they provide essential protein, which when combined with garden produce and meat from livestock (primarily pigs) when available, add up to a large portion of daily subsistence. Knowledge of the land, its virtues, limitations, and seasonal patterns, are certainly important for all agricultural societies, but "the Kentucky way" reinforces the importance of hunting, fishing and agrarian skills in combination with the mechanical skills necessary for keeping machinery, vehicles and households functioning as self-sustaining units.

Being a "good Kentucky woman" (homemaker and worker in the broadest sense of these terms) is an essential part of "the Kentucky way." Women pass down knowledge of food production (gardening), processing (canning and freezing) and storage techniques from generation to generation. For women as well as for men, knowing how to be resourceful is regarded as the essence of the good person. Women also resist specialization, but in ways that are both similar to and different from that of men. For both men and women, maintaining one's position in trade networks and social groups leads to knowledge about which marketplaces are best for selling or buying particular items. Men and women sell and trade different kinds of things, however, and they engage in different kinds of social groups. Women's social groups are often church-based. Women exchange goods, provide help with children, and donate time for home health care. Men's social groups are smaller and more informal. It is not uncommon to see men gathered in groups of two or three on porches, in the aisles of marketplaces, or almost anywhere.

On another level, "the Kentucky way" signifies certain kinds of ideal relations to the means of production, especially to the land. Owning land, "private property," however small one's plot may be, provides a buffer against dependency upon outsiders. A piece of land large enough for a large subsistence garden and tobacco plot (Tobacco, until recently, was the main cash crop.) is most desirable. In this context, ties to rural homeplaces can be understood not only as sources of land, but as reservoirs of local knowledge and the resources this knowledge provides.

The Kentucky way also indicates relationships to regional and state authorities. It is a form of identity, an attachment to rural lifestyles. Disdain for industrialism and for economic development is part of the Kentucky way. I remember being driven around the region one afternoon when my attention was directed to the posted signs that read: "Let Toyota be your neighbor." "This is terrible," said one of the region's residents. "This is ruining our farms." Many people express strong resentments concerning the defacement of the countryside by foreign industrialists. One hears negative comments about the governor's lack of sensitivity to the traditional needs of the people. In part, the negativism stems from the fact that people do not perceive jobs as providing a secure or sufficient livelihood. A disdain for industry is combined with disdain for those in power and for those who control the means of production. "People are made into machines in those factories," one man told me repeatedly. The Toyota plant, which opened within the last few years, did indeed encompass the entire horizon. I was urged to photograph one particular spot in which the plant spanned the horizon; a barn occupied the background, and a lone horse, the foreground. "See," one man said, "all the trees have been cut down; no berries and no rabbits could live there now."

Participating in the Kentucky way carries certain obligations as well as certain rights. Critical among the obligations are those to family members. Making a living must never interfere with these obligations. If, for example, a young adult chooses to take a job that is located too far for kin to visit easily, he or she will be the object of criticism. Also, staying in school too long for the pursuit of advanced degrees can be negatively regarded. Questions from parents such as, "Haven't you been in school long enough; when are you going to get a *real* job?" are frequently heard.

Perhaps one of the best ways to understand the Kentucky way is as a form of what Daniela Weinberg has called the traditional ideology of "peasant wisdom:" "the wisdom to remain free of outside control by owning and managing a variety of resources, and free of debt by running a self supporting household" (1975:196). The key component of peasant wisdom, Kentucky style, is control over one's day to day life, if not one's destiny. Control requires maintaining a network of people for support in times of need and securing sufficient private property in land such that one does not rely upon the outside for loans. Loans from kin are preferable to loans from banks or loans from non-kin. The kinsperson who is in the best position to lend money and provide work for the unemployed kin is the person who owns a farm.

The bottom line for practitioners of the Kentucky way is that work tasks are oriented towards meeting basic needs without overconsumption or conspicuous consumption. One afternoon in a produce stand the size of an eight by ten shed, people were talking about how "we don't want for anything; we live high on the hog." People are very sophisticated in knowing how to obtain "everything we need and more."

We can begin to see a subtle, but distinct ideology of equality as part of the Kentucky way. It appears in statements such as "We're all kin here" (Bryant 1981, Beaver 1986, Foster 1988). A highly respected judge in the region told me that "it takes awhile to become accepted here, but once you are, people take you in as family." It is not that people do not recognize differences in income, education, and skill, but that these differences are not emphasized. People's resistance to specialization contributes to egalitarianism. On a more subtle level, the ideology of equality operates in the form of people's willingness to give freely and generously of their time and their resources to help kin and neighbors on a regular basis, not just in times of crisis. University students whose families grow burley tobacco are expected to go home to help out with the harvesting and processing of tobacco regardless of how pressing their academic responsibilities might be. Needless to say, there are conflicts for many people who grow up with the Kentucky way. Work responsibilities must be compatible with responsibilities to family. People make constant adjustments to accommodate family needs in accordance with the basic exigencies of livelihood. People without families are objects of pity.

One of the most important features of "the Kentucky way" then, is its emphasis on the benefits of the country, whether this involves living in the country or maintaining close ties to people and land, or both. People see greater opportunities to use a variety of resources in the country. They see themselves as "belonging to the country" and as "country people," even though many of them live less than five miles from a city. Belonging to the country involves the mastery of practical knowledge through apprenticeships and close intergenerational ties. Older Kentuckians lament the proliferation of young "shut ins," a folk term for people who live in apartments, work at unskilled and low-paying wage labor jobs, and watch television and drink beer in their spare time. In analytical terms, these are people who, by refusing to engage in learning the spectrum of practical skills, prevent the production and reproduction of local practical knowledge. From the point of view of older people in the region, these young adults are putting themselves in a very vulnerable position. That is, without practical local knowledge of agrarian skills, people become completely dependent upon cash generated in the wage labor sector. When they are inevitably laid off, unless family members "help them out" they must rely upon the welfare system, something that is an anathema to "the Kentucky way" because it flies in the face of self-sufficiency and local autonomy.

People talk about not putting all your eggs in one basket, an idiom that refers not only to being a generalist, but to operating in multiple economic sectors, in this case, the agrarian, the marketplace, and the wage labor sectors. Nathan is an example of a person who uses his rural skills and his ties to his own and his wife's extended family, to resist participation in the wage labor system, and thus, to resist dependency upon capitalism.

Nathan, now 28 years old, was born on a farm in Southern Kentucky. From the age of 14, he worked as a carpenter's apprentice for a man with whom he had an excellent working relationship. The carpentry business was good, and Nathan worked extremely hard. At the age of 21, Nathan moved to Cincinnati, where he worked as a wage laborer for a wholesale food company. When the food company went out of business, he went to work as a temporary wage laborer for the Goody Company, a large manufacturing firm where he held a similar kind of job maintaining machinery, operating a fork-lift truck, and performing a variety of other tasks in the factory. He obtained this temporary job from an agency in the city. While working for the Goody Company, he met his present wife, Sue, who is also 28 years old. Shortly thereafter, all temporary employees at Goody were notified of termination. Sue quickly found another temporary job at the Rinterline plant and, after one month of employment, learned of a few openings in the machine recycling area. She told Nathan about these jobs. He applied and was immediately hired because of his machine operator's experience at the Goody facility. Because both Sue and Nathan were temporary employees, they could both be hired at Rinterline.

Nathan's job in truck part recycling at the Rinterline plant was dangerous and dirty. Everything in this area of the plant was covered with grease. As a temporary employee, Nathan had to furnish and wash his own work clothes. In this particular work area, a set of clothes lasted approximately two weeks at the most. The wage was $4 per hour with no benefits of any sort. Sue told me that Nathan was exposed to petroleum products and no mask was provided. She said also that the chemical compounds used to clean the recycled parts nearly ruined Nathan's wedding band. The floors were slippery from the grease and this made it difficult to move 70 lb parts from one station to another. Nathan's back became very sore from several bad falls on the floor. Since grinding metal was part of the job, goggles were provided by Rinterline. The metal particles were so small, however, that they still occasionally came behind the goggles. Three weeks into his employment, a piece of metal slipped into Nathan's eye. He was transported to an eye specialist in Fenwick who removed the fragment. The doctor told Nathan and Sue that the cornea was severely scratched, placed a patch over the eye, and sent Nathan back to work. The Rinterline Company paid for the physician's bill, but did not "give Nathan a break work station wise." Sue repeatedly told me that "Nathan really hates Rinterline. He would look out the back door and exclaim that Fenwick had been converted into a moonscape—all the trees plowed down and only brown grass remaining, the horizon was dotted with factories instead of farms." Nathan himself said to me that he "felt dirty, like a peon! I know I can do better for myself."

Nathan walked off the job after four months as a temporary wage laborer as Rinterline. He began self-employment as a painter and carpenter. Much of his work, especially initially was obtained through connections long established by his father-in-law, Harry Smith who is a veteran wage laborer and now market vendor.

"Country people," particularly men, who quit their wage labor jobs in favor of odd jobs, or who decide to intensify their activities in the agrarian and marketplace sectors, often see themselves as "opting out of the system" or as "working outside the system." Discussions about the dangers of factory work, the lack of concern for safety on the part of owners and managers came out in many cases. People see themselves as resistant to factory work, and their resistance takes many forms. People see their investments in kin networks as providing them with flexibility, with options to leave wage labor jobs and establish other means of livelihood.

I would like to end with the following anecdote because it illustrates some of the rawness manifested by resistance not only to dependency upon capitalism, but to urbanism and everything that urbanism represents. Again, I return to Nathan.

One day I was driven around the countryside by Nathan and Sue. They were in the front seat. I was in the back with one of the students working on this project. We had just finished lunch "Dinner," in folk terms, at a charming old restaurant in the deep rural part of the region where the old soda fountain was still in place, complete with glass goblets with Coca Cola written on them in script. Nathan took great pride in showing us the countryside, almost as though all of it belonged to him.

I knew that Nathan had been working odd jobs with his brother for some time. I also knew that he had had a series of odd jobs since quitting his job at Rinterline. I was not quite sure what kinds of jobs they were, but I know some had been obtained through his brother, and others through his father in law. Since he seemed rather relaxed, yet in full control of the situation, quite literally in the driver's seat, I took the opportunity to ask him some rather pointed questions. He and his brother had been renovating houses. Some of the work had been obtained through a contracting company. He had also told me that he had done some other jobs "on his own," and I was extremely curious to know about the work in detail. He appeared to regard the work with a degree of flippancy, which aroused my interest all the more. On the one hand, he seemed proud of his control of his working life and of his partnerships working with his brother and father in law. On the other hand, he tried to convey the impression that he did not regard the work with any degree of seriousness. When I asked about how long the renovations would take, and whether the work was difficult, he told me "not very long; it's easy work." Yet, at least at this particular time, his "easy work" occupied the better parts of his days. I could not help but think that he was purposely down-playing his efforts because he was not declaring the income. Since he seemed already to have a chip on his shoulder, I figured I had nothing to lose in pursuing the issues a bit further. He had mentioned a job refinishing floors for a woman in the next town, a job he had obtained through his uncle. "How much can you make on that floor?" I asked him directly, to which he responded, "It's none of your business."

While Nathan's wife seemed to cringe at his apparent rudeness, I was impressed by the power of his convictions—the strength of his voice and his forthrightness. I even felt that it was the first time he was being completely honest with me by resisting my question. With the question about his income, I became to him the voice of urban authority—urban power, the power of standard English. Usually he kept his anger at that authority under a veil of politeness, albeit a politeness with an edge.

The unit of economic organization here is the three generation extended family, not the individual. People in the regionally based kin networks work in the agrarian marketplace and factory economies and they coordinate their activities through informal systems of exchange. Marketing is only one piece of the Kentucky way, but it is an important piece because it is both flexible and lucrative. Gardening is the most reliable livelihood strategy, but it is not sufficient in and of itself. Cash cropping and factory work are both risky, the former because of declining prices and federal subsidies for tobacco and the latter because of the constant lay-offs and the alienating nature of the work. Resistance to dependency upon capitalism, in a system that is indeed capitalistic, requires all the creative combinations of capitalist and pre-capitalist, formal and informal economies.

The essence of the Kentucky way is not a romantic notion; it is fundamentally practical—meticulously tailored to fit the local economy, ecology, and family structure. Preparedness is essential to the Kentucky way. It is positive and represents a great deal of foresight and planning. In order to be prepared, people marshall resources (including labor through kin networks) and knowledge to deal with a range of eventualities. In the face of plant closings, plummeting tobacco subsidies, a less and less adequate minimum wage, and the seasonal vagaries of agricultural cycles, the Kentucky way represents both continuity with past forms of rural economic organization and some creative solutions to what are becoming widespread economic conditions.

In sum, the Kentucky way is a system of local, practical knowledge that is essentially rural ("country"), and that defines "the way we do things here." The essence of the Kentucky way involves making ends meet in the self reliant, steadfast, Kentucky style. The Kentucky way involves continuities as well as transformations and reinterpretations of kin and community in relationship to livelihood. Probably the most remarkable aspect of the Kentucky way is that it operates, for the people in this study, outside of traditional community contexts. The Kentucky way involves an expansion of the range of kinship ties and an expansion of the tasks of kin network members. It also involves an expanded sense of what is local, for local refers to a region, not a community or even a county. It is clear that local does not include the city. People mobilize their ties to family members in the region as a form of outreach to people with diverse skills, knowledge and resources. One part of the family network quite literally "holds on to the land" (Hall and Stack 1982) while other parts engage in a diverse set of livelihood strategies. People always maintain the option of coming back to the land, either temporarily or permanently. The most important point to realize is that the goal of economic activity is to sustain the family network.

38

by Joe Szakos

Practical Lessons in Community Organizing in Appalachia: What We've Learned at Kentuckians for the Commonwealth

Organizing for change has always been difficult in Appalachia. One of the major obstacles to effective organizing is the fact that the Appalachian economy has long been dependent on coal and other single-industry employers. Absentee owners control much of the land and resources, and decisions about their use are made in board rooms far from the mountains. This situation contributes to the high unemployment that makes workers reluctant to speak out and challenge existing power structures for fear of losing their jobs.

In addition, a long history of local political corruption, along with wrong-headed federal economic development initiatives that favor the already powerful, have bred distrust of government. The strong influence of fundamentalist churches can also discourage participation in worldly matters, by offering instead the hope of justice in the hereafter.

Poor roads, long distances between rural communities, and a lack of public transportation make organizing across county lines difficult. High rates of illiteracy and a poor educational system leave many citizens unaware of their rights and their ability to organize for change.

A lack of good leadership training programs and experienced community organizers, along with meager financial resources and competition between citizens' groups for funding and turf, have rendered many organizations weak and ineffective.

Source: From the Chapter "Practical Lessons in Community Organizing in Appalachia: What We've Learned as Kentuckians for the Commonwealth" by Joe Szakos as it appears in Fighting Back in Appalachia: Traditions of Resistance and Change edited by Stephen L. Fisher. Reprinted by permission of Temple University Press.

Given these obstacles, it is a testament to the determination of the people in the region that the history of Appalachia is rich in stories of courageous and forceful citizen resistance. But it is not surprising that most of the community-based attempts at social change in the mountains have been piecemeal, temporary, and without long-term vision.

In recent years, a combination of factors has opened up opportunities for people in the mountains to participate in community affairs. For example, the construction of more and better roads and the advent of more accessible communication media, including local cable television programming and electronic mail, have made it possible for citizens to communicate with one another across community lines.

Open meeting laws and open records laws have made it easier for citizens to learn more about their government and prevent the kind of closed-door decisions that fed corruption in the past.

Churches and charitable foundations have become interested in funding groups working for change in Appalachia, and regional and national groups have become more willing to exchange information and training resources and to work together.

Taking advantage of these and other opportunities, several strong citizens' organizations have appeared in the region that have a solid foundation, work on a variety of issues, cover a wider geographic area, are membership-run, and have developed strategies for continued growth. This chapter examines some of the lessons learned in more than eleven years of community organizing by Kentuckians For The Commonwealth (KFTC), one of the most successful of these organizations.

What Is KFTC?

Started in mid-1981 by a small group of eastern Kentucky residents who joined together to address community problems that crossed county lines, KFTC has grown into a statewide organization of more than 2,350 members in 90 (of 120) Kentucky counties.

From KFTC's early days, people like Gladys Maynard, J.D. Miller, Mary Jane Adams, and Lorraine Slone, among others, had the vision to know that building an organization for the long haul was what would really make a difference in solving the problems they were confronting in their communities. KFTC's work is directed toward achieving broader state and regional changes while emphasizing local leadership development and fostering the ability of local groups to participate in community affairs on a variety of issues. KFTC defines itself as a "citizens social justice group" that uses direct-action community organizing to improve the quality of life for all Kentuckians. "Social justice" implies long-term, fundamental change and avoids the limited scope that a tag like "environmental group" carries. "Direct-action organizing" means that members work together as a group, democratically and nonviolently, to address the root causes of the injustices experienced in Kentucky.

Concerns about social justice have involved the organization in many issues, such as surface owners' rights, inequitable property taxation, toxic and solid wastes, waste reduction and recycling, water quality, legislative democracy, education, utility reform, and the lack of community services. Through such immediate issues, KFTC addresses *long-standing* problems of the use and ownership and control of land and natural resources and the control of our democratic institutions.

In more than eleven years of organizing, concerned citizens throughout the state have built a strong, democratically run organization that is active and effective.

- KFTC led an overwhelmingly successful statewide constitutional amendment campaign in 1988 that stopped strip mining without the permission of the landowner under "broad form" mineral deeds, a practice used by coal companies since the turn of the century to destroy people's homes and land.
- KFTC members pushed through the legislature a law that gives local gov-

ernments the right to decide whether hazardous waste incinerators can locate in their communities, putting an end to outside interests and insider deals that disregarded the wishes of area residents for a clean, safe, and healthy environment.

- KFTC filed a court case that led to a ruling by the Kentucky Supreme Court that exempting wealthy mineral owners from property taxation was unconstitutional; as a result, millions of dollars in new revenue are now pumped into local school systems and county governments in the coalfields.
- Hundreds of KFTC members have learned new skills and self-confidence in areas such as public speaking, letter writing, lobbying, organizational development, and strategies and tactics for holding government officials accountable.
- KFTC chapters have achieved a long list of local victories, such as stopping unwanted incinerators, preventing industrial water pollution, getting funds for community water systems, and improving county schools.

KFTC's Organizing Goals

Many years of retreats, evaluation sessions, and organizing-training workshops led the KFTC Steering Committee to express the long-term vision of the original KFTC members in terms of five goals. Although the goals may sound simple, few other groups in the region are as systematic about analyzing their work in such terms.

TO EMPOWER PEOPLE: KFTC wants its members to have an effective voice on matters of concern to them, and so the focus of the organization is not limited to acting on issues. KFTC strives to develop members' ability to be leaders in their own communities. Training sessions on the basic skills of community leadership (running meetings, public speaking, developing strategies and tactics, and fundraising, for example) and education on the economy and government are important elements of KFTC's work.

TO BUILD THE ORGANIZATION: KFTC was founded on the belief that individuals are important, but groups get things done. KFTC encourages and enables people to put aside differences in education, religious beliefs, and personal histories, and concentrate instead on specific issues that are common to a group. Time and attention are given to building local community groups as well as the statewide organization.

TO WIN ISSUES: People do not want to keep giving energy to an organization that does not show tangible results. Issues that KFTC tackles are chosen, addressed, and solved through direct actions carried out by, and on behalf of, the membership. Victories that affect the common welfare help build momentum for longer-term social change.

TO FOSTER DEMOCRATIC VALUES: This goal is based on the fundamental tenets that all people are created equal, everyone deserves respect and equal opportunities, and everyone has a right and the ability to share in participation, leadership, power, and wealth. Many groups—even the Ku Klux Klan—claims to have the first three goals, but it is this goal that separates KFTC from many other groups.

TO CHANGE UNJUST SOCIETAL INSTITUTIONS: Unjust institutions include political systems that are corrupt and primarily serve the interests of the powerful few, economic systems that place profits before people and allow widespread unemployment and poverty, and social systems that discriminate on the basis of race, gender, or class. Long-term solutions to major problems are a vital part of KFTC's organizational thinking.

Many groups have a tendency to focus only on winning the immediate issue or building the organization. Yet these aspects of organizing should be seen not as ends in themselves, but merely as vehicles to achieve the ends that are embodied in the other goals. Effective organizations must take the time to build, in clear and deliberate steps, toward achieving the other three goals. Most Appalachian groups have failed to do this. One of the key differences is that KFTC was willing to look to some national organizing networks for training and advice during its initial years of organizing. A great deal was gleaned from Grassroots Leadership, the Industrial Areas Foundation (IAF), the Midwest Academy, and the National Training and Information Center (NTIC), through training workshops, written materials, phone consultations, and site visits.

KFTC believes that all five goals of organizing are essential and must be built into successful organizing efforts at every step of the way. Balancing these goals is an ongoing process that effective organizations must continually evaluate and refine. The solid waste issue illustrates the way in which KFTC attempts to carry out this balancing process.

The solid waste issue arose from the direct experiences of citizens faced with an alarming increase in the amount of out-of-state waste being transported into Kentucky communities for disposal, a proliferation of proposals for new and expanded solid waste landfills and incinerators, an increase in control of Kentucky land by large corporations, a growing influence by waste companies in Kentucky politics, and a rise in the incidences of water, air, and soil contamination related to waste facilities.

KFTC members quickly realized that the "waste crisis" is a modern-day expression of many of the same systemic injustices they have struggled against for years—the destruction of the land and the environment that people depend upon for water, air, food, and jobs; corporate control of land and natural resources; out-of-state decision making adversely affecting local communities; and the exploitation of people and their communities for the sake of quick profits.

Once faced with the injustices of the waste problems, and aware of the links between issues, members held meetings in their own communities and on a state level as part of KFTC's Environmental Rights Committee. After soliciting and receiving input from local groups and KFTC chapters around the state, the committee developed a document entitled "The ABCs of Environmental Management in Kentucky," which KFTC members presented to the Kentucky Natural Resources and Environmental Protection Cabinet and released to the media as a means of stimulating discussion and encouraging solutions to environmental problems in the state. KFTC used several of the report's major points to develop a series of legislative proposals that were presented to the Kentucky Waste Management Task Force.

KFTC and the Kentucky Resources Council, while serving on the task force and the Kentucky Proposed Solid Waste Regulations Consensus Group, were the only groups that actively demanded affordable solid waste rates, especially for low-income people. On one measure dealing with solid waste billing, KFTC successfully opposed the waste industry's effort to attach delinquent garbage bills to utility bills, since this would have conflicted with KFTC efforts in Jefferson County against low-income utility disconnections. Recognizing that disposal facility costs will inevitably rise as efforts are made to safeguard the environment, KFTC began working to reduce the need for new and expensive landfill capacity by promoting waste reduction, reuse, recycling, and conservation of natural resources. In addition, KFTC strongly pushed for more local control—more democratic participation—in the planning and siting of solid waste facilities. Decision-making power has been shifted from the political wheeling and dealing in the state capital to the local courthouse, which is much more accessible. All of these positions on solid waste issues were developed by KFTC members.

KFTC's Organizational Structure

Kentuckians who support KFTC's goals become members of the organization by paying dues ($10 to $25 per year, based on ability to pay). To provide the greatest number of opportunities for participation and leadership,

KFTC's membership is organized into chapters. Chapters are established in every county where KFTC has 15 or more active members (and at least 30 after two years), and they agree to chapter accountability requirements. (See Appendix.) County chapters, rather than groups organized around identified constituencies or issue interests, make the most sense for rural Kentuckians, who typically have a strong identification with their counties. Chapters have the right to petition for the use of KFTC's resources—staff, legal, technical, and financial—and members can attend and offer input at Steering Committee meetings.

When the membership structure was established, the Steering Committee determined that membership should mean more than just paying annual dues. KFTC members have the opportunity to vote each year for the organization's officers, to set the annual platform of goals and priorities, and to select a Steering Committee representative if they live in a county with a chapter. Members are encouraged to use their newly acquired skills in a contagious way. Once they learn how to do something, it is their responsibility to share their skills and knowledge with others: members are student, teacher, mentor, and trainee interchangeably.

The annual platform-setting process is of particular importance. Each September, all county chapters meet to rank the issues that they feel KFTC should work on. Members in nonchapter counties are encouraged to provide similar input. The Steering Committee compiles these rankings into a proposed platform that is circulated among the membership in KFTC's monthly newspaper, *Balancing the Scales.* The final platform is adopted at the annual meeting each October.

The *platform* guides KFTC's work. On the basis of the platform and the activities of the local chapters, the Steering Committee sets priorities for staff time. For example, the platform priorities shape KFTC's decisions on whether and how to respond to requests from local communities and groups for assistance. To help ensure control of the organization's activities by the Steering Committee, these priorities are reviewed and voted on at each bi-monthly Steering Committee meeting.

KFTC does not work on any statewide issue unless the matter cannot be solved at the local level and unless a chapter (or chapters) requests formal statewide action to help deal with it. This policy, plus the platform and continual Steering Committee review, helps keep the organization in line with the needs and energies of its members and prevents a situation common in many other groups in which a few key leaders or staff people have too much influence on the direction of the organization.

As the task of directing the operations of a rapidly growing organization expanded, the Steering Committee established several subcommittees. Executive, Personnel, Finance, and Leadership Development committees share administrative and program responsibilities. An Environmental Rights Committee, a Land Reform Committee, and a Legislative Democracy Working Group have also been formed to broaden and guide work on these issues. Most committee members come from outside the Steering Committee so as to distribute decision-making duties among a larger number of members. Including ad hoc committees (for the annual membership meeting, the annual picnic, the Fall Fundraising Campaign, and special projects like the Tenth Anniversary Campaign), more than seventy people are involved in KFTC's statewide governance structure. Each chapter also has a membership coordinator, a fundraising coordinator, and a correspondent for *Balancing the Scales,* providing additional formal leadership roles.

KFTC believes in "multiple leadership," making sure that new people are constantly given leadership opportunities. Officers can serve only two years in a row, and chapter representatives have a three-year limit. No one person or small group can control the organization, which makes decisions more responsive to the membership. This also makes it harder for anyone to destroy a chapter or the organization because there is no single point of leadership to attack.

The structure and methods that KFTC uses in its governance are flexible enough for anyone to use in organizing, yet restrictive enough so that people cannot use them for their own personal gain.

Strengths of KFTC's Organizing

One of the early lessons that KFTC learned was that to get things changed in Appalachian Kentucky, it was more important to gain the support of people throughout Kentucky than it was to solicit help from people in other Appalachian states, an approach that many citizen organizations in Appalachia have pursued in the past. With major shifts in the early 1980s from the federal to the state level for such things as the delivery of human services, funding for education, and enforcement of environmental policies, KFTC leaders realized that they had to look to the governor and the state legislature for solutions to many of the problems facing eastern Kentucky, and that support and membership had to be organized in Kentucky's non-Appalachian counties to win victories at the state level. This also meant that KFTC had to figure out how to raise money for the long haul, to make sure it was seen as a permanent fixture in the political scene rather than a fly-by-night operation. In addition, strategic thinking had to take a long-term view, and serious thought had to be given to how to integrate all five of KFTC's goals into the organization's development. Issues of concern in other parts of the state and broader training sessions were crucial to this scenario. For example, the goals of the 1988 constitutional amendment campaign were (1) to pass the amendment limiting the abuses of broad form deeds, (2) to increase membership, (3) to have more people learn organizing skills, and (4) to educate the public about landowners' rights, thc coal industry, and the economic situation in Appalachia.

KFTC's ability to work on local and statewide issues at the same time is one of its strengths. Unlike organizations devoted to one issue, KFTC is able to work on any campaign in which a significant number of members are willing to participate. Whether it is to be resolved in the bureaucracy, the courts, the legislature, the executive branch, or at a local government meeting, KFTC is willing and able to travel many different routes to deal with an issue.

By using a multi-issue approach, KFTC members can work on each other's issues, giving them a way to learn from each other. For example, through their activities in KFTC, urban blacks working on utility rate reform and rural whites pushing for landowners' rights discovered they had a lot in common when the legislature killed all their bills behind closed doors. Making the legislative process more open and democratic and pushing for long-term institutional change became their common goal. At the same time, such alliances allow the possibility of dealing with racism on a personal level.

Being a multi-issue organization has also allowed KFTC to glean valuable lessons from each issue it has addressed. One of these is that direct-action organizing groups can sometimes get sidetracked into direct service, public awareness, or advocacy. There are so many problems in the world that people try to do too much at once and can forget to stay focused on the five goals of organizing. Another lesson was that direct-action organizing combined with victories did not necessarily produce institutional change. Getting a public water system solves a problem, but may do little to prevent further damage by strip mining. KFTC members also learned that during a slow period in a major campaign on one issue, a multi-issue group can shift its focus in order to maintain members' interest and morale. The multi-issue approach also helps members understand connections between issues. In addition, issues that require a long time to resolve provide more leadership development opportunities.

One reason KFTC is able to work on so many issues is that it trains its members in leadership and organizing skills. KFTC was the first community organization in Appalachia to systematically integrate leadership training into its work. Some organizing schools, networks, and groups in other parts of the country have used these techniques for years, but most groups in the mountains have had more of a "movement" mentality rather than a commitment to the nuts and bolts of building solid organizations.

The heart of KFTC's leadership development philosophy can be found in the preface of its *Leadership Development Training Manual*. Adopted by the KFTC Steering Committee in 1985, the preface outlines the ideal of citizen leadership within the organization:

> Everyone has the potential to lead, but most people are discouraged from taking leadership roles. Our social and economic systems prevent ordinary people from recognizing and developing their talents and skills for leadership by celebrating the rich, powerful, and well-educated as leaders. Too often society ignores the contributions of homemakers, retirees, laborers and others in making their communities better places to live. To break these barriers, KFTC's leadership training program is intended to draw out an individuals potential and encourage ongoing skill development by practice and direct application in real situations.

Training sessions consist of practice, role playing, discussion, and evaluations. KFTC's training sessions are not lectures; rather, they draw ideas from the group, with a deep respect for the talents and energies of the participants. Sometimes they are led by staff, sometimes by experienced members. Through this practical and methodical group training, KFTC members learn to lobby legislators, write letters to the editor, raise money, run meetings, talk to the press, and hold public forums. KFTC believes that training is most valuable when it is applied. The leadership training has been so effective that staff control, so common in some citizens' groups, would be difficult to wield in KFTC. At the annual membership meeting, for example, the staff may not speak during the business meeting and elections unless they are asked to respond to a specific question by a member.

Training opportunities, both formal and informal, are continually available to allow KFTC members to expand their skills and leadership potential. Leaders teach skills to new members, and organizers prepare members for events. But it is the group skills training that is the backbone of KFTC's leadership development. Using the training manual described above (which is shared with more than thirty groups throughout North America), workshop topics range from recruiting members to running effective meeting to developing strategies. The workshops, ranging from one hour to an all-day session, are conducted in a variety of settings. Most occur in local communities: in community meeting rooms, libraries, churches, a member's home or backyard.

KFTC also sponsors Kentucky Leadership Schools. Held several times a year, Leadership Schools offer an intensive leadership and organizing training opportunity and are open to members of other citizens groups as well. Three or four topics are covered in one day. In addition, leadership skills workshops are offered at the annual membership meeting and other gatherings, as well as at the chapter level. Gladys Maynard, KFTC's first chairperson, had participated in training by other organizations before she became involved with KFTC. Her comments about the experience reflect KFTC's positions on leadership: "Once I went through the trainings, I realized being a leader was something I'd really been doing all along. Most people are qualified [to be leaders] but it's never having the opportunity that frightens them."

Another reason for KFTC's success is that roles are clearly drawn: members, leaders, organizers, and technical experts.

- *Members* pay dues, identify issues, elect leaders, plan actions, and do the group's work. They support each other, attend meetings and events, and provide a power base.
- *Leaders* are members who develop new leaders, provide directions, motivate and inspire others, coordinate activities, and speak for the organization. They plan meetings and events, implement group decisions, hold members accountable, resolve conflicts, and

make emergency decisions when needed. Leaders are not just the elected officers. A successful group has many members with various leadership and organizational skills that may be needed and applied at any given time.

- *Organizers* facilitate training sessions and identify and help to develop leaders. This role is often misunderstood. Organizers do not tell members what to do. They agitate, prod, and push, creating "leadership opportunities" for members to learn new skills while being supportive and offering insights from the experiences of other groups. They produce publications and reports for the organization, but never speak publicly on behalf of the group. They are in the background and not the forefront, following through on the decisions that members and leaders make as a group.

- *Technical experts* provide advice, information, and credibility. Lawyers, geologists, and land surveyors work for the members to transfer skills to them, teaching them as much as possible so that they can become "experts" themselves. Technical experts help make complicated matters digestible, but they never make decisions for members and leaders. In its eleven-year history, KFTC has had on its staff a hydrologist, who was with the organization three years, a researcher, and first one, then two, part-time attorneys, in addition to technical experts hired for short periods as needed. KFTC's attorneys handle the organization's litigation, give it legal advice, and help draft legislation. The researcher devotes most of his time to working on reports about who mines Kentucky's coal and other issues related to the economy in Kentucky.

Other KFTC strengths include its publishing program. Its monthly newspaper (*Balancing the Scales)* and its other publications (including literacy materials and an annual study on the ownership and control of coal production in Kentucky) are known for their high quality. The newspaper format of *Balancing the Scales* makes it inexpensive to print and easy to distribute to a wide audience. It allows for a variety of coverage: local chapter updates, news of statewide campaigns, feature stories, member interviews, a monthly calendar of events, photographs, cartoons, profiles of mining and waste companies, and articles on broader economic issues and organizing skills.

The organization's members use creative tactics to accomplish their goals—another strength. Some of the best tactics are those that unite and involve many people, have direct impact on the target, have media appeal and high public visibility, and involve creativity, surprise, and, ideally, fun. A full-scale funeral was held in the state capitol building to let the public know that Kentucky was becoming a dumping ground for east coast garbage. When KFTC got tired of the secretary of the Kentucky Natural Resources and Environmental Protection Cabinet's failure to protect the state and its residents, members put up "Wanted" posters with his picture on them all over the state. Knowing that the waste industry was cutting backroom deals with some legislative leaders, KFTC leaders did a live political cartoon that portrayed legislators and industry lobbyists in bed together. The KFTC Toxics Committee staged a rally in front of the Division of Waste Management office in Frankfort, where they hung a clothesline with plastic skeletons and signs declaring this an exposure of the state's dirty laundry. KFTC's tactics have been an ongoing source of organization and personal nourishment. "The worst thing that [state officials] ever did was build roads so that we can get out of eastern Kentucky," said Ruth Colvin at the Frankfort rally described above. "Now we can get up here and raise a little hell."

Providing for the future meant being farsighted about where the money to run KFTC would come from. Besides grassroots fundraising, KFTC depends on donations from foundations, churches, and individuals. Since many of these give money for only a limited period of time, KFTC decided to establish an endowment fund to provide for times when the foundation fountain might slow to a trickle or go dry.

Another very important reason for setting up an endowment was the sense of organizational permanence it gave KFTC's members. "We plan to be around for a long time," said Mary Jane Adams, introducing the campaign. "We've just begun to fight the injustices faced by the people of Kentucky and with a successful [endowment] campaign, we're going to make sure KFTC is here as long as necessary." Endowment funds will also allow the organization to defend its victories in the future and will give KFTC options for additional expansion projects or special campaigns. As of June 1, 1992, the endowment had more than $850,000 in it.

Two final strengths involve leadership and attitudes. KFTC has emphasized placing women in leadership positions, and twelve of eighteen statewide officers to date have been women. And the organizational mentality holds that a group can always refine its goals, objectives, process, and methods. KFTC's willingness to use a cyclical process of planning, acting, and evaluating allows for healthy changes and improvements in the organization. Each year, new ideas and methods from other citizens' groups are incorporated into KFTC's system.

Weaknesses of KFTC's Organizing

Although KFTC has been successful, there are still weaknesses in its model, improvements to be made, and obstacles to be overcome.

The major strength of KFTC's structure is that it is member-run and democratic. But that can sometimes pose problems. The democratic process can be slow, inefficient, and costly. It simply takes longer to make decisions in a large membership-controlled organization than it does in more hierarchical groups. Sympathetic lobbyists, legislators, funders, reporters, and others sometimes have a hard time understanding that individual members and staff people cannot make major decisions independently, but must call a chapter or Steering Committee meeting to discuss and vote on new ideas, requests, or changes in strategy.

Another structural problem is that representation is not proportional: the person representing a chapter with 300 members has the same voting power as the person representing a chapter with 30 members. (Nevertheless, limiting counties to one chapter and one Steering Committee representative favors the rural counties and ensures that the Steering Committee will always be composed predominantly of rural representatives, which is a deliberate policy of the organization and keeps it focused on rural issues.) Also, the one at-large member on the Executive Committee is the only voice for the at-large membership, those who live in counties without KFTC chapters. There is no clear way for the at-large membership to communicate their views to the at-large Executive Committee member.

KFTC's membership has increased steadily over the years, but there is reason to be concerned over its composition. Initially, KFTC's targeted constituency was rural, low- and middle-income, longtime residents of the eastern Kentucky coalfields—those most directly affected by the problems KFTC set out to address—as well as anyone else willing to support KFTC actively. For the most part KFTC was successful in recruiting this constituency, but it failed to attract in any significant numbers people with very low incomes, racial minorities, people with low literacy skills, and youth. This has remained true as KFTC has grown into more of a statewide organization. Lower-middle-income people were joining, but the very poor generally were not. KFTC ran up against several obstacles in trying to involve low-income people. Besides a lack of money, transportation, and child care and health care services, some had no telephones, while others had no utility services at all. Low reading levels often compounded these problems and made meetings and mailings appear intimidating.

To address these obstacles, KFTC offered a sliding dues scale and full dues waivers on request, travel cost reimbursement for attending regional meetings, car-pooling, scholarships for workshops and conferences, and other types of financial assistance. The organization made a more conscientious effort to be sensitive to non- or low-level readers by using less written material in leadership training workshops. In 1987 KFTC launched a three-year project staffed by a volunteer through the Mennonite Central Committee U.S. Appalachia Program to develop materials about KFTC issues specifically for those who read at low levels. Despite these efforts, few low-income people got involved.

The barriers were not only logistical. KFTC's issues may have had less appeal to those with very low incomes, even though they would have benefited if some of those campaigns were won. Why worry about getting more tax money for local governments and school systems when your own household budget is insufficient to meet basic needs? Why be concerned about strip mining's destruction of the land and displacement of people from their homes if you do not own land or a home?

In its early years, few blacks were involved in KFTC activities. This was due, in part, to the lack of racial diversity in the eastern Kentucky coalfields. Once KFTC grew into a statewide organization with urban chapters, the lack of racial diversity became more obvious. Although KFTC had active chapters in Louisville and Lexington, Kentucky's largest cities with substantial minority populations, there was no influx of minority members. Some of the reasons for this included the fact that many of the members in the urban chapters were people who had previously lived or worked in eastern Kentucky, almost all of whom were white. Since much of KFTC's recruitment still took place by word of mouth, the white urban members tended to recruit those closest to them: relatives, friends, and neighbors who were also white. Moreover, why should minorities support an issue platform that they did not develop, or join an organization with few minority members or leaders?

KFTC's staff and leaders became increasingly aware that even though they had made a strong verbal commitment to increase the involvement of minorities and the poor in their organization, this would not happen without a conscious and deliberate strategy. Thus in March 1991 the KFTC Steering Committee voted to allot a designated amount of organizing time each week specifically to work on diversifying KFTC's constituency to include more racial minorities and low-income members. Soon afterward, KFTC hosted a workshop in Louisville on multiracial organizing and began exploring other ways KFTC could be more deliberate about targeting and recruiting a broad-based multiracial constituency. In addition, KFTC's Leadership Development Committee is now required to consider such characteristics as gender, race income-level, and age when developing nominations for statewide offices and committee positions.

Despite KFTC's sophisticated leadership development efforts, there is still room for improvement. One shortcoming is that leadership skills workshops focus mainly on nuts-and-bolts organizing skills, and there is seldom the opportunity to analyze and critique the political economy or to make the links between local and statewide issues, or between local and state issues and national and global structures and events. KFTC seeks to address this problem with workshops on "Power Analysis." While it provides a very basic and sometimes simplistic picture of who holds the power and why and how to change power relationships, it has proven effective in helping members to think more about root causes and systemic changes. Newer workshops include "Approaches to Change" and "What Would a More Desirable Society Look Like?"

One of the most pressing challenges KFTC faces is to create the time and space to systematically analyze what has happened in the past and to engage in deliberate long-range planning for the future. In its relatively short history, KFTC has achieved remarkable success at the local and state level. Many of KFTC's issue campaigns have been so ambitious and demanding that it has been difficult to step back from the intense action and take time for detailed analysis of its work. This analysis is currently being undertaken by a recently created Long Range Planning Committee and is critical to KFTC's immediate and long-term effectiveness.

In addition, KFTC must pay more attention to how much energy it should devote to maintaining its existing chapters, leaders, and members and how much it should give to developing new ones. Several of KFTC's existing chapters lack focus because they no longer have a burning issue—in most cases because they have won that campaign. Should KFTC spend energy and resources helping these chapters get involved in new organizing activities? Or should KFTC go where the energy is by investing its resources in new groups working on new issues? There is increasing concern that issues may play too great a role in determining KFTC's direction. KFTC needs to develop better ways of community-based organizing (developing relationships that include common interest and promote broad social change) instead of focusing so much on desired change on specific issues.

Finally, KFTC is under constant pressure to meet the needs of the membership with limited staff, financial, legal, and technical resources; the organization sometimes tries to do too much at once, becoming overextended and ineffective with limited organizing tools. For example, finding good staff people to keep up with the expansion needs of the organization is not easy, especially when they have to work in isolated areas. KFTC has joined with other groups to form the Southern Empowerment Project, which recruits and trains new organizers.

Conclusion

The essence of organizing is to shift power relations so that the interest of the many are respected. There are various types of power: political, economic, social, cultural, moral. There is also perceived power, actual power, and potential power. Power, in other words, is often difficult to evaluate and measure.

Economic power clearly has not been KFTC's trump card. Though the organization has done some impressive fundraising and its budget and endowment expanded considerably over the years, the organization's assets pale next to those of the corporations it has challenged and continues to confront.

People power is clearly KFTC's strength—the power of numbers. Yet KFTC's highest membership count during its first eleven years was 2,500, in a state with 3.7 million people. Similarly, the most county chapters KFTC ever had was 16, fewer than 15 percent of the state's 120 counties. KFTC's ability to mobilize people and hold mass public actions has been limited. Its biggest statewide event, a rally in Frankfort, drew fewer than 250 people. So exactly how powerful and influential is KFTC?

If sheer numbers and financial clout alone are used as a measure, KFTC appears relatively insignificant. But such criteria can be deceiving. Almost every KFTC member has wide circles of relationships—families, friends, co-workers, neighbors, fellow church members. Thousands of Kentuckians have benefited from KFTC's work: residents of the coal communities who are receiving millions of dollars in new revenue from the unmined minerals tax; people whose land has been saved from destructive strip mining; citizens who have been spared the horror of unnecessary hazardous waste facilities in their communities; or families who have had their ruined water supplies replaced. All of these are part of KFTC's potential power base.

The campaign for the broad form deed amendment tested the gap between KFTC's perceived and potential power. KFTC made connections with anyone and everyone to ask for active involvement and support. Active members contacted former members and nonmembers who had benefited from KFTC's activity or who had heard of the organization but never joined, creating a ripple effect. Just how far-reaching those circles were became obvious on Election Day when the votes were tallied. The coal industry outspent KFTC three to one and made heavy use of expensive electronic media, yet 868,634 Kentuckians voted to pass the amendment. It received 82.5 percent voter approval, one of the highest winning margins for an amendment in Kentucky's history, and passed in all 120 counties.

KFTC has increasingly earned itself a place as a respected player in Kentucky's local and state political arenas. But as Herb E. Smith, a native of Whitesburg, Kentucky, conveys below, KFTC's greatest impact has been on the powerless of eastern Kentucky. KFTC's broad form deed victory, its staying power, its multi-issue approach, and its focus on democratic empowerment have given the region's people hope and an opportunity to improve and enrich their own lives on their own terms:

> I think twenty years from now people are going to be talking about the broad form deed campaign. Previous to it there was this sense that coal was king. The king would have different squabbles with some of his subjects, but generally the subjects would end up falling in line. That's what the coal industry believed. If it came to spending, they had more money. It if came to court battles, they had more lawyers.
>
> No matter how unjust or wrong the broad form deed was, it wasn't obvious at all that we were going to win. . . . But once it happened and the returns were in, the whole playing field changed. It's not so scary any more. It's one of those times when all the makeup and paint gets washed away.
>
> I don't think there's any question that KFTC will be here in ten more years. . . . I think once it has worked so clearly for people to be an effective part of the democratic process that this country is founded on, I don't think you could ever go back on that.
>
> I think there are a number of things that will have to be dealt with for the long haul. But I guess the point for me is that it's not exactly what's on my list that's important, because what's in place now is an idea. . . . And whether that idea is applied to the kinds of things that it has been today or a whole different set of things, it's a powerful idea.
>
> It's the idea that people have the responsibility and the capacity to deal with the kinds of things that affect their lives. And through coordinated efforts we can actually make some changes in this state. It's really simple, in a way.
>
> I was taught in grade school that that was what this country was about. I was given those words. But what I was really told was, "Be quiet." What you were taught probably more than anything was the power of money. Families wanted to keep their jobs. Teachers wanted to keep their paychecks even if they weren't really teaching. The idea that people have the power and the responsibility—whether that's true or not, the point is in *acting,* taking action, putting those ideas into effect. That's the radical part, that we would actually believe it enough to try to cause it to happen. Once that is working, then I don't think any of the everyday things can stop it. You know, all of the other stuff is important day to day, but the idea is the power I trust.

39

by Maxine Waller, Helen M. Lewis, Clare McBrien, and Carroll L. Wessinger

"It Has to Come from the People": Responding to Plant Closings in Ivanhoe, Virginia

In September 1986 the people of Ivanhoe, Virginia, formed the Ivanhoe Civic League for one purpose: to stop Wythe and Carroll counties from selling an abandoned, overgrown industrial park. The park had been left to the local industrial development authorities twenty years earlier, when National Carbide, long the town's major employer, closed down its operation. The announcement that the property was for sale was the signal that local economic development officials were giving up all hope of locating another industry for the community.

In response, the residents of Ivanhoe began a citizens' campaign to revitalize the dying town. Their efforts made the national news, including an emotional fundraising event called "Hands Across Ivanhoe," in which 3,000 people paid $3 each to stand in the cold rain and hold hands in support of their community.[1] People who had grown up in Ivanhoe and moved away came home or sent money. The editor of *Appalachia,* the Appalachian Regional Commission's publication, wrote, "It gives us hope that something can be done to breathe life back into our home towns—rural America."[2]

Initially, the main strategy was to recruit a major new industry, to do what the industrial development authorities had been unable to do. As this is written, the people of Ivanhoe still do not have a new industry. Nevertheless, they have accomplished a great deal: they have waged a campaign to educate themselves about the economy, to develop their own community-centered development, to start a literacy and training center, to make officials accountable to them for the development of their community.

Ivanhoe is a small rural mountain community in southwestern Virginia. It straddles Wythe and Carroll counties, and is the poorest area in both. For a hundred years Ivanhoe was a booming center for mining iron, lead, zinc, and manganese. Two of the largest industries in southwestern Virginia were located here: National Carbide and New Jersey Zinc Company. In 1966, National Carbide

Source: From "It Has to Come From the People" by Waller, Lewis, McBrien & Wessinger as it appears in *Communities in Crisis: Appalachia and the South* edited by John Gaventa, Barbara Ellen Smith and Alex Washington. Reprinted by permission of Temple University Press.

closed, taking 450 jobs with it. In 1981, 350 more jobs were lost when New Jersey Zinc closed. Closings of furniture plants and sewing factories in surrounding counties have left the area economically devastated.

At its height, in the 1940s, Ivanhoe had around 4,500 residents, racially and ethnically mixed. It had a school, railroad, hotel, stores, theater, doctor, and restaurant. Now Ivanhoe has about 1,300 residents. The school, stores, theater, and railroad are all gone. Employment opportunities are very limited. Those who found work after the factories and mines closed commute an average of 63 miles—to jobs with lower pay and fewer benefits.

The first accomplishment of the Ivanhoe Civic League was blocking the sale of the industrial park. In 1986 the local industrial development authorities agreed to delay the sale for two years, to give the league itself time to recruit an industry to the park. This was the beginning of a vigorous campaign that included trips to Richmond to talk to the governor and legislators. The community recruited a small manufacturing industry to the old Carbide building, but the company was unable to raise sufficient capital to employ more than three people. County developers steered other potentially interested industries away from Ivanhoe to the newer growth areas located along the interstates.

Ivanhoe is located on the New River, one of the cleanest fresh-water rivers in the East. When the factories in Ivanhoe were operating, a railroad ran along the river valley, through the national forest. Now the state is developing the area along the old railroad bed into the New River Trail, a state park for hiking and biking. The industrial park is located at the head of the new trail.

During the first summer, League members and community volunteers cleaned up the land along the river by the industrial park. They named it Jubilee park, from the biblical theme of the Jubilee year. Like the people in Leviticus, they claimed it as sacred land to commemorate their repossession of it, and had a week-long Fourth of July festival in 1987 to celebrate their revived determination, to raise funds, and to mobilize the community.

After the Jubilee celebration, the Civic League began a campaign to secure the land for a permanent recreation park. As it became more and more obvious that recruiting an industry to their small rural community was unlikely, they began to plan Jubilee Park as an alternative, a community-owned enterprise. The park would have camping, bike and raft rental, and a convenience store, providing both jobs and recreation for the community, and recreation for tourists. League members hoped to use the income to finance further economic development. But they soon met resistance from the local authorities. The officials had given the community two years to find an industry for the industrial park land, but they refused to count Jubilee Park as "industry," holding to the traditional view that economic development is what happens when a factory comes into a community from the outside. Furthermore, they would not allow the Civic League to lease or buy the land.

After several frustrating encounters with the local governments and industrial development boards, the Civic League experienced a sense of powerlessness. But their discouragement led to a new determination: if anything was going to happen in Ivanhoe, it would be because the people made it happen.

In the league's small office in an abandoned building they had renovated, the group organized a six-week series of economic workshops for the community, where they read and discussed studies of rural economic development.[3] They carried out a community survey, which led them to change their major focus from "chasing smokestacks"—trying to bring a factory into town—to looking at smaller local development based on their own needs and resources. They also changed their goals from industrial recruitment to broader community development. They had already organized a senior citizens' program and a youth recreation program, but during the six weeks of the workshop they began literacy classes and GED training. Later, they renovated the old company store and named it "Ivanhoe Tech," a community-controlled education center. They now see themselves working to develop a new model of community development, one that is more self-sufficient and locally based. From an initial goal of getting *any* development, they are now creating their own.

Maxine Waller is the energetic and creative leader of the Civic League. Here she tells us what happened in Ivanhoe.

"I Wanted GM and I Wanted GE and I Wanted IBM"

I started out as an idealist. I believed in everything the American system said I should believe in. I was trying to be a true American—live my life, go to work and come home, go to the grocery store and pay the bills. When we lost the mines, we lost our jobs, I thought it was because we had done something wrong. Somehow we had made this gigantic mistake and made the company look bad or do bad or be bad because we had a union.

I have learned a lot, and one of the things I learned was that the company was in the black. They were making money but they could get more money by leaving us stranded without jobs, because our government gave them all these wonderful tax breaks and all these credits. So I found out that the American system is not made for the American people, in a sense. There's more poor people than rich people but rich people are in control. And one day you wake up like me, a thirty-eight-year-old woman, and you realize that you have done all those things you are supposed to: you paid your taxes; you sent your children to school. You just accept. Then one morning you realize it was the right way for the multi-rich people, for these rich people who live in these wonderful houses, that aren't hungry and aren't cold, but it's not the right way for you. Some people just go back and accept it again—but I am not going to accept it.

I am going to bring about some changes. I know I am still going to have to pay taxes and I am still going to have to deal with the government, but I am going to bring about changes in my own life, and I am going to be in control. I am going to teach my children there is a difference between being an American and being part of the so-called system, and that the Constitution does grant us rights. But we have got to bring about some changes. I am going to bring about changes with my children and my neighbors' children and anybody else that will listen to me.

First thing that I had to do was accept the fact that I couldn't change everything overnight. We didn't get in this situation overnight. Then I realized along the line that it was a world problem. The depression is a world problem, and there are people all over the country and all over the world bringing about these little changes just like we are. We are going to work here in our community, but as time goes on, it will spread out to other communities and other people will learn from it.

I was really blind. We wanted this wonderful factory and it had to have smoke coming out of it and it would employ the people. I just knew that was the answer for us, so I went out to get this factory. I kept trying to find a factory and there wasn't none to find. I kept knocking on doors and I called people and I worried the hell out of some people trying to figure some way to get a factory to come. I wanted this white knight waving an American flag to come down the street and have all these wonderful jobs. I wanted GM and I wanted GE and I wanted IBM to come in here and save us, but that didn't happen.

"With My Bible Under One Arm and My Dictionary Under the Other"

The first thing that happened was that we were treated as radicals, as bad children. Our governments in Wythe and Carroll counties kept throwing out all these big educated words that mean nothing and all these theories that mean nothing to nobody. That's not living and eating and sleeping and walking and thinking. That's not reality. They do that to throw the poor people off. They have this other language and they think you don't understand it. But hell, I've got a dictionary and that was my main thing. I carried it under my arm. My Bible is under one arm and my dictionary under the other. I figured what the Lord didn't straighten out for me, the dictionary would.

I was always looking up these big words. I would go to all these damn meetings, and they would throw out all these big words and I would get my dictionary to look them up and that would throw them off completely. I would say, "I didn't understand what you said and I'm going to look it up and see what it means." And I'd read the damned definition to them. When I got *Robert's Rules of Order* on how to run a meeting, that really just floored them all. I was standing up before 140 people, and the Senator was beside me and the delegate beside me and the head of economic development in southwest Virginia, and they are all sitting there in their little three-piece suits. I was reading this *Robert's Rules of Order* and then I just shut it and said, "According to *Robert's Rules of Order* I can do any damn thing I want to."

So that's the way it is, because this is a people movement and we are doing what suits us and not what suits Robert or anybody else. And that's when I really got a grasp on it. It didn't make a damn if we didn't do things just exactly right as long as we did things right for us, if it was right for the people. And that's what we have been doing all this time.

I went to Tennessee to the Highlander Center in January or February of 1987. I had applied for a SALT fellowship, which is Southern Appalachian Leadership Training Program. I was really upset because I wasn't trained with anything, I didn't know what I was doing, just haphazardly doing stuff. I felt like I needed some extra school but I didn't want to go over to the college because that is the kind the political system has and they used *Robert's Rules of Order* and they were going against everything we were trying to do. Nothing had to do with the people.

I went to the Highlander Center and they asked me why I was there. I said I wanted a factory to employ the people because the people were tired and cold and hungry and they wanted a job. And I wanted a factory and that was it. If someone could find me a factory, then I would be happy. I spent the weekend out there, talking and listening to other people. They were in the same boat as me. Part of them had a factory and didn't want it because it was the wrong kind of factory. I thought, "Oh, I just want any kind of factory," and they kept saying, "No, you don't, you don't want one that kills the people," and I thought, "Are there factories that kill people?"

I got to reading wonderful articles, and resource books, and then I read the Bible. All the time I read the Bible. I read *Unexpected News: Reading the Bible with Third World Eyes.* I didn't even know there *was* a Third World. I still haven't figured out who said there was a Third World and who decided that the United States was the first world. I read *Colonialism in Modern America: the Appalachian Case.*[4] I got to reading about all these things in Appalachia and I also got to traveling around in the Appalachian mountains, so I had some eye-opening experiences. I went to Kentucky and I saw strip mining. I went to Kentucky, and I saw these beautiful, beautiful mountains that God made being destroyed by man. Only God can make a mountain and man should leave it alone. There is no reclaiming a mountain after man has destroyed it.

I saw the video of *Global Assembly Line.* I was crying because I was so mad—they were shooting people in the Philippines, and all they wanted to do was work. You know, here in Ivanhoe all we wanted to do was work but everybody says we want to be on welfare. You can go over to Wytheville and over to the government offices and they say, "All those people over there want to do is be on welfare." But you know when we did the survey here, didn't nobody say they wanted to be on welfare and didn't nobody ask to be a millionaire. But the American system is set up so that people are on welfare.

I began to see it was a world problem more than just an Ivanhoe problem and more than an Appalachian problem. I went to Dungannon, Virginia, and I went to Trammell, Virginia, and I learned a really wonderful lesson about getting independent and dependent at the same time. I learned it is easy to get dependent on someone else. I decided that we would be diversified, and that we would keep control. When outsiders came in, we would keep control. We wouldn't just let anybody come in and take charge. I had seen that happen to a lot of little places in Appalachia. They were defeated—the same people who had helped them be independent made them dependent again. So we had to be independent and we had to be in control. The people of Ivanhoe—if it is good or if it is bad, if it is a failure or if it is a huge success—the people of Ivanhoe have to be in charge. We will do it together.

I had to realize that all people are not going to see the same way, and it is going to take a while for some people to see. There is not anybody that I haven't in some way tried to work with; they are part of the community even though they go around saying we are doing wrong. "We didn't get no factory." I don't know how many times I have heard "We didn't get no factory."

"It Has to Come from the People"

We made some comparisons between the kind of development we used to have under Carbide and New Jersey Zinc and the kind of development we wanted to have. And people started talking about all the awful parts of working for these industries and how they wanted a different kind of industry. That was a change for some people in that room. M. H., in particular, came forth and said, "If we have to have that same kind of industry I don't want it. I worked for it."

That was the turning point for education. That was when everyone said that we want to get the kind of industry *we* want, one that is good for us, and one that we can live with. We don't want the kind we have had. We were uneducated then, so we better get a better education. But we don't want the education they are teaching over at the college, because that teaches us to go along with what has been done. We want something different.

People started reading those articles on the "buffalo hunt" and others.[5] See, many years ago there really were buffalos and they skinned this buffalo and they used the skin, the horns, the eyes, the head, everything, and they ate it but they didn't kill more than they needed. Then men came along with get-rich schemes—power. They could make money by selling the skins so they went out and killed the buffalo and just got the skin and left all the meat, the carcasses out on the prairie, and then there weren't any more buffalo. In the 1940s and 1950s and 1960s they went up north and they went buffalo hunting there for industries and said, "If you will come down south, we will work for you for a little bit of nothing and we will make you rich people. You just come on down south. You will have a wonderful home with us."

So the industries moved down and they left all these vacant buildings up north and that was like the carcasses and meat of the buffalo. They brought the buffalo skins down here and put them up like little teepees, little factories everywhere, and everyone went to work but we didn't have a union so they didn't treat us right and we had to this slave labor for a little bit of pay. We became dependent. And the people up north were in the same boat so some of them came down south to try and keep working. Only thing was, when they came down south they worked for about half what they worked for up north. Then because we lured them down here they knew somebody else would lure them someplace else.

So you see we went buffalo hunting and the Northern people were crippled by what we did to them. We deindustrialized them, then we industrialized the South, and now the South is almost crippled by what has happened, so this is called an economic crisis.

I don't know the answer to the economic crisis but I know that it has to come from the people. It has got to come out of the hands of the so-called system and the so-called powerful people and come back to the people—the dinner buckets of America and the dinner buckets of Korea and the dinner buckets of the Philippines.

"Who Made the Decisions?"

Another eye-awakening time in my life was in May 1987 at Highlander. I had brought two people with me, and the people at Highlander asked us, "Who was in charge of Ivanhoe, the political system in charge of the bank? Who made the decisions about Ivanhoe?" And we got to writing out and talking and asking ourselves who owned the land, what politicians voted for us or voted against us, who had control, and the rest. And we found out that the powers of the two counties were the powers in the banks, all business people, insurance, the lawyers, doctors, all those people. The people in charge are also the people we depended most on, the people that hold the life line to us. We found out that there was no separation between them; there weren't two groups of people, they were the same people. That was an eye-opener for all of us—to find out that someone who had played a big political part in our lives was the landlord here.

That was one of the reasons I wanted the classes in economics because I couldn't understand the economy of Ivanhoe. I didn't understand that none of our money stays here, so why shouldn't we be poor? I found out if you have money and put it in a place and it stays in the community and turns over two or three times, that's what makes the community economically stable. We live here but we pay rent to people outside and it goes out of Ivanhoe—we never bring it into our town. That's the reason we are economically depressed.

I don't think it is going to be a fast process to bring things around, but I am really convinced that we will do it. It is going to be a lifetime and more than my life. I think this is something that will pass on to my children and their children because this is happening all over the country. You wake up one day and these industries have gone and left these communities and there is nothing there to support them.

I've had a lot of problems being a woman, first by not being taken seriously. "Pat her on the back and she will go home." And "Hush." But I didn't—I didn't go home and I didn't hush. They patted me on the back and called me "honey" and "darling," and I resent those words, because I'm not anybody's honey and I'm not anybody's darling. I'm a person and they way they were treating me was, "Go home and make little brownies for the PTA meeting. We'll take care of this, honey, we know what we are doing." Being a woman has opened a lot of doors, but in the community it has created some resentment from mountain men, especially the older men who believe that a woman should be seen and not heard. She should go to church and she should be at home and cook the meals. My husband doesn't feel that way—I am really blessed with that. So far I have been able to turn everything around and present things in a way that people could see that it was right. They couldn't say it is because she is a woman that this happened or that happened, because it wasn't that.

"So Who Is Educated?"

Ivanhoe is what I am working for. It is hard for me to even begin to think that I could ever sit here and think like I think now, but it's because of this education process I have been through. I have some strikes against me because I am a woman and because of not being educated, not educated in the system. I don't have little papers to go with my education, but I've got an education all right. I've got a wonderful education because I read and I research and I do all these things but they are not things I can write on a piece of paper and add "XYZ" behind my name.

When I started out I thought like them: economic development was a factory. And what has happened? I have left them behind. I didn't realize that until right now, but I am superior in my thinking, and these people are in charge of economic development. I realize that you can't go out and get these little factories no more. And these are educated people in charge of economic development and they are still looking for factories, and I realize you can't get them. So who is educated?

I used to feel so inferior to these people; they had their little suits and they go to the club for lunch, but now I don't feel inferior to them. I feel superior to them. Theirs is an educated ignorance. They are educated to the point that they are ignorant. I can't feel equal to them. I can't be equal to them because I have an open mind. People in Ivanhoe are receptive to new ideas, new thoughts. But these people are not. Is it because they are not cold and hungry? Is it because they have plenty to eat and plenty of money? Is it because we don't have those things, is that why we are grasping and doing so much and being so receptive to everything and they are not? Because they are comfortable and we are uncomfortable?

They don't have to listen to us because they are not dependent on us and we are dependent on them—or they *thought* we were. But somewhere along the line, someday they are going to wake up and they are going to find out that this bunch of people here, this core bunch of people in Ivanhoe, are going to be *independent*. They keep thinking we are going to die and we are going to quit and they are going to break us apart. They have done everything to throw us off.

We questioned who the kings of the world were. How did you get so much power? Who decides? Who made these decisions and why? Did you make these decisions because it was good for us, the taxpayers, or did you make these decisions because it was good for you? And how much taxes do you pay? And who buys lunch at the club? We asked them a lot of stuff. So we have kind of shook their castle—cracked the base of it.

The political powers would like to see our group separated, because we banded together and we have stayed together for so long and have been such a strong force. If part of us stand on one side and part on the other, that's exactly what they want. And that has happened all over the world.

In August 1987 I talked with the assistant county administrator, and he said—as long as I live I will remember these words—"Maxine, what's wrong with you is you have never learned to work within the system." And I said right back to him. "If the system, the so-called system, is set up to make people cold and make people hungry and uneducated and to die in poverty, then God help the damn system. Because the system is wrong. There needs to be a new system because this one is not working."

We don't have many successful models to follow. We are brand-new at it. We are giving birth to a new way of life for the Appalachian people. I feel like we are nurturing a baby and we are going to have to be stronger than most people. I think we are progressive. We are dealing with something entirely different from what has been done before. We have been so creative. I think this is the right place to be and the right time, and I think we will be a role model in economic development. We have gone out of the system and started thinking in terms of reality. We have a stronger momentum, a stronger movement right now. The time is right.

Appendices

X

References

1. Appalachia

Appalachian Land Ownership Task Force. *Who Owns Appalachia?* Land Ownership and Its Impact. Lexington: University Press of Kentucky, 1983.

Batteau, A. W. *The Invention of Appalachia.* Tucson: University of Arizona Press, 1990, pp. 144–167.

Blair, L. Prophets without honor: A case study of two Appalachian artists. *Diversity in Appalachia: Images and Realities; Journal of the Appalachian Studies Association* 5:117–123, 1993.

Cable, S. From fussin' to organizing: Individual and collective resistance at Yellow Creek. In: Fisher, S.L., ed. *Fighting Back in Appalachia: Traditions of Resistance and Change.* Philadelphia: Temple University Press, 1993, pp. 69–84.

Campbell, J.C. *The Southern Highlander and His Homeland.* New York: Russell Sage Foundation, 1921.

Campbell, R. Modern Appalachians and "those people": The perceived validity of hillbilly stereotypes among a diverse population. Paper presented at the Appalachian Studies Conference, Johnson City, Tennessee, March 19–21, 1993.

Caudill, H. *Night Comes to the Cumberlands: A Biography of a Depressed Area.* Boston: Little, Brown and Company, 1962.

Crawford, J.R. Archetypical stereotypes: The Appalachian hillbilly and the wider world. Paper presented at the Appalachian Studies Conference, Johnson City, Tennessee. March 19–21, 1993.

Cunningham, R. *Apples on the Flood: The Southern Mountain Experience.* Knoxville: University of Tennessee Press, 1987.

Du Bois, W.E.B. *Black Reconstruction: An Essay Toward a History of the Part Which Black Folk Played in the Attempt to Reconstruct Democracy in America, 1860–1880.* New York: S.A. Russell, 1935.

Eller, R.D. *Miners, Millhands, and Mountaineers: Industrialization of the Appalachian South, 1880–1930.* Knoxville: University of Tennessee Press, 1982.

Ford, T.R. *The Southern Appalachian Region: A Survey.* Lexington: University of Kentucky Press, 1962, pp. 1–9.

Foster, S.W. Politics, expressive form, and historical knowledge in a Blue Ridge resistance movement. In: Fisher, S.L., ed. *Fighting Back in Appalachia: Traditions of Resistance and Change.* Philadelphia: Temple University Press, 1993, pp. 303–316.

Galbraith, J.K. *The Affluent Society.* Boston: New American Library, 1958, pp. 324–325.

Galbraith, J.K. *The Culture of Contentment.* Boston: Houghton Mifflin Company, 1992, pp. 13–29.

Gaventa, J. *Power and Powerlessness: Quiescence and Rebellion in an Appalachian Valley.* Urbana: University of Illinois Press, 1980.

Grigsby, J.L. A Caucasian Appalachian "hillbilly" becomes a professor in a historically black university: A personal account of working-class conflict in academe. Paper presented at the Appalachian Studies Conference, Johnson City, Tennessee, March 19–21, 1993.

Kephart, H. *Our Southern Highlanders: A Narrative of Adventure in the Southern Appalachians and a Study of Life Among the Mountaineers.* New York: Macmillan Publishing Company, 1913.

Lewis, H.M.; Johnson, L.; and Askins, D., ed. *Colonialism in Modern America: The Appalachian Case.* Boone, North Carolina: Appalachian Consortium Press, 1978.

Raitz, K.B., and Ulack, R., with Leinbach, T.R. *Appalachia—A Regional Geography: Land, People, and Development.* Boulder, Colorado: Westview Press, 1984, pp. 9–35.

Shapiro, H.D. *Appalachia on Our Mind: The Southern Mountains and Mountaineers in the American Consciousness, 1870–1920.* Chapel Hill: University of North Carolina Press, 1978.

Speer, J.H. From stereotype to regional hype: Strategies for changing media portrayals of Appalachia. In: *Diversity in Appalachia: Images and Realities; Journal of the Appalachian Studies Association* 5:12–19, 1993.

Tribe, D.L. Contemporary images of Appalachian Ohio: The view from within. In: *Diversity in Appalachia: Images and Realities; Journal of the Appalachian Studies Association* 5:26–33, 1993.

Waller, A. L. *Feud: Hatfields, McCoys, and Social Change in Appalachia, 1860–1900.* Chapel Hill: University of North Carolina Press, 1988.

Weller, J. *Yesterday's People.* Lexington: University Press of Kentucky, 1965.

Whisnant, D.E. *All That Is Native and Fine: The Politics of Culture in an American Region.* Chapel Hill: University of North Carolina Press, 1983.

Wigginton, E., ed. *The Foxfire Book.* Garden City, New Jersey: Doubleday, 1972.

2. The Sociology of Southern Appalachia

1. George E. Vincent, "A Retarded Frontier," *The American Journal of Sociology,* 4 (July 1898), 20.

2. Shapiro, *Appalachia on Our Minds* (Chapel Hill: Univ. of North Carolina Press, 1978); the book is a revision of his dissertation, "A Strange Land and Peculiar People: The Discovery of Appalachia, 1870–1920" (Rutgers, 1966). Shapiro's thesis is summarized in his "Introduction" to the reprinted edition of John C. Campbell, *The Southern Highlander and His Homeland* (New York: Russell Sage Foundation, 1921; rpt. Lexington: Univ. Press of Kentucky, 1969).

3. Blumer, "Social Problems as Collective Behavior," *Social Problems,* 18 (Winter 1971), 299.

4. See USDA Miscellaneous Publication No. 205 (1935); Frederick G. Tryon and Bushrod W. Allin, "The Southern Appalachian Coal Plateaus," Ch. 2 in Carter Goodrich, et al., *Migration and Economic Opportunity* (Philadelphia: Univ. of Pennsylvania Press, 1936), pp. 54–123; *The Southern Appalachian Region: A Survey,* ed. Thomas R. Ford (Lexington: Univ. of Kentucky Press, 1962).

5. John Fiske, *Old Virginia and Her Neighbours* (Boston: Houghton, Mifflin, 1897), II, 177–89; Arthur Estabrook, "Presidential Address: Blood Seeks Environment," *Eugenical News,* 11 (August 1926), 106–14; Nathaniel D. Hirsch, "An Experimental Study of the East Kentucky Mountaineers," *Genetic Psychology Monographs* 3 (March 1928), 183–244; Harry M. Caudill, *A Darkness at Dawn: Appalachian Kentucky and the Future* (Lexington: Univ. Press of Kentucky, 1976), Ch. 1.

6. William Goodell Frost, "Our Contemporary Ancestors in the Southern Mountains," *Atlantic Monthly,* 83 (March 1899), 311–19; Ellen Churchill Semple, "The Anglo-Saxons of the Kentucky Mountains: A Study in Anthropogeography," *The Geographical Journal,* 17 (June 1901), 588–623, rpt. *Bulletin of the American Geographical Society,* 42 (August 1910), 561–94.

7. Campbell, *Southern Highlander,* Chs. 3 and 4, Appendix B.

8. Oscar Lewis, *The Children of Sanchez* (New York: Random House, 1961), pp. xxiv–xxvii; Jack E. Weller, *Yesterday's People: Life in Contemporary Appalachia* (Lexington: Univ. of Kentucky Press, 1965); and Herbert J. Gans, *The Urban Villagers: Group and Class in the Life of Italian-Americans* (New York: Free Press, 1962).

9. David H. Looff, *Appalachia's Children: The Challenge of Mental Health* (Lexington: Univ. Press of Kentucky, 1971); Norman A. Polansky, Robert D. Borgman, and Christine DeSaix, *Roots of Futility* (San Francisco: Jossey-Bass, 1972); Richard A. Ball, "New Premises for Planning in Appalachia," *Journal of Sociology and Social Welfare,* 2 (Fall 1974), 92–101; and "The Southern Appalachian Folk Subculture as a Tension-Reducing Way of Life," in *Change in Rural Appalachia,* ed. John D. Photiadis and Harry K. Schwarzweller (Philadelphia: Univ. of Pennsylvania Press, 1970), pp. 69–79.

10. For example, Jack L. Roach and Orville R. Gursslin, "An Evaluation of the Concept 'Culture of Poverty,'" *Social Forces,* 45 (March 1967), 383–92; Charles A. Valentine, *Culture and Poverty: Critique and Counter-Proposals* (Chicago: Univ. of Chicago Press, 1968); the comments on Valentine in *Current Anthropology,* 10 (April–June 1969), 181–201; and the essays in *The Culture of Poverty: A Critique,* ed. Eleanor Burke Leacock (New York: Simon and Schuster, 1971); see Stephen L. Fisher, "Folk

Culture or Folk Tale: Prevailing Assumptions about the Appalachian Personality," in *An Appalachian Symposium: Essays Written in Honor of Cratis D. Williams* (Boone: Appalachian State Univ. Press, 1977), a revised and somewhat shortened version of "Victim-Blaming in Appalachia: Cultural Theories and the Southern Mountaineer," in *Appalachia: Social Context Past and Present,* ed. Bruce Ergood and Bruce E. Kuhre (Dubuque: Kendall/Hunt, 1976), pp. 139–148.

11. Dwight Billings, "Culture and Poverty in Appalachia: A Theoretical Discussion and Empirical Analysis," *Social Forces* 53 (December 1974), 315–23; and Thomas R. Ford, "The Passing of Provincialism," Ch. 2 in *The Southern Appalachian Region.*

12. Loyal Jones, "Appalachian Values," in *Voices from the Hills,* ed. Robert J. Higgs and Ambrose N. Manning (New York: Ungar, 1975), pp. 507–17; Mike Maloney and Ben Huelsman, "Humanism, Scientism, and Southern Mountaineers," *Peoples' Appalachia,* 2 (July 1972), 24–7.

13. See Robert Coles, *Migrants, Sharecroppers, Mountaineers,* especially Chs. 5, 6, 9, and 12, and *The South Goes North,* Ch. 6 (Boston: Little, Brown, 1971); John Fetterman, *Stinking Creek* (New York: Dutton, 1967); Anthony Dunbar, *Our Land Too* (New York: Random House, 1969), Part II; Kathy Kahn, *Hillbilly Women* (Garden City: Doubleday, 1973); and John B. Stephenson, *Shiloh: A Mountain Community* (Lexington: Univ. Press of Kentucky, 1968). The methodological basis of the humanistic approach is sketched in John R. Staude, *"The Theoretical Foundations of Humanistic Sociology," in Humanistic Society: Today's Challenge to Sociology,* ed. John F. Glass and John R. Staude (Pacific Palisades: Goodyear, 1972), pp. 262–70.

14. John Friedmann, "Poor Regions and Poor Nations: Perspectives on the Problem of Appalachia," *Southern Economic Journal,* 32 (April 1966), pp. 465–7.

15. On regional development theory, see Harvey S. Perloff et al., *Regions, Resources, and Economic Growth* (Lincoln: Univ. of Nebraska Press, 1960); E. A. J. Johnson, *The Organization of Space in Developing Countries* (Cambridge: Harvard Univ. Press, 1970); Harry W. Richardson, *Regional Growth Theory* (New York: Wiley, 1973); and *Backward Areas in Advanced Countries,* ed. E. A. G. Robinson (New York: St. Martin's, 1969).

16. Niles M. Hansen's works include *Rural Poverty and the Urban Crisis* (Bloomington: Indiana Univ. Press, 1970); *Intermediate-Size Cities as Growth Centers* (New York: Praeger, 1971); and an edited volume, *Growth Centers in Regional Economic Development* (New York: Free Press, 1972). On the ARC, see Donald Rothblatt, *Regional Planning: The Appalachian Experience* (Lexington, Mass.: Heath, 1971); and Monroe Newman, *The Political Economy of Appalachia* (Lexington, Mass.: Lexington Books, 1972).

17. Plunkett and Bowman, *Elites and Change* (Lexington: Univ. Press of Kentucky, 1973). Two good critical reviews of this work are by Billings in the *American Journal of Sociology,* 79 (May 1974), 1572–4; and Helen M. Lewis in *Social Forces,* 53 (September 1974), 139–40. The notion of a "cultural bridge," is borrowed from Harry K. Schwarzweller and James E. Brown, "Education as a Cultural Bridge between Eastern Kentucky and the Great Society," *Rural Sociology,* 27 (December 1962), 357–73, rpt. in *Change in Rural Appalachia,* ed. Photiadis and Schwarzweller, pp. 129–45.

18. The idea of "non decisions" is developed in Peter Bachrach and Morton S. Baratz, *Power and Poverty: Theory and Practice* (New York: Oxford Univ. Press, 1970), Ch. 3, pp. 39–51. See also Matthew Crenson, *The Un-Politics of Air Pollution: A Study of Non-Decisionmaking in the Cities* (Baltimore: Johns Hopkins Press, 1971); and Roger W. Cobb and Charles D. Elder, *Participation in American Politics: The Dynamics of Agenda-Building* (Boston: Allyn and Bacon, 1972).

19. Caudill, *Night Comes to the Cumberlands* (Boston: Little, Brown, 1963), p. 325; "Misdeal in Appalachia," *The Atlantic Monthly,* June 1965, p. 44 and his "Appalachia: The Dismal Land," *Dissent,* 14 November–December 1967), 718–19. See also the entire fourth issue of *People's Appalachia* (August–September 1970), organized around the theme "The Developers: Partners in Colonization."

20. Robert Blauner, "Internal Colonialism and Ghetto Revolt," *Social Problems,* 16 (Spring 1969), 393; revised and reprinted as Ch. 3 in Blauner, *Radical Oppression in American* (New York: Harper and Row, 1972). The Appalachian analogy is first developed in Helen M. Lewis and Edward E. Knipe, "The Colonialism Model: The Appalachian Case," an unpublished paper, revised draft, October 1970 (forthcoming in *The Colony of Appalachia: Selected Readings,* ed. Lewis et al., from The Appalachian Consortium Press); and an expanded version by Lewis, "Fatalism or the Coal Industry? Contrasting Views of Appalachian Problems," *Mountain Life & Work,* 46 (December 1970), 4–15; rpt. in *Appalachia: Its People, Heritage, and Problems,* ed. Frank S. Riddel (Dubuque, Iowa: Kendall/Hunt, 1974), pp. 221–38, and rpt. in *Appa-*

lachia: Social Context Past and Present, ed. Ergood and Kuhre, pp. 153–62. The application is further developed in Helen Lewis, Sue Kobak, and Linda Johnson, "Family, Religion and Colonialism in Central Appalachia; Or: Bury My Rifle at Big Stone Gap," in *Growin' Up Country,* ed. Jim Axelrod (Clintwood, Va.: Council of the Southern Mountains, 1973), pp. 131–56.

21. See, for example, Pablo González-Casanova, "Internal Colonialism and National Development," in *Studies in Comparative International Development,* 1 (1965), 27–37, rpt. in *Latin American Radicalism,* ed. Irving Louis Horowitz et al. (New York: Random House, 1969), especially pp. 130–2; and Pierre van den Berghe, "Education, Class and Ethnicity in Southern Peru; Revolutionary Colonialism," in *Education and Colonialism: Comparative Perspectives,* ed. Philip G. Altback and Gail P. Kelly (New York: McKay, forthcoming).

22. The critique of the internal colonialism model applied to Appalachia is developed at greater length by Walls in "Central Appalachia: A Peripheral Region within an Advanced Capitalist Society," *Journal of Sociology and Social Welfare,* 4 (November 1976), 232–47; "Internal Colony or Internal Periphery?" forthcoming in *The Colony of Appalachia,* ed H. Lewis, et al.; and the paper "Three Models in Search of Appalachian Development: Critique and Synthesis," August 1974, revised May 1976, ERIC no. ED125806.

23. See particularly his Frankfurt inaugural address of June 1965, published as "Knowledge and Human Interests: A General Perspective," in the appendix of Jügen Habermas, *Knowledge and Human Interests,* trans. Jeremy J. Shapiro (Boston: Beacon Press, 1971), pp. 301–17, quoted phrase from p. 311; and the brief explication of Habermas in the epilogue to Joachim Israel, *Alienation: From Marx to Modern Sociology* (1968: Boston: Allyn and Bacon, 1971), pp. 343–7. See also Habermas' essay "Technology and Science as 'Ideology,'" in *Toward a Rational Society* (Boston: Beacon, 1970), pp. 81–122.

24. Habermas, *Legitimation Crisis,* trans. Thomas McCarthy (1973; Boston: Beacon, 1975), pp. 33–41; see also John Kenneth Galbraith, *Economics and the Public Purpose* (1973; New York: Signet, 1975), pp. 38–50; and James O'Connor, *The Fiscal Crisis of the State* (New York: St. Martin's, 1973), especially Ch. 1, "An Anatomy of American State Capitalism," pp. 13–39; and Ralph Miliband, *The State in Capitalist Society: The Analysis of the Western System of Power* (New York: Basic Books, 1969).

25. See Immanuel Wallerstein, "Dependence in an Interdependent World: The Limited Possibilities of Transformation within the Capitalist World Economy," *African Studies Review,* 17 (April 1974) 1–26; and his "Class Formation in the Capitalist World-Economy," *Politics and Society,* 6 (1975), 367–75.

26. To the contrary, careful observers have described this traditional culture as a driving force in the lives of mountain people. Reporting "an urge toward self-improvement" and "a great desire to amount to something" among Beech Creekers, Harry K. Schwarzweller, James S. Brown, and J. J. Mangalam observe that "the omnipresent dissatisfaction of Beech Creek people with their present lot, their inability to be satisfied with the present situation, in a word, their emphasis upon 'becoming' rather than upon 'being,' was a manifestation of their puritan philosophy." See *Mountain Families in Transition: A Case Study of Appalachian Migration* (University Park: Pennsylvania State Univ. Press, 1971), p. 63.

27. See Ingolf Vogeler, "The Peasant Culture of Appalachia and Its Survival," *Antipode: A Radical Journal of Geography,* 5 (March 1973), 17–24; and Edward E. Knipe and Helen M. Lewis, "The Impact of Coal Mining on the Traditional Mountain Subculture," in *The Not So Solid South: Anthropological Studies in a Regional Subculture,* ed. J. Kenneth Moreland, Southern Anthropological Society Proceedings, No. 4 (Athens: Univ. of Georgia Press, 1971), pp. 25–37. The concept of peasant is limited to a particular historic type in George M. Foster, "Introduction: What is a Peasant," in *Peasant Society: A Reader,* ed. Jack M. Potter, May N. Diaz, and George M. Foster (Boston: Little, Brown, 1967), p. 7.

28. The only study of a similar (though non-Appalachian, technically speaking) community which purports to have discovered *no* social stratification is Elmora Messer Matthews, *Neighbor and Kin: Life in a Tennessee Ridge Community* (Nashville: Vanderbilt Univ. Press, 1965). She probably didn't ask the right question; compare her "Questionnaire," pp. 153–8, with Stephenson's approach in *Shiloh,* pp. 49–51.

29. *Mountain Families in Transition,* pp. 48–58, 165–74.

30. Floyd Hunter, *Community Power Structure* (Chapel Hill: Univ. of North Carolina Press, 1953); Willis D. Hawley and James H. Svara, *The Study of Community Power: A Bibliographic Review* (Santa Barbara: ABC-Clio, 1972).

31. Richard A. Ball, "Social Change and Power Structure: An Appalachian Case," in *Change in Rural Appalachia,* ed. Photiadis and Schwarzweller, pp. 147–66; Rod Harless, *The West Virginia Establishment* (Huntington: Appalachian Movement Press, 1971).

32. For example, see Susanne Bodenheimer, "Dependency and Imperialism: The Roots of Latin American Underdevelopment," *Politics and Society,* 1 (May 1971), 327–57.

33. Caudill, *Night Comes to the Cumberlands;* Richard A. Couto, *Poverty, Politics and Health Care* (New York: Praeger, 1975); Huey Perry, *"They'll Cut Off Your Project"* (New York: Praeger, 1972).

34. Richard A. Diehl, "Appalachia's Energy Elite: A Wing of Imperialism?" *Peoples' Appalachia,* 1 (March 1970), 2–3.

35. See Joseph F. Donnermeyer, Peter F. Korsching, and Rabel Burdge, "An Interpretative Analysis of Family and Individual Economic Costs Due to Water Resource Development," *Water Resources Bulletin,* 10 (February 1974), 91–100; F. Carlene Bryant, *The Social Impact of Surface Mining in a Rural Appalachian Community,* ARP Publication No. 46 (June 1976); Robert B. Cameron, *An Estimation of the Tangible Costs of Black Lung Disease,* ARP Publication No. 47 (June 1976); Si Kahn, *The Forest Service and Appalachia* (Mineral Bluff, Ga.: Cut Cane Associates, 1974).

36. Johnson and Burdge, "Sociologists and Environmental Impact Statements: What Are We Doing Here?" (August 1975), available from Sue Johnson at the Center for Development Change, Univ. of Kentucky; Kai T. Erikson, *Everything in Its Path: Destruction of Community in the Buffalo Creek Flood* (New York: Simon and Schuster, 1976).

37. Gaventa, "In Appalachia: Property is Theft," *Southern Exposure,* 1 (Summer/Fall 1973), 42–51; and his *Power and Powerlessness: Quiescence and Rebellion in an Appalachian Valley* (Oxford: Oxford Univ. Press, forthcoming).

38. Whisnant, *Missionaries, Planners and Developers in Appalachia* (forthcoming); Caudill, *The Watches of the Night* (Boston: Little, Brown, 1976).

39. U.S. Census, *General Population Characteristics, 1970;* State Volumes, Table 34: Race by Sex for Counties. The statistical reports on black Appalachians done by NAACP Legal Defense Fund (1971) and the National Urban League (1972) relied on advance census data which contained numerous minor errors in the figures for the black population in eight of 13 Appalachian states; the figures were corrected only in the final census reports. Figures on minority groups remain one of the least reliable areas within the census.

40. Darold T. Barnum, *The Negro in the Bituminous Coal Mining Industry* (Philadelphia: Univ. of Pennsylvania Press, 1970); Paul Nyden, *Black Coal Miners in the United States* (New York: American Institute for Marxist Studies, 1974).

41. John Gulick, *Cherokees at the Crossroads* (Chapel Hill: Institute for Research in Social Science, Univ. of North Carolina, 1960), reissued in 1973 with an epilogue by Sharlotte Neely Williams; *Appalachian Journal,* 2 (Summer 1975).

42. A popular discussion of mixed-race groups is Brewton Berry, *Almost White* (New York: Macmillan, 1963). For a mixture of fact and fiction, see Bonnie Ball, *The Melungeons: Their Origin and Kin,* 4th ed. (privately printed, 1972); for the facts, see Edward T. Price, "The Melungeons: A Mixed-Blood Strain of the Southern Appalachians," *The Geographical Review,* 41 (April 1951), 256–71. An ongoing study is announced in Avery Gaskins' "An Introduction to the Guineas: West Virginia's Melungeons," *Appalachian Journal,* 1 (Autumn 1973), 234–7.

43. Calvin L. Beale, "American Triracial Isolates: Their Status and Pertinence to Genetic Research," *Eugenics Quarterly,* 4 (December 1957), 187–96; his most dubious figure is a count of 2,420 Melungeons in Knott County, Kentucky!

44. Kenneth R. Bailey, "A Judicious Mixture: Negroes and Immigrants in West Virginia Mines, 1880–1917," *West Virginia History,* 34 (January 1973), 141–61.

45. August Meir and Elliot Rudwick, *CORE: A Study in the Civil Rights Movement, 1942–1968* (New York: Oxford Univ. Press, 1973); Kirkpatrick Sale, *SDS* (New York: Random House, 1973). See John D. McCarthy and Mayer N. Zald, *The Trend of Social Movements in America* (Morristown, N.J.: General Learning Press, 1973).

46. See the articles in *Appalachia in the Sixties,* ed. Walls and Stephenson (Lexington: Univ. Press of Kentucky, 1972), pp. 161–209; Hume, *Death and the Mines* (New York: Grossman, 1971); Bill Peterson, *Coaltown Revisited* (Chicago: Regnery, 1972).

47. David E. Whisnant, "Controversy in God's Grand Division: The CSM," *Appalachian Journal,* 2 (Autumn 1974), 7–45; and "The Congress for Appalachian Development," *Peoples' Appalachia,* 3 (Spring 1973), 16–22. A chapter on the Appalachian Volunteers is also included in his forthcoming collection of essays, *Missionaries, Planners and Developers in Appalachia.* Two doctoral dissertations may lead to books on Appalachian social

movements: Paul Nyden on the Miners for Democracy (Columbia, 1974), and Bennett M. Judkins on the Black Lung Associations (Univ. of Tennessee, 1976). On Highlander, see Frank Adams, *Unearthing Seeds of Fire* (Winston-Salem: Blair, 1975).

48. Selznick, *TVA* (1949; New York: Harper and Row, 1966); Whisnant's controversial chapter on TVA has been published in *The Elements,* Nos. 24 and 25 (November and December 1976).

49. See Todd Gitlin and Nanci Hollander, *Uptown: Poor Whites in Chicago* (New York: Harper and Row, 1970); and Tommie Miller, "Urban Appalachians: Cultural Pluralism and Ethnic Identity in the City" (unpublished M. A. thesis, Univ. of Cincinnati, 1976), summarized in the *Research Bulletin* (November 1976) of the Urban Appalachian Council, pp. 3–4.

50. Ford, "The Passing of Provincialism," in *The Southern Appalachian Region: A Survey.* For a methodological critique, see Billings, "Culture and Poverty in Appalachia," *Social Forces,* 53 (December 1974).

51. Wilbur Zelinsky, *The Cultural Geography of the United States* (Englewood Cliffs: Prentice-Hall, 1973), pp. 117–25.

52. Eugene Genovese, *Roll, Jordan, Roll: The World the Slaves Made* (New York: Pantheon, 1974); Richard Sennett and Jonathan Cobb, *The Hidden Injuries of Class* (New York: Vintage, 1973).

53. See *Mountain Families in Transition,* pp. 58–67; these themes reflect the society-culture-personality schema developed by Pitirim Sorokin and Talcott Parsons, with whom Brown studied at Harvard.

54. "Family, Religion and Colonialism," in *Growin' Up Country,* ed. Axelrod.

55. See Roland Warren, *The Community in America,* 2nd ed. (Chicago: Rand McNally, 1972), pp. 75–85, for an interpretation of the move to suburbia "as an attempt to preserve and restore [personalistic and familistic] values threatened with destruction" by the constellation of forces he calls "the great change."

56. *Little Smokey Ridge* (University: Univ. of Alabama Press, 1959); Gazaway, *The Longest Mile* (Garden City: Doubleday, 1969); *The Hollow* (New York: Coward-McCann, 1971). See John Photiadis, *Community Size and Social Attributes in West Virginia,* Appalachian Center Research Report 5 (Morgantown: West Virginia Univ., n.d.), for a comparative study.

57. Stephenson, *Shiloh;* Berton Kaplan, *Blue Ridge* (Morgantown: West Virginia Univ., 1971); George L. Hicks, *Appalachian Valley* (New York: Holt, Rhinehart and Winston, 1976).

58. Stephenson, *Shiloh;* Knipe and Lewis, "The Impact of Coal Mining," in *The Not So Solid South,* ed. Moreland, pp. 25–37.

59. Art Gallaher, Jr., "The Community as a Setting for Change in Southern Appalachia," in *The Public University in Its Second Century,* ed. Lloyd Davis, Public Affairs Series No. 5 (Morgantown: West Virginia Center for Appalachian Studies and Development, 1967), pp. 17–32; rpt. in *Appalachia,* ed. Riddel, pp. 291–304.

60. On the "Two Appalachias," see Harry Caudill, "O, Appalachia!" *Intellectual Digest* (April 1973), 16–19; rpt. in *Appalachia,* ed. Riddel, p. 275; and in *Voices from the Hills,* ed. Higgs and Manning, pp. 524–5. The same conclusion is reached in the face of contrary data in Roman B. Aquizap and Ernest A. Vargas, "Technology, Power, and Socialization in Appalachia," *Social Casework,* 51 (March 1970), 131–9.

61. See John C. Belcher, "Population Growth and Characteristics," and James S. Brown and George A. Hillery, Jr., "The Great Migration, 1940–1960," Chs. 3 and 4 in *The Southern Appalachian Region;* James S. Brown, "A Look at the 1970 Census," in *Appalachia in the Sixties,* pp. 130–144.

62. Gordon F. DeJong, *Appalachian Fertility Decline* (Lexington: Univ. Press of Kentucky, 1968).

63. See C. Milton Coughenour, "Measuring the Quality of Life for Rural Families," *Appalachia,* 9 (February–March 1976), 1–9.

64. Estabrook, "Presidential Address," *Eugenical News,* 11 (August 1926), 106–14; Josiah Henry Combs, *The Kentucky Highlanders from a Native Mountaineer's Viewpoint* (Lexington: J. L. Richardson, 1913), p. 43.

65. Woodrow R. Clevinger, "The Appalachian Mountaineers in the Upper Cowlitz Basin, *Pacific Northwest Quarterly,* 29 (April 1938), 115–34; and "Southern Appalachian Highlanders in Western Washington," *Pacific Northwest Quarterly,* 33 (January 1942), 3–25. See also his *Cascade Mountain Clan: The Clevengers and Stiltners and Related Families* (Seattle: Seattle Univ. Bookstore, 1971). David Looff notes his first contact with Appalachian mountaineers as a boy in the Cascades in Ch. 1 of *Appalachia's Children,* pp. 4–8.

66. Tryon and Allin, "Southern Appalachian Coal Plateaus," in Goodrich, *Migration and Economic Opportunity,* p. 66; Jerome Pickard, "Appalachian Population Estimated at 19 Million," *Appalachia,* 9 (August–September 1975), 1–9.

67. See Schwarzweller et. al., *Mountain Families in Transition,* Chs. 7–9; John Photiadis, *Migration and Occupational Adjustment of West Virginians in the City* (Morgantown: Office of Research and Development, West Virginia Univ., 1974).

68. See, for example, Rex A. Lucas, *Minetown, Milltown, Railtown: Life in Canadian Communities of Single Industry* (Toronto: Univ. of Toronto Press, 1971); Lantz, *People of Coal Town* (New York: Columbia Univ. Press, 1958).

69. Althouse, *Work, Safety, and Life Style among Southern Appalachian Coal Miners* (Morgantown: West Virginia Univ., 1974); the articles in *Appalachia in the Sixties,* pp. 69–119; Thomas N. Bethell, *The Hurricane Creek Massacre* (New York: Harper and Row, 1972); Tom Nugent, *Death at Buffalo Creek* (New York: Norton, 1973); the semi-fictionalized biographical sketch of a coal miner by George Vecsey, *One Sunset a Week* (New York: Dutton, 1974); and Meade Arble, *The Long Tunnel: A Coal Miner's Journal* (New York: Atheneum, 1976). See also the studies by Keith Dix in the Research Series of the Institute for Labor Studies at West Virginia University, and J. Davitt McAteer, *Coal Mine Health and Safety: The Case of West Virginia* (New York: Praeger, 1973).

70. See the work of Broadus and George S. Mitchell in the 1920s and 1930s; Liston Pope, *Millhands and Preachers* (New Haven: Yale Univ. Press, 1940); Glenn Gilman, *Human Relations in the Industrial Southeast* (Chapel Hill: Univ. of North Carolina Press, 1956). Billings is currently working on such a comparison, having just completed an historical analysis of textile industrialization in the Carolina piedmont; see his *Planters, Capitalists, and the Politics of Development in the New South* (Chapel Hill: Univ. of Carolina Press, forthcoming).

71. See John Stephenson's insightful discussion of this second theme in "Appalachia and the Third Century in America: On the Eve of an Astonishing Development—Again," *Appalachian Journal,* 4 (Autumn 1976), 34–8.

3. Appalachian Studies, Resistance, and Postmodernism

1. John Gaventa, "Inequality and the Appalachian Studies Industry," *Appalachian Journal* 5 (1978): 322.

2. See Jack Weller, *Yesterday's People* (Lexington: University Press of Kentucky, 1965); and Harry M. Caudill, *Night Comes to the Cumberlands: A Biography of a Depressed Area* (Boston: Little, Brown/Atlantic Monthly, 1962). Rupert Vance summarized Weller's thesis in a foreword to *Yesterday's People* (p. iv): "Thus mountain isolation, which began as physical isolation enforced by rugged topography, became mental and cultural isolation, holding people in disadvantaged areas, resisting those changes that would bring them into contact with the outside world. The effect of conditions thus becomes a new cause of conditions, but *the cause is now an attitude, not a mountain.* . . . To change the mountains is to change the mountain personality." Emphasis added.

3. Helen Lewis, "Fatalism or the Coal Industry?" *Mountain Life & Work,* December 1970.

4. For example, see Alan Banks, "Labor and the Development of Industrial Capitalism in Eastern Kentucky" (Ph.D. diss., McMaster University, 1980); Dwight B. Billings, "Religion as Opposition: A Gramscian Analysis," *American Journal of Sociology* 96 (1990): 1–31; David Alan Corbin, *Life, Work, and Rebellion in the Coal Fields: The Southern West Virginia Miners, 1880–1922* (Urbana: University of Illinois Press, 1981); Ronald D. Eller, *Miners, Millhands, and Mountaineers: Industrialization of the Appalachian South, 1880–1930* (Knoxville: University of Tennessee Press, 1982); John Hevener, *Which Side Are You On?* Urbana: University of Illinois Press, 1978).

5. Notably John Gaventa, *Power and Powerlessness: Quiescence and Rebellion in an Appalachian Valley* (Urbana: University of Illinois Press, 1980).

6. For example, Altina L. Waller, *Feud: Hatfields, McCoys, and Social Change in Appalachia, 1860–1900* (Chapel Hill: University of North Carolina Press, 1988).

7. The Appalachian Land Ownership Task Force was a coalition of scholars and activists in the region that managed to obtain funding for an impressive seven-volume participatory study of land ownership patterns in Appalachia. Members of the ALOTF produced *Landownership Patterns and Their Impacts on Appalachian Counties: A Survey of Eighty Counties,* which documents ownership patterns for both surface and mineral rights. A summary of the findings of the ALOTF study can be found in *Who Owns Appalachia? Landownership and Its Impact* (Lexington: University Press of Kentucky, 1983). Also see Pat Beaver, "Participatory Research on Land Ownership in Rural Appalachia," in Allen W. Batteau, ed., *Appalachia and America: Autonomy and Regional Dependence* (Lexington: University Press of Kentucky, 1983), 252–66.

For more on the Appalachian Alliance, see Appalachian Alliance, "Appalachia 1978: A Protest From the Colony," pamphlet (1978); and Appalachian Alliance, "National Sacrifice Area," pamphlet (1979).

8. Richard Couto, "Appalachian Innovations in Health Care," in Batteau, *Appalachia and American*, 185. Also see Karen W. Tice, "A Case Study of Battered Women's Shelters in Appalachia," *Affilia* 5 (Fall 1990): 83–100.

9. Trisha Frazen and Lois R. Helmbold, "What Is To Be Done?" *Women's Review of Books* 8 (February 1991): 29.

10. Teresa Ebert, "Postmodernism's Infinite Variety," *Women's Review of Books* 8 (January 1991): 24.

11. Jean Baudrillard, *Selected Writings*, ed. Mark Poster (Stanford, Calif.: Stanford University Press, 1988); Jean-Francois Lyotard, *The Postmodern Condition* (Minneapolis: University of Minneapolis Press, [1979] 1984).

12. For example, Fredric Jameson, "Postmodernism or the Cultural Logic of Late Capitalism," *New Left Review*, no. 146 (July–August 1984): 53–92.

13. Quoted in Ebert, "Postmodernism's Infinite Variety," 24–25.

14. Clifford Geertz, *Local Knowledge* (New York: Basic Books, 1983), 20.

15. The model for such freethinking was empirical science. Simply observing the world as it really was—rather than passively accepting the way it was described by religious or political authorities—promised liberation from ignorance, superstition, and fear. And, until the past few decades, many people have shared the Enlightenment faith that when the eye of reason judged social institutions, it would guarantee a critical vision that would lead the march to Progress.

16. Along with the loss of faith in reason's ability to perfect society, we have also become increasingly skeptical about reason's ability even to understand and represent social life. In particular, the simple, unmediated, unitary vision of reason has been called into question.

17. Quoted in W.T. Jones, *Kant and the Nineteenth Century* (New York: Harcourt Brace Jovanovich, 1975), 237.

18. Thomas S. Kuhn, *The Structure of Scientific Revolutions* (Chicago: University of Chicago Press, 1970).

19. Cornel West, "Interview," in Andrew Ross, ed., *Universal Abandon?* (Minneapolis: University of Minnesota Press, 1988), 272.

20. See Geertz, *Local Knowledge*, 19.

21. Hayden White, *The Content of the Form* (Baltimore: Johns Hopkins University Press, 1987), 14.

22. David Cattell-Gordon, "The Appalachia Inheritance: A Culturally Transmitted Traumatic Stress Syndrome?" *Journal of Progressive Human Service* 1 (1990): 41–57. Also see Karen W. Tice and Dwight B. Billings, "Appalachian Culture and Resistance," *Journal of Progressive Human Services* 2 (1991): 1–18.

23. See Todd Gitlin, "Hip Deep in Post-Modernism," *New York Times Book Review*, November 6, 1988, 35–36.

24. For example, Douglas Kellner, "Critical Theory and the Crisis of Social Theory," *Sociological Perspectives* 33 (Spring 1990): 11–17.

25. Geertz, *Local Knowledge*, 21.

26. Nancy Fraser and Linda Nicholson, "Social Criticism Without Philosophy: An Encounter Between Feminism and Postmodernism," *Theory, Culture & Society* 5 (1988): 391.

27. For example, the work of Carol Gilligan on women's moral development and Nancy Chodorow on mothering has been criticized for their failure to consider important differences between white women and women of color and the accommodations that slavery and domestic work have demanded of African-American women. See Fraser and Nicholson, "Social Criticism"; Sandra Morgan, *To See Ourselves, To See Our Sisters* (Memphis, Tenn.: Memphis State University Press/Center for Research on Women, 1986); and Carol Stack, "The Culture of Gender: Women and Men of Color," *Signs* 11 (1986): 321–24.

28. Fraser and Nicholson, "Social Criticism," 391.

29. Joan Scott, "Deconstructing Equality-Versus-Difference: Or, The Uses of Poststructuralist Theory for Feminism," *Feminist Studies* 14 (1988): 33–50.

30. Herbert Reid, "Appalachian Studies: Class, Culture and Politics—II," *Appalachian Journal* 9 (1982): 144; Ronald L. Lewis, *Black Coal Miners in America: Race, Class, and Community Conflict, 1780–1980* (Lexington: University Press of Kentucky, 1987); Sally Maggard, "Eastern Kentucky Women on Strike: A Study of Gender, Class and Political Action in the 1970s" (Ph.D. diss., University of Kentucky, 1988); and John Gaventa, Barbara E. Smith, and Alex Willingham, eds., *Communities in Economic Crisis: Appalachia and the South* (Philadelphia: Temple University Press, 1990). Also note that many of these points are raised in a special issue of *Appalachian Journal* 9,

entitled "Assessing Appalachian Studies" (Winter/Spring 1982).

31. Henry D. Shapiro, *Appalachia on Our Mind: The Southern Mountains and Mountaineers in the American Consciousness, 1870–1920* (Chapel Hill: University of North Carolina Press, 1978), 265.

32. See Herbert Reid, "Appalachian Policy, the Corporate State and American Values," *Policy Studies Journal* 9 (Special Issue no. 2, 1980–81): 622–33.

33. Rodger Cunningham, *Apples on the Flood: The Southern Mountain Experience* (Knoxville: University of Tennessee Press, 1987).

34. Gurney Norman and Lance Olsen, "Frankenstein in Palestine or: Postmodernism in Appalachia," in *Pine Mountain Sand and Gravel,* ed. Jim Webb et al. (Whitesburg, Ky.: Appalshop Productions, 1988), 83.

35. By taking the Scotch-Irish as the predominant ethnic group to settle and influence the region, Cunningham suppresses much of the diversity that can be found throughout Appalachia, essentializing it as a Scotch-Irish enclave. For a different look at early settlement patterns, see John Solomon Otto, "The Migration of the Southern Plain Folk: An Interdisciplinary Synthesis," *Journal of Southern History* 51 (1985): 183–200. For a look at the ethnic and racial diversity that came to characterize coal camp living, see Lewis, *Black Coal Miners in America.*

36. Cunningham, *Apples on the Flood,* xvii, 160, 162.

37. Jerome Bruner, *Actual Minds, Possible Worlds* (Cambridge: Harvard University Press, 1986), 94, 123.

38. Stephen William Foster, *The Past Is Another Country: Representation, Historical Consciousness, and Resistance in the Blue Ridge* (Berkeley, Los Angeles and London: University of California Press, 1988).

39. Ibid., 203.

40. Frances Mascia-Lees et al., "The Postmodernist Turn in Anthropology: Cautions from a Feminist Perspective," *Signs* 15 (1989): 12.

41. Ebert, "Postmodernism's Infinite Variety," 24.

42. Reid, "Appalachian Studies," 141.

43. Lisa Hall, "Trapped in the Ivory Tower?" *Women's Review of Books* 11 (May 1991): 25.

4. Appalachia and the Idea of America: The Problem of the Persisting Frontier

1. The principal documents of our recent "rediscovery" of Appalachia, and our redefinition of Appalachian otherness as a matter of economic rather than cultural differences, include Michael Harrington, *The Other America: Poverty in the United States* (New York: The Macmillan Co., 1962); Harry M. Caudill, *Night Comes to the Cumberlands: A Biography of a Depressed Area* (Boston: Little, Brown & Co., 1962); Thomas R. Ford, ed., *The Southern Appalachian Region: A Survey* (Lexington: Univ. of Kentucky Press, 1962); and Jack E. Weller, *Yesterday's People: Life in Contemporary Appalachia* (Lexington: Univ. of Kentucky Press, 1965). On the first discovery of Appalachia, see Henry D. Shapiro, "Strange Land and Peculiar People: The Discovery of Appalachia, 1870–1920" (Ph.D. dissertation, Rutgers University, 1966). On the first discovery and its consequences, see Henry D. Shapiro, *Appalachia on Our Mind: The Southern Mountains and Mountaineers in the American Consciousness, 1870–1920* (Chapel Hill: Univ. of North Carolina Press, 1977).

2. E.g., Thomas Wilson Humes, *The Loyal Mountaineers of Tennessee* (Knoxville: Ogden Bros. & Co., 1888); Joseph E. Roy, *Americans of the Midland Mountains* (New York: American Missionary Assn., 1891); "A Scotch-Irishman [pseud.]," *The Mountain Whites of the South* (Pittsburgh: [Banner Publishing Co.], 1893); Mrs. S. M. Davis, "The 'Mountain Whites' of America," *Missionary Review of the World,* 8 (June 1895), 422–26. A late example is William Goodell Frost, "God's Plan for the Southern Mountains," *Biblical Review,* 6 (July 1921), 405–25.

3. John Dwight Kern, *Constance Fenimore Woolson, Literary Pioneer* (Philadelphia: Univ. of Pennsylvania Press, 1934); Rayburn S. Moore, *Constance Fenimore Woolson* (New York: Twayne Publishers, 1963); James Lane Allen, "Local Color," *The Critic,* n.s., 5 (Jan. 9, 1886), 13–14, and "H. M. Alden," *The Bookman,* 50 (November 1919); 330–36; Grant Knight, *James Lane Allen and the Genteel Tradition* (Chapel Hill: Univ. of North Carolina Press, 1935); Edd Winfield Parks, *Charles Egbert Craddock (Mary Noailles Murfree)* (Chapel Hill: Univ. of North Carolina Press, 1941); Charles Dudley Warner, "On Horseback," *Atlantic Monthly,* 56 (July–October 1885), 88–100, 194–207, 388–98, 540–54, and C. D. Warner correspondence, Century Collection, New York Public Library Manuscript

Division; David Hunter Strother, "The Mountains," *Harper's Magazine,* April 1872–September 1875, *passim;* Cecil D. Eby, Jr., *"Porte Crayon": The Life of David Hunter Strother* (Chapel Hill: Univ. of North Carolina Press, 1960).

4. Carvel E. Collins, "Nineteenth Century Fiction of the Southern Appalachians" *Bulletin of Bibliography,* 17 (October 1942 and January 1943), 186–90, 215–17; Henry D. Shapiro, "Strange Land and Peculiar People," 250 ff.

5. Horace Spencer Fiske, *Provincial Types in American Prose Fiction* (Chautauqua, N.Y.: The Chautauqua Press, 1903), 1 Cf. Elizabeth Haven Appleton, "Half-Life and Half a Life," *Atlantic Monthly,* 13 (February 1864), 157–82; Edward H. Pollard, "The Virginia Tourist," *Lippincott's Magazine,* 5 (May 1870), 48–97; James Esten Cooke, "Owlet," *Harper's Magazine,* 57 (July 1878), 199–211.

6. E.g., William D. Kelley, *The Old South and the New: A Series of Letters* (New York: G. P. Putnam's Sons, 1887).

7. N. S. Shaler, "Peculiarities of the South," *North American Review,* 151 (October 1890), 447–88; George H. Vincent, "A Retarded Frontier," *American Journal of Sociology,* 4 (July 1898), 1–20; Charles Dudley Warner, "On Horseback" (1885).

8. James Lane Allen, "Through Cumberland Gap on Horseback." *Harper's Magazine,* 73 (June 1886), 50–66.

9. Cf. Joseph E. Roy, *Americans of the Midland Mountains;* William Goodell Frost, "Our Contemporary Ancestors in the Southern Mountains," *Atlantic Monthly,* 83 (March 1899), 311–19; Lillian Walker Williams, "In the Kentucky Mountains: Colonial Customs that Are Still Existing in that Famous Section of the Country," *New England Magazine,* n.s., 30 (March 1904), 37–45. It was to the problem posed by the apparent persistence of pioneer culture in the face of rapid economic and social change elsewhere in the nation that Ellen Churchill Semple and the environmentalists of the early twentieth century addressed themselves.

10. Unsigned, "Novel Notes," *The Bookman,* 2 (January 1896), 434. "A Cumberland Vendetta" was first published in *The Century,* 48 (June–August 1894), 163–78, 366–73, 496–505, and was subsequently issued as *A Cumberland Vendetta and Other Stories* (New York: Harper & Bros., 1895). On Fox's treatment of mountain lawlessness generally see the excellent short study *John Fox, Jr.,* by Warren I. Titus (New York: Twayne Publishers, 1969).

11. On mountain violence in literature, see Carvel E. Collins, "The Literary Tradition of the Southern Mountaineer, 1824–1900" (Ph.D. dissertation, University of Chicago, 1944); Isabella D. Harris, "The Southern Mountaineer in American Fiction, 1824–1910" (Ph.D. dissertation, Duke University, 1948). Early reports of feuds and moonshining include: A. H. Gernsey, "Illicit Distillation of Liquors," *Harper's Weekly,* 11 (Dec. 7, 1867), 773 and "Hunting for Stills," *Harper's Weekly,* 11 (Dec. 21, 1867), 811; unsigned, "The Moonshine Man: A Peep into His Haunts and Hiding Places," *Harper's Weekly* 21 (Oct. 21, 1877), 820–22; Young E. Allison, "Moonshine Men," *Southern Bivouac,* n.s., 2 (February 1887), 528–34; Francis Lynde, "The Moonshiners of Fact," *Lippincott's Magazine,* 57 (January 1896), 66–76; unsigned, "The Knell of the Kentucky Feud," *Scribner's Magazine,* 21 (May 1897), 660; J. Stoddard Johnston, "Romance and Tragedy of the Kentucky Feuds," *Cosmopolitan,* 27 (September 1899), 551–58; John Fox, Jr., "Manhunting in the Pound," *Outing,* 36 (July 1900), 344–50.

12. On the Kentucky feuds, see Hartley Davis and Clifford Smyth, "Land of Feuds," *Munsey's Magazine,* 30 (November 1903), 161–72; R. L. McClure, "Mazes of a Kentucky Feud," *The Independent,* 55 (Sept. 17, 1903), 2216–24; O. O. Howard, "The Feuds in the Cumberland Mountains," *The Independent,* 56 (April 7, 1904), 783–88; *New York Times,* 1901–1905, *passim;* Charles G. Mutzenburg, *Kentucky's Famous Feuds and Tragedies: Authentic Histories of the World Renowned Vendettas of the Dark and Bloody Ground* (New York: R. F. Fenno, 1917). While Kentucky was not all of Appalachia, it has traditionally received the most attention from local color writers, denominational home-mission personnel, and travel-writers, and provided the basis upon which generalizations about the region as a whole were made, at least until the organization of the Russell Sage Foundation's Southern Highland Division in 1908.

13. Carvel E. Collins notes this in "Nineteenth Century Fiction of the Southern Appalachians" (see note 4). The shift is apparent in, e.g., the emphases of William Goodell Frost's articles of 1899 and 1900. The first, "Our Contemporary Ancestors in the Southern Mountains," asks for a sympathetic understanding for "these eighteenth century neighbors and fellow countrymen of ours"; the second, "The Southern Mountaineer: Our Kindred of the Boone and Lincoln Type," *American Monthly Review of Reviews,* 21 (March 1900), 303–11, seeks to explain away the feuds by identifying mountaineer "individualism" as an historical trait.

14. Frost, "Our Contemporary Ancestors." Cf. His "Educational Pioneering in the Southern Mountains," National Education Association, *Addresses and Proceedings,* 14 (1901), 555–60, and "Our Southern Highlanders," *The Independent,* 72 (April 4, 1912), 708–14; John Fox, Jr., *The Kentuckians* (New York: Harper & Bros., 1898), and "The Southern Mountaineer," *Scribner's Magazine,* 29 (April–May 1901), 387–99, 557–70.

15. James G. Craighead, *Scotch and Irish Seeds in American Soil* (Philadelphia: Presbyterian Board of Publication, 1878).

16. Charles J. Ryder, "Our American Highlanders: Problems and Progress," *Education,* 18 (October 1897), 67, 69. Ryder coined the term in an address to the American Missionary Association in 1892 (ibid., 67), published as *The Debt of Our Country to the American Highlanders During the War* (New York: American Missionary Association, [1896]).

17. John M. Moore, *The South To-Day* (New York: Missionary Education Movement of the U.S. and Canada, 1916), 127–28, 132–33.

18. Ellen Churchill Semple, "The Anglo-Saxons of the Kentucky Mountains: A Study in Anthropogeography," *Geographical Journal* (London), 17 (June 1901), 616; reprinted in *Bulletin of the American Geographical Society,* 42 (August 1910), 561–94. See also George E. Vincent, "A Retarded Frontier," *American Journal of Sociology,* 4 (July 1898), 1–20; James Mooney, "Folk-Lore of the Carolina Mountains," *Journal of American Folk-Lore,* 2 (April–June 1889), 95–104; S. S. MacClintock, "The Kentucky Mountains and their Feuds," *American Journal of Sociology,* 7 (July–September 1901), 1–28, 171–87; McClure, "Mazes of a Kentucky Feud"; Howard, "The Feuds in the Cumberland Mountains."

19. Mary Verhoeff, *The Kentucky Mountains. Transportation and Commerce, 1750–1911: A Study in the Economic History of a Coal Field,* Filson Club Publication No. 26 (Louisville: John P. Morton & Co., 1911), 183–84; John C. Campbell, "Social Betterment in the Southern Mountains," National Conference of Charities and Correction, *Proceedings,* 36 (1909), 137.

20. John C. Campbell, "Mountain and Rural Fields in the South," *[Annual Report of the] Home Missions Council, 1916* ([New York, 1916]), 180. On Campbell, see John M. Glenn et al., *Russell Sage Foundation, 1907–1946* (New York: Russell Sage Foundation, 1947), I, 62 ff.; Henry D. Shapiro, "Introduction," in John C. Campbell, *The Southern Highlanders and His Homeland* (Lexington: Univ. Press of Kentucky, 1969), xxii–xxxi, and *Appalachia On Our Mind,* esp. ch. 7. Some discussion of Wilson's activities will be found in Betty Carol Clutts, "Country Life Aspects of the Progressive Movement" (Ph.D. dissertation, Ohio State University, 1962).

21. Walter Hines Page, ["Editorial Note"], *The World's Work,* 19 (March 1910), 12704. See also Thomas Dawley, "Our Southern Mountaineers: Removal the Remedy for the Evils that Isolation and Poverty Have Brought," *The World's Work,* 19 (March 1910), 12704–14; Walter A. Dyer, "Training New Leaders for the Industrial South," *The World's Work,* 28 (July 1914), 285–92; William L. Hall, "To Remake the Appalachians: A New Order in the Mountains that is Founded on Forestry," *The World's Work,* 28 (July 1914), 321–38.

22. Conditions in Appalachia since the 1920s are conveniently summarized in Caudill, *Night Comes to the Cumberlands.*

5. The Eastern Cherokees in Southern Appalachia: Principal People, Persistent People

1. John G. Burnett, "The Cherokee Removal Through the Eyes of a Private Soldier (December 11, 1890)," *Journal of Cherokee Studies* 3(3) (1978):180–185; Grant Foreman, *Indian Removal: The Emigration of the Five Civilized Tribes of Indians* (Norman: University of Oklahoma Press, 1932); Duane H. King and Raymond Evans, "Editor's Note, Special Edition: The Trail of Tears," *Journal of Cherokee Studies* 3(3) (1978), 147; James Mooney, "Myths of the Cherokee," *Smithsonian Institution, Bureau of American Ethnology, Nineteenth Annual Report, 1897–98,* Part I (Washington, D.C.: United States Government Printing Office, 1900), 3–576.

2. Russell Thornton, *The Cherokees: A Population History* (University of Nebraska Press, Lincoln, 1990), 289; Also see Betty J. Duggan, "Being Cherokee in a White World: The Ethnic Persistence of a Post-Removal American Indian Enclave" (Knoxville: Ph.D. dissertation, The University of Tennessee, 1998), 38.

3. Duggan, "Being Cherokee," 1998; John R. Finger, *The Eastern Band of Cherokees: 1819–1900* (Knoxville: The University of Tennesee Press, 1984); Sharon P. Flanagan, "The Georgia Cherokees Who Remained: Race, Status, and Property in the Chattahoochee Community" *The Georgia Historical Quarterly* 73(3)(1989):584–609; King and

Evans, "Editor's Note," 1978; Brett H. Riggs, "Removal Period Cherokee Households in Southwestern North Carolina: Material Perspectives on Ethnicity and Cultural Differentiation" (Knoxville: Ph.D. dissertation, University of Tennessee, 1999).

4. Qualla Boundary Library and Cherokee Enrollment Office, personal communications, 2001. Also see John R. Finger, *Cherokee Americans: The Eastern Band of Cherokees in the Twentieth Century* (Lincoln: University of Nebraska Press, 1991); Sharlotte Neely, *Snowbird Cherokees: People of Persistence* (Athens: University of Georgia Press, 1991). Eastern Cherokee lands, which were purchased by the Indians after Removal, are owned by the Eastern Band of Cherokee Indians and held in trust by the U.S. government. Right to use and improvements on particular properties can be inherited but the land cannot be sold.

5. George Roth, "Overview of Southeastern Indian Tribes Today," in *Indians of the Southeastern United States in the Late 20th Century,* ed. J. Anthony Paredes (Tuscaloosa and London: The University of Alabama Press, 1992), 183–201, see especially, 184–185; J. Anthony Paredes, personal communication, 2001.

6. Sharlotte Neely, "Acculturation and Persistence Among North Carolina's Eastern Band of Cherokee Indians," in *Southeastern Indians Since the Removal Era,* ed. Walter L. Williams (Athens: University of Georgia Press, 1979), 154–173; Neely, *Snowbird Cherokees,* 1991; Edward H. Spicer, "Types of Contact and Processes of Change," in *Perspectives in American Indian Culture Change,* ed. Edward H. Spicer (Chicago: University of Chicago Press, 1961), 517–544; Edward H. Spicer, "Persistent Cultural Systems: A Comparative Study of Identity Systems," *Science* 174(1971):795–800.

7. Charles Hudson, "The Hernando de Soto Expedition, 1539–1543, in *The Forgotten Centuries: Indians and Europeans in the American South, 1521–1704,* ed. Charles Hudson and C. Tesser (Athens: University of Georgia Press, 1994), 74–103; Charles, Hudson, *The Juan Pardo Expeditions* (Washington, DC: Smithsonian Institution Press, 1990); Gerald F. Schroedl, "Cherokee Ethnohistory and Archaeology from 1540–1838," in *Indians of the Greater Southeast: Historical Archaeology and Ethnohistory,* ed. Bonnie McEwan (Gainesville: University Press of Florida, 2000), 204–241.

8. Mooney, "Myths," 1900; Mary Rothrock, "Carolina Traders Among the Overhill Cherokees, 1690–1760," *East Tennessee Historical Society's Publications* 1(1929):3–18.

9. William H. Gilbert, "The Eastern Cherokee," *Smithsonian Institution, Bureau of American Ethnology Bulletin* 133 (Washington, DC: Government Printing Office, 1943), 169–413; Lance K. Greene, "The Archaeology and History of the Cherokee Out Towns" (Knoxville: M.A. thesis, University of Tennessee, 1996); Mooney, "Myths," 1900; Schroedl, "Cherokee Ethnohistory," 2000. In a number of historical documents the Out Towns are lumped with the Middle Towns, but contemporary archaeologists distinguish between the two adjacent locales.

10. Roy S. Dickens, Jr., *Cherokee Prehistory* (Knoxville: The University of Tennessee Press); Betty J. Duggan and Brett H. Riggs, "Cherokee Baskestry: An Evolving Tradition," in *Studies in Cherokee Baskestry,"* ed. Betty J. Duggan and Brett H. Riggs, *Occasional Paper No.* 9 (Knoxville: The Frank H. McClung Museum, The University of Tennessee, 1991), 22–52; Brian T. Egloff, "An Analysis of Ceramics from Historic Cherokee Towns" (Chapel Hill: M.A. thesis, University of North Carolina, 1967); Duane H. King, "The Origin of the Eastern Cherokees as a Social and Political Entity," in *The Cherokee Indian Nation: A Troubled History,"* ed. Duane H. King (Knoxville: The University of Tennessee Press, 1979), 164–180; Wendell H. Oswalt and Sharlotte Neely, "Eastern Cherokee Farmers," in *This Land was Theirs: A Study of Native Americans* (Mayfield Publishing Company, Mayfield, California, 1999), 447–476, sixth edition.

11. Mooney, "Myths," 1900.

12. Oswalt and Neely, "Eastern Cherokee," 1999; Also see Gilbert, "Eastern Cherokee," 1943; Mooney, "Myths," 1900.

13. Oswalt and Neely, "Eastern Cherokee," 1999; Also see Frederick O. Gearing, "Priest and Warriors: Social Structures for Cherokee Politics in the 18th Century," *American Anthropological Association Memoir* 93, *Vol.* 5, *Part* 2 (Menasha, Wisconsin: American Anthropological Association, 1962); Gilbert, "Eastern Cherokee," 1943; John Gulick, *Cherokees at the Crossroads,* (Institute for Research in Social Science, Chapel Hill: University of North Carolina, 1960); Robert K. Thomas, "Cherokee Values and World View," Manuscript on file, Institute for Research in Social Science, University of North Carolina, Chapel Hill, 1958.

14. See Wilma A. Dunaway, *The First American Frontier: Transition to Capitalism in Southern Appalachia, 1700–1860* (Chapel Hill and London: University of North Carolina Press, 1996); Eric R.

Wolf, *Europe and the People Without History* (Berkeley: University of California Press, 1982).

15. Gary C. Goodwin, "Cherokees in Transition: A Study of Changing Culture and Environment Prior to 1775," Department of Geography, *Research Paper No.* 181 (Chicago: University of Chicago Press, 1977).

16. William G. McLoughlin, *Cherokees and Missionaries, 1789–1839* (New Haven: Yale University Press, 1984); William G. McLoughlin, *Cherokee Renascence in the New Republic* (Princeton: Princeton University Press, 1986); Theda Perdue, "The Sequoyah Syllabary and Cultural Revitalization," in *Perspectives on the Southeast,* ed. Patricia B. Kwachka, *Southern Anthropological Proceedings, No.* 27 (Athens: University of Georgia Press, 1989), 116–125.

17. Theda Perdue, "The Conflict Within: Cherokees and Removal," in *Cherokee Removal: Before and After,* ed. William L. Anderson (Athens: University of Georgia Press, 1991); Also see Frank W. Porter, III, ed., *Strategies for Survival: American Indians in the Eastern United States* (Westport, Connecticut: Greenwood Press, 1986).

18. Henderson Enrollment, "Census Roll of the Cherokee Nation," Records of the Bureau of Indian Affairs, Record Group 75 (Washington, DC: United States National Archives, 1835); William G. McLoughlin and Walter H. Conser, Jr., "The Cherokees in Transition: A Statistical Analysis of the Federal Cherokee Census of 1835." *The Journal of American History* 64(December, 1977):678–703.

19. Marshall D. Sahlins, *Islands of History* (Chicago: University of Chicago Press, 1985), viii, 144.

20. Duggan, "Being Cherokee," 1998; Leslie Hewes, *Occupying the Cherokee Country of Oklahoma* (Lincoln: University of Nebraska Press, 1978); Richard Pillbury, "The Europeanization of the Cherokee Settlement Landscape Prior to Removal: A Georgia Case Study," in *Historical Archaeology of the Eastern United States, Papers from the R. J. Russell Symposium,* ed. R. W. Neuman, *Geosciences and Man, No.* 23 (Baton Rouge, Louisiana State University, 1983), 59–69; Riggs, "Removal Period," 1999.

21. Mooney, "Myths," 1900; Also see Finger, *Eastern Band,* 1984:21–28; Finger, *Cherokee Americans,* 1991; Paul Kutsche, "The Tsali Legend: Culture Heroes and Historiography," *Ethnohistory* 10(1963):329–357. In his history of the Eastern Band, John Finger (1984) provides an updated analysis of the historical events and players of the Tsali episode and the various legends that developed.

22. King, "Origin," 1979.

23. Finger, *Eastern Band,* 1984; Theda Perdue, *The Cherokee* (New York: Chelsea House Publishers, 1989).

24. Bynum, John Gray, "Journal, 1838," Manuscript on file, Southern Historical Collection, Wilson Library, University of North Carolina, Chapel Hill; Duggan, "Being Cherokee," 1998; Finger, *Cherokee Americans,* 1991; Flanagan, "Georgia Cherokees," 1989; Neely, *Snowbird Cherokees,* 1991; Henry M. Owl, "The Eastern Band of Cherokee Indians Before and after the Removal" (Chapel Hill: M.A. thesis, University of North Carolina, 1929).

25. Duggan, "Being Cherokee", 1998; Finger, *Eastern Band,* 1984

26. Mooney, "Myths," 1900; also see Finger, *Eastern Band,* 1984; Robert S. Lambert, "The Oconoluftee Valley, 1800–1860: A Study of the Sources of Mountain History." *North Carolina Historical Review* 35(1958): 415–426; Charles Lanman, *Letters from the Allegheny Mountains* (New York, 1849).

27. Duggan, "Being Cherokee," 1998; Finger, *Eastern Band,* 1984; Neely, *Snowbird Cherokees,* 1991).

28. For discussions of this issue see: Duggan, "Being Cherokee," 1998; Finger, *Eastern Band,* 1984; Neely, *Snowbird Cherokees,* 1991; Riggs, *Removal Period,* 1999.

29. See discussions of these and other such settlements in: Betty J. Duggan, "Voices from the Periphery: Reconstructing and Interpreting Post-Removal Histories of the Duck Town Cherokees," in *Responsibility and Partnership: Anthropologists Among Southern Indians in the New Millennium,* ed. Lisa J. Lefler and Frederic Gleach, *Southern Anthropological Society Proceedings, No.* 35 [Athens: University of Georgia, 2002 (in press)]; Duggan, "Being Cherokee," 1998.

30. "Alexis," "A Visit to the Cartoogechaye Indians," North Carolina University Magazine 1(3) (1852):116–118; Fogelson and Kutsche, "Cherokee Economic," 1961; Lanman, *Letters,* 1849; Neely, *Snowbird Cherokees,* 1991; Frank G. Speck and C. E. Schaeffer, "The Mutual-Aid and Volunteer Company of the Eastern Cherokee as Recorded in a Book of Minutes in the Sequoyah Syllabary, compared with Mutual-Aid Societies of the Northern Iroquois." *Journal of Washington Academy of Sciences* 35(6)(1945):169–179. James Mooney bought several ethnological objects from the Yellow Hill

town house for the Smithsonian's National Museum collections.

31. Thomas Donaldson, The Extra Census Bulletin; Indian: Eastern Band of Cherokees of North Carolina (Washington, DC: U.S. Census Printing Office, 1892); Duggan, "Being Cherokee," 1998; Finger, *Eastern Band,* 1991; Neely, *Snowbird Cherokees,* 1991.

32. Duggan, "Being Cherokee," 1998; Finger, *Eastern Band,* 1984; Neely, *Snowbird Cherokees,* 1991.

33. Duggan, "Being Cherokee," Mooney, "Myths," 1900.

34. Duggan, Being Cherokee," 1998; Also see e.g. Mooney, "Myths," 1900; Finger, *Eastern Band,* 1984; Finger, *Cherokee Americans,* 1991; Gilbert, "Eastern Cherokee," 1943; Gulick, *Cherokees,* 1960; Harriet J. Kupferer, 'The "Principal People,' 1960: A Study in Cultural and Social Groups of the Eastern Cherokee," *Smithsonian Institution, Bureau of American Ethnology Bulletin* 196, *Paper* 78 (Washington, D.C.: United States Government Printing Office, 1966), 215–325. Neely, *Snowbird Cherokees,* 1991. For exceptions to the latter statement see Flanagan, "Georgia Cherokees," 1989; Fogelson and Kutsche, "Cherokee Economic," 1961; Barbara S. McRae, The Indians of Sand Town. *The State* (February, 1987):16–17.

35. See Duggan, "Being Cherokee," 1998 for details and additional sources.

36. See Duggan, "Being Cherokee," 1998 for details and additional sources.

37. James Adair, *History of the American Indians* (London, 1775); Leonard Bloom, "The Acculturation of the Cherokee Historical Aspects," *The North Carolina Historical Review* 19(4)(1942): 323–358; David L. Bushnell, Jr., "The Sloane Collection in the British Museum," *American Anthropologist* 8(1906, n.s.):671–685; Betty J. Duggan, "Tourism, Cultural Authenticity, and the Native Crafts Cooperative: The Eastern Cherokee Experience," in *Tourism and Culture: An Applied Perspective,* ed. Erve Chambers (Ithaca: State University of New York (SUNY) Press, 1997), 31–57.

38. Duggan, "Being Cherokee," 1998; Harmon, "Eighteenth Century," 1986; William L. McDowell, Jr., ed., "Journals of the Commissioners of the Indian Trade, September 20, 1710–August 29, 1718," *Colonial Records of South Carolina* (Columbia: South Carolina Archives Department, 1955); Wayne D. Roberts, "Lithic Analysis at Chota-Tanasee," Paper presented at the 37th Southeastsern Archaeological Conference, New Orleans, 1980. Schroedl, "Cherokee Ethnohistory," 2000; John Whitthoft, "Stone Pipes of the Historic Cherokees," *Southern Indian Studies* 1(1949): 43–62.

39. Duggan and Riggs, "Cherokee Baskety," 1991; Duggan, "Tourism," 1997; Duggan, "Being Cherokee," 1998; Greene, "Archaeology," 1996; Sarah H. Hill, *Weaving New Worlds: Southeastern Cherokee Women and Their Basketry* (Chapel Hill: University of North Carolina Press, 1997); Duane King, personal communication, 1991.

40. See Duggan and Riggs, "Cherokee Basketry," 1991. Edward Palmer and James Mooney from the Smithsonian Institution's Bureau of American Ethnology, M.R. Harrington from the Heye Foundation's Museum of the American Indian, and Frank Speck, who first collected for the Milwaukee Public Museum and then the University of Pennsylvania, made many purchasing trips, often recording considerable ethnographic detail about the objects and makers.

41. Duggan and Riggs, "Cherokee Basketry," 1991; Finger, *Cherokee Americans,* 1991; Frank G. Speck and C. E. Schaeffer, "The Mutual-Aid and Volunteer Company of the Eastern Cherokee: as Recorded in a Book of Minutes in the Sequoyah Syllabary, Compared with Mutual-Aid Societies of the Northern Iroquois," *Journal of Washington Academy of Sciences* 35(6)(1945):169–179. Also see Duggan, "Tourism," 1997.

42. Jane S. Becker, "Selling Tradition: The Southern Highland Handicraft Guild and Southern Mountain Culture, 1929–1942," Paper presented at the American Folklore Society, Oakland, CA, 1990; Duggan and Riggs, "Cherokee Basketry", 1991; Duggan, "Tourism," 1997; Hill, *Weaving,* 1997. Also see Allen H. Eaton, *Handicrafts of the Southern Highlands* (New York: Dover Publications, 1937).

43. Duggan, "Tourism," 1997; also see Finger, *Cherokee Americans,* 1991. Also see Hill, *Weaving,* 1997.

44. Anonymous, personal communication, 1995; Duggan, "Tourism," 1997; Finger, *Cherokee Americans,* 1991.

45. Finger, *Cherokee Americans,* 1991; Oswalt and Neely, "Eastern Cherokee," 1999.

46. The Official Home Page of the Eastern Band of Cherokee Indians, Cherokee Indian Reservation, Tribal Travel and Tourism website, http://www.Cherokee-nc.com.

47. This two-lane highway formerly served local Cherokee and non-Indian families and timber trucks, as well as hikers, nature enthusiasts, and some day tourists, who visit the Joyce Kilmer Na-

tional Forest or a handful of upscale, rustic lodges. Now the same road as a "designated scenic highway" provides a new connecting route from southeastern Tennessee into North Carolina.

48. Joyce Dugan and David Redmond, personal communications, 2001.

49. Joyce Dugan, personal communication, 2001.

50. James Bird, personal communication, 2000; Marina Catt, personal communication, 2001; Oswalt and Neely, "Eastern Cherokee," 1999.

51. "Thomas, "Cherokee Values," 1958; also see e.g., Gulick, *Cherokees,* 1960; Kupferer, "Principal People," 1966; also see Neely, "Adapation and the Contemporary North Carolina Cherokee Indian," in *Indians of the Southeastern United States in the Late Twentieth Century,* ed. By J. Anthony Paredes (Tuscaloosa: University of Alabama Press, 1992) 29–43.

52. Finger, *Cherokee Americans,* 1991

53. Fredrik Barth, ed., *Ethnic Groups and Boundaries: The Social Organization of Culture Difference* (London: George Allen & Unwin, 1969); Raymond D. Fogelson, "Perspectives on Native American Identity, in *Studying Native America: Problems and Prospects,*" ed. Russell Thornton (Madison: University of Wisconsin Press, 1998), 40–59, 40.

54. Finger, *Eastern Cherokees,* 1984; Neely, *Snowbird Cherokees,* 1991; Brett H. Riggs, personal communication, 2001.

55. Jack Gregory and Rennard Strickland, *Adventures of an Indian Boy* (Muskogee, OK: Indian Heritage Association, 1972), 29.

6. Race and Racism in Nineteenth-Century Southern Appalachia: Myths, Realities, and Ambiguities

The author is grateful for very helpful critiques of this essay by Fitzhugh Brundage, Durwood Dunn, James Klotter, William McFeely, and Gordon McKinney.

1. U. B. Phillips, "The Central Theme of Southern History," *American Historical Review* 34 (1928): 30–43. On the debate among historians since, see John David Smith and John C. Inscoe, eds., *Ulrich Bonnell Phillips: A Southern Historian and His Critics* (Westport, Conn.: Greenwood Press, 1990). David Whisnant statement from a book review, *Journal of Southern History* 56 (1990): 566.

2. John Fox, Jr., *The Little Shepherd of Kingdom Come* (1903; reprint, Lexington: University Press of Kentucky, 1987), pp. 28, 119, 239.

3. William Faulkner, "Mountain Victory," in *Collected Stories,* by William Faulkner (1950; reprint, New York: Vintage, 1977), pp. 745–80; quote, p. 751. For a more extensive analysis of this story, see John C. Inscoe, "Faulkner, Race, and Appalachia," *South Atlantic Quarterly* 86 (Summer 1987): 244–53.

4. William Brewer, "Moonshining in Georgia," *Cosmopolitan* 23 (June 1897): 132, quoted in Nina Silber, *The Romance of Reunion: Northerners and the South, 1865–1900* (Chapel Hill: University of North Carolina Press, 1993), p. 144.

5. Ellen Churchill Semple, "The Anglo-Saxons of the Kentucky Mountains: A Study in Anthropogeography," in *Appalachian Images in Folk and Popular Culture,* ed. W. K. McNeil (Ann Arbor, Mich.: U.M.I. Research Press, 1989), pp. 150–51.

6. Nathaniel S. Shaler, "The Peculiarities of the South," *North American Review* 151 (October 1890): 483–84. See also Margaret Ripley Wolfe, "The Appalachian Reality: Ethnic and Class Diversity," *East Tennessee Historical Society Publications* 52 and 53 (1980–81): 40–60.

7. Samuel Tyndale Wilson, *The Southern Mountaineers* (New York: Presbyterian Home Missions, 1906), pp. 42, 20–21; Thomas Wolfe, *The Hills Beyond* (1935; reprint, New York: Plume, 1982), p. 263.

8. Flannery O'Connor, "The Artificial Nigger," in *The Complete Stories,* by Flannery O'Connor (New York: Farrar, Straus and Giroux, 1971), quote, p. 129. Curiously, analysts of this story fail to recognize or acknowledge the mountain context of the two characters' background. See, for example, Miles Orvell, *Flannery O'Connor: An Introduction* (Jackson: University of Mississippi Press, 1991), pp. 152–60; Kathleen Feeley, *Flannery O'Connor: Voice of the Peacock* (New York: Fordham University Press, 1982), pp. 120–24; Jill P. Baumgaertner, *Flannery O'Connor: A Proper Scaring* (Wheaton, Ill.: Harold Shaw, 1988), pp. 56–62.

9. James C. Klotter, "The Black South and White Appalachia," *Journal of American History* 66 (March 1980): 832–49; Silber, *Romance of Reunion,* pp. 143–58. See also Allen W. Batteau, *The Invention of Appalachia* (Tucson: University of Arizona Press, 1990), pp. 59–63, on other uses of Anglo-Saxonism in romanticizing Appalachia.

Even more recent studies have focused on turn-of-the-century mission work to Appalachian blacks. See Conrad E. Ostwalt, Jr., "Crossing of Cultures: The Mennonite Brethren of Boone, North Carolina," in *Environmental Voices: Cultural, Social, Physical, and Natural,* ed. Garry Barker, *Journal of the Appalachian Studies Association* 4 (1992), pp. 105–122; Conrad E. Ostwalt, Jr., and Phoebe Pollitt, "The Salem School and Orphanage [in Elk Park, N.C.]: White Missionaries, Black School," *Appalachian Journal* 20 (Spring 1993): 265–75.

10. Useful and varied anthologies on the black experience in the southern highlands, most of which focus on the twentieth century, include William H. Turner and Edward J. Cabbell, eds., *Blacks in Appalachia* (Lexington: University Press of Kentucky, 1985); Edward J. Cabbell, guest ed., "Black Appalachians," special issue of *Now and Then* 3 (Winter 1986); Lenwood Davis, *The Black Heritage of Western North Carolina* (Asheville: Southern Highlands Research Center, University of North Carolina, 1986); William H. Turner, guest ed., "Blacks in Appalachia," special issue of *Appalachian Heritage* 19 (Fall 1991).

11. On the distribution of slaves in Appalachia, see Robert P. Stuckert, "Black Populations of the Southern Appalachian Mountains," *Phylon* 48 (June 1987): 141–51; Richard B. Drake, "Slavery and Antislavery in Appalachia," *Appalachian Heritage* 14 (Winter 1986): 25–33; James B. Murphy, "Slavery and Freedom in Appalachia: Kentucky as a Demographic Case Study," *Register of the Kentucky Historical Society* 80 (1982): 151–69; John C. Inscoe, *Mountain Masters: Slavery and the Sectional Crisis in Western North Carolina* (Knoxville: University of Tennessee Press, 1989), pp. 59–63, 84–86; Wilma A. Dunaway, "Southern Appalachia's People without History: The Role of Unfree Laborers in the Region's Antebellum Economy," paper presented at the annual meeting of the Social Science History Association, November 1989, Washington, D.C., tabs. 2–5. For a nineteenth-century perspective, see William E. Barton, "The Cumberland Mountains and the Struggle for Freedom," *New England Magazine* 16 (1897): 65–87.

We are still sadly lacking in scholarly treatment of antebellum free black highlanders. Among the few works dealing with the subject are Stuart Sprague, "From Slavery to Freedom: African-Americans in Eastern Kentucky, 1864–1884," in *Diversity in Appalachia: Images and Realities,* ed. Tyler Blethen, *Journal of the Appalachian Studies Association* 5 (1993): 67–74; Marie Tedesco, "Freedman and Slave Owner: The Strange Case of Adam Waterford," paper presented at the Sixteenth Appalachian Studies Conference, March 1993, Johnson City, Tenn.

12. Sadie Smathers Patton, "The Kingdom of the Happy Land" (Asheville: Stephens, 1957); Sam Gray and Theda Perdue, "Appalachia as the Promised Land: A Freedmen's Commune in Henderson County, North Carolina, 1870–1920," paper presented at the meeting of the American Anthropological Association, 1979, Lexington, Ky.; William Lynwood Montell, *The Saga of Coe Ridge: A Study in Oral History* (Knoxville: University of Tennessee Press, 1970).

For other treatments of the postwar black population in Appalachia, see William H. Turner, "The Demography of Black Appalachia, Past and Present," in Turner and Cabbell, *Blacks in Appalachia,* pp. 237–61; Michael A. Cooke, "Race Relations in Montgomery County, Virginia, 1870–1990," in Barker, *Environmental Voices,* pp. 94–104; Sprague, "From Slavery to Freedom," pp. 72–73; and Wilson, *Southern Mountaineers,* pp. 41–42.

13. On the migration of blacks in Appalachian coalfields, see Ronald L. Lewis, *Black Coal Miners in America: Race, Class, and Community Conflict, 1780–1980* (Lexington: University Press of Kentucky, 1987), chap. 7; Ronald L. Lewis, "From Peasant to Proletarian: The Migration of Southern Blacks to the Central Appalachian Coalfields," *Journal of Southern History* 55 (1989): 77–102; Emily Jones Hudson, "The Black American Family in Southeastern Kentucky: Red Fox, Kodak, and Town Mountain," in *Reshaping the Image of Appalachia,* ed. Loyal Jones (Berea, Ky.: Berea College Appalachian Center, 1986), pp. 136–45; Joe William Trotter, Jr., *Coal, Class, and Color: Blacks in Southern West Virginia, 1915–1932* (Urbana: University of Illinois Press, 1990), pt. 1; Wayne Flynt, *Poor but Proud: Alabama's Poor Whites* (Tuscaloosa: University of Alabama Press, 1989), chap. 5. None of these works speaks to the issue of local reaction of white Appalachians to this influx of black migrants, though Flynt has a perceptive discussion of race relations between black and Appalachian white workers in northern Alabama's coalfields (pp. 121, 136–38, 257–61).

14. Stuckert, "Black Populations of Southern Appalachian Mountains," pp. 141 (tab. 1), 145.

15. W. J. Cash, *The Mind of the South* (New York: Knopf, 1941), p. 219.

16. John Eaton, *Grant, Lincoln, and the Freedman: Reminiscences of the Civil War* (New York: Longmans, Green, 1907), p. 119. See also John Cimprich, "Slavery's End in East Tennessee," *East Tennessee Historical Society Publications* 52 and 53 (1980–81): 85.

17. John C. Campbell, *The Southern Highlander and His Homeland* (New York: Russell Sage Foundation, 1921), p. 95; Muriel E. Sheppard, *Cabins in the Laurel* (Chapel Hill: University of North Carolina Press, 1935), p. 60.

18. Raymond Andrews, *The Last Radio Baby: A Memoir* (Atlanta: Peachtree, 1990), p. 79; William Styron, *The Confessions of Nat Turner* (New York: Random House, 1967), pp. 326–27.

19. Loyal Jones, "Appalachian Values," in *Voices from the Hills: Selected Readings of Southern Appalachia,* ed. Robert J. Higgs (New York: Ungar, 1975), pp. 507–17.

20. Quoted in William H. Turner, "Between Berea (1904) and Birmingham (1908): The Rock and Hard Place for Blacks in Appalachia," in Turner and Cabbell, *Blacks in Appalachia,* p. 13.

The whole notion of Appalachia as a center of Underground Railroad activity is suspect. Most major treatments of the Underground Railroad make no reference to southern highland locales. See Larry Gara, *The Liberty Line: The Legend of the Underground Railroad* (Lexington: University Press of Kentucky, 1961); William Still, *The Underground Railroad* (Philadelphia: Porter and Coates, 1872); Eber M. Pettit, *Sketches in the History of the Underground Railroad* (Fredonia, N.Y.: W. McKinstry and Son, 1879). The only such account to refer to even the possibility that Appalachians provided regular routes is Wilbur H. Siebert, *The Underground Railroad from Slavery to Freedom* (New York: Macmillan, 1899), pp. 118–19, but its map (facing p. 113) indicates no routes anywhere in the region.

21. Leon F. Williams, "The Vanishing Appalachian: How to 'Whiten' the Problem," in Turner and Cabbell, *Blacks in Appalachia,* p. 201.

22. Barbara J. Fields, "Ideology and Race in American History," in *Region, Race, and Reconstruction: Essays in Honor of C. Vann Woodward,* ed. J. Morgan Kousser and James M. McPherson (New York: Oxford University Press, 1982), p. 157; Samuel C. Williams, ed., "Journal of Events (1825–1873) of David Anderson Deaderick," *East Tennessee Historical Publications* 8 (1936): 121–37.

23. Frederick Douglass, *The Life and Times of Frederick Douglass* (1892; reprint, New York: Macmillan, 1962), pp. 273–74. See also William S. McFeely, *Frederick Douglass* (New York: Norton, 1991), pp. 186–87, 190–92.

24. Richard Hinton interview with John Brown and John Kagi in August 1858, in *John Brown,* ed. Richard Warch and Jonathan F. Fauton (Englewood Cliffs, N.J.: Prentice-Hall, 1973), p. 54 (second quote). For other treatments of the southern highlands as central to Brown's insurrection plan, see Siebert, *Underground Railroad,* p. 118; and Jules Abel, *Man of Fire: John Brown and the Cause of Liberty* (New York: Macmillan, 1971), pp. 245–48.

25. James W. Taylor, *Alleghania: A Geographical and Statistical Memoir* (St. Paul, Minn.: James Davenport, 1862), pp. 1–2, 15–16.

26. William Goodrich, *God's Handiwork in the Sea and the Mountains: Sermons Preached after a Summer Vacation* (Cleveland, Ohio: Privately published, n.d.), quoted in Jan Davidson's introduction to Frances Lousia Goodrich, *Mountain Homespun* (Knoxville: University of Tennessee Press, 1989), p. 13.

27. Batteau, *Invention of Appalachia,* p. 78.

28. Harry M. Caudill, *Night Comes to the Cumberlands: A Biography of a Depressed Area* (Boston: Little, Brown, 1962), pp. 38–39.

29. Asa Earl Martin, "The Anti-Slavery Societies of Tennessee," *Tennessee Historical Magazine* 1 (1915): 261–81; Cratis D. Williams, "The Southern Mountaineer in Fact and Fiction" (Ph.D. diss., New York University, 1961), 1:74–75; North Callahan, *Smoky Mountain Country,* ed. Erskine Caldwell (New York: Duell, Sloan, and Pearce, 1952), pp. 37–49; Thomas W. Humes, *The Loyal Mountaineers of Tennessee* (Knoxville: Ogden Bros., 1888), pp. 31–33; David W. Bowen, *Andrew Johnson and the Negro* (Knoxville: University of Tennessee Press, 1989), pp. 15–16.

30. Durwood Dunn, *Cades Cove: The Life and Death of a Southern Appalachian Community, 1818–1937* (Knoxville: University of Tennessee Press, 1988), pp. 124–25. On opposition to East Tennessee abolitionists, see Chase C. Mooney, *Slavery in Tennessee* (Bloomington: Indiana University Press, 1957), pp. 70–73; Bowen, *Andrew Johnson and the Negro,* p. 16; Drake, "Slavery and Antislavery in Appalachia," pp. 31–32. On postwar commitment to biracial education at Maryville, see Lester C. Lamon, "Ignoring the Color Line: Maryville College, 1868–1901," in *The Adaptable South: Essays in Honor of George Brown Tindall,* ed. Elizabeth Jacoway et al. (Baton Rouge: Louisiana State University Press, 1991), pp. 64–89.

31. Henry Ruffner, *Address to the People of West Virginia: Showing That Slavery is Injurious to the Public Welfare and That It May Gradually Be Abolished Without Detriment to the Rights and Interests of Slaveholders* (Lexington, Va.: R. C. Noel, 1847), cited and discussed in Fitzhugh Brundage, "Shifting Attitudes towards Slavery in Antebel-

lum Rockbridge County," *Rockbridge Historical Society Proceedings* 10 (1980–89): 333–44. There is no indication that the abolition of slavery was ever a factor in intrastate sectional battles waged by highlanders in antebellum legislatures in North Carolina, Kentucky, or even Tennessee.

32. Richard D. Sears, *"A Practical Recognition of the Brotherhood of Man": John G. Fee and the Camp Nelson Experience* (Berea, Ky.: Berea College Press, 1986), p. 46; Semple, "Anglo-Saxons of the Kentucky Mountains," p. 151. See also Richard D. Sears, *The Day of Small Things: Abolitionism in the Midst of Slavery* (Lanham, Md.: University Press of America, 1986). Broader studies of abolitionism in Kentucky include Asa Earl Martin, *The Anti-Slavery Movement in Kentucky Prior to 1850* (Louisville, Ky.: Filson Club Publication no. 25, 1918); Lowell H. Harrison, *The Antislavery Movement in Kentucky* (Lexington: University Press of Kentucky, 1978); Gordon E. Finnie, "The Antislavery Movement in the Upper South before 1840," *Journal of Southern History* 35 (1969): 319–42; Jeffrey Broke Allen, "Were Southern White Critics of Slavery Racists? Kentucky and the Upper South, 1791–1824," *Journal of Southern History* 44 (1978): 169–90; Stanley Harrold, "Violence and Nonviolence in Kentucky Abolitionism," *Journal of Southern History* 57 (1991): 15–38. None of these works acknowledges any significant abolitionist activity in the state's eastern mountain region. (Another Appalachian institution that embraced biracial education after the war was Tennessee Wesleyan College in Athens, under the auspices of the Northern Methodist Church).

33. Quoted in Sears, *"Practical Recognition of the Brotherhood of Man,"* p. 46. On Berea's move away from its commitment to black education, see Klotter, "Black South and White Appalachia," pp. 846–48; Turner, "Between Berea and Birmingham," pp. 13–14; Jacqueline G. Burnside, "Suspicion Versus Faith: Negro Criticisms of Berea College in the Nineteenth Century," in Jones, *Reshaping the Image of Appalachia,* pp. 102–25.

34. Carter G. Woodson, "Freedom and Slavery in Appalachia," *Journal of Negro History* 1 (April 1916): 132–50. Much the same ground is covered in Finnie, "Antislavery Movement in the Upper South." See also Barton, "Cumberland Mountains and the Struggle for Freedom."

35. Don West, *Freedom in the Mountains* (Huntington, W.Va.: Appalachian Movement Press, 1973), pp. 3–4, 9.

36. Woodson, "Freedom and Slavery in Appalachia," p. 147; Don West interview in *Refuse to Stand Silently By: An Oral History of Grass-Roots Social Activism in America, 1921–1964,* ed. Eliot Wigginton (New York: Doubleday, 1992), p. 68.

37. Frederick Law Olmsted, *A Journey through the Back Country in the Winter of 1853–54* (New York: Mason Brothers, 1860), pp. 239, 237, 263–64. On Olmsted's schedule and route, see Charles E. Beveridge, ed., *The Papers of Frederick Law Olmsted,* vol. 2, *Slavery and the South, 1852–1857* (Baltimore: Johns Hopkins University Press, 1981), pp. 309 (map), and 481–82 (itinerary). For a fuller discussion of his mission and findings, see John C. Inscoe, "Olmsted in Appalachia: A Connecticut Yankee Encounters Slavery and Racism in the Southern Highlands," *Slavery and Abolition* 9 (September 1988): 171–82.

38. Humes, *Loyal Mountaineers,* p. 30.

39. Julian Ralph, "Our Appalachian Americans," *Harper's Monthly Magazine,* June 1903, p. 37.

40. Lillian Smith, *Killers of the Dream,* rev. ed. (New York: Norton, 1961), p. 171.

41. Kenneth W. Noe, *Southwest Virginia's Railroad: Modernization and the Sectional Crisis* (Urbana: University of Illinois Press, 1994), p. 17.

42. See, for example, Smith, *Killers of the Dream,* p. 170; Daniel R. Hundley, *Social Relations in Our Southern States* (1860; reprint, Baton Rouge: Louisiana State University Press, 1979), pp. 258–60; Eugene D. Genovese, "Yeomen Farmers in a Slaveholder's Democracy," *Agricultural History* 49 (1975): 331–42; Steven Hahn, *The Roots of Southern Populism: Yeoman Farmers and the Transformation of the Georgia Upcountry, 1850–1890* (New York: Oxford University Press, 1983), pp. 88–91; J. William Harris, *Plain Folk and Gentry in a Slave Society: White Liberty and Black Slavery in Augusta's Hinterlands* (Middleton, Conn.: Wesleyan University Press), pp. 72–77; F. N. Boney, *Southerners All* (Macon, Ga.: Mercer University Press, 1984), chap, 2. On the commonality of southern and Appalachian values, see Richard B. Drake, "Southern Appalachia and the South: A Region within a Section," in *Southern Appalachia and the South: A Region within a Region,* ed. John C. Inscoe, *Journal of the Appalachian Studies Association* 3 (1991): 18–27.

43. Carl N. Degler, *The Other South: Southern Dissenters in the Nineteenth Century* (Boston: Northeastern University Press, 1982). Quote is title of chap. 2.

44. Alexis de Tocqueville, *Democracy in America,* 4th ed. (New York: Henry G. Langley, 1845), 1:389–90.

45. Eugene H. Berwanger, *The Frontier against Slavery: Western Anti-Negro Prejudice and the Slavery Extension Controversy* (Urbana: University of Illinois Press, 1967); Rodger Cunningham, *Apples on the Flood: The Southern Mountain Experience* (Knoxville: University of Tennessee Press, 1987), p. 99.

46. Oliver P. Temple, *East Tennessee and the Civil War* (Cincinnati, Ohio: Robert Clarke, 1899), pp. 196–97.

47. Humes, *Loyal Mountaineers,* p. 31. See also Arthur W. Spaulding, *The Men of the Mountains: The Story of the Southern Mountaineer and His Kin of the Piedmont* (Nashville: Southern Press, 1915), pp. 40–41.

48. Alexander H. Jones, *Knocking at the Door* (Washington, D.C.: McGill and Witherow, 1866), p. 14; Inscoe, *Mountain Master,* pp. 236–38.

49. Vernon M. Queener, "William G. Brownlow as an Editor," *East Tennessee Historical Society Publications* 4 (1932): 80; W. G. Brownlow, *Sketches of the Rise, Progress and Decline of Secession* (Philadelphia: George W. Childs, 1862), p. 109; Nelson quoted in Richard Current, *Lincoln's Loyalists: Union Soldiers from the Confederacy* (Boston: Northeastern University Press, 1992), p. 50. For a comparison of attitudes in two sections of Appalachia, see John C. Insoe, "Mountain Unionism, Secession, and Regional Self-Image: The Contrasting Cases of Western North Carolina and East Tennessee," in *Looking South: Chapters in the Story of an American Region,* ed. Winfred B. Moore, Jr., and Joseph F. Tripp (Westport, Conn.: Greenwood Press, 1989), pp. 115–29.

50. Inscoe, *Mountain Masters,* pp. 244–46.

51. Altina L. Waller, *Feud: Hatfields, McCoys, and Social Change in Appalachia, 1860–1900* (Chapel Hill: University of North Carolina Press, 1988), p. 30.

52. Etheleve Dyer Jones, *Facets of Fannin: A History of Fannin County, Georgia* (Dallas: Curtis Media, 1989), p. 32; Jonathan Sarris, "Anatomy of an Atrocity: The Madden Branch Massacre and the Guerrilla War in North Georgia, 1861–1865," *Georgia Historical Quarterly* 77 (Winter 1993): 679–710.

53. Henry T. Shanks, "Disloyalty to the Confederacy in Southwestern Virginia, 1861–1865," *North Carolina Historical Review* 21 (1944): 118–19. For more recent confirmation of Shanks's conclusions, see Kenneth W. Noe, "Red String Scare: Civil War Southwest Virginia and the Heroes of America," *North Carolina Historical Review* 59 (1992): 301–22.

54. Theodore F. Davidson, "The Carolina Mountaineer: The Highest Type of American Character," in *First Annual Transactions of the Pen and Plate Club of Asheville, N.C.,* by Theodore F. Davidson (Asheville: Hackney and Mole, 1905), pp. 84–85. For variations of this theme, see Spaulding, *Men of the Mountains,* pp. 41–43; Humes, *Loyal Mountaineers,* pp. 30–31; Caudill, *Night Comes to the Cumberlands,* pp. 37–39; Waller, *Feud,* pp. 30–31.

55. Quoted in Michael P. Johnson, *Toward a Patriarchal Society: The Secession of Georgia* (Baton Rouge: Louisiana State University Press, 1977), p. 50.

56. Circular by W. W. Avery and Marcus Erwin, quoted in Insco, *Mountain Masters,* p. 226; Richard O. Curry, *A House Divided: A Study of Statehood Politics and the Copperhead Movement in West Virginia* (Pittsburgh: University of Pittsburgh Press, 1964), chap. 9, esp. pp. 91–92.

57. Drake, "Slavery and Antislavery in Appalachia," 28. For more extensive discussion of the slave trade in Appalachia, see Dunaway, "People without History," pp. 4–8; Noe, *Southwest Virginia's Railroad,* chap. 1.

58. G. W. Featherstonaugh, *Excursion through the Slave States* (New York: Harper and Brothers, 1844), pp. 36–37, 46.

59. Joseph John Gurney, *A Journey in North America, Described in Familiar Letters to Amelia Opie* (Norwich: J. Fletcher, 1841), pp. 53–54.

60. Sarah Gudger and Mary Barbour interviews in *The American Slave: A Composite Autobiography,* ed. George P. Rawick, vol. 14, *North Carolina Narratives* (Westport, Conn.: Greenwood Press, 1972), pt. 1, pp. 354–55 (Gudger), p. 79 (Barbour). Aunt Sophia quoted in Drake, "Slavery and Antislavery in Appalachia," p. 27. For other examples of Appalachian ex-slave testimony, see Dunaway, "People without History," pp. 5, 7, 36–37.

61. Eric J. Olson, "Race Relations in Asheville, North Carolina: Three Incidents, 1868–1906," in *The Appalachian Experience: Proceedings of the 6th Annual Appalachian Studies Conference,* ed. Barry M. Buxton (Boone, N.C.: Appalachian Consortium Press, 1983), pp. 153–56.

62. Edward L. Ayers, *Vengeance and Justice: Crime and Punishment in the Nineteenth-Century American South* (New York: Oxford University Press, 1984), pp. 159–61.

63. William F. Holmes, "Moonshining and Collective Violence: Georgia, 1889–1895," *Journal of American History* 67 (December 1980): 589–611; W. Fitzhugh Brundage, *Lynching in the New South: Georgia and Virginia, 1880–1930* (Urbana:

University of Illinois Press, 1993), chap. 5. See also Wilbur R. Miller, *Revenuers and Moonshiners: Enforcing Federal Liquor Law in the Mountain South, 1865–1900* (Chapel Hill: University of North Carolina Press, 1991), pp. 52–53. It is perhaps noteworthy that the only black informant Miller cites as a victim of whitecappers was a Georgian.

64. George C. Wright, *Racial Violence in Kentucky, 1865–1940: Lynchings, Mob Rule, and "Legal Lynching"* (Baton Rouge: Louisiana State University Press, 1990), chap. 2 (see particularly tab. 4, p. 73).

65. Robert P. Stuckert, "Racial Violence in Southern Appalachia, 1880–1940," *Appalachian Heritage* 20 (Spring 1991): 35–41.

66. Brundage, *Lynching in the New South,* chap. 4.

67. Charles Lanman, *Letters from the Alleghany Mountains* (New York: Putnam, 1849), p. 314; Olmsted, *Journey through the Back Country,* pp. 226–27. It is worth noting that the mountain slaves to whom Gurney reacts are the first he encountered during his tour of the United States, whereas both Lanman and Olmsted moved into the southern highlands after extensive travel elsewhere in the South and thus had a basis for comparison of slave life that Gurney lacked.

68. Inscoe, *Mountain Masters,* chap. 5. Some reviewers of the book found this section less than convincing. See Shane White, "Feeling 'Awful Southern' or Slavery on the Periphery," *Reviews in American History* 18 (June 1990): 197–201; and reviews by Altina L. Waller, in *Register of the Kentucky Historical Society* 88 (1990): 346–48; John Schlotterback, in *Journal of Southern History* 57 (1991): 330–31; and Lynda Morgan, *American Historical Review* 96 (1991): 262–63. It is admittedly a slippery point to prove, and the evidence must remain, by its nature, circumstantial and impressionistic.

69. Van Beck Hall, "The Politics of Appalachian Virginia, 1790–1830," in *Appalachian Frontiers: Settlement, Society, and Development in the Preindustrial Era,* ed. Robert D. Mitchell (Lexington: University Press of Kentucky, 1991), pp. 184–86.

70. Gordon B. McKinney, "Southern Mountain Republicans and the Negro, 1865–1900," *Journal of Southern History* 41 (1975): 493–96.

71. Cimprich, "Slavery's End in East Tennessee," pp. 84–85. Cimprich also indicated that antiblack sentiment among East Tennesseeans did indeed intensify after emancipation, just as Eaton had complained.

72. Olson, "Race Relations in Asheville," pp. 163–64.

73. J. Morgan Kousser, *The Shaping of Southern Politics: Suffrage Restriction and the Establishment of the One-Party South, 1880–1910* (New Haven: Yale University Press, 1974), pp. 112, 224, 248, 264.

74. Fields, "Ideology and Race in American History," pp. 144, 146. For further expansion of her arguments, see Fields, "Slavery, Race, and Ideology in the United States of America," *New Left Review,* no. 181 (1990): 118. See also John B. Boles, "Cycles of Racism in Southern History," paper presented at conference, "Black and White Perspectives on the American South," 29 September 1994, University of Georgia, Athens.

75. Fields, "Ideology and Race in American History," p. 155.

7. Gender, Class and Self-Image

Ball, R.A. 1968. A poverty case: The analgesic subculture of the southern Appalachians. *American Sociological Review* 33:855–95.

Beaver, P.D. 1976. Symbols and social organization in an Appalachian community. Ph.D. diss., Duke University, Durham, N.C.

Beaver, P.D. 1986. *Rural community in the Appalachian South.* Lexington: University Press of Kentucky.

Cavender, A. 1981. An ethnographic inquiry into social identity, social stratification, and premature school withdrawal in a rural Appalachian school. Ph.D. diss., University of Tennessee, Knoxville.

Coles, R. 1971. *Children of crisis,* vol. 2, *Migrants, sharecroppers, mountaineers.* Boston: Little, Brown.

Fisher, S.L. 1977. Folk culture or folk tale: Prevailing assumptions about the Appalachian personality. In *An Appalachian symposium: Essays written in honor of Cratis D. Williams,* 14–27. Boone, N.C.: Appalachian State University Press.

Fitchen, J.M. 1981. *Poverty in rural America: A case study.* Boulder, Colo.: Westview Press.

Gaventa, J. 1980. *Power and powerlessness: Quiescence and rebellion in an Appalachian valley.* Urbana: University of Illinois Press.

Glaser, B.G., and A.L. Strauss. 1967. *The discovery of grounded theory: Strategies for qualitative research.* Chicago: Aldine.

Heller, P.L., and G.M. Quesada. 1977. Rural familism: An interregional analysis. *Rural Sociology* 42(2):220–39.

Hicks, G.L. 1976. *Appalachian valley.* New York: Holt, Rinehart, and Winston.

Kahn, K. 1972. *Hillbilly women.* New York: Avon.

Kaplan, B.H. 1971. *Blue Ridge: an Appalachian community in transition.* Morgantown, W.Va.: Office of Research and Development, Appalachian Center, University of West Virginia.

Keefe, S.E., U.M.L. Reck, and G.G. Reck. 1985. Family and education in southern Appalachia. Paper presented at the annual meeting of the Appalachian Studies Conference, Berea, Ky.

Lewis, H.M., and E.E. Knipe. 1978. The colonialism model: The Appalachian case. In *Colonialism in modern America: The Appalachian case,* eds. H.M. Lewis, L. Johnson and D. Askins, 9–31. Boone, N.C.: The Appalachian Consortium Press.

Lewis, H.M., S. Kobak, and L. Johnson. 1978. Family, religion and colonialism in central Appalachia. In *Colonialism in modern America: The Appalachian case,* eds. H.M. Lewis, L. Johnson, and D. Askins, 113–139. Boone, N.C.: The Appalachian Consortium Press.

Lewis, H.M., L. Selfridge, J. Merrifield, S. Thrasher, L. Perry, and C. Honneycutt, eds. 1986. *Picking up the pieces: Women in and out of work in the rural South.* New Market, Tenn.: Highlander Research and Educational Center.

Looff, D.H. 1971. *Appalachia's children: The challenge of mental health.* Lexington: University Press of Kentucky.

Parenstedt, E. 1965. A comparison of the childrearing environment of upper-lower and very low-income class families. *American Journal of Orthopsychiatry* 35:89–98.

Petchesky, R.P. 1983. Reproduction and class divisions among women. In *Class, race and sex: The dynamics of control,* eds. A. Swerdlow and H. Lessinger, 221–241. Boston: G.K. Hall.

Photiadis, J.D. n.d. *An overview of the processes of social transition in rural Appalachia.* Morgantown: Office of Research and Development, Center for Extension and Continuing Education, West Virginia University.

Photiadis, J.D. 1970. Rural southern Appalachia and mass society. In *Change in rural Appalachia: Implications for action programs,* ed. J.D. Photiadis and H.K. Schwarzweller, 5–22. Philadelphia: University of Pennsylvania Press.

Photiadis, J.D. 1986. *Community and family change in rural Appalachia.* Morgantown: West Virginia University Center for Extension and Continuing Education.

Polansky, N.A., R.A. Borgman, and C. De Saix. 1972. *Roots of futility.* San Francisco: Jossey-Bass.

Schwarzweller, H.K., J.S. Brown, and J.J. Mangalam. 1971. *Mountain families in transition: A case study in Appalachian migration.* University Park: Pennsylvania State University Press.

Smith, B.E. 1986. Women in the South: Economic survival. In *Picking up the pieces: Women in and out of work in the rural South,* ed. H.M. Lewis, L. Selfridge, J. Merrifield, S. Thrasher, L. Perry, and C. Honeycutt, 4–5. New Market, Tenn.: Highlander Research and Education Center.

Stephenson, J.B. 1968. *Shiloh: A mountain community.* Lexington: University Press of Kentucky.

Tennessee Advisory Commission on Intergovernmental Relations. 1985. *Fiscal, economic and social profiles of county areas in Tennessee.*

Tickamyer, A.R., and C. Tickamyer. 1987. Gender, family structure, and poverty in central Appalachia. In *The land and economy of Appalachia: Proceedings from the 1986 conference on Appalachia,* 80–90. Lexington: Appalachian Center, University of Kentucky.

U.S. Bureau of the Census. 1982. *Census of population: 1980, general, social and economic characteristics.* Washington, D.C.: U.S. Government Printing Office.

Walls, D.S., and D.B. Billings. 1977. The sociology of southern Appalachia. *Appalachian Journal* 4:131–44.

Weeks, J.S. 1980. Is the mountain woman unique? A debate. In *The Appalachian woman: Images and essence,* ed. P.B. Cheek, 22–26. Mars Hill, N.C.: Council on Appalachian Women.

Weller, J.E. 1965. *Yesterday's people: Life in contemporary Appalachia.* Lexington: University of Kentucky Press.

8. Out in the Mountains: Exploring Lesbian and Gay Lives

1. Ed. Note: "Gaydar" is a "sixth sense" many gay people have developed and is a pun on the word "radar."

Interviews Cited

1. 1993. Female, twenty-eight years old. Interview with authors. Lexington, Ky., 16 December.

2. 1993. Female, forty-five years old. Interview with authors. Lexington, Ky., 27 October.

3. 1994. Male, thirty-seven years old. Interview with authors. Lexington, Ky., 23 January.

4. 1994. Female, twenty-one years old. Interview with authors. Lexington, Ky., 15 February.

5. 1993. Female, twenty-eight years old. Interview with authors. Lexington, Ky., 12 August.

6. 1993. Female, forty-three years old. Interview with authors. Lexington, Ky., 19 October.

7. 1993. Male, twenty-eight years old. Interview with authors. Lexington, Ky., 15 December.

8. 1993. Male, twenty years old. Interview with authors. Lexington, Ky., 10 December.

9. 1993. Male, twenty-three years old. Interview with authors. Lexington, Ky., 14 September.

9. New Paths and Patterns of Appalachian Migration, 1975–1990

1. This was the era of an international oil embargo and a concomitant energy crisis in the U.S. that put a premium on the value of coal and brought many miners and their families back into the central Appalachian coalfields. Net inmigration to Appalachia also ended with the resolution of that crisis.

2. The urbanization of Appalachia is an increasingly important phenomenon in the study of the region. In 1990 nearly half of the residents in the Appalachian region lived in what the census bureau defines as a metropolitan county. But urbanization is not evenly distributed across the region: for instance, many of the counties in eastern Tennessee are classified as metropolitan, while there are relatively few such counties in southeastern Kentucky (see Maloney, 1987; Satterwhite, 1999).

3. From an Appalachian perspective, Gregory's research is seriously flawed because he consistently confuses Appalachians with white Southerners. With one exception, Appalachians are aggregated in Gregory's 1995 analysis with white migrants from the South as defined by the census bureau, i.e. sixteen southern states and the District of Columbia. In the one instance where "Appalachian" migrants are broken out of the data for special consideration, Gregory defines them as being born in the states of Kentucky, Tennessee, and West Virginia. In point of fact West Virginia is the only state that lies entirely within the ARC region along with portions of twelve other states.

4. Participants in the Great Migration have reached retirement age and may be returning to their home counties; other retirees may simply be amenity migrants, seeking the economic and environmental benefits of mountain life (Armas, 2000; Rowles, Watkins and Pauer, 1992; Schnell, 1996). In either case, the aging of Appalachia is a critical issue: Couto (1994:120) documents a significant growth in the over-65 population in the region between 1980 and 1990 (Appalachia 18.47% vs U.S. 11.16%).

5. The African-American population in the region has generally grown apace with that of the U.S. (c.f. Turner and Cabbell, 1985). However, southern and central Appalachia are losing black residents, while northern Appalachia accounts for most of the gain (Couto, 1994:108). Moreover, new enclaves of Hispanic residents have been established in the region during the 1990s (Lexington Herald Leader, 2000; Hartshorn, 1997; Turner et. al., 1996).

6. Halperin (1990) notes a preference among Appalachians to live in peripheral areas where they can commute to industrial work while maintaining rural pursuits such as gardening, farming, and raising livestock. Obermiller and Maloney, (1990) found evidence of the same phenomenon among migrants locating in smaller towns near Pittsburgh.

7. There is extensive documentation of "step migration" occurring among African-American southerners who moved to the North in the first half of this century (c.f. Alexander, 1998).

8. The 1980 data were made available by the Inter-University Consortium for Political and Social Research. The authors would like to thank Mark Carrozza at the University of Cincinnati's Institute for Policy Research for his assistance in identifying and acquiring this data set. Neither of these institutions nor their staff members bear any responsibility for the analyses or interpretations presented here.

9. For the purposes of this study the data for the minor civil divisions in New England are aggregated at the county level whenever possible.

10. The net proportions used here and elsewhere in this study are calculated for migrants over age 5 in relation to the 1990 census population of the area in question.

11. Caution should be used in interpreting the data on Hispanics. Because of the relatively small base populations of Hispanics in Appalachia, small numbers of migrants can result in large percentages.

12. Although no exact figure exists, an estimate based on the compilation of available data indicates there are about a million students enrolled in the community colleges, colleges, and universi-

ties located in the Appalachian region (c.f. National Center for Educational Statistics, 2000).

13. Caution should be used in interpreting the data on income. Because they represent persons 15 and older they may be skewed, for instance, by large numbers of students, retirees, people in the early stages of their working careers, or those receiving public assistance.

14. Poverty thresholds are determined by a federal formula that included 1989 income, size of family, and the number of related children under 18 years of age in the family. The average poverty threshold for a family of four persons was $12,674 in 1989.

15. The imbalance of migration by sex and race to Maryland appears to be a function of the penal institutions and military installations in or adjacent to the state's three Appalachian counties.

16. The authors used Beale Code (BC) definitions to create the following county categories (Butler and Beale, 1994):

Metro: (BC 0) Central counties of metropolitan areas of 1 million population or more; (BC 1) Fringe counties of metropolitan areas of 1 million population or more; (BC 2) Counties in metropolitan areas of 250,000–1,000,000 population; and (BC 3) Counties in metropolitan areas of less than 250,000 population.

Urban: (BC 4) Urban population of 20,000 or more, adjacent to a metropolitan area; (BC 5) Urban population of 20,000 or more, not adjacent to a metropolitan area; and (BC 6) Urban population of 2,500–19,999, adjacent to a metropolitan area.

Rural: (BC 7) Urban population of 2,500–19,999, not adjacent to a metropolitan area; (BC 8) Completely rural (no places with a population of 2,500 or more) adjacent to a metropolitan area; (BC 9) Completely rural (no places with a population of 2,500 or more) not adjacent to a metropolitan area.

17. Readers wishing to examine the complete tabular data upon which this article is based may access them at http://arc.gov/research/pdf/migrat.pdf

References

Alexander, J. Trent. 1998. "The Great Migration in Comparative Perspective: Interpreting the Urban Origins of Southern Black Migrants to Depression-Era Pittsburgh," *Social Science History,* 22:349–376.

Appalachian Regional Commission. 1979a. *Appalachia—A Reference Book.* Washington, D.C.

———. 1979b. *A Report to Congress on Migration.* Washington, D.C.

———. 1999. "Population Change in Appalachia." from www.arc.gov/data/pop/popmain.htm accessed 11/04/99.

Armas, Genaro C. 2000. "Luring retirees is lucrative for states." Associated Press. December 27. (Naples Daily News).

Bishop, C.E. *et al.* 2000. *The State of the South 2000.* MDC, Inc., Chapel Hill, NC.

Brown, James S. and George A. Hillery, Jr. 1962. "The Great Migration, 1940–1960," p. 54–78 in Thomas R. Ford, ed., *The Southern Appalachian Region: A Survey.* University of Kentucky Press.

———. 1972. "A Look at the 1970 Census," pp. 130–143 in David S. Walls and John B. Stephenson, eds., *Appalachia in the Sixties: A Decade of Reawakening.* Lexington: University of Kentucky Press.

Butler Margaret A. and Calvin L. Beale. 1994. "Rural-Urban Continuum Codes for Metro and Non-Metro Counties, 1993." Agriculture and Rural Economy Division, Economic Research Service, U.S. Department of Agriculture. Staff Report No. 9425.

Couto, Richard A. 1994. *An American Challenge: A Report on Economic Trends and Social Issues in Appalachia.* Dubuque, IA.: Kendall/Hunt Publishing Co.

———. 1997. "What Makes Mountains Move? Social Capital in Appalachia," a paper read at the Twentieth Annual Appalachian Studies Conference, March 14–16, Fort Mitchell, KY.

——— with Catherine S. Guthrie. 1999. *Making Democracy Work Better: Mediating Structures, Social Capital, and the Democratic Prospect.* Chapel Hill: University of North Carolina Press.

Doyle, Rodger. 2000. "The U.S. Population Race," *Scientific American,* (August) 283:26.

———. 2000. "Going the Distance," *Scientific American,* (January) 282:24.

Goodrich, Carter, Bushrod W. Allin, C. Warren Thornthwaite, et.al., 1936. *Migration and Economic Opportunity: The Report of the Study of Population Redistribution.* Philadelphia: University of Pennsylvania Press.

Gregory, James N. 1995. "The Southern Diaspora and the Urban Dispossessed: Demonstrating the Census Public Use Microdata Samples," *Journal of American History,* 82:111–134.

Halperin, Rhoda H. 1990. *The Livelihood of Kin: Making Ends Meet the "Kentucky Way."* Austin: University of Texas Press.

Hartshorn, Truman A. 1997. "The Changed South, 1947–1997," *Southeastern Geographer*, 37 (November): 122–139.

Lewandowski, James P. and Mark E. Reisinger. 1996. "Pennsylvania Migration 1985–1995: Responses to the State's Changing Space-Economy," *The Pennsylvania Geographer*, 34 (Spring/Summer): 5–21.

Lexington Herald Leader. 2000. "Perpetuating poverty at taxpayer expense: Low-wage plants do state more harm than good," unsigned editorial, December 3. from www.kentuckyconnect.com/heraldleader/news/120300/editorialdocs/1203cagle_s.htm

Maloney, Michael E. 1987. "Urban Appalachia: A Neglected Field of Study," *Urban Resources*, 4:5–7.

McCoy, Clyde B. and James S. Brown. 1981. "Appalachian Migration to Midwestern Cities," pp. 35–78 in William W. Philliber and Clyde B. McCoy, eds., *The Invisible Minority: Urban Appalachians*. Lexington: University Press of Kentucky.

National Center for Educational Statistics. 2000. "Integrated Postsecondary Education Data System (IPEDS)." from http://caspar.nsf.gov accessed 8/6/2000.

Obermiller, Phillip J. and Robert W. Oldendick. 1987. "Moving On: Recent Patterns of Appalachian Migration," pp. 51–62 in Phillip J. Obermiller and William W. Philliber, eds., *Too Few Tomorrows*. Boone, NC: Appalachian Consortium Press.

——— and Michael E. Maloney. 1990. "Looking for Appalachians in Pittsburgh: Seeking 'Deliverance' and Finding the 'Deer Hunter'," *Pittsburgh History*, 73:160–169.

Pandit, Kavita. 1997. "The Southern Migration Turnaround and Current Patterns," *Southeastern Geographer*, 37 (November): 238–250.

Picard, Jerome. 1981a. "A Decade of Change in Appalachia," *Appalachia*, 14:1–9.

———. 1981b. "Appalachia's Decade of Change—A Decade of Immigration," *Appalachia*, 15: 24–28.

Rand McNally. 1990. *City / County Finder*. Chicago: Rand McNally.

Rowles, Graham D. and John F. Watkins. 1995. *Demographic Change in Appalachia: Patterns and Trends*. Washington, D.C.: Appalachian Regional Commission.

———. John F Watkins, and G. Pauer. 1992. *Impact of Migration of the Elderly*. Washington, D.C.: Appalachian Regional Commission.

Satterwhite, Emily. 1999. "Seeing Appalachian Cities," *Southern Changes*, 21:20–22.

Schnell, George A. 1996. "Pike County's Location, Second-Home Population, and Retired In-Migrants: A Prescription for Rapid Growth," *Pennsylvania Geographer*, 35 (Spring): 23–37.

Turner, John, Erin Molenda, and Bernie Westendorff. 1996. "Migrants in Appalachia," *Journal of Appalachian Studies*, 2 (Spring): 123–130.

Turner, William H. and Edward J. Cabbell, eds. 1985. *Blacks in Appalachia*. Lexington: University Press of Kentucky.

U.S. Congress. 1940. House Select Committee to Investigate the Interstate Migration of Destitute Citizens, Interstate Migration: *Hearings*, 76th Congress, 3rd session, Vol. 3.

U.S. Department of Agriculture. 1935. *Economic and Social Problems of the Southern Appalachians*. Bureau of Agricultural Economics Miscellaneous Publication 205, Washington, DC: U.S. Government Printing Office.

———. 1999. "Economic Research Service's Revised County Typology," from www.econ.ag.gov/epubs/other/typolog accessed 11/17/99.

U.S. Department of Commerce. 1986. *Census of Population and Housing, 1980 (United States): County Migration by Selected Characteristics, 1975–1980*. Washington, DC: Bureau of the Census.

U.S. Department of Commerce. 1995. *Census of Population, 1990: County to County Migration Flow File on CD-ROM, Special Project (SP) 312*. Washington, DC: Bureau of the Census.

Woodson, Carter G. 1916. "The Negroes of Cincinnati Prior to the Civil War," *The Journal of Negro History*, 1:1–22

10. "We ain't agoin' back": A Retrospective Look at Urban Appalachians in Greater Cincinnati

1. See Carter G. Woodson. 1916. "The Negroes of Cincinnati Prior to the Civil War," and "Freedom and Slavery in Appalachian America," *Journal of Negro History*, 1, pages 1–22 and 132–150; see also The Carter G. Woodson Institute for Afro-American and African Studies at http://www.virginia.edu/~woodson/welcome/name.html.

2. The term 'urban Appalachians' is also used to describe the population of urban centers within Appalachia like Pittsburgh and Knoxville, but this usage is less frequent. For more information on Appalachian migration and urban Appalachians see the selected bibliography at http://www.uacvoice.org/bibliography.html

3. See Thomas Shaw. 2001. "The Greater Cincinnati Survey, Project Report for the Urban Appalachian Council," Institute for Policy Research, University of Cincinnati. Hamilton County encompasses the city of Cincinnati and for the purposes of this chapter we consider Hamilton County and greater Cincinnati to be coterminous.

4. For the analysis of census data see Michael E. Maloney and Janet R. Buelow. 1997. *The Social Areas of Cincinnati: An Analysis of Social Needs*. Third Edition—Patterns for Three Census Decades 1970–1990. University of Cincinnati, School of Planning; for a participant-observer study of an integrated urban Appalachian neighborhood see Rhoda Halperin. 1998. *Practicing Community: Class Culture, and Power in an Urban Neighborhood.* University of Texas Press.

5. Their low numbers in each of the survey samples (1980 N=36, 1989 N=20, 2001 N=50) make the cohort of black Appalachians too small for reliable statistical analysis in any given survey year. Consequently, in the balance of this chapter black Appalachians are included in neither the Appalachian cohort nor the black cohort to avoid confounding race with ethnicity. See William W. Philliber and Phillip J. Obermiller, 1987. "Black Appalachian Migrants: The Issue of Dual Minority Status," pp. 111–116 in Obermiller and Philliber, eds., *Too Few Tomorrows: Urban Appalachians in the 1980's*. Appalachian Consortium Press. For other sources of information on black Appalachians see John C. Inscoe, ed., 2001. *The Mountain South from Slavery to Segregation*. Lexington: University Press of Kentucky; William H. Turner and Edward J. Cabbell, eds., 1985. *Blacks in Appalachia*. Lexington: University Press of Kentucky.

6. If a second-generation Appalachian respondent had children living in Hamilton County, OH, he or she was asked five demographic questions about up to four of those children. In this way information was gathered for 184 third-generation Appalachians.

7. Cincinnati's predominantly Appalachian neighborhoods include Lower Price Hill, South Fairmount, Camp Washington, East End, Sedamsville-Riverside, Linwood, East Price Hill, Carthage, and census tract ten in Over-the-Rhine. For more information, especially on Appalachian enclaves in the wider metropolitan area, see Maloney and Buelow, op.cit.

8. See Cincinnati Department of City Planning, "Cincinnati Population Change by Race," at http://www.rcc.org/cplanning/census/change_race.pdf.

9. Shaw, op.cit.

10. Maloney and Buelow, op.cit., p. 50.

11. Ibid., see especially chapter six.

12. Timm, Patricia Ziegel. 1994. "Early School Leaving: An Analysis Across Three Generations of Urban Appalachian Women." D.Ed. dissertation, University of Cincinnati.

13. Ibid., p. 62.

14. Maloney, Michael, Pauletta Hansel and Ed Burdell. 1991. "East End Community Report." (Mimeo) Cincinnati: Legal Aid Society and the Urban Appalachian Council.

15. Halperin, op.cit.

16. Ibid., p. 1–2.

17. For more information about the Urban Appalachian Council see Thomas E. Wagner and Phillip J. Obermiller. 1999. *Valuing Our Past, Creating Our Future: The Founding of the Urban Appalachian Council*. Berea College Press; On other urban Appalachian organizations in Cincinnati see Phillip J. Obermiller. 1999. "Paving the Way: Urban Organizations and the Image of Appalachians," pages 251–266 in Billings, Norman, and Ledford, eds., *Confronting Appalachian Stereotypes: Back Talk from an American Region*. University Press of Kentucky; On urban Appalachian organizations in other cities see Thomas E. Wagner and Phillip J. Obermiller, 2000. "Going Home Without the Trip: Appalachian Migrant Organizations," pp. 215–230 in Obermiller, Wagner, and Tucker, eds., *Appalachian Odyssey: Historical Perspectives on the Great Migration*. Praeger.

11. Seeing Appalachian Cities

1. "Core Appalachia" is defined by Appalachian historian John Alexander Williams as consisting of the 164 counties which are included in all six of the major historical definitions of the region. These influential definitions were authored by W.G. Frost (1890s), John C. Campbell (1921), the US Department of Agriculture (1935), Thomas Ford (1962), the Appalachian Regional Commission (1965), and Raitz/Ulack (1984).

2. Calculations are based on the Appalachian Regional Commission's 1965 and 1997 annual reports, the US Bureau of the Census "Standard Metropolitan Statistical Areas: 1965," and metropolitan statistical areas as defined in the 1984 *County and City Data Book*. 1990 city population figures are taken from the 1997–98 *State and Metropolitan Area Data Book*.

Castells, Manuel. *The Information Age—Economy, Society, and Culture Volume II: The Power of Identity.* Malden, MA: Blackwell, 1997.

Rowles, Graham D. and John F. Watkins, "Demographic Change in Appalachia: Patterns and Trends." Report funded by the Appalachian Regional Commission, January, 1995.

Williams, John Alexander. "Counting Yesterday's People: Using Aggregate Data to Address the Problem of Appalachia's Boundaries." *Journal of Appalachian Studies.* 2, 1 (Spring 1996): 3–27.

12. "Hillbilly Culture": The Appalachian Mountain Folk in History and Popular Culture

Bare, Bobby. "Detroit City," RCA Victor, 8183, 1957.

Barron, Hal. S. "A Case for Appalachian Demographic History." *Appalachian Journal* 4 (Spring–Summer 1977): 208–15.

Bradley, William A. "Hobnobbing with Hillbillies." *Harper's Magazine* 132 (Dec. 1915): 91–103.

Brown, James, and George Hillery, Jr. "The Great Migration, 1940–1960." *The Southern Appalachian Region: A Survey.* Ford 54–78.

Brown, William P. "A Peculiar People." *Overland Monthly* 12 (Nov. 1888): 505–08.

Carawan, Guy and Candie. *Voices from the Mountains.* New York: Knopf, 1975.

Carr, Patrick, ed. *The Illustrated History of Country Music.* Garden City: Doubleday, 1979.

Caudill, Harry M. *Night Comes to the Cumberlands: A Biography of a Depressed Area.* Boston: Little, Brown, 1963.

———. "The Appalachian Future." *Appalachian Notes* 4 (Fourth Quarter 1976): 49–55.

Combs, Josiah H. *The Kentucky Highlanders from a Native Mountaineer Viewpoint.* Lexington: J. L. Richardson, 1913.

DeJong, Gordon F. "Ebb in the Exodus?" *Mountain Life and Work.* 45(Oct. 1969): 6–11, 22.

Dickey, James. *Deliverance.* Boston: Houghton Mifflin, 1970.

Eller, Ronald D. "Industrialization and Social Change in Appalachia, 1880–1930: A Look at the Static Image." *Colonialism in Modern America: The Appalachian Case.* Ed. Helen Lewis, Linda Johnson, and Donald Askins. Boone, N.C.: Appalachian Consortium, 1978. 35–46.

Flynt, J. Wayne. *Dixie's Forgotten People: The South's Poor Whites.* Bloomington: Indiana UP, 1979.

Ford, Thomas, ed. *The Southern Appalachian Region: A Survey.* Lexington: U of Kentucky. P, 1962.

Frost, William G. "The Southern Mountaineer: Our Kindred of the Boone and Lincoln Type." *American Monthly Review of Reviews* 21 (March 1900): 308–11.

Gibbard, Harold A. "Extractive Industries and Forestry." *The Southern Appalachian Region: A Survey.* Ford: 102–19.

Gray, L. C. "Economic Conditions and Tendencies in the Appalachians." *Mountain Life and Work* 9 (July 1933): 7–12.

Green, Archie. "Hillbilly Music: Source and Symbol." *Journal of American Folklore* 78 (July–Sept. 1965): 204–28.

Haney, William H. *The Mountain People of Kentucky.* Cincinnati: Rossler, 1906.

Harrington, Michael. *The Other America: Poverty in the United States.* New York: MacMillan, 1962.

Hilliard, Sam B. *Hog Meat and Hoecake: Food Supply in the Old South.* Carbondale: Southern Illinois UP, 1972.

Horn, Maurice, ed. *The World Encyclopedia of Comics.* New York: Chelsea House, 1976.

Kephart, Horace. *Our Southern Highlanders.* New York: Outing, 1913.

Klotter, James C. "The Black South and White Appalachia." *Journal of American History* 66 (Mar. 1980): 832–49.

McDonald, Forrest, and Grady McWhiney. "The South from Self-Sufficiency to Peonage: An Interpretation." *American Historical Review* 85 (Dec. 1980): 1095–1118.

Malone, Bill C. *Country Music U.S.A.: A Fifty-Year History.* Austin: American Folklore Society, 1968.

May, Ernest R. *American Imperialism: A Speculative Essay.* New York: Atheneum, 1968.

Morton, Oren F. *Land of the Laurel: A Story of the Alleghanies.* Morgantown, W.V.: Acme, 1903.

Newton, Milton B., Jr. "Cultural Preadaptation and the Upland South." *Man and Cultural Heritage: Papers in Honor of Fred B. Kniffen* Ed. H. J. Walker and W. G. Haag. Baton Rouge: Louisiana State U, School of Geoscience, 1974, 143–54.

Otto, John S. "Oral Traditional History in the Southern Highlands." *Appalachian Journal* 9 (Fall 1981): 20–31.

———. "Upland South Folk Culture." *Mid-America Folklore* 9 (Winter 1981): 73–88.

Owsley, Frank L. "Plain Folk and their Role in Southern History." *The South: Old and New Frontiers.* Ed. Harriet C. Owsley. Athens: U of Georgia P., 1969. 30–48.

Semple, Ellen C. "The Anglo-Saxons of the Kentucky Mountains." *Geographical Journal* 17 (June 1901): 558–623.

Shackelford, Laurel, and Bill Weinberg, eds. *Our Appalachia: An Oral History.* New York: Hill and Wang, 1977.

Smith, J. Russell, "Farming Appalachia." *American Review of Reviews* 53 (Mar. 1916): 329–36.

Taylor, Alva W. "Sub-Marginal Standards of Living in the Southern Mountains." *Mountain Life and Work* 14 (July 1938): 12–14.

Terrace, Vincent. *The Complete Encyclopedia of Television Programs.* 2 vols. South Brunswick, N.J.: A. S. Barnes, 1976.

Tribe, Ivan M. "The Hillbilly Versus the City: Urban Images in County Music." *John Edwards Memorial Foundation Quarterly* 10 (Summer 1974): 41–51.

U.S. Department of Agriculture. "Message from the President of the United States, Transmitting a Report of the Secretary of Agriculture in Relation to the Forests, Rivers, and Mountains of the Southern Appalachian Region." *Senate Document No. 84.* Washington, D.C.: Government Printing Office, 1902.

———. "Economic and Social Problems of the Southern Appalachians." *Miscellaneous Publications* No. 205. Washington, D.C.: Government Printing Office, 1935.

Vincent, George E. "A Retarded Frontier." *American Journal of Sociology* 4 (July 1898): 1–20.

Votaw, Albert N. "The Hillbillies Invade Chicago." *Harper's Magazine* 216 (Feb. 1958): 64–67.

Wilgus, D. K. "Country-Western Music and the Urban Hillbilly." *Journal of American Folklore* 83 (Apr.–June 1970): 157–79.

Williams, Cratis D. "Who Are the Southern Mountaineers?" *Appalachian Journal* 1 (Winter 1972): 48–55.

13. From Stereotype to Regional Hype: Strategies for Changing Media Portrayals of Appalachia

Belcher, Anndrena. 1991. "Relatively Strange: On the Set of *Next of Kin.*" *Now and Then* 8 (Fall): 22, 25–26.

Branscome, James. 1971. "Annihilating the Hillbilly: The Appalachians' Struggle with America's Institutions." *Katallagete* (Winter): 25–32.

"Hollywood in the Hills: An Interview with Tom Rickman." 1983. *Appalachian Journal* 10 (Summer): 335–349.

Montgomery, Kathryn. 1989. *Target Prime Time.* Oxford: Oxford University Press.

Newcomb, Horace. 1979. "Appalachia on Television: Region as Symbol in American Popular Culture." *Appalachian Journal* 6 (Autumn/Winter): 155–164.

Reed, John Shelton. 1986. *Southern Folk, Plain and Fancy.* Athens: University of Georgia Press.

Seltzer, Curtis. 1976. "The Media vs. Appalachia: A Case Study." *Mountain Review* 2 (May): 10–11.

Speer, Jean Haskell. 1977. "The Urban Hillbilly." Paper presented for the American Folklore Society. Detroit.

Turow, Joseph. 1992. *Media Systems in Society.* New York: Longman.

Whisnant, David. 1973. "Ethnicity and the Recovery of Regional Identity in Appalachia: Thoughts Upon Entering the Zone of Occult Instability." *Soundings* 56 (Spring 1973): 124–38.

14. Beyond Isolation and Homogeneity: Diversity and the History of Appalachia

1. Will Wallace Harney, "A Strange Land and Peculiar People," *Lippincott's Magazine* 12 (Oct. 1873): 430–31.

2. William Goodell Frost, "Our Contemporary Ancestors in the Southern Mountains," *Atlantic Monthly* 83 (March 1899): 311–19, quotations on 311.

3. Darlene Wilson, "The Felicitous Convergence of Mythmaking and Capital Accumulation: John Fox Jr. and the Formation of An (Other) Almost-White American Underclass," *Journal of Appalachian Studies* 1 (Fall 1995): 8, 6, 7.

4. Henry D. Shapiro, *Appalachia on Our Mind: The Southern Mountains and Mountaineers in the American Consciousness, 1870–1920* (Chapel Hill: Univ. of North Carolina Press, 1978); Allen W. Batteau, *The Invention of Appalachia* (Tucson: Univ. of Arizona Press, 1990); Dwight B. Billings, Mary Beth Pudup, and Altina L. Waller, "Taking Exception with Exceptionalism: The Emergence and Transformation of Historical Studies of Appalachia," in *Appalachia in the Making: The Mountain South in the Nineteenth Century,* ed. Mary Beth Pudup, Dwight

B. Billings, and Altina L. Waller (Chapel Hill: Univ. of North Carolina Press, 1995), 3.

5. The line between preindustrial and industrial Appalachia is sharply drawn at the turn of the twentieth century by some scholars. See, for example, Ronald D Eller, *Miners, Millhands, and Mountaineers: Industrialization of the Appalachian South, 1880–1930* (Knoxville: Univ. of Tennessee Press, 1982). Others argue that the critical changes were already taking place in the 1850s. See, for example, Kenneth W. Noe, *Southwest Virginia's Railroad: Modernization and the Sectional Crisis* (Urbana: Univ. of Illinois Press, 1994).

6. Gene Wilhelm Jr., "Appalachian Isolation: Fact or Fiction?" in *An Appalachian Symposium,* ed. J.W. Williamson (Boone, N.C.: Appalachian State Univ. Press, 1977), 77–78.

7. Ibid., 79–80.

8. Eller, *Miners, Millhands, and Mountaineers,* 100.

9. Steven Hahn, *The Roots of Southern Populism: Yeoman Farmers and the Transformation of the Georgia Upcountry, 1850–1890* (New York: Oxford Univ. Press, 1983). See also Steven Hahn, "The 'Unmaking' of the Southern Yeomanry: The Transformation of the Georgia Upcountry, 1860–1890," in *The Countryside in the Age of Capitalist Transformation,* ed. Steven Hahn and Jonathan Prude (Chapel Hill: Univ. of North Carolina Press, 1985), 179–203.

10. Lacy K. Ford Jr., *Origins of Southern Radicalism: The South Carolina Upcountry, 1800–1860* (New York: Oxford Univ. Press, 1988), 219–77.

11. Durwood Dunn, *Cades Cove: The Life and Death of a Southern Appalachian Community, 1818–1937* (Knoxville: Univ. of Tennessee Press, 1988), 85, 99, 115, 143, 145.

12. Wilma Dunaway, *The First American Frontier: Transition to Capitalism in Southern Appalachia, 1700–1860* (Chapel Hill: Univ. of North Carolina Press, 1996), 10, 198–99, 204–11.

13. Altina L. Waller, *Feud: Hatfields, McCoys, and Social Change in Appalachia, 1860–1900* (Chapel Hill: Univ. of North Carolina Press, 1988), 103, 20–23.

14. Dwight Billings, Kathleen Blee, and Louis Swanson, "Culture, Family, and Community in Preindustrial Appalachia," *Appalachian Journal* 13 (Winter 1986): 155, 161.

15. David C. Hsiung, "How Isolated Was Appalachia? Upper East Tennessee, 1780–1835," *Appalachian Journal* 16 (Summer 1989): 336–49. See also Hsiung's *Two Worlds in the Tennessee Mountains: Exploring the Origins of Appalachian Stereotypes* (Lexington: Univ. Press of Kentucky, 1997), 1–73.

16. Robert Tracy McKenzie, *One South or Many? Plantation Belt and Upcountry in Civil War-Era Tennessee* (Cambridge: Cambridge Univ. Press, 1994), 3–4.

17. Robert Tracy McKenzie, "Wealth and Income: The Preindustrial Structure of East Tennessee in 1860," *Appalachian Journal* 21 (Spring 1994): 262–63.

18. John C. Inscoe, *Mountain Masters, Slavery, and the Sectional Crisis in Western North Carolina* (Knoxville: Univ. of Tennessee Press, 1989), 11; Mrs. John C. [Olive Dame] Campbell, "Flame of a New Future for the Highlands," *Mountain Life and Work* 1(1925): 9.

19. Inscoe, *Mountain Masters,* 12–13.

20. The essay that touched off this debate is James A. Henretta, "Families and Farms: Mentalité in Pre-Industrial America," *William and Mary Quarterly* 35 (Jan. 1978): 3–32. See also Christopher Clark, *The Roots of Rural Capitalism: Western Massachusetts, 1780–1860* (Ithaca, N.Y., Cornell Univ. Press, 1990); Allan Kulikoff, *The Agrarian Origins of American Capitalism* (Charlottesville: Univ. Press of Virginia, 1992); Winifred Barr Rothenberg, *From Market-Places to a Market Economy: The Transformation of Rural Massachusetts, 1750–1850* (Chicago: Univ. of Chicago Press, 1992).

21. Robert D. Mitchell, *Commercialism and the Frontier: Perspectives on the Early Shenandoah Valley* (Charlottesville: Univ. Press of Virginia, 1977), 8.

22. Eller, *Miners, Millhands, and Mountaineers,* 3–38, quote on 3.

23. McKenzie, "Wealth and Income," 270–71.

24. Ibid., 271.

25. Ibid., 273–74, 272; Morton Rothstein, "The Antebellum South as a Dual Economy: A Tentative Hypothesis," *Agricultural History* 41 (1967): 375.

26. Billings, Blee, and Swanson, "Culture, Family, and Community," 154–70. For Beech Creek, see also Harry K. Schwarzweller, James S. Brown, and J.J. Mangalam, *Mountain Families in Transition: A Case Study of Appalachian Migration* (University Park: Pennsylvania State Univ. Press, 1971).

27. Paul Salstrom, *Appalachia's Path to Dependency: Rethinking a Region's Economic History, 1730–1940* (Lexington: Univ. Press of Kentucky, 1994).

28. Richard K. MacMaster, "The Cattle Trade in Western Virginia, 1760–1860," in *Appalachian*

Frontiers: Settlement, Society and Development in the Preindustrial Era, ed. Robert D. Mitchell (Lexington: Univ. Press of Kentucky, 1991), 127–49. See also Paul C. Henlein, *Cattle Kingdom in the Ohio Valley, 1783–1860* (Lexington: Univ. of Kentucky Press, 1959); John E. Stealey III, "Notes on the Ante-Bellum Cattle Industry from the McNeill Family Papers," *Ohio History* 75 (Winter 1966): 38–47, 70–72; Eugene J. Wilhelm, "Animal Drives: A Case Study in Historical Geography," *Journal of Geography* 66 (Sept. 1967): 327–34.

29. MacMaster, "Cattle Trade," 132–49; Stealey, "Notes on the Ante-Bellum Cattle Industry," 38–47, 70–72; Wilhelm, "Animal Drives," 327–34; Henlein, *Cattle Kingdom,* chap. 1.

30. Inscoe, *Mountain Masters,* 45–52, quotations on pp. 45, 52. See also H. Tyler Blethen and Curtis W. Wood, "A Trader on the Western Carolina Frontier," in *Appalachian Frontiers,* Mitchell, 150–65.

31. Tyrel G. Moore, "Economic Frontiers: Settlement, Society, and Development in the Preindustrial Era," in *Appalachian Frontiers,* Mitchell, 223, 227.

32. Gordon B. McKinney, "Economy and Community in Western North Carolina, 1860–1865," quote on 168, in *Appalachia in the Making,* Pudup, Billings, and Waller, 171–72.

33. Ibid., 166.

34. Turk McClesky, "Rich Land, Poor Prospects: Real Estate and the Formation of a Social Elite in Augusta County, Virginia, 1738–1770," *Virginia Magazine of History and Biography* 98 (July 1990): 449–86; Sara Shaver Hughes, *Surveyors and Statesmen: Land Measuring in Colonial Virginia* (Richmond: Virginia State Library, 1979); Warren Hofstra, "Land Policy and Settlement in the Northern Shenandoah Valley," in *Appalachian Frontiers,* Mitchell, 105–26; Barbara Rasmussen, *Absentee Landowning and Exploitation in West Virginia, 1760–1920* (Lexington: Univ. Press of Kentucky, 1994); Wilma A. Dunaway, "Speculators and Settler Capitalists: Unthinking the Mythology about Appalachian Landholding, 1790–1860," in *Appalachia in the Making,* Pudup, Billings, and Waller, 50–75.

35. Mary Beth Pudup has written on social stratification in "Social Class and Economic Development in Southeast Kentucky, 1820–1880," in *Appalachian Frontiers,* Mitchell, 235–60; "The Boundaries of Social Class in Preindustrial Appalachia," *Journal of Historical Geography* 15 (April 1989): 139–62; and "The Limits of Subsistence: Agriculture and Industry in Central Appalachia," *Agricultural History* 64 (Winter 1990): 61–89; "Town and Country in the Transformation of Appalachia," in *Appalachia in the Making,* Pudup, Billings, and Waller, 270–96. See also Dwight B. Billings and Kathleen M. Blee, "Appalachian Inequality in the Nineteenth Century: The Case of Beech Creek, Kentucky," *Journal of the Appalachian Studies Association* 4 (1992): 113–23.

36. McKenzie, "Wealth and Income," 175.

37. Ralph Mann, "Diversity in the Antebellum South: Four Farm Communities in Tazewell County, Virginia," in *Appalachia in the Making,* Pudup, Billings, and Waller, 137–62.

38. Chief of Engineers Report, *Index to the Executive Documents of the House of Representatives,* 45th Cong., 2d sess., vol. 3, part 1 (Washington, D.C.: Government Printing Office, 1878), 664.

39. John E. Stealey III, *The Antebellum Kanawha Salt Business and Western Markets* (Lexington: Univ. Press of Kentucky, 1993).

40. Moore, "Economic Frontiers," 230; Ronald L. Lewis, *Coal, Iron, and Slaves: Industrial Slavery in Maryland and Virginia, 1715–1865* (Westport, Conn.: Greenwood Press, 1979); Lester J. Cappon, "Iron-Making: A Forgotten Industry of North Carolina," *North Carolina Historical Review* 9 (Oct. 1932): 331–48; R. Bruce Council, Nicholas Honerkamp, and M. Elizabeth Will, *Industry and Technology in Antebellum Tennessee: The Archaeology of Bluff Furnace* (Knoxville: Univ. of Tennessee Press, 1992).

41. Gordon B. McKinney, *Southern Mountain Republicans, 1865–1900: Politics and the Appalachian Community* (Chapel Hill: Univ. of North Carolina Press, 1978), chap. 2. See also Dunn, *Cades Cove,* chap. 5.

42. Inscoe, *Mountain Masters,* 209–57.

43. Kenneth W. Noe, *Southwest Virginia's Railroad: Modernization and the Sectional Crisis* (Urbana: Univ. of Illinois Press, 1994), 6–8.

44. Ibid., 7–8. For similar influences and conclusions for East Tennessee see W. Todd Groce, "The Social Origins of East Tennessee's Confederate Leadership," in *The Civil War in Appalachia: Collected Essays,* eds. Kenneth W. Noe and Shannon H. Wilson (Knoxville: Univ. of Tennessee Press, 1997), 30–54.

45. Van Beck Hall, "The Politics of Appalachian Virginia, 1790–1830," in *Appalachian Frontiers,* Mitchell, 166.

46. Ibid., 169. For similar conclusions for a slightly earlier period in the Virginia backcountry, see Warren R. Hofstra and Robert D. Mitchell, "Town and Country in Backcountry Virginia: Win-

chester and the Shenandoah Valley, 1730–1800," *Journal of Southern History* 59 (Nov. 1993): 619–46.

47. Hall, "Politics of Appalachian Virginia," in *Appalachian Frontiers,* Mitchell, 172–73. See also Charles Henry Ambler, *Sectionalism in Virginia from 1776 to 1861* (Chicago: Univ. of Chicago Press, 1910).

48. Hall, "Politics of Appalachian Virginia," 186, in *Appalachian Frontiers,* Mitchell, 186.

49. Ronald L. Lewis, *Black Coal Miners in America: Race, Class, and Community Conflict, 1780–1980* (Lexington: Univ. Press of Kentucky, 1987), 122; Charles Bias, "The Completion of the Chesapeake and Ohio Railroad to the Ohio River, 1869–1873," *West Virginia History* 40 (Summer 1979): 393–403.

50 Lewis, *Black Coal Miners,* 123; Joseph T. Lambie, *From Mine to Market: The History of Coal Transportation on the Norfolk and Western Railway* (New York: New York Univ. Press, 1957), chap. 1–2.

51. Eller, *Miners, Millhands, and Mountaineers,* 140–53; Maury Klein, *History of the Louisville and Nashville Railroad* (New York: Macmillan, 1972), 23.

52. Eller, *Miners, Millhands, and Mountaineers,* 101; Ina Woestermeyer Van Noppen, *Western North Carolina since the Civil War* (Boone, N.C.: Appalachian Consortium Press, 1973).

53. John H. Stanfield, "The Sociohistorical Roots of Black/White Inequality in Urban Appalachia: Knoxville and East Tennessee," in *Blacks in Appalachia,* eds. William H. Turner and Edward J. Cabbell (Lexington: Univ. Press of Kentucky, 1985), 133.

54. Margaret Ripley Wolfe, *Kingsport Tennessee: A Planned American City* (Lexington: Univ. Press of Kentucky 1987), chaps. 2, 4; V.N. Phillips, *Bristol, Tennessee/Virginia: A History, 1852–1900* (Johnson City, Tenn.: The Overmountain Press, 1992), chaps. 10, 12.

55. For the impact of railroads on American society see, for example. Albro Martin, *Railroads Triumphant: The Growth, Rejection and Rebirth of a Vital American Force* (New York: Oxford Univ. Press, 1992). For their impact in the Appalachians see also Allen W. Trelease, *The North Carolina Railroad, 1849–1871, and the Modernization of North Carolina* (Chapel Hill: Univ. of North Carolina Press, 1991); William Price McNeel, *The Durbin Route: The Greenbrier Division of the Chesapeake and Ohio Railway* (Charleston, W.Va.: Pictorial Histories, 1985); Mary Verhoeff, *The Kentucky Mountains: Transportation and Commerce, 1750–1911* (Louisville, Ky.: Filson Club, 1911).

56. Corbin, *Life, Work, and Rebellion,* 7.

57. There are divergent interpretations on the nature of coal company-owned towns. One view grants exceptions to the rule, but holds that generally they oppressed their inhabitants. See Eller, *Miners, Millhands, and Mountaineers,* chap. 5; Corbin, *Life, Work, and Rebellion,* chap. 3. The opposing view also grants exceptions, but generally argues that life was better in company towns than what their inhabitants had known before. See Crandall A. Shifflett, *Coal Towns: Life, Work, and Culture in Company Towns of Southern Appalachia, 1880–1960* (Knoxville: Univ. of Tennessee Press, 1991). For the Americanization movement see John C. Hennen Jr., *The Americanization of West Virginia* (Lexington: Univ. Press of Kentucky, 1995).

58. U.S. Census of Population, 1880–1920; Randall G. Lawrence, "Appalachian Metamorphosis: Industrializing Society on the Central Appalachian Plateau" (Ph.D. diss., Duke Univ., 1983), 51–52; Ronald L. Lewis, "From Peasant to Proletarian: The Migration of Southern Blacks to the Central Appalachian Coalfields," *Journal of Southern History* 55 (Feb. 1989): 81.

59. Lewis, "Peasant to Proletarian," 82; Joe William Trotter Jr., *Coal, Class, and Color: Blacks in Southern West Virginia, 1915–32* (Urbana: Univ. of Illinois Press, 1990), chap. 3.

60. Margaret Ripley Wolfe, "Aliens in Southern Appalachia: Catholics in the Coal Camps, 1900–1940," *Appalachian Heritage* 6 (Winter 1978): 45; Kenneth R. Bailey, "A Judicious Mixture: Negroes and Immigrants in the West Virginia Mines, 1880–1917," in *Blacks in Appalachia,* Turner and Cabbell, 118–120.

61. Lewis, *Black Coal Miners,* 156.

62. See Herbert G. Gutman, *Work, Culture, and Society in Industrializing America* (New York: Vintage Books, 1977), 3–78.

63. Anonymous observation quoted in Wolfe, "Aliens in Southern Appalachia," 43. For an example of cross-cultural exchange see Barry O'Connell, "Doc Boggs, Musician and Coal Miner," *Appalachian Journal* 1–2 (Autumn–Winter 1983–84): 44–57.

64. See, for example, Dunaway, *First American Frontier;* N. Brent Kennedy, *The Melungeons: The Resurrection of a Proud People* (Macon, Ga.: Mercer Univ. press, 1994); John R. Finger, *The Eastern Band of Cherokees, 1819–1900* (Knoxville: Univ. of Tennessee Press, 1986).

15. Diversity in the Mountains and Regional and Cultural Identity

1. George M. Fredrickson, "America's Diversity in Comparative Perspective," *Journal of American History,* LXXXV (December 1998), 859–875.

2. Nancy J. Gentile, "Survival Behind Barbed Wire: The Impact of Imprisonment on Japanese-American Culture in World War II," *Maryland Historian,* XIX (Fall/Winter 1988), 15–31; Andrew Gyory, *Closing the Gate: Race Politics, and The Chinese Exclusion Act* (Chapel Hill: University of North Carolina Press, 1998); Robert Shaffer, "Opposition to Internment: Defending Japanese American Rights during World War II," *Historian,* LXI (Spring 1999), 597–619; Michi Nishiura Weglyn, *Years of Infamy: The Untold Story of America's Concentration Camps* (New York: Morrow, 1976); John R. Wunder, "The Chinese and the Courts in the Pacific Northwest: Justice Denied?" *Pacific Historical Review,* LII (May 1983), 191–211.

3. Jean H. Baker, *Ambivalent Americans: The Know-Nothing Party in Maryland* (Baltimore: Johns Hopkins University Press, 1977); Patricia Fanning, "Boycott!: Louis Imogen Guiney and the American Protective Association," *Historical Journal of Massachusetts,* XXVIII (Summer 1999), 166–180; John R. Mulkern, *The Know-Nothing Party in Massachusetts: The Rise and Fall of a People's Movement* (Boston: Northeastern University Press, 1991); Stephen R. Prescott, "White Robes and Crosses: Father John Conoley, the Ku Klux Klan, and the University of Florida," *Florida Historical Quarterly,* LXXI (July 1992), 18–40; James R. Sweeney, "Rum, Romanism, and Virginia Democrats: The Party Leaders and the Campaign of 1928," *Virginia Magazine of History and Biography,* XC (October 1982), 403–431.

4. Leonard Dinnerstein, *The Leo Frank Case* (New York: Columbia University Press, 1968; Robert S. Frey, "Christian Responses to the Trial and Lynching of Leo Frank: Ministers, Theologians, and Laymen," *Georgia Historical Quarterly,* LXXI (Fall 1987), 461–476; John Higham, "Anti-Semitism in the Gilded Age: A Reinterpretation," *Mississippi Valley Historical Review,* XLIII (March 1957), 557–578.

5. John Bodnar, *The Transplanted: A History of Immigrants in Urban America* (Bloomington: Indiana University Press, 1985); Richard H. Bradford, "Religion and Politics: Alfred E. Smith and the Election of 1928 in West Virginia," *West Virginia History,* XXXVI (April 1975), 213–221; Peter D'Agostino, "The Scalabrini, the Italian Immigrant Church, and Ethnic Nationalism in America," *Religion and American Culture,* VII (Winter 1997), 121–159; Matthew E. Mason, "The Hands Here Are Disposed to Be Turbulent: Unrest among the Irish Trackmen of the Baltimore and Ohio Railroad, 1829–1851," *Labor History,* XXXIX (August 1998), 253–272; Timothy J. Meagher, "Irish All the Time: Ethnic Consciousness among the Irish in Worcester, Massachusetts, 1880–1905," *Journal of Social History,* XIX (Winter 1985), 273–303; Donald Pienkos, "Politics, Religion, and Change in Polish Milwaukee, 1990–1930," *Wisconsin Magazine of History,* VI (Spring 1978), 179–209; William Toll, "Ethnicity and Stability: The Italians and Jews of South Portland, 1900–1940," *Pacific Historical Review,* LIV (May 1985), 161–189.

6. Nicola Beisel, "Class, Culture, and Campaigns against Vice in Three American Cities, 1872–1892," *American Sociological Review,* LV (February 1990), 44–62; John Higham, *Strangers in the Land: Patterns of American Nativism* (New Brunswick: Rutgers University Press, 1994).

7. Robert E. Bionaz, "Trickle-Down Democracy: The Commission Government Contest in Des Moines, 1905–1908," *Annals of Iowa,* LVIII (Summer 1999), 241–272; Arthur E. DeMatteo, "The Progressive as Elitist: 'Golden Rule' Jones and the Toledo Charter Reform Campaign of 1901," *Northwest Ohio Quarterly,* LXIX (Winter 1997), 8–30; Ari Hoogenboom, *Outlawing the Spoils: A History of the Civil Service Reform Movement, 1865–1883* (Urbana: University of Illinois Press, 1961); Shelton Stromquist, "The Crucible of Class: Cleveland Politics and the Origins of Municiple Reform in the Progressive Era," *Journal of Urban History,* XXIII (January 1997), 192–220.

8. Russell Korobin, "The Politics of Disfranchisement in Georgia," *Georgia Historical Quarterly,* LXXIV (Spring 1990), 20–58; J. Morgan Kousser, *The Shaping of Southern Politics: Suffrage Restriction and the Establishment of the One-Party South, 1880–1910* (New Haven: Yale University Press, 1974); Karl L. Rodabaugh, "Fusion, Confusion, Defeat, and Disfranchisement: The 'Fadeout of Populism' in Alabama," *Alabama Historical Review,* XXXIV (Summer 1973), 131–153.

9. Francesca Morgan, "'Regions Remote from Revolutionary Scenes': Regionalism, Nationalism, and the Iowa Daughters of the American Revolution, 1890–1930," *Annals of Iowa,* LVI (Winter/Spring 1997), 46–79; Alison M. Parker, "'Hearts Uplifted and Minds Refreshed': The Woman's Christian Temperance Union and the Production

of Pure Culture in the United States, 1880–1930," *Journal of Women's History,* XI (Summer 1999), 135–158; Anastatia Sims, *The Power of Femininity in the New South: Women's Organizations and Politics in North Carolina, 1880–1930* (Columbia: University of South Carolina Press, 1997).

10. Henry D. Shapiro, *Appalachia On Our Mind: The Southern Mountains and Mountaineers in the American Consciousness, 1870–1920* (Chapel Hill: University of North Carolina Press, 1978); Patricia D. Beaver and Helen M. Lewis, "Uncovering the Trail of Ethnic Denial: Ethnicity in Appalachia," in Carole E. Hill and Patricia D. Beaver (eds.), *Cultural Diversity in the U.S. South: Anthropological Contributions to a Region in Transition* (Athens: University of Georgia Press, 1998), pp. 51–68; Stephen P. Hanna, "Three Decades of Appalshop Films: Representational Strategies and Regional Politics," *Appalachian Journal,* XXV (Summer 1998), 372–413; Ronald L. Lewis," "Beyond Isolation and Homogeneity: Diversity and the History of Appalachia," in Dwight B. Billings, Gurney Norman, and Katherine Ledford (eds.), *Confronting Appalachian Stereotypes: Back Talk from an American Region* (Lexington: University Press of Kentucky, 1999), 21–43; Tommy R. Thompson, "The Image of Appalachian Kentucky in Popular Magazines," *Register of the Kentucky Historical Society,* XCI (Spring 1993), 176–202; Cratis D. Williams, "The Southern Mountaineer in Fact and Fiction: Fictional Stereotypes of the Southern Mountaineer," *Appalachian Journal,* III (Spring 1976), 186–208; J. W. Williamson, *Hillbillyland: What the Movies Did to the Mountains & What the Mountains Did to the Movies* (Chapel Hill: University of North Carolina Press, 1995).

11. John Fiske, *Outlines of Cosmic Philosophy,* vol II (London: The Macmillan Company, 1874), p. 196.

12. Henry Cabot Lodge, *A Short History of the English Colonies in America* (New York: Harper & Brothers, 1981), pp. 70–72, 154–155.

13. James S. Brown, "An Appalachian Footnote to Toynbee's *A Study of History,*" *Appalachian Journal,* VI (August 1978), 29–32.

14. William Goddell Frost, "Our Contemporary Ancestors in the Southern Mountains," *Appalachian Heritage,* IV (Fall 1976), 80–90; Betty N. Smith, *Jane Hicks Gentry: A Singer Among Singers* (Lexington: University Press of Kentucky, 1998).

15. Grady McWhiney and Forrest McDonald, "Celtic Origins of Southern Herding Practices," *Journal of Southern History,* LI (May 1985), 165–182; Grady McWhiney, *Cracker Culture: Celtic Ways in the Old South* (Tuscaloosa: University of Alabama Press, 1988).

16. David Hackett Fischer, *Albion's Seed: Four British Folkways in America* (New York: Oxford University Press, 1989); Cratis D. Williams, "The Southern Mountaineer in Fact and Fiction: Who Are the Southern Mountaineers?" *Appalachian Journal,* III (Autumn 1975), 11–19.

17. Rowland Berthoff, "Celtic Mist Over the South," *Journal of Southern History,* LI (November 1986), 523–546; H. Tyler Blethen and Curtis W. Wood Jr., *From Ulster to Carolina: The Migration of the Scotch-Irish to Southwestern North Carolina* (Cullowhee: Mountain Heritage Center, 1983); Blethen and Wood (eds.), *Ulster and North America: Transatlantic Perspectives on the Scotch-Irish* (Tuscaloosa: University of Alabama Press, 1997); Donald Edward Davis, "Before Albion's Seed: Other Influences on Appalachian Culture," *Journal of the Appalachian Studies Association,* VII (1995), 57–66; Michael Ellis, "On the Use of Dialect as Evidence: Albion's Seed in Appalachia," *Appalachian Journal,* XIX (Spring 1992), 278–297; James G. Leyburn, *The Scotch-Irish: A Social History* (Chapel Hill: University of North Carolina Press, 1962); Gordon B. McKinney, et al, "Culture Wars: David Hackett Fisher's *Albion's Seed,*" *Appalachian Journal,* XIX (Winter 1992), 161–201; Michael Montgomery, "The Roots of Appalachian English: Scotch-Irish or British Southern?" *Journal of the Appalachian Studies Association,* III (1991), 177–191; J. Scott Plaster, "An Enduring Voice: Celtic Influences on the Appalachian Ballad 'Black Jack Davy," *Journal of Appalachian Studies,* II (Spring 1996), 87–102.

18. Harriette Arnow, *The Dollmaker* (New York: Avon Books, 1954); Chad Berry, *Southern Migrants, Northern Exiles* (Urbana: University of Illinois Press, 2000): Katheryn M. Borman and Phillip J. Obermiller, *From Mountain to Metropolis: Appalachian Migrants in American Cities* (Westport: Bergin and Garvey, 1994); Carl E. Feathers, *Mountain People in a Flat Land: A Popular History of Appalachian Migration to Northeast Ohio, 1940–1965* (Athens: Ohio University Press, 1998); Thomas J. Wagner and Obermiller, *Valuing Our Past, Creating Our Future: The Founding of the Urban Appalachian Council* (Berea: Berea College Press, 1999).

19. Kathryn M. Borman and Phillip J. Obermiller (eds.), *From Mountains to Metropolis: Appalachian Migrants in American Cities* (Westbrook: Bergin & Garvey, 1994); Theresa Myadze, "Rethinking Urban Appalachian Ethnicity," *Jour-*

nal of Appalachian Studies, III (Fall 1997), 243–252; Obermiller and Thomas E. Wagner, "Cincinnati's 'Second Minority': The Emergence of Appalachian Advocacy, 1953–1973," *Appalachian Journal,* XXIV (Spring 1997), 274–295; Obermiller and William W. Philliber (eds.). *Too Few Tomorrows: Urban Appalachians in the 1980s* (Boone: Appalachian Consortium Press, 1987); Philliber and Clyde B. McCoy (eds.), *The Invisible Minority: Urban Appalachians* (Lexington: University Press of Kentucky, 1981).

20. Charles B. Dew, *Band of Iron: Master and Slave at Buffalo Forge* (New York: W. W. Norton & Company, 1994); John C. Inscoe, *Mountain Masters, Slavery, and the Sectional Crisis in Western North Carolina* (Knoxville: University of Tennessee Press, 1989); Ronald L. Lewis, *Coal Iron, and Slaves: Industrial Slavery in Maryland and Virginia, 1715–1865* (Westport: Greenwood Press, 1979); Edward W. Phifer, "Slavery in Microcosm: Burke County, North Carolina," *Journal of Southern History,* XXVIII (May 1962), 137–165; John E. Stealey, III, *The Antebellum Kanawha Salt Business and Western Markets* (Lexington: University Press of Kentucky, 1993).

21. Ann Field Alexander, "'Like an Evil Wind': The Roanoke Riot of 1893 and the Lynching of Thomas Smith," *Virginia Magazine of History and Biography,* C (April 1992), 173–206; Paul G. Beers, "The Wythe County Lynching of Raymond Bird: Progressivism vs. Mob Violence in the 20s," *Appalachian Journal,* XXII (Fall 1994), 34–59; Jacqueline Burnside, "A Delicate and Difficult Duty: Interracial Education at Maryville College, Tennessee, 1868–1901," *American Presbyterians,* LXXII (Winter 1994), 229–240; Dan T. Carter, *Scottsboro: A Tragedy of the American South* (Baton Rouge: Louisiana State University Press, 1969); Mark Curriden and Leroy Phillips Jr., *Contempt of Court: The Turn-of-the-Century Lynching That Launched a Hundred Years of Federalism* (New York: Faber and Faber, 1999); Nancy L. Grant, *TVA and Black Americans: Planning for the Status Quo* (Knoxville: University of Tennessee Press, 1990); Brian Kelley, "Policing the Negro Eden: Racial Paternalism in the Alabama Coalfields, 1908–1921," *Alabama Review,* LI (July, October 1998), 163–183, 243–265; Lester C. Lamon, "Tennessee Race Relations and the Knoxville Riot of 1919," *East Tennessee Historical Society's Publications,* XLI (1969), 67–85; Gordon B. McKinney, *Southern Mountain Republicans, 1865–1900: Politics and the Appalachian Community* (Chapel Hill: University of North Carolina Press, 1978); William L. Montell, *The Saga of Coe Ridge: A Study in Oral History* (Knoxville: University Press, 1970), Nancy J. Potts, "Unfulfilled Expectations: The Erosion of Black Political Power in Chattanooga, 1865–1911," *Tennessee Historical Quarterly,* XLIX (Summer 1990), 112–128; Melissa Walker, African Americans and TVA Reservoir Property Removal: Race in a New Deal Program," *Agricultural History,* LXXII (Spring 1998), 417–428; Michael D. Webb, "'God Bless You All—I am Inoocent': Sheriff Joseph E. Johnson, Chattanooga, Tennessee, and the Lynching of Ed Johnson," *Tennessee Historical Quarterly,* LVIII (Summer 1999), 156–179.

22. June N. Adamson, "Few Black Voices Heard: The Black Community and the Desegregation Crisis in Clinton, Tennessee, 1956," *Tennessee Historical Quarterly,* LIII (Spring 1994), 30–41; Kathleen M. Blee and Dwight B. Billings, "Race Differences in the Origins and Consequences of Chronic Poverty in Rural Appalachia," *Social Science History,* XX (Fall 1996), 345–374; Alice E. Carter, "Segregation and Integration in the Appalachian Coalfields: McDowell County Responds to the *Brown* Decision," *West Virginia History,* LIV (1995), 239–253; Henry Louis Gates, *Colored People* (New York: Alfred A. Knopf, 1994); Janice M. McClelland, "A Structural Analysis of Desegregation: Clinton High School, 1954–1958," *Tennessee Historical Quarterly,* LVI (Winter 1997), 294–309; Timothy J. Minchin, "Color Means Everything: Black Pioneers, White Resistance and Interracial Unionism in the Southern Textile Industry, 1957–1980," *Labor History,* XXXIX (May 1998), 109–133.

23. Michael H. Burchett, "Promise and Prejudice: Wise County, Virginia, and the Great Migration, 1910–1920," *Journal of Negro History,* LXXXII (Summer 1997), 312–327.

24. Cynthia G. Fleming, "White Lunch Counters and Black Consciousness: The Story of the Knoxville Sit-Ins," *Tennessee Historical Quarterly,* XLIX (Spring 1990), 40–52; Henry Louis Gates, *Colored People;* William H. Turner and Edward J. Cabbell (eds.), *Blacks in Appalachia* (Lexington: University Press of Kentucky, 1985); Frank X. Walker, *Affrilachia* Lexington: Old Cove Press, 2000).

25. Brian Kelley, "Policing the Negro Eden: Racial Paternalism in the Alabama Coalfields, 1908–1921," *Alabama Review,* LI (July, October 1998), 163–183, 243–265; Daniel Letwin, *Alabama Coal Miners, 1878–1921: The Challenge of Interracial Unionism* (Chapel Hill: University of North Carolina Press, 1998); Henry M. McKiven Jr., *Iron & Steel: Class, Race, and Community in Birming-*

ham, Alabama, 1875–1920 (Chapel Hill: University of North Carolina Press, 1995); Rebecca H. Moulder, "Convicts as Capital: Thomas O'Conner and the Leases of the Tennessee Penitentiary System, 1871–1883," *East Tennessee Historical Society's Publications,* XLVIII (1976), 40–70; Karin Shapiro, *A New South Rebellion: The Battle Against Convict Labor in the Tennessee Coalfields, 1871–1896* (Chapel Hill: University of North Carolina Press, 1998).

26. Kenneth R. Bailey, "A Judicious Mixture: Negroes and Immigrants in the West Virginia Mines, 1880–1917," *West Virginia History,* XXXIV (January 1973), 141–161; Doug Cantrell, "Immigrants and Community in Harlan County, 1910–1930," *Register of the Kentucky Historical Society,* LXXXVI (Spring 1988), 119–141; Ronald L. Lewis, "From Peasant to Proletarian: The Migration of Southern Blacks to the Central Appalachian Coalfields," *Journal of Southern History,* LV (February 1989), 77–102; Charles H. McCormick, "The Death of Constable Riggs: Ethnic Conflict in the World War I Era," *West Virginia History,* LII (1993), 33–58; Russell D. Parker, "The Black Community in a Company Town: Alcoa, Tennessee, 1919–1939," *Tennessee Historical Quarterly,* XXXVII (Summer 1978), 203–221; Connie L. Rice, "The 'Separate but Equal' Schools of Monogalia County's Coal Mining Communities," *Journal of Appalachian Studies,* II (Fall 1996), 323–335; Crandall A. Shifflett, *Coal Towns: Work and Culture in Company Towns of Southern Appalachia, 1880–1960* (Knoxville: University of Tennessee Press, 1991); Joe William Trotter Jr., *Coal, Class, and Color: Blacks in Southern West Virginia, 1915–32* (Urbana: University of Illinois Press, 1990); Robert David Ward and William W. Rogers, *Convicts, Coal, and the Banner Mine Tragedy* (University: University of Alabama Press, 1987); Deborah R. Weiner, "Middlemen of the Coalfields: The Role of Jews in the Economy of Southern West Virginia Coal Towns, 1890–1950," *Journal of Appalachian Studies,* IV (Spring 1998), 29–56; Margaret Ripley Wolfe, "Aliens in Southern Appalachia, 1900–1920: The Italian Experience in Wise County, Virginia," *Virginia Magazine of History and Biography,* LXXXVII (October 1979), 455–472; Wolfe, "The Appalachian Reality: Ethnic and Class Diversity," *East Tennessee Historical Society's Publications,* LII–LIII (1980–1981), 40–60.

27. See the special issue on Hispanics in the South: *Southern Exposure,* XXVII (Summer 1999); Loida Velazquez, "Finding a Voice: Latinas in the South," in Barbara E. Smith (ed.), *Neither Separate nor Equal: Women, Race, and Class in the South* (Philadelphia: Temple University Press, 1999), 125–137.

28. Ibid.

29. See: Abraham Verghese, *My Own Country: A Doctor's Story of a Town and Its People in the Age of AIDS* (New York: Simon and Schuster, 1994), pp. 161–167.

30. Marilou Awiakta, *Selu: Seeking the Corn Mother's Wisdom* (Golden: Fulcrum Publishing, 1993); Ginney Carney, "Cherokee/Appalachian Communities: Remembering the Pattern, Re-Spinning the Web," Journal of Appalachian Studies, II (Spring 1996), 115–121; John R. Finger, *Cherokee Americans: The Eastern Band of the Cherokees in the Twentieth Century* (Lincoln: University of Nebraska Press, 1991); Laurence French and Jim Hornbuckle (eds.), *The Cherokee Perspective: Written by Eastern Cherokees* (Boone: Appalachian Consortium Press, 1981); French, *The Qualla Cherokee Surviving in Two Worlds* (Lewiston: L. Mellen Press, 1998); Sarah R. Hill, *Weaving New Worlds: Southeastern Cherokee Women and Their Baskets* (Chapel Hill: University of North Carolina Press, 1997); Sharlotte Neely, *Snowbird Cherokees: People of Persistence* (Athens: University of Georgia Press, 1991).

31. Avery F. Gaskins, "An Introduction to the Guineas: West Virginia's Melungeons," *Appalachian Journal,* I (Autumn 1973), 234–237; N. Brent Kennedy and Robyn V. Kennedy, *The Melungeons—The Resurrection of a Proud People: An Untold Story of Ethnic Cleansing in America* (Macon: Mercer University Press, 1994).

32. Kate Black and Marc A. Rhorer, "Out in The Mountains: Exploring Lesbian and Gay Lives," *Journal of the Appalachian Studies Association,* VII (1995), 18–28; Mary K. Anglin, "Stories of AIDS in Appalachia," in Dwight B. Billings, Gurney Norman, and Katherine Ledford (eds.), *Confronting Appalachian Stereotypes: Back Talk from an American Region* (Lexington: University Press of Kentucky, 1999), pp. 267–280; Jeff Mann, "Stonewall and Matewan: Some Thoughts on Gay Life in Appalachia," *Journal of Appalachian Studies,* V (Fall 1999), 207–214; Verghese, *My Own Country.*

33. Wilma A. Dunaway, "Rethinking Cherokee Acculturation: Women's Resistance to Agrarian Capitalism and Cultural Change, 1800–1838," *American Indian Culture and Research Journal,* XXI (1997), 155–192; Thomas Hatley, "Cherokee Women Farmers Hold Their Ground," in Robert D. Mitchell (ed.), *Appalachian Frontiers: Settlement, Society, and Development in the Preindustrial Era*

(Lexington: University Press of Kentucky, 1991), 37–51; Theda Perdue, *Cherokee Women: Gender and Cultural Change, 1700–1835* (Lincoln: University of Nebraska Press, 1998).

34. Wilma A. Dunaway, "Diaspora, Death, and Sexual Exploitation: Slave Families in the Mountain South," *Appalachian Journal,* XXVI (Winter 1999), 128–149; Ann Short Chirhart, "Gardens of Education: Beulah Rucker and African-American Culture in the Twentieth-Century Georgia Upcountry," *Georgia Historical Quarterly,* LXXXII (Winter 1998), 829–847.

35. Howard Dorgan, "Comfort in Confinement: Gender Roles in the Old Regular Baptist Church," in Carl Ross (ed.), *Contemporary Appalachia: In Search of a Usable Past* (Boone: Appalachian Consortium Press, 1987), 11–20; Gordon B. McKinney, "Women's Role in Civil War Western North Carolina," *North Carolina Historical Review,* LXIX (January 1992), 37–56; Ann M. Oberhauser, Towards a Gendered Regional Geography: Women and Work in Rural Appalachia," *Growth and Change,* XXVI (Spring 1995), 217–244; Mary Beth Pudup, "Women's Work in the West Virginia Economy," *West Virginia History,* XLIX (1990), 7–20; Shaunna L. Scott, "Gender among Appalachian Kentucky Farm Families: The Kentucky Farm Family Oral History Project and Beyond," *Journal of Appalachian Studies,* II (Spring 1996), 103–113.

36. Karen Beckwith, "Collective Identities of Class and Gender: Working Class Women in the Pittston Coal Strike," *Political Psychology,* XIX (March 1998), 147–167; Mary Beth Bingham, "Women in Appalachian Community Organizations: Sites of Learning and Change," *Journal of Appalachian Studies,* V (Fall 1999), 215–226; Anne Wallace Effland, "A Profile of Political Activists: Women of the West Virginia Woman Suffrage Movement," *West Virginia History,* XLIX (1990), 103–114; Carol A B. Giesen, *Coal Miners' Wives: Portraits of Endurance* (Lexington: University Press of Kentucky, 1995); Jacqueline D. Hall, "Disorderly Women: Gender and Labor Militancy in the Appalachian South," *Journal of American History,* LXXIII (September 1986), 354–382; Sally Ward Maggard, "Gender and Schooling in Appalachia: Lessons for an Era of Economic Restructuring," *Journal of the Appalachian Studies Association,* VII (1995), 140–151; Ann M. Oberhauser and Anne-Marie Turnage, "A Coalfield Tapestry: Weaving the Socioeconomic Fabric of Women's Lives," in Barbara E. Smith (ed.), In *Neither Separate nor Equal: Women, Race and Class in the South* (Philadelphia: Temple University Press, 1999), 109–122; Virginia Rinaldo Seitz, *Women, Development, and Communities for Empowerment in Appalachia* (Albany: State University of New York Press, 1995); Donna J. Spindel, "Women's Legal Rights in West Virginia, 1863–1984," *West Virginia History,* LI (1992), 29–44.

16. Appalachian Music and American Popular Culture: The Romance That Will Not Die

1. Henry Shapiro, chapter ten, "The Folksong Revival," in *Appalachia On Our Mind: The Southern Mountains and Mountaineers in the American Consciousness, 1870–1920* (Chapel Hill: University of North Carolina Press, 1978), pp. 244–65.

2. Emma Bell Miles, "Some Real American Music," in *The Spirit of the Mountains* (Knoxville: The University of Tennessee Press, 1975. Orig. pub. in 1905), pp. 146–71.

3. Cecil Sharp and Olive Dame Campbell, *English Folk Songs from the Southern Appalachians* (New York: Putnam's, 1917).

4. Howard Brockway spoke of the "poise and innate dignity" of mountain people in "The Quest of the Lonesome Tunes," in Hazel Gertrude Kinscella, *Music On the Air* (Garden City, NY: Garden City Publishing Co., 1934), p. 162.

5. See Edwin T. Arnold, "Al, Abner, and Appalachia," *Appalachian Journal,* 17 (Spring, 1990), p. 266.

6. Bradley Kincaid, *My Favorite Mountain Ballads and Old-Time Songs* (Chicago: WLS, 1928) and *Favorite Old-Time Songs and Mountain Ballads* (Chicago: WLS, 1930), and Kincaid, letter to H.E. Taylor of Berea College, November 24, 1932 (Berea Archives, Berea College, Kentucky).

7. Folklorist Archie Green notes that Anglo-Saxon attributions "were used by Harvard rhetoricians as well as by Kentucky mountain settlement school teachers to give American folksong a blue ribbon pedigree" and that "patriotism and purity formed a banner which waved over folksong, and eventually over country music," in Loyal Jones, *Radio's "Kentucky Mountain Boy" Bradley Kincaid* (Appalachian Center: Berea College, rev. ed., 1988), p. 4.

8. Sharp came to the mountains imbued with the conviction that people were actually singing the ballads collected by Francis James Child. He therefore searched for no other kind of musical material.

9. See David Whisnant, *All That Is Native and Fine: The Politics of Culture in an American Region* (Chapel Hill: The University of North Carolina Press, 1983); William Tallmadge, "The Folk Banjo and Clawhammer Performance Practice in the Upper South: A Study of Origins," in Barry M. Buxton, ed., *The Appalachian Experience:* Proceedings of the Sixth Annual Studies Conference (Boone, N.C.: Appalachian Consortium Press, 1983); Robert B. Winans, "The Folk, the Stage, and the Five-String Banjo in the Nineteenth Century," *Journal of American Folklore,* 89 (October–December, 1976), pp. 406–37.

10. The catholic receptivity of mountain singers to non-traditional material, as well as their ability to adapt such material to older melodic forms, was brought home to me dramatically and delightfully when I heard the great North Carolina ballad singer, Doug Wallin, sing "After the Ball" in a modal style at a conference on traditional music in Chapel Hill, North Carolina, April, 1989.

11. The name of the Ritchie songbook suggests the range of songs that were included: *Lover's Melodies, A Choice Collection of Old Sentimental Songs Our Grandmother Sang, and Other Popular Airs.* Jean Ritchie, *Singing Family of the Cumberlands* (New York: Geordie Music Publishing, 1980; Orig. pub. 1955, Oak Publications), pp. 73–76.

12. *Mountain Music: Bluegrass Style,* Folkways FA2318, was produced and edited in 1959 by Mike Seeger.

13. Robert Cantwell, *Bluegrass Breakdown: The Making of the Old Southern Sound* (Urbana: University of Illinois Press, 1984), p. 143.

17. Dialect As a Deterrent to Cultural Stripping: Why Appalachian Migrants Continue to Talk That Talk

Adler, S. 1993. *Multicultural Communication Skills in the Classroom.* Boston: Allyn & Bacon.

Blanton, L. 1985. "Southern Appalachian: Social Considerations of Speech." In *Toward a Social History of American English,* ed. J.L. Dillard, 73–90. New York: Mouton Publishers.

Chambers, J.K. 1993. "Sociolinguistic Dialectology." In *American Dialect Research,* ed. D.R. Preston, 133–164. Philadelphia: John Benjamin Publishing.

D'Anglejan, A., and G.R. Tucker. 1973. "Sociolinguistic Correlates of Speech Style in Quebec." In *Language Attitudes: Trends and Prospect,* ed. R. Shuy and R. Fasold. Washington, D.C.: Georgetown University Press.

Dayton Public Schools Publishing Service. 1995. *Just the Facts: 1994–1995.* Dayton, Ohio: Dayton Public Schools.

Dillard, J.L., ed. 1985. *Toward a Social History of American English.* New York: Mouton Publishers.

Edwards, J. 1989. *Language and Disadvantage.* London: Cole and Whurr.

Fishman, J.A. 1989. *Language and Ethnicity in Minority Sociolinguistic Perspective.* Philadelphia: Multilingual Matters Ltd.

Hymes, D.H. 1991. Afterword to *Language, Self, and Society: A Social History of Language,* ed. P. Burke and R. Porter. Cambridge, Mass.: Basil Blackwell.

Kahn, K. 1973. *Hillbilly Women.* New York: Doubleday.

Labov, W. 1966. *The Social Stratification of English in New York City.* Arlington, Va.: Center for Applied Linguistics.

———. 1972. *Language in the Inner City: Studies in Black English Vernacular.* Philadelphia: University of Pennsylvania Press.

Milroy, J., and L. Milroy. 1985. "Linguistic Change, Social Network, and Speaker Innovation." *Journal of Linguistics* 21: 339–384.

Montgomery, M., and C. Chapman. 1992. "The Pace of Change in Appalachian English." In *History of Englishes: New Methods and Interpretations in Historical Linguistics,* ed. M. Rissanen, O. Ihalainen, T. Nevalainen, and I. Taavitsainen, 624–639. New York: Mouton de Gruyter.

Obermiller, P.J., and M.E. Maloney. 1994. "Living City, Feeling Country: The Current Status and Future Prospects of Urban Appalachians." In *From Mountain to Metropolis: Appalachian Migrants in American Cities,* ed. K. M. Borman and P.J. Obermiller, 3–12. Westbrook, Conn.: Bergin & Garvey.

Philipsen, G. 1991. *Speaking Culturally: Explorations in Social Communication.* Albany, N.Y.: SUNY Press.

Ryan, E.B. 1979. "Why Do Low-Prestige Language Varieties Persist?" In *Language and Social Psychology.* Baltimore: Basil Blackwell.

Ryan, E.B. and M.A. Carranza. 1977. "Ingroup and Outgroup Reactions to Mexican American Language Varieties." In *Language, Ethnicity and Intergroup Relations,* ed. H. Giles. London: Academic Press.

Walton, J.W. 1996. "Talking Proper: The Rise of Accent as Social Symbol." Review of *Talking Proper: The Rise of Accent as Social Symbol,* by L. Mugglestone. *Journal of Social History* (Fall): 284–286.

Wardhaugh, R. 1992. *An Introduction to Sociolinguistics*. Cambridge, Mass.: Blackwell Publishing.
Wolfram, W., and D. Christian. 1989. *Dialect and Education: Issues and Answers*. Englewood Cliffs, N.J.: Prentice-Hall.

18. Some Observations

1. Photiatis, John and B. B. Maurer, *Religion in an Appalachian State*. 1974. Appalachian Center, Division of Personal and Family Development. Morgantown, WV: University of West Virginia.

20. Constructing and Staffing the Cultural Bridge: The School as Chance Agent in Rural Appalachia

1. Braxton has two weekly papers with much greater out-of-county subscriptions than in-county ones, for out-migrants seeking news of home is the largest percentage of each paper's readership.

2. Part of the 1990 Kentucky Education Reform Act was specifically targeted at reforming alleged nepotism and patronage in the eastern (Appalachian) part of that state (Kannapel 1990).

References Cited

Anderson, James
1988 The Education of Blacks in the South, 1860–1935. Chapel Hill: University of North Carolina Press.
Bender, Louis, Bernal Green, Thomas Hady, John Kuehn, Marlys Nelson, Leon Perkinson, and Peggy Ross.
1985 The Diverse Social and Economic Structure of Nonmetropolitan America. Rural Development Research Report, 49. Washington, DC: Economic Research Service, USDA.
Billings, Dwight
1988 The Rural South in Crisis: A Historical Perspective. *In* The Rural South in Crisis: Challenges for the Future. Lionel Beaulieu, ed. Pp. 13–29. Boulder, CO: Westview Press.
Bogdan, Robert, and Sari Biklen
1982 Qualitative Research for Education. Boston: Allyn and Bacon.
Children's Defense Fund
1992 Falling by the Wayside: Children in Rural America. Washington, DC: Children's Defense Fund.
CEDaR (Council for Educational Development and Research)
1987 Building on Excellence: Regional Priorities for the Improvement of Small, Rural Schools. Washington, DC: CEDaR.
Cremin, Lawrence
1977 Traditions of American Education. New York: Basic Books.
Cubberly, Elwood
1914 Rural Life and Education: A Study of the Rural School Problem as a Phase of the Rural Life Problem. New York: Houghton Mifflin.
DeYoung, Alan
1991 Struggling with Their Histories: Economic Decline and Educational Improvement in Four Rural Southeastern School Districts. Norwood, NJ: Ablex Publishers.
1995 The Life and Death of a Rural American High School: Farewell Little Kanawha. New York: Garland Publishers.
DeYoung, Alan, and Craig Howley
1992 The Political Economy of Rural School Consolidation. Peabody Journal of Education 67(4):63–89.
Dorgan, Howard
1993 The Airwaves of Zion: Radio and Religion in Appalachia. Knoxville: University of Tennessee Press.
Dreeben, Robert
1968 On What Is Learned in School. Reading, MA: Addison-Wesley.
Eller, Ronald D.
1982 Miners, Millhands and Mountaineers: Industrialization of the Appalachia South, 1880–1930. Knoxville: University of Tennessee Press.
Ergood, Bruce, and Bruce Kuhre
1991 Appalachia: Social Context, Past and Present. Dubuque, IA: Kendall/Hunt.
Fuller, Wayne
1982 The Old Country School. Chicago: University of Chicago Press.
1989 The Teacher in the Country School. *In* American Teachers: Histories of a Profession at Work. Donald Warren, ed. Pp. 98–117. New York: Macmillan.
Gaventa, John
1980 Power and Powerlessness: Quiessence and Rebellion in an Appalachian Valley. Urbana: University of Illinois Press.
Gjelten, Tom
1982 A Typology of Rural School Settings. Washington, DC: U.S. Department of Education.
Haas, Toni
1991 Why Reform Doesn't Apply: Creating a New Story about Education in Rural America. *In*

Rural Education: Issues and Practice. Alan DeYoung, ed. Pp. 413–446. New York: Garland Publishers.
Hartford, Ellis
1977 The Little White Schoolhouse. Lexington: University of Kentucky Press.
Heath, Shirley Brice
1983 Ways with Words: Language, Life and Work in Communities and Classrooms. Cambridge, England: Cambridge University Press.
Hollingshead, August
1975 Elmstown's Youth and Elmstown Revisited. New York: Wiley.
Inkeles, Alex, and David Smith
1974 Becoming Modern. Cambridge, MA: Harvard University Press.
Kannapel, Patricia
1990 Educational Reform in Kentucky: Expert Theory, Folk Theory and the Kentucky Educational Reform Act of 1990. Unpublished thesis, University of Kentucky, Lexington, KY.
Katz, Michael
1971 Class, Bureaucracy, and Schools. New York: Praeger.
Kleinfeld, Judith
1979 Eskimo Village on the Andreafsky. New York: Praeger.
Kliebard, Herbert
1986 The Struggle for the American Curriculum: 1893–1958. Boston: Routledge and Kegan Paul.
Lee, Howard
1968 The Burning Springs and Other Tales of the Little Kanawha. Parsons, WV: McClain Printing.
Lewis, Helen, Linda Johnson, and Don Askins
1978 Colonialism in Modern America: The Appalachian Case. Boone, NC: Appalachian Consortium Press.
Link, William
1986 A Hard Time and a Lonely Place: Schooling, Society and Reform in Rural Viginia, 1870–1920. Chapel Hill: University of North Carolina Press.
Merriam, Sharan
1988 Case Study Research in Education. San Francisco: Jossey Bass.
Page, Ann, and Donald Clelland
1978 The Kanawha County Textbook Controversy: A Study of the Politics of Lifestyle Concern. Social Forces 57(1):265–281.
Parsons, Talcott
1959 The School Class as a Social System: Some of Its Functions in American Society. Harvard Educational Review 29:297–313.
Perkinson, Henry
1991 The Imperfect Panacea: American Faith in Education, 1865–1990. New York: Random House.
Peshkin, Alan
1978 Growing Up American. Chicago: University of Chicago Press.
1982 The Imperfect Union: School Consolidation and Community Conflict. Chicago: University of Chicago Press.
Schwarzeller, Harry, and James Brown
1962 Education as a Cultural Bridge between Eastern Kentucky and the Great Society. Rural Sociology 27 (December):357–373.
Shapiro, Henry
1978 Appalachia on Our Mind. Chapel Hill: University of North Carolina Press.
1983 The Place of Culture and the Problem of Identity. *In* Appalachia and America: Autonomy and Regional Dependence. Alan Batteau, ed. Pp. 111–141. Lexington: University of Kentucky Press.
Sher, Jonathan
1977 Education in Rural America: A Reassessment of the Conventional Wisdom. Boulder, CO: Westview Press.
Spring, Joel
1980 Educating the Worker Citizen: The Social, Economic and Political Foundations of Education. New York: Longman.
1993 Conflict of interests. New York: Longman.
Stake Robert
1978 The Case Study Method in Social Inquiry. Educational Researcher (February):5–8.
Stern, Joyce
1994 The Condition of Education in Rural Schools. Washington, DC: Office of Educational Research and Improvement, U.S. Department of Education.
Theobald, Paul
1991 Historical Scholarship in Nineteenth Century Rural Education. *In* Rural Education: Issues and Practice. Alan DeYoung, ed. Pp. 3–25. New York: Garland Publishers.
Tyack, David
1974 The One Best System. Cambridge, MA: Harvard University Press.
Walters, Wanda Exline
1986 Outside . . . Inside Appalachia. Weston, WV: McClain Publishing.
Wax, Murray, Rosalie Wax, and Robert Dumont
1964 Formal Education in an American Indian Community. Social Problems 2(4):1–126.

West, James
1945 Plainville, U.S.A. New York: Columbia University Press.
Whisnant, David
1980 Modernizing the Mountaineer. Boone, NC: Appalachian Consortium Press.
Wirt, Frederick, and Michael Kirst
1982 Schools in Conflict. Berkeley, CA: McCutchan.

21. There Ain't No Starbucks in Appalachia

Material from an earlier article in the Spring 2001 issue of the *Appalachian Journal* has been incorporated into this piece.

1. Technically Gore only received 266 electoral votes in 2000 because a District of Columbia elector pledged to him returned an unmarked ballot.

2. Michael Barone, *Our Country: The Shaping of America from Roosevelt to Reagan* (New York: Free Press, 1980, p. xi.)

3. Quoted in Charlie Cook, "Economics, Geography, and the 2000 Race," *National Journal*, December 23, 2000, p. 3983.

4. Burt Solomon, "Disunity for All," *National Journal*, December 16, 2000, p. 3873.

5. Quoted in *The Big Lever: Party Politics in Leslie County Kentucky*, prod. Frances Morton, Appalshop Films, 1982, videocassette.

6. Jack W. Germond and Jules Witcover, "Who'd You Rather Have a Beer With?," *National Journal*, October 28, 2000, p. 3440.

7. Quoted in Tom Hamburger, "A Coal-Led Crusade Helped Bring Bush a Crucial Victory," *Wall Street Journal*, June 13, 2001, p. A1.

8. Phil Kabler, "Governor's Race 2000: What a Long, Stange Campaign It Has Been," *Charleston Gazette*, November 7, 2000, p. 1A.

9. Peter Carlson, "In Coal Country, a Third Party Candidate Is Out to Save Her World," *Washington Post*, October 25, 2000, p. C1.

22. Bringing Modern Medicine to the Mountains: Scientific Medicine and the Transformation of Health Care in Southern West Virginia, 1880–1910

1. The best recent scholarship on the region has been collected in Mary Beth Pudup, Dwight E. Billings, and Altina L. Waller, *Appalachia in the Making: The Mountain South in the Nineteenth Century* (Chapel Hill: Univ. of North Carolina Press, 1995).

2. Ronald L. Lewis, "Railroads, Deforestation, and the Transformation of Agriculture in the West Virginia Back Counties, 1880–1920," in *ibid.*, 303.

3. John Hennen, *The Americanization of West Virginia* (Lexington: Univ. Press of Kentucky, 1996).

4. Claude Frazier with F. K. Brown, *Miners and Medicine: West Virginia Memories* (Norman: Univ. of Oklahoma Press, 1992), 59.

5. Sarah Stage, *Female Complaints: Lydia Pinkham and the Business of Women's Medicine* (New York: W. W. Norton, 1979), 27 and Leonard W. Roberts, *Up Cutshin and Down Greasy: Folkways of a Kentucky Mountain Family* (Lexington: Univ. Press of Kentucky, 1959), 96.

6. "State vs. Ragland," in West Virginia Board of Health, *Biennial Report, 1887–88* (Charleston: Moses W. Donnally, 1888), 65–68.

7. Emma Bell Miles, *The Spirit of the Mountains* (Knoxville: Univ. of Tennessee Press, 1975), 24; Roberts, *Up Cutshin and Down Greasy*, 95; and Laurel Shackelford and Bill Weinberg, eds., *Our Appalachia: An Oral History* (Lexington: Univ. Press of Kentucky, 1988), 127.

8. Edward Van Liere and Gideon Dodd, *History of Medical Education in West Virginia* (Morgantown: West Virginia Univ. Library, 1965), 18.

9. Susan Ritchie, "A Comparison of Infant Mortality in Logan County, West Virginia in 1872 and 1910," unpublished paper in possession of the author.

10. "The Early Physicians of Sandy River District," Claude Frazier Collection, Eastern Regional Coal Archives, Craft Memorial Library, Bluefield, WV, hereafter referred to as Frazier Coll., ERCA.

11. *Ibid.*

12. *Ibid.*

13. Frazier, *Miners and Medicine*, 64.

14. Ritchie, "A Comparison of Infant Mortality in Logan County."

15. Carolyn Clay Turner and Carolyn Hay Traum, *John C. C. Mayo: Cumberland Capitalist* (Pikeville: Pikeville College Press, 1983), 32–33.

16. Department of Commerce, Bureau of the Census, *Thirteenth Census of the United States, 1910*, vol. 3: *Population* (Washington, D.C.: GPO, 1913), 1018–24, hereafter referred to as 1910 Census, vol. 3.

17. West Virginia Department of Mines, *Annual Report, 1910* (Charleston: News Mail Company, 1911), 306.

18. *Ibid.*, 334–35.

19. Stuart McGehee, "Sawbones: The Company Doctor Gets His Due," *Coal People* (August 1990): 11.

20. Frazier, *Miners and Medicine,* 65.

21. "The Early Physicians of the Sandy River District," Frazier Coll., ERCA.

22. Department of the Interior, Census Office, *Report on Population of the United States at the Eleventh Census: 1890,* vol. 2, pt. 2 (Washington, D.C.: GPO, 1897), 337, hereafter referred to as 1890 Census.

23. *Ibid.,* 337; U.S. Census Office, *Twelfth Census of the United States, 1900,* vol. 2, part 2: *Population* (Washington, D.C.: GPO 1902), 541, hereafter referred to as 1900 Census; and Department of Commerce, Bureau of the Census, *Thirteenth Census of the United States, 1910,* vol. 4: *Population, Occupation Statistics* (Washington, D.C.: GPO, 1914), 151, hereafter referred to as 1910 Census, vol. 4.

24. 1890 Census, 337; 1900 Census, 541; 1910 Census, vol. 3, 1012, 1018, 1020 and vol. 4, 151; and Board of Health, *Report of the Secretary, 1881–83* (Wheeling: Moses Donnally, 1884), 94–102, *Biennial Report, 1889–90* (Charleston: Moses Donnally, 1890), 31–36, and *Biennial Report, 1908–09* (Charleston: News Mail Company, 1909), 21–30.

25. Board of Health, *Biennial Report, 1889–90,* 31–36 and 1910 Census, vol. 3, 1018, 1020.

26. Board of Health, *Biennial Report, 1889–90,* 31–36 and 1910 Census, vol. 3, 1018, 1020.

27. Board of Health, *Report of the Secretary, 1881–83,* 94–102, *Biennial Report, 1889–90,* 31–36, and *Biennial Report, 1908–09,* 21–30.

28. Board of Health, *Biennial Report, 1889–90,* 31–36 and *Biennial Report, 1908–09,* 21–30; and 1910 Census, vol. 3, 1018, 1020.

29. "The Early Physicians of the Sandy River District," Frazier Coll., ERCA.

30. *Ibid.*

31. Stuart McGehee, "A Century of Care: A History of Bluefield Regional Medical Center, Bluefield Community Hospital, Bluefield Sanitarium," unpublished manuscript, ERCA.

32. *Ibid.*

33. "Hospitalization Facilities of the Region," *Bluefield Daily Telegraph,* Semi-Centennial Anniversary Edition, 14 December 1939.

34. McGehee, "A Century of Care," ERCA.

35. Van Liere and Dodd, *History of Medical Education in West Virginia,* 17–18; Board of Health, *Biennial Report, 1887–88,* 59 and *Biennial Report, 1891–92,* 54.

36. Board of Health, *Report of the Secretary, 1881–83,* 89–90 and *Biennial Report and Report of Vital and Mortuary Statistics, 1903–04* (Charleston: Tribune Printing Company, 1904), 53–54.

37. Board of Health, *Biennial Report and Report of Vital and Mortuary Statistics, 1903–04,* 53–54.

38. Board of Health, *Biennial Report and Report of Vital and Mortuary Statistics, 1898–99* (Charleston: Tribune Company, 1901), 160–63.

39. Board of Health, *Biennial Report and Report of Vital and Mortuary Statistics, 1903–04,* 53–54.

40. Board of Health, *Biennial Report and Report of Vital and Mortuary Statistics, 1898–99,* 160–63.

41. "The Early Physicians of the Sandy River District," Frazier Coll., ERCA.

42. Cathy Melvin Efird, "A Geography of Lay Midwifery in Appalachian North Carolina: 1925–1950" (Ph.D. diss., University of North Carolina, 1985), 6.

43. "The Early Physicians of the Sandy River District," Frazier Coll., ERCA.

44. Crandall Shifflet, *Coal Towns: Life, Work, and Culture in Company Towns of Southern Appalachia, 1880–1960* (Knoxville: Univ. of Tennessee Press, 1991), 23.

45. Mary Kegley, *Wythe County, Virginia: A Bicentennial History* (Salem, WV: Don Mills, Inc., 1989), 105.

46. Henry D. Hatfield to Walter S. Hallanan, 15 June 1929, Henry D. Hatfield Papers, West Virginia and Regional History Collection, West Virginia University, Morgantown.

47. Rebecca Bailey, "Liberty and License: The Ascendance to Power of the Investors of the Williamson-Thacker Coalfield," unpublished paper in possession of the author.

48. Richard Shryock, *Medicine and Society in America: 1660–1860* (Ithaca: Cornell Univ. Press, 1960), 148–49.

49. Ronald L. Numbers and John Harley Warner, "The Maturation of American Medical Science," in *Sickness and Health in America: Readings in the History of Medicine and Pubic Health,* ed. by Judith Walzer Leavitt and Ronald L. Numbers (Madison: Univ. of Wisconsin Press, 1985), 116–17.

50. Homeopaths, building on the teachings of German doctor Samuel Hahnemann, insisted that sickness could be cured by the administration of minute quantities of substances that actually provoked the offensive symptom from the patient. "Like cures like," a phrase often used to describe homeopathic medicine, reflected the belief that the body would heal itself if forced to respond to

external stimuli. Chiropractors and their osteopathic predecessors insisted that illness rested in the maladjustment of bones and relied on manual alignment to remedy disease. Charles Rosenberg, "The Therapeutic Revolution: Medicine, Meaning, and Social Change in 19th Century America," in *Sickness and Health in America,* 100; Martin Kaufman, *Homeopathy in America: The Rise and Fall of a Medical Heresy* (Baltimore: Johns Hopkins Univ. Press, 1971), 7; and Norman Gevitz, *The D. O.s: Osteopathic Medicine in America* (Baltimore: Johns Hopkins Univ. Press, 1982), 12.

51. Paul Starr, *The Social Transformation of American Medicine* (New York: Basic Books, 1982), 90–91.

52. *Transactions of the Medical Society of the State of West Virginia, Instituted April 10, 1867, Together with the Code of Ethics, Constitutions, and Bylaws* (Wheeling: Frew, Hagans, and Hall, 1868), 8–9.

53. *Ibid.,* 9.

54. C. H. Maxwell, "Pennsylvania and West Virginia Medical Associations—A Comparison," *West Virginia Medical Journal* (October 1907): 106.

55. *Ibid.,* 107.

56. William W. Golden, "The Evolution of Medical Legislation in West Virginia," *West Virginia Medical Journal* (April 1918): 362; Virginia State Medical Examining Board, "Minutes of Board From Organization in 1884, Together with Results of Examinations from 1884 to December 16–18 1902," 14 April 1899, Virginia State Medical Examining Board Records Collection, Library of Virginia, Richmond; and *Dent vs. West Virginia, United States Reports, Cases Adjudicated in the Supreme Court at October Term, 1888,* Vol. 3 (New York: J. C. Bancroft Davis Banks Law Publishing Co., 1904), 114.

57. Golden, "The Evolution of Medical Legislation in West Virginia," 362.

58. Numbers and Warner, "The Maturation of American Medical Science," 116–17 and Rosenberg, "The Therapeutic Revolution," 100.

59. Maxwell, "Pennsylvania and West Virginia Medical Associations," 105.

23. Family Health in a Rural Appalachian Ohio County

Anderson, K.H., and P.S. Tomlinson. 1992. "The Family Health System as an Emerging Paradigmatic View for Nursing." *Image* 24, no. 1: 57–63.

Backett, K. 1992. "The Construction of Health Knowledge in Middle Class Families." *Health Education Research* 7, no. 4: 497–507.

Berman, P., C. Kendall, and K. Bhattacharyya. 1994. "The Household Production of Health: Integrating Social Science Perspectives on Micro-Level Health Determinants." *Social Science Medicine* 38, no. 2: 205–215.

Blecke, J. 1990. "Exploration of Children's Health and Self-Care Behavior Within a Family Context Through Qualitative Research." *Family Relations* 39: 284–291.

Bomar, P.J., ed. 1989. *"Nurses and Family Health Promotion: Concepts, Assessment, and Interventions."* Baltimore: Williams and Wilkins.

Bomar, P.J. 1990. "Perspectives of Family Health Promotion." *Family and Community Health* 12, no. 4: 1–11.

Bronfenbrenner, U. 1979. *The Ecology of Human Development: Experiments by Nature and Design.* Cambridge: Harvard University Press.

Campbell, T.L. 1986. "Family's Impact on Health: A Critical Review." *Family Systems Medicine* 4, no. 2–3: 135–191.

Duffy, M.E. 1988. "Health Promotion in the Family: Current Findings and Directives for Nursing Research." *Journal of Advanced Nursing* 13: 109–117.

Garbarino, J. 1992. *Children and Families in the Social Environment (2nd Ed.).* New York: Aldine De Gruyter.

Gillis, C.L. 1991. "Family Nursing Research, Theory and Practice." *Image* 23: 19–22.

Grey, M. 1993. "Stressors and Children's Health." *Journal of Pediatric Nursing* 8, no. 2: 85–91.

Harkness, S., and C.M. Super. 1994. "The Developmental Niche: A Theoretical Framework for Analyzing the Household Production of Health." *Social Science Medicine* 38, no. 2: 217–226.

Keltner, B. 1992. "Family Influences on Child Health Status." *Pediatric Nursing* 18, no. 2: 128–131.

Kelly, R.B., S.J. Zyzanski, and A.S. Alemagno. 1991. "Prediction of Motivation and Behavior Change Following Health Promotion: Role of Health Beliefs, Social Support, and Self-Efficacy." *Social Science Medicine* 32, no. 3: 311–320.

Lau, R.R., M.J. Quadrel, and K.A. Hartman. 1990. "Development and Change of Young Adults' Preventive Health Beliefs and Behavior: Influence from Parents and Peers." *Journal of Health and Social Behavior* 31: 240–259.

Mclead, J.D., and M.J. Shanahan. 1993. "Poverty, Parenting, and Children's Mental Health." *American Sociological Review* 58: 351–366.

National Center for Health Statistics. 1993. *Health, United States, 1992.* Hyattsville, Md.: Public Health Service.

Nelson, M.A. 1994. "Economic Impoverishment as a Health Risk: Methodological and Conceptual Issues." *Advances in Nursing Science* 16, no. 3: 1–12.

Patterson, J.M. 1990. "Family and Health Research in the 1980s: A Family Scientist Perspective." *Family Systems Medicine* 8, no. 4: 421–434.

Ransom, D.C. 1986. "Research on the Family in Health, Illness and Care: State of the Art." *Family Systems Medicine* 4, no. 2–3: 329–335.

Spradley, J.P. 1980. *Participant Observation.* Fort Worth, Tex.: Holt, Rinehart and Winston.

Thomas, R.B. 1990. "A Foundation for Clinical Family Assessment." *Children's Health Care* 19, no. 4: 244–250.

Whall, A.L., and C.J. Loveland-Cherry. 1993. "Family Unit-Focused Research: 1984–1991." *Annual Review of Nursing Research* 11: 227–247.

Wierenga, M.E., J.M. Browning, and J.L. Mahn. 1990. "A Descriptive Study of How Clients Make Life-Style Changes." *Diabetes Educator* 16, no. 6: 469–473.

Wise, P.H., and J.A. Lowe. 1992. "Noise or Fugue: Seeking the Logic of Child Health Indicators." *Mental Retardation* 30, no. 6: 323–329.

Yin, R.K. 1994. *Case Study Research: Design and Methods (2nd Ed.).* Thousand Oaks, Calif.: Sage Publications.

25. Poverty

Children's Defense Fund. 1992. *City Child Poverty Data from 1990 Census.* Washington, D.C.: Children's Defense Fund.

26. Four Perspectives on Appalachian Culture and Poverty

Austin, Richard C. 1967. "A Search for Appalachian People." In *Parish Studies.* San Francisco, Ca.: San Francisco Theological Seminary.

Ball, Richard A. 1968. "A Poverty Case: The Analgesic Subculture of the Southern Appalachians." *American Sociological Review* 33: 6, 884–894.

Bassett, Jeffrey E. 1973. *Regional Delineation of Poverty Levels in Appalachia.* Thesis. Lexington, Ky: University of Kentucky.

Billings, Dwight. 1974. "Culture and Poverty in Appalachia: A Theoretical Discussion and Empirical Analysis." *Social Forces* 53: 2, 315–232.

Blair, John P. 1973. "A Review of the Filtering Down Theory." *Urban Affairs Quarterly* 8: 3, 303–316.

Bould Sally. 1977. "Rural Poverty and Economic Development: Lessons from the War on Poverty." *Journal of Applied Behavioral Science* 13: 471–488.

Clarkson, Ray B. 1964. *Tumult on the Mountains—Lumbering in West Virginia, 1770–1920.* Parsons, WV: McClain Publishing Co.

Coles, Robert. 1971. *Migrants, Sharecroppers and Mountaineers.* Boston: Little, Brown & Co.

Cloward, Richard and Frances Fox Piven. 1971. *Regulating the Poor.* New York: Free Press.

Dial, Wylene. "Appalachian Culture" (mimeo)

Eller, Robert D. 1982. *Miners, Millhands and Mountaineers: Industrialization of the Appalachian South, 1880–1930.* Knoxville: University of Tennessee Press.

Fenton, John H. 1957. *Politics in the Borders States.* New Orleans: Hauser Publishing.

Friedmann, John R. 1966. "Poor Regions and Poor Nations: Perspectives on the Problem of Appalachia." *Southern Economic Journal* 32: 465–477.

Gaventa, John. 1980. *Power and Powerlessness: Quiescence and Rebellion in an Appalachian Valley.* Hagerstown MD: University of Illinois Press.

Gaventa, John and Bill Horton. 1982. "Who Owns Appalachia? Digging the Facts." *Southern Exposure.* January–February, 34–35.

Harrington, Michael. 1984. *The New American Poverty.* New York: Macmillan.

Hennon, Charles B. and John Photiadis. 1979. "The Rural Appalachian Low-Income Male: Changing Role in a Changing Family." *The Family Coordinator* 28: 4, 608–615.

Irelan, Lola M. 1966. Low Income Life Styles. Washington: U.S. Welfare Administration. Washington D.C.

Kahn, Si. 1970. "New Strategies for Appalachia." *New South* 25: Summer, 57–64.

Kenkel, William F. 1980. "Occupational Saliency and Age at Marriage Plans of Low Income High School Girls." *Sociological Forum* 3: Fall, 62–74.

Lewis, Helen. 1978. *Colonialism in Modern America: The Appalachian Case.* Boone, N.C.: Appalachian Consortium Press.

Miernyk, William. 1982. "The West Virginia Economy." Prepared for the West Virginia Legislative Tax Study Commission (mimeo).

Miller, Tom D. 1982. "Who Owns West Virginia?" Huntington, WV: series of newspaper articles (paperbound, undated).

Orshansky, Mollie. 1968. "Shape of Poverty in 1966." Washington: *Social Security Bulletin* 31: March 1968, 3–32.

Parsons, Kenneth H. 1969 "Poverty as an Issue in Development Policy: A Comparison of United States and Underdeveloped Countries." *Land Economics* 45: February, 52–65.

Perry Charles, S. 1979. "Income and Poverty in Kentucky, 1959–1976: A Comparative County-Level Analysis." Paper presented to the Rural Sociological Society, Lexington, KY.

Peterson, Gary W., Mary E. Stivers and David F. Peters. 1986. "Family Verses Nonfamily Significant Others for the Career Decisions of Low-Income Youth." *Family Relations* 35: 3, 417–424.

Philliber, William W. 1982. "Wife's Absence from the Labor Force and Low Income Among Appalachian Migrants." *Rural Sociology* 47: 4, 705–710.

Photiadis, John D. 1970. "The Economy and Attitudes Toward Government in Appalachia." John Photiadis and Harry Schwartzweller, eds. *Change in Rural Appalachia: Implications for Action Programs.* Philadelphia: University of Pennsylvania Press, 115–127.

Piven, Frances Fox and Richard Cloward. 1972. "Enforcing Low Wage Work: Administrative Methods." *Public Welfare . . . Right or Privilege: System Under Attack.* Wil J. Smith and Frederick, eds. Morgantown, W.Va.: West Virginia University, Office of Research and Development, 24–54.

Pierce, Diana. 1978. "The Feminization of Poverty: Women, Work and Welfare." *Urban and Social Change Review* 11: 28–36.

Pierce, Neil. 1975. "West Virginia: The Saddest State." *The Border South States.* New York: W.W. Norton.

Rabow, Jerome, Sherry L. Berkman and Ronald Kessler. 1983. "The Culture of Poverty and Learned Helplessness: A Social Psychological Perspective." *Sociological Inquiry* 53: 4, 419–434.

Rosenberg, Bernard and Joseph Bensman. 1968. "Sexual Patterns in Three Ethnic Subcultures of an American Underclass." *Annals of the American Academy of Political and Social Science* 376: 61–75.

Shapiro, Henry O. 1978. *Appalachia On Our Mind: The Southern Mountains and Mountaineers in the American Consciousness: 1870–1920.* Chapel Hill, N.C.: University of North Carolina Press.

Simon, Richard. 1981. "Uneven Development and the Case of West Virginia: Going Beyond the Colonialism Model." *Appalachian Journal* 8: 3, 165–186.

Smith, Wil J., ed. 1971. *Critical Issues in Pubic Finance in an Underdeveloped Region.* Morgantown, W.Va.: West Virginia University, Office of Research and Development.

Stephens, L.F. 1972. "Media Exposure and Modernization among the Appalachian Poor." *Journalism Quarterly* 49: 2, 247–257.

Tickamyer, Ann R. and Cecil Tickamyer. 1987. *Poverty in Appalachia.* Appalachian Data Bank Report #5. Lexington, Ky: University of Kentucky, Appalachian Center.

Trent, Roger B., Nancy S. Weigand and Dennis K. Smith. 1985. "Attitudes Toward Development in Three Appalachian Counties." *Rural Sociological Society.*

U.S. News and World Report. 1965. "New Ways to Beat Poverty—the Plan for Appalachia." 59: 27 September 1965, 68–70.

U.S. National Advisory Commission on Rural Poverty. 1967. The People Left Behind. *A Report.* Washington, D.C.: U.S. Gov. Print. Off.

Walls, David S. 1976. "Central Appalachia: A Peripheral Region within an Advanced Capitalist Society." *Journal of Sociology and Social Welfare* 4: 2, 232–247.

Weller, Jack. 1967. "Who Is the Target Group?" *Appalachian Review* 1: Winter, 15–20.

Weller, Jack. 1965. *Yesterday's People: Life in Contemporary Appalachia.* Lexington, Ky: Kentucky University Press.

West Virginia Governor's Office of Economic and Community Development. 1980. *State Development Plan.* Charleston, W.Va.

West Virginia Governor's Office of Economic and Community Development. 1983. *State Plan Update.* Charleston, W.Va.

West Virginia Human Resources Association, Inc. 1988. *Children In Crises, State at Risk.* Charleston: HRA.

Whisnant, David E. 1974. "Growing Old by Being Poor: Some Cautionary Notes About Generalizing from a Class Phenomenon." *Soundings* 57: Spring, 101–112.

White, David B. 1987. "A Social Epidemiological Model of Central Appalachia." *Arete* 2: 1, 47–66.

White, Theodore. 1960. "The Art of the Primary: Wisconsin and West Virginia." *The Making of the President - 1960.* New York: Atheneum Press, 93–138.

Whitman, Gloria. 1968. "Economic Development." *Trends in Human Services.* Kevin Meeghan, Roger Lohmann and Barry Locke, eds. Morgantown, W.Va.: West Virginia University School of Social Work.

Wilensky, Harold and Charles LeBeaux. 1965. *Industrial Society and Social Welfare.* New York: Free Press.

Zeller, Fred and Robert Miller. 1969. *Manpower Development in West Virginia.* Morgantown, W.Va.: West Virginia University.

27. From Farm to Coal Camp to Back Office and McDonald's: Living in the Midst of Appalachia's Latest Transformation

1. See Fisher for excellent, exhaustive bibliographies on the Appalachian Region (1991) and on social protest in Appalachia (1993).

2. See Corbin (1981, 61–86) on the contradictions in efforts to construct company towns which would discipline workers but which actually contributed to the development of class solidarity and class consciousness. For a discussion of social institutions, social ties, and amenities in company towns see Shifflett (1991).

3. See James Still's (1978) *River of Earth* for a powerful fictional account of what this period of economic restructuring in Appalachia meant to women. Moving into the coal camps stripped away a bottom line security for Still's character Alpha Baldridge. Even in the worst of times if she were on her own land she knew she could grow food to feed her children.

4. See Hartmann (1981) on the value of unpaid women's economic activity and Beneria (1981) on the need to re-conceptualize the labor force in order to count and assign economic value to the "invisible" work of women, children, and others. See Pudup (1990) for a discussion of these issues in assessing the economic history of West Virginia women.

5. See May (1982, 1985) and Kessler-Harris (1980) on ideological forces which shaped expectations about women's work from colonial days to the present. See Bradley (1989) for the preindustrial genesis of such ideas and a review of contemporary sex segregation in a wide variety of occupations.

6. In 1972 Congress amended the 1965 Civil Rights Act to prohibit discrimination in federal, state, and local government on the basis of race, color, religion, sex, or national origin. In the mid-1970s, through the pioneering work of the Coal Employment Project, women entered mining jobs. Discrimination suits forced coal companies with federal coal supply contracts to recruit and hire women. Still, evidence exists of women "coal diggers" early in this century (Donohue 1989; Pudup 1990) and more recently in family "dog hole" operations (*Mountain Life & Work* 1975).

7. Pudup (1990, 19–20) argues that these trends also reflect the persistence of a significant rural household economy. She argues for more inclusive economic measures to capture home-based production statistics, localized exchange of goods and services, intermittent wage labor, and the value of unpaid women's labor.

8. The state's service sector grew more slowly than national growth trends in terms of real growth in receipts, payroll, or jobs created. Between 1982 and 1987 West Virginia added 28 percent more service jobs compared to a 41 percent national increase (Center for Economic Research 1991b).

9. The national male labor force participation rate also fell, but at a slower rate (–1.3 percent); similarly the national female rate rose, but at a slower rate (6 percent) (U.S. Bureau of Census 1990).

10. For a review of this and similar state sponsored development initiatives see Parker and Hudson (1992).

Works Cited

Appalachian Regional Commission. 1979. *Appalachia—A Reference Book.* 2nd ed. Washington, D.C.: Appalachian Regional Commission.

Bailey, K.R. 1973. "A Judicious Mixture: Negroes and Immigrants in the West Virginia Mines, 1880–1917." *West Virginia History* 34(2):141–161.

Beneria, Lourdes. 1981. "Conceptualizing the Labor Force: The Underestimation of Women's Economic Activities." *Journal of Development Studies* 17:10–28.

Billings, Dwight, Kathleen Blee, and Louis Swanson. 1986. "Culture, Family, and Community in Preindustrial Appalachia." *Appalachian Journal* 13(2):154–170.

Bradley, Harriet. 1989. *Men's Work, Women's Work.* Minneapolis: University of Minnesota Press.

Center for Economic Research. 1991a. "Bearfacts: West Virginia 1979–89" and Bulletin 7. Morgantown: West Virginia University.

______. 1991b. "West Virginia Service Industries." Morgantown: West Virginia University.

______. 1993. "Long-Term Economic Forecasts for West Virginia: 1993–2002." *West Virginia Business and Economic Review.* Issue 1.

Coles, Robert and Jane Hallowell Coles. 1978. *Women of Crisis: Lives of Struggle and Hope.* New York: Delta.

Conway, Mimi. 1979. *Rise Gonna Rise: A Portrait of Southern Textile Workers.* Garden City: Anchor.

Corbin, David Alan. 1981. *Life, Work, and Rebellion in the Coal Fields: The Southern West Virginia Miners, 1880–1922.* Urbana: University of Illinois Press.

Culp, Linda, Fred Bingaman, Tom Witt. 1991. "State of the West Virginia Economy." Prepared for Governor's Office of Community and Industrial Development. August 27. Center for Economic Research. Morgantown: West Virginia University.

Curran, Daniel. 1993. *Dead Laws for Dead Men: The Politics of Federal Coal Mine Health and Safety Legislation.* Pittsburgh: University of Pittsburgh Press.

Dickstein, Carla. 1992. "Back Offices and West Virginia." *West Virginia Public Affairs Reporter* 9(2):1–7.

Dix, Keith. 1988. *What's a Miner to Do? The Mechanization of Coal Mining.* Pittsburgh: University of Pittsburgh Press.

Donohue, Jean. 1989. "From the Shadows of Power." Videotape. Media Working Group, Inc.

Drury, Doris M. 1965. "A Study of the Literature on Accidents in Coal Mines of the United States with Comparisons of the Records in Other Coal-Producing Countries." Ph.D. dissertation, Indiana University.

Eller, Ronald D. 1982. *Miners, Millhands, and Mountaineers: Industrialization of the Appalachian South, 1880–1930.* Knoxville: University of Tennessee Press.

Ewen, Lynda. 1989. "All God's Children Ain't Got Shoes: A Comparison of West Virginia and the Urban 'Underclass'." *Humanity & Society* 13(2): 145–64.

Fisher, Steven L. 1991. "A Selective Bibliography for Appalachian Studies." In *Appalachian: Social Context Past and Present,* ed. Bruce Ergood and Bruce E. Kuhre. Dubuque, Iowa: Kendall/Hunt. 3rd ed.

Fisher, Steven L. ed. 1993. *Fighting Back in Appalachia: Traditions of Resistance and Change.* Philadelphia: Temple University Press.

Fladung, Tom. 1992. "West Virginia Shakes off Two Decades of Hard Economic Times." *Southeast Regional Review* March/April: 16:170, 172–173.

Flynt, J. Wayne. 1986. "The South's Poor Whites." In *Reshaping the Image of Appalachia,* ed. Loyal Jones. Berea, Ky.: Berea College Appalachian Center.

Gonzalez, Suronda. 1991. "Talking Like My Grandmothers: Spanish Immigrant Women in Spelter, West Virginia." Master's Thesis. West Virginia University.

Groneman, Carol and Mary Beth Norton, eds. 1987. *"To Toil the Livelong Day": America's Women at Work, 1780–1980.* Ithaca, N.Y.: Cornell University Press.

Hall, Betty Jean. 1980. "Women Miners Can Dig It, Too!" In *Communities in Economic Crisis: Appalachia the South,* ed. John Gaventa, Barbara Ellen Smith, Alex Willingham. Philadelphia, Pa.: Temple University Press.

Hartmann, Heidi I. 1981. "The Family as the Locus of Gender, Class, and Political Struggle: The Example of Housework." *Signs: Journal of Women in Culture and Society* 6(3):366–394.

Harvey, Curtis E. 1986. *Coal in Appalachia: An Economic Analysis.* Lexington: University Press of Kentucky.

Kahn, Kathy. 1972. *Hillbilly Women.* New York: Doubleday.

Kessler-Harris, Alice. 1980. *Out to Work: A History of Wage-Earning Women in the United States.* New York: Oxford University Press.

Lewis, Ronald L. 1987. *Black Coal Miners in America: Race, Class and Community Conflict 1780–1980.* Lexington: University Press of Kentucky.

______. 1989. "From Peasant to Proletarian: The Migration of Southern Blacks to the Central Appalachian Coalfields." *Journal of Southern History* 60(1):77–102.

______. 1992. "Appalachian Restructuring in Historical Perspective: Coal, Culture, and Social Change in West Virginia." Research Paper 9102. Regional Research Institute. Morgantown: West Virginia University.

McAteer, Davitt. 1973. *Coal Mine Health and Safety: The Case of West Virginia.* New York: Praeger.

McAteer, Davitt and L. Thomas Galloway. 1980. "A Comparative Study of Miners' Training and Supervisory Certification in the Coal Mines of

Great Britain, the Federal Republic of Germany, Poland, Romania, France, Australia and the United States: The Case for Federal Certification of Supervisors and Increased Training of Miners." *West Virginia Law Review* 82: 937–1018.

Maggard, Sally Ward. 1981. "From Farmers to Miners: The Decline of Agriculture in Eastern Kentucky." In *Science and Agricultural Development,* ed. Lawrence Busch. Totowa, Canada: Allanheld, Osmun.

______. 1988. "Eastern Kentucky Women on Strike: A Study of Gender, Class, and Political Action in the 1970s." Ph.D. dissertation, University of Kentucky.

May, Martha. 1982. "The Historical Problem of the Family Wage: The Ford Motor Company and the Five Dollar Day." *Feminist Studies* 8:399–424.

______. 1985. "Bread Before Roses: American Workingmen, Labor Unions, and the Family Wage." In *Women, Work and Protest: A Century of U.S. Women's Labor History,* ed. Ruth Milkman. Boston: Routledge & Kegan Paul.

Milkman, Ruth, ed. 1985. *Women, Work and Protest: A Century of U.S. Women's Labor History.* Boston: Routledge & Kegan Paul.

Mountain Life & Work. 1975. "In the Mines . . . Two Women Remember." 51(2):35–37.

National Research Council. 1982. *Toward Safer Underground Coal Mines.* Washington, D.C.: National Academy Press.

Nyden, Paul. 1989. "Collapse of Coal Employment: Why Are the Jobs Vanishing?" *Sunday Gazette-Mail,* Charleston, W. Va. October 15.

Parker, Edwin B. and Heather E. Hudson. 1992. *Electronic Byways: State Policies for Rural Development through Telecommunications.* Boulder: Westview Press.

Pitcher, David K. 1992. *West Virginia: The Location for Your "Office of the Future."* Arlington, Va.: Bell Atlantic Business Research.

Pudup, Mary Beth. 1990. "Women's Work in the West Virginia Economy." *West Virginia History* 49:7–20.

Scott, Frank E. 1997. "A Woman's Place is . . . in the Mines?" *Coal Mining and Processing.* November: 63–67, 80.

Seltzer, Curtis. 1985. *Fire in the Hole: Miners and Managers in the American Coal Industry.* Lexington: University Press of Kentucky.

Shifflett, Crandall A. 1991. *Coal Towns: Life, Work, and Culture in Company Towns of Southern Appalachia, 1880–1960.* Knoxville: University of Tennessee Press.

Simon, Rick and Betty Justice. 1981. "The Economy of West Virginia and the Oppression/Liberation of Women." In *Appalachia/America: Proceedings of the 1980 Appalachian Studies Conference,* ed. Wilson Somerville. Johnson City: Appalachian Consortium Press and East Tennessee State University.

Smith, Michal. 1989. *Behind the Glitter: The Impact of Tourism on Rural Women in the Southeast.* Lexington, Ky.: Southeast Women's Employment Coalition.

Steel, Edward M., ed. 1988. *The Speeches and Writings of Mother Jones.* Pittsburgh, Pa.: University of Pittsburgh Press.

Still, James. 1978. *River of Earth.* Lexington: University Press of Kentucky.

Trotter, J.W. Jr. 1990. *Coal, Class, and Color: Blacks in Southern West Virginia, 1915–32.* Urbana: University of Illinois Press.

United Mine Workers of America. 1976. "Proud to be a Miner: a Special Bicentennial Issue." *United Mine Workers Journal* 87(11) (June 15–July 15).

United States Bureau of the Census. 1983. *Detailed Population Characteristics.* Part 50. West Virginia. Washington, D.C.: Government Printing Office.

______. 1990. *Characteristics of the Population.* Washington, D.C.: Government Printing Office.

United States Bureau of Labor Statistics. 1961. *Technological Change and Productivity in the Bituminous Coal Industry, 1920–1960.* Bulletin No. 1305. Washington, D.C.: Government Printing Office.

United States Department of Labor. 1925. *Home Environment and Employment Opportunities of Women in Coal-Mine Workers' Families.* Bulletin No. 45. Washington, D.C.: Government Printing Office.

Verhoeff, Mary. 1917. *The Kentucky River Navigation.* Filson Club Pubs. No. 28. Louisville, Ky.: John P. Morton and Company.

Weise, Robert. 1993. "Selling Mineral Rights on Beaver Creek, Kentucky." Paper presented at the Appalachian Studies Annual Conference. Johnson City, Tenn.

WVBEIS (West Virginia Business and Economic Information Service). 1991. Average Employment, Total Wages, Average Annual and Weekly Wages by 2 Digit Industry: Calendar Year 1990. Morgantown: West Virginia University.

West Virginia Women's Commission. 1993. *Women and WV Economy.* West Virginia Women's Commission. Charleston, West Virginia.

Yoder, Delmar R. 1993. "State Employment Update." *Community and Economic Development Newsletter* 2(1):6.

28. Social Class and Economic Development in Southeast Kentucky, 1820–1880

The author gratefully acknowledges the financial support granted to this research by the University of California, the University of Kentucky James Still Fellowship program, and Berea College Appalachian Center. Permission to quote from the R.G. Dun and Company Collection was granted through the Baker Library of the Harvard University Business School.

1. George E. Vincent, "A Retarded Frontier," *American Journal of Sociology* 4 (1898): 1–20.

2. Others who based their descriptions of Appalachia on conditions in southeast Kentucky include James Lane Allen, "Through the Cumberland Gap on Horseback," *Harper's New Monthly Magazine* 76 (1886): 50–66; Grace Ryan, "The Highlands of Kentucky," *Outlook* 58 (1896), 363–68; Ellen Churchill Semple, "The Anglo-Saxons of the Kentucky Mountains: A Study in Anthropogeography," *Geographical Journal* 17 (1901): 588–623; and Charles Dudley Warner, "Comments on Kentucky," *Harper's New Monthly Magazine* 78 (1888–89); 255–71.

3. William Goodell Frost, "Our Contemporary Ancestors in the Southern Mountains," *Atlantic Monthly* 83 (1899): 311–19.

4. Ibid., 312.

5. Vincent, "A Retarded Frontier," 20.

6. Some of the best descriptions of this year are in the form of oral histories collected in Laurel Shackelford and Bill Weinberg, eds., *Our Appalachia* (New York, 1977).

7. Some exemplary works in this regard are Mary Jean Bowman and W. Warren Haynes, *Resources and People in East Kentucky* (Baltimore, 1963); Harry M. Caudill, *Theirs Be the Power* (Urbana, Ill., 1983); David Alan Corbin, *Life, Work, and Rebellion* (Urbana, Ill., 1981); John Gaventa, *Power and Powerlessness* (Urbana, Ill., 1980); John Hevener, *Which Side Are You On?* (Urbana, Ill., 1977).

8. Antimodernism in American culture is analyzed by T.J. Jackson Lears, *No Place of Grace* (New York, 1981).

9. One of the earliest efforts to discredit the culture of poverty thesis is Dwight B. Billings, "Culture and Poverty in Appalachia: A Theoretical Discussion and Empirical Analysis," *Social Forces* 53 (1974): 315–23.

10. Helen Lewis, Linda Johnson, and Donald Askins, eds., *Colonialism in Modern America: the Appalachian Case* (Boone, N.C., 1978).

11. The most coherent statement along these lines is Edward E. Knipe and Helen M. Lewis, "The Impact of Coal Mining on the Traditional Mountain Subculture," in J. Kenneth Moreland, ed., *The Not So Solid South* (Athens, Ga., 1971), 35–37.

12. Ronald D. Eller, *Miners, Millhands, and Mountaineers: Industrialization of the Appalachian South, 1880*–1930 (Knoxville, Tenn., 1982), 3.

13. Ronald D. Eller, "Land and Family: An Historical View of Preindustrial Appalachia," *Appalachian Journal* 6 (1979): 83–109.

14. Douglas Arnett, "Eastern Kentucky: The Politics of Dependency and Underdevelopment" (Ph.D. diss., Duke University, 1978), 46.

15. Eller, *Miners, Millhands, and Mountaineers,* 57.

16. Eugene Conti, "Mountain Metamorphosis: Culture and Development in East Kentucky" (Ph.D. diss., Duke University, 1979), 17.

17. Allen Batteau, "Contradictions of a Kinship Community," in Robert Hall and Carol Stack, eds., *Holding on to the Land and the Lord* (Athens, Ga., 1971), 32.

18. Harry Caudill, "The Strange Career of John C.C. Mayo," *Filson Club Quarterly* 56 (1982): 258–89.

19. Robert Brenner, "Agrarian Class Structure and Economic Development in Preindustrial Europe," *Past and Present* 70 (1976): 31; and see Brenner, "The Agrarian Roots of European Capitalism," *Past and Present* 97 (1982): 16–113.

20. The Appalachian farm economy differed greatly from that of agricultural regions to the north and south. Compare, for example, Harriet Friedmann, "World Market, State, and Family Farm: Social Bases of Household Production in an Era of Wage Labor," *Comparative Studies in Society and History* 20 (1978): 545–86; and Gavin Wright, *The Political Economy of the Cotton South* (New York, 1978).

21. A fuller discussion of preindustrial economic development in southeast Kentucky is contained in Mary Beth Pudup, "Land before Coal: Class and Regional Development in Southeast Kentucky" (Ph.D. diss., University of California, Berkeley, 1987).

22. Robert Lively, "The American System," *Business History Review* 29 (1955): 81–96.

23. John Barnhart, "Frontiersmen and Planters in the Formation of Kentucky," *Journal of Southern History* 7 (1941): 19–36.

24. E. Merton Coulter, "Early Frontier Democracy in the First Kentucky Constitution," *Political Science Quarterly* 39 (1924): 665–77.

25. E. Merton Coulter, *Civil War and Readjustment in Kentucky* (Gloucester, Ky., 1966).

26. Sally Ward Maggard, "From Farmers to Miners: The Decline of Agriculture in Eastern Kentucky," in Lawrence Busch, ed., *Science and Agricultural Development* (Totowa, N.J., 1981), 25–66.

27. Robert M. Ireland, *The County in Kentucky History* (Lexington, Ky., 1976), 2.

28. Robert M. Ireland, *Little Kingdoms: The Counties of Kentucky* (Lexington, Ky., 1977), 1.

29. Ireland, *Little Kingdoms,* 1.

30. Numbers were computed by using totals from the annual reports of the state auditor as a baseline for the assessed acreages and numbers of taxpayers. From these totals were subtracted the number of absentee owners, identified as "NR" (nonresident) on the manuscript schedules, and their assessed acreage.

31. Although some speculative investments in mountain resources had already been made by 1880, most postdate that year.

32. Competing views on slavery in Appalachia can be found in Carter Woodson, "Freedom and Slavery in Appalachian America," *Journal of Negro History* 1 (196): 132–50; and John Inscoe, "Mountain Masters; Slaveholding in Western North Carolina," *North Carolina Historical Review* 61 (1984): 143–73.

33. Both Hazard, the seat of Perry County, and Mount Pleasant, the seat of Harlan County, were incorporated by (separate) acts of the state legislature in 1884. The name of the latter town was changed to Harlan in 1912.

34. James S. Brown, "Social Class, Intermarriage, and Church Membership in a Kentucky Community," *American Journal of Sociology* 56 (1951): 233; see also idem, "The Farm Family in a Kentucky Mountain Neighborhood," *Kentucky Agricultural Experiment Station Bulletin* 587 (1952); and idem, "The Family Group in a Kentucky Mountain Farming Community," *Kentucky Agricultural Experiment Station Bulletin* 587 (1952).

35. John Egerton, *Generations: An American Family* (Lexington, Ky., 1983).

36. There exists no definitive history of Kentucky land law. The best summary is the first chapter in Willard Rouse Jillson's compendium *Kentucky Land Grants* (Baltimore, 1971).

37. Ireland, *County in Kentucky History,* 2.

38. Hazard Chapter of the Daughters of the American Revolution, *A History of Perry County, Kentucky* (Privately published, 1953), 4–7.

39. Mabel Green Condon, *A History of Harlan County* (Nashville, Tenn., 1962), 15–16.

40. Ireland, *County in Kentucky History,* 3–4.

41. Shackelford and Weinberg, eds., *Our Appalachia,* 37.

42. Ibid., 54.

43. Supplement to the *Harlan Enterprise,* 10 April 1908, Appalachian Collection, University of Kentucky Library, Lexington.

44. Kentucky, 16: 154, R.G. Dun & Co. Collection, Baker Library, Harvard University Graduate School of Business, Cambridge, Mass.

45. R.G. Dun & Co. Collection, 37:45; Perry County Tax Assessor Books, 1860.

46. R.G. Dun & Co. Collection, 37:51.

47. Floyd County, R.G. Dun & Co. Collection, 12:168.

48. R.G. Dun & Co. Collection 37:44, 43.

49. Share-rent agreements, William Webb and F.A. Hopkins, 15 Nov. 1883, T.M. Nesbitt and Wesley Callahan and W.S. Harkins, 15 Oct. 1884, box 1, file 8, Harkins Family Papers, Special Collections, University of Kentucky Library.

50. In western North Carolina, for example, Inscoe reported that most slave owners were chiefly engaged in commercial occupations. See Inscoe, "Mountain Masters."

51. Frederick Law Olmsted, *A Journey in the Back Country* (New York, 1863), 226.

52. Floyd County Tax Assessor Book, 1860.

53. Perry County Tax Assessor Book, 1860; Dun Collection, 37:43.

54. R.G. Dun & Co. Collection, 12:158; Judge Charles Kerr, *History of Kentucky,* 4 vols. (Chicago, 1922), 4:612–13.

55. Kerr, *History,* 4:632–33.

56. Ibid., 227–28.

57. Ibid., 579.

58. Ibid., 612.

59. George B. Turner, "From Harlan County—Big Trees and Remarkably Old People," clipping, n.d., *Lexington Herald,* in scrapbook ca. 1890, Filson Club, Louisville, Ky.

30. The Mountain Crafts: Romancing the Marketplace

Davidson, Jan. [1931] 1990. Introduction to reprint of *Mountain Homespun,* by Frances Louisa Goodrich. Knoxville: University of Tennessee Press.

Eaton, Allen H. 1937. *Handicrafts of the Southern Highlands.* New York: Russell Sage Foundation. Reprinted 1973. New York: Dover Books.

Miller, Jim W. 1980. *The Mountains Have Come Closer.* Boone, N.C.: Appalachian Consortium Press. (Used with author's permission).

Whisnant, David. 1983. *All That is Native and Fine.* Chapel Hill: University of North Carolina Press.

31. A New Wave of Colonization: The Economics of the Tourism and Travel Industry in Appalachian Kentucky

Applalachian Regional Commission (ARC). 1998. "Appalachian Regional Commission Homepage." [On-line]. Available: http://www.arc.gov/.

Commonwealth of Kentucky. 1999. "Commonwealth of Kentucky Homepage." Available online at: http://www.state.ky.us/.

Diamond, J. 1977. "Tourism's Role in Economic Development." *Economic Development and Cultural Change* 25: 539–553.

Eller, Ronald D. 1982. *Miners, Millhands, & Mountaineers: Industrialization of the Appalachian South, 1880–1930.* Knoxville: University of Tennessee Press.

Gaventa, John. 1980. *Power & Powerlessness: Quiescence & Rebellion in an Appalachian Valley.* Champaign: University of Illinois Press.

Hoivik, Tord, and Turidd Heiberg. 1980. "Centre-Periphery Tourism and Self-Reliance." *International Social Science Journal* 32: 69–98.

Hsiung, David. 1997. *Two Worlds in the Tennessee Mountains: Exploring the Origins of Appalachian Stereotypes.* Lexington: University Press of Kentucky.

Lanfant, M. 1980. "Introduction: Tourism in the Process of Internationalization." *International Social Science Journal* 32: 14–43.

Lewis, Helen Matthews. 1983 [1970]. "Fatalism or the Coal Industry?" In *Appalachia: Social Context, Past and Present,* ed. B. Ergood and B. Kuhre, 221–229. Dubuque, Iowa: Kendall/Hunt Publishing Company.

Maggard, Sally Ward. 1994. "Will the Real Daisy Mae Please Stand Up? A Methodological Essay on Gender Analysis in Appalachian Research." *Appalachian Journal: A Regional Studies Review* (Winter): 136–150.

Oliver-Smith, Anthony, Francisco Jurdao Arrones, and Jose Lison Arcal. 1989. "Tourist Development and the Struggle for Local Resource Control." *Human Organization* 48: 345–351.

Olsen, Barbara. 1997. "Environmentally Sustainable Development and Tourism: Lessons from Negril, Jamaica." *Human Organization* 56: 285–293.

Salstrom, Paul, and Steve Hollenhorst. 1994. "Increasing Dependency and the Tourisitization Rag." *Appalachian Journal: A Regional Studies Review* (Summer): 410–420.

Shapiro, Henry. 1983 [1977]. "Appalachia and the Idea of America: The Problem of the Persisting Frontier." In *Appalachia: Social Context, Past and Present,* ed. B. Ergood and B. Kuhre, 74–80. Dubuque, Iowa: Kendall/Hunt Publishing Company.

Walls, David S. 1978. "Internal Colony or Internal Periphery? A Critique of Current Models and an Alternative Formulation." In *Colonialism in Modern America: The Appalachian Case,* ed. H. M. Lewis, L. Johnson, and D. Askins, 319–349. Boone, N.C.: Appalachian Consortium Press.

Whitaker, Stephen Paul. 1994. "Tourist Commission Promotes Region at Boat/Travel Shows." *Pulaski Week* (January 22–28): 1. Somerset, Ky.: The Counties Group.

Wood, Robert. 1980. "International Tourism and Cultural Change in Southeast Asia." *Economic Development and Cultural Change* 28: 561–581.

32. Prospects for the UMWA

1. As is true of the majority of historians, I do not accept Price Fishback's benign view of the company town.

2. See Coal Mines Administration, *A Medical Survey of the Bituminous-Coal Industry* (Washington, D.C.: GPO, 1947).

3. Arthur E. Suffern, *Conciliation and Arbitration in the Coal Industry of America* (Boston: Houghton Mifflin, 1915).

4. *Proceedings of Joint Convention of N.P.U. and N.T.A. 135, K. of L., January 23–27, 1890* (Pennsylvania State University, Pattee Library, The Pennsylvania Historical Collections and Labor Archives, United Mine Workers of America Papers; hereafter, UMWA Papers).

5. Uji Ichioka, "Asian Immigrant Coal Miners and the United Mine Workers of America: Race and Class in Rock Springs, Wyoming, 1907," *Amerasia* 6 (Fall 1979): 1–23.

6. UMWA Papers, CIO collection.

7. W. Jett Lauck Papers, University of Virginia Library, Special Collections Department. For a review of the legislative development of this idea, see Maier B. Fox, *United We Stand: The United Mine Workers of America, 1890–1990* (United Mine Workers of America, 1990), 307–12.

8. See the *UMW Journal* and the *Proceedings* of the UMWA national conventions for the period 1900–1912, especially.

9. *Labor Radical: From the Wobblies to CIO: A Personal History* (Boston: Beacon, 1971), 217.

10. See, among others, Singer, Chapter 5, and Phelan, Chapter 4.

11. See *UMWJ* (March–April 1995).

12. Interview with Richard Trumka, January 5, 1995.

13. See, for example, the discussion of the Rushton experiment in the *UMWJ* (December 16–31, 1976).

14. This (and following material) is based on coverage in the *UMWJ* (May 1993).

15. Interview with Trumka, January 5, 1995.

16. Available through the UMWA or the BCOA.

17. See *UMWJ* (April 1994).

18. See *UMWJ* (August–September 1994), on the decision handed down June 30, 1994.

19. Unless otherwise indicated, all material in the rest of this essay is drawn from the Trumka interview of January 5, 1995.

20. Early examples of the "comprehensive campaign" are reported in many sources, including the *UMWJ;* John Brophy, *A Miner's Life* (Madison: University of Wisconsin Press, 1964); and Lynda Ann Ewen, *Which Side Are You On?* (Chicago: Vanguard Books, 1979).

33. Policies and Programs

Anderson, Jack and Michael Binstein. 1993. Prisoners and Poverty in Appalachia. *The Washington Post* (May 6):B23.

Bellah, Robert N., Richard Madsen, William M. Sullivan, Ann Swidler and Steven M. Tipton. 1985. *Habits of the Heart: Individualism and Commitment in American Life.* Berkeley: University of California Press.

Berger, Peter and Richard J. Neuhaus. 1977. *To Empower People: The Role of Mediating Structures in Public Policy.* Washington, D.C.: American Enterprise Institute for Public Policy Research.

Couto, Richard A. 1991. Heroic Bureaucracies. *Administration & Society* 23(1):28–43.

Drape, Joe. 1991. Through the Mill. *Southern Exposure.* (Fall):8–12.

Dreier, Peter and John Atlas. 1992. Housing. In *Changing America: Blueprints for the New Administration,* ed. Mark Green. New York: Newmarket Press: 383–398.

Edelman, Marian Wright. 1992. In *Changing America: Blueprints for the New Administration,* ed. Mark Green. New York: Newmarket Press, 431–442.

Fisher, Steve, ed. 1993. *Fighting Back in Appalachia: Traditions of Resistance and Change.* Philadelphia: Temple University Press.

Gilbert, Pamela and Susannah Goodman, 1992. In *Changing America: Blueprints for the New Administration,* ed. Mark Green. New York: Newmarket Press, 589–603.

Gray, Peter. 1992. Nuclear Weapons: Build Down/Clean Up. In *Changing America: Blueprints for the New Administration,* ed. Mark Green. New York: Newmarket Press, 273–82.

Green, Mark ed. 1992. *Changing America: Blueprints for the New Administration.* New York: Newmarket Press.

Greenstein, Robert. 1992. Reducing Poverty. In *Changing America: Blueprints for the New Administration,* ed. Mark Green. New York: Newmarket Press, 415–430.

Greider, William. 1992. *Who Will Tell the People: The Betrayal of American Democracy.* New York: Simon & Schuster.

Gund, Agnes. 1992. Arts and Culture. In *Changing America: Blueprints for the New Administration,* ed. Mark Green. New York: Newmarket Press, 472–79.

Horton, Bill. 1989. Review of *Highlander: No Ordinary School, 1932–1962. Appalachian Journal* (16): 368–70.

Kamarck, Elaine. 1992. In *Changing America: Blueprints for the New Administration,* ed. Mark Green. New York: Newmarket Press, 443–56.

Kuttner, Robert. 1992. Labor Policy. In *Changing America: Blueprints for the New Administration,* ed. Mark Green. New York: Newmarket Press, 154–69.

Littlefield, Nick. 1992. In *Changing America: Blueprints for the New Administration,* ed. Mark Green. New York: Newmarket Press, 457–471.

Marlin, John Tepper. 1992. In *Changing America: Blueprints for the New Administration,* ed. Mark Green. New York: Newmarket Press, 249–60.

Marmor, Theodore and Michael S. Barr. 1992. Health. In *Changing America: Blueprints for the New Administration,* ed. Mark Green. New York: Newmarket Press, 399–414.

Marshall, Will and Martin Schram. 1993. *Mandate for Change.* New York: Berkley Books.

McIntyre, Robert S. 1992. Tax Policy. In *Changing America: Blueprints for the New Administration,* ed. Mark Green. New York: Newmarket Press, 29–45.

Osborne, David and Ted Gaebler. 1990. *Reinventing Government.* Reading, MA: Addison-Wesley.

Passall, Peter. 1994. Public Schools for Profit, Phase 2: The Sales Pitch. *The New York Times* (January 19):B9L.

Salamon, Lester. 1981. Rethinking Public Management: Third-Party Government and the Changing Forms of Government Action. *Public Policy* 29:3 (Summer): 266–72.

——— and Alan J. Abramson. 1982. *The Federal Budget and the Nonprofit Sector.* Washington, D.C.: Urban Institute Press.

Schorr, Lisbeth B. 1988. *Within Our Reach: Breaking the Cycle of Disadvantage.* New York: Doubleday.

Seminario, Margaret M. 1992. Workplace Safety and Health. In *Changing America: Blueprints for the New Administration,* ed. Mark Green. New York: Newmarket Press, 578–88.

Shapiro, Robert. 1992. Fiscal Policy. In *Changing America: Blueprints for the New Administration,* ed. Mark Green. New York: Newmarket Press, 74–87.

Social Policy. 1989. Democratic Dilemma: From Local Victories to National Impact? Parts I and II. (Spring) 22–40 and (Summer): 34–57.

Steinbrunner, John. 1992. Conventional and Nuclear Defense. In *Changing America: Blueprints for the New Administration,* ed. Mark Green. New York: Newmarket Press, 231–48.

Toch, Thomas. 1993. Whittling the Future Schools. *U.S. News and World Report* (August 16): 50–53.

34. A Political Approach to Regional Development

Appalachian Land Ownership Task Force. 1983. *Who Owns Appalachia?* Lexington: Univ. Press of Kentucky.

Appalachian Regional Commission. 1985a. *Appalachia: Twenty Years of Progress.* Washington, D.C.: Appalachian Regional Commission.

———. 1985b. "ARC Workshop Showcases Practical Programs for Dropout Prevention," *Appalachia* 18, no. 6; 19, no. 1:1–21.

Bradshaw, M.J. 1985. "Public Policy in Appalachia: The Application of a Neglected Geographical Factor?" *Transactions of the Institute of British Geographers,* N.S. 10:385–400.

Schwarz, J. 1983, 1987. *America's Hidden Success.* New York: Norton.

White, S. 1989. "America's Soweto: Population Redistribution in Appalachian Kentucky, 1940–86," *Appalachian Journal,* Summer, 350–60.

36. The Grass Roots Speak Back

1. This discussion draws heavily from the introduction and conclusion in Stephen L. Fisher, ed., *Fighting Back in Appalachia: Traditions of Resistance and Change* (Philadelphia: Temple Univ. Press, 1993); and Stephen L. Fisher, "Lessons from Change Efforts in Appalachia," in *Sowing Seeds in the Mountains: Community-Based Coalitions for Cancer Prevention and Control,* eds. Richard A. Couto, Nancy K. Simpson, and Gale Harris, (Washington, D.C.: National Institutes of Health, 1994), 81–95.

2. Ronald D Eller, *Miners, Millhands, and Mountaineers: Industrialization of the Appalachian South, 1880–1930* (Knoxville: Univ. of Tennessee Press, 1982); John Gaventa, *Power and Powerlessness: Quiescence and Rebellion in an Appalachian Valley* (Urbana: Univ. of Illinois Press, 1980).

3. James C. Scott, *Domination and the Arts of Resistance: Hidden Transcripts* (New Haven, Conn.: Yale Univ. Press, 1990).

4. Helen Lewis, Sue Kobak, and Linda Johnson, "Family, Religion, and Colonialism in Central Appalachia or Bury My Rifle in Big Stone Gap," in *Colonialism in Modern America: The Appalachin Case,* eds. Helen Lewis, Linda Johnson, and Don Askins (Boone, N.C.: Appalachian Consortium Press 1978), 113–39.

5. Kathleen Blee and Dwight Billings, "Reconstructing Daily Life in the Past: An Hermeneutical Approach to Ethnographic Data," *Sociological Quarterly* 27 (winter 1986): 443–62.

6. Altina L. Waller, *Feud: Hatfields, McCoys, and Social Change in Appalachia, 1860–1900* (Chapel Hill: Univ. of North Carolina Press, 1988).

7. See "Dissent in Appalachia: A Bibliography," in *Fighting Back in Appalachia: Traditions of*

Resistance and Change, ed. Stephen L. Fisher (Philadelphia: Temple Univ. Press, 1993), 339–60.

8. Bill Allen, "Save Our Cumberland Mountains: Growth and Change within a Grassroots Organization," in *Fighting Back in Appalachia,* Fisher, 85–99.

9. Melanie Zuercher, ed., *Making History: The First Ten Years of KFTC* (Prestonsburg, Ky.: Kentuckians for the Commonwealth, 1991).

10. Hal Hamilton and Ellen Ryan, "The Community Farm Alliance in Kentucky: The Growth, Mistakes, and Lessons of the Farm Movement of the 1980s," in *Fighting Back in Appalachia,* Fisher, 123–47.

11. David E. Wisnant, *Modernizing the Mountaineer: People, Power, and Planning in Appalachia* (Boone, N.C.: Appalachian Consortium Press, 1981). Pierre Clavel, *Opposition and Planning in Wales and Appalachia* (Philadelphia: Temple Univ. Press, 1983); John M. Glen, "Like a Flower Slowly Blooming: Highlander and the Nurturing of an Appalachian Movement," in *Fighting Back in Appalachia,* Fisher, 31–55.

12. Bill Horton, review of *Highlander: No Ordinary School, 1932–1962,* by John Glen, *Appalachian Journal* 16 (summer 1989): 370; Glen, "Like a Flower Slowly Blooming."

13. Horton, review of *Highlander.*

14. Helen Lewis, "Backwoods Rebels: Resistance in the Appalachian Mountains," in *Conflict and Peacemaking in Appalachia,* Coalition for Appalachian Ministry (Amesville, Ohio: Coalition for Appalachian Ministry, 1987), 22.

15. The following discussion draws from a variety of sources that are part of a vigorous debate in community organizing circles during the past decade over what organizational instruments and strategies are best suited for building progressive citizen groups and political movements. Stephen L. Fisher, "Conclusion: New Populist Theory and the Study of Dissent in Appalachia," in *Fighting Back in Appalachia,* Fisher, 317–36.

16. Jim Green, "Culture, Politics, and Workers' Response to Industrialization in the U.S.," *Radical America* 16 (Jan.–Feb. 1982): 114, 117.

17. Mary Beth Bingman, "Stopping the Bulldozers: What Difference Did It Make?" in *Fighting Back in Appalachia,* Fisher, 17–30.

18. Allen, "Save Our Cumberland Mountains," 96.

19. David E. Wisnant, "Brief Notes toward a Reconsideration of Appalachian Values," *Appalachian Journal* 4 (Autumn 1976): 46.

20. Laura A. Schwartz, "Immigrant Voices from Home, Work, and Community: Women and Family in the Migration Process, 1890–1938" (Ph.D. diss., State Univ. of New York at Stony Brook, 1983), 78.

21. Guy Carawan and Candie Carawan "Sowing on the Mountain: Nurturing Cultural Roots and Creativity for Community Change," in *Fighting Back in Appalachia,* Fisher, 245–61.

22. James C. Scott, *Weapons of the Weak: Everyday Forms of Resistance* (New Haven, Conn.: Yale Univ. Press, 1985), 45.

23. Mary Anglin, "'A Lost and Dying World': Women's Labor in the Mica Industry of Southern Appalachia" (Ph.D. diss., New School for Social Research, 1990); Sally M. Maggard, "Gender Contested: Women's Participation in the Brookside Coal Strike," in *Women and Social Protest,* eds. Guida West and Rhoda Blumberg (New York: Oxford Univ. Press, 1990), 75–98.

24. Michael Yarrow, "The Gender-Specific Class Consciousness of Appalachian Coal Miners: Structure and Change," in *Bringing Class Back In: Historical and Contemporary Perspectives,* eds., Scott G. McNall, Rhonda F. Levine, and Rick Fantasia (Boulder, Colo.: Westview Press, 1991), 285–310.

25. Richard A. Couto, "Failing Health and New Prescriptions: Community-Based Approaches to Environmental Risks," in *Current Health Policy Issues and Alternatives: An Applied Social Science Perspective,* ed. Carole E. Hill (Athens: Univ. of Georgia Press, 1986), 53–70.

26. Dwight Billings, "Religion as Opposition: A Gramscian Analysis," *American Journal of Sociology* 96 (July 1990): 1–31.

27. Don Manning-Miller, "Racism and Organizing in Appalachia," in *Fighting Back in Appalachia,* Fisher, 57–68.

28. D.E. Wisnant, "Farther Along: The Next Phase of Cultural Work in the South," *Southern Change* 13 (May 1991): 7–8.

29. Barry Goldberg, "A New Look at Labor History," *Social Policy* 12 (winter 1982): 61.

30. Prudence S. Posner, introduction to *Dilemmas of Activism: Class, Community, and the Politics of Local Mobilization,* eds. Joseph M. King and Prudence S. Posner (Philadelphia: Temple Univ. Press, 1990), 5.

31. Green, "Culture, Politics, and Workers' Response."

32. Jim Sessions and Fran Ansley, "Singing across Dark Spaces: The Union/Community Takeover of Pittston's Moss 3 Plant," in *Fighting Back in Appalachia,* Fisher, 217.

37. The Kentucky Way

Beaver, Patricia, Rural Community in the Appalachian South. (Lexington: University Press of Kentucky, 1986.)

Bryant, Carlene, We're All Kin: A cultural study of an East Tennessee Mountain Neighborhood. (Knoxville: University of Tennessee Press, 1981.)

Foster, Stephen William, The Past is Another Country. (Berkeley: University of California Press, 1988.)

Gaventa, John, Power and Powerlessness: Quiescence and Rebellion in an Appalachian Valley. (Urbana: University of Illinois Press, 1980.)

Hall, Robert and Carol Stack (eds.), Holding on the Land and the Lord. (Athens: University of Georgia Press, 1982.)

Halperin, Rhoda H., The Livelihood of Kin: Making Ends Meet "The Kentucky Way." (Austin: University of Texas Press, 1990.)

Hicks, George, Appalachian Valley. (New York: Holt, Rinehart and Winston, 1976.)

Lewis, Helen, The Colony of Appalachia. In Colonialism in Modern America: The Appalachian Case, edited by Helen Matthews Lewis, Linda Johnson, and Donald Askins. (Boone, N.C.: Appalachian Consortium Press, 1978.)

Precourt, Walter, The Image of Appalachian Poverty in Allen Batteau (ed.) Appalachia and America. (Lexington: University of Kentucky Press, 1983.) Pp. 86–110.

Scott, James, Weapons of the Weak. (New Haven: Yale University Press, 1985.)

Walls, David, Internal Colony or Internal Periphery: A Critique of Current Models and an Alternative Formulation. In Colonialism in Modern America: The Appalachian Case. Helen Matthews Lewis, Linda Johnson, and Donald Askins. (Boone, N.C.: Appalachian Consortium Press, 1978.)

Weinberg, Daniela, Peasant Wisdom: Cultural Adaptation in a Swiss Village. (Berkeley: University of California Press, 1975.)

Whisnant, Modernizing the Mountaineer: People, Power and Planning in Appalachia. (New York: Burt Franklin and Company, 1980.)

Notes

1. Scholars are just beginning to address heterogeneity within the Appalachian culture area. While there is no question that Appalachian people have experienced political, economic, and cultural domination, the assumption has been that their responses have necessarily been negative (Gaventa 1980; Whisnant 1980, 1983, Lewis 1978, Walls 1978).

39. "It Has to Come from the People"

1. For an example of national news coverage, see "Virginia Town Staves Off Disaster," *Washington Post,* February 11, 1987.

2. Jack Russell, *Appalachia* 20, no. 2 (Fall 1987).

3. The discussions began when the members of the Ivanhoe Civic League contacted Carroll L. Wessinger, a Lutheran minister, and Clare McBrien, a local Catholic church worker, for assistance. In turn, they contacted Helen M. Lewis of the Highlander Research and Education Center because of her work in economic education in other communities. Highlander's approach to economic education is described in Chapter 18 and in several publications available from the center (see Resources).

4. Robert McAfee Brown, *Unexpected News: Reading the Bible with Third World Eyes* (Philadelphia: Westminster Press, 1984). Helen Matthews Lewis, Linda Johnson, and Donald Askins, *Colonialism in Modern America: The Appalachian Case* (Boone, N.C.: Appalachian Consortium Press, 1978).

5. This is a reference to a report discussed during the six-week economics class, *Shadows in the Sunbelt,* prepared by MDC, Inc., an economic development research group in North Carolina (Chapel Hill, 1986). In the report, MDC compares the strategy of industrial recruitment or "smokestack chasing" to "the great buffalo hunts of the last century. . . . The stampede of plants to the South is definitely over—especially in rural areas that lack a skilled workforce, transportation, infrastructure, and cultural amenities. Yet the hunters continue in their pursuit, hoping to bag one of the remaining hides" (p. 10). The report urges the South to go "beyond the buffalo hunt" to seek new strategies for community-based economic development.

XI

by Stephen L. Fisher

A Selected Bibliography of Books on Appalachia, 1991–2001

This highly selective bibliography of 200 books supplements the bibliography published in the 1991 edition of this anthology edited by Bruce Ergood and Bruce E. Kuhre (Steve Fisher, "A Selective Bibliography for Appalachian Studies, Revised, Summer 1990"). The works presented here were chosen to inform those teaching or taking Appalachian courses with a social science, political economy, and grassroots perspective. Because of space limitations and a desire to cover a variety of topics and issues, a number of relevant books could not be included. For additional sources, readers are encouraged to consult Jo B. Brown's "Annual Bibliography" in the *Journal of Appalachian Studies* (1995–present) and Marie Tedesco's bibliography on the Appalachian Studies Association website (www.appalachianstudies.org)

Abbreviations

CASS, ETSU (Center for Appalachian Studies and Services, East Tennessee State U.); JASA (Journal of the Appalachian Studies Association); SUNY (State U. of New York); TUP (Temple U. Press); U. (University); UGP (U. of Georgia Press); UIP (U. of Illinois Press); UNCP (U. of North Carolina Press); UPK (U. Press of Kentucky); UTP (U. of Tennessee Press)

Bibliography

Anderson, William L., ed. *Cherokee Removal: Before and After.* Athens: UGP, 1991.

Atkins, Jonathan M. *Parties, Politics, and the Sectional Conflict in Tennessee, 1832–1861.* Knoxville: UTP, 1997.

Ayers, Harvard, Jenny Hager, & Charles E. Little, eds. *An Appalachian Tragedy: Air Pollution and Tree Death in the Eastern Forests of North America.* San Francisco: Sierra Club Books, 1998.

Bailey, Jason, & Liz Natter. *Kentucky's Low Road to Economic Development: What Corporate Subsidies Are Doing to the Commonwealth.* Lexington: Democracy Resource Center, 2000.

Baker, Chris, ed. *Appalachian Studies: Syllabus Guide and Teaching Materials.* 2nd ed. Washington, D. C.: American Sociological Association Teaching Resources Center, 2000.

Barker, Garry. *Notes from a Native Son: Essays on the Appalachian Experience.* Knoxville: UTP, 1995.

———, ed. *Environmental Voices: Cultural, Social, Physical, and Natural.* *JASA* 4. Johnson City: CASS, ETSU, 1992.

Barney, Sandra Lee. *Authorized to Heal: Gender, Class, and the Transformation of Medicine in Appalachia, 1880–1930.* Chapel Hill: UNCP, 2000.

Bartlett, Richard A. *Troubled Waters: Champion International and the Pigeon River Controversy.* Knoxville: UTP, 1995.

Beatty, Bess. *Almanance: The Holt Family and Industrialization in a North Carolina County, 1837–1900.* Baton Rouge: Louisiana State U. Press, 1999.

Beaver, Patricia D., ed. "Appalachia and the South: Place, Gender, Pedagogy." Special Issue, *NWSA Journal* 11:3 (Fall 1999).

Becker, Jane S. *Selling Tradition: Appalachia and the Construction of an American Folk, 1930–1940.* Chapel Hill: UNCP, 1998.

Beik, Mildred A. *The Miners of Windber: The Struggles of New Immigrants for Unionization, 1890s–1930s.* University Park: Pennsylvania State U. Press, 1996.

Bell, Augusta G. *Circling Windrock Mountain: Two Hundred Years in Appalachia.* Knoxville: UTP, 1998.

Berry, Chad. *Southern Migrants, Northern Exiles.* Urbana: UIP, 2000.

Besmann, Wendy L. *A Separate Circle: Jewish Life in Knoxville, Tennessee.* Knoxville: UTP, 2001.

Best, Bill, ed. *One Hundred Years of Appalachian Visions, 1897–1996.* Berea: Appalachian Imprints, 1997.

Bickley, Ancella R., & Lynda Ann Ewen, eds. *Memphis Tennessee Garrison: The Remarkable Story of a Black Appalachian Woman.* Athens: Ohio U. Press, 2001.

Billings, Dwight B., & Kathleen M. Blee. *The Road To Poverty: The Making of Wealth and Hardship in Appalachia.* New York: Cambridge U. Press, 2000.

Billings, Dwight B., Gurney Norman, & Katherine Ledford, eds. *Confronting Appalachian Stereotypes: Back Talk from an American Region.* Lexington: UPK, 1999.

Blatz, Perry K. *Democratic Miners: Work and Labor Relations in the Anthracite Coal Industry, 1875–1925.* Albany: SUNY Press, 1994.

Blethen, Tyler, ed. *Diversity in Appalachia: Images and Realities. JASA* 5. Johnson City: CASS, ETSU, 1993.

Blethen, H. Tyler, & Curtis W. Wood, Jr., eds. *Ulster and North America: Transatlantic Perspectives on the Scotch-Irish.* Tuscaloosa: U. of Alabama Press, 1997.

Bolgiano, Chris. *The Appalachian Forest: A Search for Roots and Renewal.* Mechanicsburg, PA: Stackpole Books, 1998.

Boone, D. Daniel, & Gregory H. Aplet. *Sustaining Biodiversity in the Southern Appalachians.* Washington, D. C.: Wilderness Society, 1994.

Borman, Kathyrn M., & Phillip J. Obermiller, eds. *From Mountain To Metropolis: Appalachian Migrants in American Cities.* Westport, CT: Bergin & Garvey, 1994.

Botsch, Robert E. *Organizing the Breathless: Cotton Dust, Southern Politics, & the Brown Lung Association.* Lexington: UPK, 1993.

Bradshaw, Michael. *The Appalachian Regional Commission: Twenty-Five Years of Government Policy.* Lexington: UPK, 1992.

Bragg, Rick. *All Over But The Shoutin'.* New York: Pantheon, 1997.

———. *Ava's Man.* New York: Knopf, 2001.

Brown, Fred W., & Jeanne McDonald. *The Serpent Handlers: Three Families and Their Faith.* Winston-Salem, NC: John F. Blair, 2000.

Brown, Margaret L. *The Wild East: A Biography of the Great Smokey Mountains.* Gainesville: U. Press of Florida, 2000.

Brundage, W. Fitzhugh. *Lynching in the New South: Georgia and Virginia, 1880–1930.* Urbana: UIP, 1993.

Burton, Thomas. *Serpent-Handling Believers.* Knoxville: UTP, 1993.

Bush, Florence C. *Dorie: Woman of the Mountains.* Knoxville: UTP, 1992.

Camp, Scott D. *Worker Response To Plant Closings: Steelworkers in Johnstown and Youngstown.* New York: Garland, 1995.

Cecil-Fronsman, Bill. *Common Whites: Class and Culture in Antebellum North Carolina.* Lexington: UPK, 1992.

Clark, Daniel J. *Like Night & Day: Unionization in a Southern Mill Town.* Chapel Hill: UNCP, 1997.

Colignon, Richard A. *Power Plays: Critical Events in the Institutionalization of the Tennessee Valley Authority.* Albany: SUNY Press, 1997.

Cook, Samuel R. *Monacans and Miners: Native American and Coal Mining Communities in Appalachia.* Lincoln: U. of Nebraska Press, 2000.

Cooper, Leland R., & Mary Lee Cooper. *The Pond Mountain Chronicle: Self-Portrait of a Southern Appalachian Community.* Jefferson, NC: McFarland, 1998.

Couto, Richard A. *An American Challenge: A Report on Economic Trends and Social Issues in Appalachia.* Dubuque, IA: Kendall/Hunt, 1994.

———. *Making Democracy Work Better: Mediating Structures, Social Capital, and the Democratic Prospect.* Chapel Hill: UNCP, 1999.

Couto, Richard A., Nancy K. Simpson, & Gale Harris, eds. *Sowing Seeds in the Mountains: Community-Based Coalitions for Cancer Prevention and Control.* Washington, D.C.: National Cancer Institute, 1994.

Covington, Dennis. *Salvation on Sand Mountain: Snake Handling and Redemption in Southern Appalachia.* Reading, MA: Addison-Wesley, 1995.

Crass, David C., Steven D. Smith, Martha A. Zierden, & Richard D. Brooks, eds. *The Southern Colonial Backcountry: Interdisciplinary Perspectives on Frontier Communities.* Knoxville: UTP, 1998.

Crissman, James K. *Death and Dying in Central Appalachia: Changing Attitudes and Practices.* Urbana: UIP, 1994.

Curran, Daniel J. *Dead Laws for Dead Men: The Politics of Federal Coal Mine Health and Safety Legislation.* Pittsburgh: U. of Pittsburgh Press, 1993.

Davis, Donald E. *Where There Are Mountains: An Environmental History of the Southern Appalachians.* Athens: UGP, 2000.

Derickson, Alan. *Black Lung: Anatomy of a Public Health Disaster.* Ithaca: Cornell U. Press, 1998.

DeRosier, Linda S. *Creeker: A Woman's Journey.* Lexington: UPK, 1999.

Dew, Charles B. *Bond of Iron: Master and Slave at Buffalo Forge.* New York: Norton, 1994.

Dews, Carlos L., & Carolyn L. Laws, eds. *Out in the South.* Philadelphia: TUP, 2001

DeYoung, Alan J. *The Life and Death of a Rural American High School: Farewell Little Kanawha.* New York: Garland, 1995.

DiCiccio, Carmen. *Coal and Coke in Pennsylvania.* Harrisburg: Pennsylvania Historical and Museum Commission, 1996.

Dorgan, Howard. *The Airwaves of Zion: Radio and Religion in Appalachia.* Knoxville: UTP, 1993.

———. *In the Hands of a Happy God: The "No-Hellers" of Central Appalachia.* Knoxville: UTP, 1997.

Drake, Richard B. *A History of Appalachia.* Lexington: UPK, 2001.

Dublin, Thomas. *When The Mines Closed: Stories of Struggles in Hard Times.* Ithaca: Cornell U. Press, 1998.

Dunaway, Wilma A. *The First American Frontier: Transition to Capitalism in Southern Appalachia, 1700–1860.* Chapel Hill: UNCP, 1996.

Duncan, Cynthia M. *Worlds Apart: Why Poverty Persists in Rural America.* New Haven: Yale U. Press, 1999.

Dunn, Durwood. *An Abolitionist in the Appalachian South: Ezekiel Birdseye on Slavery, Capitalism, and Separate Statehood in East Tennessee, 1841–1846.* Knoxville: UTP, 1997.

Eller, Ronald D., ed. *Communities of Hope: Preparing for the Future in Appalachian Kentucky.* Frankfort, KY: Kentucky Appalachian Task Force, 1995.

Epstein, Robin. *Citizen Power: Stories of America's New Civic Spirit.* Lexington: Democracy Resource Center, 1999.

Ergood, Bruce, & Bruce E. Kuhre, eds. *Appalachia: Social Context Past and Present.* 3rd ed. Dubuque, IA: Kendall/Hunt, 1991.

Eslinger, Ellen. *Citizens of Zion: The Social Origins of Camp Meeting Revivalism.* Knoxville: UTP, 1999.

Fagge, Roger. *Power, Culture and Conflict in the Coalfields: West Virginia and South Wales, 1900–1922.* Manchester: Manchester U. Press, 1996.

Feather, Carl E. *Mountain People in a Flat Land: A Popular History of Appalachian Migration to Northeast Ohio, 1940–1965.* Athens: Ohio U. Press, 1998.

Fine, Elizabeth C., ed. *Appalachia and the Politics of Culture. JASA* 7. Johnson City: CASS, ETSU, 1995.

Finger, John R. *Cherokee Americans: The Eastern Band of Cherokees in the Twentieth Century.* Lincoln: U. of Nebraska Press, 1991.

Fischer, David H., and James C. Kelly. *Bound Away: Virginia and the Westward Movement.* Charlottesville: U. Press of Virginia, 2000.

Fishback, Price V. *Soft Coal, Hard Choices: The Economic Welfare of Bituminous Coal Miners, 1890–1930.* New York: Oxford U. Press, 1992.

Fisher, Noel C. *War at Every Door: Partisan Politics and Guerrilla Violence in East Tennessee, 1860–1869.* Chapel Hill: UNCP, 1997.

Fisher, Stephen L., ed. *Fighting Back in Appalachia: Traditions of Resistance and Change.* Philadelphia: TUP, 1993.

Flamming, Douglas. *Creating the Modern South: Millhands and Managers in Dalton, Georgia, 1884–1984.* Chapel Hill: UNCP, 1992.

Friend, Craig T., ed. *The Buzzel About Kentuck: Settling the Promised Land.* Lexington: UPK, 1999.

Gates, Henry Louis, Jr. *Colored People.* New York: Knopf, 1994.

Giesen, Carol A. B. *Coal Miners' Wives: Portraits of Endurance.* Lexington: UPK, 1995.

Glen, John. *Highlander: No Ordinary School.* 2nd ed. Lexington: UPK, 1996.

Glick, Patricia. *The Toll from Coal: How Emissions from the Nation's Coal-Fired Power Plants Devastate Wildlife and Threaten Human Health.* Washington, D.C.: National Wildlife Federation, 2000.

Gorn, Elliott J. *Mother Jones: The Most Dangerous Woman in America.* New York: Hill and Wang, 2001.

Grammich, Clifford A., Jr. *Local Baptists, Local Politics: Churches and Communities in the Middle and Uplands South.* Knoxville: UTP, 1999.

Groce, W. Todd. *Mountain Rebels: East Tennessee Confederates and the Civil War, 1860–1870.* Knoxville: UTP, 1999.

Halperin, Rhoda H. *Practicing Community: Class Culture and Power in an Urban Neighborhood.* Austin: U. of Texas Press, 1998.

Hargrove, Erwin C. *Prisoners of Myth: The Leadership of the Tennessee Valley Authority, 1933–1990.* Princeton: Princeton U. Press, 1994.

Hartigan, John, Jr. *Racial Situations: Class Predicaments of Whiteness in Detroit.* Princeton: Princeton U. Press, 1999.

Hathaway, Dale A. *Can Workers Have a Voice? The Politics of Deindustrialization in Pittsburgh.* University Park: Pennsylvania State U. Press, 1993.

Haynes, Ada F. *Poverty in Central Appalachia: Underdevelopment and Exploitation.* New York: Garland, 1997.

Hennen, John C. *The Americanization of West Virginia: Creating a Modern Industrial State, 1916–1925.* Lexington: UPK, 1996.

Higgs, Robert J., Ambrose N. Manning, & Jim Wayne Miller, eds. *Appalachia Inside Out: A Sequel to "Voices from the Hills".* 2 vols. Knoxville: UTP, 1995.

Hill, Sarah H. *Weaving New Worlds: Southeastern Cherokee Women and Their Basketry.* Chapel Hill: UNCP, 1997.

Hinsdale, Mary Ann, Helen M. Lewis, & S. Maxine Waller. *It Comes from the People: Community Development and Local Theology.* Philadelphia: TUP, 1995.

Hoffschwelle, Mary S. *Rebuilding the Rural Southern Community: Reformers, Schools, and Homes in Tennessee, 1900–1930.* Knoxville: UTP, 1998.

Howard, John, ed. *Carryin' On in the Lesbian and Gay South.* New York: New York U. Press, 1997.

Hsiung, David C. *Two Worlds in the Tennessee Mountains: Exploring the Origins of Appalachian Stereotypes.* Lexington: UPK, 1997.

Inscoe, John C., ed. *Appalachians and Race: The Mountain South from Slavery to Segregation.* Lexington: UPK, 2001.

———. *Southern Appalachia and the South: A Region Within a Region. JASA* 3. Johnson City: CASS, ETSU, 1991.

Inscoe, John C., & Gordon B. McKinney. *The Heart of Confederate Appalachia: Western North Carolina in the Civil War.* Chapel Hill: UNCP, 2000.

Inscoe, John C., & Robert C. Kenzer, eds. *Enemies of the Country: New Perspectives on Unionists in the Civil War South.* Athens: UGP, 2001.

Irons, Janet. *Testing the New Deal: The General Textile Strike of 1934 in the American South.* Urbana: UIP, 2000.

Jones, Jacqueline. *The Dispossessed: America's Underclass from the Civil War to the Present.* New York: BasicBooks, 1992.

Jones, Loyal. *Faith and Meaning in the Southern Uplands.* Urbana: UIP, 1999.

Juravich, Tom, & Kate Bronfenbrenner. *Ravenswood: The Steelworkers' Victory and the Revival of American Labor.* Ithaca: ILR Press, 1999.

Keith, Jeanette. *Country People in the New South: Tennessee's Upper Cumberland.* Chapel Hill: UNCP, 1995.

Kelly, Brian. *Race, Class, and Power in the Alabama Coalfields, 1908–21.* Urbana: UIP, 2001.

Kennedy, N. Brent. *The Melungeons: The Resurrection of a Proud People.* 2nd ed. Macon: Mercer U. Press, 1997.

Kenny, Kevin. *Making Sense of the Molly Maguires.* New York: Oxford U. Press, 1998.

Kimbrough, David L. *Taking Up Serpents: Snake Handlers of Eastern Kentucky.* Chapel Hill: UNCP, 1995.

Kingsolver, Ann E., ed. *More than Class: Studying Power in U.S. Workplaces.* Albany: SUNY Press, 1998.

Koons, Kenneth E., and Warren R. Hofstra, eds. *After the Backcountry: Rural Life in the Great Valley of Virginia, 1800–1900.* Knoxville: UTP, 2000.

Krajcinovic, Ivana. *From Company Doctors to Managed Care: The United Mine Workers' Noble Experiment.* Ithaca: ILR Press, 1997.

La Lone, Mary B., ed. *Appalachian Coal Mining Memories: Life in the Coal Fields of Virginia's New River Valley.* Blacksburg, VA: Pocahontas Press, 1997.

Laslett, John H. M., ed. *The United Mine Workers of America: A Model of Industrial Solidarity?.* University Park: Pennsylvania State U. Press, 1996.

Leloudis, James L. *Schooling the New South: Pedagogy, Self, and Society in North Carolina, 1880–1920.* Chapel Hill: UNCP, 1996.

Leonard, Bill J., ed. *Christianity in Appalachia: Profiles in Regional Pluralism.* Knoxville: UTP, 1999.

Letwin, Daniel. *The Challenge of Interracial Unionism: Alabama Coal Miners, 1878–1921.* Chapel Hill: UNCP, 1998.

Lewis, Johanna M. *Artisans in the North Carolina Backcountry.* Lexington: UPK, 1995.

Lewis, Ronald L. *Transforming the Appalachian Countryside: Railroads, Deforestation, and Social Change in West Virginia, 1880–1920.* Chapel Hill: UNCP, 1998.

Lichtenstein, Alex. *Twice the Work of Free Labor: The Regional Economy of Convict Labor in the New South.* New York: Verso Press, 1997.

Lieber, James B. *Friendly Takeover: How an Employee Buyout Saved a Steel Town.* New York: Viking Penguin, 1995.

Little, Charles E. *The Dying of the Trees: The Pandemic in America's Forests.* New York: Viking, 1995.

Lockard, Duane. *Coal: A Memoir and Critique.* Charlottesville: U. Press of Virginia, 1998.

Mancini, Matthew J. *One Dies, Get Another: Convict Leasing in the American South, 1866–1928.* Columbia: U. of South Carolina Press, 1996.

McCauley, Deborah V. *Appalachian Mountain Religion: A History.* Urbana: UIP, 1995.

McElroy, James T. *We've Got the Spirit: The Life and Times of America's Greatest Cheerleading Team.* New York: Simon & Schuster, 1999.

McFarland, Andrew S. *Cooperative Pluralism: The National Coal Policy Experiment.* Lawrence: U. Press of Kansas, 1993.

McKenzie, Robert T. *One South or Many? Plantation Belt and Upcountry in Civil War-Era Tennessee.* New York: Cambridge U. Press, 1994.

McKiven, Henry M, Jr. *Iron and Steel: Class, Race, and Community in Birmingham, Alabama, 1875–1920.* Chapel Hill: UNCP, 1995.

McNeil, W. K., ed. *Appalachian Images in Folk and Popular Culture.* 2nd ed. Knoxville: UTP, 1995.

Merrifield, Juliet, et al. *Life at the Margins: Literacy, Language, and Technology in Everyday Life.* New York: Teachers College Press, 1997.

Meyers, Norma, ed. *Appalachian Adaptations to a Changing World. JASA* 6. Johnson City: CASS, ETSU, 1994.

Michrina Barry P. *Pennsylvania Mining Families: The Search for Dignity in the Coalfields.* Lexington: UPK, 1993.

Miller, Wilbur R. *Revenuers & Moonshiners: Enforcing Federal Liquor Law in the Mountain South, 1865–1900.* Chapel Hill: UNCP, 1991.

Miller, Zane L., & Bruce Tucker. *Changing Plans For America's Inner Cities: Cincinnati's Over-the-Rhine and Twentieth-Century Urbanism.* Columbus: Ohio State U. Press, 1998.

Minchin, Timothy J. *Hiring the Black Worker: The Racial Integration of the Southern Textile Industry, 1960–1980.* Chapel Hill: UNCP, 1999.

———. *What Do We Need a Union For? The TWUA in the South, 1945–1955.* Chapel Hill: UNCP, 1997.

Mitchell, Robert D., ed. *Appalachian Frontiers: Settlement, Society, & Development in the Preindustrial Era.* Lexington: UPK, 1991.

Moore, Marat. *Women in the Mines: Stories of Life and Work.* New York: Twayne, 1996.

Mulcahy, Richard P. *A Social Contract for the Coal Fields: The Rise and Fall of the United Mine Workers of America Welfare and Retirement Fund.* Knoxville: UTP, 2000.

Murphy, Arthur D., Colleen Blanchard, & Jennifer A. Hill, eds. *Latino Workers in the Contemporary South.* Athens: UGP, 2001.

Nash, Steve. *Blue Ridge 2020: An Owner's Manual.* Chapel Hill: UNCP, 1999.

Neely, Sharlotte. *Snowbird Cherokees: People of Persistence.* Athens: UGP, 1991.

Noe, Kenneth W. *Southwest Virginia's Railroad: Modernization and the Sectional Crisis.* Urbana: UIP, 1994.

Noe, Kenneth W., & Shannon H. Wilson, eds. *The Civil War in Appalachia: Collected Essays.* Knoxville: UTP, 1997.

Nolt, John, et al. *What Have We Done? The Foundation for Global Sustainability's State of the Bioregion Report for the Upper Tennessee Valley and the Southern Appalachian Mountains.* Washburn, TN: Earth Knows, 1997.

Norris, Randall, & Jean-Philippe Cypres. *Women of Coal.* Lexington: UPK, 1996.

Obermiller, Phillip J., ed. *Down Home, Downtown: Urban Appalachians Today.* Dubuque, IA: Kendall/Hunt, 1996.

Obermiller, Phillip J., & William W. Philliber, eds. *Appalachia in an International Context: Cross-National Comparisons of Developing Regions.* Westport, CT: Praeger, 1994.

Obermiller, Phillip J., Thomas E. Wagner, & E. Bruce Tucker, eds. *Appalachian Odyssey: Historical Perspectives on the Great Migration.* Westport, CT: Praeger, 2000.

O'Brien, John. *At Home in the Heart of Appalachia.* New York: Knopf, 2001.

O'Brien, Sean M. *Mountain Partisans: Guerrilla Warfare in the Southern Appalachians, 1861–1865.* Westport, CT: Praeger, 1999.

Patterson, Beverly Bush. *The Sound of the Dove: Singing in Appalachian Primitive Baptist Churches.* Urbana: UIP, 1995.

Patton, Randall L., with David B. Parker. *Carpet Capital: The Rise of a New South Industry.* Athens: UGP, 1999.

Pearce, John Ed. *Days of Darkness: The Feuds of Eastern Kentucky.* Lexington: UPK, 1994.

Perdue, Theda. *Cherokee Women: Gender and Culture Change, 1700–1835.* Lincoln: U. of Nebraska Press, 1998.

Perdue, Theda, & Michael D. Green. *The Columbia Guide to American Indians of the Southeast.* New York: Columbia U. Press, 2001.

Perkins, Elizabeth A. *Border Life: Experience and Memory in the Revolutionary Ohio Valley.* Chapel Hill: UNCP, 1998.

Pierce, Daniel S. *The Great Smokies: From Natural Habitat to National Park.* Knoxville: UTP, 2000.

Portelli, Alessandro. *The Death of Luigi Trastulli and Other Stories: Form and Meaning in Oral History.* Albany: SUNY Press, 1991.

Pudup, Mary Beth, Dwight B. Billings, & Altina L. Waller, eds. *Appalachia in the Making: The Mountain South in the Nineteenth Century.* Chapel Hill: UNCP, 1995.

Puglisi, Michael J., ed. *Diversity and Accommodation: Essays on the Cultural Composition of the Virginia Frontier.* Knoxville: UTP, 1997.

Purcell-Gates, Victoria. *Other People's Words: The Cycle of Low Literacy.* Cambridge: Harvard U. Press, 1995.

Rasmussen, Barbara. *Absentee Landowning and Exploitation in West Virginia, 1760–1920.* Lexington: UPK, 1994.

Richman, Ann F., ed. *The Plow Reader: Selections from an Appalachian Alternative Newsmagazine of the Late 1970's.* Abingdon, VA: Sow's Ear Press, 1996.

Roberts, Ron E., & Carol Cook-Roberts. *Mother Jones and Her Sisters: A Century of Women Activists in the American Coal Fields.* Dubuque, IA: Kendall/Hunt, 1999.

Salmond, John A. *Gastonia 1929: The Story of the Loray Mill Strike.* Chapel Hill: UNCP, 1995.

Salstrom, Paul. *Appalachia's Path to Dependency: Rethinking a Region's Economic History, 1730–1940.* Lexington: UPK, 1994.

Schmidt, Ronald G., & William S. Hooks. *Whistle Over The Mountain: Timber, Tracks & Trails in the Tennessee Smokies.* Yellow Springs, OH: Graphicom Press, 1994.

Schwartz, Scott W. *Faith, Serpents, and Fire: Images of Kentucky Holiness Believers.* Jackson: U. of Mississippi Press, 1999.

Scott, Shaunna L. *Two Sides To Everything: The Cultural Construction of Class Consciousness in Harlan County, Kentucky.* Albany: SUNY Press, 1995.

Seitz, Virginia R. *Women, Development, and Communities for Empowerment in Appalachia.* Albany: SUNY Press, 1995.

Shapiro, Karin A. *A New South Rebellion: The Battle against Convict Labor in the Tennessee Coalfields, 1871–1896.* Chapel Hill: UNCP, 1998.

Shifflett, Crandall A. *Coal Towns: Life, Work, and Culture in Company Towns of Southern Appalachia, 1880–1960.* Knoxville: UTP, 1991.

Simon, Bryant. *A Fabric of Defeat: The Politics of South Carolina Millhands, 1910–1948.* Chapel Hill: UNCP, 1998.

Smith, Barbara Ellen, ed. *Neither Separate Nor Equal: Women, Race, and Class in the South.* Philadelphia: TUP, 1999.

Smith, Danna. *Chipping Forests & Jobs: A Report on the Economic and Environmental Impacts of Chip Mills in the Southeast.* Brevard, NC: Dogwood Alliance, 1997.

Speer, Allen P. *Voices From Cemetery Hill: The Civil War Diary, Reports, and Letters of Colonel William Henry Asbury Speer (1861–1864).* Johnson City: Overmountain Press, 1997.

Speer, Allen P., & Janet Barton Speer, eds. *Sisters of Providence: The Search for God in the Frontier South (1843–1858).* Johnson City: Overmountain Press, 2000.

Spence, Beth. *The Story of the Politics of Education in West Virginia! Whatever Happened to Pauley vs. Bailey?.* Charleston: Covenant House, 1998.

Stealey, John E., III. *The Antebellum Kanawha Salt Business and Western Markets.* Lexington: UPK, 1993.

Steel, Edward M., Jr. *The Court-Martial of Mother Jones.* Lexington: UPK, 1995.

Stewart, Kathleen. *A Space on the Side of the Road: Cultural Poetics in an "Other" America.* Princeton: Princeton U. Press, 1996.

Stoddart, Jess, ed. *The Quare Women's Journals: May Stone and Katherine Pettit's Summers in the Kentucky Mountains and the Founding of the Hindman Settlement School.* Ashland: Jesse Stuart Foundation, 1997.

Sutherland, Daniel E., ed. *Guerrillas, Unionists, and Violence on the Confederate Home Front.* Fayetteville: U. of Arkansas Press, 1999.

Thomas, Jerry Bruce. *An Appalachian New Deal: West Virginia in the Great Depression.* Lexington: UPK, 1998.

Tillson, Albert, H., Jr. *Gentry and Common Folk: Political Culture on a Virginia Frontier, 1740–1789.* Lexington: UPK, 1991.

Tolnay, Stewart E., & E. M. Beck. *A Festival of Violence: An Analysis of Southern Lynchings, 1882–1930.* Urbana: UIP, 1995.

Trotter, Joe W., Jr. *River Jordan: African American Urban Life in the Ohio Valley.* Lexington: UPK, 1998.

Verghese, Andrew. *My Own Country: A Doctor's Story of a Town and Its People in the Age of Aids.* New York: Simon & Schuster, 1994.

Wagner, Thomas E., & Phillip J. Obermiller. *Valuing Our Past, Creating Our Future: The Founding of the Urban Appalachian Council.* Berea: Berea College Press, 1999.

Waldrep, G. C., III. *Southern Workers and the Search for Community: Spartanburg County, South Carolina.* Urbana: UIP, 2000.

Walker, Melissa. *All We Knew Was to Farm: Rural Women in the Upcountry South, 1919–1941.* Baltimore: Johns Hopkins U. Press, 2000.

Webb, Samuel L. *Two-Party Politics in the One-Party South: Alabama's Hill Country, 1874–1920.* Tuscaloosa: U. of Alabama Press, 1997.

Weidensaul, Scott. *Mountains of the Heart: A Natural History of the Appalachians.* Golden, CO: Fulcrum, 1994.

Weise, Robert S. *Grasping at Independence: Debt, Male Authority, and Mineral Rights in Appalachian Kentucky, 1850–1915.* Knoxville: UTP, 2001.

Williamson, J W. *Hillbillyland: What the Movies Did to the Mountains and What the Mountains Did to the Movies.* Chapel Hill: UNCP, 1995.

Williamson, J. W., & Edwin T. Arnold, eds. *Interviewing Appalachia: The "Appalachian Journal" Interviews, 1978–1992.* Knoxville: UTP, 1994.

Wolensky, Robert P., Kenneth C. Wolensky, & Nicole H. Wolensky. *The Knox Mine Disaster, January 25, 1959: The Final Years of the Northern Anthracite Industry and the Effort to Rebuild a Regional Economy.* Harrisburg: Pennsylvania Historical and Museum Commission, 1999.

Wolfe, Margaret Ripley. *Daughters of Canaan: A Saga of Southern Women.* Lexington: UPK, 1995.

Zuercher, Melanie, ed. *Making History: The First Ten Years of KFTC.* Prestonsburg, KY: Kentuckians For The Commonwealth, 1991.

XII

by Jack Wright

Selected Filmography

The following are film and video titles categorized by subject and available on VHS tape:

Economics

BEYOND MEASURE

58 M. VHS/16 mm 1995 Directed by Herb E. Smith

Since the 1980s communities in the Appalachian coalfields have lost thousands of their best-paying jobs. *Beyond Measure* places these economic challenges in a larger historical context and documents efforts of citizens to rebuild their communities. Mountain people describe how the mutual aid and support of extended families and attachments to the land are more important than the things economics usually measures.—Appalshop

Environment

BUFFALO CREEK FLOOD

40 M. VHS/16 mm 1975 Directed by Mimi Pickering

On February 26, 1972, a coal-waste dam owned by the Pittston Company collapsed at the head of a crowded hollow in southern West Virginia. A wall of sludge, debris and water tore through the valley below, leaving in its wake 125 dead and 4,000 homeless. Interviews with survivors, representatives of union and citizen's groups, and officials of the Pittston Company are juxtaposed with actual footage of the flood and scenes of the ensuing devastation. As reasons for the disaster are sought out and examined, evidence mounts that company officials knew of the hazard in advance of the flood, and that the dam was in violation of state and federal regulations.—Appalshop

CHEMICAL VALLEY

58 M. VHS 1991 Directed by Mimi Pickering

A toxic gas known as MIC leaked from a Union Carbide pesticide plant in Bhopal, India. At least 3,500 people were killed, and over 50,000 were permanently disabled. *Chemical Valley* begins with Bhopal and the immediate response to the tragedy in the Kanawha Valley of West Virginia, an area once dubbed by residents "the chemical capital of the world" because of the many plants operated by such industrial giants as Monsanto, DuPont, FMC and Union Carbide. The program follows events in the valley over five years as lines are drawn and all sides are heard in the debate between those who fear for their livelihood and those who fear for their lives.—Appalshop

ON OUR OWN LAND

29 M. VHS 1988 Directed by Anne Lewis

In the Appalachian coalfields broadform deeds were used, beginning around 1900, to sever the ownership of mineral rights from the ownership of the surface land. Although surface mining was virtually unheard of at the time most of these deeds were signed, Kentucky courts ruled years later that the owners of such deeds could strip mine the land without the consent of the surface owners. The video chronicles the citizens' fight to have the broadform deed declared unconstitutional in the state of Kentucky.—Appalshop

TIME ON THE RIVER

60 M. VHS 1988 Directed by John Morgan

The Kentucky River has played a critical role in the settlement and growth of Kentucky. Boonesborough, Kentucky's first permanent settlement, was established on its banks in 1775; later, it carried steamboats and logs for the timber industry. In the 19th century, Frankfort was designated the state capital because the river provided easy access. Author Gurney Norman brings the story up to date by exploring the contemporary uses of the river and investigating the controversies that swirl around it. His guided tour takes viewers from the river's headwaters in the Eastern Kentucky mountains to its confluence with the Ohio River near Carrollton.—Kentucky Educational Television

YELLOW CREEK, KENTUCKY

29 M. VHS 1984 Directed by Anne Lewis

This show documents the efforts of the Yellow Creek Concerned Citizens to stop a commercial tannery from dumping toxic wastes into the creek that flows through their small community near Middlesboro, Kentucky.—Appalshop

Women

BELINDA

29 M. VHS 1992 Directed by Anne Lewis

A native of eastern Kentucky, Belinda Mason was, as she says, "a small-town journalist, a young mother, a reliable Tupperware party guest" until she became infected with the HIV virus in 1987. She decided to go public with her condition and spent the rest of her life as a powerful advocate for AIDS prevention, education, and treatment and human rights.—Appalshop

COALMINING WOMEN

40 M. VHS/16 mm 1982 Directed by Elizabeth Barret

Interviewed at home and on the job, women coal miners tell of the conditions that led them to seek employment in this traditionally male-dominated industry—and the problems they encountered once hired. Watching these women bolt mine roofs, shovel beltlines, haul rock dust and build ventilation barriers leaves little doubt that they can, indeed, do the work. The movie traces women's significant contributions to past coalfield struggles and the importance of their newer position as working miners.—Appalshop

DREADFUL MEMORIES: THE LIFE OF SARAH OGAN GUNNING

38 M. VHS 1988 Directed by Mimi Pickering

For decades, Sarah Gunning wrote and performed hauntingly beautiful ballads about the lives of working people. Born in the eastern Kentucky coalfields in 1910, Gunning lived through the organizing drives and coal mine strikes of the 1920s and '30s and the bitter poverty of the Depression. This program intercuts Sarah's most affecting songs with rare documentary film clips and photographs of early mining life.—Appalshop

EVELYN WILLIAMS

28 M. VHS 1995 Directed by Anne Lewis

Evelyn Williams is a portrait of a woman who is many things: a coalminer's daughter and wife; a domestic worker and mother of nine; a college student in her fifties and community organizer; an Appalachian African-American. Above all, she is a woman whose awareness of class and race oppression has led her to a lifetime of activism. In her eighties, she battled to save her land in eastern Kentucky from destruction by a large oil and gas firm.—Appalshop

FAST FOOD WOMEN

28 M. VHS 1991 Directed by Anne Lewis

This video takes an inside look at the lives of the women who fry chicken, make pizzas and flip burgers at four different fast food restaurants in eastern Kentucky. These women, mostly middle-aged with children to raise, are often the sole source of income for their families. They work for wages barely above the minimum wage, have trouble getting full-time hours because of their employers' scheduling policies, and are without health insurance and other benefits.—Appalshop

Media and Cultural Identity

DANCING OUTLAW

30 M. VHS 1991 Directed by Jacob Young

Dancing Outlaw, one of nine video documentaries from the series "Different Drummer," focuses on

Jesco White, a "real-life" storyteller and flat-foot dancer from Boone County, West Virginia. A revealing portrait of the nearly extinct "hillbilly" culture, the video traces White's uphill battle against abject poverty, drug abuse, petty crime and mental instability. In his struggle to live up to his father's legacy as the finest mountain dancer in Appalachia, he leans on Jesus, Elvis Presley, and his wife.—Flower Films

THE PICTURE MAN

58 M. VHS/16 mm 1998 Directed by Wolfgang Hastert

Each year, "Picture Man" Shelby Lee Adams returns to the places of his childhood home in the Appalachian mountains to photograph stark and striking family portraits. The film follows Shelby's footsteps through remote areas of rural eastern Kentucky to discover a reclusive world of mystery, sorrow and love tangled within strong familial bonds.—Hastert Films

STRANGERS & KIN

58 M. VHS/16 mm 1984, Directed by Herb E. Smith

Using funny, often poignant examples, *Strangers & Kin* shows the development and effect of stereotypes in a region where technological change collides with tradition. The film traces the evolution of the "hillbilly" image through Hollywood films, network news and entertainment shows, dramatic renderings of popular culture and interviews with contemporary Appalachians to demonstrate how stereotypes are created, reinforced and often used to rationalize exploitation.—Appalshop

STRANGER WITH A CAMERA

60 M. VHS/16 mm 2000 Directed by Elizabeth Barret

During the 1960s, filmmakers from around the world came to Appalachia to document the dire conditions of the region's poorest residents. The use of striking images of poverty raised questions about whether media-makers with otherwise good intentions exploited and perpetuated long-held stereotypes of Appalachia. In 1967 tension between media and community led to an extreme and tragic response, when eastern Kentuckian Hobart Ison shot and killed Canadian filmmaker Hugh O'Connor. *Stranger With A Camera* revisits this tragedy as a way to examine the relationship between media-makers and the communities they portray in their work.—Appalshop

TO RENDER A LIFE

60 M. VHS/16 mm 1992 Directed by Ross Spears

To Render a Life is a detailed and dramatic portrait of a contemporary poor, rural family as seen through the eyes of James Agee and Walker Evans' literary classic *Let Us Now Praise Famous Men*. The film also reflects on the documentary process with comments by acclaimed social documentarians such as Fred Wiseman and Robert Coles.—Agee Films

Coal Mining History and Culture

CLINCHCO, STORY OF A MINING TOWN

30 M. VHS/35 mm slides 1982 Directed by Susie Baker

Interviews and photographs, many from family albums, chronicle the boom and bust of a biracial coal camp in the hills of Virginia.—Appalshop

LONG JOURNEY HOME

58 M. VHS/16 mm 1987 Directed by Elizabeth Barret

This work explores the ethnic diversity of the Appalachian region, the economic forces that cause people to migrate into and out of the area, and the personal choices individuals make to stay, to leave and to come back.—Appalshop

ROVING PICKETS

28 M. VHS 1991 Directed by Anne Lewis

The decade of the 1950s was a period of massive change in the coal industry. Small coal operators were unable to keep up with the mechanization taking place in large mines owned by auto, steel and energy conglomerates and began to abrogate their union contracts to reduce costs. *Roving Pickets* looks at the consequences of these changes in eastern Kentucky.—Appalshop

Politics

PEACE STORIES

28 M. VHS 1991 Directed by Anne Lewis

Three men from the South recount their war experiences and discuss how their views of war were affected by participation. William Farmer, a North Carolinian, served in an armored tank battalion in France in World War I; Connie Bolling, a schoolteacher from Flat Gap, Virginia, was recruited by the Department of Defense during World War II to train cyclotron operators in Oak Ridge, Tennessee, where they were secretly making the enriched uranium which went into the first atomic bomb; and Jack Wright, a Vietnam veteran from Wise, Virginia, describes an experience where he felt he was responsible for killing a prisoner of war, and how difficult it has been for him to recover.—Appalshop

BIG LEVER: PARTY POLITICS IN LESLIE COUNTY, KENTUCKY

53 M. VHS/16 mm 1982 Directed by Frances Morton

In 1978 Richard Nixon chose Hyden, Kentucky, for his first public appearance since resigning the presidency. Priceless footage of his visit introduces us to this incisive and sometimes hilarious look at the engines that drive American politics. The film explores the machinations of party politics in rural, and staunchly Republican, Leslie County, Kentucky.—Appalshop

THE ELECTRIC VALLEY

90 M. VHS/16 mm 1984 Directed by Ross Spears

This feature film tells the history of the Tennessee Valley Authority—the TVA—as both political parable and human drama. *The Electric Valley* puts a human face on the nation's largest energy producer and one of the remarkable institutions of our time. A journal of the American political soul.—Agee Films

Religion

IN THE GOOD OLD FASHIONED WAY

29 M. VHS /16 mm 1973 Directed by Herb E. Smith

The Old Regular Baptist Church is one of the oldest denominations in the Appalachian mountains, and its followers cherish its traditional practices and its sense of everlasting values in a changing world. This film documents a riverside baptism, foot-washing ceremonies, an Association Meeting, the "lined-out" music of the church, and memorial services held at a family cemetery.—Appalshop

RAISE THE DEAD

53 M. VHS 1998 Directed by James Rutenbeck

Raise the Dead is an uncritical yet revealing look at three Pentecostal ministers who subscribe to a literal interpretation of a Biblical promise: True believers may partake of any of the nine gifts of the spirit—among them healing the sick, speaking in tongues, and raising the dead. None of the three ministers actually claims to have brought anyone back to life, yet Rutenbeck resists any temptation to lampoon their belief that such a thing is possible. —Icarus Films

SIGNS, CURES, & WITCHERY: APPALACHIAN COSMOLOGY AND BELIEF

58 M VHS 2001 Directed by Gerald Milnes

A fascinating glimpse of some little-known Appalachian beliefs and practices among descendants of early German pioneers. These traditions merged in the New World with Anglo/Celtic influences. The documentary traces Germanic belief systems from Europe to West Virginia, from the fifteenth century to present day practitioners.—Augusta Heritage Center

Education

CRATIS WILLIAMS: LIVING THE DIVIDED LIFE

58 M. VHS 1999 Directed by Fred Johnson

Balladeer, linguist, cultural activist, and storyteller, Cratis Williams was an eloquent defender of Appalachian culture and one of the most important scholars of the post-war era. In this hour-long documentary, Cratis visits his ancestral homeland on Caines Creek in eastern Kentucky's Big Sandy Valley. He reminisces about confronting the stereotypes of Appalachian culture and personalities while growing up among descendants of "Kentucky Long Hunters, veterans of the American Revolution, Tories escaped to the backwoods, refugees from the Whisky Rebellion, and Kentucky Mountain feudists."—Media Working Group

KINGDOM COME SCHOOL

22 M. VHS/16 mm 1973 Directed by Dianna Ott

This work follows teacher Harding Ison and his twenty-two students as they work, study and play together during a typical day at the last one-room schoolhouse in Letcher County, Kentucky. Students are seen doing cross-age tutoring, fixing lunch, working at the chalkboard and receiving one-on-one instruction from the teacher. Ison's views on the value of one-room schools are contrasted with the county school superintendent's rationale for further consolidation.—Appalshop

Literature

AGEE

60 M. VHS/16 mm 1980 Directed by Ross Spears

The life and work of Pulitizer-Prize-winning novelist, poet, journalist, screenwriter and film critic James Agee are examined in this highly acclaimed film biography.—Agee Films

COAL BLACK VOICES

60 M. VHS 2001 Directed by Jean Donohue and Fred Johnson

An intimate mosaic of images, poetry, and storytelling by the Affrilachian Poets as they give glimpses of life in the American Black South and Appalachian region. The ensemble of African-American writers challenge simple notions of an all white Appalachian region and culture while drawing on traditions such as the Harlem Renaissance, the Black Arts Movement, and experiences of the African Diaspora. The writing of the Affrilachian Poets celebrates their African heritage and rural roots while encompassing themes of racism and black identity.—Media Working Group

FAT MONROE

29 M. VHS/16 mm 1990 Directed by Andy Garrison

In this narrative film, Ned Beatty plays the title role of Fat Monroe, a gruff, unshaven mountain man with the gift of gab and a merciless sense of humor. He offers a ride in his pickup truck to nine-year-old Wilgus Collier. Most of the film is a battle of wits between the overwhelming Monroe, who seems to twist everything the boy says, and the steadfast Wilgus, who stands up to Monroe's devilment.—Appalshop

HARRIETTE SIMPSON ARNOW: 1908-1986

35 M. VHS/16 mm 1988 Directed by Herb E. Smith

This work introduces readers of *The Dollmaker* to its author—a feisty, funny, outspoken, talented and hardworking woman. In interviews filmed not long before her death, Mrs. Arnow describes the biographical details of her life and reveals the difficulties of being a writer, a wife and a mother—three roles that she balanced for much of her career.—Appalshop

JAMES STILL'S RIVER OF EARTH

60 M. VHS 1997 Directed by Heather Lyons

An Alabama native who fell in love with Eastern Kentucky as a young man, the late James Still is known as the dean of Appalachian literature. While living and working in a simple cabin in the woods for more than 70 years, he created a body of work reflecting the natural beauty, rich cultural heritage, and often harsh social realities of the region, ranging from the novel *River of Earth* to poetry collections and children's books. This production profiles Still through his own words, interviews with fellow writers, and readings.—Kentucky Educational Television

Grassroots Organizing

ROUGH SIDE OF THE MOUNTAIN

58 M. VHS 1997 Directed by Anne Lewis

In the last 20 years, mining companies and factories have closed, leaving behind rural communities with crumbling infrastructures, unemployment and inexperience in self-governance. *Rough Side of the Mountain* documents the efforts of citizens to rebuild their communities in two company towns in southwest Virginia, Ivanhoe and Trammel.—Appalshop

TO SAVE THE LAND AND PEOPLE

57 M. VHS 1999 Directed by Anne Lewis

In the 1960s, unregulated strip mining heavily damaged land and water resources in Appalachia. During this critical time in coal mining history, an eastern Kentucky citizen activist group, the Appalachian Group to Save the Land and People, organized to fight strip mining. *To Save The Land and People* tells the story of resistance in the voices of people who were directly involved and demonstrates the creativity and energy that indigenous and working class people bring to the environmental justice movement.—Appalshop

Health

CATFISH: MAN OF THE WOODS

27 M. VHS/16 mm 1974 Directed by Alan Bennett

Clarence "Catfish" Gray is a fifth-generation herb doctor living near Glenwood, West Virginia. In this day-in-the-life visit, Catfish reads letters from around the world seeking health advice, gathers herbs and roots from the woods around his house, receives visitors and, finally, relaxes by skinny dipping with hippies in a nearby stream.—Appalshop

MUD CREEK CLINIC

29 M. VHS 1986 Directed by Anne Lewis

The Mud Creek Clinic is a primary health clinic that was started in 1973 by a community in Floyd County, Kentucky, with the idea that health care is a right, not a privilege. *Mud Creek Clinic* explores the formation of the clinic, gives voice to the feelings among the patients and community that the facility belongs to them, and draws a portrait of remarkable clinic director Eula Hall.—Appalshop

NATURE'S WAY

22 M. VHS/16 mm 1974 Directed by John Long with Elizabeth Barret

Most early mountain settlers did without professional medical help and learned to cure their own ailments by using herbs, Indian folklore and home remedies. M. D. Machen is shown selling his cures in the traditional style of the patent medicine man while Scoop and Willie Westbrook talk about their remedies for flu; Etta Banks takes the viewer through the preparation of her family's special salve; Kern Kiser is seen preparing his cancer cure medicine and describes how it saved his wife's life; and Lena Stephens, a midwife who has delivered more than 5,000 babies, chats about her work as she calmly delivers twins.—Appalshop

Traditional Life/Rural Values

APPLEWISE

29 M. VHS 1997 Directed by Anthony Slone

This work is an insider's portrait of the Mullins family and their struggle to maintain and manage one of only two remaining family-run apple orchards in southwest Virginia. Set in the high country of Wise County, *Applewise* is a study of family apple farming, a traditional way of life rapidly giving way to strip mines, highway construction and corporate farming.—Appalshop

FEATHERED WARRIOR

12 M. VHS/16 mm 1973 Directed by Ben Zickafoose

Feathered Warrior portrays the various aspects of the widely practiced, but illegal, sport of cockfighting. Troy Muncie, a seasoned cock breeder and fighter who has won over 65 percent of his fights, outlines the rules of the game, describes the breeding techniques and fighting skills needed to win, and talks about why people enjoy the sport.—Appalshop

MOUNTAIN FARMER

9 M. 1973 VHS/16 mm Directed by Shelby Lee Adams

Mountain Farmer is a visit with Lee Banks, one of the last of the old-style mountain farmers—a man who grew his own food and "never bought." A horse and a wooden plow, a vegetable garden, and a few hogs sustain Lee and his family.—Appalshop

WATERGROUND

16 M. VHS/16 mm 1977 Directed by Frances Morton

Walter Winebarger is the fifth generation of his family to operate Winebarger's Mill, a waterpowered gristmill located at Meat Camp, near Boone, North Carolina. He continues to grind flour and meal using a process that has changed very little since the mill was built a hundred years ago.—Appalshop

Music and Dance

THE HIGH LONESOME SOUND

28 M VHS/16 mm 1963 Directed by John Cohen

The High Lonesome Sound weaves a portrait of a region and way of life with the story of Roscoe Holcomb, the extraordinary singer-guitarist whom Eric Clapton once called "his favorite country musician." Images of Roscoe singing on his back porch or working a hoe against stubborn soil are intercut with scenes of coal miners, passionate church services, a riverside baptism, Bill Monroe and his Bluegrass Boys singing on the Hazard, Kentucky, courthouse steps, and stark, intense visions of life in eastern Kentucky.—Shanachie

IT'S HARD TO TELL THE SINGER FROM THE SONG

58 M. VHS 2000 Directed by Mimi Pickering

West Virginia native Hazel Dickens' repertoire of feminist country ballads, bluegrass tunes, union anthems, and blue collar laments combines the traditional and the political to fashion a grassroots music for working people everywhere. Interwoven with her life story are her most affecting compositions like "Black Lung," "Working Girl Blues," and "Mama's Hand."—Appalshop

MORGAN SEXTON: BANJO PLAYER FROM MUD CREEK

28 M. VHS 1991 Directed by Anne Lewis

Eighty-year-old Morgan Sexton talks about his life and music, and shares his ethereal versions of the old songs. Morgan and his nephew Lee Boy Sexton describe the process of learning from their elders and each other. They talk of the old days when, after a hard day's work, they would "roll up the rug" to play music and dance with neighbors.—Appalshop

MOUNTAIN BORN: THE JEAN RITCHIE STORY

60 M.VHS 1994 Directed by H. Russell Farmer and Guy Mendes

Through interviews and recordings, this program not only chronicles the life of one folk singer and songwriter, but also introduces viewers to broader issues regarding the role of the traditional musician in contemporary society. Teachers will also find the program useful for generating classroom discussions about general topics such as life in Appalachia in the early part of the 20th century and the changing role of music in our lives, as well as more specific issues including the recent folk music revival and the influence of Appalachian music on performers from Johnny Cash to Bob Dylan.—Kentucky Educational Television

NIMROD WORKMAN: TO FIT MY OWN CATEGORY

35 M. VHS/16 mm 1975 Directed by Scott Faulkner and Anthony Slone

This film takes viewers on an extended visit at the home of Nimrod Workman as he and his family prepare meals, build an addition to the house, dig for yellow root, swap jokes with the neighbors and enjoy each other's company. Nimrod's reminiscences about coal mining, early union organizing in the 1920s and '30s, and eighty-three years in the mountains are intercut with impromptu performances of the traditional ballads and original songs for which he won a National Heritage Award.—Appalshop

THE RALPH STANLEY STORY

80 M. VHS/16 mm 2000 Directed by Herb E. Smith

For over 50 years now, Ralph Stanley's banjo playing and powerful singing have represented the wealth of musical treasures that can be found deep in the southern Appalachian mountains. The documentary tells of the creation of "bluegrass music" and relates the story of Ralph and Carter Stanley. It includes performances from Ralph's 1995, '96 and '97 Hills of Home Festival with Patty Loveless, Dwight Yoakam, Ricky Skaggs, Larry Sparks, and others.—Appalshop

SUNNY SIDE OF LIFE

58 M. VHS/16 mm 1985 Directed by Jack Wright, Scott Faulkner, and Anthony Slone

In the 1920s, A. P. Carter, his wife Sara, and sister-in-law Maybelle began recording the songs of the people of southwestern Virginia. Their records and radio shows brought them international fame and spread the music of the southern mountains around the world. *Sunny Side of Life* celebrates the legacy of this country music dynasty by focusing on the Carter Family Fold in Hiltons, Virginia—an old-time music hall founded in 1975 by Janette, Joe and Gladys (the children of A.P. and Sara Carter) to carry on the family tradition.—Appalshop

Art and Artists

CHAIRMAKER

22 M. VHS/16 mm 1975 Directed by Rick DeClemente

Chairmaker follows 80-year-old Dewey Thompson from Sugarloaf Hollow, Kentucky, as a rough- hewn rocking chair takes form under his experienced hands and well-worn knife. Thompson's philosophy and insights into his character are gently interwoven with the depiction of his work.—Appalshop

HAND CARVED

88 M. VHS/16 mm 1981 Directed by Herb E. Smith

Chester Cornett has made chairs for Presidents, and his work is displayed in museums across the country. In *Hand Carved*, Chester fells a tree on the site of his family's homeplace on Pine Mountain in southeastern Kentucky, and transports it back to his small apartment and workshop in inner-city Cincinnati. Intricate camerawork illustrates the process as he uses simple hand tools to chop, whittle and carve the wood into an exquisite, eight-legged "two in one" rocker he designed especially for the film.—Appalshop

QUILTING WOMEN

28 M. VHS/16 mm 1976 Directed by Elizabeth Barret

Quilting Women traces the process of traditional Appalachian quilting from cutting out and piecing together the patterns to the quilting bee. Quilters comment on the origins of the generations-old patterns, the time and patience required, the satisfaction of accomplishment, the quilts as art and the companionship offered by women working together over a quilting frame.—Appalshop

UNBROKEN TRADITION

28 M. VHS/16 mm 1989 Directed by Herb E. Smith

Jerry Brown of Hamilton, Alabama, is the ninth generation of his family to sit behind the potter's wheel and turn out churns, jugs, pitcher, pots and bowls. *Unbroken Tradition* follows Jerry as he digs his own clay, prepares it with a mule-driven pug mill, works the clay into a twenty-seven pound churn on his wheel, and glazes and fires it in his wood-powered, "groundhog"-style kiln.—Appalshop

Storytelling

FIXIN' TO TELL ABOUT JACK

25 M. VHS/16 mm 1975 Directed by Elizabeth Barret

Ray Hicks is a mountain farmer from Beech Mountain, North Carolina, with a genius for telling traditional folktales or "Jack tales"—stories with details and histories that have been passed down in his family for generations. This film shows Ray at work on his farm and gathering herbs in the woods as this National Heritage Award winner describes his family's tradition of storytelling and his theories of human and natural continuity.—Appalshop

HOMEMADE TALES: SONGS & SAYINGS OF FLORIDA SLONE

28 M. VHS 1993 Directed by Anthony Slone

Florida Slone is a singer and storyteller who lives in Knott County, Kentucky. As a child, she contracted typhoid fever and was pronounced dead. Because of the doctor's diagnosis of brain damage and because she did not speak, Florida's parents kept her at home. These early years of isolation, cut off from spoken communication with even the closest members of her family, prompted Florida to develop a keen sense of observation. She eventually learned to talk and began to tell stories and sing songs that she had made up during her years of silence.—Appalshop

RED FOX/SECOND HANGIN'

90 M. VHS 1984 Directed by Don Baker

A video version of Roadside Theater's highly acclaimed play, it is the story of M. B. "Doc" Taylor, called "the Red Fox"—a red-headed, red-bearded popular preacher, medical doctor, herb doctor, philosopher, mystic and U.S. marshal. His execution, the second in the history of Wise County, Virginia, followed that of a local troublemaker. Both had been implicated in murders resulting from a feud that began during the Civil War. The hangings kicked off a law-and-order campaign that Northern speculators considered essential to expanding their coal mining operations in turn-of-the-century Appalachia.—Appalshop

Performing Arts/Performers/ Folk Collectors

ARTUS MOSER OF BUCKEYE COVE

29 M. VHS 1985 Directed by Anne Lewis

"A Renaissance man of the mountains," Artus Moser was born in 1894 and grew up on the Biltmore Estate near Asheville, North Carolina, where his father was a forester. This program explores the richness and variety of his long life as an early collector of ballads for the Library of Congress, and as a teacher, singer, storyteller, actor, painter, sculptor, gardener, naturalist, and husband and father.—Appalshop

TELL ME A STORY, SING ME A SONG

29 M. VHS 1985 Directed by Dudley Cocke, Anne Lewis and Susan Wehling

This video showcases the work of three theater companies that performed together in the mid-1980s as a way to celebrate cultural pluralism and bring theater from diverse cultural traditions to underserved audiences. Junebug Productions, A Traveling Jewish Theater and Appalshop's Roadside Theater are featured. —Appalshop

Film/Video Resources

In addition to the addresses listed below many titles, both listed and unlisted here, can be located in many libraries such as East Tennessee State University, University of Kentucky, West Virginia University, and the West Virginia Public Library. For a listing of films and videos on Appalachian migration and urban Appalachians go to http://uacvoice.org/bibliography.html.

Agee Films
P.O. Box 3441
Charlottesville, VA 22903
804/971-2921
http://www.ageefilms.org

Appalshop Films
306 Madison Avenue
Whitesburg, KY 41858
606/633-0108
http://www.appalshop.org

Augusta Heritage Center
Davis and Elkins College
Elkins, WV 26241
304/637-1209
http://www.augustaheritage.com

Flower Films
10341 San Pablo Avenue
El Cerrito, CA 94530
510/525-0942
http://www.lesblank.com

Hastert Films
3510 Pershing Avenue
San Diego, CA 92103
619/299-3874

Icarus Films
153 Waverly Place
6th Floor
New York, NY 10014

Kentucky Educational Television
600 Cooper Drive
Lexington, KY 40502-2296
800/945-9167
http://www.ket.org

Media Working Group
525 W. Fifth Street
Suite 321
Covington, KY 41011
859/581-0033
http://www.mwg.org

Shanachie Entertainment Corp.
13 Laight Street 6th Floor
New York, NY 10013
212/334-0284
http://www.shanachie.com

XIII

by Roy Silver
www.secc.kctcs.net/Roy

Selected Websites

This list of websites provides an introductory gateway to assist those with an interest in Appalachian Studies.

A. Appalachian Centers provide a range of services from community development to scholarship:

Appalachian State University's *Center for Appalachian Studies* coordinates and promotes curriculum offerings, public programs and research activities to illuminate and sustain the region's history, communities, and ecology. www1.appstate.edu/dept/appstudies/index.html

Berea College's *Appalachian Center* gives leadership to Appalachian activities, working to stimulate student and scholarly interest, brings together existing outreach programs, and guides the creation of new services. www.berea.edu/ApCenter

Carson-Newman College's *Center for Educational Service to Appalachia* is a center for the study and a forum for the discussion of issues and challenges related to Appalachia, its history, culture, and problems. www.cn.edu/academics/special/steeples/appalachian/appcenter.html

Eastern Kentucky University's *Center for Appalachian Studies* coordinates and promotes a multi-disciplinary approach to teaching, research and service on issues about Appalachia. www.appalachianstudies.eku.edu

East Tennessee State University's *Center for Appalachian Studies and Services* provides educational, public service, and artistic projects addressing the needs and interests of Appalachia. Programs include Appalachian Scottish and Irish Studies, Appalachian Studies Curriculum, Archives of Appalachia, Bluegrass and Country Music Program, *Encyclopedia of Appalachia*, Governors School for Tennessee Heritage, Reece Museum and *Now & Then Magazine*. cass.etsu.edu

Emory & Henry College's *Appalachian Center for Community Service* initiates sustainable community-college partnerships. Programs include the Bonner Scholars Program, the Appalachian Center Associates, the AmeriCorps Program, the Public Policy and Community Service major, the Office of Volunteer Services, and the Emory & Henry Student Tutoring Program. www.ehc.edu/appcenter

Marshall University's Center for the Study of Ethnicity and Gender in Appalachia provides fellowships for humanities scholars who study some aspect of gender and/or ethnicity in Appalachia. www.marshall.edu/csega

Morehead State University's *Institute for Regional Analysis and Public Policy* provides applied research and organized public service meeting the needs of eastern and northeastern Kentucky. irapp.morehead-st.edu/index.htm

The ***Ohio Appalachian Center for Higher Education*** is a consortium of ten public colleges and universities in Appalachian Ohio seeking to increase the level of educational attainment in this region. www.oache.org

Radford University's *Appalachian Regional Studies Center* serves as an information clearinghouse. Programs include an Appalachian Events Committee, Selu Living History Museum, the Highland Summer Conference, the Appalachian Teachers' Network, the Assembly on the Literature and Culture of Appalachia, and Appalachian Arts and Studies in the Schools. www.radford.edu/~arsc

Southeast Community College's *Appalachian Center* is a resource for the region's history and cultural traditions and fosters community development. It provides a forum for the arts through cross cultural experiences, and promotes the arts in education. Programs include an archive, the Harlan Area Performing Series, the Center Gallery and a Professional Pottery Program. www.secc.kctcs.net/AppalachianCenter

The **University of Kentucky's *Appalachian Center*** links resources with Appalachian communities in programs of research, instruction, and service. It supports citizens seeking positive change and community-based solutions to regional problems; nurtures awareness of Appalachian Kentucky, the mountain region, its history and people; and provides technical support to citizens and colleagues. www.appalachiancenter.org

Virginia Tech's *Appalachian Studies Program* supports teaching, research, and service on issues pertaining to Appalachia. www.cis.vt.edu/appalachia/apphome.html

Western Carolina University's *Mountain Heritage Center* celebrates the natural and cultural heritage of the southern Appalachian region. Through exhibitions, publications, educational programs, and demonstrations the Center promotes the rich traditions of the mountains. www.wcu.edu/mhc

West Virginia University's *Regional Research Institute* creates learning opportunities and provides research support for faculty members and students while serving as an internationally prominent center for the advancement of regional science. www.rri.wvu.edu

B. **Discussion Lists** provide current information on issues and ideas in the Appalachian region:

Appalnet is the un-moderated list of the Appalachian Studies Association, devoted to providing a forum on contemporary, historical, and social issues for students, scholars, activists and others. To subscribe, email APPALNET-request@LSV.UKY.EDU

H-Appalachia is a moderated list devoted to the discussion of issues relating to the life and culture, both past and present, of Appalachia. To subscribe visit www2.h-net.msu.edu/~appalach

C. **Government** plays a critical role in Appalachian health, safety, and development:

The ***Appalachian Regional Commission*** seeks to develop an informed and skilled population, strengthen the region's physical infrastructure, build local and regional capacity, create a dynamic economic base and foster healthy people. www.arc.gov

FedWorld is a generic gateway for information provided by Federal Government. www.fedworld.gov

The ***Office of Surface Mining*** is a bureau of the U.S. Department of the Interior with responsibility to protect citizens and the environment during coal mining and reclamation, and to reclaim mines abandoned before 1977. www.osm.gov

U.S. Census Bureau collects and distributes data about the people and economy of the United States. It contains links to regional and state data centers. www.census.gov

U.S. Mine Safety and Health Administration www.msha.gov

D. **Non-Profit and Grassroots Organizations** operate some of the most innovative and effective programs in the region:

The ***Appalachian Center for Economic Networks (ACEnet)*** is a community economic development group in southeastern Ohio helping communities create a dynamic, sustainable regional economy with opportunities for all. www.acenetworks.org

The ***Appalachian Community Fund*** is a regionally based and controlled grant-making organization for working on economic, environmental, social, and racial justice issues. www.korrnet.org/appafund

Appalachian Focus is committed to providing citizens the tools and information they need to analyze their problems, design actions, and to communicate directly with others. www.appalachianfocus.org

Appalachian Voices is a grassroots organization committed to protecting and restoring the fragile and threatened native ecosystems of Appalachia. www.appvoices.org

Appalshop is a media arts and a cultural center that produces and presents work celebrating the culture and voicing the concerns of people living in the Appalachian Mountains. appalshop.org

The ***Canary Coalition*** works to improve the air quality in western North Carolina and the southern Appalachian region. www.canarycoalition.org

The ***Democracy Resource Center*** is a multiracial, anti-racist organization whose mission is to help citizens and grassroots groups participate in public decision-making and to make government more democratic. kydrc.org

The ***Highlander Research and Education Center*** aims to overcome poverty, bigotry and economic injustice in Appalachia and the South through building grassroots movements for change led by those most affected by oppression. www.highlandercenter.org

Kentuckians For The Commonwealth is a membership led organization that works for economic, environmental and social justice. www.kftc.org

Save Our Cumberland Mountains is a grassroots citizen's organization working for environmental, social, and economic justice. www.socm.org

The ***Southern Appalachian Biodiversity Project*** is a regional citizen's organization dedicated to the defense and restoration of the native biodiversity of Southern Appalachia. www.sabp.net

The ***Southern Appalachian Forest Coalition*** creates accurate biological inventory data and maps of wilderness areas, old-growth fragments, recreation areas, streams and rivers, sensitive habitats and other valuable resources. www.safc.org

The Urban Appalachian Council is a community-based organization providing coordination and sponsorship of service projects, community schools, cultural events, and research for Appalachian migrants and urban Appalachians. www.UACvoice.org

The ***Virginia Organizing Project*** is a statewide grassroots organization that challenges injustice by empowering people in local communities to address issues that affect their lives. www.virginia-organizing.org

The ***Western North Carolina Alliance*** is a grassroots organization that brings people together to address critical environmental issues. www.main.nc.us/wnca/index.htm

E. Research and Scholarship are sources for developing an accurate understanding of Appalachia:

American Memory is a generic gateway to primary source materials relating to the history and culture of the United States offering more than seven million digital items from more than 100 historical collections. memory.loc.gov

The ***Appalachian Bibliography*** lists more than 8,000 citations to books, journal articles, and documents, is subject-indexed, and contains descriptive annotations. www.libraries.wvu.edu/appalachian/bibliography.htm

The ***Appalachian Education Laboratory*** is an education research, development, and service institution. It links knowledge from research with the wisdom from practice to improve teaching and learning. www.ael.org

The ***Appalachian Journal: A Regional Studies Review*** publishes reviews, poems, essays, and current news items dealing with Appalachia. www.acs.appstate.edu/orgs/appjournal

Appalachian Life is a source of history, stories and folklore found in the mountains of East Tennessee, Southwest Virginia and Western North Carolina. www.appalachianlife.com

The ***Appalachian Studies Association*** encourages study, advances scholarship, distributes information, and heightens communication between Appalachian people, their communities, governmental organizations, and educational institutions. AppalachianStudies.org

The ***Archives of Appalachia*** is concerned with the collection, preservation, and public use of historical materials from the region. cass.etsu-tn.edu/archives

The ***Center for Virtual Appalachia*** portrays and describes Appalachia through the medium of the world wide web. cva.morehead-st.edu

John Jacob Niles Center for American Music provides a comprehensive focus for research and performance, with special emphasis on the native culture of the southeastern United States. www.uky.edu/Libraries/NilesCenter

The ***Journal of Appalachian Studies*** is a refereed journal published twice per year by the Appalachian Studies Association. www.appalachianstudies.org/jas/index.htm

The ***Library of Congress* Online Catalog** contains more than 12 million bibliographic records representing books, serials, computer files, manuscripts, cartographic materials, music, sound recordings, and visual materials from the Library's collections. lcweb.loc.gov/homepage/lchp.html

Manuscript Resources for Appalachian History is a part of the special collection in the Virginia Tech Libraries. scholar2.lib.vt.edu/spec/appal/apunindx.htm

MountainLit is sponsored by the Bridgeport Public Library in Bridgeport, West Virginia. Its purpose is to serve as a vehicle for the collection and distribution of information about past and present West Virginia authors and their writing. www.mountainlit.com

National Archives and Records Administration helps preserve our nation's history by overseeing the management of all Federal records. www.nara.gov

The ***New Deal Network*** is a database of photographs, political cartoons, and texts speeches, letters, and other historic documents from the New Deal period. newdeal.feri.org

Tending the Commons: Folklife and Landscape in Southern West Virginia incorporates 679 excerpts from original sound recordings and 1,256 photographs from the American Folklife Center's 1992–99 Coal River Folklife Project. memory.loc.gov/ammem/cmnshtml

About the Contributors

Alan Banks is a professor of sociology at Eastern Kentucky University.

Gary Barker is the author of *The Handicraft Revival in Southern Appalachia, 1930–1990.*

Sandra Barney is an associate professor of history at Lock Haven University.

Kate Black is a librarian at the University of Kentucky who also teaches in the Appalachian Studies and Women's Studies programs at UK.

Dwight Billings is a professor of sociology at the University of Kentucky.

Michael Bradshaw is the author of *The Appalachian Commission: Twenty-Five Years of Government Policy.*

Richard A. Couto is a professor of leadership studies at the Jepson School of the University of Richmond.

Ron Crouch is the director of the Kentucky State Data Center.

Sharon A. Denham is an assistant professor in the school of nursing at Ohio University.

Betty J. Duggan is a research affiliate at Harvard University's Peabody Museum of Archaeology and Ethnology.

Alan De Young is a professor of education at the University of Kentucky.

Judith Ivy Fiene is a professor of social work at the University of Tennessee.

Stephen L. Fisher is Hawthorne Professor of Political Science at Emory & Henry College.

Maier B. Fox a co-author of *Employer Tactics and Labor Law Reform.*

Rhoda H. Halperin is a professor of anthropology at the University of Cincinnati.

Steven R. Howe is an associate professor of psychology at the University of Cincinnati.

John C. Inscoe is an associate professor of history at the University of Georgia.

Loyal Jones is the former director of the Berea College Appalachian Center and author of books on Appalachian humor, values, and religion.

Patricia Smith Jones is an advocate for urban Appalachians in the Dayton, Ohio, area and does research on the subject of dialect.

Carl G. Kilbourne is a retired professor of industrial arts and a long-time tree farmer.

Helen M. Lewis is a co-editor of *Colonialism in Modern America: The Appalachian Case.*

Ronald L. Lewis is Eberly Professor of History at West Virginia University.

Roger A. Lohmann is professor of social work at West Virginia University.

Sally Ward Maggard is a national program leader at the U.S. Department of Agriculture and a past president of the Appalachian Studies Association.

Bill C. Malone is the author of *Country Music USA.*

Michael E. Maloney, an urban Appalachian from Eastern Kentucky, is a scholar, activist and consultant based in Cincinnati. His consulting practice focuses on work with rural and urban Appalachians.

Claire McBrien works with the education programs of the Ivanhoe, Virginia, Civic League.

Gordon B. McKinney is professor of Appalachian studies and director of the Appalachian Center at Berea College.

Michael Miskowiec is an attorney in Charleston, West Virginia, who specializes in Social Security, SSI disability, and federal black lung claims.

Phillip J. Obermiller has written or edited six books on Appalachian topics.

John Solomon Otto is a former research associate at the International Center for Development Policy in Washington, D.C.

David Sutton teaches Appalachian politics at Appalachian State University.

Mary Beth Pudup is an assistant professor of community studies at the University of California, Santa Cruz.

Jedediah S. Purdy is a senior correspondent for *The American Prospect*.

Marc A. Rhorer is the Director of Undergraduate Studies for the College of Business at Florida Atlantic University where he also teaches sociology.

Emily Satterwhite is a graduate student in American studies at Emory University.

Henry D. Shapiro is author of *Appalachia on Our Mind: The Southern Mountains and Mountaineers in the American Consciousness, 1870–1920.*

Roy Silver is a professor of sociology at Southeast Community College in Kentucky.

Jean Haskell Speer is director of the center for Appalachian studies and services at East Tennessee State University.

Joe Szakos has been staff coordinator for Kentuckians for the Commonwealth since 1982.

Karen Tice is the former director of women's studies and assistant professor of social work at Western Kentucky University.

Maxine Waller is president of the Ivanhoe, Virginia, Civic League and a former Southern Appalachian Leadership Fellow.

David S. Walls is the former dean of extended education and summer session at Sonoma State University.

Carroll L. Wessinger is a Lutheran minister with a long-time involvement in Appalachian community development.

Stephen Paul Whittaker is a Yates fellow at the center for women's studies at the University of Cincinnati.

Jack Wright is an assistant professor in the school of film at Ohio University.